Department of Economic and Social Affairs
Population Division

ST/ESA/SER.N/44-45

Population Bulletin of the United Nations

Policy Responses to Population Decline and Ageing

Special Issue Nos. 44/45 2002

 United Nations   New York, 2004

NOTE

The designations employed and the presentation of the material in the present publication do not imply the expression of any opinion whatsoever on the part of the United Nations Secretariat concerning the legal status of any country, city or area, or of its authorities, or concerning the delimitation of its frontiers or boundaries.

The term "country" as used in the text of this publication also refers, as appropriate, to territories or areas.

The designations "developed" and "developing" for countries and "more developed" and "less developed" for regions are intended for statistical convenience and do not necessarily express a judgement about the stage reached by a particular country or area in the development process.

The views expressed in signed papers are those of the individual authors and do not imply the expression of any opinion on the part of the United Nations Secretariat.

Papers have been edited and consolidated in accordance with United Nations practice and requirements.

ST/ESA/SER.N/44-45

UNITED NATIONS PUBLICATION
Sales No. E.02.XIII.4

ISBN 92-1-151364-2

PREFACE

The Population Division of the Department of Economic and Social Affairs of the United Nations Secretariat is responsible for providing the international community with up-to-date and scientifically objective information on population and development. The Population Division provides guidance to the United Nations General Assembly, the Economic and Social Council and the Commission on Population and Development on population and development issues and undertakes regular studies on population levels and trends, population estimates and projections, population policies and population and development interrelationships.

The Population Division organized the United Nations Expert Group Meeting on Policy Responses to Population Ageing and Population Decline at United Nations Headquarters in New York from 16 to 18 October 2000. The purpose of the Meeting was to investigate the consequences of expected population decline and population ageing as well as the policy responses to cope with such demographic changes. The Meeting brought together national experts from eight countries, namely, France, Germany, Italy, Japan, the Republic of Korea, the Russian Federation, the United Kingdom of Great Britain and Northern Ireland and the United States of America, as well as the two regions of Europe and the European Union. The Meeting improved the knowledge base and identified priorities for future research in order to enhance informed policy development and programme planning.

Thanks are due to the experts and other participants who prepared invited papers and contributed to discussions, and also to Ms. Gallya Lahav who assisted in preparing the report.

The papers for this Meeting as well as other population information may be accessed on the Population Division's World Wide Web site at *http://www.un.org/esa/population/popdecline.htm*. To discuss the present publication, or population issues in general, please contact Mr. Joseph Chamie, Director, Population Division, United Nations, New York 10017, USA, at telephone (212) 963-3179 or fax (212) 963-2147, or e-mail to *population@un.org*.

CONTENTS

PART ONE.   REPORT OF THE UNITED NATIONS EXPERT GROUP MEETING ON POLICY RESPONSES TO POPULATION AGEING AND POPULATION DECLINE

ANNEXES

PART TWO.   BACKGROUND PAPER

PART THREE.   CONTRIBUTED PAPERS

Explanatory notes

Symbols of United Nations documents are composed of capital letters combined with figures.

Various symbols have been used in the tables throughout the present publication, as follows:

Two dots (..) indicate that data are not available or are not separately reported.

An em dash (—) indicates that the population is less than 500 persons.

A hyphen (-) indicates that the item is not applicable.

A minus sign (-) before a figure indicates a decrease.

A full stop (.) is used to indicate decimals.

Years given refer to 1 July.

Use of a hyphen (-) between years, for example, 1995-2000, signifies the full period involved, from 1 July of the beginning year to 1 July of the end year.

Details and percentages in tables do not necessarily add to totals because of rounding.

Countries and areas are grouped geographically into six major areas: Africa, Asia, Europe, Latin America and the Caribbean, Northern America and Oceania. Those major areas are further divided geographically into 21 regions. In addition, the regions are classified as belonging, for statistical convenience, to either of two general groups: more developed and less developed regions. The less developed regions include all regions of Africa, Asia (excluding Japan), Latin America and the Caribbean, Melanesia, Micronesia and Polynesia. The more developed regions comprise Northern America, Japan, Europe and Australia/New Zealand.

Part One

REPORT OF THE UNITED NATIONS EXPERT GROUP MEETING ON POLICY RESPONSES TO POPULATION AGEING AND POPULATION DECLINE

REPORT OF THE EXPERT GROUP MEETING

I. OPENING

The Population Division of the Department of Economic and Social Affairs of the United Nations Secretariat, with financial support from the United States National Institute on Ageing, organized a meeting of experts from 16 to 18 October 2000 to discuss policy responses related to population ageing and decline. The meeting was inspired by an earlier report entitled "Replacement Migration: Is It a Solution to Declining and Ageing Populations?", issued by the Population Division in March 2000. The report was issued as a United Nations publication in 2001 (United Nations, 2001). Projecting a trend towards "smaller and older" populations in a growing number of countries, the report identified migration as one possible partial solution. In the context of growing public resistance to migrants in the developed countries, the conclusions generated a flurry of news activity. The proposals raised critical questions concerning contemporary demographic trends, and prompted an intensive debate among scholars and policy makers. In response, the United Nations invited experts from countries experiencing rapid population ageing and facing population decline to survey the implications of these changes.

In a number of advanced industrialized countries, the fertility rates have remained below replacement level (in other words, women are having fewer than two children). Given current levels of immigration, this rate could lead to a 25 per cent decline in the populations of countries such as Italy and Spain by the year 2050. This trend towards smaller populations is accompanied by population ageing. For example, while 18 per cent of Italy's population is now above age 65, it is estimated that approximately 35 per cent would be in that age bracket by 2050. Smaller and older populations have diverse societal implications, since they affect the size and composition of the labour force, including the reduction in the ratio of persons of working age to the elderly, pensions, social security systems and care services. A serious policy re-evaluation of established economic, social and political policies and programmes is warranted to respond to the substantial consequences at stake. These trends also bring into question current restrictive immigration policies.

The three-day meeting was opened by Mr. Joseph Chamie, Director of the Population Division. He emphasized that the two most important objectives of the gathering were: (*a*) to consider the demographic prospects for the countries and regions affected by ageing trends during the next half-century; and (*b*) to identify the consequences of ageing and population decline. Within the context of these expected changes, it would be essential to assess various related issues and policy options. These included topics such as migration and fertility, the modification of retirement age and pension systems. Concerned mostly with issues of population decline from the perspective of the labour force, the meeting focused on eight countries, namely, France, Germany, Italy, Japan, the Republic of Korea, the Russian Federation, the United Kingdom of Great Britain and Northern Ireland and the United States of America. Among the invited guests were members of the Permanent Missions to the United Nations, representatives of non-governmental organizations and members of the press.

The present report, prepared by the Rapporteur, Ms. Gallya Lahav, includes a summary of the main points that emerged in the general discussions and conclusions of the meeting. It not only contains the comments, questions and responses, but also captures some of the major themes of the papers.

II. PANEL DISCUSSION

This panel discussion was designed to create a framework for discussion, by identifying the critical issues and policy responses related to changing demographics. The panellists included Mr. Makoto Atoh, Director-General, National Institute of Population and Social Security Research, Japan; Ms. Charlotte Höhn, Director and Professor, Federal Institute for Population Research, Germany; and Mr. Paul Demeny, Distinguished Scholar, Population Council, United States. Ms. Isabel Piquer, a correspondent of *El País*, was the moderator.

Mr. Atoh began the panel discussion with a summary of the main findings on fertility decline in Japan described in his paper. He reported that the total fertility rate (TFR) in Japan has been declining since the mid-1970s owing, first, to an increase in the proportion of single women and, second, since the 1990s, to a decline in marital fertility. Among possible explanations are: (a) women's status (that is to say, women's labour-force participation has increased while family roles have remained traditional); and (b) "parasite/aristocratic singles", applicable to all developed countries. What is specific to Japan is the postponement of marriage, which is not compensated by an increase in cohabitation.

Assessing policy responses, Mr. Atoh reported that the Japanese Government has taken direct and indirect measures to address fertility decline. Since the aged dependency ratio (ADR) has doubled in 25 years, and will increase to 60 per cent in 2050, it is necessary to adopt policy responses to cope with the demographic change. In this vein, the public pension scheme is being restructured, and policies to ensure long-term care for the elderly are being developed. Labour-force policies for different population segments are also being adopted. The Government is targeting the elderly by encouraging companies to increase the retirement age from 60 to 65. It is also trying to incorporate women by introducing a one-year parental leave with compensation and improved childcare. Foreign workers are also a consideration. While the foreign population constitutes only 1.4 per cent of the total population, the Government is still cautious with respect to softening migration policies. Replacement migration seems to be an economically unviable and politically unacceptable option.

4

The second panellist, Ms. Höhn, reported that population ageing also has been high in the Germany political agenda since the mid-1970s. Although the German media have shown considerable interest in the report entitled *Replacement Migration*, it is clear that migration cannot solve the problem of ageing. Economic forces need to be figured into the demographic equation. In Germany, for instance, unemployment is very high among the young, and immigration needs to be restricted to certain professions. Structural unemployment is the main issue, and migration will be limited to economic areas where foreign labour is needed. Labour-force policy may be an effective response to ageing. Once unemployment is reduced (in 10 to 30 years), depending on demand, global economic forces, and changes in productivity, the German Government could promote women's participation in the labour force and increase the age at retirement, an unpopular measure. According to Ms. Höhn, Germany is still not ready to consider itself an "immigration country". There are severe problems that are politically sensitive and therefore lack policy appeal to decision makers. Older people, for example, have significant electoral weight and can oppose changes directed against them.

The third panellist, Mr. Demeny, noted that although there are more immediate population concerns, it is important to look at these issues as long-term problems, whereby population decline and ageing may be by-products. He identified some responses to ageing, such as modifications of pension systems, open doors to immigration, and support for fertility increases. Mr. Demeny identified both short- and long-term goals of increasing birth rates. He proposed a more radical but less expensive approach than current family support programmes in many European countries: rearing children as a career. Because standard pronatalist policies usually fail, Mr. Demeny favoured a bifurcated regime: in such a system, 70 per cent of women would have the desired number of children (assumed to be 1.2) and 30 per cent of women would have the number of children required to reach replacement at the national level (4). At present, having children is an unpaid job. Governments need to develop competitive material compensations. To participate, "rearers" should meet certain criteria (that is to say, they should be young and married, should share the same ethnic distribution as the total population etc.). Societies not willing to accept population decline should consider this option.

Ms. Piquer, the moderator of the forum session, questioned how these issues could be presented in a convincing manner so as to appeal to public opinion. Clearly, public awareness of these problems needs to be taken into account. Mr. Atoh and Ms. Höhn reinforced the sentiment that pronatalist measures were difficult to address publicly owing to national histories. Also, the thinking of policy makers may be compared to prisms that refract light within short-term contexts; they are reluctant to impose unpopular measures, particularly when they will not harvest the results. Furthermore, Governments conceive choices of fertility to be an individual matter, and having the number of children desired to be a human right. Thus, they do not wish to interfere. Nonetheless, in countries such as Singapore and Hungary these issues have been widely debated, and even in countries such as Germany, Governments have begun to deliberate on adopting family measures as a means to deal with the shortage of skilled workers.

In the discussion it was mentioned that, according to Eurobarometer public opinion polls, in almost all European countries, the individual's first choice is to have two children; the second choice is for three children; and the third choice varies from zero to four. The question is: Do Governments take these preferences into consideration? According to Mr. Antonio Golini, while Demeny's provocative solution may not be entirely unrealistic in the South, where women are the only labour-force reserve, low fertility must be framed as a cultural and behavioural issue in terms of the "mystique of leisure" and a decreasing sense of social responsibility. One participant was optimistic that an end to fertility postponement among young people had begun in Western Europe.

A key question centres on whether an approach other than a laissez-faire one can be realistic at the global level. Women's participation in the labour force could be increased to respond to ageing. Men may take rearing responsibilities over in the future. Mr. Demeny agreed that male involvement was necessary to his proposal; after all, rearers are couples. In his scheme, fertility preferences are inconsequential, because possibilities are what matters. It was pointed out however, that economic incentives to have children would be very expensive, especially in terms of replacing opportunity costs of working mothers to stay home. In any case, the impact of fertility changes would take 30 years to be realized. It would be best to persuade people to have children earlier.

III. REVIEW OF DEMOGRAPHIC TRENDS AND PROSPECTS

In her introduction, Ms. Hania Zlotnik, Chief of the Population Estimates and Projections Section of the Population Division, provided an overview of demographic trends and implications. Participants discussed the results presented by the Population Division and compared them with their national estimates.

Ms. Zlotnik addressed future changes in population ageing. In her assessment, despite the fact that the population pyramids for the less developed regions are projected to change even more quickly, the current issues of ageing relate mostly to the more developed regions. Underlying causes include the change in fertility patterns in the most developed regions, which was not anticipated by most demographers. Many countries in these regions are projected to experience population decline. More specifically, 58 countries are expected to undergo a population decline by 2050, an increase from the 21 countries that are currently witnessing this decline. This development marks the first population diminution during times of economic prosperity.

The median age of the population has notably changed. Lower fertility and mortality rates increase the median age of the population in the more developed regions from 38 years in 2000 to 46 years in 2050. In the less developed regions, this age is projected to increase from 24 years in 2000 to 37 years in 2050. These calculations are based on the assumption that the TFR in more developed countries will stabilize at about 1.7 to 1.9. If the TFR declined to 1.5, the median age in 2050 would be 53 years. By 2050, the working-age population will have declined in absolute terms in developed regions. In the developing regions, the levels of ageing will not be as extreme as in the developed regions. Thus, the more developed regions will lose populations, while the less developed regions are expected to increase their population bases. The question, therefore, is how much potential there is for movement from the less developed to the more developed regions. In the 1990s, migration from the developing regions accounted for nearly half the growth in the developed regions. In fact, in the period 1995-2000, 61 per cent of the total growth in developed regions stemmed from migration.

Comments/questions. The experts reacted to the Population Division's projections by raising methodological issues. Some participants considered the projection time-span of 50 years to be too long. For example, no one anticipated the start or end of the baby boom; forecasting migration for five years alone would be a difficult task. Differences between low migration assumptions of the United Nations and those posited by the European Union (EU) were noted. For example, according to United Nations projections, migration figures were estimated to be roughly 200,000 between 2020 and 2025. In comparison, the Statistical Office of the European Communities (Eurostat) figures suggested a minimum figure of 660,000 per year. Discussants questioned the modest assumptions of the United Nations, especially as they do not follow observed trends.

One participant suggested that, in order to forecast for the more developed countries and recommend policies, it is necessary to assume a global perspective, rather than a narrow one. A macro view would uncover overpopulation problems and lack of resources in some areas. In fact, the population at the world level is still increasing fast, and stabilization, decline and low fertility are actually necessary for the survival of the planet. This situation may be detrimental for the more developed countries, but beneficial for the world at large.

The magnitude of the economic and demographic effects is unclear. Several participants argued that the big unknowns for social security systems are economic, not demographic. One of the key issues is labour productivity. If it increased at a rate of 4-5 per cent per year, as at present, migration would not be needed. Clearly, the solution is contingent upon the speed of technological innovation. It was noted that Europe receives many different types of migrant flows, including family reunification, refugees, illegal migration and skilled labour migration. The choice of the type of migrants the economy would "need" is an elusive one. If fertility increased in the next 20 years, the labour effects would not be felt until 2040. Furthermore, the opportunity costs of having children, for example, depend on trends in real incomes. The costs increase when real income increases. In this case, fertility will further decline. Participants who embraced this view argued that demography alone was not sufficient, and urged for the inclusion of economic and social theories in projection analysis.

Others argued that population momentum is not an unknown. For example, even if fertility is not forecast correctly, it would not change the outcome of projections much, because the current age structure is the main factor. It was suggested that demographers tend to be conservative in their assumptions, and are thus often blamed by economists for faulty projections. However, it would be erroneous to consider that fertility differences could be explained by economic theories. Fertility, for example, was lower in countries with lower opportunity costs. Economics does not explain why the TFR was lower in Italy and Spain than in the United Kingdom. One participant cautioned against over-simplifying the relationship between opportunity costs of childbearing and real income. There are quality issues involved. Children may become more costly or spending preferences may change. They are tantamount to luxury goods and, as such, demand for them may increase, as does income.

Ms. Zlotnik agreed that the United Nations has been conservative in migration assumptions, but indicated that changes had been made in the 1998 revision, and migration assumptions will be extended in the 2000 revision. There was consensus that the economic and political nature of the migration phenomenon often impeded projections. United Nations demographers were also conservative in projecting mortality decline, because forecasting radical changes or technological innovation and its effects is difficult. Although these flaws are inevitable, the worthiness of population projections, and especially of the use of three variants, is inescapable. Conservatism may lead to biases, but its consequences may have less impact than other approaches. In any case, the Expert Group Meeting was intended to be used as feedback on the work conducted by the Population Division.

The value of extending projections to populations over age 80 or 100 was discussed. Unfortunately, to date, new and sound data with which to test models are non-existent. One participant argued that while there was much talk about the top of the pyramid, the changes were at the base. It is essential to consider the total support ratio, including young plus old, rather than only the old. Together, both do not change so much, so why adopt such an exaggerated view? Another participant retorted that changes in the base or top were not comparable, since they had different economic effects. For example, these changes may not have an effect on the number of consumers, but they do affect the number of producers. An increase in the number of aged (consumers) has consequences for savings: it requires more societal savings for future consumption. This raises questions of how and where to save. These are important issues, given reduced investments and possible recessions.

The impact of population decline is contentious. Some participants believe the demographic community might be underestimating the impact of population decline on competitive advantages. Population decline has serious repercussions for the entire business community. Others recalled that demographers had talked about population decline in the 1930s and 1940s. Concerns did not materialize, and the discipline stepped back. It appears that we have been raised in a culture where population growth is the norm; but this does not have to be so. Our era of population growth may be exceptional. Population stabilization or even decline may be the norm.

IV. CONSEQUENCES AND PROBLEMS

The major question informing this session was to what extent Governments should be concerned about population ageing and population decline. Deliberations focused on broad socio-economic consequences.

Mr. Jean-Claude Chesnais, Directeur de Recherche at the Institut National d'Études Démographiques, France, summarized the findings of his paper on policy responses to the inversion of the age pyramid and future population decline. There are various types and levels of below-replacement fertility. These patterns range from the most modest cases, which demand slight revisions in population policy, to the more extreme cases with rapid ageing processes, which threaten the structural base and compromise the future of societies at large. In each case, the consequences vary in terms of demographic and non-demographic repercussions.

In terms of demographic factors, we should consider reproductive potential; that is to say, the number of women in reproductive ages (20-35, in practice) is declining. In addition, with the age structure becoming older, the number of births is declining while the number of deaths is increasing. This creates a natural deficit. The elderly population will nearly double but, at the same time, the base of the pyramid becomes smaller. This creates an inversion of the age pyramid, beyond simple ageing. These phenomena impact on the median age. Clearly, small differences in fertility have large consequences in the long term.

The second set of factors involves the non-demographic consequences of population ageing and decline. There is a fiscal debate about retirement pensions and social security systems. Questions include whether to decrease benefits, increase contributions, or increase retirement age. In many countries, the social security systems are substantial and constitute a significant proportion of the gross domestic product (GDP). The need for a labour force to take care of old people may require immigration. There is a lack of consensus on responses to the decline of the labour force. According to some experts, it is necessary to increase participation rates and employment. To others, the answer is to increase productivity. The important question is to what extent current productivity increases are sustainable in the long term. Productivity increases cannot be expected to solve ageing problems. New techniques usually come with young people. Ageing threatens to slow down the pace of modernization. There are obvious political and cultural consequences of ageing (namely, conservatism).

With regard to global policy responses to these trends, Mr. Chesnais identified the variations that continue to distinguish countries. Some countries have experienced TFR below replacement for a long time (approximately 20-25 years). In others, the decline has been more recent. In addition, the TFR is close to replacement in some cases, and much lower in others. In all cases, Chesnais claimed that migration is only a partial solution to the reversal of the age pyramid. Immigration has always been a political or economic tool, not a demographic one.

Comments/questions. The discussion covered a wide range of topics ranging from the nature of the ageing problem to the extent to which migration could be a solution to it. Some participants felt that insufficient attention had been paid to the question whether ageing was due to changes in fertility or in mortality. The economic and social effects of fertility decline and those of mortality improvements are very different. It was also argued that productivity increases could not be a permanent solution to ageing, particularly if pensions were indexed on the basis of wages, as has usually been the case. The need to consider different time-horizons was also raised. In the middle term (5-10 years), population decline does not necessarily cause a decline in the labour supply. It is only in the very long term that demographic factors matter.

Regarding solutions, it was mentioned that increases in labour-force participation can have only short-term effects, and thus cannot be a long-term solution. The Population Division presented a note on the impact of economic activity rates on potential support ratios. The main conclusion of the note was that possible future increases in economic activity rates in ages 25-64 cannot, on their own, offer a solution to the decline of potential support ratios. In order to keep support ratios at levels close to current ones without turning to migration, consideration will have to be given to increasing labour-force participation beyond age 65.

The costs of immigration and long-term growth are substantial. It was felt by some that migration does not necessarily meet labour-market needs (especially those that stem from asylum or family reunification) or solve pension problems, since migrants will eventually become receivers as well. The different views of the business sector, which defends the need for more immigrants, and the academic sector were mentioned. Some noted that while increasing migration provides the business sector with more choice, this fact does not define it as a positive or a negative factor at large. Regional and sectoral issues need to be considered, because unemployment and labour shortages are not mutually exclusive, and can occur simultaneously. More importantly, to what extent is it really ethical or possible to select migrants?

The nature of the pension/ageing crisis is controversial. There was some debate whether the crisis was political (in other words, one of resource redistribution) or inherently economic, in terms of total output. Those who viewed the crisis as political argued that productivity did not resolve problems of *how* to share the societal pie. Increases in productivity are not a solution, if they do not benefit or represent the different groups: resource distribution is a political decision, and it is important to consider additional public burdens on future generations. Those who thought that the issue was economic noted that ageing, through the reduction in the number of young people, was a major cause of economic recession.

In an effort to frame the discussion, Mr. Chamie posed five questions regarding population projections: 1. Are population estimates and projections reasonable, and if not, why? 2. Should the Governments be concerned about ageing and population decline? 3. Are there serious consequences of population ageing and decline to address at present? 4. Should issues of retirement, pensions and health care be currently addressed, or are they not relevant now? 5. What are the three most important policy actions that Governments are advised to embrace?

A general discussion ensued around a number of questions, ranging from the limitations of population estimates to the practical relevance to current policy makers of issues such as retirement, pensions, health care and other consequences of population ageing or decline. Some concerns were raised about the impact of divergent migration assumptions among the United Nations, the United States and other Organisation for Economic Co-operation and Development (OECD) member countries. Given that United Nations projections are more conservative than those of the United States Census Bureau, which expects ageing to occur at a more rapid pace, we may anticipate different outcomes.

There was some enquiry about political pressures to project mortality changes or other demographic estimates. One participant suggested that officials may be motivated by their complicity with life insurance companies, which have stakes in underestimating life expectancy improvements. Despite disagreement about the influence of political forces, there was consensus that life expectancy underestimates reflected the conservative nature of such projections. Difficulties in the political domain are relevant only insofar as political decisions are unilinear or rarely reversed; that is to say, policies regarding retirement, for instance, are marked by gains that are rarely withdrawn.

Issues of terminology were also raised. It is important to distinguish between fertility postponement and fertility decline. For example, although there has been a TFR decline since the 1990s in Eastern Europe, the picture is more complex. Some countries experienced a decline in quantum, while others, namely, those in Central Europe, witnessed postponements (Slovenia and the Czech Republic). Also, since there is an increase in age at marriage, the TFR may be only temporarily depressed, as the youngest generations are still postponing fertility.

Regarding migration, data for some European countries reveal that life expectancy and mortality differ among immigrant groups and native populations. This is due to selection bias effects, namely, the selection of immigrants by health status or the fact that sick people tend not to migrate. It should be noted, however, that the selection bias is relevant for labour immigration only, not other types of immigration. In any case, comparative migrant and native projections need to be treated with some caution. Statistics for foreigners leaving the country tend to be underestimated, and are not always reliable. The nature of illegal migration inherently impedes data analysis. Many foreigners return home when they become ill, and they prefer to die in their countries of origin. These factors combined explain the apparent lower reported mortality of foreigners. They also point to the value of using census instruments to verify the accuracy of these trends. It was reported, for example, that a study based on the census in Belgium had revealed that the mortality of Turkish and Moroccan foreigners was similar to that of Belgian citizens, after corrections were made for the undercounted emigrants. Leaving statistical limitations aside, studies deal with past migration processes. In other words, in order to migrate, one needed medical clearance. Thus, health is one of those dimensions that characterized past migration processes.

V. POLICY OPTIONS

The session on policy options was divided into two sections, and was introduced by Mr. Anatoly Zoubanov, of the Population Division of the United Nations Secretariat. The first part of the discussions focused on policies relating to determinants of demographic changes, including fertility, health and mortality, and international migration. The second half addressed policies relating to consequences of demographic changes.

The Population Division has monitored population policies since the adoption of the World Population Plan of Action (United Nations, 1975, chap. I) in 1974. Data derive from official inquiries sent to Governments on population and development, national reports and other official statements by government agencies. Mr. Zoubanov reported some of the key findings on government views and policies related to population ageing and decline.

There are several noteworthy trends in the period spanning 1974 to 1999. An increasing number of Governments consider their population growth rate to be too low. In 1998-1999, 66 countries were concerned with this issue. Ageing has also become a major concern. Although awareness of the problem is growing, action is not yet in place. In fact, there appears to be an inverse relation subsisting between the magnitude of the problem and political action (that is to say, regarding pension systems, age of retirement). Policy responses to other issues, such as unemployment, have sometimes created detrimental effects for the ageing problem. In terms of fertility, the number of children desired in developed countries is frequently higher than the actual number. Nonetheless, in some countries, some measures may negatively affect fertility. Governments need to think more seriously about how to help couples achieve a desired family size.

Unemployment is particularly high among the youth, and the young frequently postpone marriage and childbearing. Are there measures in place to support the young? Are there any surveys on the desired number of children? Certain conditions are required in order to have children. Are Governments ensuring or facilitating any of them?

According to the enquiries, measures to respond to ageing include raising the age at retirement, encouraging higher labour participation and enabling participation of retirees. Fertility incentives involve fiscal measures and childcare facilities. Governments have also developed various measures to manage migration flows and stocks. In all cases, practices vary. There cannot be one single solution, but rather a set of measures in place, which are defined according to the social, economic and cultural characteristics of the country. It is important to find a common denominator for effective strategies, but policies need to be adapted to each case.

A. Policies related to determinants of demographic changes

This session aimed to gauge Governments' views and policies on causal factors of demographic changes, including fertility, international migration, health and mortality. It surveyed whether Governments had adopted programmes and legislative measures to cope with population ageing and population decline. Participants discussed recent changes in Governments' views as well as other related policy and legislative developments. The actual and potential impact of these measures was considered in terms of effectiveness and efficiency, as well as the possibility and feasibility of alternative initiatives.

1. Fertility

In presenting his paper on the Italian case, Mr. Antonio Golini, Professor, University of Rome, provided a schema of determinants and consequences of the ageing process. He urged the experts to talk about the absolute number of births, rather than fertility, when discussing ageing. Although fertility is the main factor, it is births, not fertility per se, that determine the ageing process. One expert objected. Maintaining that stable population theories are based on fertility, not on the number of births, he suggested that in order to understand trends in birth figures, one needed to analyse fertility.

Mr. Golini stated that an important question was whether the recovery of fertility was essential and whether policies were a necessity. In order to evaluate desirability and/or sustainability of fertility levels in the medium and long terms, several parameters should be considered. First, regarding population size and decline, defining optimum population size is difficult. However, there may be a minimum desirable population size. Social and economic structures require a certain number of people. Second, speed of change of total population and of specific groups affects the capacity of society to adapt. Certain speeds of change appear too high, particularly if certain age groups are increasing at considerably higher rates. The third factor is age distribution, particularly the ageing of working-age populations. The aged populations in older countries will have to compete with young populations in other countries. Factors that should be considered from both a national and an international perspective include: ratio of past-working-age population to working-age population; family structure, in particular ratio of older people to children; ratio of the young old to the old old (80+); and ratio of younger to older working-age population. The ratio of deaths to births is also a critical factor in the policy equation. In some populations, the ratio is moving towards 4 deaths per 1 birth.

Taking these parameters into consideration, Mr. Golini questioned the severity of the demographic situation. Evaluating the urgency of fertility policy, he referred to Mr. Chesnais's classification of fertility levels by length of projections. In cases where fertility was almost at replacement level (1.8 to 2.1) for more than 15 years (long time-span), and ageing occurred at a moderate rate, small adjustments were required. A TFR of less than 1.2 can create political waves if it persists for under 5 years, but severe problems if its duration is longer than 15 years. If countries experience very low fertility for a long time, intense ageing and rapid population decline create a possible "point of no return" situation, especially in areas with no consistent immigration. This point of no return means a strong reduction of women in fertile ages, to a point where even high fertility could not produce as many births as deaths, and population decline would continue. Such a scenario may prompt rapid ageing and even disappearances of small communities, and thus requires great financial flexibility in social policies. Fertility policy should be implemented according to the severity of the situation.

Solutions for fertility recovery require a comprehensive assessment of the problem. Removal of all disincentives to childbearing, and the implementation of incentives to have children were recommended. These policies should respect the rights of couples to have the number of children they want. Improvement of cultural, social and economic environments for having children is also warranted. Cultural values that penalize large families and individualism should be modified. Attitudes and behaviour of men in couples and expectations of women's roles need to be modified in view of the necessity of reconciling the desired versus the actual number of children and the social need to encourage a certain number of births. Incentives may be indirect, such as through services, or direct in nature, by being oriented towards economic or fiscal rewards. They may be universal or targeted. If targeted, we may consider Demeny's proposal of paid professional child-rearers. Eventual recovery should be gradual, continuity in social policies should be secured, and convergence in subnational differences should be assured.

Whether or not it matters if a community becomes extinct was considered debatable. Some observers perceived the disappearance of certain groups to be beneficial. Others, however, noted that societies reacted to threats to their survival, so that measures would inevitably be needed. The central problem with respect to the disappearance of communities relates to its unplanned nature.

In the discussion, a participant asked whether changes in family forms and practices over the last 30 years helped to explain fertility dynamics. For example, marriage prevalence has decreased, while divorce has increased with fertility decline. Can these trends explain fertility decreases? Although these phenomena are worthy of examination, the trends may not necessarily be related. After all, marriage has decreased throughout Western European countries with very different fertility levels.

The relationship between marriage and children has changed, that is to say, marriage no longer plays a "regulating" role in determining the choice of number of children. Married women do not have children immediately after marrying. Fifty years ago, a non-wed pregnant woman married before giving birth in order to legitimize her child within the marriage. Today, this is not the case in many countries of Europe, although in some countries women still marry when pregnant. Two different images of family prevail in Europe. In countries where the legal status of the child requires a marriage, fertility is very low. In contrast, in countries where there is no discrimination against children born out of wedlock, fertility is higher, or only slightly below replacement. Hence, the legal status of children is an important variable with consequences for fertility. To advise policy makers, one has to clearly understand these dynamics.

The participants discussed the question who takes care of the home in a situation where, when both women and men work, two adults have the responsibilities of three jobs (including an unpaid one) to fulfil. Mr. Demeny's early proposal of paid professional mothers may resolve this dilemma; but it begs the question: Who would raise the children, the couple or someone else? There is a need to revamp social rules, in order to fulfil society's requirements in respect of number of children. As long as the costs of raising children are private ones, parents will not have enough children, because it threatens to lower their living standards. We need to consider public pay for raising children if we want to increase the supply. Mr. Chamie hypothesized that, if the State paid for children, then the West would observe strong migration flows.

There are other options that individuals may prefer which may not imply radical choices. For example, part-time career jobs were suggested. The possibility of developing a full career with part-time work may get us away from thinking in binomial terms. For example, we need a structure that allows people to retire gradually, not abruptly, so as to be partly retired and partly active. These options are mostly neglected, but they merit consideration, because some individuals may prefer to work 60 per cent of the time for 60 per cent of their salary. In the United Kingdom, for example, part-time work is increasingly discussed, and women are taking such jobs. Some observers contend, however, that it is detrimental to their career progress. In cases of gradual retirement, there are still imbalances in earnings.

The critical question is which policies would work. Should the costs of caring for old people and those related to increasing fertility be evaluated on an equal footing? Beyond the economic arena, how can we conceptualize measures that influence "culture"? Are there leaders in a young culture to promote behaviours? There was some sentiment expressed that discourse on economic incentives and disincentives overshadowed cultural considerations. In order to reduce disincentives, one needs to understand how the desired size relates to reality. Demographers are not traditionally well informed about the mass media and cultural leaders who have great influence on the attitudes and behaviours of the populations. Responding to the participants, Mr. Golini noted that the differing situations in Southern, Central and Northern Europe were not necessarily a product of cultural variables, as cohabitation is fully accepted but not practised in Southern Europe. Families invested a lot in their daughters, and women sought economic and social rewards in return.

2. Health and mortality

Mr. Namhoon Cho, Korea Institute of Health and Social Affairs, provided an overview of his paper on health and mortality in the Republic of Korea. A recent study showed an increase in life expectancy over age 65 at a rate of 40 per cent for males and 60 per cent for females. In many countries, health programmes are facing funding problems, because of the increase in the number of old people, and the rise of health service costs. While most countries have universal health insurance, they need to put more emphasis on preventive aspects. Health prevention programmes and cost-saving home care need to be developed. Health services for the elderly should also be integrated within welfare programmes. Long-term care policy needs to be sensitive to home and community-based interests. Although Western countries were successful in reducing mortality, in countries such as the United Kingdom, trends in health have not been as successful. It appears that most of the extended longevity comprises years with chronic illness. Thus, an increase in life expectancy should not only include the question of numbers but also figure in the years of disease.

Socio-economic analyses consider that, in the future, if longevity accompanies longer healthy living, retired people will be willing to work. It was suggested that, at present, women live longer but have fewer healthy years than men. The extension of active life through gradual retirement programmes was favoured in lieu of early retirement schemes. The differences between legal and actual retirement are noteworthy. Assuming 60+ for the aged dependency ratio (ADR), we may expect that it will double from 2000 to 2050. If we take 65+ as a measure, we may also expect that the ratio will double. However, comparing the actual real age (60) with the legal age (65) in 2050 makes a difference in the ADR. As long as early retirement schemes are in place, measures to change the age at retirement cannot be effective.

Lifelong learning is important because companies do not generally invest in training, especially small companies whose life expectancy is shorter. After prime age, enterprises do not invest in education, and if people lose their jobs after age 45, it is extremely difficult for them to find another job. Seniority payments also make this more difficult, because they increase with age, making it more expensive to hire older workers. Nevertheless, if these incentives were lacking, other incentives would need to be implemented in order for senior staff to continue to work in a productive way. Status needs to be granted to senior citizens who are willing to work past their normal retirement age. Another related issue is mobility. Aged people are usually less mobile than younger ones, and ways could be found to help them to be more mobile.

Ending discrimination towards aged workers is imperative. A representative from the Division for Social Policy and Development of the Department of Economic and Social Affairs of the United Nations Secretariat announced that the Second World Assembly on Ageing would be held in Madrid from 8 to 12 April 2002. This conference underscores a recognition that the world has experienced significant demographic and political changes since the first conference held in Vienna in 1982. The United Nations is responsible for three simultaneous tasks: to analyse what has happened since the Vienna conference; to revise the International Plan of Action on Ageing (United Nations, 1982, chap. VI, sect. A); and to identify the priorities for member States in facing the issue of ageing. They will seek policy recommendations that may tackle ageing issues on the macrolevel by addressing lifelong and society-wide processes.

3. International migration

Ms. Ellen Brennan-Galvin, Chief of the Population Policy Section of the Population Division of the United Nations Secretariat, discussed the finding that replacement migration was not a solution to ageing. Large-scale replacement migration is socially and politically unacceptable. In any case, migration processes involve family reunification and other specific categories, where skills cannot be selected. Current movements of high-skilled workers are temporary and involve small numbers. There are also new phenomena such as trafficking. More importantly, few countries have emigration control. Migration trends are likely to continue in the future, including illegal migration, which constitutes part of the de facto labour force. Demographic differentials in the world remain large. This means that we may expect countries to become increasingly polarized. International migration will not go away, but it is certainly not a solution to the ageing problem.

The experts lauded the United Nations report entitled *Replacement Migration* for stimulating discussions. There was a consensus among participants that migration in its current form could not be a global solution. Although historically, migration has had an impact on the labour market and has contributed to the implementation of social security or pay-as-you-go systems in Europe, this will not be the case in the future. International migration has a limited impact on population dynamics unless there is a continuous flow, and the median age of migrants is lower than that of the population. Numbers would have to be very large for a very long time in order to be consequential. Replacement migration numbers need to be high and considered for their cumulative effect because migration is a process and not a number per year. At a certain stage, a proportion of migrants, for example, acquire citizenship, and so on. The real interest is net migration.

Some variations of migration initiatives were discussed. The utility of creating selective or temporary labour migration programmes was considered. In light of the fact that ageing would create a demand for caregivers or labour in health care, it may be beneficial to revisit temporary migration schemes. A rejoinder to this proposal was that, if implemented, trafficking would become rampant. Furthermore, it was pointed out that temporary schemes had not worked in Europe. In recent history, high-fertility countries had more migrants. There is also the social aspect of this dynamic to consider, that is to say, how would migrants integrate? Integration of migrants would be difficult in the context of low fertility. While migration can contribute somewhat to fertility, its impact is very limited. Temporary labour migrants tend to become permanent residents, so such a policy is difficult to promote.

The suggestion that trafficking was a function of unorganized immigration prompted a discussion about the effective management of immigration. Some questions were raised with regard to the linkage between lack of organized immigration and trafficking. It was pointed out, for example, that countries such as Canada and the United States had managed migration for a long time, and had nonetheless experienced large-scale illegal migration and trafficking. Although social scientists tend to agree that liberal democracies are limited in their capacity to influence fertility, they often underestimate the State's effectiveness in areas such as migration. While emigration regulations have been relaxed in most countries, some countries—including the largest one, China—still regulate the exit of their citizens. The effects of China's opening its borders could be enormous.

There was disagreement on the extent to which migration could be controlled. One participant noted that, although countries might try to regulate entries, they could not control exits. Furthermore, even if countries could regulate entries, there would be significant overstaying. Also, in order for this to be effective, it would be necessary to control migration by age and gender. No country could devise and implement such a policy. Monitoring and fine-tuning net immigration are neither feasible nor practical.

EU was developing a global European migration policy. Principles involve the right to seek asylum, fair treatment of third-country nationals, and cooperation with countries of origin. While partnerships based on trade and other agreements exist with most countries, there is still a need to identify conditions that allow regulated migration in these agreements and to ensure that sending countries will collaborate in controlling illegal migration. The underlying principle behind such cooperation is the notion that zero migration is not realistic. Past zero-migration policy in EU was a failure, and implicitly encouraged trafficking. Nonetheless, stopping illegal migration and trafficking, conditions which fuel xenophobia, is critical. Although a zero-migration policy is not recommended, migration should be controlled.

The nature of partnerships with sending countries was questioned. Sending countries are highly diverse and the nature of the partnerships often remains vague. Even in clear cases, such as those of Morocco and Tunisia, for example, agreement excludes key sectors such as agriculture, and thus the impact of agreements on sending economies is minimal. Further scepticism about cooperation stemmed from the fact that Europe was still lacking an entity such as a congress to take political decisions, and sovereign representation was absent.

The impact of migration schemes on developing countries is also important to consider. With 1 billion people in rich countries and 5 billion in the poorer countries, future migration is determined by the politics not only of rich countries. It is worth recalling that the vast majority of people who are migrating are moving among the developing countries rather than into more developed ones. An argument was posed that the numbers involved in replacement migration are too small to have a strong impact on countries of origin. In EU, only 1-1.5 million a year are needed, which means that there would be no problem for developing countries in terms of brain drain. Problems, however, may be more relevant to Eastern European countries that would lose populations to Western Europe, especially if they join EU. These countries themselves need replacement migration, but, if they joined, would experience emigration instead.

The application of migration as a replacement tool in Central and Eastern Europe, where labour markets are more challenged, is debatable. Eastern European countries are experiencing unemployment, declines in output, and losses in labour productivity. It was argued that these economies did not need migration as much as they needed to make their labour-force potential fully productive. Some participants disagreed with the notion that the Russian Federation did not need migration. The situation is contradictory, because developing an economy of vast regions requires larger populations. The Russian Federation has low-density areas and highly populated neighbours. This opens up the possibility of immigration as a solution, despite the fact that massive immigration is not realistic because public opinion would oppose it.

Alternatives to migration in Eastern Europe could come in the form of fertility and labour-force adjustments. Theoretically, fertility could be increased and mortality decreased. In practice, however, there are not enough resources dedicated to improving public health. Indeed, there are patriotic speeches about fertility, but populations will not have more children simply based on speeches. As long as there are economic and political crises in the Russian Federation, we should not expect a boom in fertility. If the Russian Federation emerges from crisis, fertility may be expected to rise. Analogously, it was noted that, after the reunification of Germany, women from East Germany had had the opportunity to earn substantial income. The outcome, however, was a sudden and sharp drop in fertility. Similarly, if the Russian Federation experienced economic recovery, fertility might decline. The official position of the Russian Federation, however, is that the low level of fertility is a consequence of persistent socio-economic crisis. In 1992, a survey of 14,000 families in 22 regions of the Russian Federation revealed that 85 per cent of young people preferred two or more children. Only 3 per cent declared that the Government could not influence their fertility decisions. Stabilization of the population and increase in fertility were placed as high priorities in the national policy agenda. Many ministries in the Russian Federation welcomed the United Nations report on replacement migration, and expressed great interest in it. They agreed that, in order to prevent further decline of the demographic situation, it was incumbent upon them to estimate both quantitatively and qualitatively the number of needed migrants, and to modify policies accordingly.

The role of public attitudes as a constraint on policy-making, particularly in respect of promoting migration, prompted a lively discussion. In some areas of Germany, for example, the native population is expected to become a minority, a trend that public opinion will reject. According to a German poll, a majority (two thirds) of Germans perceive migration to be too high and are already resistant to migration. It was pointed out that, while the poll correctly captured the general feeling that there were too many migrants, those living in areas with more migrants espoused a less negative attitude (similar to the American case). Ms. Höhn reported that the conservative party had won elections in her state (*Land*) owing to its endorsement of a more restrictive migration policy. Could attitudes in general be altered to recognize migration's beneficial effects? Future immigration prospects will depend on economic factors, not demographic interests.

B. *Policies related to consequences of demographic changes*

These discussions focused on other non-demographic policy options, such as increasing labour-force participation, retirement age, productivity of labour, and self-reliance of the elderly and reducing retirement benefits.

The session was introduced by Mr. Michael Teitelbaum, who discussed his paper on long-range demographic projections and their implications for the United States. Mr. Teitelbaum reminded the meeting participants that the issues being debated are consequences of success: that is to say, the increase of life expectancy, and the control over mortality and fertility. He urged the group to take four factors into account.

First, current policies on age and age structure had been created long ago, and defined when age and age structure were very different. At that time, they

19

had a different meaning than they do today, yet they have not been adapted to the current realities. In the past, retirees received a "very good deal"—returns that were far superior to their contribution. This is not bound to happen again. Current retirees are thus situated within a transitional phenomenon, unlikely to be observed in the future.

Second, the adjustment of policies can best be effected with minor revisions, not radical transformations. This may involve, for example, increase of taxation, immigration, productivity, the percentage of economically active persons, age at retirement, and laws on retirement pensions (as well as no penalties for later retirements). Gradual changes may also be encouraged by facilitating gradual retirement and part-time careers, investing social security funds in higher-yielding investments, changing the way pensions are actualized, liberalizing trade (that is to say, increasing national specializations and comparative advantages) and exporting services that are geographically bound. If implemented together, small changes in each domain would be sufficient. No single large change will work as well as a number of combined minor ones.

Third, migration should not be perceived as an adequate solution. The age-structure effects are limited. Economic effects depend on migrant productivity and integration. And migrants also retire. A deficit in the number of births can be balanced by an increase in migration, if one thinks of migrants as units with desired age and other characteristics. Migrants, however, may also have "undesired" attributes. While deficiency in births can be replaced by immigration, immigrants are less acceptable where fertility is low, and the costs of social tensions have to be factored into the equation. Thus, the paradox is that increasing migration may be less acceptable when fertility is low. A liberal migration policy is one approach, but it must be contextualized against other measures.

Finally, demographers need to be more sceptical about the indicators they use. Demographic measures are as outdated as the policies that we claim must be modified. The aged dependency ratio is anachronistic; for example: age 60 or 65 is not an appropriate boundary marker. One suggestion is that the ADR be renamed and alternative series of indicators should be included in the analysis. Measures must change when reality changes.

Comments/discussion. Mr. Teitelbaum's assertion that the consequences under discussion stem from success was questioned. If the population decreases sharply, how does this qualify as success?

A reference was made to a recent call by the Governor of the Italian Central Bank for having more children as a solution to the dilemma lying between demographic decline and increased migration. In rejecting this approach, it was claimed that the priority in places such as the Russian Federation was not to increase births but to ensure that those who did get born were granted decent living conditions. According to some, this is the major issue in the Russian Federation, where the conditions for giving birth are far from ideal and reproductive health standards are very low. In cases such as these, pronatalist policies cannot be considered, from an ethical point of view.

Organization is pivotal in Mr. Teitelbaum's migration scheme to offset fertility trends. There is a perceived need to "control" migration in EU, but to offer an opportunity for migrants to enter (in other words, establish quotas etc.). There was agreement that immigrants were less accepted when fertility was lower. Given that integration starts in school, it is hindered when the proportion of immigrants is too large. On the other hand, in many countries, low fertility was a by-product of government failures to create the conditions that allowed people to have the number of children they wanted.

A number of other issues were also discussed. The fruitfulness of extensive fertility discussions was questioned, given reported policy limitations in changing fertility level. There are time-factor issues: political decision-making requires decades; and it takes a long time for reforms to be implemented. Economic constraints include public debts, and shortage of resources to be devoted to increasing fertility or to health care. EU constraints that are related to fiscal policy limit the resources available for increasing fertility, as countries with public debts are trying to reduce them in the coming years. Age-at-retirement issues involve questions of competitiveness and of familiarity with new technologies, and the existence of public pressures not to increase retirement age.

In terms of health care or long-term care, it must be noted that ageing is not free of charge. We need to create awareness among the youth of the need to be healthier. Could the community do this? In fairness to the younger generation, pay-as-you-go systems will not be sufficient. The younger generations should be advised now about how to invest and in what. The solution of investing surplus funds in the stock market was viewed sceptically. In considering the rate of return in support systems, we need to distinguish between payroll taxes which are similar to investments (that is to say, you contribute, and you receive in return) and income taxes. In a mature system, there is a return rate of equilibrium. The notion of return rates in pay-as-you-go systems was rejected, given the absence of a funded system. In the United States, the pension system has always been presented as a funded system. Payroll taxes are called "contributions", a wording that reflects a deliberate political decision to make this appear to be a voluntary exercise. The past "rate of return" would be seen as a right in the future.

Mr. Constantinos Fotakis, General Directory of Employment and Social Affairs, European Commission, presented some findings on demographic ageing, employment growth and pension sustainability in EU. Since 1997, EU has made improvement of the employment situation in Europe its main priority. This could ameliorate, but not solve, the retirement/ageing issue. There is a clear political aim of supporting pensions (funded schemes), while minimizing the risk of savings losses. There are also increasing trends towards dissociating wages from pensions, towards increasing contributions, and towards adopting other measures such as taxes on the environment, and migrant quota systems. A combination of measures, which should be enforced gradually, and adapted to each national situation, was recommended.

Mr. Fotakis displayed a series of graphs of comparative trends in demographic dependency ratios (assuming all persons 65+ have pension rights) and economic dependency ratios in Europe. The empirical analysis suggests that an increase in employment could avoid the problem in some countries up to 2040. Nonetheless, there is a need to be more realistic about increases in the participation rate in the short term. For example, would older generations of women join the labour market? The data also revealed that pensions as a percentage of GDP are highest in Italy (14.5 per cent), Greece and France. The public debt is also highest in Italy (110 per cent), Belgium and Greece (70 per cent) and Spain (62 per cent).

Some participants noted that Mr. Fotakis's graphs were compelling, and showed that there will be time to adjust. Nonetheless, there is a gap between real wages and real pensions, which will be very visible by 2020. In addition, age boundaries are seemingly arbitrary, and should be made more flexible. There was wide consensus that age brackets of 60+ or 65+ are not meaningful.

Speaking to the issue of dependency ratios, the lack of discussion about the physical dependency of the oldest old, which is bound to increase as ageing progresses, was noted. It was foreseen that this will have become an issue at a time when the forms of the family have changed. Policies can alter the age at retirement, but not the age of physical dependency. It was noted that the ADR is fixed, while "natural" boundaries are changing. The ratio should not be called a "dependency" ratio. According to one participant, there is a wage-incentive problem, and a tendency to embrace a "we cannot change" position. He suggested that it is better to adjust early than late.

The notion of liberalizing trade through increase in comparative advantages met with questions whether low-skilled work could be exported. Measures such as increasing national specializations are being adopted in the sense that low-wage work is already being exported. Nonetheless, it is not favourable to the national unskilled labour. It is better to have flexibility in the national labour markets.

VI. FUTURE RESEARCH

A number of research gaps and initiatives were identified. They ran the gamut from terminology to data-collection issues and cost-benefit analyses. The demand to contextualize population ageing and decline against the backdrop of dramatic global changes was echoed throughout the deliberations. In Europe, it appears that medical analysis prevails, at the expense of analyses of social and economic consequences of ageing. It is important to recognize that the older person of today is different than he/she may have been 30 years ago. Expectancy of life without disability is a crucial variable. These are issues that merit further study.

More data on intergenerational informal transfers are warranted. Although earlier theories suggested that one could transfer resources from the young to the old, rigidity in the system hinders such transfers. Age-related costs in the health sector should be studied. Pharmaceutical companies should be advised to examine cost-saving measures rather than simply work towards maximizing profit.

Fertility behaviour must be studied more systematically. Research on changes in family norms is also welcomed. Although some participants lauded the active pursuit by EU of proposals and funding possibilities for research on ageing, some experts felt that EU continues to place low priority on family issues. This ambivalence is believed to result from divergent national opinions. For example, the United Kingdom does not want EU to intrude in this area, and Germany does not want to pay for such research. Methodological approaches for family projections also need to be improved in order to answer many of the unresolved questions noted in the discussions. What are the effects of family norms on fertility?

Meeting participants also addressed definitional and data needs. They urged for the development of new measures of ageing, health and disabilities. More general indicators for the elderly and for aspects of the labour market related to ageing and retirement are also welcomed. Many existing surveys are underutilized, and could be more conducive to the study of skills, flows and so on.

Several participants noted the lack of dialogue between policy makers and academic researchers, a gap that needs to be bridged. Policy makers require evidence that there are impediments to families' having the number of children they would like to have. They need more academic research on this topic.

The relative costs of young versus old dependants were also inconclusive and controversial, begging more questions. Are the old more expensive to sustain than the young? We need more empirical data to substantiate these theories.

The effects of the population momentum at the subnational level are also worthy of examination. There are interesting subnational developments in ageing and in the numbers of elderly people, which demand an evaluation of regional trends in the working-age population, particularly those between 20 and 40 years of age, who are more prone to migrate. The trends in the old and oldest old merit more attention, and further study as well.

VII. CONCLUSIONS

Mr. Joseph-Alfred Grinblat, Chief of the Mortality and Migration Section of the Population Division of the United Nations Secretariat, summarized some of the main points discussed in the meeting. He reminded the participants that the purpose of the gathering was to discuss policy responses to population ageing and decline. The population projections prepared by the Population Division indicate that a major aspect of the future of the world population is an ageing process that will occur in all countries. The ageing process is expected to be most pronounced when it is accompanied by a decline in the total population, which is projected to occur in 58 countries between 2045 and 2050. The median age of the more developed regions will increase from 38 years in 2000 to 46 years in 2050.

The combination of population ageing and decline stems from a prolonged history of below-replacement fertility, and a continuous increase in life expectancy which magnifies the increase in the proportion of the elderly in the population. These are the results of the medium variant of the projections prepared by the Population Division. How reliable are these predictions? Obviously, no one can predict the future and, understandably, there are a number of questions regarding the future assumptions made by the Population Division. In particular, a number of participants mentioned that the future net immigration into Europe was underestimated, as well as the prospective increase of life expectancy at older ages. It is also impossible to forecast the course of fertility. However, there is some general agreement that fertility rates will remain below replacement level in the foreseeable medium term. The population momentum resulting from the current age structure cannot be changed. The main point is that complete consensus exists on the fact that there will be, in the next 50 years, a combination of sharp population ageing and population decline in most industrialized countries.

Why is population decline and ageing a problem? In the very long perspective of mankind, population stabilization or even temporary decline is the normal course, and a long positive growth rate as experienced in the last century is the exception. A decline in population, total or labour-force, is not always perceived as a problem in the short term, especially in countries that suffer from current high levels of unemployment. Nonetheless, significant future reduction in population resulting from long-term population decline is unacceptable in most societies, even though some decline may not be a negative phenomenon at the global level.

Notwithstanding these considerations, it is important to recognize that population ageing is a cause of various social and economic problems. A major concern is the viability of pension systems. If current rules continue to apply, the decreasing ratio of numbers of workers to numbers of retirees threatens to bring most pension systems to the brink of bankruptcy. This is especially so because in the past, very favourable age-structure situations encouraged Governments to create rules that gave retirees very generous benefits, which are no longer sustainable. Even if per capita income increased and there were no global economic problems of insufficient resources, political issues about the proper distribution of the available resources would emerge.

In the context of social and economic issues, we need to consider that the sharp increase in the number of old people will make it more difficult to face the cost of providing adequate health services to the elderly population. This will be particularly the case if a large proportion of the added years of life expectancy is spent in poor health. Another concern is that ageing of the overall population is accompanied by ageing of the labour force. This threatens to reduce the productivity of the country, as a result of two factors. First, older people are usually paid more, even if they do not produce more, and this increases the cost of production. Second, new techniques usually accompany the labour of young people, and ageing may slow down the pace of modernization, reducing the productivity of the labour force.

The question is what can be done to prevent population decline and population ageing. Several approaches of varying duration were mentioned. In the short term, migration can slow down the process of population ageing and prevent population decline. The volumes of migrants that would be necessary to prevent population decline are relatively small in demographic terms, sometimes smaller than those reflected in past experiences of migration. However, even in the short term, these levels of immigration are often considered untenable and unacceptable, socially and politically. This is a major drawback, since, empirically, migration seems to be socially less acceptable in areas where local fertility is lower, which are also the areas where it is the most needed. In the long term, the accumulated number of migrants needed to prevent population decline would result in the presence of a large proportion of population of foreign origins, a phenomenon that would be widely rejected, both socially and politically.

Concerning population ageing, migration can only decelerate the ageing process; it cannot be a solution. In demographic terms, an increase in fertility is the only way to prevent population ageing in the long term. Moreover, in the absence of significant migration levels, a return of fertility to near-replacement levels is the only answer to total population decline. Nonetheless, there is a consensus that Governments lack the capacity to change the behaviour of individual couples towards increasing their fertility. Economic incentives do not appear to be realistic options, and they generate effects reflecting ambivalence. It was observed that, in some cases, income drops prompted couples to desire fewer children. However, it was also mentioned that an increase in income influences couples to opt for fewer children. One of the few optimistic signs is that, in all countries, couples declare that they desire more children on average than they actually have. Hence, it seems that there may be some room for improvement in this regard. Increasing parental leave, making available more and better nursery care to couples and, generally, facilitating women's ability to have children while averting income loss and strengthening career development may generate some increase in fertility.

In the absence of any clear policy that might so affect behaviour of couples as to raise fertility and bring it back to replacement levels, there were some proposals for extreme government policies, such as paying salaries to a large number of women to become professional mothers. This scenario would entail the recruitment of professional mothers who gave birth to, and raised, with their husbands, large numbers of children (four or more) for the sake of bringing back the average fertility of society to replacement levels.

Given all these proposed solutions, it is noteworthy that a possible sharp upturn in fertility would not yield a significant impact before at least 25 to 30 years, owing to the population momentum created by the current age structure. Thus, we may conclude that population ageing is unavoidable. All countries will have to face the consequences and search for the means to cope with them.

This pessimistic conclusion begs the question what can be done to manage the consequences. No single action can adequately address the problem. Policy adjustments need to be implemented in small increments within several domains. Early revisions are much easier and more effective than the delaying of action until crisis occurs.

Several arenas where action may be taken were identified. One goal would be to increase the labour-force participation. In the short term, increasing the labour-force participation, particularly that of women, which is currently much lower than that of men, could offset the decrease in the ratio of the numbers of employed people to the numbers of retired people. However, it has been shown that, in the long term, even a 100 per cent labour-force participation rate would only restore a small part of the loss in the support ratio caused by ageing. Immigration, particularly in areas needed by elderly people, can help somewhat in reducing the impact of ageing, but only in a very modest way.

Increasing the retirement age is another policy goal. The contemporary system, which was established long ago, has not kept pace with biological changes. In 1950, one was physically old at age 65. Today, a person aged 65 is physically still young, and has a much longer life expectancy ahead. We may anticipate the acceleration and consolidation of this trend in the coming decades. A number of measures could be adopted to increase both the legal and the real age at retirement. They may include prohibiting compulsory retirement, facilitating gradual retirement, encouraging part-time old-age employment and amending regulations that penalize later retirement. Increasing the real age at retirement, even by a relatively small amount, offers a strong impact, as it increases the number of active people at the same time that it decreases the number of inactive persons. Furthermore, a decrease in benefits paid to retirees to more sustainable levels will have a double impact. It will decrease the burden of payments by the active population, and simultaneously inspire more people to remain active longer.

Among other measures mentioned were increasing the contribution of workers to the social security system. As part of balancing the burden equitably among the different sectors of the population, the following principle could be considered: if benefits to retirees should decrease, contributions by workers should increase. In addition, proposals to change social security systems from pay-as-you-go to capitalization schemes may be considered. This offers the possibility of helping to solve government budgetary problems, but it may create other problems in the economy, related to the amount of needed savings.

Finally, an important strategy to consider is based on nurturing the successes of this decade more systematically. More particularly, it is important to promote increases in productivity and the development of technological innovations.

Comments/questions. In the concluding remarks, there were some comments made by the meeting participants. Mr. Teitelbaum questioned the causal linkage between declines in productivity and the ageing of the labour force. He remarked that this was not a uniform experience and not a cardinal rule. In fact, older workers may be more productive with other compensatory characteristics, such as better judgement and greater reliability. As long as there is investment in training to keep the elderly up to date, decreases in productivity should not exist. Instead, the promotion of non-economic, non-political measures, such as revising cultural norms, produced by the mass media and leadership, may serve to better orient behaviour. It was also suggested that the prospect of excess in the number of professors might be useful in developing long-life education.

Other experts reinforced the concept of lifelong learning as a solution. The need for heightened awareness of the "human factor" as a strategic tool for future development is critical: that is to say, the contemporary shortage is one of labour, not—as was the case in the past—one of capital. A useful policy practice is to dissociate pension increases from wage increases, because this allows for slow adjustment. One expert also proposed a two- or three-pillar system of pensions, including pay-as-you-go and partially funded schemes. Fully funded pension systems could be as dangerous as pay-as-you-go ones. Clearly, more research and new methodologies are warranted.

Some questions arose with regard to the impact of ageing and subsequent policy measures on developing countries, particularly in the transition from antinatalist to pronatalist policies. The implementation of pronatalist policies in developed countries can have an impact on developing countries, both culturally/politically and financially, particularly with regard to the funding provided by developed countries. Ageing will occur in developing countries at lower stages of development. Are the policies discussed applicable? We still know very little about the situation of the elderly in the developing world. Finally, we lack more systematic analysis of labour migration from the point of view of developing countries. To what extent is labour migration cost-effective? Indeed, several developing countries are expected to face rapid ageing over the next two decades. Ageing at lower stages of development is a true problem to be addressed.

As a final comment, it was underscored that despite the necessity for global measures, these policy solutions remained nationally driven. States notably operate according to their own national interests. Different problems require distinct solutions. Perhaps the most valuable consequence of these trends is that the less developed countries may profit from the experiences and lessons of the more developed countries.

The Expert Group Meeting was concluded in the afternoon of 18 October 2000. The experts expressed their satisfaction with the constructive discussions that had taken place during the three days, and their hope that these would help in future research and decision-making in this difficult area.

REFERENCES

United Nations (1975). *Report of the United Nations World Population Conference, 1974, Bucharest, 19-30 August 1974.* Sales No. E.75.XIII.3.

_____ (2001). *Replacement Migration: Is It a Solution to Declining and Ageing Populations?* Sales No. E.01.XIII.19.

_____ (1982). *Report of the World Assembly on Ageing, Vienna, 26 July–6 August 1982.* Sales No. E.82.I.16.

ANNEXES

ANNEX I

Agenda

1. Opening of the Expert Group Meeting
2. Panel discussion
3. Review of demographic trends and prospects
4. Consequences and problems
5. Policy options
6. Future research
7. Consultations, discussion and follow-up
8. Conclusion and closing of the formal sessions

ANNEX II

List of participants

Experts

Makoto Atoh, National Institute of Population and Social Security Research, Tokyo, Japan

Herwig Birg, Institute for Population Research and Social Policy, University of Bielefeld, Germany

Jean-Claude Chesnais, Institut National d'Études Démographiques (INED), Paris, France

Namhoon Cho, Korea Institute of Health and Social Affairs, Seoul, Republic of Korea

David Coleman, University of Oxford, Oxford, United Kingdom of Great Britain and Northern Ireland

Paul Demeny, Population Council, New York, New York, United States of America

Karen Dunnell, Socio-economic Statistics and Analysis Group, Office for National Statistics, London, United Kingdom of Great Britain and Northern Ireland

Patrick Festy, Institut National d'Études Démographiques (INED), Paris, France

Constantinos Fotakis, European Commission, General Directory of Employment and Social Affairs, Brussels, Belgium

Antonio Golini, Università di Roma, Rome, Italy

Charlotte Höhn, Bundesinstitut für Bevölkerungsforschung, Wiesbaden, Germany

Yukiko Katsumata, National Institute of Population and Social Security Research, Tokyo, Japan

Ik Ki Kim, Dongkuk University, Department of Sociology, Seoul, Republic of Korea

Gallya Lahav, Department of Political Science, State University of New York, Stony Brook, New York, United States of America

Ron Lesthaeghe, Interface Demography, Vrije Universiteit Brussel, Brussels, Belgium

Svetlana V. Nikitina, Population Projections Division, State Committee of the Russian Federation on Statistics, Moscow, Russian Federation

Georges Tapinos, Institut d'Études Politique de Paris, Paris, France

28

Michael Teitelbaum, Alfred P. Sloan Foundation, New York, New York, United States of America

Maria Rita Testa, Department of Statistics, University of Milan-Bicocca, Milan, Italy

Judith Treas, Department of Sociology, University of California, Irvine, California, United States of America

Anatoly Vishnevsky, Institute for Economic Forecasting, Russian Academy of Sciences, Moscow, Russian Federation

Agencies

Kevin Kinsella, Committee on Population, National Research Council, Washington, D.C., United States of America

Rose Maria Li, National Institute on Aging, Bethesda, Maryland, United States of America

Miroslav Macura, United Nations Economic Commission for Europe, Geneva, Switzerland

Mohammed Nizamuddin, United Nations Population Fund, New York, New York, United States of America

Robert Paiva, International Organization for Migration, New York, New York, United States of America

Ann Pawliczko, United Nations Population Fund, New York, New York, United States of America

Victoria Velkoff, International Programs Center, United States Census Bureau, Washington, D.C., United States of America

Peter Way, International Programs Center, United States Census Bureau, Washington, D.C., United States of America

Population Division of the United Nations Secretariat

Joseph Chamie, Director

Birgitta Bucht, Assistant Director

Larry Heligman, Assistant Director

Ellen Brennan-Galvin, Chief, Population Policy Section

Joseph A. Grinblat, Chief, Mortality and Migration Section

Armindo Miranda, Interregional Adviser, Population Programmes and Projects

Hania Zlotnik, Chief, Population Estimates and Projections Section

Keiko Osaki, Population Affairs Officer

Patience Stephens, Population Affairs Officer

Marta Roig, Population Affairs Officer

Anatoly Zoubanov, Population Affairs Officer

Alice Samuel, Administrative Support Assistant

Division for the Advancement of Women of the United Nations Secretariat

Emanuela Calabrini, Junior Professional Officer, Gender Analysis Section

Division for Social Policy and Development of the United Nations Secretariat

Alexandre Sidorenko, Chief, Programme on Ageing

Rosemary Lane, Social Affairs Officer, Programme on Ageing

Statistics Division of the United Nations Secretariat

Hermann Habermann, Director

Alice Clague, Chief, Demographic Statistics Section

*Division for Public Economics and Public Administration
of the United Nations Secretariat*

Larry Willmore

*Outreach Programme Fellows of the Population Division
of the United Nations Secretariat*

Dirgha J. Ghimire, Population Studies Center, University of Michigan, Ann Arbor, Michigan,
United States of America

Ismael Ortega-Sanchez, Department of Agricultural Economics, Penn State University, University
Park, Pennsylvania, United States of America

Padma Srinivasan, Department of Sociology, Bowling Green State University, Bowling Green,
Ohio, United States of America

ANNEX III

List of documents

Symbol	Title/author
Background papers	
UN/POP/PRA/2000/1	Replacement migration: is it a solution to declining and ageing populations? (Population Division of the United Nations Secretariat)
UN/POP/PRA/2000/2	Population ageing and population decline: government views and policies (Population Division of the United Nations Secretariat)
UN/POP/PRA/2000/3	The inversion of the age pyramid and the future population decline in France: implications and policy responses (Jean-Claude Chesnais)
UN/POP/PRA/2000/4	Policy responses to population ageing and population decline in France (Georges Tapinos)
UN/POP/PRA/2000/5	Demographic ageing and population decline in twenty-first-century Germany: consequences for the systems of social insurance (Herwig Birg)
UN/POP/PRA/2000/6	Policy responses to population ageing and population decline in Germany (Charlotte Höhn)
UN/POP/PRA/2000/7	Possible policy responses to population ageing and population decline: the case of Italy (Antonio Golini)

Symbol	Title/author
UN/POP/PRA/2000/8	Fewer and older Italians: more problems? Looking for solutions to the demographic question (Maria Rita Testa)
UN/POP/PRA/2000/9	Population policies and the coming of a hyper-aged and depopulating society: the case of Japan (Makoto Atoh)
UN/POP/PRA/2000/10	The impact of population decline and population ageing in Japan from the perspectives of social and labour policy (Yukiko Katsumata)
UN/POP/PRA/2000/11	Policy responses to population ageing and population decline in the Republic of Korea (Namhoon Cho)
UN/POP/PRA/2000/12	Policy responses to low fertility and population ageing in the Republic of Korea (Ik Ki Kim)
UN/POP/PRA/2000/13	Population decline and population ageing in the Russian Federation (Svetlana V. Nikitina)
UN/POP/PRA/2000/14	Replacement migration: is it a solution for the Russian Federation? (Anatoly Vishnevsky)
UN/POP/PRA/2000/15	Who's afraid of low support ratios? An unofficial response from the United Kingdom to the report of the Population Division of the United Nations Secretariat on replacement migration (David Coleman)
UN/POP/PRA/2000/16	Policy responses to population ageing and population decline: United Kingdom of Great Britain and Northern Ireland (Karen Dunnell)
UN/POP/PRA/2000/17	Long-range demographic projections and their implications for the United States of America (Michael S. Teitelbaum)
UN/POP/PRA/2000/18	Population ageing in the United States of America: retirement, reform and reality (Judith Treas)
UN/POP/PRA/2000/19	Looking for European demography, desperately? (Patrick Festy)
UN/POP/PRA/2000/20	Europe's demographic issues: fertility, household formation and replacement migration (Ron Lesthaeghe)
UN/POP/PRA/2000/21	Demographic ageing, employment growth and pension sustainability in the European Union: the option of migration (Constantinos Fotakis)
UN/POP/PRA/2000/22	Demographic change and the potential contribution of international migration (International Organization for Migration)
UN/POP/PRA/2000/23	On policy responses to population decline (Paul Demeny)

Symbol	Title/author

Information papers

UN/POP/PRA/2000/INF.1	Organization of work
UN/POP/PRA/2000/INF.2	List of participants
UN/POP/PRA/2000/INF.3	List of documents

Part Two

BACKGROUND PAPERS

POPULATION AGEING AND POPULATION DECLINE: GOVERNMENT VIEWS AND POLICIES

Population Division of the United Nations Secretariat

INTRODUCTION

The present background paper for the United Nations Expert Group Meeting on Policy Responses to Population Ageing and Population Decline discusses government views and policies on population growth, age composition of the population, and levels of fertility, mortality and international migration. The information is derived from a variety of sources: official replies of Governments to the United Nations Inquiries among Governments on Population and Development, national reports, official statements at population conferences, and material provided by government agencies as well as the world press. The data analysed cover the period of the last quarter of a century, from 1974 to 1999. The paper focuses on the eight countries considered in the report on replacement migration (United Nations, 2001a), namely, France, Germany, Italy, Japan, the Republic of Korea, the Russian Federation, the United Kingdom of Great Britain and Northern Ireland and the United States of America. Some general trends in government views and policies are discussed for the whole world and especially for 56 countries where the total fertility rate (TFR) was below replacement level in 1995-2000, and where 44 per cent of the world population currently lives.

The group of eight selected countries represents different regions: Asia, Europe and Northern America. It includes mostly developed countries, as well as a country in transition (the Russian Federation) and a developing country (the Republic of Korea). There is great diversity among these countries in many respects. They are different in terms of the way the labour market is regulated, employment, the size of the labour force and the size of elderly population, saving patterns, culture and institutional arrangements. Demographic parameters of ageing differ in terms of speed and intensity. In half of these countries, Italy, Germany, Japan and the Republic of Korea, ageing is proceeding particularly rapidly, while in the other half, the United States, France, the United Kingdom and the Russian Federation, it is proceeding more slowly. The group includes countries with some of the lowest fertility (Italy), lowest mortality (Japan) and highest immigration (the United States and Germany) in the world.

I. GOVERNMENT VIEWS ON THE POPULATION GROWTH RATE, THE AGE COMPOSITION OF THE POPULATION AND LEVELS OF FERTILITY, MORTALITY AND INTERNATIONAL MIGRATION

In response to very low levels of fertility in a growing number of countries, and the social and economic consequences of resultant population ageing and the potential for population decline, more countries are expressing concern about low rates of population growth (see tables 1 and 2). The proportion of Governments perceiving their growth rate to be too low, which had fallen from 25 per cent in 1974 to 11 per cent in 1993, increased to 15 per cent in 1999 (see table 1). These changes in government views since 1993—with more countries expressing concern about low rates of population growth—correspond to the changing demographic situation. During the last decade, in more and more countries, first the developed countries and lately some of the developing countries in Eastern and South-eastern Asia, couples are having on average fewer births than are necessary for generations to replace themselves. Hence, more and more countries are experiencing below replacement level fertility. As a result, population growth has begun declining in many of these countries, both in relative and in absolute terms.

TABLE 1.   GOVERNMENT VIEWS OF POPULATION GROWTH RATE, 1974-1999
(*Percentage of countries*)

Year	Too high	Satisfactory	Too low	Total	Number of countries
World					
1974	27.6	47.4	25.0	100.0	156
1983	36.3	45.2	18.5	100.0	168
1993	43.7	45.3	11.0	100.0	190
1999	41.0	44.0	15.0	100.0	193

Source: Population Policy Data Bank maintained by the Population Division of the United Nations Secretariat.

TABLE 2.   GOVERNMENT VIEWS OF POPULATION GROWTH RATE, BY LEVEL OF DEVELOPMENT, 1983-1999
(*Percentage of countries*)

Year	Too high	Satisfactory	Too low	Total	Number of countries
More developed regions					
1983	0.0	69.2	30.8	100.0	39
1993	1.8	85.7	12.5	100.0	56
1999	2.1	62.5	35.4	100.0	48
Less developed regions					
1983..............	47.3	38.0	14.7	100.0	129
1993..............	61.2	28.4	10.4	100.0	134
1999..............	53.8	37.9	8.3	100.0	145

Source: Population Policy Data Bank maintained by the Population Division of the United Nations Secretariat.

Almost two thirds of countries, which viewed population growth as too low in 1999, have below replacement level fertility. They are primarily located in Europe: nine countries in Eastern Europe, four in Southern Europe, three in Northern Europe and one country in Western Europe. The other third of the countries viewing their population growth as too low are scattered in Oceania (four countries), Western Asia (three countries), Africa (two countries) and Latin America (one country). In Europe, the Governments of Austria, Lithuania, the Russian Federation and Slovakia, which considered population growth to be satisfactory in 1993, shifted to a view of it as too low in 1999 (see table 3). The greatest shift in views with regard to population growth occurred among the successor countries of the former Union of Soviet Socialist Republics (USSR) and in Eastern Europe. Many of these countries considered their population growth to be satisfactory in 1993 but, by 1999, all countries of Eastern Europe (except the Czech Republic) and two thirds of the countries of the former USSR considered it to be too low. Among the eight selected countries, the Government of the Russian Federation, where population size has been declining since the early 1990s, views population growth as too low, and the Governments of Italy and the Republic of Korea view it as satisfactory, while the other five Governments express no official position.

During recent decades, in addition to Governments' growing dissatisfaction with declining population growth, an increasing number of countries are concerned with issues of population ageing. In the most recent (eighth) United Nations Inquiry among Governments on perceptions and policies in reference to population and development (United Nations, 2001b), for the first time, a question was asked regarding Governments' views on population ageing. Of the 90 countries that responded to the Inquiry, 66 countries (81 per cent) were concerned with population ageing. Among them, 31 countries (38 per cent) considered the ageing of the population to be a major concern. The developed countries were most concerned with population ageing. Among them, Australia, Austria, Belarus, Belgium, Croatia, Estonia, Germany, Greece, Japan, Latvia, Lithuania, Poland, Romania, the Russian Federation, Slovakia and Yugoslavia (53 per cent) all indicated that population ageing was a major concern. All of these countries have below-replacement fertility. Among the developing countries, seven countries with below replacement level fertility (Armenia, China, Cyprus, Mauritius, Thailand, Trinidad and Tobago and Republic of Korea) and seven countries with higher fertility (Bangladesh, Brazil, Dominica, the Dominican Republic, Ghana, Iraq and Kazakhstan) (29 per cent) indicated that population ageing was of major concern.

Among the eight selected countries, there is great variety in how ageing is regarded. Germany, Japan, the Republic of Korea and the Russian Federation have significant concern, while Italy and the United Kingdom indicated minor concern. France and the United States expressed no official position. At the same time, France, as well as Germany, Japan, the Republic of Korea and the Russian Federation, has major concern with older age groups and their special needs. Half of the countries—Germany, Japan, the Republic of Korea and the Russian Federation—had major concern with the working-age group (see table 4).

For the German Government, for example, the problem of population ageing presents a major political challenge, since changes in age structure

TABLE 3. GOVERNMENT VIEWS OF POPULATION GROWTH RATE IN EIGHT COUNTRIES, 1974-1999

Year	France	Germany	Italy	Japan	Republic of Korea	Russian Federation	United Kingdom	United States
1974	Too low	Satisfactory	Satisfactory	Satisfactory	Too high	Too low	Satisfactory	Satisfactory
1983	Too low	Too low	Satisfactory	Satisfactory	Too high	Too low	Satisfactory	Satisfactory
1993	Satisfactory	Satisfactory	Satisfactory	Satisfactory	Satisfactory	Satisfactory	Satisfactory	Satisfactory
1999	Satisfactory	Satisfactory	Satisfactory	Satisfactory	Satisfactory	Too low	Satisfactory	Satisfactory

Source: Population Policy Data Bank maintained by the Population Division of the United Nations Secretariat.

TABLE 4. GOVERNMENT VIEWS OF THE AGE COMPOSITION AND THE AGEING OF THE POPULATION IN EIGHT COUNTRIES, 1999

Variable	France	Germany	Italy	Japan	Republic of Korea	Russian Federation	United Kingdom	United States
Age group								
Youth	Minor concern	Major concern	Not a concern	Major concern	Minor concern	Major concern	Minor concern	Not a concern
Working-age population	Minor concern	Major concern	Not a concern	Major concern	Major concern	Major concern	Minor concern	Not a concern
Older persons	Major concern	Major concern	Minor concern	Major concern	Major concern	Major concern	Minor concern	Not a concern
Population ageing	No official position	Major concern	Minor concern	Major concern	Major concern	Major concern	Minor concern	No official position

Source: Population Policy Data Bank maintained by the Population Division of the United Nations Secretariat.

will have repercussions in many areas. The Government considers it of critical importance that the number of years people work be increased, and early retirement restricted. The Government also considers that older workers must remain part of the labour force longer than today through lifelong learning, greater flexibility and mobility, and options for gradual transition to retirement. Also, for the Japanese Government, population ageing is the first priority among population issues. Faced with a rapidly ageing population, Japan considers it essential to provide services for the elderly.

The Government of the United Kingdom is especially concerned with an anticipated steadily increasing demand for long-term care, related to the growth in number of the oldest old, and significant increases in costs in coming years, especially after 2020. There is considerable debate over whether future cohorts of elderly people will be more or less healthy than elderly people today. In Italy, while there is no special attention being paid to population growth and population size in relation to economic and social development, ageing has recently become an issue of Government concern, particularly in relation to a possible crisis of the social security system and health-care system. Attention is paid to enhancing the ability of families to take care of elderly people according to Italian value systems.

In the United States, the Government has not sought to determine the most desirable balance among population age groups or to design policies to influence the balance. However, President Clinton in his State of the Union address in 1998 proposed a "dialogue" on the future of Social Security. The politics of social security were at the centre of debate during the year 2000 presidential campaigns in the United States as well as in many European parliaments. Some politicians in the United States want to address the low rate of personal savings and to encourage more private savings as well as private investing (within Social Security or outside of it).

In the Russian Federation, President Putin in his 2000 State of the Nation address to the Federal Assembly characterized the current demographic situation in the country as most alarming. He referred to the fact that many people found it difficult to bring up their children and ensure a befitting old age to their parents, and that the number of citizens of the Russian Federation was becoming smaller and smaller with every passing year. He concluded: "If the current trend persists, the nation's survival will be threatened. We are facing a real threat of becoming an ageing nation" (Putin, 2000).

Regarding perceptions of fertility, the proportion of Governments that viewed their fertility as too low increased from 11 per cent in 1976 to 17 per cent in 1999. In addition to one country in Africa (Gabon), one in South America (Uruguay), one in South-central Asia (Kazakhstan), two in South-eastern Asia (Japan and Singapore) and four in Western Asia (Armenia, Cyprus, Georgia and Israel), all of the other countries that viewed their fertility level as too low were located in various subregions of Europe: Belarus, Bulgaria, the Czech Republic, Hungary, Poland, Romania, the Russian Federation, Slovakia and Ukraine in Eastern Europe; Estonia, Latvia and Lithuania in Northern Europe; Bosnia and Herzegovina, Croatia, Greece, Italy, Portugal, Slovenia and Spain in Southern Europe; and Austria, France, Germany, Luxembourg and

Switzerland in Western Europe (see table 5). Some 52 per cent (29 countries) of the group with below replacement level fertility consider fertility to be too low. The other four countries, which have the same view, despite their higher fertility, are Gabon, Israel, Kazakhstan and Uruguay. Five of the eight selected countries view their fertility level as too low, while the Republic of Korea, the United Kingdom and the United States view it as satisfactory (see table 6).

The German Government does not, however, regard it as necessary to adopt a target for future birth rates, and considers it important to maintain freedom of decision for parents about the number and spacing of their children, and to eliminate impediments to having additional children. The Japanese Government considers that the tendency of the young to delay marriage, related to difficulties of balancing work and child-rearing, is the direct cause of the country's declining fertility rate. Therefore, the Government considers it necessary to make concerted efforts both to alleviate problems arising from the strains of balancing work and childcare and to enhance society's support for raising children.

Declining mortality is becoming increasingly important as a determinant of further population ageing. Life expectancy has improved greatly over the last half-century in the countries examined, with the exception of the Russian Federation. For example, Japan, from 1950-1955 to 1995-2000, has experienced a 16-year increase in life expectancy at birth. However, despite the considerable progress that has been made in combating morbidity and mortality, the percentage of countries worldwide that consider their level of mortality to be unacceptable has decreased very little during the last quarter of a century. Obviously, the target level of countries with regard to life expectancy is increasing. Among the eight countries considered, only half view their life expectancy as acceptable (France, Germany, Italy and Japan) (see table 7). The United States in 1976 and 1983 considered its life expectancy to be acceptable, but later shifted its view to "unacceptable". This view is shared by three other countries: the Republic of Korea, the Russian Federation and the United Kingdom.

International migration was a topic of secondary concern for most Governments in the early 1970s. However, with the economic recession that followed the first oil shock, Governments' concerns over the consequences of both immigration and emigration significantly increased. The proportion of Governments that viewed immigration as too high rose from 7 per cent in 1976 to 20 per cent in 1986 and remained at this level in 1999. Migration concerns were strongest in the developed countries in which, by 1999, 27 per cent of Governments considered immigration levels to be too high, compared with 17 per cent in 1976. Thirty per cent (17 countries) of the group with below-replacement fertility considered immigration to be too high and only 2 countries viewed it as too low (the Republic of Moldova and Ukraine), while the remaining countries viewed it as satisfactory. Among the eight selected countries, France, Germany and the Russian Federation viewed immigration as too high; the United Kingdom for a long period considered immigration to be too high and shifted to a view of it as satisfactory in 1999, joining the other four countries holding this view (see tables 8 and 9).

TABLE 5. POPULATION GROWTH RATES, TOTAL FERTILITY RATES, AND GOVERNMENT VIEWS AND POLICIES ON POPULATION GROWTH, FERTILITY AND IMMIGRATION

Country	Annual growth rate (percentage) 1995-2000	Total fertility rate (per woman) 1995-2000	Population growth View 1999	Population growth Policy 1999	Fertility View 1999	Fertility Policy 1999	Immigration View 1999	Immigration Policy 1999
Africa								
Eastern Africa								
Mauritius.........	0.8	1.9	Satisfactory	Lower	Satisfactory	No intervention	Satisfactory	No intervention
Asia								
Eastern Asia								
China............	0.9	1.8	Too high	Lower	Satisfactory	Maintain	Satisfactory	Maintain
Japan............	0.2	1.4	Satisfactory	No intervention	Too low	No intervention	Satisfactory	Maintain
DPR of Korea[a]	1.6	2.1	Satisfactory	No intervention	Satisfactory	Maintain	Satisfactory	Maintain
Republic of Korea ..	0.8	1.7	Satisfactory	No intervention	Satisfactory	No intervention	Satisfactory	Maintain
Sri Lanka.........	1.0	2.1	Too high	Lower	Satisfactory	Lower	Satisfactory	Lower
South-eastern Asia								
Singapore	1.4	1.7	Satisfactory	Maintain	Too low	Raise	Satisfactory	Raise
Thailand	0.9	1.7	Satisfactory	No intervention	Satisfactory	Maintain	Too high	Lower
Western Asia								
Armenia..........	-0.3	1.7	Too low	Raise	Too low	Raise	Too high	Lower
Azerbaijan........	0.5	2.0	Satisfactory	No intervention	Satisfactory	Maintain	Satisfactory	No intervention
Cyprus	1.1	2.0	Too low	No intervention	Too low	Raise	Too high	Lower
Georgia	-1.1	1.9	Too low	No intervention	Too low	Raise	Satisfactory	No intervention
Europe								
Eastern Europe								
Belarus	-0.3	1.4	Too low	Raise	Too low	Raise	Too high	Lower
Bulgaria..........	-0.7	1.2	Too low	Raise	Too low	Raise	Satisfactory	Maintain
Czech Republic.....	-0.2	1.2	Satisfactory	No intervention	Too low	Raise	Too high	Maintain
Hungary..........	-0.4	1.4	Too low	Raise	Too low	Raise	Too high	Maintain
Poland...........	0.1	1.5	Too low	Raise	Too low	Raise	Satisfactory	Maintain
Republic of Moldova	0.0	1.8	Too low	Raise	Satisfactory	No intervention	Too low	Raise

TABLE 5 (continued)

Country	Annual growth rate (percentage) 1995-2000	Total fertility rate (per woman) 1995-2000	Population growth View 1999	Population growth Policy 1999	Fertility View 1999	Fertility Policy 1999	Immigration View 1999	Immigration Policy 1999
Romania	-0.4	1.2	Too low	Raise	Too low	Raise	Satisfactory	Maintain
Russian Federation	-0.2	1.4	Too low	Raise	Too low	Raise	Too high	Raise
Slovakia	0.1	1.4	Too low	Raise	Too low	Raise	Satisfactory	Lower
Ukraine	-0.4	1.4	Too low	Raise	Too low	Raise	Too low	Maintain
Northern Europe								
Denmark	0.3	1.7	Satisfactory	No intervention	Satisfactory	No intervention	Too high	Lower
Estonia	-1.2	1.3	Too low	No intervention	Too low	No intervention	Satisfactory	Maintain
Finland	0.3	1.7	Satisfactory	No intervention	Satisfactory	No intervention	Satisfactory	Maintain
Iceland	0.9	2.1	Satisfactory	Maintain	Satisfactory	Maintain	Satisfactory	No intervention
Ireland	0.7	1.9	Satisfactory	No intervention	Satisfactory	Maintain	Satisfactory	Maintain
Latvia	-1.5	1.3	Too low	No intervention	Too low	Maintain	Too high	Maintain
Lithuania	-0.3	1.4	Too low	Raise	Satisfactory	Raise	Satisfactory	Maintain
Norway	0.5	1.9	Satisfactory	No intervention	Satisfactory	No intervention	Satisfactory	Maintain
Sweden	0.3	1.6	Satisfactory	No intervention	Satisfactory	No intervention	Satisfactory	Maintain
United Kingdom	0.2	1.7	Satisfactory	No intervention	Satisfactory	No intervention	Satisfactory	Lower
Southern Europe								
Bosnia and Herzegovina	3.0	1.4	Too low	No intervention	Too low	No intervention	Satisfactory	No intervention
Croatia	-0.1	1.6	Satisfactory	Raise the rate	Too low	Raise	Satisfactory	No intervention
Greece	0.3	1.3	Too low	No intervention	Too low	No intervention	Satisfactory	Lower
Italy	-0.0	1.2	Satisfactory	No intervention	Satisfactory	No intervention	Satisfactory	Maintain
Malta	0.7	1.9	Satisfactory	No intervention	Too low	No intervention	Satisfactory	Lower
Portugal	0.0	1.4	Too low	No intervention	Too low	No intervention	Satisfactory	Lower
Slovenia	-0.1	1.3	Satisfactory	Raise the rate	Too low	Raise	Too high	Lower
Spain	0.0	1.2	Satisfactory	No intervention	Too low	No intervention	Satisfactory	Maintain
TFYR Macedonia[b]	0.6	2.1	Too high	Lower the rate	Too high	Lower	Too high	Lower
Yugoslavia	0.1	1.8	Satisfactory	Maintain the rate	Satisfactory	Maintain	Too high	No intervention

Western Europe								
Austria	0.5	1.4	Too low	No intervention	Too low	Raise	Too high	Lower
Belgium	0.1	1.6	Satisfactory	No intervention	Satisfactory	No intervention	Satisfactory	Maintain
France	0.4	1.7	Satisfactory	No intervention	Too low	No intervention	Too high	Lower
Germany	0.1	1.3	Satisfactory	Maintain the rate	Too low	Raise	Too high	Lower
Luxembourg	1.1	1.7	Satisfactory	No intervention	Satisfactory	No intervention	Too high	Lower
Netherlands	0.4	1.5	Satisfactory	No intervention	Too low	No intervention	Satisfactory	No intervention
Switzerland	0.7	1.5	Satisfactory	No intervention	Too low	No intervention	Too high	Lower
Latin America and the Caribbean								
Barbados	0.5	1.5	Satisfactory	No intervention	Satisfactory	No intervention	Satisfactory	No intervention
Cuba	0.4	1.6	Satisfactory	No intervention	Satisfactory	No intervention	Satisfactory	Maintain
Trinidad and Tobago	0.5	1.7	Too high	Lower	Too high	Lower	Satisfactory	Maintain
Northern America								
Canada	1.0	1.6	Satisfactory	No intervention	Satisfactory	No intervention	Satisfactory	Maintain
United States of America	0.8	2.0	Satisfactory	No intervention	Satisfactory	No intervention	Satisfactory	Maintain
Oceania								
Australia	1.0	1.8	Satisfactory	No intervention	Satisfactory	No intervention	Satisfactory	Maintain
New Zealand	1.0	2.0	Satisfactory	No intervention	Satisfactory	No intervention	Satisfactory	Maintain

Sources: World Population Prospects: The 1998 Revision, vol. I, Comprehensive Tables (United Nations publication, Sales No. E.99.XIII.9); and Population Policy Data Bank maintained by the Population Division of the United Nations Secretariat.

a Democratic People's Republic of Korea.

b The former Yugoslav Republic of Macedonia.

TABLE 6. GOVERNMENT VIEWS OF FERTILITY LEVEL IN EIGHT COUNTRIES, 1976-1999

Year	France	Germany	Italy	Japan	Republic of Korea	Russian Federation	United Kingdom	United States
1976	Too low	Too low	Satisfactory	Satisfactory	Too high	Satisfactory	Satisfactory	Satisfactory
1983	Too low	Too low	Satisfactory	Satisfactory	Too high	Satisfactory	Satisfactory	Satisfactory
1993	Too low	Too low	Satisfactory	Too low	Satisfactory	Too low	Satisfactory	Satisfactory
1999	Too low	Too low	Too low	Too low	Satisfactory	Too low	Satisfactory	Satisfactory

Source: Population Policy Data Bank maintained by the Population Division of the United Nations Secretariat.

TABLE 7. ACCEPTABILITY OF LIFE EXPECTANCY IN EIGHT COUNTRIES, 1976-1999

Year	France	Germany	Italy	Japan	Republic of Korea	Russian Federation	United Kingdom	United States
1976	Unacceptable	Acceptable	Unacceptable	Acceptable	Unacceptable	Unacceptable	Unacceptable	Acceptable
1983	Acceptable	Acceptable	Unacceptable	Acceptable	Unacceptable	Acceptable	Unacceptable	Acceptable
1993	Acceptable	Acceptable	Acceptable	Acceptable	Unacceptable	Unacceptable	Unacceptable	Unacceptable
1999	Acceptable	Acceptable	Acceptable	Acceptable	Unacceptable	Unacceptable	Unacceptable	Unacceptable

Source: Population Policy Data Bank maintained by the Population Division of the United Nations Secretariat.

TABLE 8. GOVERNMENT VIEWS OF IMMIGRATION LEVEL IN EIGHT COUNTRIES, 1976-1999

Year	France	Germany	Italy	Japan	Republic of Korea	Russian Federation	United Kingdom	United States
1976	Satisfactory	Satisfactory	Satisfactory	Satisfactory	Satisfactory	Satisfactory	Too high	Satisfactory
1983	Too high	Too high	Too high	Satisfactory	Satisfactory	Satisfactory	Too high	Too high
1993	Too high	Too high	Satisfactory	Satisfactory	Satisfactory	Too high	Too high	Satisfactory
1999	Too high	Too high	Satisfactory	Satisfactory	Satisfactory	Too high	Satisfactory	Satisfactory

Source: Population Policy Data Bank maintained by the Population Division of the United Nations Secretariat.

TABLE 9. GOVERNMENT VIEWS AND POLICIES ON INTERNATIONAL MIGRATION IN EIGHT COUNTRIES, 1999

Variable	France	Germany	Italy	Japan	Republic of Korea	Russian Federation	United Kingdom	United States
Immigration								
View	Too high	Too high	Satisfactory	Satisfactory	Satisfactory	Too high	Satisfactory	Satisfactory
Policy								
Immigration for permanent settlement	Lower	Lower	Maintain	Maintain	Maintain	Raise	Maintain	Maintain
Entry of persons on non-permanent work permits	Maintain	Lower	Raise	Maintain	Maintain	Maintain	Maintain	Maintain
Entry of dependants of persons on work permits	Maintain	Lower	Maintain	Maintain	Maintain	No intervention	Maintain	Maintain
Entry of refugees	Maintain	Lower	Maintain	Maintain	Maintain	Lower	Maintain	Maintain
Entry of asylum-seekers	Maintain	Lower	Maintain	Maintain	Maintain	Halt	Maintain	Maintain
Entry of undocumented or illegal migrants	Halt	Halt	Halt	Halt	Halt	Halt	Halt	Halt
Integration of non-nationals	Yes	Yes	Yes	No intervention	No intervention	Yes	Yes	Yes
Emigration								
View	Satisfactory	Satisfactory	Satisfactory	Satisfactory	Satisfactory	Satisfactory	Satisfactory	Satisfactory
Policy	Raise	No intervention	No intervention	No intervention	Maintain	No intervention	No intervention	No intervention
Encouraging the return of nationals	No intervention	No intervention	No intervention	No intervention	No intervention	Yes	No intervention	No intervention

Source: Population Policy Data Bank maintained by the Population Division of the United Nations Secretariat.

The United Kingdom considered it to be important to have firm control over immigration and to make sure that all staff applying the government immigration policy observed central principles of being fair, fast and firm. The German Government felt that, in the light of the causes for increasing global migration, efforts should be made to control and limit immigration into the European Union (EU) and particularly into Germany. This applied primarily to preventing foreigners from entering the country illegally in order to settle therein permanently.

This view was shared by the European Commission. In 1994, a Communication by the Commission on asylum law highlighted the necessity of limiting the admission of foreigners. It said that, in the light of the economic situation and the situation on the labour market, the admission of foreigners must continue to be restrictive. In the short term, quotas did not represent a suitable measure. It also held that a longer-term strategy for employment-related immigration would have to take into account economic development and the situation in the labour market. In the view of the Commission, there was at that time no demand for the admission of foreigners into the member States of EU.

Immigration has not been considered in relation to population ageing. Only recently have Governments started to consider immigration as an instrument to offset fiscal burdens and to solve labour-market problems associated with ageing populations. However, some Governments realize that immigration as a strategy to deal with population ageing will have to remain at high levels permanently in order to reduce the fiscal burden of ageing, because migrants will also retire. Moreover, large immigration flows will require social adjustments.

II. POLICY INTERVENTIONS IN RESPONSE TO POPULATION DECLINE AND POPULATION AGEING

A. *Population growth policies*

The proportion of Governments that had policies aimed at influencing population growth increased from 45 per cent in 1974 to 63 per cent in 1993 (see table 10). By 1999, this proportion had declined to 58 per cent mainly owing to the fact that the proportion of Governments of developed countries intervening to influence population growth declined between 1983 and 1999: a number of countries with policies to raise or maintain the rate of population growth shifted to a policy of non-intervention (see table 11). Among the eight countries considered, there are no countries, with the exception of the Russian Federation, that have a pro–population growth policy (see table 12). France and Italy shifted to a policy of non-intervention and five other countries in the group, Germany, Japan, the Republic of Korea, the United Kingdom and the United States, do not have any explicit policy in relation to population growth.

TABLE 10. GOVERNMENT POLICIES ON POPULATION GROWTH RATE, 1974-1999

(*Percentage of countries*)

Year	Lower	Maintain	Raise	No intervention	Total	Number of countries
World						
1974.	25.0	0.0	19.9	55.1	100.0	156
1983	25.6	13.5	19.0	41.9	100.0	168
1993	37.9	13.1	11.6	37.4	100.0	190
1999	38.8	8.3	10.5	42.4	100.0	193

Source: Population Policy Data Bank maintained by the Population Division of the United Nations Secretariat.

TABLE 11. GOVERNMENT POLICIES ON POPULATION GROWTH RATE, BY LEVEL OF DEVELOPMENT, 1983-1999

(*Percentage of countries*)

Year	Lower	Maintain	Raise	No intervention	Total	Number of countries
More developed regions						
1983	0.0	28.2	30.8	41.0	100.0	39
1993	1.8	33.9	16.1	48.2	100.0	56
1999	2.1	10.4	22.9	64.6	100.0	48
Less developed regions						
1983	33.3	9.3	15.5	41.9	100.0	129
1993	53.0	4.5	9.7	32.8	100.0	134
1999	51.0	7.6	6.2	35.2	100.0	145

Source: Population Policy Data Bank maintained by the Population Division of the United Nations Secretariat.

In contrast, the Russian Federation and many other Governments, especially in Eastern Europe (Bulgaria, Poland, the Republic of Moldova, Romania and Slovakia) as well as some in Southern Europe (Slovenia) and Asia (Armenia and Kazakhstan) have recently inaugurated policies to modify the current demographic situation, increase population growth and reverse population decline. All of these countries had below-replacement fertility in 1995-2000, except Kazakhstan.

In 1999, 75 Governments (39 per cent) had policies aimed at lowering population growth, while 20 (11 per cent) had policies aimed at increasing population growth (see table 10). The proportion of Governments that had policies aimed at increasing population growth had declined from 19 per cent in 1983 to 11 per cent in 1999. However, in more developed regions, it increased from 16 per cent in 1993 to 23 per cent in 1999 (see table 11). Government policies do not always match their satisfaction with demographic parameters. For example, the proportion of Governments that had policies aimed at raising population growth was less than the proportion of those that viewed population growth as too low (see tables 1 and 10). Many Governments with below-

TABLE 12. GOVERNMENT POLICIES ON POPULATION GROWTH IN EIGHT COUNTRIES, 1974-1999

Year	France	Germany	Italy	Japan	Republic of Korea	Russian Federation	United Kingdom	United States
1974.........	Raise	No intervention	No intervention	No intervention	Lower	Raise	No intervention	No intervention
1983.........	Raise	No intervention	Maintain	No intervention	Lower	Raise	No intervention	No intervention
1993.........	Raise	No intervention	No intervention	No intervention	Lower	No intervention	No intervention	No intervention
1999.........	No intervention	No intervention	No intervention	No intervention	No intervention	Raise	No intervention	No intervention

Source: Population Policy Data Bank maintained by the Population Division of the United Nations Secretariat.

49

replacement fertility, including France and the Republic of Korea, pointed out that the chief objective in modifying the fertility level was to improve family well-being, not to modify the rate of population growth.

B. *Ageing policies*

According to the fourth United Nations review and appraisal of the implementation of the International Plan of Action on Ageing (United Nations, 1982, chap. VI, sect. A), the majority of developed countries and an increasing number of developing countries have in place a range of policies and programmes that respond to population ageing. In addition, non-governmental organizations have increased efforts to address ageing issues in those countries (United Nations, 1997). At the same time, there are still many countries that do not have effective policies to address ageing, especially in the areas of social security benefits, specific health needs and public recognition of lifelong and continuing contributions of older people to the human, social and economic capital of countries. The observance of the International Year of Older Persons in 1999 offered a further incentive for the application of such a policy framework. Therefore, many countries are currently re-examining their policies in the light of the principle that elderly people constitute an important component of a society's human resources. They are also seeking to identify how best to assist elderly people with long-term support needs.

Employment and income security policies

In order to reduce the cost pressure associated with population ageing, and to slow the rate of growth in demand placed on public pension systems, some countries are gradually increasing the age at which workers become eligible for retirement benefits. In Japan, 1994 legislation increased in stages the age of eligibility for the full flat benefit (the "National Pension") from 60 to 65, by 2013 for men and by 2018 for women. In 1999, the Government announced its intention to institute a similar increase with respect to the other part of the retirement benefit—the earnings-related pension, fully effective in 2025 for men and in 2030 for women. Germany has raised the age for full benefits from age 60-63 (depending on the circumstances surrounding retirement) to age 65. The Government allows many people to collect reduced benefits at the earlier age. It intends to gradually raise the age of initial eligibility for retirement benefits to 62 by 2012, and only those with 35 years of service will be eligible for reduced benefits. In the United States, the 1983 amendments to the Social Security Act raised the age of eligibility for full Social Security benefits from 65 to 67. However, the increase will be phased in over a 27-year period beginning with workers turning age 62 in the year 2000.

Among other common adjustments to population ageing have been: equalizing retirement ages for men and women by raising the retirement age for women (United Kingdom), tightening eligibility requirements for full benefits (France) or for early retirement benefits (Germany, Italy), reducing full benefit levels (France, Germany, Italy, Japan, United Kingdom) or early retirement pensions (Germany, Italy) and increasing contribution rates (Japan).

A variety of benefit reductions have been introduced. Germany and Japan have changed the index used to adjust benefits after retirement and switched from indexing benefits to the rate of growth of gross wages to indexing them to the rate of growth of net wages (earnings net of taxes and social insurance contributions). A demographic factor was added in 1997 (to be effective in 1999) that gradually reduced the replacement rates of newly retiring workers to reflect gains in life expectancy; however, that provision has since been suspended. In Italy, a demographic adjuster has been introduced according to which the benefit schedule is to be adjusted every 10 years to fully offset projected changes in life expectancy after retirement. Also, benefits for the self-employed are reduced relative to those of employees to correspond more closely to the lower contribution rate paid by the self-employed.

To reduce the size of the benefit associated with retirement at the normal age, France is increasing the number of years (to 25 by 2008) over which earnings are averaged. Japan intends to phase in a 5 per cent reduction. Germany has announced an increase in the retirement age from 63 to 65, while introducing permanently reduced benefits available at the previous ages. In Italy and the United Kingdom, benefits under the State earnings-related scheme have begun to be based on lifetime earnings, rather than on the previous five years (in Italy) or the 20 highest years (in the United Kingdom). One of the key elements of pension reforms in Italy and the United Kingdom is a shift from defined benefits (the computation rules produce a monthly benefit that is paid for the life of the retiree and the initial impact of rising life expectancies is an increase in the total cost of the pension programme) to defined contribution arrangements (the computation rules spread the available account balance over the expected remaining life of the retiree and the initial impact of rising life expectancies is a reduction in the monthly income of the retiree). The latter approach is likely to be more effective in constraining costs because it produces automatic benefit reductions (Thompson, 1999).

To offset the impact of population ageing, some countries increase the amount of revenue going into the pension system. Japan increased combined employer-employee rates (to 17.35 per cent in 1994-1996) and intends to moderately increase them every five years until 2025 in order to finance scheduled benefits. In order to avoid or reduce the pension contribution increases, Germany has increased the budget subsidy for its pension programme from 20 to 25 per cent of outlays. The 1999 reform package announced by the Japanese Government also includes an increase in the budget subsidy intended to support the flat benefit portion of its retirement income system.

Some countries are moving towards a greater reliance on advance funding of the pension promises. This involves acquiring financial assets that generate investment returns and provide an ongoing source of revenue for covering pension payments. It allows a given level of future pensions to be financed with lower contribution rates. Many current reforms shift a portion of the responsibility for managing pension arrangements from the Government to private enterprises or to individuals. The United States has one of the world's most extensive private pension systems, and funded private pensions are relatively common there (Peterson, 1999). Greater use of advance funding is being encouraged in the private pension sectors of Germany and Japan, which had previously relied heavily on book reserve financing. The Government of the United Kingdom also proposed to establish a "stakeholder pension scheme", which appears to be an advance-funded, defined-contribution arrangement with low administrative costs.

In the Russian Federation, there has also been reform of the State pension system. It originally assumed a full replacement of the distributive system of pension provision with an accumulative system. However, in 1998, the Government adopted the programme of pension provision of mixed type: obligatory State pension provision and additional non-State pension provision. The later system appeared in the country in the early 1990s and its successes have been very modest. A major concern in the Russian Federation has been over the low level of and delays in pension payments, high inflation and loss of tax-collecting capacity. An effective pension reform will require macroeconomic stabilization, renewed economic growth, and development of legal and administrative systems adapted to a market economy based on private enterprise. The implementation of the pension reform also requires a lot of preparatory educational and informative work with the entire population on the part of the Government. The Russian Federation is currently preparing a policy to address the needs of senior citizens. The policy under consideration would focus on property, land and housing concerns, as well as improved social services for the elderly.

Many Governments try to increase incentives for people either to delay accepting retirement benefits or to continue working after they have started to receive them. For example, special reductions are introduced that apply only to workers who take benefits before the normal retirement age. In Italy, a schedule of adjustment factors is implemented that scales monthly benefits to the worker's expected remaining lifespan at the time benefits are first received. Some countries that limit the earnings of persons receiving retirement benefits have reduced the penalty on continued work to increase incentives for people to work and to make continued pension contributions after having started receiving benefits.

Despite government efforts to encourage people to work longer, there is a trend towards ever earlier retirement in Europe, as in the United States. Generous public pensions together with high unemployment in many European countries have increased the appeal of early retirement and expanding employment opportunities for younger people. In France, for example, during the 1970s, there was a large increase in the specific allowance for people aged 65 years or over, which guaranteed a minimum level of income for older people. Many people at about age 60 have benefited from pre-retirement contracts with good financial conditions. In addition, the proportion of retired women who receive their own pension has increased. Currently, the mean income per capita is higher for retired persons than for people aged 20-59 (Hourriez and Legris, 1995). In fact, in some countries, ageing people are even encouraged to retire early. Because of high unemployment, there is still an active policy of sending people into retirement earlier. Governments subsidize businesses for retiring older people and replacing them with younger workers. They subsidize the difference between full retirement benefits and the reduced benefits, for people who retire earlier.

Some Governments and businesses are already trying to adapt to a labour market in which many new jobs will have to be filled with retrained older workers instead of newly trained young ones. They are considering introducing "lifelong learning" policies to help older workers keep up with the increasing demands of the economy. A lifelong learning approach would have an impact on the labour market. For example, the pattern of working throughout the life cycle would be modified, since more time would be devoted to learning at all ages and workers would retire later. Some countries have already taken active measures in this direction. The United Kingdom has raised the maximum age of access to its "Training for Work" programme from 59 to 63 years (Whitting and others, 1995). In Japan, different subsidies have been introduced to employers who extend the employment of workers until age 65, or who maintain a specified minimum proportion of older workers (Organisation for Economic Cooperation and Development, 1995). In France and Germany, wage subsidies to encourage hiring older workers also exist (Whitting and others, 1995).

A number of Governments are going further and trying to introduce greater flexibility and mobility. Workers over age 65 are healthier and more educated than, for example, 30 years ago and can use their expertise and contribute intellectually. There are many people who do not want to retire but would prefer a more flexible organization of work. Germany, for example, is moving in this direction and looking for appropriate work organization and options for gradual transition to retirement. Other Governments have adopted a national policy of reducing the average workweek. This measure will provide workers with more time for the family, and a healthier life, and may lead to longer working years. France has recently had a campaign to cap the workweek at 35 hours (Peterson, 1999), though with the original intention of creating more employment opportunities for youth. Given the large international disparity in work habits, there is ample room for change in many countries. Average manufacturing work-hours in the United States are 20 per cent longer than in France; in Japan, they are 40 per cent longer than in Sweden (Peterson, 1999). Time is worth a lot more than money to many workers. In a recent national survey of the United States (by a Harris Poll that was commissioned by Fleet Boston Financial), by a margin of almost two to one, respondents said they would rather have more time off than be paid more money. According to the Bureau of Labor Statistics, the average employee works almost two more hours a week than in 1982. Over the same period, the proportion of married couples whose members both work has risen to 47 from 39 per cent, putting even more time pressure on families.

Governments can change retirement ages as a strategy to cope with labour shortages, but the role of the State in deciding when people retire is declining, and what really matters are the employment policies of transnational corporations. Currently, in the United States, businesses have begun to discover the value of hiring or retraining older workers. Those placements have been for specialized high-income as well as low-income jobs. The tight labour market, which has created intense competition for qualified employees at every level, is a new reality conditioned by intensive technological progress as well as shrinking numbers of young workers. Indeed, members of the baby-boom generation are approaching age 55 and soon will reach retirement age. They are healthier than their parents, and will live longer. Recent surveys by *Fortune* magazine and the American Association of Retired Persons (AARP) found that 74-80 per cent of them expect to still be working in retirement. A Harris Poll estimated that there are 4 million people over age 65 in the United States who would like to be working. People over age 65 could work at temporary jobs, or at home, using the Internet; moreover, companies would have a workforce that did not require office space, fixed salaries, pensions or health-care insurance.

Traditional biases of the recent past against older workers—that they are slow, less motivated than younger people, and technologically deficient—are gradually disappearing. A survey by Louis Harris pollsters of the human resource directors at some 800 American companies showed that 80 per cent of them agreed that there was less turnover among older workers than among younger ones; 74 per cent said that older workers had as much ability as younger workers in acquiring new skills; 62 per cent agreed that younger workers were actually less creative and less innovative than older workers; and 80 per cent said that younger workers had more absenteeism. Still, as a cost-saving mechanism, older workers are being let go because they are paid more than younger ones.

Some countries, such as Italy, Germany and the Republic of Korea, are trying to get working-age people to work in greater numbers, especially young adults and women. The French Government in the last decade started to implement measures to provide temporary jobs and part-time jobs, and to encourage enterprises to employ young people at lower salaries. The Italian Government also intends to alleviate increasing ageing costs without changing the social security system through a number of measures to increase employment of the youth. In the Republic of Korea, many highly educated women still become housewives instead of getting a job because of gender discrimination; the Government is working to create a more favourable working environment for women.

The Republic of Korea has experienced labour shortages of production workers, and especially of unskilled workers. In response, the Government has followed a policy of gradually phasing out low value added labour-intensive industries in favour of more capital-intensive industries. Also, the Government adopted the Employment Insurance system in 1995 as a way of solving the problems connected with unemployment and on-the-job training through offering job placement services, vocational training, and employment promotion programmes to unemployed workers. To solve the issue of shortages of skilled workers, economists in the Republic of Korea have proposed building flexible production systems and increasing investment for training multi-skilled workers. They also have emphasized the importance of on-the-job training of workers, and especially of learning from older, more experienced workers.

Past efforts of the Government with respect to older persons' employment (focused mainly on introducing various laws and regulations) have had limited success. Some employers, for example, prefer to pay fines rather than to employ the stipulated number of the elderly. Therefore, the Government intends to initiate stronger measures to enable a greater portion of the healthy and active elderly population to continue working, and to retrain older workers so that they can take up new occupations and cope with rapid technological change. In addition, in order to augment the labour supply, the Government is making efforts to further increase female participation in the labour force, especially in higher-skilled and better-paid jobs; and to support and complement private efforts to provide childcare facilities for female employees.

Health and long-term care policies

Policies to improve older people's health and well-being vary according to the particular country's economic, epidemiological, demographic, infrastructural and cultural conditions that influence the feasibility and effectiveness of public-health interventions. Most developed countries are experimenting with home health benefits. The Italian Government is now increasing both home care and day hospital care, in order to avoid the institutionalization of older persons, particularly those with physical or mental problems. It also intends to allow deductions for nurses and home health workers. The German Government has set up a separate agency with its own payroll tax revenue to provide long-term care benefits, and Japan intends to do something similar.

The United Kingdom published a Green Paper entitled "Our Healthier Nation" in 1998, setting out proposals for a new health strategy for England. It has two aims: to improve the health of the population as a whole by increasing the length of people's lives and the number of years free from illness; and to improve the health of the worst off and to narrow the health gap. To succeed, the strategy will need action at all levels—government, local and individual. The strategy proposes national targets on reducing deaths from particular causes. For each target, a national contract will suggest what each level can do to improve people's health. The strategy identifies three key settings for action: healthy schools, healthy workplaces and healthy neighbourhoods. Health Impact Assessments will monitor the effect on health of appropriate policies across levels of government.

An important policy direction of many Governments is the promotion of community participation in older people's health-care and social services. Some Governments encourage older persons to take responsibility for becoming the principal promoters of their own health. There is a rising tendency on the part of Governments to emphasize the role of the family in informal care in contrast with more formal and institutionalized care (United Nations, International Institute on Ageing, 1999). The trend towards shifting responsibilities from public support systems back to the family has increased the demand put on informal caregivers. Women are often caught in the middle of the needs of their children and their ageing parents. Furthermore, since women are increasingly entering the labour market, they have to cope with the double or triple burdens of caregiving, household work, and the needs of their families and the workplace.

In Germany, the family is regarded as the source of help of first recourse, and assistance is available from the welfare State only where that has failed. The responsibility of families, furthermore, is encoded in laws. In Austria, a "new old age policy" aims at a holistic intergenerational approach, which is to meet the need for social participation by the older as much as by the younger people. Priority is given to strengthening and extending intergenerational solidarity. Family members who provide long-term care to disabled or elderly family members and give up their job for this reason have the employer's share of the pension insurance paid from public funds, which reduces their pension insurance payments by about half. With the growing need for medical, social and nursing care, especially by the oldest old, and with the rise in the number of women holding full-time jobs, older people will have to make greater use of professional services in the future. The long-term care benefit provides the financial basis that allows people to have an independent life for as long as possible. Special support given to those who provide long-term care to the oldest old within the family is crucial, both to ensure the well-being of women (and some men) who provide care, and to meet the needs of older persons who depend upon care.

Some other developed countries have also introduced care insurance schemes, which compensate caregivers for the work they do. Finland, France and Sweden are willing to see caring as a form of work, and possibly as a form of paid work. The Governments of Canada and the United Kingdom are promoting an equal sharing of caregiving responsibilities between men and women and a better reconciliation of working and caregiving responsibilities. The Australian Government has passed a number of amendments to existing legislation to address discrimination on the grounds of family responsibilities, and to promote adoption of family-friendly employment practices that assist workers in successfully balancing their employment and family responsibilities. The amendments involve insertion of a provision for the Australian Industrial Relations Commission to determine standards for leave to care for sick family members. It allows employees to use their own sick leave to care for ill family members. It also allows employers and employees to negotiate more flexible access to up to one week's annual leave, to be taken in single days, make-up time arrangements, and unpaid leave. The Government has been working with caregivers to improve assistance through such measures as the income-tested Careers Pension and the Domiciliary Nursing Home Benefit, which provide assistance for people caring at home for those with nursing home-level care needs.

Although almost all industrialized countries provide old-age pensions for their elderly populations, most countries have shown considerable reluctance to pay cash benefits to the relatives who care for elderly or handicapped family members through the social security system. Australia, Canada and Sweden have cash payments for care providers, though the means or income tests applied to establish eligibility are tight. Germany is one of a few countries that have introduced a long-term care insurance programme targeted at the elderly and the chronically disabled. It provides to eligible persons medical and custodial care, either at home or in recognized institutions. For home care, the disabled person may choose to receive a cash benefit and to pay a family member for services provided, or alternatively to receive these services from a community-based system.

A.   *Fertility policies*

The steepness of the fertility decline determines the speed of the ageing process; it has been occurring fastest in Eastern Asia and in Southern and Eastern Europe. The pace of change is critical to the development of appropriate responses. Some Governments make direct or indirect policy interventions aimed at increasing fertility, though the measures applied to increase fertility had often only temporary effects. Other Governments try only to ease adaptation to the new circumstances. Only recently, some Governments have started to take multiple and more comprehensive actions to increase fertility, although these sometimes involve enormous costs. In addition, Governments have begun to realize the importance of removing existing obstacles to childbearing and child-rearing. This is certainly feasible, and there is considerable potential for it in many countries.

In 1999, two thirds of Governments worldwide had policies to modify the level of fertility. Thirteen per cent had policies aimed at raising fertility, and 9 per cent had policies aimed at maintaining the current level of fertility, while 45 per cent still had policies aimed at lowering fertility. It is worth noting that a Government's view of its level of fertility as too low or too high does not necessarily mean that a policy has been formulated to alter the level. A number of Governments, for example, that consider their level of fertility to be too low (Bosnia and Herzegovina, Estonia, France, Germany, Greece, Italy, Japan, Portugal, Spain and Switzerland) do not intervene to affect the fertility level. Among the eight countries considered, France, which consistently had a policy to raise fertility, and the Republic of Korea, which had, in 1993, a policy to maintain fertility, have both shifted to a policy of non-intervention, joining the other five countries in the group. In contrast, the Russian Federation has shifted its policy from no intervention to a policy to raise fertility (see table 13).

Some European countries have centred on helping families and working mothers by government-subsidized education and housing, and giving tax reductions according to the number of children. In the Scandinavian countries, for example, Sweden has been working for decades to identify and solidify policy interventions to reduce gender differences and enable both women and men to combine productive and reproductive lives, together or alone. Norway was one of the few developed countries not projected to experience fertility decline over the next 50 years. Over the past decade, the TFR has remained close to replacement level. The Government's "family-friendly" policies, aimed at both men and women, included: one year of parental leave with pay after each birth, at least one month of which had to be taken by the father; arrangements for reduced or flexible work hours for parents; and child allowances. It is not surprising that Scandinavian fertility has risen to levels somewhat above those prevailing elsewhere in Europe. However, even in these countries, more profound structural factors had contributed to restraining the rise of fertility to a higher level, including the persistence of gender inequalities that were

TABLE 13.   GOVERNMENT POLICIES ON FERTILITY IN EIGHT COUNTRIES, 1976-1999

Year	France	Germany	Italy	Japan	Republic of Korea	Russian Federation	United Kingdom	United States
1976	Raise	No intervention	No intervention	No intervention	Lower	Maintain	No intervention	No intervention
1983	Raise	No intervention	No intervention	No intervention	Lower	Raise	No intervention	No intervention
1993	Raise	No intervention	No intervention	No intervention	Maintain	No intervention	No intervention	No intervention
1999	No intervention	No intervention	No intervention	No intervention	No intervention	Raise	No intervention	No intervention

Source: Population Policy Data Bank maintained by the Population Division of the United Nations Secretariat.

entrenched in the overall social dynamics of a post-industrialized affluent society, and were not easy to change within democratic political systems. In Sweden, the educational campaign encouraging fathers to stay at home with their children was effective. Similar to those made by the Scandinavian countries, the Government of the Netherlands has made many recent strides in the areas of family-formation policy and addressing the problem of ageing and gender. It considers that it is now important to move away from an exclusive focus on the role of women and to include men, thus emphasizing a more couple-oriented approach. In that regard, the Government has developed several policy measures to guarantee men's involvement in childcare and child-rearing responsibilities.

The Government of France has had a family policy for several decades, more pronatalist than many other developed countries (with allowances increasing with the number of children and decreasing with the age of the children) (Bradshaw and others, 1993). The Government's 1997 decision that the family allowances were to become means-tested has brought the family policy once again to the centre of social and political debate. There are many facilities that enable women to continue working when they become mothers (maternity leave, part-time jobs and nursery schools). The labour-participation rate in France for women aged 25-49 is one of the highest in Europe; indeed, it was already 76 per cent in 1988. However, the proportion of working women employed part-time in 1992 was 24 per cent, which was lower than in the United Kingdom (45 per cent) and in Germany (31 per cent). However, temporary work is increasing in France, and 8 per cent of working women and 7 per cent of working men in 1994 had a temporary contract, a government-assisted job, paid training or a "non-standard" contract (Institut National de la Statistique et des Études Économiques, 1995).

At the same time, beginning in the 1980s, the relative economic situation of young adults became more difficult. It is reflected in the higher unemployment rate of people aged 15-29, which was recently about 20 per cent, as against 10 per cent for the active population over age 30. Overall inequality has been on the increase, partially owing to the emergence of underemployment, and of government-assisted jobs, often paid under the minimum legal level for wages (Toulemon, 1998). In France, as in a number of other European countries, the proportion of married people has decreased. Cohabitation without marriage has been becoming a lifestyle and a common type of union among young people. In addition, more and more young people live with their parents or relatives and remain unmarried.

The family policy of the German Government is devoted to creating a framework in which families enjoy the freedom to have and raise children as they see fit. The promotion of family planning activities is designed to enable young couples to determine for themselves when they want to have children. The Government introduced a child-raising allowance and child-raising leave to enable the parents to reconcile their child-raising duties with gainful employment. Since 1996, single parents bringing up at least one child and married couples with at least two children could deduct from their income, for tax purposes, the costs of household help. Since 1997, the monthly family allowance for the first and the second child and the annual tax abatement for dependent children were raised.

Recently, the family-related measures of tax law and transfer law have been supplemented and further developed. In the case of the equalization of family benefits and the promotion of homeownership, they have been basically reformed. In their entirety, these measures constitute an essential and effective contribution to helping families in raising children. New regulations of the Reform Law of the Childhood Law came into effect in 1998, removing any legal differences between children born in and out of wedlock. To equalize the burdens of families, the child allowance for the first and second child was increased. The Supreme Constitutional Court instructed the legislature to introduce stronger fiscal relief measures for families, and in particular to grant all families additional tax-free allowances for raising children, to be implemented not later than early 2000. Before 2002, married couples with children should receive the same tax-free allowance for household management, which is currently granted only to a non-married parent.

In Italy, the Government has not been able to keep pace with a rapid increase in jobs for women in terms of legislation, facilities and the organization of work and services to cater to the new position of women. In addition, family allowances for children have practically disappeared, while the economic cost of children has become much higher. The structure of the welfare State has provided strong incentives to couples with very few or no children, while families with children experienced an extra tax burden. Only recently, the Government has become concerned with the problems the country is facing due to the very low fertility rate (Golini, 2000). Currently, the Italian Government gives priority to the implementation of social transfers in favour of children and youth, and of interventions in favour of families.

Throughout Eastern Europe, with political collapse and economic uncertainty, many women almost immediately stopped having children or decided to delay motherhood. Real incomes have declined in the region and are only slowly recovering, with larger gaps between rich and poor. At the same time, Governments have cut back support for families with children, while services such as day-care centres have been privatized or have become more expensive. The demographic behaviour of the population in countries of Eastern Europe experienced a marked change after 1990 owing to major societal shifts. A big shock has been the emergence of unemployment, accompanied by a decline in social and family services. This contributed to a dramatic decrease in fertility rates in the mid-1990s. In response, some Governments have recently adopted a family policy aimed at consolidating women's roles as mothers and workers.

In the Russian Federation, where the number of marriages has declined and the number of divorces has risen, the TFR declined from 2.1 children per woman in 1985-1990 to 1.3 children per woman in 1995-2000. The Government has taken measures to strengthen the family as an institution as well as to protect mothers and children. Currently, the Russian Federation has a State policy that addresses the needs of women, children and families with a focus on replacing State paternalism with the principle of partnership and equal representation. The Government has created a national action plan for women.

A Family Code was adopted in 1995, which established norms in the area of family life, marriage protection, and the rights of children and orphans, and also ensured access to basic educational tools and facilities. Maternity leave has been extended and the number of women examined early in pregnancy has been increasing. Grants given to children and to women who look after children have been increased.

Since the 1960s, the Government of the Republic of Korea has implemented a successful family planning programme, with a view to breaking the "vicious cycle" of poverty caused by high population growth and low economic development. In the 1980s, however, as population growth slowed and the economy blossomed, new problems appeared, such as the disintegration of the family and population ageing. In response, the Government established its "New Population Policy" in 1996. The main concerns of the national family planning programme were shifted from the past policy of fertility reduction to a qualitative approach—the enhancement of quality of life and welfare services for the people. Among the directions of the New Population Policy are the maintenance of a balanced sex ratio through improvement of women's social status and gender equality, and a reduction in induced abortion.

In Japan, although opportunities for women in the workplace continue to be limited, they have more freedom to hold careers and thus have become more economically independent. As a result, more are choosing careers over marriage and parenting. The proportion never married in the female population of Japan has risen conspicuously since the mid-1970s, and continues to rise. Among women aged 25-29, it has more than doubled in two decades (1975-1995) (Kaneko, 2000). Other factors such as the cost of education and the lack of day-care centres and small homes in the cities are problems discouraging many young couples from raising large families. The Government has adopted a number of measures in response to the trend of the country's falling fertility rate. The Angel Plan for children was formulated along with the Gold Plan for the elderly several years ago. Thus, the measures to cope with the two interrelated demographic trends (ageing and the trend towards fewer children) have become a policy agenda (Kojima, 2000). Among other steps taken were the enactment of the Basic Law for a Gender-Equal Society, the reinforcement of the Equal Employment Opportunity Law, and the improvement of public childcare support systems. Actions such as these contributed to securing equal treatment for women and men in the area of employment and ensured that women would be more fully able to realize their potential. In addition, many Japanese companies provide financial gifts for first and second children. Some companies have begun offering a much higher financial bonus to any employee celebrating the birth of their third or later child.

B. *Mortality crisis in countries of Eastern Europe and the former USSR*

With fertility being near-constant, the extent of ageing and population growth will be determined by mortality shifts. The future of mortality rates is unknown. Will the very large increases in expectations of life that have occurred in the past quarter-century continue? Or will they reverse?

Recently, mortality rates have increased in large parts of the European region, which includes the Russian Federation and the European successor parts of the former Union of Soviet Socialist Republics (USSR). The Russian Federation's population is dropping by almost 1 million per year not just because of very low fertility, but also because of sharply higher levels of mortality. The low life expectancy in these countries is due to a number of factors such as stress, pollution, malnutrition and the reappearance of epidemic diseases such as diphtheria and cholera. Among conditions currently of major concern from the standpoint of health policy are infectious and parasitic diseases, acquired immunodeficiency syndrome (AIDS), syphilis, circulatory diseases, and high levels of morbidity related to accidents, injuries and poisoning. Thousands of persons die every day in the Russian Federation from the consumption of low-quality alcohol. The quality of many food products has deteriorated as well.

In the Russian Federation, as in some other countries of Eastern Europe and the former USSR, the Government is particularly concerned with rising mortality among males in the economically active ages: in the Russian Federation, male mortality is four to five times as high as female mortality. The Russian Federation has the lowest life expectancy for males among developed countries and the largest disparity in the world between male and female life expectancy, which recently was 13.5 years.

The current health situation in these countries has been adversely affected by the complex economic situation. The material base of the health sector is obsolete and health-care services have deteriorated sharply. During the transition period, these countries have come up against the problem of large-scale poverty and growing social stratification. Difficulties exist in providing adequate social protection and health care because of structural changes in those sectors and widespread disruption of supplies of medical equipment and medicine. Many medical research centres have been left without proper financial support.

The Russian Government has attempted to reform the health-care sector through privatization and promoting the private medical sector. Since 1993, the Russian Federation has been undergoing a transition from universal free medical services to a public-health system based on compulsory and voluntary insurance. One of the main goals of reform is to establish compulsory health insurance financed through taxes and operated by both the State and the private sector. In 1997, the Government adopted a programme of action for overcoming the existing demographic crisis in the country. Policy on health, morbidity and mortality has been further developed in recent years in several decisions of the Government: on "The concept of improvement of the status of women in the Russian Federation", "The Plan of Action for the improvement of the status of children in the Russian Federation in 1995-1997" and "The national plan of action for the improvement of the status of women and enhancement of their role in society till 2000"; and the Decree of the President of the Russian Federation on "The extension of the President's Programme: children of the Russian Federation".

C. Migration policies

Permanent migration policies

The current policies of most countries are not favourable towards permanent migration. Those countries that accept permanent migrants have become increasingly selective in deciding which types of immigrants to admit. A characteristic policy of many developed countries has been to restrain migration. Moreover, until recently, ageing has not triggered any change in restrictive policies. Among the 56 countries with below replacement level fertility, only 3 countries (Singapore, the Republic of Moldova and the Russian Federation) reported that they had a policy to raise immigration, 46 per cent (26 countries) had a policy to maintain it and 32 per cent (18 countries) had a policy to lower immigration, while 16 per cent (9 countries) reported a policy of no intervention (see table 5). In 1999, of the eight selected countries, with the exception of the Russian Federation, which seeks to increase the inflow of former compatriots, emigrants, and migrant-investors, four countries—Italy, Japan, the Republic of Korea and the United States—had a policy to maintain and three other countries—France, Germany and the United Kingdom—had a policy to lower permanent immigration (see tables 9 and 14). Views and policies of these countries on emigration are given in tables 15 and 16.

The immigration policies in the traditional countries of immigration, Australia, Canada, New Zealand and the United States, have changed over the years and continue to evolve. Their policies also have a tendency towards greater selectivity and increased emphasis on economic needs and conditions in the receiving country. Higher priority is being given to skilled, educated immigrants; fewer slots are available for unskilled workers. Even in the family reunification category, employability is becoming a more important consideration.

In a number of countries, especially in Europe, foreigners have been permitted to bring family members to join them in the host country, and they have established communities and ethnic networks, but most are not allowed full participation in the social and political life of the host country. Another type of permanent migration consists of repatriation of certain foreign residents who emigrated at some earlier time. The descendants of these emigrants may qualify for admission. Among the countries that accept immigrants according to ethnic origin are Germany, Italy and Japan. A final category of permanent migrants consists of investors, or business immigrants, who bring capital to the country of destination. Programmes in most traditional countries of immigration seek to attract investors and entrepreneurs, provided that they meet financial requirements and establish businesses that create jobs for native workers.

In the 1990s, all the countries that traditionally receive immigrants made adjustments in their immigration policies, often as a response to the popular perception that immigrants are a net cost to the receiving society. Most of the changes have reinforced the tendency to limit immigrant intakes. Some countries have imposed more selective admissions criteria, while others have addressed qualifications for family reunification, either by limiting the categories of eligible relatives or by requiring family sponsors to accept more responsibility for their immigrating relatives.

TABLE 14. GOVERNMENT POLICIES ON IMMIGRATION IN EIGHT COUNTRIES, 1976-1999

Year	France	Germany	Italy	Japan	Republic of Korea	Russian Federation	United Kingdom	United States
1976	Maintain	Maintain	Maintain	Maintain	Maintain	Maintain	Lower	Maintain
1983	Lower	Lower	Raise	Maintain	Maintain	Maintain	Lower	Maintain
1993	Lower	Lower	Maintain	Maintain	Lower	Lower	Lower	Maintain
1999	Lower	Lower	Maintain	Maintain	Maintain	Raise	Lower	Maintain

Source: Population Policy Data Bank maintained by the Population Division of the United Nations Secretariat.

TABLE 15. GOVERNMENT VIEWS OF EMIGRATION LEVEL IN EIGHT COUNTRIES, 1976-1999

Year	France	Germany	Italy	Japan	Republic of Korea	Russian Federation	United Kingdom	United States
1976	Satisfactory	Satisfactory	Too high	Satisfactory	Too low	Satisfactory	Satisfactory	Satisfactory
1983	Satisfactory	Satisfactory	Satisfactory	Too low	Too low	Satisfactory	Satisfactory	Satisfactory
1993	Satisfactory	Satisfactory	Satisfactory	Satisfactory	Too low	Too high	Satisfactory	Satisfactory
1999	Satisfactory	Satisfactory	Satisfactory	Satisfactory	Satisfactory	Satisfactory	Satisfactory	Satisfactory

Source: Population Policy Data Bank maintained by the Population Division of the United Nations Secretariat.

TABLE 16. GOVERNMENT POLICIES ON EMIGRATION IN EIGHT COUNTRIES, 1976-1999

Year	France	Germany	Italy	Japan	Republic of Korea	Russian Federation	United Kingdom	United States
1976.........	Maintain	Maintain	Lower	Maintain	Raise	Maintain	Maintain	Maintain
1983.........	Maintain	Maintain	Lower	Raise	Raise	Maintain	Maintain	Maintain
1993.........	Maintain	No intervention	No intervention	No intervention	Raise	Lower	No intervention	No intervention
1999.........	Raise	No intervention	No intervention	No intervention	Maintain	No intervention	No intervention	No intervention

Source: Population Policy Data Bank maintained by the Population Division of the United Nations Secretariat.

Germany, like many other European countries, does not pursue a policy aimed at the permanent settlement of foreigners. When the federal Government started to recruit foreign workers in 1955, all persons concerned assumed that the workers would stay for a limited period of time. However, the Government realized that many foreigners intended to stay in the country permanently. In 1973, the Federation and the federal Länder decided that, as a rule, the recruitment of foreign workers was to be discontinued. In 1981, the federal Cabinet decided to prevent the further immigration of non-EU nationals. When the asylum compromise was reached in 1992, the parliamentary groups agreed that ways of limiting and controlling immigration should be considered nationally and that negotiations regarding immigration should be continued on the European level.

German policy towards ethnic Germans has also changed significantly. Before 1990, their home Governments were urged to let ethnic Germans emigrate. In the 1990s, the ethnic Germans have been given assistance so they can remain where they are. Eligibility to return has been narrowed several times. In 1993, an annual quota of 220,000 a year was introduced, and only ethnic Germans from the former USSR were presumed to have been persecuted because of their German heritage; ethnic Germans from other countries would have to prove persecution individually. In 1996, a German language test was introduced as a measure of German identity, with no possibility of repeating the test. One reason for tightening restrictions on the arrival of ethnic Germans was the perception that the 1990s arrivals were not "sufficiently German" and were likely to have difficulty integrating into Germany. Unemployment rates that were often as high as those of foreign guest workers led some Germans to consider ethnic Germans to be difficult-to-integrate foreigners.

Very recently, some countries have come to realize the significance of attracting immigrants to offset the effects of an ageing population, low birth rate and shrinking workforce. Some Governments have introduced policies to increase the inflow of skilled workers. The French Government wishes to increase the inflow of qualified migrants, particularly in the scientific, cultural and technological fields. The German Government wishes to increase the inflow of students. The policy of the Government of the United Kingdom on immigration is also to welcome students and, in addition, to support family life by admitting the spouses and minor dependent children of those already settled in the United Kingdom.

The Government may also relax immigration rules for some immigrants. Under current rules, foreigners must buy a British company for at least 200,000 pounds (£) which they will actively manage, or must invest £ 1 million, in order to reside in Great Britain. The Government is considering implementing a limited version of the Canadian points system. The Canadian system awards points for occupation, education and knowledge of English and French; some foreigners can immigrate even if they do not have a job offer from a Canadian employer. The Government of the United Kingdom believes that the system is fairer than the American green card system (Burrell, 2000).

To address the problem of ageing, the Canadian Government has set an ambitious target of 300,000 immigrants a year, a 50 per cent increase from the current level. The new legislation to make it easier for immigrants to enter Canada is expected to pass this year. It would drop the "occupations list", which awards points to immigrants with specific skills. The changes would put a higher premium on family reunification by increasing the dependent children category to include youths as old as 22 (the current limit is age 19). The Government is also promoting a proposal that would give each Canadian a one-time "free pass" card to sponsor any blood relative, no matter how far removed on the family tree. Some Canadian provinces that are in particular need of workers are making use of the 1998 measures that let provinces accept immigrants based on local needs even if the applicants do not meet the federal test.

Labour migration policies

In 1999, of the eight countries considered, only Italy had a policy to raise the entry of persons on non-permanent work permits; six others—France, Japan, the Republic of Korea, the Russian Federation, the United Kingdom and the United States—had a policy to maintain the flow, while Germany had a policy to lower the entry of persons on work permits as well as their dependants. Six countries in the group had a policy to maintain the entry of dependants of persons on work permits, while the Russian Federation had a policy of non-intervention (see table 9).

Major policy issues in the area of labour migration in the 1990s included controlling the number of immigrants admitted as foreign workers and ensuring that contract workers returned to their home countries after the expiration of their contracts. Short of integration efforts, protecting the rights of migrant workers has also been a major policy concern. Policy considerations in countries of both origin and destination are weighed heavily against the cost-benefit analyses of importing and exporting labour. Recourse to temporary foreign workers is designed to meet immediate manpower shortages related to specific activities. In certain countries, this type of migration serves as a means of counteracting undocumented migration, with its accompanying integration costs.

For receiving countries, the benefits of unskilled and semi-skilled foreign labour that fills dirty, dangerous, demanding and low-paying jobs, often unwanted by the local population, are offset by some costs. In sending countries, the benefits—potential knowledge transfer and remittances—are weighed against the numerous costs—particularly the brain drain. Indeed, the drain of students and highly educated individuals may compromise the establishment of an intellectual and research pool in the sending country.

In EU, an immigration plan has been proposed that would open a labour migration channel with the goal of reducing the number of asylum-seekers: countries could decide whether to accept labour migrants as workers or as immigrants. All labour migrants would have to have identity papers and work contracts with EU employers who paid taxes on their wages. It is believed that an active immigration policy could reduce the number of asylum-seekers and illegal refugees (Smith, 2000). EU has prepared an expansive family unification regulation that would recommend that member States permit spouses and minor children to join settled foreigners abroad after one year's residence, as well as grandparents, aunts and uncles in some cases.

In Germany, high illegal employment has disturbed the order in the labour market and thus has been an obstacle to the improvement of the employment situation of the unemployed. Therefore, apart from sanctions against illegal workers themselves, there are above all a wide range of sanctions against employers who illegally employ workers. Recently, an Immigration Commission has been established to introduce an "active immigration policy" in order to have greater control over those entering the country (Atkins, 2000). The Government would like to give immigration a predictable form and favour those immigrants who can make a contribution to the economy rather than be a burden on the taxpayers.

Chancellor Schroeder announced this year that his Government intends to issue special work permits (green cards) to computer specialists from Asia and Eastern Europe to ease the shortage of such specialists in German industry, while the country still had more than 4 million people unemployed. Business leaders claim that there are about 75,000 vacancies in the information technology (IT) sector that cannot be filled with specialists available on the German or EU labour market. The Government intends to start by giving work permits to up to 30,000 foreign specialists from EU member countries, with contracts limited to a period between three and six years. The Government planned to issue five-year residence and work permits for foreign computer professionals arriving in Germany, so that a foreigner could change jobs and remain in Germany. However, some states announced that foreigner computer specialists there would receive "blue cards" which would link the duration of their residence permits to their work contracts (Associated Press, 2000).

In Italy, although the unemployment rate is 11 per cent, the Government believes that all conditions exist for the country to increase the quota of immigrants. This perception is based on the fact that the country needs a labour force and its population is growing old very rapidly. Italy granted legal status to 56,500 unauthorized foreigners in 1999 after they found an employer to provide them with a formal sector job, or found a sponsor to provide them with housing and at least $3,000 a month in support. The quota for 2000 is 63,000 regularizations, and it was reached already in June 2000. The Italian Parliament, under pressure from northern Italian businesses complaining of labour shortages, is expected to increase that number by another 30,000. Some politicians assert that Italy needs immigration, and should accept immigrants via front-door legal immigration rather than legalize some of the illegals in the country. Others assert that, if Italy does not open the door wider to legal immigrants, it will be strengthening the hand of smugglers and traffickers. Finally, rightist opposition parties oppose legal immigration and amnesties, referring to the amount of crime committed by immigrants (Reuters, 2000).

The policy of the United Kingdom is to grant entry to persons on non-permanent work permits and to their dependants who qualify for periods of work. Regarding entry of undocumented or illegal migrants, the Government aims to detect and remove those entering or remaining in the United Kingdom without authority and take firm action against those profiting from abuse of the immigration laws. The United Kingdom intends to resume "economic migration" this year for the first time since 1971. The immigration Minister declared that the United Kingdom and Europe must "be ready to think imaginatively about how migration can meet economic and social needs". The United Kingdom Department for Education and Employment's overseas labour division started advertising a fast-track entry to Great Britain for people with IT and other specialist skills (Burrell, 2000).

In the Republic of Korea, in 1994, the Government introduced an "industrial trainee system" to fill vacant 3D (dirty, dangerous and difficult) jobs, under which foreigners come to the Republic of Korea for three years as trainees. The ruling Millennium Party, over the objections of the Korea Federation of Small Businesses (KFSB), intends to convert the current system for foreign trainees into a migrant worker programme. KFSB argues that converting trainees, who are paid less than the minimum wage, into guest workers would increase labour costs and reduce their competitiveness. The Government has released a policy direction report intended to "lay an institutional groundwork to allow foreigners to work as regular employees". A Committee for Employment of Foreign Workers would be established to regulate the new programme (Korea Times, 2000; Korea Herald, 2000).

In Japan, with respect to terms of entry and stay of migrant workers (and their dependants), the Government adopted the Eighth Employment Measures Basic Plan in 1995. According to this Plan, from the viewpoint of activating and internationalizing Japanese economy and society, the Government would give as much consideration as possible to accepting foreign workers in professional or technical fields. Also, the Government intends to review the examination criteria of qualifications for residence in Japan in accordance with changes in the economic and social situation. On the other hand, concerning the acceptance of unskilled workers, there is anxiety that it could exert a wide range of effects on the Japanese economy and society such as pressure on older Japanese workers, for whom employment opportunities are rather limited; a new dual structure in the labour market; unemployment as a result of business fluctuations; and new social expenses.

Based on these policies, the Government is making an effort to regulate enterprises employing foreign workers. It is also trying to improve the system for accepting foreign workers by elaborating and improving systems of employment placement, providing counselling for foreign job seekers in public employment offices, and providing guidance and assistance to employers in improving employment management. For workers of Japanese descent, in particular, the Government is trying to secure proper employment by improving public employment channels and employment management.

CONCLUSION

The analysis of government views and policies shows that more and more countries are concerned with the potential consequences of population decline and the significant increase in the population of their older citizens. The recent report on replacement migration based on the United Nations estimates and projections has increased the awareness of Governments of the coming challenges in the near and long-term future, namely, that societies could suffer profound economic, social and political consequences. Governments are especially concerned with the current and growing potential issues of social security, health-care costs, and labour shortages.

Past policies and measures related to population ageing show that demographics were not taken into consideration when economic and social policies were formulated, for example, in relation to pension payments or retirement age. Therefore, some measures taken in this regard have often been inconsistent and brought results opposite to the countries' interests. For example, many Governments desire to increase the retirement age, although the trend has been towards its decreasing. Many countries want to solve ageing issues, but at the same time experience high unemployment. In some countries, the existing tax burdens have been higher for families with children, in conditions of rapidly falling fertility.

Earlier policies are still in place that will make the problem worse; but awareness on the part of Governments is increasing and may lead to adjustments to policies that will improve the situation. Among the current common adjustments to population ageing have been: gradually increasing the age at which workers become eligible for retirement benefits (Japan, Germany); equalizing retirement ages for men and women by raising the retirement age for women (United Kingdom); restricting access to early retirement benefits (Germany, Italy); reducing retirement benefits (Germany, Italy, Japan and United Kingdom); and increasing contribution rates (Japan). In addition, some countries are changing the social security system from pay-as-you-go to capitalization. They are moving to a greater reliance on advance funding of the pension promises.

Many Governments try to increase incentives for people either to delay accepting retirement benefits or to continue working at least part-time after they have started to receive them. Also, incentives are offered to companies to employ older workers (France, Germany, Japan, United Kingdom). Governments and businesses are trying to adapt to a labour market in which many new jobs will have to be filled with retrained older workers instead of newly trained young ones. They are considering introducing "lifelong learning" policies to help older workers keep up with the increasing demands of the economy (Germany, Republic of Korea, United Kingdom). Seeking a more comprehensive approach to the issues, they are also trying to introduce training of multi-skilled workers, greater flexibility and mobility, changing job structures, the building of flexible production systems, appropriate work organization and options for gradual transition to retirement.

In the area of health and long-term care, most developed countries are experimenting with home health benefits. They try to reduce the cost of older people's health care by improving home health care. An important policy direction of many Governments is the promotion of community participation in social and health services for older people. Others have also introduced care insurance schemes, which compensate caregivers for the work they do.

A number of Governments consider it preferable to raise fertility rather than to substantially increase the flow of immigrants. However, previous attempts in this direction were not effective and usually had only a temporary effect. Survey results in terms of preferences regarding the number of children show that there is a gap between the number of children people want and the number they actually have, and this gap is even increasing. Obstacles to the fulfilment of reproductive desires confronted by people should be identified and removed to permit the expression of existing demand for children. Recently, government policies have been shifting to a more comprehensive approach towards the family and fertility. The Governments are becoming more concerned with enabling parents to have as many children they want, and with helping them more substantially in raising and educating children.

Among different types of government interventions are fiscal incentives to have children: child-raising allowances, tax incentives, education subsidies, housing subsidies etc. Labour-market policies that encourage parenthood include: parental leave for both parents, flexible working hours etc. Social policies that make it easier for parents to combine work and child-rearing duties include: childcare services, pre-school and after-school arrangements etc. Young people could be helped more by the State as well as by the firms that may be potential employers. Some Governments also see the importance of equalizing gender relations both in the family and at work and, in particular, encouraging both parents to participate in child-rearing (Norway, Sweden). Moreover, they also see it as necessary to change the attitude of society towards children, so as to enhance the value of children.

A number of Governments are turning to international migration to help stem various negative consequences arising from declines in population size, especially of the working-age population. A characteristic policy of many developed countries has been to restrain migration and, until recently, ageing has not triggered any change in restrictive policies. Some Governments and EU as a whole are shifting towards more open borders and, at the same time, better regulation, in order to attract immigrants who are more suitable to their economies, as well as moving towards a more selective approach to accepting immigration. In EU, an immigration plan has been proposed that would open a labour migration channel with the goal of reducing the number of asylum-seekers and illegal migrants.

The changing labour market is pushing the developed countries towards such a change in policies. Recently, some countries have come to realize the importance of attracting immigrants to offset the effects of an ageing population, low birth rates and a shrinking workforce and have introduced policies to increase the inflow of skilled workers, and to use age-related selection criteria for some categories of immigrants. Immigration is sometimes perceived by Governments as an easier solution because they can see the results more quickly and with less cost. However, it is recognized by many Governments that, to ease the issues of ageing, permanent large immigrant flows would be needed. Therefore, temporary contract arrangements are being introduced, which may nonetheless lead to permanent settlement. At the same time, the Governments are concerned with the issues of integrating large numbers of immigrants. In many cases, public perception of migration is a critical issue that drives the government policy.

Other Governments prefer to rely more on non-demographic options that aim at attenuating the consequences of ageing, such as increasing productivity by introducing labour-saving technologies, improving the use of existing labour resources (particularly, youth, women and older persons) and effecting better coordination of education and labour demand.

Obviously, the various policy measures are as multiple and complex as the issue of ageing itself, which affects all aspects of society and includes all stages of human life. Therefore, there cannot be a single solution to the complex issue of population ageing. In each case, there should be a balanced mix of different approaches and measures. Clearly, it is necessary to study in greater detail the factors and consequences of the ageing process in each particular country, and the effectiveness of current policy measures, and, on this basis, formulate policy recommendations that best fit cultural and socio-economic settings.

REFERENCES

Associated Press (2000). Germany approves "green card" law for high-tech immigrants. *Associated Press*, July 14.

Atkins, Ralph (2000). Panel launched to plan overhaul of German immigration and asylum rules. *Financial Times*, July 13.

Bradshaw, J., and others (1993). *Support for Children: A Comparison of Arrangements in Fifteen Countries*. Department of Social Security, Research Report, No. 21, London: HM Stationery Office.

Burrell, Ian (2000). New open door policy for "skilled" immigrants. *The Independent* (London), July 21.

Golini, Antonio (2000). Levels and trends of fertility in Italy: are they desirable or sustainable? In United Nations, *Population Bulletin of the United Nations: Below Replacement Fertility*. Special Issue, Nos. 40/41 (1999). New York. Sales No. E.99.XIII.13.

Hourriez, J. M., and B. Legris (1995). Le niveau de vie relatif des personnes âgées (The relative standard of living among senior citizens). Économie et Statistique, Nos. 283-284.

Institut National de la Statistique et des Études Économiques (1995). *Les femmes. Portrait social, Serie Contours et Caractères*. Paris: INSEE.

Kaneko, Ryuichi (2000). Below-replacement fertility in Japan: trends, determinants and prospects. In United Nations, *Population Bulletin of the United Nations: Below Replacement Fertility*. Special Issue, Nos. 40/41 (1999). New York. Sales No. E.99.XIII.13.

Kojima, Hiroshi (2000). Ageing and social welfare policies in Japan. In *Low Fertility and Policy Responses to Issues of Ageing and Welfare*. Seoul: Korea Institute for Health and Social Affairs.

Korea Herald (2000). Disputes escalate over equal treatment of foreign workers. *Korea Herald*, July 7.

Korea Times (2000). Gov't Plan to Adopt Work Permit System to Protect Foreign Workers. *Korea Times*, July 15.

Organisation for Economic Co-operation and Development (1995). *The Transition from Work to Retirement*. Social Policy Studies, No. 16. Paris.

Peterson, Peter G. (1999). Gray Dawn: *How the Coming Age Wave Will Transform America—and the World*. New York: Random House.

Putin, Vladimir (2000). *The State of Russia: A Way to an Effective State*. The state of the nation address to the Federal Assembly of the Russian Federation, 8 July 2000. Moscow: Russian Information Agency Novosti.

Reuters (2000). Italy mulls opening doors to more immigrants. *Reuters*, July 13.

Smith, Jeffrey R. (2000). Europe bids immigrants unwelcome. *Washington Post*, 23 July.

Thompson, Lawrence H. (1999). Pension reform in industrialized countries. In *Encuentro Latino-americano y Caribeño sobre las Personas de Edad*. Seminario tecnico. Santiago de Chile, 8 al 10 de septiembre, 1999. Santiago: Centro Latinoamericano y Caribeño de Demografía (CELADE).

Toulemon, Laurent (1998). Demographic trends and family policy in France. Paper presented at the International Symposium on Population and Development Policies in Low Fertility Countries organized by the Korea Institute for Health and Social Affairs and the United Nations Population Fund (UNFPA), Seoul, 7-12 May.

United Nations (1982). *Report of the World Assembly on Ageing, Vienna, 26 July–6 August 1982.* Sales No. E.82.I.16.

_____ (1997). Report of the Secretary-General on the fourth review and appraisal of the implementation of the International Plan of Action on Ageing. E/CN.5/1997/4.

_____ (2001a). *Replacement Migration: Is It a Solution to Declining and Ageing Populations?* Sales No. E.01.XIII.19.

_____ (2001b). *Results of the Eighth United Nations Inquiry among Governments on Population and Development*. Sales No. E.01.XIII.2.

United Nations, International Institute on Ageing (1999). *Care-Giving and Older Persons: Gender Dimensions*. Malta: International Institute on Ageing.

Whitting, G., and others (1995). Employment policies and practices towards older workers: an international overview. *Employment Gazette* (April).

Part Three

CONTRIBUTED PAPERS

Part Three

CONTRIBUTED PAPERS

THE INVERSION OF THE AGE PYRAMID AND THE FUTURE POPULATION DECLINE IN FRANCE: IMPLICATIONS AND POLICY RESPONSES

*Jean-Claude Chesnais**

INTRODUCTION

The demographic landscape is changing dramatically; the industrialized world is facing unprecedented population trends: extended longevity is combining with low fertility, thus producing a progressive reversal of the age pyramid.

But the notion of "below-replacement" fertility is vague. From a theoretical point of view, it comprises all levels of total fertility rates (TFRs) between zero (extinction) and 2.1 children per woman (stationarity, or equilibrium). The impact of the emerging new trends is not familiar, but it is powerful; if we put aside the role of the population momentum inherited from past fertility, a TFR of 1 (child per woman) is the symmetrical value of a TFR of at least 4 children per woman or, more precisely, of a net reproduction rate (NRR) of 2 surviving daughters per woman. Let us push the argument further: if in some regions or cities, the TFR drops to 0.5 children per woman and then stabilizes, the population is subject to a division by 8 after 2 generations; the symmetrical value on the demographic scale is a NRR of 4 (that is to say, an average family size of at least 8 children). The well-known mechanism of population explosion (multiplication) gives place to a population implosion (division, or exponential decrease).

The modern fertility decline usually took place from the mid-1960s to the mid-1970s but it sometimes occurred earlier (Japan) or later (Southern and Eastern Europe). Since that fall, the fertility level has tended to remain constant or to decline slowly. Such is the case for France and Germany, for example, where, contrary to Easterlin's hypothesis[1] or to the supposed timing impact, fertility did not recover and, as a consequence, did not describe a cyclic curve. Short-term fluctuations can exist but they are small and, until now, the long-term trend seems to be rather linear, structural. No sign of long-standing upturn has appeared since the 1970s.

The ultimate or "final" value of the stabilization level is widely differentiated from country to country. Some (few) populations will probably remain stationary (zero growth) while others could experience a massive decline, or even be reduced to one half of their size, every 30 years.

*Institut National d'Études Démographiques (INED), France.

I. THE FOUR PATTERNS OF BELOW-REPLACEMENT FERTILITY

At present, with current international data, we can, at least provisionally, make a distinction between four patterns of below-replacement fertility depending on the stabilization level during the latest stage:

- *First scenario*: 1.8 to 2.1 children per woman. Slightly insufficient fertility, which can return to replacement level if the population policy is modernized and adapted to the needs of young couples in terms of money, space and time. This is especially true in countries where surveys show a wide discrepancy between the actual and the desired number of children. Under this scenario, the number of migrants required (possible labour shortage) is relatively low, and migration will therefore be easier to master in the long run;

- *Second scenario*: 1.5 to 1.8 children per woman. Strong dearth calling for a deep revision of the population policy. In the longer term (from 2005 to 2010 onwards), higher risk of labour shortage and reduced capacity to integrate new immigrants; since the main engine of integration of foreigners is the school, this integration cannot happen if a certain fertility level is not reached among the resident population;

- *Third scenario*: 1.2 to 1.5 children per woman. Heavy and structural contraction, which digs a deep hole at the base of the age pyramid and consequently compromises the future of the society at large. Limited chance to secure a return to equilibrium; strong population decline. The prolongation of such a scenario could imply a massive renewal of the population on the given territory; the resident population is progressively replaced by a continuous and bulky inflow of immigrants;

- *Fourth scenario*: less than 1.2 children per woman. Increasingly frequent extreme case, particularly in Southern Europe and in the former Eastern bloc. A severe amputation of the base of the age pyramid is taking place in front of our eyes; this vacuum can be aggravated if fertility remains depressed. Acute and rapid ageing process; deep and long-lasting migratory dependency, which could be unbearable or unmanageable without social tensions.

To each of these scenarios is associated a given range of reversal of the age pyramid: the lower the fertility, the narrower the base of the age pyramid.

Let us consider the French case. Since the mid-1970s, the TFR has been at the lowest limit of scenario 1 and the upper limit of scenario 2, but we have to take into account the magnitude of the fluctuation; in the former time-span, France experienced an intense and long baby boom covering all of the period 1946-1973. The shift of fertility is important, thus creating a big swing. Hence, scenario 2 is more relevant.

We will first examine the demographic consequences of population ageing, then we will consider the financial, the economic and political impact, and finally envisage policy responses.

II. THE DEMOGRAPHIC CONSEQUENCES OF AGEING

The first consequence of population ageing is the loss of reproductive potential. The number of women of childbearing age will peak and then decline. This number had increased by 40 per cent between 1950 and 1990, then it reached a maximum of 14 million during the 1990s; a decrease will occur during the next decades, bringing this figure back to lower values. Let us recall the latest United Nations population prospects (United Nations, 1999):

- The low variant: small and regular fertility decline; the TFR reaches 1.56 in 2005-2010, then remains constant;

- The medium variant: regular fertility increase from the present level (1.71 in the 1990s) to 1.96 in 2015-2020, then stabilization;

- The high variant: sustained fertility recovery, bringing the TFR to a value that does not exist any more in the advanced parts of the world: 2.36 children per woman at the end of the projection period (2030-2050); as mentioned above, we will not use it in our comments.

Of these three fertility assumptions, only two have been envisaged, because they seem more or less realistic now, namely, the medium and the low variants; the high variant should be used only for the purpose of comparison or illustration.

Under the first assumption (low variant) the number of women at childbearing age falls below the threshold of 10 million in 2050 (table 1); this is below the value of 1950, which was historically very weak because of structural sub-fertility and the adverse impact of the First World War and the Great Depression on natality. In the middle of the twenty-first century, the number of

TABLE 1. POPULATION TRENDS IN FRANCE: PAST (1950-2000) AND PROSPECTIVE (2000-2050)

Indicator	1950	1970	1990	2000	2010 A	2010 B	2030 A	2030 B	2050 A	2050 B
Total population (millions) . . .	41.8	50.8	56.7	59.1	59.7	60.6	57.8	61.6	51.7	59.9
Number of women aged 15-49 (millions). . . .	10.3	12.0	14.1	14.4	13.8	13.8	11.6	12.4	9.5	11.8
Population aged 60 years or over (millions). . . .	6.8	9.2	10.8	12.1	13.9	13.9	18.2	18.2	18.8	18.8
Median age (years)	34.5	32.3	34.7	37.6	40.3	40.8	43.6	46.1	43.9	49.8
Age 60 or over/age 0-24 (ratio) . .	0.43	0.44	0.54	0.64	0.77	0.81	1.04	1.30	1.12	1.63

Source: *World Population Prospects: The 1998 Revision*, vol. I, *Comprehensive Tables* (United Nations publication, Sales No. E.99.XIII.9).

NOTE: A: Low variant: total fertility rate falling from 1.71 children per woman in the 1990s to 1.56 during the period 2005-2010, then remaining constant. This is a scenario of slight fertility decrease.

B: Medium variant: total fertility rate rising from 1.71 children per woman in the 1990s to 1.96 during the period 2015-2020, then remaining constant. This is a scenario of slight fertility increase.

young women should be affected by the influence of the long-lasting depression of fertility levels; if no change occurs, it should continue to decline.

Under the second assumption (medium variant)—which, as compared with the prevailing fertility of the post-transitional period 1973-2000, seems rather high—the fertility rate increases moderately (table 2).

Whatever the fertility trend, the number of women at childbearing age will diminish during the coming two or three decades. The shift has a strong meaning for the future of the population; the annual number of births can fall back to the historically low levels of the pre-war period: about 600,000 per year, instead of 850,000 per year as during the baby-boom phase. A spiral of decline can eventually emerge and reinforce itself from decade to decade.

Ageing influences vital rates; typically an older population will have not only fewer births but also more deaths. The potential for demographic decline is already inscribed in the age distribution: the baby-boom cohorts will age and the number of deaths will grow. Negative natural increase will occur by 2020 or so, and it will continue in an older population, even if fertility moves to around the replacement level: the small number of women of reproductive age and the larger number at older ages would still imply fewer births than deaths. Even if France does not reflect the bottom pattern described above, the potential for population decline will be difficult to reverse: the population momentum is declining below unity, thus working against any spontaneous recovery.

Whether European, North American or East Asian, industrialized countries will experience a radical change in the age distribution of their populations; the classical triangle profile of the age distribution shaped by high mortality and high fertility of the pre-transitional era progressively gives way to a pagoda shape when fertility comes close to replacement. In a third stage, which is now beginning, the transformation goes still further. The base of the age pyramid becomes narrower and narrower while the top enlarges. The so-called pyramid progressively takes a bonsai-like shape. The corresponding structure is an inverted pyramid; the contemporary population trends tend to produce a more or less profound reversal of the age pyramid.

France is no exception. The demographic weight of a strong and sustained baby boom has limited the impact of the fertility depression on the number of births. When the baby-bust cohorts born from 1974 onward reach age 20-34, this protecting screen will disappear and, other things being equal, the number of births could drop by 15 per cent. The history of French population was atypical; the secular fertility decline began one century before the rest of the West; as a consequence, all through the period 1850-1950, France had the oldest population in the world; the share of the elderly was the highest ever seen in the history of mankind; the baby boom created a parenthesis, but the transition phenomenon is resuming. With the ongoing stages of the post-transition (much below replacement fertility and increased life expectancy), population ageing will reach new summits which will be much higher than past ones.

The process of population ageing is in fact the combination of two phenomena: the ageing of the cohorts born during the above-replacement fertility regime which inflates the upper part of the age distribution and the amputation of the base of the pyramid associated with the below-fertility regime. The second

TABLE 2. FERTILITY DIFFERENTIAL AND THE PIVOTING AGE STRUCTURE[a]

Indicator	1995		2000		2010		2020		2030		2040		2050	
	B	A	B	A	B	A	B	A	B	A	B	A	B	A
Fertility...............	1.72	1.72	1.73	1.63	1.86	1.56	1.96	1.56	1.96	1.56	1.96	1.56	1.96	1.56
Ratio (65 or over/0-14)	0	0	0.85	0.85	0.95	1.01	1.16	1.41	1.37	1.76	1.53	2.13	1.51	2.33
Differential (B - A)														
In fertility.........	0		0.10		0.30		0.40		0.40		0.40		0.40	
In ratio	0		0		0.06		0.25		0.39		0.60		0.81	

Source: Calculated from *World Population Prospects: The 1998 Revision,* vol. I, *Comprehensive Tables* (United Nations publication, Sales No. E.99.XIII.9).

[a]See table 1 for description of variants A (low variant) and B (medium variant).

phenomenon was unanticipated since the model of the demographic transition theory usually announced a post-transitional fertility equal or close to the replacement level. Therefore, all calculations made on numbers, rates and ratios (population size, renewal of the labour force, dependency ratio, percentage of the elderly etc.) have to be reconsidered.

In the three sets of projections made by the United Nations, there is only one single mortality variant (and three fertility variants, as described above); the same is true for net migration rates. These rates are 0.7 per 1,000 population at the beginning of the period 1995-2000, then they diminish: 0.3 in 2000-2005, and 0.2 in 2005-2010, finally to become nil.

By the year 2000, the population of France was 59 million; under the medium-variant projection, it would peak at about 61 million–62 million between 2020 and 2030 then slowly decline (60 million in 2050); the fluctuation is small: fertility is supposed to increase by 15 per cent to come back closer to the replacement line.

Under the low-variant projection, the maximum population is a bit lower (59.6 million) and the decline begins earlier (2005-2010). The difference is rather small; in both cases, the peak is similar. However, the percentage aged 60 years or over differs greatly; when all the baby boomers have entered this age group (60+), that is to say, by 2030-2035, the number of elderly is maximal (it could nearly double between now and that period); but the corresponding share continues to grow since the new depleted generations continue to shrink, thus changing the global age profile converging towards a bonsai or mushroom shape. According to the medium-variant assumption, the proportion of the population aged 60 years or over which was 20.2 per cent in 1995 would cross the 25 per cent mark by 2015, and the 30 per cent mark in 2030 finally to reach approximately one third in 2050 (32.5 per cent). The pace of ageing is even more striking under the low-variant assumption; the progression becomes much steeper at the end of the period of projection: in 2050, the percentage of elderly is 38 per cent and the process does not end there. The inversion of the age pyramid is so acute that the number of the elderly (age 60 years or over) is nearly twice as large as the number of "young" (population aged 0-24). The impact of a small fertility difference on the age structure in the long run (half a century) is huge. For the next few decades, the findings are the following: the older the population, the faster the increase; the younger the population, the stronger the decrease. Thus, the difference is maximal between the two extremes of the age scale. The residual population increase (if any) will be unbalanced: progression of the elderly, notably the oldest old; regression of the youth, notably the very young. At the two extremes, the trends tend to be exponential, but opposite. The digging of demographic deficits at the youngest ages has begun; these deficits will become more acute in the coming decades (table 2).

III. THE NON-DEMOGRAPHIC IMPACTS OF AGEING

The consequences of population ageing are manifold and covered by an extensive literature. In this short essay, we shall try to summarize briefly only three points: the financial aspect, the economic aspect and the political aspect.

A. *The financial dimension*

This aspect is a matter of arithmetic and therefore largely consensual. It has been studied by international agencies (Organisation for Economic Co-operation and Development, 1998; World Bank, 1994) and national bodies (social security authorities, government councils) and individual experts (Blanchet and Chanut, 1998; Calot, 1997; Kotlikoff and Leibfritz, 1998; Peterson, 1999).

The growing transfer of resources for the elderly (pension and health costs) to the detriment of younger workers can have a feedback effect, creating a disincentive to fertility. At present, three decades before the peak of population ageing, the composition of the social security budget is already affected by the reversal of the age pyramid. The main branch of social security in France is the pension system, with a total amount of 1,000 billion French francs (FF) for a total social budget of 2,200 billion; the second function which is predominantly devoted to the elderly is the health cost: FF 600 billion. The childhood and family get a meagre amount, FF 200 billion.

The pension system is PAYG (pay-as-you-go).

The basic equation between contributions (left) and outlays (right) is then the following:

$$Aowr = Eip$$

with A: adult population (potentially active population)

o: proportion occupied; Ao is the employed or contributing population

w: mean wage

r: rate of contribution

E: number of elderly

i: proportion of inactive people among the elderly

p: mean pension

The key political variable is the rate of contribution r, where

$$r = \frac{Aow}{Eip}$$

This rate is the product of three factors: the demographic one, $\frac{A}{o}$ (age structure); the economic one, $\frac{o}{i}$, which expresses the division of labour along the age/sex structure, the retirement age being a crucial factor in this division of labour; and the institutional (or political) one, $\frac{w}{p}$. The last ratio is the replacement ratio of the wage by the pension; it is a matter of public choice or of trade-off between workers and pensioners. Demographics can be considered a given (at least provisionally). Only the four other variables can be changed, and one of the major elements of adaptation will be the rise of the effective age at retirement, which is exceptionally low (58.5 years). The mechanism will probably be largely spontaneous, directly influenced by the dynamics of generation renewal. New generations entering the labour market now have a median age of about 22.5, as compared with 13 for the present generation of retirees: the beginning of the professional career is delayed, the career itself is frequently discontinuous (unemployment), and the rise of the retirement age will occur by necessity. This argument is reinforced by the possible decline of the relative level of pensions: the present low retirement age is partly induced by the high level of pension (retirees have a higher standard of living than workers); reciprocally, the reduction of the relative level of pension to a more reasonable standard should work in the opposite direction.

B. *The economic aspects*

These aspects are much more open to debate. Let us mention a few arguments. The early stages of ageing produce net economic benefits: with the reduction of the young population, there is a high proportion of the population of working age (this phenomenon is called the "demographic bonus"); there is also less need for family allowances or specific budget for childhood; and, at the same time, there are more double-income families, hence a broader fiscal base.

However, after a while, adverse effects tend to appear: an older labour force means more rigidity, less geographical and occupational mobility, and smaller capacity to adapt to economic change; this could represent a threat to innovativeness, which is so important in global competition.

Another crucial issue is the linkage between demographic recession and economic growth. The changing size and structure of the population can have a negative impact on demand. This is the case for large sectors of the economy, like housing, infrastructure, equipment etc. As the number of young households diminishes, many related segments of investment should contract, thus creating a negative pressure on economic growth.

Another aspect of the demographic crisis is the downward pressure on the value of assets; this holds true for the housing market. In a shrinking and greying population, the supply of vacant houses grows faster than demand, thus reducing prices. For the majority of French people, main property is their own housing. The implicit consequence is obvious: the demographic change means that their family capital could melt.

However, the greying of the baby boomers during the next few decades will pave the way to the emerging market of seniors; in parallel, there will be an explosion of the market of solitude, with its corresponding needs (flats, food processing, health care, safety etc).

C. *The political aspects*

The political implications of population ageing are difficult to measure quantitatively: they are mainly qualitative. The main point relates to the risk of conservatism. A population that is numerically dominated by elders should—others things being equal—be less open to change and more prone to maintain the status quo. Moreover, as the number of elderly expands, the senior lobbies could become ever more powerful and lay claim to an ever larger share of public budgets. Hence an unavoidable tension: the opposition of interest between the pensioners and the taxpayers could lead to a clash between generations. The growing reluctance to accept necessary reforms (even now, the Government does not dare to harmonize the pension benefits between the public and the private sectors) could have a major impact not only on the rise of costs but also on the improvement of productivity. The experience of France in a past period of ageing (Third Republic: 1870-1945) shows a country progressively lagging in terms of growth and innovation (Sauvy, 1984). Older generations tend to hold on to the knowledge of their generation; their opposition to reform is pernicious, since an ageing population requires more adaptation. A rapidly ageing society could ignore this at its peril, thus losing its position in the international ranking, whether demographic, economic or cultural.

IV. POLICY RESPONSES: STRENGTHS AND WEAKNESSES OF THE FRENCH POPULATION POLICY

The French population policy is commonly viewed as "pronatalist". This was true for the first decades covering the period 1938-1962; this is not the case any more; only rhetoric has subsisted. The social expenditures devoted to family welfare now rank fourth, after pensions, health care and unemployment benefits (their share in the social security budget is 9 per cent); they ranked first until the 1960s. Other countries of EU (Scandinavia, United Kingdom of Great Britain and Northern Ireland) spend more on children. The population policy did not change in accordance with deep social change such as was reflected by the end of the predominance of agriculture, the priority of career in women's status, the explosion of the cost of children etc.

The French system has two main relative advantages: the existence of a successful, universal pre-elementary school (for age group 2-5); and the fiscal system called *quotient familial*, which creates substantial child-related rebates. However, one has to keep in mind that the threshold is so low that only half of households pay income tax. The efficiency of pre-elementary schooling is appreciated by the public and also by the parents who find therein a good alternative to a career break or the use of child-minders. At the beginning of the 1980s, the fiscal system was hotly debated; now there is a consensus between the left and the right on the principle of taxation (the principle that was voted in December 1945 by the Parliament with full unanimity). It is considered a matter of general orientation, based on the *Déclaration des Droits de l'Homme et du Citoyen*: taxation has to be calculated not on incomes, but on the contributive capacity, that is to say, on a relative income, taking household composition into account.

Now, there are weaknesses, since no major breakthrough has been decided during the last three decades. The purchasing power of family allowances has regularly deteriorated. Many income-tested allowances (about 20) have been created, so that the system lacks transparency and seems more dedicated to poverty alleviation than to compensation of family costs. The distribution of the minimum income to the unemployed (*revenu minimum d'insertion* (RMI)) is managed by the Caisse Nationale d'Allocations Familiales (CNAF); this is the strongest argument showing this bias.

Let us mention other discrepancies:

- The greater investment by women born since the 1970s than by men in education. They take the decision to have a partner and build a family only when their professional career has begun and seems to be stabilized. A growing share of them work full-time in the private sector, often in qualified jobs. Thus, the opportunity cost of children is much higher now than in former generations; this requires a reconsideration of childhood policy. As mentioned above, children have access to publicly subsidized pre-elementary school from the age of two onward. There is a missing chain between maternity leave and early schooling. The access to parental leave is limited by parity (only for high-parity children) and by income (only to poor couples). The distance between Nordic countries and France becomes considerable; parental leave is exceptional and not related to the wages of the parents: it is a social minimum, and thus penalizes the couples who are both engaged in professional life and decide to become parents. This factor is probably the most serious obstacle to childbearing;

- The inadequate supply of reasonably priced housing in big urban centres, namely, the Paris region. Many official reports have underlined the need to revise the system of moderate rental housing; the access to this stock is in practice granted more to a political clientele or to middle-class couples than to families in need of space;

- The absence of consideration of the expenditures linked to older dependent children, whether students or unemployed. These children have come of age, but they are not financially autonomous; their parents face the most expensive years (the fiscal law is adapted to this new reality, but it is not the case for the social security system; there are many similar contradictions);

- The absence of clear doctrine on the responsibilities both of the State and of the private sector, and on the role of the State, of the system of social welfare and of supranational (European) authorities. The pension system continues to be prosperous, probably because older people are more likely to vote and become a majority. Since children have no lobby, they do not exist politically.

Public policy has to address the needs of children who now have a higher rate of poverty than the elderly. Potential parents are waiting for a framework opening the way to a real "free choice" in terms of number of children.

Another direction that is still taboo in France as well as in many countries of Western Europe is renouncing the so-called "zero immigration policy", which, given the demographic and economic international imbalances between the two rims of the Mediterranean Sea (and particularly the situation of sub-Saharan Africa), is totally unrealistic. The country needs labour at the two extremes of the levels of qualification: low-skilled and highly skilled labour. The Government might favour admitting more young immigrants, along the lines of a quota policy; French history and international experience call for such a reconsideration.

CONCLUSION

A demographic benchmark will soon be created. By the year 2010, people aged 65 years or over will outnumber people aged 0-14. In spite of the peculiarity of French history in the field of population ageing (due to the early fertility decline), the ratio of youth (0-14) to the elderly (65 years or over) was 2.5 in 1950. This ratio will continue to diminish from approximately 1 by the year 2010 to 0.6-0.7 by the year 2030 and finally to 0.4-0.7 by the year 2050. The fact that the elderly outnumber the young is new in human history. This will take place in a context of declining population: if fertility remains low, population numbers will decline progressively; under the low-fertility assumption, the population could decrease by 13.5 per cent over the period 2010-2050 (to 59.7 million and 51.7 million, respectively).

The unprecedented association of hyper-longevity and hypo-fertility will induce a massive reversal of the age structure, that is to say, an inversion of the age pyramid. The median age will rise to unprecedented values of about 45 to 50 years. The change is impressive: in the year 1945, the median age of the population in France was 35 years and it was then the world record. As described above, in the future, the elderly will become predominant in number over the young, thus creating a major challenge for society. With a persisting sub-fertility, the age distribution is pivoting around a dividing line which will be marked by the generations born around 1974-1975 (the period when fertility fell below replacement). All institutions established since time immemorial for "normal" (that is to say, triangular) age distribution will have to be reconsidered. Special measures could be envisaged to avoid gridlock if the grey vote is organized into a political lobby; it could represent half of the total vote and become a majority not only at the local level ("communes") but also at the national level (Parliament and Government).

Immigration is not the appropriate response to this challenge (United Nations, 2000). From the middle of the nineteenth century until the Second World War, France experienced both immigration and population ageing. Immigration is basically an economic regulator, used to meet the labour needs of employers. The immigration policy does not take into account demographic considerations like the will to repair or rectangularize the age distribution. Such an imperative would need a solution totally opposed to basic human rights: the import of children without their parents.

NOTE

[1]Easterlin's hypothesis assumed that fertility follows a cyclic pattern, depending on the weight of young adults relative to older adults (Easterlin, 1987).

REFERENCES

Blanchet, Didier, et J. M. Chanut (1998). Les retraites à long terme: une projection par microsimulation, *Économie et Statistique* (Paris), No. 5, pp. 95-117.

Calot, Gérard (1997). *Le Vieillissement Démographique dans l'Union européenne à l'Horizon 2050: Une Étude d'Impact.* Paris: Futurible International.

Chesnais, Jean-Claude (1990). Demographic transition patterns and their impact on the age structure. *Population and Development Review* (New York), No. 2.

Easterlin, Richard A. (1987). *Birth and Fortune. The Impact of Numbers on Personal Welfare.* Chicago, University of Chicago Press.

Kotlikoff, L. J., and W. Leibfritz (1998). An International Comparison of Generational Accounts. National Bureau of Economic Research (NBER) Working Paper No. 6447 (March). Cambridge, Massachusetts: NBER.

Malabouche, G. (1987). L'évolution à long terme du système de retraites: une nouvelle méthode de projection. *Population*, vol. 42, No. 1, January-February. Paris: Institut National d'Études Démographiques.

Organisation for Economic Co-operation and Development (1998). *Maintaining Prosperity in an Ageing Society.* Paris: OECD.

Peterson, Peter G. (1999). *Gray Dawn: How the Coming Age Wave Will Transform America and the World.* New York: Times Books, Random House.

Sauvy, Alfred (1984). *Histoire économique de la France entre les deux guerres*, vol. II. Paris: Economica.

United Nations (1999). *World Population Prospects: The 1998 Revision*, vol. I, *Comprehensive Tables.* Sales No. E.99.XIII.9.

_____ (2000). *Below Replacement Fertility. Population Bulletin of the United Nations* (New York), Special Issue Nos. 40/41. Sales No. E.99.XIII.13.

Wattenberg, Ben J. (1987). *The Birth Dearth.* New York: Pharos Books.

World Bank (1994). *Averting the Old Age Crisis.* New York: Oxford University Press.

POLICY RESPONSES TO POPULATION AGEING AND POPULATION DECLINE IN FRANCE

*Georges Tapinos**

INTRODUCTION

In most developed countries, the decline in fertility and the increase in longevity have raised three concerns for the future: the decrease in the supply of labour, the socio-economic implications of population ageing, and the long-term prospects of population decline and demise.

The population debate has a particular relevance in the case of France, where the early decline in fertility has prompted a deep and ongoing concern, which goes back to the last decades of the nineteenth century, and led to the implementation of population policies, favouring immigration and natality. The debate regained strength from the late 1960s on, when fertility started to decline, as in most Western European countries, though the current and projected fertility levels remain above the average level of the other member States of the European Union (EU).

Over this long span, however, the way that the population debate was formulated changed in a significant way—from a philosophical debate on the future of the French nation and a political concern in relation to Germany, to one on the socio-economic implications of demographic ageing and, in particular, the endangering of the welfare State. Indeed, inasmuch as economic variables are related to the size, rate of growth and age distribution of the population, the projected changes in these parameters might impact economic welfare. The concern is legitimate but, in order to set out what is at stake, we need to assess the nature, the extent and the timing of the issues stemming from the projected demographic trends and to consider, in a comparative way, the relevance and efficiency of the policy responses available in order to meet the desired targets, whether population policies or other instruments of intervention.

First, considering the demographic parameters involved, to preclude the demise of population and to ensure a stationary population is an unquestionable end for any society, and in that respect fertility is an inescapable means for attaining that given target. Immigration, except for settlement countries, is not an end per se, though it might be a means, in order to respond to the needs of the labour market with respect to achieving a more balanced age structure or to slowing down the decrease of the population. The age structure itself is a constraint, which can be altered through policy only to a limited extent.

---

*Institut d'Études Politique de Paris, Paris, France.

Secondly, there is an interrelation between the type of issues involved, their timing, and the appropriate policy measures and their efficiency. For that purpose, it is appropriate to envisage, as a working device, three time-horizons and the specific reference systems, that is to say, the set of variables to be considered relevant for a given issue at a given point in time in the future.

In the medium run, the next 10 years or so, the labour market is the main focus of concern. The reference system comprises here the set of supply and demand variables that determine the employment equilibrium. The impact of fertility and mortality changes is for that purpose at this time-horizon very limited. Conversely, international migration could play a decisive role, as well as other socio-economic variables.

For the long run, from 2020 to the population projections horizon 2040-2050, structural imbalances of the age distributions are elements to worry about. Now, the equilibrium of the social security system depends not only on demographic trends and structure but also on a number of variables, social, economic and institutional, that might just as well strengthen as dampen the demographic impact.

In the very long run, beyond the next 50 years, the concern is total population decline. The relevant framework of analysis for that concern is population dynamics and there is no other meaningful option than an increase in fertility in order to sustain a stationary population. Indeed, the 2050 horizon is acceptable but arbitrary. From the base year of the projection, it represents a time-span of roughly two generations. It may be seen as being too long, since behaviour may change from one generation to the next. This space of time is too short for the full effect of population dynamics to work through, assuming stable fertility.

Sorting the issues according to different deadlines is necessary in order to relate them to the relevant variables; however, as policy changes need time to produce a significant effect, and the timing of the issues and the policy responses differ, choices have to be made at an early stage.

The United Nations report on replacement migration (United Nations, 2001) focuses on the prospects of a negative growth rate of the population, a decrease in the supply of labour and an increase in the burden put on the population of working age by the increase of the population retired from the labour force. This exercise shows, indeed, the arithmetical impact of population prospects, which is precisely and solely what the exercise is about, but this is only one dimension of the issue and it remains to demonstrate in which cases, under which conditions and for which time-horizon population changes can be considered a relevant and determinant factor.

The following sections of the present paper deal first with the assumptions of the projection and the appropriate age grouping, then with the three major issues raised by the decline in the growth rate and the ageing of the population: the labour-market adjustment, the social security system equilibrium, and the prospect of a declining population. A final section considers specifically the replacement migration issue.

At this time, a presentation of future trends of the French population is constrained by the absence of recent projections by l'Institut National de la Statistique et des Études Économiques (INSEE). The statistical office, pending the exploitation of the 1999 census, has not yet updated its projections that date back to the early 1990s.

A. Fertility, mortality and migration assumptions

The latest available population projections produced by INSEE are based on the 1990 census and the previous intercensal trends (Dinh, 1994 and 1995). They cover the period 1990-2050. They assume one pattern for mortality, one for international migration and three levels of fertility (high: 2.1; "central": 1.8; low: 1.5). How do they compare with the latest United Nations projections (table 1)? The United Nations 1998 medium variant upon which the replacement migration report is based is close to the INSEE "central" projection, except for international migration.

TABLE 1.   POPULATION PROJECTIONS FOR FRANCE (2050)[a]

	Projections		
	Low	Central	High
	INSEE projections, 1992		
Total fertility rate (per woman)	1.5	1.8	2.1
Life expectancy (years)			
Males	77.9	77.9	77.9
Females	86.4	86.4	86.4
Net migration per year (thousands)	50	50	50
	United Nations projections, 1998		
Total fertility rate (per woman)	1.56	1.96	2.36
Life expectancy (years)			
Males	78.9	78.9	78.9
Females	86.0	86.0	86.0
Net migration per year (thousands)[b]			

Sources: Dinh (1994 and 1995); and United Nations (1999).

[a]Values are those of the end point of projections (2050).

[b]Net migration declining from 30,000 per year in 1995-2000 to 0 in 2020 and after.

The medium/central fertility assumptions are nearly the same. Both assume a slight increase in the fertility level, with minor differences in the time path. For INSEE, fertility is supposed to stabilize at 1.8 from 2005 on, whereas the United Nations assumes a stabilization at 1.96 from 2015-2020 on, which amounts on the whole to a total fertility rate (TFR) of 1.9. The patterns of mortality are quite similar and, in both cases, there is only one mortality assumption, which is regrettable, taking into account the impact of increasing longevity on the number and proportion of older people.

The international migration assumption is, in both cases, somehow ad hoc. INSEE assumes a 50,000 net immigration per year over the entire projection period, a mere extrapolation of the balance inferred from the comparison between the 1982 and 1990 censuses. The United Nations assumes a 525,000 net immigration from 1995 to 2020, that is to say, 21,000 per year and none after 2020. Unfortunately, the preliminary results of the 1999 census which show a zero net migration over the period 1990-1999—indeed a highly surprising and questionable outcome considering the level of entries during this period—are not of great help in arguing for a better choice. The INSEE labour-force projections based on total population projections and covering the period 1995-2040 have added a variant of net migration that could be induced by an increased labour demand (158,000 per year over the period 2007-2025), a level close to the observed net migration during the years of high growth and migration (129,000 per year between 1963 and 1974) (Brondel and others, 1996).

The sensitivity of the INSEE projection to the assumptions is given in table 2. As a matter of fact, INSEE has also run the central projection assuming either constant mortality or no migration. Table 3 shows the respective impact of fertility, mortality and migration assumptions on the total population and the age structure at the end point of the projection. Fertility has the strongest impact on the level of the population, and mortality on the ageing indices; migration, that is to say, the assumed level of net immigration plus the natural increase of immigrants, slows down the ageing process to a limited extent.

It should be stressed that this brief comparative exercise between the two sets of projection has no other purpose than to help explain some differences in the results, but cannot be regarded in any way as an argument strengthening the predictive value of the choices made for the projection of the future levels and trends. Indeed, the logic of the projection and the methodology are the same. In both cases, the values of the parameters are based on past and current trends, independently of any theory on the determinants of fertility, mortality and international migration, and exclude by construction any possibility of reversal in trends, notwithstanding the fact that comparisons between expected and observed trends in contemporary population history show great discrepancies, and in particular cycles in fertility, when dealing with periods that stretch over half a century. The record for population projections, considered reasonably good over the span of one generation, is rather poor for the long run, though this is its main target. Working with the best available calculations does not preclude considering these cum grano salis.

B. *The population indicators*

Among the targets already mentioned, the age grouping relevant for assessing the implications of the projections on the supply of labour and the potential support ratio, in relation to the time-span of the projection, needs some qualification. The United Nations follows the usual 0-15, 15-64, and 65 or over age groupings. For France, this cluster does not appear very relevant, taking

	Population in 2050	Percentage 20 years or younger	Percentage 20-59 years	Percentage 60 or older	Percentage 65 or older
INSEE, 1992					
Central projection	65 098 000	20.7	45.6	33.7	17.2
High projection	73 602 000	24.3	45.8	29.8	15.2
Low projection	56 804 000	16.7	44.8	38.7	19.7
Central projection without migrants	59 633 470	19.8	44.9	35.3	18.3
Central projection with constant mortality	58 044 640	22.8	49.9	27.3	11.0
United Nations, 1998					
Medium variant.	59 883 000			31.4	25.5
High projection	67 413 000			27.9	22.7
Low projection	58 020 000			36.4	29.6

Sources: Dinh (1994 and 1995) and United Nations (1999).

TABLE 3. REPLACEMENT MIGRATION FOR FRANCE, BY SCENARIO

	I	II	III	IV	V
	Medium variant	Medium variant with zero migration	Constant total population	Constant age group 15-64	Constant ratio 15-64/65 years or older
Net number of migrants, 1995-2050 (thousands)	525	0	1 473	5 459	93 794
Potential support ratio in 2050 (number of persons aged 15-64 per person aged 65 or older)	2.26	2.26	2.33	2.49	4.36
Average annual net number of migrants between 2000 and 2050, per million inhabitants in 2000	110	0	500	1 854	30 430
Percentage of post-1995 migrants and their descendants in total population in 2050	0.9	0	2.9	11.6	68.3
Total population and growth rates Population in 2050 (thousands) . . .	59 883	59 357	61 121	67 130	187 193
Average annual growth rate 1995-2050 (percentage)	0.06	0.04	0.09	0.27	2.13

Source: United Nations (2001).

into account the shortening of the length of the working life. At one end, with more years of schooling and increasing difficulties for young people in finding a job, the average age at entry into the labour force increased by 2.5 years from 1969 to 1993 (Brondel and others, 1996); at the other end, the reduction of the legal age for retirement down to 60 years and the reluctance of employers to hire older persons led to a decrease in the average age of retirement by 3.5 years, from 62 to 58.5 years, between 1968 and 1995 (Blanchet and Marioni, 1996). A later age at entry into the labour force coupled with an earlier retirement age makes the age bracket 20-60, instead of 15-65, more appropriate for the working-age population and the age bracket 60 or over more appropriate for the retired persons. Clearly, whatever the index, there is not much difference between the projected trends of the potential support ratio, but there is a significant difference in the levels; and, thus, when it comes to the absolute numbers required to keep the ratio constant at its initial level, the differences are significant.

These are demographic ratios that compare age groups, whereas the indicators have to be related to a given concern. The relevant ratio for the social security system is the ratio of retired persons to employed persons. For macroeconomic purposes, one should consider the ratio of all persons out of the labour force (young and old, inactive and unemployed) to employed persons. Depending on assumptions on female labour-force participation rates and even more on unemployment rates, there may be significant differences between the "demographic" and the "economic" ratios. Indeed, in France, the employment rate (employed population compared with population of working ages) is well below and the unemployment rate above the level observed in the other more advanced countries of EU.

Besides, and more importantly, the baseline ratios reflecting the demographic history of a very specific period, characterized by the upturn and downturn of fertility, the improvement of life expectancy, a strong immigration component and, finally, an exceptional population growth in French history cannot therefore be used as the long-run steady-state ratios. A more meaningful reference would be the stationary population. Thus, according to the United Nations, the 15-64/65-plus ratio in France was 4.36 to 1 in 2000 and this is the target for 2050 (United Nations, 2001). According to Didier Blanchet (in Tapinos, 1992), the ratio of employed to elderly inactive was 2.7 to 1 in 1990; on the basis of a stationary population, this ratio would have been 1.7 to 1. Reference to a stationary population is all the more interesting considering that stable population theory shows that, with fertility below replacement level, and a constant number of immigrants with a constant age structure, the total population ultimately becomes stationary.

Also, with the lengthening of the retirement period, and the improvement of health and living conditions of the elderly, a distinction between those aged 60-70 or so and those over these ages becomes important. The former, relatively more well off, in good health, and with more free time, are holding a key position in the intergenerational links, bearing responsibility for their older parents and at the same time helping raise their grandchildren; the latter, whatever their economic conditions, are often physically dependent and isolated, and a significant proportion of them are left with fewer or no living children and grandchildren, reduction in biological kinship being due to the decline in fertility, even though the new patterns of divorce and remarriage somehow compensate.

THE IMPACT OF DEMOGRAPHIC CHANGES

A. *Demographic projections and the labour market*

The impact on the labour market is the first concern of population projections. The population of working age (20-59 years) continues to increase by 150,000 per year up to 2005; but from then on, the baby-bust cohorts will start reaching the working age (fertility declined between the 1964 birth cohorts and the 1974 birth cohorts), while—and this effect is much stronger—the baby-boom cohorts will be reaching the age of retirement. Thus, the working-age population, after reaching a peak in 2005 (32.85 million as against 31.5 million in 1995), will decline steadily, down to 29.7 million in 2050. As has been the case in previous decades, the demographic component will dominate over the changes in participation rates. Between 1968 and 1995, the average participation rate remained nearly stable (a 1 percentage point change, from 54.4 to 55.4 per cent) as a result of the compensating effect of declining rates for young and older persons and increasing rates for adult women (Brondel and others, 1996). For the future, the central labour-force projection assumes in the main a prolongation of past tendencies in participation rates, and demographic projections will shape labour-force trends, but with a significant change in trends and levels: a much slower growth in the first phase followed by a decrease in the population of working age and, on the whole, a much smaller variation than in the pre-1990 period.

The projected decrease in the rate of growth and in the level of the working-age population has prompted a debate on a possible labour shortage—a strong departure, indeed, from the current concern about the high level of unemployment. However, we are a long way from changes in the numbers and proportion of the population of working ages and employment. The equilibrium of the labour market results from labour supply and labour demand conditions which involve a set of determinants that range well beyond the demographic variables and are related to a limited extent to these variables (the cost of labour, entrepreneurs' anticipations, productivity, changes in the production process and induced changes in the structure skills, the global demand etc.). Moreover, the impact of demographic changes on the determinants of labour demand remains elusive.

To infer a labour shortage from the predictable changes in the population of working age is totally unwarranted. Indeed, considering the past, an accounting decomposition of the way changes in the population of working ages translates into changes in employment, participation rates and unemployment, shows a great diversity in the adjustment processes. In France, between 1975 and 1985, a 12.2 per cent variation in the population of working ages was associated with a slight increase in employment (0.8 points), a strong increase in unemployment (7.0 points) and a decrease in activity rates (3.9 points); during the period 1985-1996, for a 6.2 per cent decrease in the population of working age, the equivalent figures were 3 points for employment, 3 points for unemployment and a negligible change in participation rates. The same decomposition for other European countries shows a wide range of adjustment processes. It is clear that an increase in the population of working age can result in an increase of employment as well as of unemployment, and the same is true in the case of a decrease of the population of working ages (G. P. Tapinos, 1996).

Now, let us assume that the projected decrease in the population of working ages will induce a labour shortage; if that happens, the order of magnitude of the increase in the labour force required to adjust the labour market is within reach of manageable changes in the supply of labour determinants, among which immigration could be one possibility. In the extreme case where the adjustment would rely only on immigration, in order to stabilize the active population after 2006, net immigration per year would have to increase from the assumed constant level of 50,000 to approximately 100,000 in 2010 (and should increase from then on) (Brondel and others, 1996). The spectrum of global labour shortage is unwarranted. In fact, barring the unlikely combination of very low fertility, high mortality, low immigration and constant labour-force participation rates, almost all the EU countries will have in 2020 the same-sized total population and labour force as now (Feld, 2000).

B. *Demographic projections and the social security system*

Undoubtedly, amid the current concern in France about future population trends, the implications of ageing for the pension system are at the heart of the debate. Indeed, France is not the only European country where the pay-as-you-go scheme predominates, but putting aside the arguments on the relative merits of pay-as-you-go and funded systems, which are not to be discussed here, it is a country where the pay-as-you-go system is viewed as a fundamental element of intergenerational solidarity and social cohesion. Indeed, the implementation of social security, the extension in coverage to all categories of the population and the increases in pensions have contributed to a significant improvement of the economic conditions of retirees, whose income compares favourably with that of the active young, though it contains a larger share of capital income.

The demographic stylized facts are well known. Taking into account the decrease of fertility and the progress in longevity and, more specific to the French case, the shortening of the working lifespan, as already mentioned, all things being equal, population projections show a reduction by two of the old age dependency ratio at the horizon of the projection (2050). There is no way to escape from a fundamental reform of the system and some steps have been already taken for that purpose (in 1993)—increasing the number of years of work required to secure a full pension from 37.5 to 40 and indexing pensions on prices rather than on wages. However, there is still a long way to go. The question and the ensuing heated debate are about the policy mix. What is more feasible, more efficient and more desirable?

Let us consider first the financial aspect. With a projected division by two (or more) of the 20-59/60 years or over ratio at the end year of the projection, the fact that, in a system with defined contributions, the benefits would be divided by two, and in a system of defined benefits, the contributions should be multiplied by two, means that the return would be divided by two.

Assuming a 2.1 fertility (instead of 1.8) would increase the number of active population by 2.2 million by 2040. For migration to compensate for the decline in the old age dependency ratio, net migration should be at each point in time roughly three times the number of persons reaching retirement. This will be discussed more appropriately in the next section.

What can we expect from changes in labour-force participation? Assuming a convergence of the participation rates of women aged 30-49 with those of men (that is to say, 90 instead of 87.5 per cent) would increase the active population by 900,000 persons by the year 2020, a surplus that would remain constant from then on until 2040.

Increasing the age of retirement by five years over the period 2000-2020 will, in the stable state (approximately 2020), increase the active population by 3 million persons (Blanchet and Marioni, 1996). This has the strongest impact on the old age dependency ratio, the projected increase of the ratio resulting mainly from the increase of the number of retired persons and only to a much lesser extent from the decrease of the active population. Indeed, postponing the age of retirement increases the active population and decreases the retired population by an equivalent amount. Though the progress in longevity gives a rationale in favour of an increase in the retirement age, it is strongly opposed by trade unions. Roughly speaking, a one-year postponement of the age of retirement is equivalent to one year of contributions.

Finally, the most powerful adjustment could come from productivity. A 3 per cent productivity growth per year would totally compensate for the increase of the support ratio, assuming that all progress is allocated to retired persons (Blanchet, in Tapinos, 1992).

There is indeed a wide range of possible adjustments. If assuming all factors constant except for one does not make sense, the solution is evidently in a policy mix. However the possible adjustments differ not only by their specific difficulties in implementation (for instance, the strong reluctance to a later age of retirement), but also by their impact on intergenerational equity, inasmuch as they tend to shift the burden between generations. In that respect, the pay-as-you-go system raises a specific intergenerational distribution problem. Defining the conditions of the cross-section accounting equilibrium between contributions and benefits is one thing; assessing the impact of demographic trends on the equity of the system for contributors and recipients is another. For that we need a longitudinal perspective and some measure of intra- and intergenerational equity (for instance, for each generation, the ratio of contributions to benefits, or between generations, the equivalence between contributions and the equivalence of benefits). Thus, beyond accounting exercises, what is most feasible and what is most desirable entail a political choice according to the social values of the society and the vision about social cohesion and intergenerational equity. The preferred choice is itself related to the age distribution and might reflect the interests of the groups with more electoral weight. Indeed, if the average age of the labour force increases with ageing by a few years, the increase in longevity increases the number and proportion of the elderly and brings a radical change in the average age of the electorate. In France, from 1988 to 1995, the average age of the electors increased from 45.1 to 46.6 years; the increase will be much more pronounced at the 2050 horizon.

C. *Fertility below replacement and declining population*

According to the INSEE projections (which include a 50,000 net immigration per year), the total population will continue to increase up to 2020 in any case. After that and at the horizon of the projection, the trend will depend mainly on the fertility assumption. With fertility below replacement, in the most extreme case, a TFR of 1.5 and no immigration, the population would start declining between 2010 and 2015; immigration would postpone the turning point by 10 years or so. Assuming a TFR of 1.8 (and net migration), the population continues to grow until 2040.

The prospect of a declining population and its demise, though far remote, is the most challenging aspect of population policies, increase in fertility being the only option. It is indeed a legitimate and desirable objective for a nation, independently of any considerations of the socio-economic implications of population prospects. Is it feasible in the case of France? On the one hand, the intensity and tempo of completed fertility across generations do not suggest a catching-up process for the younger generations; on the other hand, the difference between the current levels and the replacement level is not considerable and might be amenable to policies. However, in a situation of controlled fertility, when observed fertility comes close to desired fertility, the rationale of a pronatalist population policy is at stake. One could argue that preferences of individuals do not give much weight to the future of the society or that their choices reflect their ignorance of the long-run implications at the aggregate level of their own behaviour, or that the future of a nation being a public good, the demand for children may be suboptimal. Policies aiming at an alleviation of the private costs of child-raising have shown some efficiency at the margin; more is required in order to induce a significant behavioural change. This raises issues well beyond the limited scope of this paper.

REPLACEMENT MIGRATION

We focus more specifically in this last section on replacement migration as a means to reach the three targets stated initially.

Recourse to immigration has the advantage of producing an immediate and relatively large impact on the labour force owing to the characteristics of the new arrivals, who are younger and more mobile. In addition, the fact that fertility rates among female immigrants tend to be high contributes to population growth, albeit to a limited degree. At the same time, there are a number of practical and political constraints on formulating a migration policy aimed at achieving demographic change.[1] We first consider the dynamics of the levels of immigration required to meet these targets, in particular a stable support ratio, then the feasibility of migration policy as a response to demographic changes and the constraints on the social process of integration of immigrants in the society. Is a policy that relies solely on migration to achieve demographic adjustment feasible? Is it desirable? There are three kinds of limitations that call into question the soundness of the approach. They involve immigration policies, population dynamics and social dynamics.

A. *Replacement migration and population dynamics*

The simulations that attracted the most attention, at least in the media, involving a constant old age dependency ratio until 2050, imply a very large volume of arrivals and departures and fluctuations in migration (table 3). These translate into an exceptional increase in total population and in the proportion of immigrants. The level of annual net migration needed to hold the old age dependency ratio constant is huge and disproportionate with respect to the data on record.

Given the age structure and dynamics of immigrant populations, the number and proportion of foreign-born persons and their descendants would reach disproportionately high levels, compared with the current ones, by the scenario's horizon date of 2050. In 1990, the recorded proportion of foreign-born persons was 10.4 per cent in France. At the scenario horizon, on the other hand, the proportion of immigrants who arrived in 1995 and their descendants would be 68.3 per cent of the total population in France (United Nations, 2001).

In addition, an unchanged dependency ratio over time presupposes huge fluctuations not only in migration flows (arrivals and departures) but also in net immigration, given age structures and population dynamics (Blanchet, 1988). This point is disregarded in the United Nations study, which assumes continuous inward migration with no outflows.

B. *Migration policies and social dynamics*

The implicit, but critical, assumption of the scenario is that immigration, or rather the aforementioned net immigration, is a control variable. It could be argued that, the supply of emigrants worldwide exceeding the demand for immigrants, the countries willing to accept a level of immigration that meets the replacement targets would have no difficulty in achieving their objective. These arguments need to be qualified.

Is the control of the volume and age structure of migration inflows and outflows feasible? Migration policies could make entry more dependent on age requirements, which are already explicitly or implicitly present. However, there are still many factors that limit, or complicate, the ability to control and select migration flows: the agreements on free movement of persons, the persistence of illegal immigration, humanitarian grounds, and other constraints like admission for reasons of family reunification. The acceptance of refugees cannot, by definition, be governed by demographic and economic criteria.

Similarly, the selectivity applied to close relatives and other family members has its limits; and if immigration targets emphasize age or fertility patterns, this may be seen as a form of discrimination and hence a political issue. In the last analysis, all will depend on the philosophy underlying each country's migration policy and on its proper characteristics. Besides, monitoring immigration for labour-market needs implies a distribution of immigrants by skills, a much harder goal to achieve if the projected labour requirements deal with highly qualified workers, which was not the case in the past when most immigrants were unskilled.

Whatever the efficiency of migration policies with respect to the number and characteristics of immigrants, they have virtually no effect on return migration, hence the difficulty of controlling the volume and characteristics of net migration. Even in the case of countries that favour settlement, the returns are far from negligible and their determinants are not amenable to policy, as evidenced by the attempts to implement return policies. One way around this difficulty would be to introduce programmes for admitting temporary workers in order to increase labour supply in periods of rapid growth in the elderly population or decline in the population of working age. Experience has shown, however, that such programmes are difficult to implement. Although most countries have legislation for the admission of temporary foreign workers,[2] it has been found that a proportion of the immigrants admitted on this basis settle permanently in the host country. This they do either legally, by applying for a change of status or having their permits regularly renewed, or illegally. Furthermore, other than in cases where the authorized stay is very short, some countries' temporary employment programmes offer the worker's dependants and close relatives the right to reside in the host country.

There is still some uncertainty whether policy targets are actually attained. The means available to monitor the trends of net migration differ across countries. The measurement of entries in France is far from accurate, the measurement of exits is non-existent and the data on stocks cannot, for the present, be of great help for this purpose. The necessary lag for estimating net migration and, in any case, the absence of linkage between individual data on entries and those on exits preclude any form of fine-tuned migration policy.

Beyond the population dynamics and policy management issues, there is the fundamental question of social dynamics. The history of immigration in France as elsewhere shows that immigrants have a better chance of integrating into the host society if the native population is experiencing a natural increase. Fertility and immigration are, to a large extent, complementary, not substitutable.

To conclude, the goal of migration policy may be to ensure sustainability of the nation, to adjust labour supply to demand by volume and by structure, or to bring pay-as-you go pension systems into financial equilibrium. There is also the humanitarian approach in the acceptance of a certain number of immigrants regardless of political or economic considerations. Immigration can certainly help to prevent population decline for a time. It has only a marginal impact on the cited imbalances in age structure. Immigration is clearly not the solution to population ageing. It can even be said that the simulations made to date demonstrate the impossibility of a migration solution, and the analysis of migration processes reinforces this assessment.

The equilibrium of social welfare systems depends on a set of demographic and institutional parameters (age of entry into the active labour force, participation rates and unemployment rates, contribution rates and benefit levels, economic growth rates, productivity growth rates etc.). Given the predicted drastic change in the old age dependency ratio, it is quite impossible to count on just one variable to achieve the necessary adjustment and treat all the others as constants; but although replacement migration cannot be the answer to the problem, immigration can possibly contribute, inter alia, to labour-market adjustment, and balancing of the population's age structure and population decline.

CONCLUSION

The demographic regime of France, like that of most developed countries, has changed drastically in the last decades. Most analyses show that these fundamental changes are of a permanent nature and that, in particular, the prospects of a reversal in fertility trends and the return to demographic growth logic are totally unwarranted.

The pattern and level of fertility reflect fundamental behavioural changes and it appears irrelevant to consider the conditions resulting from high population growth as the baseline and the target for the future.

The challenge posed by demographic prospects calls for new types of adjustments. Indeed, as has been shown by sociologists as well as economists, a stationary population makes necessary an acceleration of changes of the production system, while at the same time tending naturally to reinforce rigidities, in particular with respect to professional and social mobility.

(This paper draws upon a previous note on replacement migration prepared for the Organisation for Economic Co-operation and Development (OECD) Working Party on Immigration. I would like to thank Jean-Pierre Garson for his comments).

NOTES

[1] A number of these difficulties were outlined in *Migration: The Demographic Aspects* (Organisation for Economic Co-operation and Development, 1991).

[2] See the special chapter on temporary employment of foreigners in selected OECD countries in *Trends in International Migration* (Paris, Organisation for Economic Co-operation and Development, 1998).

REFERENCES

Blanchet, Didier (1988). Immigration et régulation de la structure par âge d'une population. *Population* (Paris), vol. 2, pp. 293-309.

_____, and P. Marioni (1996). L'activité après 55 ans : évolutions récentes et éléments de prospective. *Économie et Statistique* (Paris), No. 300, pp. 105-119.

Brondel, D., and others (1996). La population active devrait encore augmenter pendant une dizaine d'années. *Économie et Statistique* (Paris), No. 300, pp. 13-37.

Charpin, J. M. (1998). *L'avenir de nos retraites*. Paris: La documentation française.

Dinh, Q. C. (1994). La population de la France à l'horizon 2050. *Économie et Statistique* (Paris), vol. 4, No. 274, pp. 7-32.

_____ (1995). Projection de population totale pour la France métropolitaine. Base RP 90. Horizons 1990-2050. *Démographie Société* (Paris), No. 44, p. 139.

Feld, S. (2000). Active population growth and immigration hypotheses in Western Europe. *European Journal of Population* (Amsterdam, Holland), vol. 16, pp. 3-40.

Organisation for Economic Co-operation and Development (1991). *Migration: the Demographic Aspects*. Paris: OECD.

_____ (1998). *Trends in International Migrations*. Paris: OECD.

Tapinos, Georges P. (1996). *Europe méditerranéenne et changements démographiques*. Turin, Italy: Fondazione Giovanni Agnelli.

_____ (1996). *La démographie. Population, économie et sociétés*. Paris: Ed. de Fallois, le Livre de poches.

_____ (2000). *The Role of Migration in Moderating the Effects of Population Ageing*. Paris: OECD.

Tapinos, G. P., ed. (1992). *La France dans deux generations: Population et société dans le premier tiers du XXIe siècle*. Paris: Fayard.

United Nations (1999). *World Population Prospects: The 1998 Revision*, vol. I, *Comprehensive Tables*. Sales No. E.99.XIII.19.

_____ (2001). *Replacement Migration: Is It a Solution to Declining and Ageing Populations?* Sales No. E.01.XIII.19.

DEMOGRAPHIC AGEING AND POPULATION DECLINE IN TWENTY-FIRST-CENTURY GERMANY: CONSEQUENCES FOR THE SYSTEMS OF SOCIAL INSURANCE

*Herwig Birg**

INTRODUCTION

There is a fundamental link in most societies between economic production (that is to say, output) and demographic *re*production. A population's total fertility rate (TFR), expressed as the number of live births per woman, tends to be lower, the higher a country's level of development. I shall discuss the main causes of this "demo-economic paradox" in section B, and show its adverse consequences for the system of social insurance in Germany. Section C will summarize the main findings of our demographic projections computed for Germany in the twenty-first century, and section D will analyse the impact of these projected demographic developments on the social insurance system and set out the consequent policy options. Section E will sum up the conclusions to be drawn on the impact of economic globalization on population change and on the ability of social insurance systems to function properly in the future.

THE DEMO-ECONOMIC PARADOX AND ITS SIGNIFICANCE FOR GERMANY'S SOCIAL INSURANCE SYSTEM

In theoretical biology, evolution is explained in terms of competition between different biological species, and between individuals of the same species, to attain optimum conditions for their life and reproduction. In human populations, too, competition among individuals and groups is an important principle determining action, so the principle's prominence in theoretical demography is similar to that in theoretical biology. Competitive behaviour has both positive and negative impacts on how we live together in human societies. Modern societies endeavour to make the best of the positive impact exerted by the competition for political power and economic success, by developing appropriate rules for democracy and the market economy. In social market economies like Germany, the negative impacts are restrained by means of comprehensive social welfare legislation.

_____
*Institute for Population Research and Social Policy, University of Bielefeld, Germany.

The more successful modern societies are in utilizing the beneficial effects of competition while avoiding its adverse effects, the less people need to rely on their own families, which always performed these tasks before the emergence of modern societies, and the larger is the fall in the value of having children "as an investment". So there is indeed an underlying logic to the inverse relationship that emerges between a country's level of development and its TFR. Yet it still appears a paradoxical outcome that people should be less willing to have children the more they can afford them. In Germany, for example, the number of live births per woman was twice as high in the 1960s as it is today (a TFR of 2.4 versus one of 1.3) even though real incomes have quadrupled since that time.

For decades, the positive net cost/benefit outcome of the German-style model of the social market economy appeared beyond dispute. However, in the last quarter of the twentieth century, it became increasingly clear that the economic success generated by this type of society was counterbalanced by a demographic failure that may yet prove destructive for both economy and society in future. The cause of this adverse trend lies in the demo-economic paradox which affects most countries of the world. Whether the comparison is made longitudinally, that is to say, by viewing the same country at different points in time, or as a cross section of countries at the same point in time, the same inverse correlation is found between live births per woman and the level of development, as expressed by indicators such as life expectancy, the United Nations Development Programme (UNDP) human development index, and per capita income.

This cross-section comparison is shown in figure I, which covers the world's 30 most populous countries, together accounting for 80 per cent of the world population. If the correlation is carried out for other points in time, the same falling curve appears. Evidently, this pattern of correlation is valid across the globe: it holds for most countries in the world, regardless of what kind of economic system or form of society they have and regardless of their histories, religions and cultures. So this has to be a fundamental mechanism, the stringency and force of which derive from the unbridgeable antagonism between the two basic human principles of action, namely, competition and the *ex*clusion of rivals on the one hand and solidarity with and the *in*clusion of fellow human beings on the other.

Economic globalization is pushing outward the boundaries of national labour and goods markets. Although individuals still primarily compete as employees with others in their own national labour market, this direct competitive relationship is now supplemented by a less obvious and more indirect one which results from global competition in the markets for goods and services. National goods have to compete on the world market with similar goods and services from elsewhere, and these are likely to be all the more competitive, the lower the labour costs related to social insurance contributions to cover retirement pensions, health care and unemployment. These are the so-called non-wage labour costs that, in Germany, include the additional component of long-term care insurance. As far as the real, demographically generated cost burden is concerned, it is immaterial whether these costs are charged as a percentage

Figure I. Correlation between life expectancy in 1980-1985 and the number of children per woman (total fertility rate), 1985-1990, for the 30 most populous countries, covering 80 per cent of the total world population

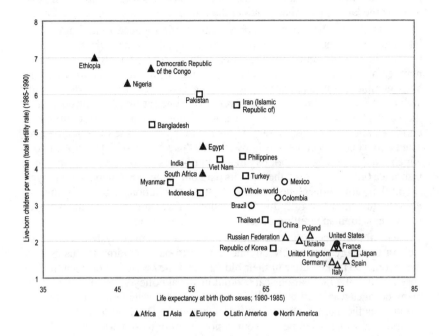

Source: Author's own calculations based on United Nations (1999).

of wages and salaries or as a percentage of corporate profits: the increase in costs and the adverse impact on competitiveness are the same either way, and the difference is purely one of economic accounting.

Non-wage costs are a fundamental determinant of prices. The older the society, the greater the per capita expenditure on social insurance systems; hence, the greater the non-wage costs and, thus, the lower the country's global competitivity. However, developed countries with high per capita incomes and high demographically determined non-wage labour costs will not automatically be swept out of the world markets by countries where both incomes and non-wage labour costs are lower. High incomes are based on higher productivity which can make up for, or perhaps even surpass, their less favourable labour-cost situation. Thus, high-wage countries will not necessarily be driven out of their markets by less developed countries. In fact, every country has scope to improve its position with regard to productivity and per capita income.

This competition among economies to obtain a favourable position en-courages employees to invest in their skills and qualifications, so the average real wage level rises continually. On the other hand, the opportunity cost to a parent of turning down work for the sake of bringing up a child also increases just as fast as this real wage level. In developed countries, the resulting low birth rate has created an "inverse" age structure: instead of the classic pyramid shape in which the youngest age groups make up the largest cohorts, these are now the middle-aged; and in Germany's case, those aged 70-74 are destined to become the largest five-year group in the future.

In Germany, the modern welfare State was introduced as far back as the late nineteenth century with the Bismarckian social reforms, which were continually improved upon during the twentieth century. The system now has a number of different features, including retirement pension, health, accident, and unemployment insurance, as well as provision for surviving dependants and, most recently, long-term care insurance. When it was first introduced in the 1880s, the social insurance system was tailored to an age structure based on the classic "population pyramid" form with a broad base of young people. The system operates on what is known as the "pay-as-you-go" principle, under which those currently in work pay their contributions into the various statutory insurance branches to fund the benefits paid out to the pensioners, unemployed etc. at that same time. Benefit payments and contributions take place simultaneously, in contrast to fully funded pensions in which capital is built up over many years to finance future benefits for the same generation.

For almost a century, this statutory benefits insurance system worked so well in Germany that hardly anyone needed to have children to ensure that they would be looked after in their old age or if they were in poor health. The very fact that the innovations carried out in social policy were so effective for many decades was itself one of the reasons why the system ultimately stopped working as the age structure changed owing to the low birth rate. Of course, the modern social insurance system is not the only reason why the birth rate has declined, but it is certainly one of the factors that influenced the demo-economic paradox, with all its consequences for a declining birth rate.

POPULATION PROJECTIONS FOR GERMANY IN THE TWENTY-FIRST CENTURY

To show how uncertain forecasts are, people often point out that weather forecasters repeatedly get it wrong. Yet weather forecasting offers a useful means to illustrate the use of demographic projections, which differ in nature from economic forecasts and various other predictions of future trends: seasonal changes, and associated aspects such as changes in average temperatures, can be predicted months in advance with greater reliability than, say, temperatures in the coming week. Though it may be generally true that predictions grow more uncertain the further into the future they look, the fields of climatology and demography offer some major exceptions to this rule. One of the most important of such exceptions is the phenomenon of demographic inertia, that is to say, the inbuilt momentum of population growth and decline: once the absolute number of births in a population has fallen owing to a change in reproductive patterns rather than to any change in the number of women of childbearing age, this will lead to a further reduction in future births, even if reproductive patterns remain constant following their initial change. Thus the initial change is triggered by a change in reproductive behaviour, but subsequent downward movements in the absolute number of births, in a series of waves each a generation apart, are due not to any further behavioural change but rather to the simple fact that people who have not been born cannot have any offspring of their own. This impact on future births created by the reduction in the number of potential parents can be forecast with a similar degree of certainty to that of the seasonal changes in years to come, in other words, almost 100 per cent. Thus, it ought not to surprise us that demographic forecasts are substantially more reliable than, say, economic ones. For example, the forecast changes in the population of former West Germany up to the pre-unification period (1985) based on the 1970 census produced an error of 1.2 per cent.

The number of live births per woman (TFR) in Western Europe initially rose slightly after the Second World War, but fell back sharply thereafter. The TFR had increased from 2.39 in 1950-1955 to 2.66 in 1960-1965, but had fallen to just 1.48 by 1995-2000. In Germany (East and West combined), the rate went up from 2.16 in 1950-1955 to 2.49 in 1960-1965, before falling back to 1.30 in 1995-2000. In the whole of Europe, whose population in 2000 was 729 million, the corresponding figures are 2.57 (1950-1955), 2.56 (1960-1965) and 1.42 (1995-2000) (United Nations, 1999).

The general downward trend in the TFR in Europe after the period 1960-1965 was due to a change in reproductive behaviour which in turn had a broad range of causes, including a shift away from traditional "family values", greater sexual permissiveness, women's liberation, the growing number of working women (meaning that those who chose to raise children would miss out on greater earning opportunities, known as the "opportunity cost of children") and the increasingly effective cover against key life risks provided by the modern welfare State (making children dispensable as a form of family-based social insurance), and extending all the way through to such factors as the advent of modern contraceptives. Strictly speaking, these factors do not properly explain the change in reproductive behaviour because they are mutually dependent and because they themselves require explanation. However, no matter how the explanatory factors are fitted together to compose a cogent theory of reproductive behaviour, the impact of the changes that really have occurred on the number of potential parents growing up and the number of children they will have in the coming decades can be computed relatively precisely. The collection of essays by Voland (1992) offers an interdisciplinary review of modern theories of reproduction. This also includes the present author's biographical fertility theory, which endeavours to achieve a synthesis of the approaches of a number of disciplines (Birg, 1995, chap. 3, p. 45).

If no migration occurred in either direction, Europe's population would fall substantially by the year 2050, even if one were to assume, as the United Nations does, that the number of live births per woman will recover somewhat, from 1.42 in 1995-2000 to 1.78 in 2040-2050. On this assumption, the population would fall from 729 million in 2000 to 628 million in 2050 (United Nations, 2001, table 26). The United Nations projections also assume that the TFR in Germany will pick up from 1.30 in 1995-2000 to 1.64 in 2040-2050; yet even assuming the birth rate does grow to this extent, the population net of any migration would then fall from 81.7 million (1995) to 58.8 million (2050) (ibid., table A.4).

The reasons given above for past changes in reproductive behaviour will not lose their validity in future, so there is nothing to suggest that these factors will cease to operate and allow the TFR to increase again, as the United Nations assumes in its projections. Thus, it is interesting to analyse how the population will develop if different assumptions are applied. The main findings of the author's projections based on these differing assumptions (Birg, 1998) will be presented below as well as in figures II and III. Two variants have been computed, one with and one without migration, and each is divided into six sub-variants. The sub-variants are intended to show projected population sizes on a purely hypothetical assumption, like that of the United Nations, that the number of children per woman will again increase. However, the approach differs from that of the United Nations in that a choice of start dates for this increase is given, from the year 2000, the year 2010, the year 2020 etc., with the last alternative assuming that the increase does not begin until 2050, the end of the projection period. In each case, the number of children per woman (TFR) is assumed to increase from 1.25 (1995) to 1.50 over a 15-year period. The last of the sub-variants, in which the TFR remains constant until 2050, tells us how the population would develop up to 2050 if we rejected the assumption of the United Nations that the birth rate will rise: net of all migration, the population of Germany would shrink to 50.7 million by 2050 and to 24.3 million by 2100. Even if we assume annual net immigration of 250,000 young people, the population would still be set to fall to 66.1 million in 2050 and to 50.0 million by 2100. The assumed net migration figure of 250,000 immigrants is in fact quite high relative to the average of 170,000 in recent decades. If net inward migration was lower, the shrinkage in the population would be correspondingly more acute.

The severity of the decline in population despite assumed net immigration of 250,000 people per annum demonstrates the momentum involved in the process, due to the compound impact in each generation of the potential parents who were never born. This momentum of population decline substantially multiplies the birth deficit (that is to say, the excess of deaths over births in a given year) from about 100,000 at present to a peak of some 700,000 in the mid-twenty-first century. Even if net immigration is, say, 225,000 and the TFR holds its level of the last quarter-century at about 1.4 live births per woman, the increase in the birth deficit to approximately 700,000 is still inevitable (figure IV). So if one sought to counteract the birth deficit by net immigration, as has happened so far, this would call for an ever-increasing number of immigrants each year, rising to between 700,000 and 800,000—depending on the assumed TFR—by the year 2050 (figure V). This figure is substantially higher than the uniquely high rate of net immigration into Germany following the collapse of the Soviet bloc.

Figure II. Population of Germany in the twenty-first century excluding migration effects, assuming an increase in the number of births per woman (TFR) from 1.25 to 1.50 over 15 years, starting from alternative points in time

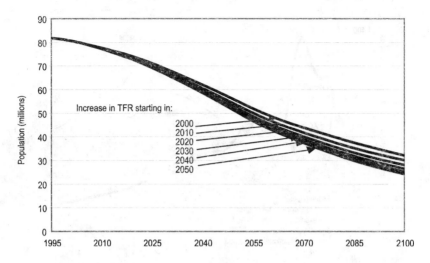

Source: Author's own calculations based on United Nations (1999).

NOTE: Assumed life expectancy: increasing to 81 years (men) and 87 years (women) by 2080.

Figure III. Population of Germany in the twenty-first century including migration effects, assuming annual net migration of 250,000 and an increase in the number of births per woman (TFR) from 1.25 to 1.50 over 15 years, starting from alternative points in time

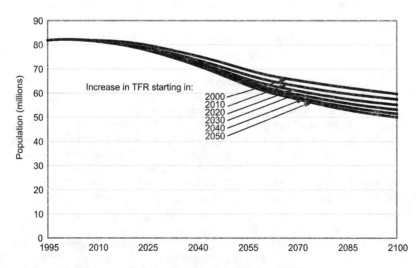

Source: Author's own calculations based on United Nations (1999).

NOTE: Assumed life expectancy: increasing to 81 years (men) and 87 years (women) by 2080.

Figure IV. Absolute number of births and deaths and the gap between the two in Germany, 1946-1997 and 1998-2100

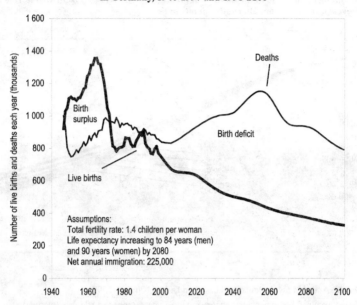

Source: H. Birg and others, *Simulationsrechnungen der Bevölkerungsentwicklung in den alten und neuen Bundesländern im 21. Jahrhundert* (Bielefeld, Germany, University of Bielefeld, 1999).

NOTE: The curves plotted up to 1997 are based on actual figures.

THE CONSEQUENCES OF DEMOGRAPHIC TRENDS FOR GERMANY'S SOCIAL INSURANCE SYSTEMS AND THE POLICY OPTIONS AVAILABLE

1. *The extent of demographic ageing and the population decline in the twenty-first century*

The decline in absolute population size and the change in the age pro-file both have their own different impacts on our economy and society. As far as social insurance systems are concerned, the change in the make-up of the population in terms of age groups is a problem that is foreseeable and can be budgeted decades in advance. The impact of the fall in the absolute population size is rather more difficult to estimate, particularly as the number of older peo-ple in society will continue to rise while the number of younger ones is already in decline, leaving a relatively small net reduction in population size over the next 20 years. However, as time goes on, the shrinkage will gain ever more momentum. This will have a growing adverse impact on economic growth, thus creating an additional impact on the ability to finance welfare spending, for example, from tax revenues. Exactly how demographic changes will affect economic growth, and how severely, cannot be forecast precisely. By way of contrast, the effect an ageing society will have on the income and expenditure

110

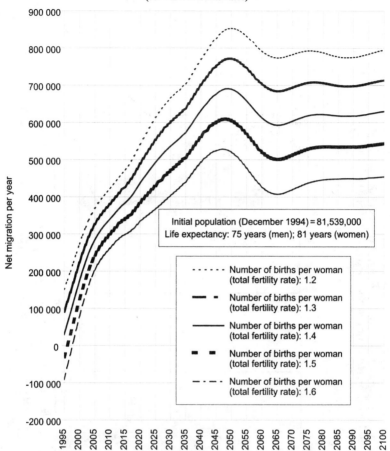

Figure V. Hypothetical net migration rate for a constant population number in Germany (for various birth rates)

Net migration per year

Initial population (December 1994) = 81,539,000
Life expectancy: 75 years (men); 81 years (women)

- - - - - Number of births per woman
(total fertility rate): 1.2

━ ━ Number of births per woman
(total fertility rate): 1.3

─── Number of births per woman
(total fertility rate): 1.4

■ ■ Number of births per woman
(total fertility rate): 1.5

─ · ─ Number of births per woman
(total fertility rate): 1.6

Source: H. Birg and others (1998).

of the social insurance system (retirement pensions, health and long-term care insurance) is clearly apparent even now. The comments that follow will concentrate on the latter issue.

The term "demographic ageing" refers to the increase in a society's average age or, to be more precise, in its median age. The present median age in Germany is 38 years: one out of two males in the population is over age 37, while one out of two females is over age 40. Median age is set to grow not only because of the declining numbers in successive newly born age groups as the years move on but also because life expectancies are increasing. By the year 2050, one out of two males in Germany will be older than age 51, and one out of two females older than age 55. These estimates even include the assumption that there will be a net immigration of 150,000 younger people into Germany; if the immigration effect is ignored, the estimated median ages in 2050 will be 53 years for males and 58 for females (see figure VI, and Birg and others, 1998).

Figure VI. Development of the age profile in former West Germany (Federal Republic of Germany) and East Germany (German Democratic Republic) (population projection variant No. 5: including migration and economic feedback)

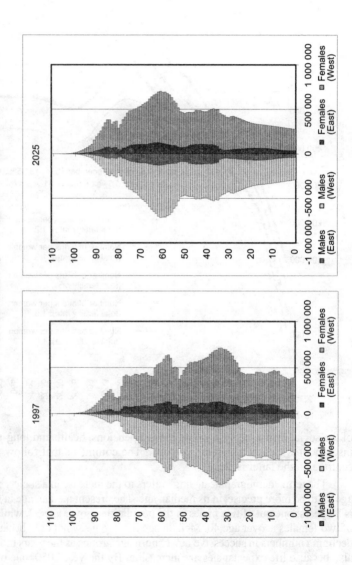

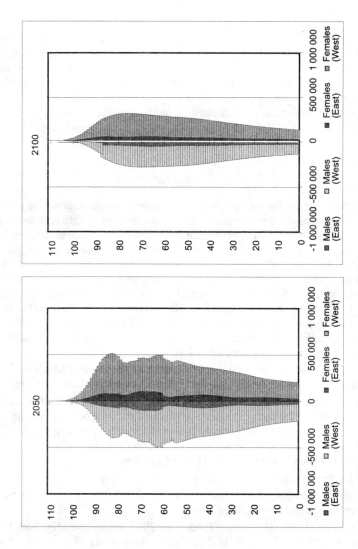

Source: H. Birg and others, *Simulationsrechnungen der Bevölkerungsentwicklung in den alten und neuen Bundesländern im 21. Jahrhundert* (Bielefeld, Germany, University of Bielefeld, 1999).

To make the impact of demographic ageing on social insurance systems as clear as possible, we can measure it not just via median age but also via the "ageing index": this is normally expressed as the number of persons aged 60 or over for every 100 people aged 20-59. The inverse value of the ageing index is referred to as the "potential support ratio". Depending on what happens to the birth rate, life expectancy and net immigration, Germany's ageing index will increase to a value between two and three times today's figure by 2050. Even on the hypothetical assumption that life expectancy remains constant, the index will nevertheless at least double. The demographic projections commissioned by the German Insurance Association to address the pension reforms in 2000 offer the following key figures: the number of persons over age 60 will increase from 17.9 million in 1998 to 27.8 million in 2050, while the number of people in age group 20-59 will fall from 46.5 million to 30.4 million in the same period, which means that the ageing index is projected to rise from 38.6 to 91.4, by a factor of 2.4 (middle variant: see Birg and Börsch-Supan, 1999, p. 162).

2. *The changing age profile*

In the report for the German Insurance Association cited above, the author computed dozens of demographic variants incorporating different assumptions regarding the birth rate, net immigration levels and future changes in life expectancy. The account given below summarizes the changes in age profile computed for the middle variant (population projection variant No. 5), also shown in figure VI. The population projections and the assumptions applied are subdivided into four groups, namely, German citizens in former West Germany (Federal Republic of Germany) and in former East Germany (German Democratic Republic), and immigrants in former West Germany and in former East Germany. For Germany as a whole, the assumptions applied to these four subpopulations can be summarized as follows:

(*a*) The mean number of live-born children per woman, which changes over the course of time, is 1.25 for German citizens and 1.64 for immigrants;

(*b*) Life expectancy at birth rises steadily from 74.0 to 80.9 years for males and from 80.8 to 86.9 years for females. Life expectancy among the immigrants is assumed to be initially approximately five years higher than for German citizens, owing to the favourable selection effect of migration, but to gradually fall back to the same level as for Germans;

(*c*) Net immigration is assumed to average 170,000 per annum.

These assumptions also include the feedback effects of economic growth on the birth rate and net migration.

The number of young people (under age 20) decreases steadily from 17.7 million in 1998 to 9.7 million in 2050, while the number of people aged 80 years or over increases in the same period from 3.0 million to approximately 10.0 million. The number of persons under age 40 in 1998 was still substantially higher than that of persons aged 60 years or over (42.3 million versus 17.9 million). In future, this relative picture will be reversed, and there will be more people aged 60 years or over than under age 40 (tables 1 and 2).

The proportion of the population under age 20 is set to decline from 21.6 to only 14.3 per cent by 2050 while the proportion of persons aged 60 years or over will increase from 21.8 to 40.9 per cent by 2050. The increase in an age group's proportion of the total population is most pronounced for the oldest population group, aged 80 years or over, which in 1998 accounted for only 3.7 per cent of the population but in 2050 is projected to constitute 14.7 per cent of the total. From 2050 onwards, the proportion of persons aged 80 years or over remains similar to that of persons under age 20.

TABLE 1.   POPULATION AT START OF THE YEAR
(*Millions*)

Age (years)	1998	2030	2050	2080
Under 20	17.7	12.0	9.7	7.8
20-39	24.6	16.3	13.4	10.4
40-59	21.9	19.9	17.1	13.1
60 or over	17.9	29.4	27.8	21.7
80 or over	3.0	6.6	10.0	7.6
TOTAL POPULATION	82.1	77.5	68.0	53.1

TABLE 2.   SHARE OF TOTAL POPULATION TAKEN UP BY VARIOUS AGE GROUPS
(*Percentage*)

Age (years)	1998	2030	2050	2080
Under 20	21.6	15.5	14.3	14.6
20-39	30.0	21.0	19.7	19.6
40-59	26.7	25.7	25.2	24.7
60 or over	21.8	37.9	40.9	40.9
80 or over	3.7	8.5	14.7	14.3
TOTAL POPULATION	100.0	100.0	100.0	100.0

3.   Consequences for the statutory pension system

(a)   How the "pay-as-you-go" system works

For by far the most part, Germany's statutory pension insurance operates on the "pay-as-you-go" system. In other words, those contributing to the system today are effectively not saving up for their own retirement pensions, but directly financing the amounts being disbursed to today's pensioners. By the time current contributors have reached retirement age, the contributions that they have made during their working lives will already have been spent, so that their pensions will have to be funded by the younger generations still engaged in work.

If the ratio of people requiring pensions to those effectively paying the pensions increases over a period of time by a factor such as 2.4, the result is either that contribution rates to the statutory pension have to be raised by that same factor or that the level of pensions paid out (expressed as the average pension in relation to average earned income) has to be cut by 1/2.4. Thus, the core dilemma facing policy makers is to choose between either more than doubling the contribution rate (currently 20 per cent) over that period of time, more than halving the pension level from the present 70 per cent, or funding even more of the statutory pensions system out of general taxation than is already the case.

These alternative prospects, though politically untenable, are nevertheless objectively inevitable. This being so, measures have already been taken over the past 10 years, unnoticed by most of the general public, to chip away at the level of benefits paid out by the statutory pension system and hence reduce the size of the necessary increase in contributions. Among the little-known benefit changes now legislated are measures such as heavier deductions in pensions paid to early retirees, the crediting of only a maximum of three years for school education instead of the previous seven, a reduction in the value now attached to a contributor's early working years, cuts in the pensions paid for partial occupational disability, and overall reductions in the proportionate pension level over time in accordance with the "*demographic factor*", intended to automatically cut real pensions in line with increased demographic ageing.

(b) Policy option I: increased contribution rate or lower pensions

Figure VII illustrates the fundamental interrelationship, inherent in the pay-as-you-go principle, between the statutory pension contribution rate, the ageing index and the pension level as defined above. If policy makers wish to cut the contribution rate, they also have to cut the proportionate pension level, or vice versa. The options available are shown as points on a straight line, the gradient of which is determined by the ageing index. At present, demographic ageing has not yet shown through very strongly, so the lowest of the straight lines with the shallowest gradient applies. However, that gradient will increase over time in proportion to the ageing index itself. This increase will certainly occur, simply because of the declining number of people in age group 20-60. In other words, the gradient will increase even if there is no change whatever in life expectancy. Yet in practice, life expectancy at birth actually doubled during the twentieth century, and it is still increasing at an average rate of six to eight weeks each year. So even if the increase tails off in the future, a further growth in life expectancy by at least five to six years is quite likely. In the report we were commissioned to prepare in connection with the pension reforms, the middle variant envisaged an increase from 74.0 to 80.9 years for males and from 80.8 to 86.9 years for females. The increasing life expectancy (variant "b") makes the gradients in figure VII even steeper, raising the contribution rate required to maintain the same pension level even higher than under constant life expectancy.

Even under the unrealistic assumption that life expectancy will not rise any further, the Scientific Advisory Council to Germany's Federal Ministry of Economics has calculated that the contribution rate would need to rise from today's approximately 20 to about 40 per cent if the Government wished to maintain the present proportionate pension level of 70 per cent (Bundesministerium für Wirtschaft, 1998, p. 37). Figure VII shows a similar result. However, if life expectancy does go on rising, the rate needed to maintain pension levels will

Figure VII. Relationship between the statutory pension contribution rate, the pension level and increased life expectancy

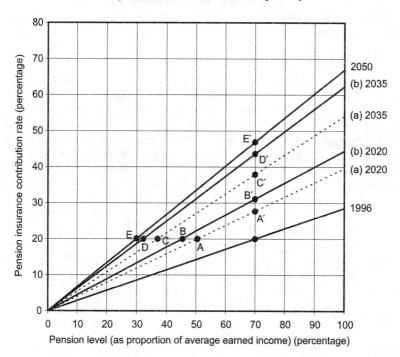

Source: "Simulations, scenario 4", *Materialien des IBSs* (Bielefeld, Germany: University of Bielefeld), vol. 45 (1999).

NOTE: Assumed life expectancy increases since 1994-1996 and ageing index (AI) for chosen years:

    1994-1996: males 73.3 years, females 79.7 years; AI = 37.5

    2020 (a): no increase; AI = 51.0

    2020 (b): plus 3.7 years; AI = 58.4

    2035 (a): no increase; AI = 71.0

    2035 (b): plus 5.3 years; AI = 81.8

    2050: plus 6.7 years; AI = 87.9

need to increase much more, to some 46 per cent. An alternative would be to maintain today's contribution rate but cut the pension disbursed to about 30 per cent of average earned income. This makes explicit the covert contribution increase implied by using general taxation to help finance the statutory pension.

The general public is largely unaware that the last round of pension reforms was based on demographic projections produced by the Federal Statistical Office (in its eighth coordinated population projection) that worked on the unrealistic assumption of no further increase in life expectancy from 1 January 2000 onward. The expert report by the Scientific Advisory Council is also based on these unrealistic figures. It was not until its next projection published in July 2000 (the ninth coordinated population projection) that the Federal Statistical Office also built in the assumption of further increases in life expectancy, which our figure VII has already catered for.

(*c*) *Policy option II: raising the retirement age*

If the options of cutting the level of pensions or raising contribution rates are not acceptable, a drastic increase in the retirement age will be unavoidable. By calculating age indices with a moving retirement age at one-year intervals (61, 62, 63, ... , 73), we can establish in which years the retirement age would need to be raised, and by how much, so as to maintain the ageing index constant by virtue of this boundary shift. The dates at which retirement age would need to be raised as ascertained in variant 5 of the projections made for the German Insurance Association are shown in table 3.

TABLE 3.   INCREASE IN RETIREMENT AGE NEEDED TO MAINTAIN A CONSTANT
AGEING INDEX BY SHIFTING THE AGE GROUP BOUNDARY

Increase in the retirement age from ... to ...	This increase will be needed in the year ...
60 ⇨ 61	2000
61 ⇨ 62	2002
62 ⇨ 63	2006
63 ⇨ 64	2014
64 ⇨ 65	2018
65 ⇨ 66	2022
66 ⇨ 67	2026
67 ⇨ 68	2029
68 ⇨ 69	2031
69 ⇨ 70	2036
70 ⇨ 71	2039
71 ⇨ 72	2042
72 ⇨ 73	2074

The retirement age, currently about 60 years in practical terms (though formally for men it is still 65 years), would have to be steadily raised to really be 65 years by 2018, 70 years by 2036 and, finally, 73 years by 2074: if this were not done, the ageing index with its crucial impact on increased contribution rates would inevitably increase (figure VIII). Even if the immigration rate of younger people is high, the ageing index will increase at least by 100 per cent for a constant life expectancy (figure IX) or by up to 200 per cent for a parallel increase of life expectancy (figure X).

An increase in the retirement age is not only unpopular but also unrealistic. For one thing, only a minority of the elderly population would be in good enough health to keep working right through to age 65, or indeed 73—male life expectancy is currently 74 years, and assumed to rise in future to 80 years; and for another, businesses mainly prefer to employ younger people. There are many occupations today, not just that of pilot or information technology (IT) expert, in which employees 40 or 50 years of age are already considered

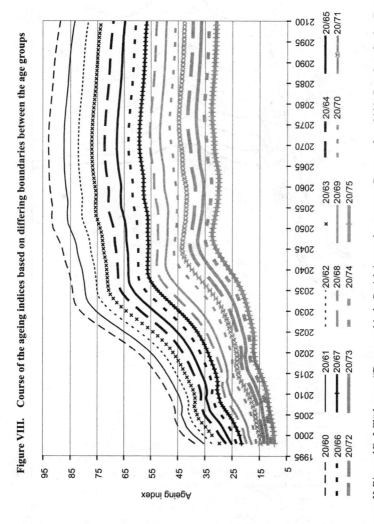

Figure VIII. Course of the ageing indices based on differing boundaries between the age groups

Source: H. Birg and E.-J. Flöthmann, "Demographische Projektionsrechnungen zur Rentenreform 2000: Gutachten für den Gesamtverband der deutschen Versicherungswirtschaft" (projection variant 5), Berlin, 1999.

119

Figure IX. Course of the ageing index taking account of differing annual rates of net immigration (assumptions: TFR = 1.358; expectancy at birth (eo) = 75 years (males), 81 years (females))

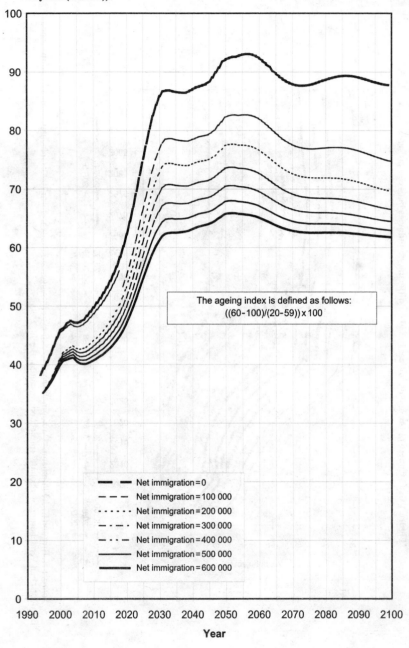

The ageing index is defined as follows:
$$((60-100)/(20-59)) \times 100$$

Net immigration = 0
Net immigration = 100 000
Net immigration = 200 000
Net immigration = 300 000
Net immigration = 400 000
Net immigration = 500 000
Net immigration = 600 000

Year

Source: Own calculations.

Figure X. Course of the ageing index taking account of differing annual rates of net immigration (assumptions: TFR = 1.358; expectancy at birth (eo) = 84 years (males), 90 years (females))

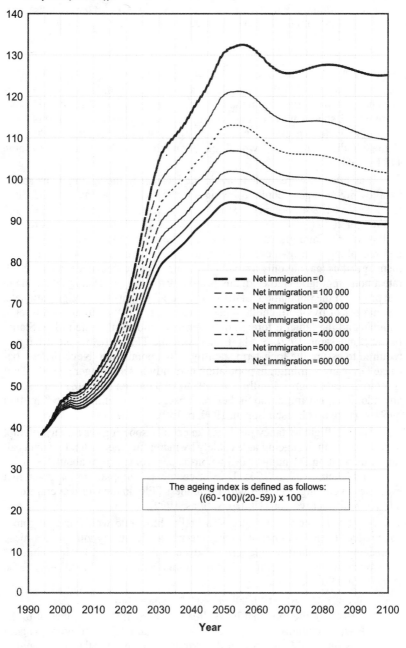

Source: Own calculations.

rather old for the job. The more dynamically economies develop in the wake of globalization, the more rapidly the relevance of the knowledge acquired in occupational training will decline, and the less value will be placed on experience, a form of capital that grows with age.

(*d*)   *Policy option III: immigration and an increased birth rate*

High levels of net immigration adding 600,000 or more per annum to the population cannot prevent an increase in the ageing index, even if life expectancy ceases to rise, let alone if it does keep growing as expected. If net immigration stayed at the level of recent decades (approximately 170,000 per annum) and life expectancy went on rising to 84 years (males) and 90 years (females), the ageing index would roughly treble from the current 38 to some 115 by 2050.

If an attempt were made to avoid the increase in the ageing index solely by allowing younger people to immigrate, the United Nations has calculated that a total of 188 million people (net) would need to immigrate into Germany by the year 2050 (United Nations, 2001, table A.4). The reason this figure is so high is that the immigrants would cut back the ageing index only temporarily, before making their own contribution to its increase once they reached retirement age, thus leaving only a small net easing effect, especially since the birth rate among immigrants to Germany is too low to have any lasting effect on the age profile of the population. Statistically, if both parents are foreign nationals, the number of live-born children per woman is 1.5. If the mother is a foreign national and the father a foreign or a German national, the rate is 1.9 (Statistische Bundesamt, 1999, p. 51). Either way, the TFR is below the 2.1 figure required to assure the long-term stability of the population. Nevertheless, because Germany's immigrant population currently has a younger age profile, it is set to increase from 7.4 million in 1998 to 10.0 million in 2050, even without any additional net immigration, before subsequently declining to 6.8 million by 2100 (Birg and Börsch-Supan, 1999, p. 150).

Another flight of fancy produces an equally sobering result: any attempt to halt the rise in the ageing index solely by increasing the birth rate would call for an increase in the number of live births per woman from about 1.3 to 3.8 (Birg and Koch, 1987, p. 174). This, of course, is a utopian notion given that even the developing countries with the highest TFRs in the world average only 3.0 live births per woman (United Nations, 1999).

As already shown in figure V, a higher birth rate would indeed somewhat reduce the net number of immigrants needed for the hypothetical purpose of keeping a constant population, but even with a TFR of 1.6 live children per woman the annual net immigration in mid-century would still have to be 300,000-500,000 people.

Thus, to summarize some of the conclusions so far:

- Because the falls that have already occurred in the number of births will inevitably give rise to further substantial falls in future years, it is impossible to prevent demographic ageing whether by changing policy to encourage larger families or by moderately increasing the net number of relatively young people immigrating into Germany. The demographic ageing of society can only be alleviated a little by demographic measures; it cannot be brought to a halt;

• Germany's system of retirement pension insurance was designed in the late nineteenth century for a population that had a young age profile. The decline in the birth rate during the twentieth century will markedly increase the ratio of elderly people to those of working age in the twenty-first century. The only way of retaining the present pay-as-you-go system of statutory pension insurance without increasing contribution rates and/or lowering the pension level is to raise the retirement age to 70 years and beyond.

The ultimate conclusion is that the statutory pension system, currently based on the pay-as-you-go principle, has to be reformed and adapted to the changing age profile of the population. To avoid both excessive increases in contribution rates and all-too-drastic cuts in the pensions paid out, additional provision for old age on an individual basis via private savings is needed: this will be substantially less dependent on demographic factors than the current statutory system. However, the statutory pay-as-you-go pension insurance system cannot be totally replaced by fully funded individual retirement provision—it can only be supplemented by it. Total substitution would imply replacing the demographically derived security implicit in raising children by a form of provision totally dependent on the capital markets. By its very nature, this would provide less and less security, the more profitable the investments needed to be, since these would then involve greater risk and increasingly have to be placed in foreign markets.

4. *Impact on statutory health insurance*

At least hypothetically, the lost revenues and increased expenditure for the statutory retirement pension scheme can be restrained by raising the retirement age. However, the health and long-term care insurance systems do not even have this purely theoretical avenue open to them: increasing per capita expenditure on health care as the population grew older would still be just as inevitable, even if raising the retirement age were not a problem.

People at a very advanced age need, on average, about eight times more spent on their health than do people age 20, as the North Rhine–Westphalian health ministry has found (Ministerium für Gesundheit und Soziales NRW, 1995, p. 174). This is partly because older people tend to need more medical attention in the normal course of their lives than younger ones, and partly also because the older the age group, the greater the number of deaths, hence the rise in health-care costs. In 1997, just one man aged 20-25 years died per 1,000 in this age group, whereas the figure was 111 per 1,000 in age group 80-85, and 256 per 1,000 in age group 90 or over. Moreover, technical progress in the medical field means that the "centre of gravity" in the age profile of per capita health-care spending is continually pushing upward. While the ratio of per capita health spending on young age groups to such spending on old age groups was 1:8 in 1992, these shifts could alter the ratio to 1:20 by the year

2040, according to the German Parliamentary Commission of Enquiry on Demographic Change, based on the findings of a study by the Prognos Institute (Enquete-Kommission, 1998, p. 230).

Demographic ageing increases the expenditure and lowers the revenues of the statutory health insurance system. Because of the reduced number of people of working age resulting from demographic factors, the system will have less contributors and hence suffer a loss of revenue, amounting to some 30 per cent by 2040. Simultaneously, expenditure is set to increase owing to two factors, namely, an increase in the pure number of older people coupled with the increase in the per capita expenditure on health care needed for older age groups. Our own simulations estimate that these two factors will generate additional expenditure needs at constant prices of some 22 per cent by 2040.

The widening gulf between rising expenditure and falling revenues will require contribution rates to the statutory health insurance organizations to rise from the present average of approximately 12 to about 21 per cent, unless either standards of care are reduced or participants are required to fund a substantially greater proportion of costs themselves. These findings operate on the assumption that future technological advances in medicine will not push up costs at all or, in other words, that there will be no upward shift in the age profile of per capita health-care expenditure. If the ratio of per capita expenditure was indeed to rise from 1:8 to, say, 1:20, as discussed above, the contribution rate would have to be further increased from 21 to 24 per cent. This relatively small additional margin of 3 percentage points for such a drastic shift in the age profile due to medical progress shows that the need for higher future contribution rates is driven much more by falling revenue than by increased expenditure, the momentum of which is reduced by the fact that the number of persons aged 60 years or over begins to fall back again after rising in the period up to 2030-2035 (figure XI).

5.   Impact on long-term care insurance

As in the case of health insurance, the statutory long-term care insurance programme will also be affected by demographic ageing as it lowers revenues and increases expenditure. A similar pattern emerges insofar as the per capita expenditure on long-term care increases steeply with age. In 1996, for example, 4 out of 1,000 participants in the statutory scheme in age group 35-39 received benefits from it, compared with 24 per 1,000 in age group 65-69 and 280 per 1,000 in the age group 80 or over. Demographic simulations conducted by a number of institutes have calculated that the contribution rate for long-term care insurance would need to rise from the current 1.7 per cent to between 3 and 6 per cent by 2040 (Enquete-Kommission, 1998, p. 126). Yet even the upper projection of 6 per cent will probably be insufficient, as the following computations on the increase in the "demographic senior citizens' care index" shows.

The demographic senior citizens' care index used here consists of the number of people of advanced old age (where the need for care is most prevalent) per 100 people in the age group that is 20-40 years younger than they are, who normally take responsibility for caring for the elderly. The index has been calculated using alternative borderlines, initially treating "advanced old age" as meaning 80 years or over, then 81 years or over, and so on up to 90 years or over. Correspondingly, the age groups assumed to be responsible for providing care are 40-59, 41-60, and so on. The first alternative is expressed in the formula

$$\text{Care index } P_{80/(40\text{-}60)} = \frac{\text{Population aged 80+}}{\text{Population aged 40-60}} \times 100$$

The calculations made on the basis of the middle projection variant for the German Insurance Association produced the following results (figures XII and XIII):

(*a*) Age group 80 years or over, in which the largest number of people requiring care are found, will treble in size between 1998 and 2050, from 3.0 million to 9.9 million, as the large cohorts born in the 1960s reach their old age;

(*b*) The number of men over age 80 is at present considerably smaller than the number of women over age 80, owing to wartime losses (0.8 million men versus 2.2 million women). In future, the number of men in this age group will return to normal, growing to 3.9 million in 2050, while the number of women increases to 6.0 million;

(*c*) The demographic senior citizens' care index for persons aged 80 years or over (relative to 100 people in age group 40-60) is set to quadruple from 12.6 in 1998 to 55.0 in 2050. In other words, one person in every two aged 40-60 years will be "matched" by a person aged 80 years or over with the much higher likelihood of requiring care. The increase among men will be more marked than among women;

(*d*) The care index relating the number of people aged 90 years or over to 100 persons aged 50-70 years was 2.3 in 1998; this is projected to grow to 10.8 in 2050, and, by a factor of six, to 14.1 in 2059;

(*e*) The further life expectancy of people who have already reached age 70, 80 or 90 has increased much more significantly in recent decades than the further life expectancy of younger people, where marked advances already occurred some years ago. This trend will continue in the twenty-first century. The number of people in the German population aged 100 or over—a significant figure from the care point of view—was estimated at 11,000 in 1998, but is set to increase to 70,000 by 2050 and to peak at 115,000 in 2067 (figures XIV and XV).

The care index applied above measures only the direct, demographically determined increase in the cost burden for long-term care associated with the shift in the population's age profile. However, another demographically induced set of costs involving a slightly less direct route flows from the dramatic increase in the number of people who remain childless throughout their lives. In younger generations, one woman in three now lives her life without having children. The upward trend is a continuing one. By far, the major part of care for the elderly is still provided by members of their family and those members' children. In future, the number of people requiring care who are childless and

Figure XI. Simulations of the demographically induced rise in health-care expenditure and of the impact on health insurance contributions in the twenty-first century

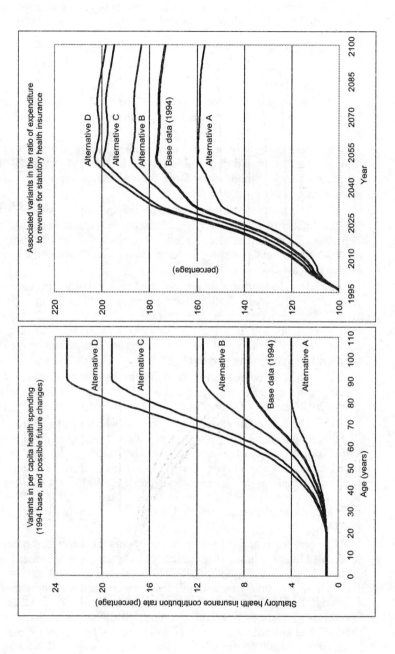

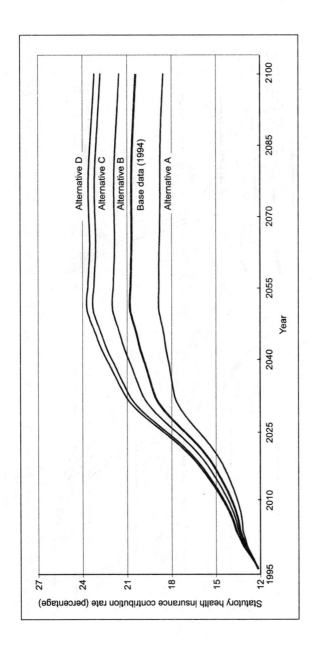

Source: Own calculations.

NOTE: Assumptions: Gradual increase in life expectancy from 73 to 81 years (males) and from 80 to 87 years (females) by 2080; TFR = 1.4; annual net immigration = 150,000.

Figure XII.   Changes in the demographic senior citizens' care indices, using different delineation ages

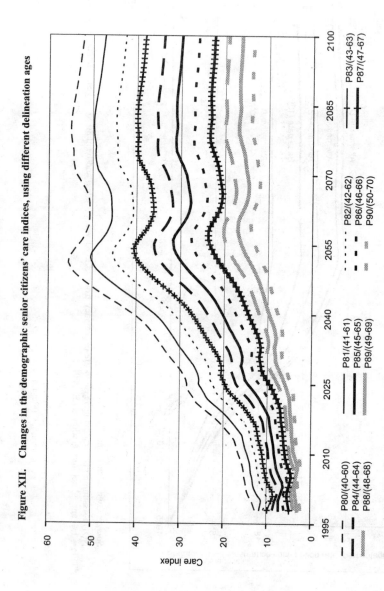

Source: H. Birg and E.J. Flöthmann, "Demographische Projektionsrechnungen zur Rentenreform 2000" (report to the German Insurance Association (Gesamtverband der deutschen Versicherungswirtschaft)) (projection variant 5), Berlin, 1999.

Figure XIII. Changes in the demographic senior citizens' care indices, using different delineation ages
(all variants indexed to 1998 = 100)

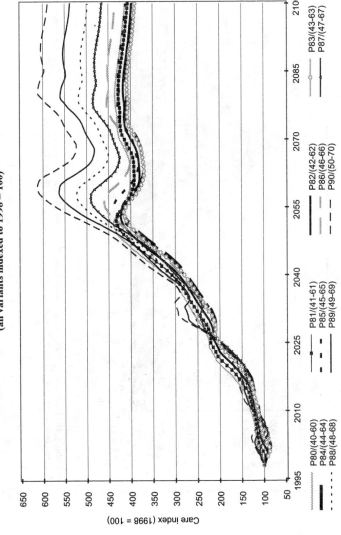

Source: H. Birg and E.-J. Flöthmann, "Demographische Projektionsrechnungen zur Rentenreform 2000" (report to the German Insurance Association (Gesamtverband der deutschen Versicherungswirtschaft)) (projection variant 5), Berlin, 1999.

Figure XIV. Estimate of the future number of people aged 100 years or over in Germany (projection variant 5)

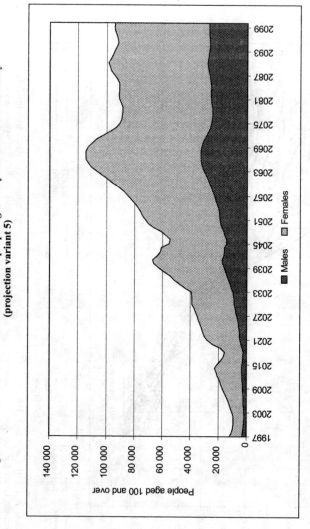

Source: H. Birg and others, *Simulationsrechnungen der Bevölkerungsentwicklung in den alten und neuen Bundesländern im 21. Jahrhundert* (Bielefeld, Germany, University of Bielefeld, 1999).

Figure XV. Estimate of the future share of the total population taken up by people aged 100 years or over in Germany (projection variant 5)

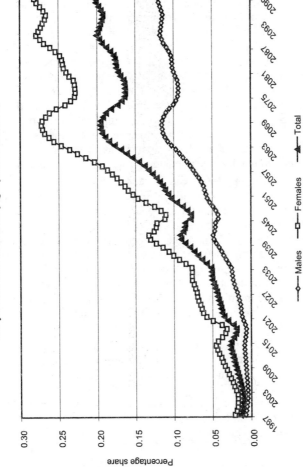

Source: H. Birg and others, *Simulationsrechnungen der Bevölkerungsentwicklung in den alten und neuen Bundesländern im 21. Jahrhundert* (Bielefeld, Germany, University of Bielefeld, 1999).

have to obtain their care outside the family will increase especially strongly. This raises a problem in that the principle of equity in relation to contributions paid will be breached unless contribution rates somehow take account of how many descendants people have and what part they will play in providing care.

CONCLUSIONS

In the last three decades of the twentieth century, the worldwide decline in birth rates and increased life expectancy generated demographic ageing not only in the populations of industrialized countries, but in developing ones, too. The worldwide process of demographic ageing will continue in the twenty-first century. By mid-century, the ageing index in Germany will have doubled or trebled. This is largely attributable to the ever-decreasing numbers in the younger age cohorts, and due only secondarily to increasing life expectancy. Demographic ageing so thoroughly undermines the effectiveness of the statutory insurance system, including the solidarity between generations encapsulated in the pay-as-you-go method of financing State benefits, that it is becoming a matter of ever-growing urgency to develop other forces of cultural integration between younger and older generations as a substitute for the solidarity formerly underpinned by the population's demographic structure.

Yet in practice, the opposite trend is operating. Now that competition among economies predominates on a global scale and economic action in general is increasingly driven solely by the competitive principle, the link between economic competitors and their responsibility towards society, based on a principle of solidarity, is steadily on the wane. Indeed, there is even a tendency for the normal competitive principle to be perverted in the phenomenon of hyper-competition, in which cooperation and coexistence are no longer regarded as a worthy aim, but the destruction of a competitor's entire trading basis is so regarded. The demo-economic paradox of a declining number of live births per woman while the level of economic development and per capita incomes increase is one of the key consequences of this underlying trend.

Economic globalization leads to demographic destabilization, compelling drastic reforms to be made in statutory welfare insurance systems. Nor can the pressure for social reform exerted by demographic change be resisted by allowing high levels of immigration of well-qualified people. Indeed, large-scale, uncontrolled immigration of relatively unskilled people into Germany—representing several times the number of "permanent" immigrants to the United States of America per 1,000 of population (Organisation for Economic Co-operation and Development, 1997, p. 15)—has actually exacerbated the demographically driven problems by laying large additional burdens on the welfare State instead of helping to alleviate them.

In Germany, the "pact between the generations"—that is to say, the demographically underpinned basis of solidarity for the statutory social insurance system—has already been so critically weakened that the pay-as-you-go system of funding retirement pensions can now be maintained only with the aid of substantial grants out of general taxation to boost the revenue side. Without these subsidies, the current contribution rate would be 24 per cent, not 20 per cent as it actually is. In future, the pay-as-you-go system will inevitably have to be supplemented by individual private pension plans, in other words, set up on a "fully funded" basis for each future pensioner. The investment yield inherent in such fully funded pensions will then be able to accompany (but not fully replace) the demographic guarantee of solidarity inherent in the pay-as-you-go system.

In the wake of globalization, national capital markets are increasingly merging together into a single world capital market, the main rationale of which is to maximize returns. Yet to seek to provide a secure living in old age on the strength of this risk-dependent principle of yield maximization, of all things, is a strategy destined to become all the more dangerous the more countries forfeit their national "sheltered areas" in the wake of globalization.

REFERENCES

Birg, H. (1992). Differentielle Reproduktion aus der Sicht der biographischen Theorie der Fertilität. In *Fortpflanzung: Natur und Kultur im Wechselspiel - Versuch eines Dialogs zwischen Biologen und Sozialwissenschaftlern*, E. Voland, ed. Frankfurt am Main, Germany: Campus, pp. 189-215.

_____ (1995). *World Population Projections for the 21st Century: Theoretical Interpretations and Quantitative Simulations*. Frankfurt am Main, Germany: Campus; and New York: St. Martin's Press.

_____ (1998). Demographisches Wissen und politische Verantwortung: Überlegungen zur Bevölkerungsentwicklung Deutschlands im 21. Jahrhundert. *Zeitschrift für Bevölkerungswissenschaft*, No. 3, pp. 221-251.

_____ (2000). 188 Millionen Einwanderer zum Ausgleich? *Frankfurter Allgemeine Zeitung*, 12 April.

_____, and A. Börsch-Supan (1999). *Für eine neue Aufgabenverteilung zwischen gesetzlicher und privater Altersversorgung: eine demographische und ökonomische Analyse*. Berlin: German Insurance Association (Gesamtverband der deutschen Versicherungswirtschaft).

_____, and E.-J. Flöthmann (1996). Entwicklung der Familienstrukturen und ihre Auswirkungen auf die Belastungs- bzw. Transferquotienten zwischen den Generationen. Study report on behalf of the Federal Parliamentary Commission of Enquiry on Demographic Change. *Materialien des Instituts für Bevölkerungsforschung und Sozialpolitik* (Bielefeld, Germany: University of Bielefeld), vol. 38.

_____, and I. Reiter (1991). *Biographische Theorie der demographischen Reproduktion*. Frankfurt am Main, Germany: Campus; and New York: St. Martin's Press.

Birg, H., and H. Koch (1987). *Der Bevölkerungsrückgang in der Bundesrepublik Deutschland*. Frankfurt am Main, Germany: Campus.

Birg, H., and others (1998). *Simulationsrechnungen zur Bevölkerungsentwicklung in den alten und neuen Bundesländern im 21. Jahrhundert. Materialien des Instituts für Bevölkerungsforschung und Sozialpolitik*. Bielefeld, Germany: University of Bielefeld, vol. 45.

Bundesministerium für Wirtschaft (Federal Ministry of Economy) (1998). *Grundlegende Reform der gesetzlichen Rentenversicherung. Gutachten des Wissenschaftlichen Beirats beim Bundesministerium für Wirtschaft*. Studienreihe des BMW, No. 99. Bonn: Bundesministerium für Wirtschaft.

Enquete-Kommission (1998). *"Demographischer Wandel" des Deutschen Bundestages*, Zweiter Zwischenbericht (second interim report). Berlin: Die Bundesregierung.

Ministerium für Gesundheit und Soziales Nordrhein-Westfalen (NRW) (1995). *Gesundheitsreport, 1994*. Bielefeld, Germany: University of Bielefeld.

Organisation for Economic Co-operation and Development (OECD) (1997). *Trends in International Migration: Annual Report, 1996.* Paris: OECD.

Statistisches Bundesamt (Federal Office of Statistics) (1999). *Gebiet und Bevölkerung 1997.* Wiesbaden, Germany: Statistische Bundesamt.

United Nations (1999). *World Population Prospects: The 1998 Revision,* vol. I, *Comprehensive Tables.* Sales No. E.99.XIII.19.

_____ (2001). *Replacement Migration: Is It a Solution to Declining and Ageing Populations?* Sales No. E.01.XIII.19.

Voland, E. (1992). *Fortpflanzung: Natur und Kultur im Wechselspiel - Versuch eines Dialogs zwischen Biologen und Sozialwissenschaftlern.* Frankfurt am Main, Germany: Campus.

POLICY RESPONSES TO POPULATION AGEING AND POPULATION DECLINE IN GERMANY

*Charlotte Höhn**

A. POPULATION PROSPECTS

1. *Comparing the assumptions of two recent German population prospects with the United Nations population prospects*

Recently the German Federal Statistical Office published its ninth co-ordinated population prospects (Statistisches Bundesamt, 2000) and the German Federal Ministry of Interior a new set of model calculations of population (Bundesministerium des Innern, 2000), both up to 2050. While the assumptions of the first are coordinated between the Federal Statistical Office and the 16 State Statistical Offices, the latter are agreed upon by a ministerial working group on population matters under the competence of the Ministry of the Interior with the advice of the Federal Statistical Office and the Federal Institute for Population Research.

(a) Subpopulations

The two sets of recent German population prospects differentiate between the populations in east and west Germany, and those of the Federal Ministry of the Interior differentiate also between foreigners and Germans since there are still enormous differences in demographic behaviour, in age structure and in regional distribution of these subpopulations. East Germany displays lower fertility, life expectancy and immigration than west Germany. Foreigners live mainly in west Germany and there in urban areas, where they have a higher fertility, life expectancy and immigration surplus than Germans.

One major criticism of the United Nations study on replacement migration (United Nations, 2001) is the neglect of distinguishing between native and immigrant population both in the base population and in the assumptions on their respective demographic behaviours. Of course, this would increase data needs. But the results would be much more instructive because the stock of immigrants matters in the debate as well as adaptations in demographic behaviour and the trends in naturalizations. Here lies room for improvement of further United Nations studies in this field.

---

*Federal Institute for Population Research (BiB), Wiesbaden, Germany. Both sets of German population prospects are based on the population as of 1 January 1998.

(*b*) *Fertility*

Both sets of German population prospects assume a constant low fertility. The Federal Statistical Office assumes 1.4 births per woman, a level that, increasing from 1.1 in 1998, will be reached by east Germans in 2005. The Federal Ministry of the Interior assumes for west Germans a small fall from 1.4 to 1.35 until 2000, an increase for east Germans from 1.1 to 1.35 in 2005, and for foreigners a constant level of 1.5, which is indeed remarkably low for Germany.

The assumption of our distinguished United Nations colleagues in the medium variant of the 1998 revision (United Nations, 1999, part one, table A.2) of an increase in fertility in Germany of up to 1.64 is already much more modest than that in earlier revisions, and has been criticized, inter alia, by Höhn and Dorbritz (2000). German demographers do not share this optimism. As a matter of fact, the two German official projections discussed here are the first without differing fertility assumptions. The constant low fertility level in west Germany for nearly 30 years is a purely demographic, though strong argument. Theoretical and empirical survey-based deliberations do not leave room for assuming an increasing fertility in Germany.

(*c*) *Mortality*

Both sets of German population prospects assume an increase of life expectancy. The ninth coordinated population projection assumes life expectancy to increase from 74.4 (males)/80.5 (females) years in west Germany and 71.8/79.6 years in east Germany (1998) to 78.1/84.5 years in Germany in 2050. Also, it adds a variant with an additional increase of life expectancy up to 80.1/86.4 years in 2050. In the population prospects of the Federal Ministry of the Interior, life expectancy increases from 73.6/80.5 years in 1998 to 78.1/84.5 years (west Germans), and for the east Germans, from 71.8/79.6 years in 1998 also to 78.1/84.5 years in 2050. Foreigners have a higher life expectancy (81.5/87.6 years) which is to hold constant.

The main mortality assumption of the German population prospects is very much in line with those of the 1998 revision of the United Nations population prospects: 78.9/84.5 years in 2040-2050.

(*d*) *Migration*

Both sets of German population prospects assume several variants to reflect the uncertainty about the dimension of international migration and to show the impact of migration on the age structure. Therefore, there is a variant without any migration. The immigration of Germans (ethnic Germans in the main) is expected to level out from 80,000 in 1998 to reach 0 in 2040. For foreigners, the ninth coordinated population projection assumes two variants: starting from minus 50,000 in 1998 (!) and over (assumed) 20,000 in 1999, immigration increases to 100,000 in 2003, and to 200,000 in 2008, and then remains constant up to 2050. The model calculation of the Federal Ministry of the Interior adds a third variant with an increase of immigration to 300,000 in 2013, with immigration then remaining constant. Also, the population prospects of the Federal Ministry of the Interior assume naturalization, taking into consideration the new legislation and the levels of immigration.

The migration assumption of the 1998 revision is hence rather close to the "200,000 variant" in the two sets of German population prospects. The temporal distribution is different, however, since the United Nations assumes 240,000 per annum up to 2005 with the figure then shifting to 200,000 per annum up to 2050.

2. Comparing the results of the two recent sets of German population prospects with the United Nations population prospects

(a) The medium variant

In table 1, we have compiled the German variants with a migration assumption close to the medium variant of the 1998 revision. The German "200,000" migration assumptions are identical. From the ninth coordinated population projections, we added the variant assuming a more substantial increase of life expectancy ("$e_0 + 2$").

TABLE 1.   MEDIUM-VARIANT POPULATION PROSPECTS FOR GERMANY

	Annual net migration (thousands)	Total net migration 1995-2050 or 1998-2050 (thousands)	Population 2050 (thousands) (1995: 81,661,000)	Potential support ratio 2050 (1995: 4.41)	Foreign population 2050 (percentage) (1999: 8.9 per cent)
Ninth coordinated, var. 2	90-200	10 360[a]	70 381	1.92	..
Ninth coordinated, var. 2, $e_0 + 2$ . .	90-200	10 360[a]	72 012	1.8	..
Fed. Min.of the Interior, var. B	90-200	10 360[a]	70 265	1.87	17.1
Scenario I	207	11 400[b]	73 303	2.05	20

Sources: Bundesministerium des Innern (2000); and Statistisches Bundesamt (2000).

[a]1998-2050.

[b]1995-2050.

The (small) differences in population size and the potential support ratio (PSR) in 2050 between the ninth coordinated population prospects, variant 2, and the Federal Ministry of the Interior's population projection B emanate from structural effects, since the ninth coordinated prospects are the sum of 16 states' results, and the projection of the Federal Ministry of the Interior is a direct calculation. Assuming a larger increase in life expectancy yields an additional 1.8 million inhabitants but lowers the PSR, since it increases the number of the elderly.

United Nations scenario I adds more immigrants mainly in the first years of calculation when the real migration surpluses were much smaller in Germany. Here we have an age structure and migration effect. The PSR was 3.93 in Germany in 1999, thus already less favourable than in 1995 (4.41).[1] United

Nations scenario I assumes that fertility increases from 2020 to 2050, so there is also a fertility-induced positive effect on population size and the PSR. In any case, the PSR falls to more than half its value:

- Ninth coordinated population prospect, variant 2: 43.5 per cent;
- Ninth coordinated population prospect, variant 2 with e_0+2: 40.8 per cent;
- Federal Ministry of the Interior population prospect, variant B: 42.4 per cent;
- United Nations scenario I: 46.5 per cent.

This dramatic deterioration of the age structure is the main message.

The small difference in the percentage of post-1995 migrants and their descendants (United Nations scenario I) and of foreign population (Federal Ministry of the Interior) should not allow room for complacency. The calculation of the Federal Ministry of the Interior considers not only the stock of foreigners (8.9 per cent in 1999), but also naturalization.

(b) The variant with zero migration

Table 2 shows the rather similar results of projecting population in Germany without any international migration. Population declines and ages much more rapidly. Without immigration, the proportion of foreigners in Germany would fall from 8.9 to 5.4 per cent but not to nil. What is even more important, the proportion of foreigners aged 65 or over would rise from a modest 4.1 to 53.2 per cent, while the proportion of Germans aged 65 or over would rise from 17.1 to 31 per cent.

The PSR would fall to:

- Ninth coordinated population prospect, variant K: 38.3 per cent;
- Federal Ministry of the Interior, variant K: 37.2 per cent;
- United Nations scenario II: 39.7 per cent.

The differences in the decline of the PSR without or with migration are not negligible, but neither are they spectacular. The loss in population, however, is much stronger as compared with that of the medium variants.

(c) The impact of migration

In table 3, we bring together the three migration variants in the Federal Ministry of the Interior's population prospects with scenarios I, III, IV and V. The main message is that the ageing process is inevitable unless one lets Germany's population grow to 300 million inhabitants (scenario V).

These are the impacts of immigration on the PSR:

- Federal Ministry of the Interior, variant A: 39.7 per cent with "100,000" net migration per annum;
- Federal Ministry of the Interior, variant B: 42.4 per cent with "200,000" net migration per annum;

	Annual net migration (thousands)	Total net migration 1995-2050 or 1998-2050 (thousands)	Population 2050 (thousands) (1995: 81,661,000)	Potential support ratio 2050 (1995: 4.41)	Foreign population 2050 (percentage) (1999: 8.9 per cent)
Ninth coordinated, var. K.	0	0[a]	59 031	1.69	..
Fed. Min. of the Interior, var. K	0	0[a]	58 624	1.64	5.4
Scenario II	0	0[b]	58 812	1.75	..

Sources: Bundesministerium des Innern (2000); and Statistisches Bundesamt (2000).
[a]1998-2050.
[b]1995-2050.

- Federal Ministry of the Interior, variant C: 44.4 per cent with "300,000" net migration per annum;

- Scenario I: 46.5 per cent with 207,000 net migration per annum;

- Scenario III: 51.2 per cent with 324,000 net migration per annum;

- Scenario IV: 55.3 per cent with 458,000 net migration per annum;

- Scenario V: 100 per cent with 3,427,000 net migration per annum.

Immigration can mitigate the ageing process, but cannot realistically be expected to stop it.

B.   CONSEQUENCES OF POPULATION DECLINE AND POPULATION AGEING

1.   *The issue of population decline*

There is no fear of population decline in Germany. In its national reports for the European Population Conference held in Geneva in 1993 and for the International Conference on Population and Development held in Cairo in 1994, Germany never considered its imminent population decline a problem. Likewise, in answering the United Nations Inquiries among Governments on Population and Development, Germany never expressed concern about its growth rate (which was negative in most years of the 1970s and 1980s in the Federal Republic of Germany).

During the 25 years that I have been asked to advise our Government, some wanted to know whether population decline would not be beneficial ecologically. It is consumption and production patterns, not population size, that have the decisive impact on ecology in an industrialized country like Germany.

So scenario III was not debated at all in Germany.

TABLE 3.   POPULATION PROSPECTS WITH SEVERAL MIGRATION VARIANTS FOR GERMANY

	Annual net migration (thousands)	Total net migration 1995-2050 or 1998-2050 (thousands)	Population 2050 (thousands) (1995: 81,661,000)	Potential support ratio 2050 (1995: 4.41)	Foreign population 2050 (percentage) (1999: 8.9 per cent)
Fed. Min. of the Interior, var. A.	90-100	5 960[a]	64 791	1.75	12.2
Fed. Min. of the Interior, var. B.	90-200	10 360[a]	70 265	1.87	17.1
Fed. Min. of the Interior, var. C.	90-300	14 260[a]	74 864	1.96	21.4
Scenario I	207	11 400	73 303	2.05	20
Scenario III	324	17 838	81 661	2.26	28
Scenario IV	458	25 209	92 022	2.44	36
Scenario V	3 427	188 497	299 272	4.41	80

Sources: Bundesministerium des Innern (2000); and Statistisches Bundesamt (2000).

[a] 1998-2050.

2. The issue of population ageing

Population ageing has been the issue debated in (west) Germany since the mid-1970s. When the fourth coordinated population prospects (published in 1974) revealed the future ageing of population, an interministerial working group on population issues was founded under the responsibility of the Federal Ministry of the Interior. This interministerial working group prepared population prospects with different fertility assumptions, fertility being rightly considered the main determinant of ageing. It did not foresee an increase of life expectancy, the second determinant of ageing. Moreover, it was cautious as to immigration of foreigners in the years after the recruitment stop in 1973; the three migration assumptions were: zero, 20,000 annual net immigration and 55,000 annual net immigration.

As to fertility, the medium variant assumed a constant net reproduction rate (NRR) of 0.627 for Germans and of 0.84 for foreigners. For the German population, a fall of the NRR to 0.5 and a rise to 0.8 were also considered. The results were sobering: the proportion of Germans aged 60 years or over would rise from 21 per cent in 1982 to 34 per cent in 2030 (to 40 per cent with lower fertility and to 31 per cent with higher fertility) (Bundesministerium des Innern, 1984, pp. 135-139). For comparison: the most recent population prospects of the Federal Ministry of the Interior show an increase of the proportion of Germans aged 60 years or over from 23.9 per cent in 1999 to 35.7-36 per cent in 2030 and 36.5-37.6 per cent in 2050, varying with the level of immigration and related naturalization of foreigners (Bundesministerium des Innern, 2000, p. 39). The persistence of the issue is remarkable. In addition, the proportion of the foreign population aged 60 years or over would rise from 7.2 per cent in 1999 to 41 per cent (variant A), 34 per cent (variant B) or 31.4 per cent (variant C) in 2050 (Bundesministerium des Innern, 2000, p. 41), offering a small demonstration that migrants age too.

The interministerial working group published its first projections in 1984 together with a comprehensive report on the consequences of population change on the various sectors of the State and economy[2] (Bundesministerium des Innern, 1984). The report deals with consequences of population change/ ageing on:

- Family and youth (with a number of interesting remarks on single children, but also on familial support and care of the elderly);

- Foreigners (maintain recruitment stop, support integration, improve education and vocational training of youth);

- The economy (the economic trends and structures, for example, increased productivity and lifelong learning, were considered more decisive than demographic change; the assessment did not go beyond the year 2000);

- The labour market (here unemployment was foreseen for the 1980s and was to disappear gradually in the 1990s (!); the assessment did not go beyond the year 2000);

- The pension system (a major problem to be studied by a commission; a report by the council of social economists to the Federal Minister of Labour found that in order to maintain the pay-as-you-go system either the contribution rate would have to be doubled or the pension level halved, two extremes to be avoided);

- Health insurance and provision (the increase of health costs was driven much more by medical progress than by ageing, an assessment partly due to the assumption of constant life expectancy);

- Education (small cohorts of students followed big cohorts at different times; fewer teachers were needed);

- Infrastructure and public finance (no major problems).

The report does not suggest any options for political action, it "only" assessed possible consequences of population ageing.

The report of the interministerial working group was presented to the German Parliament and initiated a debate. The main problem of population ageing was seen to be the maintenance of the pension system, but other issues were also analysed. Teitelbaum and Winter (1985, p. 125) correctly summarize the situation: "Apart from German sangfroid regarding economic issues, there has been some discussion of the implications for the social security system of changes in the age structure." Indeed, a pension reform law was passed by Parliament in 1989. In 1992, the first part of the pension reform law became effective: the annual adaptation of the pension level to the development of net incomes (instead of to gross incomes). The demographically more important part—the gradual extension of age at retirement to 65 years—will become effective as of 2001.

The interministerial working group is still active, but after 1984 only updated population prospects were published (the most recent one was presented in sec. A above). Neither a review of the possible consequences, nor an effort to provide recommendations for action, was made. So in 1992, the German Parliament established the Ad Hoc Study Committee (Enquete-Kommission) on Demographic Change composed of parliamentarians and experts to investigate the "challenge of our ageing society to the individual and politics" (subtitle of the committee). The committee published an interim report at the end of legislative period in 1994 (Deutscher Bundestag, 1994). This interim report of 630 pages covers:

- The demographic situation including population prospects;
- The family and social networks;
- The income situation;
- Active ageing;
- Housing;
- The health and medical situation.

All the chapters (most of them on the microlevel) provide options for political action except with regard to demographic processes. We will comment on some of them in the next section. The committee recommended that a new committee be established in the next legislative period to approach fields not yet studied, namely, demographic change in the European Union (EU), elderly foreigners, migration and integration of migrants, and the social security system and macrolevel aspects of ageing.

Thus, another Ad Hoc Study Committee on Demographic Change started its work in 1995. The report was to assess the following themes:

- Demographic trends in Germany and EU;
- The economy and the labour market;
- The pension system;
- The health and care insurance system;
- The family and social networks;
- Social services;
- Migration and integration.

As it had proved impossible to discuss policy options (except those concerning the family and social networks[3] and migration and integration), the Ad Hoc Study Committee decided to publish a second interim report of 830 pages in 1998. In the meantime, a Third Ad Hoc Study Committee is grappling with the task of elaborating recommendations on political action.

C. POLICY OPTIONS

1. *Demographic options*

(a) *Fertility*

None of the federal Governments of west Germany have any intention of influencing fertility. While they agree that fertility is too low, when responding to the United Nations Inquiries among Governments on Population and Development, they have stated that they will undertake no interventions.

Already in 1983, Alison McIntosh (1983, pp. 211-212) had summarized the attitude of the German Government: "On the basis of interviews conducted in 1978, it appeared that the Federal government lacked convincing evidence that population decline constitutes a serious threat to economic growth. The government was also aware that expert opinion is doubtful of the lasting effect of traditional pronatalist incentives. Under these circumstances, the Federal government was reluctant to embark on a costly program of incentives to childbearing, the more so since such a program violates the ruling parties' ideological belief about the family and the individual and might be interpreted as an infringement of civil liberties." McIntosh quite ingeniously labels west Germany a "prisoner of the past" in that respect. Indeed, the legacy of the racist pronatalist policy of the Nazis still provides an additional and unspoken rationale for refraining from any pronatalist measure.

The assessment of McIntosh not only correctly captures the situation in the 1970s under the social-liberal Governments, but also characterizes the attitude of the Christian-liberal Governments from 1982 to 1998 and the present social-green Government. This does not exclude an interest in developing a family policy which in the meantime is a rather broad and generous one. In their national report for the International Conference on Population and Development, we read: "For the German Government, family policy in general and family-relevant political measures have a significance of their own which need not be justified through population-relevant considerations; nevertheless, side effects considered demographically desirable might occur" (report of the Government of the Federal Republic of Germany for the International Conference on Population and Development, 1994). Such "side effects", however, did not occur—and this small sentence was never repeated.

It is therefore typical and according to expectations in Germany that the two Ad Hoc Study Committees on Demographic Change unanimously agreed not to add any policy options to influence demographic trends or, more precisely, fertility. Also, the recommendations concerning the family and social networks do not mention any measure to influence fertility. They aim at the further improvement of living conditions of children and parents without any preference for the family form, and at measures to reconcile job and family for both mothers and fathers.

Finally, it is fair to remember that the Population Division of the United Nations Secretariat prepared its study on replacement migration because "the recent experience of low-fertility countries suggests that there is no reason to assume that their fertility will return any time soon to the above-replacement level" (United Nations, 2001, chap. II, second paragraph).[4]

(b) Immigration

In (west) Germany, immigration was never regarded as a measure to shape the size or age structure of population. Though Germany so far has never pursued any immigration policy in the strict sense, there are three main reasons for immigration:

- Constitutional (Germans and ethnic Germans);
- Humanitarian (asylum-seekers);
- Economic (foreign workers).

After the Second World War, millions of German refugees and displaced persons came to the Federal Republic of Germany (west Germany). In the 1950s until 1961, Germans from the German Democratic Republic (east Germany) followed until "the wall" stopped this immigration. In the 1960s, labour-force needs led to the recruitment of foreign workers (called "guest workers" at that time); the recruitment stop was launched in 1973 and is, in principle, still in force. Exceptions relate to family members, and to persons from EU countries. Recently, a new type of immigration for a limited number of information technology specialists has been introduced. It is called the "green card"—or (in Bavaria) the "blue card"—initiative. Chancellor Schröder announced such a measure at the opening of the Hannover fair in March 2000 to overcome the apparent shortage of computer specialists. Whether Chancellor Schröder was also inspired by the United Nations study on replacement migration it is difficult to say. The discussion of this measure of temporary immigration of highly qualified foreigners, however, took on a much higher profile in Germany than did the discussion of the United Nations study.

With Gorbachev's glasnost policy, the influx of ethnic Germans from Central and Eastern Europe started in 1987. These ethnic Germans had settled in those regions (mainly the Russian Federation, Poland and Romania) 200 years ago and now wished to return to the country of their forefathers. A peak of this immigration of ethnic Germans coincided with the hasty east-west migration of persons from east Germany after the opening of the wall, which was increased by a larger number of asylum-seekers. This constitutional right of asylum of political refugees was limited in 1993 to those not arriving from "safe third countries". Also, ethnic Germans had to apply with the German embassies in their country of origin to enter Germany. Once in Germany they receive the German passport; children born to foreigners in Germany (second and third generation), however, are still foreigners. As of 2000 they have the option, however, of acquiring German nationality in addition to their foreign nationality, and they have to decide thereon after reaching the age of majority.

Germany also accepted large numbers of refugees from civil war in the former Yugoslavia who are supposed to return once there is peace again in their region of origin. Finally, one should know that only a small fraction of asylum-seekers are granted asylum, but many of those refused are nevertheless tolerated as de facto refugees.

To sum up, the varieties of situations of migrants in Germany are very complex. The present Government intends to launch an immigration law. The Minister of the Interior has established an independent immigration committee which is to submit its proposals until mid-2001. The major problem will be how to reconcile economic, humanitarian and constitutional reasons for immigration. There is no controversy either regarding whether immigration will continue, or regarding whether it must be regulated.

2. *Options of adaptation and reform policies*

(a) *Options to adapt to the decline in working-age population*

As noted in the previous section, Germany does not pursue any direct population policies, with respect either to raising fertility or to using immigration to prevent a decline in the total population size or in the size of the population of active age.

The fact that the number of persons in working ages between 20 and 65 years would decline strongly after 2010-2015 was already noted by the inter-ministerial working group when preparing its report on the consequences of demographic change at the beginning of the 1980s. The representatives of the Ministry of Labour, however, convinced the working group that it was not the demographic change that was decisive but the economic constellations; and since it would be extremely difficult to project economic trends longer than 20 years, they stopped their analysis with the year 2000 (Bundesministerium des Innern, 1984). It should be noted that they expected a shortage of apprentices in the 1990s; but the true and sad fact is that youth unemployment is appallingly high in Germany—and this is structural unemployment.

The First Ad Hoc Study Committee on Demographic Change of the German Parliament looked at the labour market up to 2030 under status quo assumptions of economic behaviour[5] and stated that there would be an increasing imbalance with a shortage of labour after 2010. The Ad Hoc Study Committee came up with five options of adaptation:

- Increase of labour productivity (use the benefits of computerization and lean production);

- Flexibility of working time (start working earlier, sabbatical years in the family phase, part-time work for the elderly);

- Increase of age at retirement (also of advantage for the social security system);

- Promotion of labour-force participation of women (a positive trend anyway);

- Controlled immigration.

These five options are reported in the order in which they were given (Deutscher Bundestag, 1994). Qualification and lifelong learning were considered to be of great importance for the ageing labour force as well as for the foreign population in Germany. The First Ad Hoc Study Committee also felt that more differentiated models of the labour market with an array of possible economic developments should be studied, a task that it transmitted to the next ad hoc study committee.

The Second Ad Hoc Study Committee on Demographic Change of the German Parliament availed itself of more recent, and more sophisticated studies with plausible alternative models of the future labour market. The sobering common denominator was that unemployment would persist well beyond 2010. As for the non-economic trends, namely, the demographic trends, this study group saw the effect of *demographic relief* of the labour market after 2010 (Deutscher Bundestag, 1998, p. 291). There were no more concerns of a labour shortage in the shadow of structural unemployment. The Ad Hoc Study Group could not agree on options: this should be done by the Third Ad Hoc Study Group.

It seems that we have reverted to the assessment of the early 1980s that, in respect of the size of the working-age population, it is economic determinants that matter most, not the demographic decline. We demographers have to note that assessments in this field go beyond population numbers and take into account plausible economic developments as to employment and unemployment and economic growth. The pure population numbers are only a first indicator of possible problems. We have returned to a state of affairs that I summarized at the Expert Group Meeting on the International Transmission of Population Policy Experience in 1988: "The modern economies will need less (expensive) labour that can be (and is) replaced by capital-intensive technology" (Höhn, 1990, p. 157).[6] The reaction of German experts to the United Nations study on replacement migration, and, in particular, to our media's interpretation of imminent economic decay without immediate large-scale immigration to balance the shrinking working-age population in Germany, was therefore to dispel these fears of current and persistent unemployment (also of foreigners) and to indicate the availability of other options to overcome an eventual shortage of labour. The main arguments were economic, and also concerned the needed qualifications of migrant workers.

(b)   Options to reform the pension system

The issue of population ageing cannot be solved by immigration. The undesired consequences of ageing for the social security system must be solved by reform of this system and hence by adaptation to population change. However, "a policy of adaptation requires a long period of launching and an observation of mechanisms so far unknown" (Höhn, 1990, p. 157).

This period of observation is now quite long in Germany, some 20 years. Already the interministerial working group had regarded the need to reform the German pay-as-you-go pension system as the biggest challenge. They regarded the introduction of a capital accumulation system of old age income security as less promising (Bundesministerium des Innern, 1984). In Germany, "the existing social security system is, however, so generous and so flexible that a reform policy with an objective of reducing the level of pensions and increasing contributions by the working population together with an increase in the age at retirement appears feasible. The theoretical alternative, either to halve the pensions or to double the social security contributions, is politically unacceptable" (Höhn, 1990, p. 156). Indeed, the age at retirement was to be raised, starting, however, only in 2001.

The First Ad Hoc Study Committee on Demographic Change of the German Parliament did not analyse the pension system, and the Second did not provide any policy options. Their analysis, however, clearly shows that there are in principle several options, but unfortunately none where the whole population would benefit financially. And here we come to the crucial problem of acceptance: politicians that take away instead of providing more risk not to be elected. Of course, if one had started reforms earlier, the acceptance might have been easier.

The introduction of a "demographic factor" (concerning increase of life expectancy at age 60 with an effect of gradually decreasing the pension level of *future* pensioners) by the Kohl Government in 1998 was immediately abolished by the new Government. Some observers believe that Kohl and the Christian Democrats lost the elections in 1998, inter alia, because of this pension reform, which was called by the Social Democrats a measure of "social chill". In the meantime (first in 2000), the pensions are no longer adjusted to the increase of net income but to the (lower) inflation rate. For the last two years, the Social Democrat Government and the trade unions have been discussing retirement at age 60 (of course, with a view to decreasing unemployment), and this idea has now been dropped. The plans to reform the German pension system that are under discussion foresee a sizeable decrease of the pension level in order to keep the contribution rate at 20 per cent of gross income; they also intend to make an additional private pension scheme compulsory (to be supported by income tax benefits); and there are rumours of an extension of the age at retirement beyond 65 years. The discussions within the Government and between the parties are vivid and controversial. Nothing definite has been decided, but the conviction grows that something must be decided. Strangely enough, the media are still rather mute on the topic of pension reform. The German system of securing old age income is too complex to be easily understood in respect of its repercussions on the different generations. Along these lines, it may be noted that:

- The majority of the population are covered by the compulsory pay-as-you-go system. Half of the contributions of the active population is paid by the employer. A growing part of pensions is assured from federal taxes;

- A number of big corporations voluntarily pay pensions to their former employees;

- Civil servants have their own system of pensions (from federal taxes);

- The self-employed acquire life insurance, investment funds or shares or contribute to pension funds;

- Many Germans own a house or a flat.

A shift from the pay-as-you-go system to a combination with a capital accumulation system is only relatively easy for the younger generations. Middle-aged and older persons in the labour force have already contributed to the pension system and acquired pension rights, and they would have fewer years for building up private pensions. The acquired pension rights, however, are related to future age structure imbalance between the elderly and the working-age population as well as to the future level of employment and income.

(c) *Options to reform the health-care system*

Health insurance is compulsory for the employed and pensioners; contributions are related to gross income. Hence, contributions become smaller after retirement. The self-employed and civil servants usually are in a private health insurance plan where the contribution rate depends on age at entering the insurance plan, current age and sex. Here insurance rate increases slightly with age.

In addition, there is compulsory long-term care insurance for everybody.

The growing expenditures in the health sector are driven by medical progress and a self-service mentality of patients, doctors, hospitals and the pharmaceutical industry. Numerous measures to limit and control expenditures have been tried in the past. Not long ago all medical services were reimbursed. In the meantime, flat rates have to be paid for medicine or for each day in hospital. Doctors have fixed budgets for their services that are not to be exceeded. Dissatisfaction is growing among patients and doctors.

It seems that the problem of maintaining the provision of general health care is related not only to the ageing process but also, and even predominantly, to medical progress and the existing health-care system. This analysis is contained in the second interim report of the Ad Hoc Study Committee, which does not, however, offer any political options (Deutscher Bundestag, 1998).

[1]The question of an optimal PSR remains to be investigated. The assumption of the highest observed PSR is quite insufficient.

[2]The recent population prospects of the Federal Ministry of the Interior do not provide comments on the consequences.

[3]Recommendations already in the first interim report were slightly modified.

[4]This statement ends with a reference to the United Nations publication on below-replacement fertility (United Nations, 2001) based on the Expert Group Meeting in 1997.

[5]These assumptions were rather optimistic shortly after the economic boom owing to reunification, and definitely underestimated structural unemployment.

[6]Where I also quote the same opinion of the Italian delegation to the Economic Commission for Europe (ECE) Meeting on Population and Development held in Budapest in 1987.

References

Bundesministerium des Innern (1984). *Bericht über die Bevölkerungsentwicklung in der Bundesrepublik Deutschland 2. Teil: Auswirkungen auf die verschiedenen Bereiche von Staat und Gesellschaft*. Bonn: Bundesministerium des Innern (Bundestags-Drucksache 10/863).

_____ (2000). *Modellrechnungen zur Bevölkerungsentwicklung in der Bundesrepublik Deutschland bis zum Jahr 2050*. Berlin: Bundesministerium des Innern.

Deutscher Bundestag, Referat Öffentlichkeitsarbeit (1994). *Zwischenbericht der Enquete-Kommission "Demographischer Wandel": Herausforderung unserer älter werdenden Gesellschaft an den einzelnen und die Politik*. Bonn: Deutscher Bundestag, Referat Öffentlichkeitsarbeit.

_____ (1998). *Zweiter Zwischenbericht der Enquete-Kommission "Demographischer Wandel": Herausforderung unserer älter werdenden Gesellschaft an den einzelnen und die Politik*. Bonn: Deutscher Bundestag, Referat Öffentlichkeitsarbeit.

Höhn, Charlotte (1990). International transmission of population policy experience in Western Europe. In *International Transmission of Population Policy Experience*. Sales No. E.91.XIII.10. New York: United Nations.

_____, and Dorbritz, Jürgen (2000). The future of the family and future fertility trends in Germany. In *Population Bulletin of the United Nations: Below Replacement Fertility*, Special Issue, Nos. 40/41 (1999), pp. 218-234. Sales No. E.99.XIII.13. New York: United Nations.

McIntosh, C. Alison (1983). *Population Policy in Western Europe*. New York: M. E. Sharpe.

Report of the Government of the Federal Republic of Germany for the International Conference on Population and Development, 1994.

Statistisches Bundesamt (2000). *Bevölkerungsentwicklung Deutschlands bis zum Jahr 2050: Ergebnisse der 9. koordinierten Bevölkerungsvorausberechnung*. Wiesbaden, Germany: Statistisches Bundesamt.

Teitelbaum, Michael S., and Jay M. Winter (1985). *The Fear of Population Decline*. London: Academic Press.

United Nations (1999). *World Population Prospects: The 1998 Revision*, vol. I, *Comprehensive Tables*. Sales No. E.99.XIII.9.

_____ (2000). *Population Bulletin of the United Nations: Below Replacement Fertility*, Special Issue, Nos. 40/41 (1999). Sales No. E.99.XIII.13.

_____ (2001). *Replacement Migration: Is It a Solution to Declining and Ageing Populations?* Sales No. E.01.XIII.19.

POSSIBLE POLICY RESPONSES TO POPULATION AGEING AND POPULATION DECLINE: THE CASE OF ITALY

*Antonio Golini**

It is widely known that population ageing is a demographically inevitable process, since it is linked to the demographic transition and therefore to the fall in births and in mortality rates, mostly at older ages, as is presently occurring in the more developed countries. Depending on the onset, speed and intensity of the demographic transition, the ageing process will vary both in speed and in extent on a geographical basis, both at the international level and within each country. It is likewise known that ageing is the positive result of two victories that humanity has sought for centuries and is still seeking: the victory over unwanted births and that over premature deaths.

Because of the sharp, prolonged fall of the fertility rates, and consequently of births, that has coincided with a sharp, prolonged rise in longevity, Italy has now become the "oldest" country in the world, recording the highest proportion of population aged 65 years or over, and the lowest proportion of people under age 15. Up to now, the fall in fertility and the increase in the mean length of life have almost perfectly compensated one another in the dynamics of population, since for many years the number of births—approximately 530,000-550,000 per year—has been more or less the same as the number of deaths. The number of the deaths has exceeded the number of the births for just a few years, and the Italian population is undergoing a natural decline that is very modest for the moment. In the near future, the speed of population ageing will probably be greater than the rate of increase in the length of life. Therefore, over the next decades, the number of deaths should rise drastically, reaching the possible figure of 750,000-800,000 deaths per year in 2050, compared with a possible number of 200,000-300,000 births, and thus to a possible deaths/births ratio equal to 2.5-4.0 (United Nations, 1999).

For the Italian population, the processes of decline and ageing have already started. Based on the United Nations projections, the population will fall from 57.3 million in 2000 to 36.8 million in 2050 according to the low-fertility scenario (continuation of the current level of 1.1-1.2 children per woman) or to 46.8 million according to the high-fertility scenario (recovery to 2.1 children per woman). At the same time, the proportion of the population aged 60 years or over would rise from the current 24.2 to between 36.3 and 46.2 per cent (United Nations, 1999). As is well known, the faster the population decline,

*Università di Roma, Rome, Italy.

the faster the ageing process and vice versa. Thus, in any case, there would be an extraordinary upsetting in the population, which would be all the greater if fertility remained very low, all other factors being equal.

The ageing process is widespread and involves individuals, households, population and subpopulations (the elderly and the working-age population in particular). This will have a series of demographic as well as psychological, cultural, economic, social and environmental consequences both at the micro-level, for individuals and households, and at the macrolevel, for populations and subpopulations (Golini, 1999). The more advanced the process of population ageing and decline becomes, the greater and more profound the consequences will be; the faster the process takes place, the greater the necessity of a prompt and adequate response from the society as a whole and from individuals. Therefore, the difficulties derived from ageing, and to a lesser extent those derived from the population decline, are linked to the intensity and speed of the process. Society does not always respond adequately to these problems because demographic changes are hard to perceive in the short term. Political decision-making processes in Western democracies are the product of long, complex negotiations and compromises, and they rarely look at the long term. Sometimes societies fail to achieve the most suitable and acceptable solutions in a timely manner, especially in processes such as ageing, which are new in the history of humankind.

Therefore, when the process is intensive and fast, there is a need to dynamically "restructure" the whole society in response to the sharp fall in the number of young people and the simultaneous sharp increase of the elderly. Figure I shows observed and expected growth rates by major age groups (for the population aged 0-19 and 60 or over) in a population like Italy's between 1950 and 2050. There have been periods, for example, around 1985, when the number of young people decreased at an average annual rate of over 3 per cent. It is obvious that a population will have serious difficulties if that population has to shift financial, physical and human resources from one segment of the population to another in just a few years.

The average annual rates of increase for various age groups produced by simulation[1] (figure II) help to understand the ageing process. It is clear that the differential trends in the young population compared with the old one depend on three values identified in the segments called a, b, c:

- Segment a indicates the excess growth of the older population when the younger population, owing to the fall in fertility rates, reaches a growth rate of zero;
- Segment b indicates how long the older population continues to grow once the younger population starts to decrease;
- Segment c indicates the excess decline of the younger population when the older population is about to decrease, having reached a growth rate of zero.

The differences in the growth rates at any given time and the time lag between the onset of the decline of the young population and the onset of the decline of the old population produce the various demographic transitions of

151

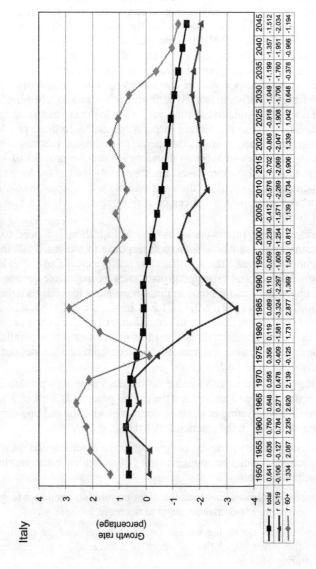

Figure I. Growth rate by major age groups (population aged 0-19, 60 or over, and total population), Italy, 1950-2050, low variant

Italy

Growth rate (percentage)

	1950	1955	1960	1965	1970	1975	1980	1985	1990	1995	2000	2005	2010	2015	2020	2025	2030	2035	2040	2045
r total	0.641	0.636	0.750	0.648	0.595	0.356	0.119	0.089	0.110	-0.059	-0.238	-0.412	-0.576	-0.702	-0.808	-0.918	-1.049	-1.199	-1.357	-1.512
r 0-19	-0.106	-0.127	0.784	0.271	0.478	-0.409	-1.581	-3.324	-2.297	-1.609	-1.254	-2.047	-2.269	-1.908	-1.706	-1.760	-1.951	-2.034
r 60+	1.334	2.087	2.235	2.620	2.139	-0.125	1.731	2.877	1.369	1.503	0.812	1.139	0.734	0.906	1.339	1.042	0.648	-0.378	-0.966	-1.194

Source: Own elaborations on data from United Nations (1999).

Figure II. Growth rate by major age groups (population aged 0-19, 20-59, 60 or over, and total population): simulation over a period of 200 years

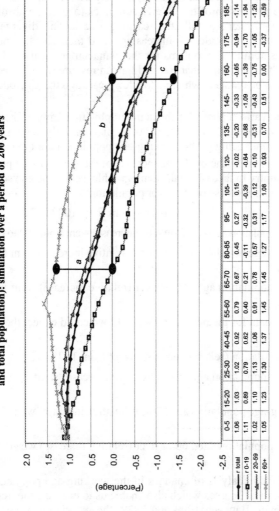

	0-5	15-20	25-30	40-45	55-60	65-70	80-85	95-	105-	120-	135-	145-	160-	175-	185-
r total	1.06	1.03	1.02	0.92	0.79	0.67	0.45	0.27	0.15	-0.02	-0.20	-0.33	-0.65	-0.94	-1.14
r 0-19	1.11	0.89	0.79	0.62	0.40	0.21	-0.11	-0.32	-0.39	-0.64	-0.88	-1.09	-1.39	-1.70	-1.94
r 20-59	1.02	1.10	1.13	1.06	0.91	0.78	0.57	0.31	0.12	-0.10	-0.31	-0.43	-0.75	-1.05	-1.26
r 60+	1.05	1.23	1.30	1.37	1.45	1.45	1.27	1.17	1.08	0.93	0.70	0.51	0.00	-0.37	-0.59

Source: Own elaborations starting from data of Coale and Demeny (South model) (1966).

153

the three population segments, with highly differentiated rates appearing as clearly shown in Figure III. Figure IV shows how this mechanism is linked with the ageing of all the subpopulations with different timing and rates; those rates should be the basic elements for formulating and implementing political responses to ageing.

Trends in the elderly segment of the simulated population are reflected in the projections of the population of an Italian region, Liguria.[2] Figure V clearly shows that while the proportion of the elderly continues to rise, the absolute number of elderly people starts to fall after reaching a peak. This divergence between the proportion of the elderly—increasing—and their absolute number—falling—creates additional problems for the management of the elderly since, at some point, the physical, financial and human resources dedicated to the elderly will have to be reduced, while up to a few years ago these resources should have been growing.

In relation to the various phases of the demographic transition of the different subpopulations, a new development is taking place in Italy: a considerable fall and a significant ageing of the working-age population are forecast.

Between 1950 and 2000, the moderate increase of the working-age population enabled the country to face (from the demographic, economic and social points of view) the sharp increase of the older population:[3]

- The total population (relative increase) went from 100 to 122;
- The young population aged 0-19 (relative increase) went from 100 to 68;
- The working-age population aged 20-59 (relative increase) went from 100 to 130;
- The elderly population aged 60 or over (relative increase) went from 100 to 241.

Referring to the data for the period 2000-2050,[4] we could expect the following changes:

- The total population (relative increase) went from 100 to 72;
- The younger population aged 0-19 (relative increase) went from 100 to 61;
- The working-age population aged 20-59 (relative increase) went from 100 to 54;
- The elderly population aged 60 or over (relative increase) went from 100 to 122.

For a more detailed analysis of changes in the working-age population, we should refer to national sources which also enable us to examine the trends at the subnational level. Between 1999 and 2029, the working-age population, considered here to be between ages 15 and 64, could vary in the amounts shown in table 1. Some brief observations:

(a) The fall in the working-age population may accelerate over time: 8.3 million in 30 years, an annual average of -173,000 in the first decade, -248,000 in the second and -404,000 in the third;

Figure III. Index numbers (year zero = 100) of total population and subpopulations (population aged 0-19, 20-59, 60 or over, and total population): simulation over a period of 200 years

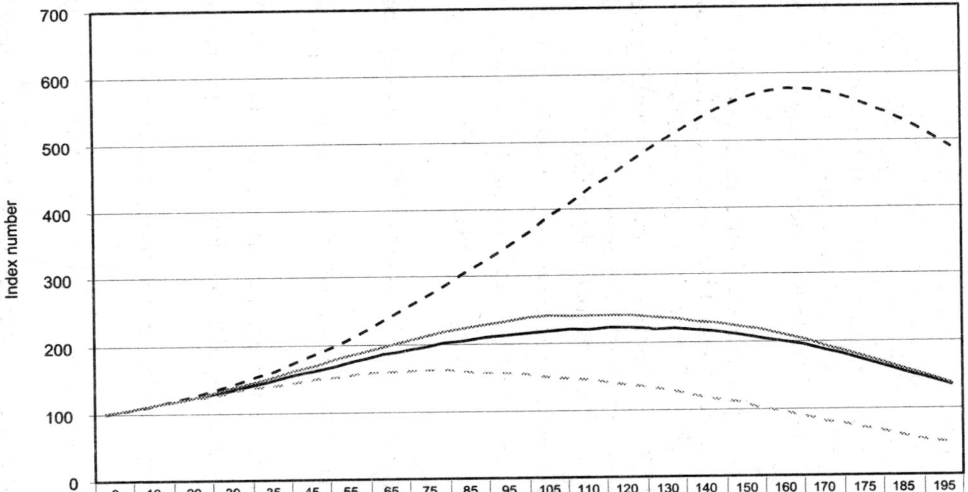

	0	10	20	30	35	45	55	65	75	85	95	105	110	120	130	140	150	160	170	175	185	195
Pop. total	100.0	111.0	123.0	136.2	143.0	157.1	171.2	184.7	196.8	206.7	213.9	219.2	220.8	222.4	221.3	217.7	211.3	201.4	187.8	179.9	162.9	144.6
Pop. 0-19	100.0	111.1	121.8	131.8	136.9	146.2	153.7	159.3	161.9	161.0	156.9	151.7	148.8	141.5	132.2	121.7	109.6	96.7	83.7	77.3	64.7	52.9
Pop. 20-59	100.0	110.8	123.4	138.4	146.1	162.5	179.4	195.6	210.7	223.9	233.9	240.2	241.6	241.8	238.6	232.0	222.8	210.2	194.0	185.0	165.5	145.1
Pop. 60+	100.0	111.5	125.9	143.0	152.7	174.9	201.0	233.5	268.4	304.9	344.1	385.9	407.2	450.4	492.2	529.9	560.4	575.1	571.1	563.6	540.0	506.6

Source: Own elaborations starting from data of Coale and Demeny (South model) (1983).

Figure IV. Births and deaths in total population, and entrance and exit flows to and from various subpopulations (aged 0-19, 20-59, and 60 or over)

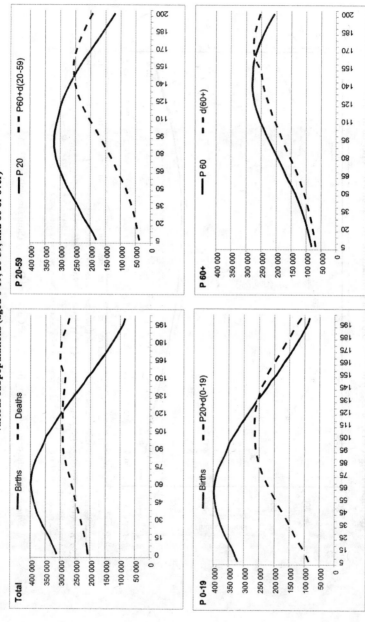

Source: Own elaborations starting from data of Coale and Demeny (South model) (1983).

Figure V. Size (thousands) and proportion of total population aged 65 years or over, Liguria, 1999-2049

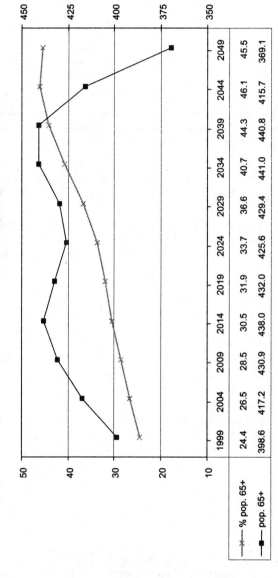

	1999	2004	2009	2014	2019	2024	2029	2034	2039	2044	2049
% pop. 65+	24.4	26.5	28.5	30.5	31.9	33.7	36.6	40.7	44.3	46.1	45.5
pop. 65+	398.6	417.2	430.9	438.0	432.0	425.6	429.4	441.0	440.8	415.7	369.1

Source: Own calculations from unpublished projections by A. Golini and A. De Simoni (constant fertility, slight reduction in mortality, zero migration).

(Thousands)

Division/gender/age group	Value in 1999	Change 1999-2029	
		Absolute	*Percentage*
North M+F, aged 15-64	17 578	-5 151	-29.3
Central M+F, aged 15-64................	7 497	-2 055	-27.4
South M+F, aged 15-64	13 993	-1 051	-7.5
Italy M+F, aged 15-64................	**39 068**	**-8 257**	**-21.1**
Italy M, aged 15-64	19 534	-3 959	-20.3
Italy F, aged 15-64...................	19 534	-4 298	-22.0
Italy M+F, aged 15-34	16 362	-6 815	-41.7
Italy M+F, aged 35-64	22 706	-1 442	-6.4

Source: Own calculations from unpublished projections by A. Golini and A. De Simoni (constant fertility, slight reduction in mortality, zero migration).

(*b*)   The fall is much sharper in north-central Italy (27-29 per cent), in other words, in the area with the greatest economic development and the lowest unemployment;

(*c*)   A decrease (7.5 per cent) is also expected in the most economically backward part of the country, which is experiencing high unemployment, especially among youth. This means that the gaps created by demographic trends in north-central Italy cannot be compensated with internal south-north migrations, as occurred in the 1950s and 1960s, when about 4 million people emigrated from the south, half to the rest of Italy and half abroad. The south was thus largely deprived of its human capital. In 1999, 64 per cent of the total working-age population in Italy lived in the north-central area, while in 2029 this proportion should fall to 58 per cent;

(*d*)   The expected decrease is slightly greater for women (4.3 million) than for men (4.0 million); that is to say, women's employment has increased sharply in recent years, while men's has fallen;

(*e*)   The expected decrease is much greater for the younger segment of the working-age population (6.8 million, -42 per cent) than for the older segment (1.4 million, -6 per cent). The lack of young people will be serious and the ageing of the working-age population will therefore be considerable.

In the medium term, the most serious problem for the Italian population, society and economy will stem from this sharp fall and ageing of the working-age population, with a persistent decline of the younger population and the increase of the older population.

A study recently conducted by the Population Division of the United Nations Secretariat (United Nations, 2001) has helped highlight all the weaknesses of the structure of the Italian population, and has had a greater impact in the press and among politicians than all the numerous and frequent analyses conducted in Italy on the same topic and with the same results. The sharp fall in fertility over recent decades brought Italian births down from 1 million in the mid-1960s to just over 500,000 in the mid-1990s. In about 30 years, the number of potential parents will also fall by half and, at that point, the population decline will become inevitable and very intense. At the same time, the mean length of life has increased beyond all expectations (1 woman of 3 could reach 90 years of age) and thus the increase in the number of the elderly and the very old, owing to old cohorts with numerous births, is significant and currently unstoppable. Therefore, Italy is now the "oldest" country in the world and, in the future, it will likely remain among the oldest ones.

One solution to ensure fewer demographic—and therefore economic-social—imbalances in the Italian system (as well as in other countries with a very low fertility rate) could be "replacement migration" (United Nations, 2001), with a substantial annual immigration, ranging from 235,000 (if we wanted to keep the total population constant) to 357,000 (if we wanted to keep the working-age population constant) for all the years from 1995 to 2050.[5] If we wanted to maintain a constant ratio between the working-age population and people aged 65 years or over, then annual immigration would have to amount to 2,176,000 people for the entire period. In my view, these figures, proposed from the demographic point of view *alone*, have reached a substantial goal: they have made politicians and public opinion realize how negative the Italian demographic panorama is currently and what it can look like in the near future.

However, from the professional and political points of view, the debate and the responses to population decline and ageing must be more fully articulated.

1. The *first response* should consist of an attempt to raise the fertility rate of Italian women and couples, which is now very low and stable at 1.1-1.2 children per woman and has been so for many years (Golini, 2000). The most recent surveys have once more shown that the number of children wanted by Italian women is just over two, that is to say, the replacement level, and that the four main reasons for not planning and having a child or two are economic (18 per cent) and work-related (17 per cent), not feeling ready (17 per cent) and being satisfied with the number of children they have (17 per cent).[6] However, if the structural problems mentioned in point 4 below are not solved, Italian women will necessarily continue to keep the number of their children low or very low; the desire for motherhood is therefore satisfied with the first child and very often stops there. In order to achieve a total fertility rate of 1.7-1.8 children per woman, at least 30 per cent of women would have 3 or more children. In present conditions, this goal seems very difficult to pursue since, in the recent survey cited, only 4 per cent of couples with two children were thinking of having a third child within the next two years; and this was not only for economic reasons (just two children already drastically reduced a couple's standard of living), but also for cultural reasons. Today, a couple with four children is seen as being heterodox and eccentric.[7] The policy makers should therefore try to remove all the elements penalizing women and couples who decide to have a child or another child. This action would, among other things, also have the advantage of showing that society is concerned with the social value of procreation and children, which for some time have been regarded exclusively as something absolutely private pertaining to women and to couples.

2. The *second response* must be to favour immigration, which for Italy is advantageous and actually necessary from the economic and demographic point of view, and is in any case unstoppable, considering on the one hand the extraordinary and in many cases growing population pressure in the countries of origin, especially in Africa, and on the other the vulnerability of our country's borders which provide access not only to Italy but also to the rest of the European Union (EU). However, from the social point of view, immigration would be highly unlikely to reach the levels mentioned in the report on replacement migration. This is, inter alia, because European countries, and therefore also Italy, host *historical ethnic minorities* who have fought for centuries, and in some cases are still fighting, to gain autonomy and independence and to obtain full recognition of their ethnic identity.[8] The immigrant flow will necessarily be relatively modest and in any case gradual in order for these *new minorities* to be able to coexist in the best possible conditions with the older ones. Even if Europe is historically based on migrations, which have played an absolutely vital role for the continent's development and history, it should be recalled that Europe today is a continent with long-established populations and not, like the Americas, a continent that was populated by migrations.

Moreover, Italy is a country of recent immigration, which started in the 1970s. In the 1990s, there were approximately 50,000-70,000 immigrants per year but, despite this moderate inflow, there were already problems with xenophobia. An increase to, say, 300,000 immigrants per year could lead to the outburst of serious racism and could further foster the political growth of the reactionary right, as has already happened in France, Germany and Austria.

3. The *third response* could be to favour a complete reabsorption of the high youth unemployment in Italy (among young people aged 15-24 years, the unemployment rate in 1998 was 33 per cent for Italy as a whole and 57 per cent for the economically most backward regions of the south). Therefore, the expected fall of the young segment of the working-age population (aged 15-39) could be, in the short and medium term, an advantage and the fall of the workforce and of the employed could be much lower than that in the working-age population. However, in the long term, this fall could prove to be a serious blow to the country's international competitiveness, unless the human capital of this young population increases significantly.

A profound overhaul of the entire education and training system is necessary. The sharp fall in the number of young people and students could provide a positive opportunity to utilize the surplus of teachers that will occur for the following: (*a*) a better quality of schools, in order to ensure that the majority of students reach the levels of excellence reached today only by a minority; (*b*) serious refresher courses for teachers; (*c*) cultural and vocational retraining courses for adults, "young" old people expelled early from the labour market; (*d*) acceptance of a considerably higher and growing number of foreign students; and (*e*) addressing the work of professors who obtain significant research funds exclusively for scientific research.

4. The *fourth response* lies in optimizing the role of women in the labour market, especially since at present they are more likely than men to obtain a school or a university degree, and their participation in the labour market is

increasing.[9] In Italy, women, together with young people, undoubtedly represent the most important human capital resource, and their skills are still underused. However, they must also be able to work and to advance in their career; they must therefore be able to count on men who fully share work at home, on public and private facilities for the necessary help in caring for children and the elderly, on a much more family-oriented labour market and on new instruments, including taxation, to provide economic support to the family.

5. The retirement age, *fifth response*, must necessarily be raised above the present thresholds,[10] while providing for a gradual retirement process to take place between ages 65 and 70; there must be full compatibility between any type of further work and pensions. This could be another way of overcoming the sharp contrast between the need to raise the retirement age and the trend towards early retirement, which leads to a fall in the age of retirement. Among other things, this could help dampen the increasingly widespread and unsustainable mystique of leisure time in favour of growing social responsibility, and also of a full implementation of the response mentioned in point 7 below.

6. The *sixth response*, closely connected to the three previous ones, could involve an increase of work productivity and a growth of the entire Italian economic system. This must certainly be the road to take, although the weaknesses of the infrastructures (in particular the transportation system), the weight of bureaucracy and the often rigid response of the trade unions often block an adequate increase of productivity in Italy. This year, in his traditional public speech at the end of May—the most important one of the year—the Governor of the Bank of Italy stressed the difficulties of the Italian economy in keeping up with the pace of growth of both the world economy and the European economy, due, inter alia, to the slowdown in the increase of productivity in the 1990s; this increase was 2.1 per cent in Italy compared with 3.7 per cent in France, 3.0 per cent in Germany and 3.4 per cent in the United States of America.

7. The *seventh response* may lie in substantial, increasing and voluntary social and health support for the elderly who have physical and/or psychological and/or cognitive problems, by other wholly self-sufficient older people who will therefore have to commit time and energy for the less fortunate (as already occurs today in many small, peripheral and very aged towns). One can imagine also the creation of a compulsory civil service for young people of both sexes, of, for instance, from 6 to 12 months' duration, which could substitute for the compulsory military service where it is still in force. This service again should be in favour of the elderly and the oldest old people who need assistance (and also in favour of the environment). The service could have several positive aspects: to reduce the wave of individualism and increase the spirit of sacrifice and team spirit; to reinforce or recreate intergenerational links not in a family environment, but in a societal one; to bring, through an enormous amount of low- or zero-cost work, relief to welfare expenses. In the future, it will not be possible for the support to elderly and oldest old people who need assistance to be provided, as it is today, almost exclusively by their children: in the near future, there will not be enough children. A rough preliminary estimate of the future ratio between parents and adult children shows that in about 20 years,

the number of people aged 75 years or over, in other words, the cohort of elderly parents, could be greater than that of people aged 50-64, in other words, the cohort of their adult children.

The first two responses are structural and should affect population trends substantially. However, the effects of the first response (recovery of fertility), *though necessary*, will not be felt for a long time (assuming it can be implemented). Moreover, it is unlikely that the Italian fertility rate will rise to replacement level, although this would be desirable; at the same time, it is unlikely and undesirable that the length of life will stop increasing.[11] The second solution (acceptance of migration flows), *though necessary*, must be gradual and requires "reasonable dosage". This means that if the two responses are applied, they may not be able to substantially change, in the short and medium term, demographic trends, already mostly determined by the past trends.

In the short and medium term, education and the labour market seem to be the key areas for governing some consequences of these demographic trends, which threaten to upset the structure of Italy's society and economy. Politicians have the difficult task of finding the right formulas for handling a challenging present and a no less challenging near future.

In order to assess the impact of the three possible responses stated in points 3, 4 and 5 above, simulations have been carried out based on the hypothesis of constant activity and employment rates at current levels, on the one hand, and sharp increases over the next 30 years, on the other hand.[12]

Simulations are based on the following hypotheses: the activity and employment rates of the central and southern regions converge towards those of the northern regions which already have almost full employment; the rates for females converge towards those for males; and, finally, there is a significant rise in rates for the "young" old, which in practice means that there is an increase in the retirement age. In particular, the hypothesis states that:

(*a*)   For the young population aged 15-24, the especially low rates in the southern areas will converge towards those of the northern regions, though still remaining about 43-47 per cent for the activity rates and 40-44 per cent for the employment rates. This takes into account the fact that, in this age group, the rates should not be particularly high, considering the need to raise educational standards;

(*b*)   For the female population of the mid-age group, from 25 to 54 years, the rates—though rising considerably compared with the present ones—will reach the values of "only" 76 per cent for activity rates and 72 per cent for employment rates. This takes into account the fact that rates in the south are very low and thus likely to increase gradually, and the fact that women will devote a certain number of years to childbearing. However, looking at the higher female activity rates among women in Northern Europe, a stronger-than-assumed increase in Italy is also possible;

(*c*)   Rates among those aged 55-64 should experience a very sharp increase, bringing male activity rates from the current 37-52 per cent towards 70 per cent, and female rates from 15-19 per cent towards 55 per cent. The hypotheses are conservative in this case as well; higher rates are also possible.

162

Current and future activity and employment rates are shown in table 2 (*a*) and (*b*). The complete results of the simulation are shown in table 3 (*a*), (*b*) and (*c*). These tables highlight the unsustainability of the current and short-term situation, that is to say, low activity rates associated with a sharp decrease of the working-age population. In particular, it can be seen that:

- Under the assumption of constant employment rates (hypothesis A), the number of employed males would fall between 1999 and 2029 by 3 million (from 13.0 million to 10.0 million), that is to say, by 32 per cent; the number of employed women would fall by 2.3 million (from 7.5 million to 5.2 million), that is to say, by 30 per cent. The situation seems totally unsustainable from the economic point of view, also because for the males and females as a whole the ratio between the population aged 65 years or over and the employed would rise from 50 to 97 per cent (line (*j*) of table 3 (*c*));

- Under the assumption of rising employment rates (hypothesis B), in 2029 there would be an additional number of employed males totalling 2.1 million and of employed females totalling 4.2 million. Nevertheless, for the males and females as a whole, the ratio between the population aged 65 years or over and the employed would rise all the same, though less under hypothesis A, from 50 to 68 per cent (line (*k*) of table 3 (*c*)).

These simulations aim only at clearly showing the need for a labour policy that contributes to an increase in the activity and employment rates. This objective must be pursued not only for many macroeconomic reasons, some of which have been mentioned here, but also for microeconomic reasons regarding the well-being of individuals and families.

This is not all; moves towards much lower unemployment and continuous economic growth would most probably lead to the dampening of all or most xenophobic feeling towards foreign immigration. I am convinced that only the full perception of the need for immigrants to maintain economic prosperity will lead to their full acceptance.

To conclude, it should be stressed that the more complex and developed a society and an economy become, the more their growth and adaptation—harmonious, prompt and continuous—to changing structural conditions depend on a complex balance and interaction of factors and policies related to administration, education, politics (in the broad sense), culture and individual and collective psychology, and therefore also to the system of expectations, as well as the economy, of course. Population factors remain part of the background in the long and very long term but, like all structural factors, they certainly cannot be ignored. If these trends continue unchecked, they would in the end unhinge all the social and economic structures.

TABLE 2 (*a*). ACTIVITY RATES BY SEX, AGE GROUP AND DIVISION: OBSERVED, 1999, AND PROJECTED, 2009–2029

Age group	Males				Females			
	1999	2009	2019	2029	1999	2009	2019	2029
Northern regions								
15-24	47.1	47.0	47.0	47.0	43.0	43.0	43.0	43.0
25-35	91.5	91.5	91.5	91.5	76.3	76.0	76.0	76.0
35-54	92.5	92.5	92.5	92.5	60.7	65.8	70.9	76.0
55-64	36.6	47.7	58.9	70.0	15.0	28.3	41.6	55.0
Central regions								
15-24	37.4	40.6	43.8	47.0	31.4	35.3	39.1	43.0
25-35	85.9	87.7	89.6	91.5	64.2	68.1	72.1	76.0
35-54	93.0	93.0	93.0	93.0	59.2	64.8	70.4	76.0
55-64	45.5	53.7	61.8	70.0	19.3	31.2	43.1	55.0
Southern regions and islands								
15-24	37.0	40.3	43.6	47.0	26.9	32.3	37.6	43.0
25-35	82.1	85.2	88.4	91.5	44.3	54.9	65.4	76.0
35-54	91.2	91.6	92.1	92.5	42.5	53.7	64.8	76.0
55-64	52.1	58.1	64.0	70.0	14.9	28.3	41.6	55.0

Source: Own calculations.

TABLE 2 (b). EMPLOYMENT RATES BY SEX, AGE GROUP AND DIVISION: OBSERVED, 1999, AND PROJECTED, 2009-2029

Age group	Males				Females			
	1999	2009	2019	2029	1999	2009	2019	2029
Northern regions								
15-24	41.4	42.3	43.1	44.0	34.8	36.5	38.3	40.0
25-35	87.9	88.3	88.6	89.0	69.3	70.2	71.1	72.0
35-54	91.0	91.0	91.0	91.0	57.3	62.2	67.1	72.0
55-64	35.6	46.4	57.2	68.0	14.3	27.2	40.1	53.0
Central regions								
15-24	28.2	33.5	38.7	44.0	20.2	26.8	33.4	40.0
25-35	77.3	81.2	85.1	89.0	53.1	59.4	65.7	72.0
35-54	90.6	90.7	90.9	91.0	54.8	60.5	66.2	72.0
55-64	44.0	52.0	60.0	68.0	18.5	30.0	41.5	53.0
Southern regions and islands								
15-24	18.2	26.8	35.4	44.0	9.5	19.7	29.8	40.0
25-35	63.3	72.0	80.6	89.0	25.9	41.3	56.6	72.0
35-54	83.2	85.8	88.4	91.0	35.5	47.5	59.8	72.0
55-64	48.3	54.9	61.4	68.0	13.7	26.8	39.9	53.0

Source: Own calculations.

TABLE 3 (a). POPULATION AGED 65 YEARS OR OVER, WORKING-AGE POPULATION, LABOUR FORCE, EMPLOYED AND INDICATORS, MALES, ITALY, 1999-2029

(*Thousands*)

Population and indicator	1999	2009	2019	2029	Change 1999-2029			
					Total	Yearly	Percentage	Yearly rate
Population								
(a) Aged 65 or over	4 141	4 984	5 668	6 352	2 211	73.7	53.4	1.44
(b) WAP (aged 15-64)	19 535	18 757	17 573	15 575	-3 960	-132.0	-20.3	-0.75
(c) Labour force, hypothesis A	14 300	13 881	12 763	10 951	-3 349	-111.6	-23.4	-0.89
(d) Labour force, hypothesis B	14 300	14 320	13 679	12 393	-1 907	-63.6	-13.3	-0.48
(e) Employed, hypothesis A	13 026	12 707	11 692	10 003	-3 023	-100.8	-23.2	-0.88
(f) Employed, hypothesis B	13 026	13 416	13 085	12 072	-954	-31.8	-7.3	-0.25
Indicator								
(g) 100 (a)/(b)	21.2	26.6	32.3	40.8	19.6	0.7	92.4	-
(h) 100 (a)/(c)	29.0	35.9	44.4	58.0	29.0	1.0	100.3	-
(i) 100 (a)/(d)	29.0	34.8	41.4	51.3	22.3	0.7	77.0	-
(j) 100 (a)/(e)	31.8	39.2	48.5	63.5	31.7	1.1	99.7	-
(k) 100 (a)/(f)	31.8	37.1	43.3	52.6	20.8	0.7	65.5	-

Source: Own calculations.

NOTE: WAP = working-age population with no migration (unpublished projections by Golini and De Simoni, base 1999).

Hypothesis A, labour force and employed: constant 1999 rates.

Hypothesis B, labour force and employed: projected activity and employment rates assuming a rise in the retirement age, a convergence of rates of central and southern regions towards rates of northern regions, and a convergence of rates for females towards rates for males (see table 2 (*a*) and (*b*)).

TABLE 3 (b). POPULATION AGED 65 YEARS OR OVER, WORKING-AGE POPULATION, LABOUR FORCE, EMPLOYED AND INDICATORS, FEMALES, ITALY, 1999-2029

(Thousands)

Population and indicator	1999	2009	2019	2029	Change 1999-2029 Total	Change 1999-2029 Yearly	Change 1999-2029 Percentage	Change 1999-2029 Yearly rate
Population								
(a) Aged 65 or over	6 049	6 995	7 711	8 370	2 321	77.4	38.4	1.09
(b) WAP (aged 15-64)............	19 534	18 578	17 281	15 236	-4 298	-143.3	-22.0	-0.82
(c) Labour force, hypothesis A.	8 883	8 262	7 380	6 167	-2 716	-90.5	-30.6	-1.21
(d) Labour force, hypothesis B	8 883	9 654	10 091	9 952	1 069	35.6	12.0	0.38
(e) Employed, hypothesis A	7 479	7 006	6 265	5 212	-2 267	-75.6	-30.3	-1.20
(f) Employed, hypothesis B.	7 479	8 601	9 332	9 452	1 973	65.8	26.4	0.78
Indicator								
(g) 100 (a)/(b)	31.0	37.7	44.6	54.9	24.0	0.8	77.4	-
(h) 100 (a)/(c)	68.1	84.7	104.5	135.7	67.6	2.3	99.3	-
(i) 100 (a)/(d)	68.1	72.5	76.4	84.1	16.0	0.5	23.5	-
(j) 100 (a)/(e)	80.9	99.8	123.1	160.6	79.7	2.7	98.6	-
(k) 100 (a)/(f)	80.9	81.3	82.6	88.6	7.7	0.3	9.5	-

Source: Own calculations.

NOTE: WAP = working-age population with no migration (unpublished projections by Golini and De Simoni, base 1999).

Hypothesis A, labour force and employed: constant 1999 rates.

Hypothesis B, labour force and employed: projected activity and employment rates assuming a rise in the retirement age, a convergence of rates of central and southern regions towards rates of northern regions, and a convergence of rates for females towards rates for males (see table 2 (a) and (b)).

167

TABLE 3 (c). POPULATION AGED 65 YEARS OR OVER, WORKING-AGE POPULATION, LABOUR FORCE, EMPLOYED AND INDICATORS, MALES AND FEMALES, ITALY, 1999-2029

(Thousands)

Population and indicator	1999	2009	2019	2029	Change 1999-2029			
					Absolute	Absolute per year	Percentage	Rate
Population								
(a) Aged 65 or over............	10 190	11 980	13 378	14 722	4 532	151.1	44.5	1.23
(b) WAP (aged 15-64)...........	39 068	37 336	34 853	30 811	-8 257	-275.2	-21.1	-0.79
(c) Labour force, hypothesis A.........	23 183	22 143	20 143	17 118	-6 065	-202.2	-26.2	-1.01
(d) Labour force, hypothesis B.........	23 183	23 974	23 770	22 344	-839	-28.0	-3.6	-0.12
(e) Employed, hypothesis A.........	20 505	19 713	17 957	15 215	-5 290	-176.3	-25.8	-0.99
(f) Employed, hypothesis B.........	20 505	22 016	22 417	21 523	1 018	33.9	5.0	0.16
Indicators								
(g) 100 (a)/(b)............	26.1	32.1	38.4	47.8	21.7	0.7	83.2	-
(h) 100 (a)/(c)............	44.0	54.1	66.4	86.0	42.0	1.4	95.7	-
(i) 100 (a)/(d)............	44.0	50.0	56.3	65.9	21.9	0.7	49.9	-
(j) 100 (a)/(e)............	49.7	60.8	74.5	96.8	47.1	1.6	94.7	-
(k) 100 (a)/(f)............	49.7	54.4	59.7	68.4	18.7	0.6	37.6	-

Source: Own calculations.

NOTE: WAP = working-age population with no migration (unpublished projections by Golini and De Simoni, base 1999).

Hypothesis A, labour force and employed: constant 1999 rates.

Hypothesis B, labour force and employed: projected activity and employment rates assuming a rise in the retirement age, a convergence of rates of central and southern regions towards rates of northern regions, and a convergence of rates for females towards rates for males (see table 2 (*a*) and (*b*)).

168

[1]The simulation starts from a stable population in which, over 200 years, the fertility rate has fallen from 4.2 to 1.2 children per woman, and the mean length of life has increased from 45 to 75 years.

[2]Liguria is in the north-west part of Italy and its capital is Genoa; in 1999, it had a population of 1,633,000. With 24.4 per cent of people aged 65 years or over and 10.3 per cent of the population under age 15, it is Italy's "oldest" region; in 1998, it recorded 11,000 births and 22,000 deaths.

[3]Data from the Population Division of the United Nations Secretariat (United Nations (1999), medium variant).

[4]Data from the Population Division (United Nations (1999), medium variant, forecasting an increase of the total fertility rate from 1.2 to 1.7 and a moderate immigration falling to nil in 2020-2025).

[5]Italian researchers already reached similar conclusions previously, for example, Gesano (1994).

[6]The average number of wanted children per woman is 2.17, falling to 1.99 for women in northern Italy and rising to 2.38 for those in the south. The figure is 2.05 for working women and 2.38 for housewives. This is therefore not a particularly large variability. These data, like all the others appearing in the text, refer to the results of a survey conducted in January 2000 on a sample of just over 1,500 by the *Istituto di Ricerche sulla Popolazione* (IRP) (National Institute for Population Research) (Gesano and others, 2000). The survey is not yet available and the information shown is that published in a magazine (*L'Espresso*, July 2000; web site: http://www.espressoedit.kataweb.it). These results substantially confirm the findings of the Fertility and Family Survey conducted in 1996-1997 (De Sandre, Pinnelli and Santini, 1999).

[7]In a recent letter to a weekly magazine, a father of four children complained about being "made fun of" because he had four children and hadn't managed to stop before (*Famiglia Cristiana*, No. 30, 2000).

[8]Just to cite some examples, we can mention the bloody fighting undertaken in Spain by the Basques, who demand their autonomy, or the struggles in a war of religion in Northern Ireland; then, there is the tragic situation in the Balkans. But even when matters have been wholly agreed and peaceful, as in the case of the recent formation of two separate States, the Czech Republic and Slovakia, there has been a net reaffirmation of ethnic and cultural identity. In Italy, the German-speaking minority living in South Tyrol (the Italian region called Alto Adige) has been assured of wide-ranging autonomy and guarantees for preserving its ethnic identity, so that an Italian who wants to settle in Alto Adige has to reside there for at least four years before obtaining the right to permanent residence.

[9]Between 1994 and 1998, the ratio of women graduates to total graduates rose from 52 to 54 per cent; between 1995 and 1999, the number of employed males aged 15-54 increased by 141,000 and that of employed females by 482,000, resulting in a ratio of 1 to 3.4.

[10]Currently, there are moves towards a retirement age of 65 for men and 60 for women; but those who have 35-40 years of pension accumulation could also retire earlier, for example, at age 57 for men.

[11]A further option for slowing down the population decline and ageing, namely, a significant and prolonged increase in mortality, especially in the adult and very elderly age groups, has not even been taken into consideration here. This type of measure has been "tested" in the formerly communist European countries, in particular in the first half of the 1990s. The hard transition stage towards a market economy led, in fact, to a collapse of individual and social defence against disease, so that the mean length of life underwent drastic reductions. Socio-economic crises and the epidemiological crisis due to acquired immunodeficiency syndrome (AIDS) are playing an extraordinarily negative role in sub-Saharan Africa, where a drastic reduction of the mean length of life is occurring.

[12]The complex balance between population factors, affecting the working-age population, and socio-economic factors, affecting the workforce and workers, are analysed for Europe in the current situation and for the future in Punch and Pearce (2000). Exercises to evaluate the possible

impact of a substantial growth of employment rates are very frequent both at the national and at the international levels.

REFERENCES

Coale, Ansley J., and P. Demeny (1966). *Regional Model Life Tables and Stable Populations.* Princeton, New Jersey: Princeton University Press.

De Sandre, P., A. Pinnelli and A. Santini (1999). *Nuzialità e fecondità in trasformazione: percorsi e fattori del cambiamento.* Bologna, Italy: Il Mulino.

Gesano, G. (1994). Nonsense and unfeasibility of demographically-based immigration policies, *Genus* (Rome), vol. 50, Nos. 3/4.

_____, and others (2000). Le intenzioni, i desideri e le scelte delle donne italiane in tema di fecondità: l'osservatorio italiano sulle aspettative di fecondità. Roma: Istituto di ricerche sulla popolazione. W.P. 01/2000.

Golini, A. (1999). Population ageing: current demographic setting and the future. Paper presented to the Economic Commission for Europe International Conference on Status of the Older Population: Prelude to the Twenty-first Century, Sion, 13-15 December.

_____ (2000). Levels and trends of fertility in Italy: are they desirable or sustainable? *Population Bulletin of the United Nations: Below Replacement Fertility*, Special Issue, Nos. 40/41 (1999). Sales No. E.99XIII.13. New York: United Nations.

Punch, A., and D. L. Pearce (2000). *La population et le marché du travail en Europe au-delà de l'an 2000.* Strasbourg, France: Council of Europe.

United Nations (1999). *World Population Prospects: The 1998 Revision,* vol. I, *Comprehensive Tables.* Sales No. 99.XIII.9.

_____ (2001). *Replacement Migration: Is It a Solution to Declining and Ageing Populations?* Sales No. E.01.XIII.19.

FEWER AND OLDER ITALIANS: MORE PROBLEMS? LOOKING FOR SOLUTIONS TO THE DEMO-GRAPHIC QUESTION

*Maria Rita Testa**

A. DEMOGRAPHIC OUTLOOK

A fertility decline and life expectancy gains in the old ages have brought about the ageing of the population in all the developed countries. Although this consequence of the demographic evolution was, in a way, predictable, its quickness and magnitude make it nonetheless shocking. With one of the lowest total fertility rates (1.2 children per woman) and one of the highest life expectancies at birth (75 years and 81.2 years, respectively, for men and women) at the end of 1990s, Italy will be the vanguard of ageing populations. Moreover, as a result of its below-replacement fertility, the Italian population is projected to stop growing in size and start decreasing, with the highest pace and intensity within the European context.

According to the United Nations population projections, medium variant, the Italian population will decrease by about 28 per cent over the next 50 years (table 1). The decline will go along with a transition in the age structure, owing to the change in size of different age groups. Indeed, the youngest generations (age group 0-14) will fall by 40 per cent, and the working-age population (age group 15-64) will decrease by 44 per cent, while only the older cohorts will increase, by 50 per cent for persons in age group 65-79 and by 160 per cent for persons aged 80 years or over.

The new proportions among different segments of the population are better understood if one considers that the potential support ratio (that is to say, ratio of the population aged 15-64 to the population aged 65 years or over) will go from 4.1 in 1995 to 1.4 in 2050, that is to say, in the mid-2000s "one and a half" persons in the working-age group will have to support one person in old age. It is the lowest value among the European countries, since France, Germany, the United Kingdom of Great Britain and Northern Ireland and the Russian Federation will have a potential support ratio of about 2 at the same date (United Nations, 1999, medium variant). Furthermore, the ratio of the working-age population to the retired population is bound to decline even in the presence of net migration flows countering the decrease of working or total Italian population size (United Nations, 2001).

*University of Milan-Bicocca, Department of Statistics, Milan, Italy.

TABLE 1. POPULATION PROJECTIONS: 1995-2050

	Base: 1995	United Nations			Base: 1996	Istituto Nazionale di Statistica (ISTAT)		
		Medium	High	Low		Medium	High	Low
Population (millions) ...	57.3	41.2	46.8	36.8	57.3	46.0	54.3	38.0
Population growth rate (percentage)	0.11[a]	-0.60	-0.37	-0.81	0.19[a]	-0.40	-0.10	-0.76
Percentage of total population								
0-14	14.7	12.0	15.6	8.3	14.9	11.7	14.4	8.4
15-64	64.8	53.1	53.7	52.6	68.3	56.0	55.7	55.5
65-79	16.7	20.9	18.4	23.4	12.7	20.4	18.4	23.2
80 or over	3.8	14.0	12.3	15.7	4.1	11.9	11.5	12.9
PSR[b]	4.1	1.5	1.8	1.4	4.1	1.7	1.9	1.5

Sources: United Nations (1999); and ISTAT (1997).
[a]Covering the period 1990-1995.
[b]Potential support ratio: ratio between population aged 15-64 and population aged 65 or over.

Differences among the three scenarios of the United Nations projections exist (table 1), but they do not alter the conclusions on population ageing and decline: there is a considerable degree of certainty on the developments concerning the working-age population and the old population in the next three decades. The demographic outlook does not change substantially if one refers to the last population projections provided by Italy's National Statistical Institute (Istituto Nazionale di Statistica (ISTAT), 1997, and table 1).

The implications of the population pyramid changes are enormous and pervasive: they will impact on all levels, from the global to the family level, and will produce far-reaching effects in all fields, such as the economic, social and political fields. They pose new problems for the solutions to which no lessons can be learned from the past. Moreover, the rapidity of these changes requires that suitable policy measures be adopted urgently.

In the present paper, we will try to focus on the most important consequences of the future demographic evolution, seeking several policy responses useful for coping with the oncoming demographic challenges. Particular attention will be given to "pensions and fertility" because they will probably play a key role in facing population ageing in a country—Italy—where the large majority of social expenditures are on old-age pensions, and fertility has reached very low levels.

Only recently have policy makers become more aware of the implications of such demographic changes. The analysis of policy responses to future population challenges will start with a description of the measures already adopted.

B. THE CONSEQUENCES OF AN AGEING POPULATION

1. *Labour-market evolution*

An older and slower-growing population will result in a smaller and older proportion of the population in the working age (table 2) and, assuming constant participation rates, in a smaller and older labour force. Under this hypothesis, the working population will have to support an increasing burden in the coming decades, as the rising number of old people will be only partially offset by the decreasing number of children, with consequent pressure on budgetary positions and output.

Nonetheless, the labour-market implications of future demographic evolution acquire a different relevance if they are considered also in terms of their qualitative aspects. In fact, the expected changes could be less severe if the age thresholds defining the working population were sufficiently flexible, as seems convenient in the light of recent improvements in health conditions in the old ages. In a context of demographic ageing, overall labour-force numbers will be more and more influenced by activity patterns of the older generations who actually show a very weak participation in the labour market.

Over the past 30 years, activity rates in the old ages have been declining considerably in Italy, especially among males (figures I and II). Several factors may help explain this trend: increases in incomes per capita and greater demand for leisure, which cause workers to wish to retire earlier; expansion of public old-age pension arrangements; the early retirement option; and pre-retirement schemes[1] relating to: (*a*) the firms' desire to get rid of expensive older workers while preserving a wage profile steeply rising with ages; and (*b*) the policy makers' belief that fewer older workers would imply more jobs available for the young unemployed.

Therefore, there exists a wide scope for pushing activity rates up, in order to counterbalance the working-age population decline and ageing. This is particularly true if one considers that women represent a huge unused potential workforce at all ages in Italy: even in their thirties women's activity rates are merely about 60 per cent.[2]

A contracting labour force will probably reduce growth in material living standards (Turner and others, 1998), and will result in lower economic growth unless it is offset by sustained improvements in factor productivity growth.

TABLE 2. WORKING-AGE POPULATION PROJECTIONS: 1995-2050

	1995	2005		
		Medium	High	Low
Total (millions)	39.2	21.9	25.1	19.4
Age structure[a]	85.4	128.9	109.1	159.0
Turnover[b]	95.6	142.6	104.2	209.0
Median age (years)	38.1	43.2	41.1	45.5

Source: United Nations (1999).
[a]Ratio between population aged 40-64 and population aged 15-39.
[b]Ratio between population aged 60-64 and population aged 15-19.

Figure I. Activity rates (*a*) in the adult and old ages: males
(Percentage)

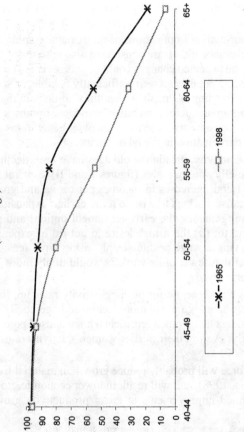

Source: ISTAT, labour-force surveys.

[a]Activity rates are calculated as the ratio of labour force to resident population. As the definition of labour force changed (in 1986 and 1992), the two series are not exactly comparable. In 1986, "other persons seeking employment" (for example, persons with no professional status who stated that they were seeking employment only after being questioned twice) were added to the total of persons seeking employment. In 1992, only the individuals who were trying to find a job during the month before the interview (no longer six months) were considered "persons seeking a first job".

Figure II. Activity rates (*a*) in the adult and old ages: females
(Percentage)

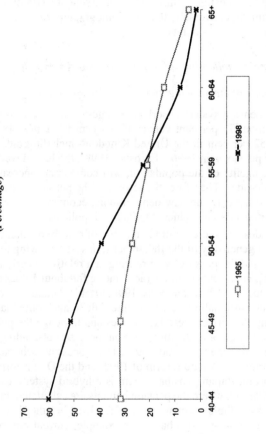

Source: ISTAT, labour-force surveys.

^aActivity rates are calculated as the ratio of labour force to resident population. As the definition of labour force changed (in 1986 and 1992), the two series are not exactly comparable. In 1986, "other persons seeking employment" (for example, persons with no professional status who stated that they were seeking employment only after being questioned twice) were added to the total of persons seeking employment. In 1992, only the individuals who were trying to find a job during the month before the interview (no longer six months) were considered "persons seeking a first job".

However, the implications of a shrunken and aged labour force are manifold and not easily predictable. An aged labour force may be a less dynamic and productive one, but at the same time, the scarcity of a workforce may accelerate human capital formation with potentially favourable long-run effects on economic growth rates. Higher aggregate savings could also counterbalance the negative effects of ageing by increasing productive investments and long-run growth; but it is not clear whether ageing implies a reduction in saving. Recent projections on the future dynamics of aggregate savings in Italy (Ministero del Tesoro, 1998) point out that imbalances between supply and demand of funds mainly stem from the negative contribution of the public sector, while the private contribution should not change significantly. Other scholars (Baldini and Mazzaferro, 2000) estimate, conversely, that the demographic transition will result in falling Italian household savings.

2. Macroeconomic implications of welfare provisions for ageing

(a) The financial burden of the growing number of older persons

Since in Italy the pension system absorbs the largest share of social protection expenditure[3] (about 73 per cent versus 49 per cent in France, 48 per cent in Germany and 52 per cent in the United Kingdom, including old age, disability and survivor pensions, in 1996) (Eurostat, 1999), the Italian welfare system, because of the ageing of the population, will come under increasing pressure in the future decades. Therefore, the reform of the pension system is at the core of the adjustments to the new demographic, economic and social conditions that Italy will need to introduce into its social policies.

Over the last decades, the increase in the number of elderly people, coupled with the increasing generosity of the Italian pension system, owing to the high replacement rates and the possibility of retiring at a relatively early age, resulted in a growth of pension expenditures (accounting for about 15 per cent of gross domestic product (GDP) in the early 1990s) (table 3) that is inconsistent with the long-run sustainability of government debt, and some blatant inequities. In the attempt to correct these imbalances and to hedge the public pension system against the gloomy demographic outlook, an outstanding reform process was triggered in the early mid-1990s. The process was characterized by two major reforms: the Amato reform of 1992[4] and the Dini reform of 1995.[5] In short, the current Italian pension system is a hybrid system, called *notional-defined contribution*, where the pension benefits are calculated on the basis of contributions as if the system were fully funded,[6] but the financial mechanism is still on a pay-as-you-go basis, for example, current contributions are used to pay current benefits. Furthermore, an *actuarial fairness* was introduced in the benefit computation formula: the pension benefits, calculated on the stock of contributions (virtually) capitalized at the rate of real GDP growth, are made available from age 57 onward with adjustments reflecting life expectancy (at the age of retirement) and expected GDP growth rates, both parameters being included in the "transformation coefficients" used to convert the lifetime payroll contributions into a lifetime annuity pension (to calculate the annuity value of the "capitalized fund" of each worker).

TABLE 3. EXPENDITURES FOR PENSIONS AND HEALTH IN ITALY AND
THE EUROPEAN UNION, 1980-1996

(Percentage of GDP)

	1980	1982	1984	1986	1988	1990	1992	1994	1996
				Italy					
Pension[a]	11.42	12.96	13.74	14.48	14.70	15.41	16.97	17.56	17.35
Health.......	7.0	7.0	6.9	7.0	7.6	8.1	8.5	8.4	7.8
				EU[b]					
Pension......	11.80	12.56	12.63	12.44	12.50	12.36	13.13	13.87	13.97
Health.......	7.0	7.2	7.1	7.2	7.3	7.4	7.9	7.9	8.0

Source: De Vincenti (2000).

[a]Old age, disability and survivor pensions.

[b]Twelve States members of the European Economic Community (EU-12) until 1990, 15 States members of the European Union (EU) (EU-15) after 1990.

The new pension system takes into account the demographic evolution and tries to face up to the effects of the future ageing of the population basically through three mechanisms, as follows:

(*a*)   The periodic revision of transformation coefficients should counterbalance the financial effects of the increase of life expectancy. These revisions will push down the transformation coefficients,[7] owing to the expected growth of life expectancy; this could give rise, however, to problems of low average replacement rates and "poor pensions";

(*b*)   The reduction of working people should be included in the GDP dynamic, so that it is already discounted in the return rate of the system (Padoa Schioppa Kostoris, 1996);

(*c*)   The new scheme, similar to an insurance mechanism (in principle, each retiree benefits as much as he has contributed during his working life), is based on individual responsibility and, for this reason, could stimulate the participation in the labour market of all persons who want to be entitled to an adequate pension benefit. Therefore, it could be more adequate to the new family types (for example, elderly women living alone) than the previous scheme based on the model of the male breadwinner, which often left insufficient pension cover to older women.

Nonetheless, the new system could not face the population ageing challenge, because it is fundamentally based upon a pay-as-you-go scheme (the funded components being so far negligible), and therefore its financial balance is still based on the ratio of the number of retirees to the number of workers, which will be subject to future deterioration.

Official projections (Ministero del Tesoro, 1999) suggest that pension spending will still increase by 0.5 per cent of GDP up to 2031, before falling back to 13 per cent of GDP by around 2050. The analysis of the future evolution of several pension schemes (table 4) shows the unfavourable trend of both the dependency rate and the replacement rate, and the reduction in pension expenditure as a share of GDP over the next 50 years.

TABLE 4.   SOME INDICATORS OF THE MAIN COMPULSORY
PENSION SCHEMES, 2000-2050

Years	Payroll tax (percentage)	Expenses (percentage of GDP)	Dependency rate[a]	Replacement rate[b]
		State employees		
2000	45.0	7.43	89.3	54.0
2025	48.5	7.91	116.2	43.4
2050	34.5	5.62	123.5	29.9
		Farmers and share-farmers		
2000	69.1	0.37	126.0	71.6
2025	92.9	0.31	156.7	71.0
2050	38.8	0.09	89.2	42.3
		Craftsmen		
2000	21.3	0.58	65.8	36.6
2025	33.9	0.85	111.3	40.2
2050	22.9	0.56	108.8	25.1
		Traders		
2000	18.5	0.47	60.4	33.4
2025	30.0	0.71	94.9	40.0
2050	21.3	0.49	102.6	24.6

Source: National Institute for Social Security (INPS), *Modello previsionale, 1998* (Rome, Coordinamento Generale Statistico Attuariale, December 1998).

[a]Calculated as ratio of pensions to contributors.
[b]Ratio of average pension to average income.

Demand for additional age-related spending, such as that for health and care for the frail elderly (geriatric treatments and other social services, including medical services) will increase, as a consequence of the growing number of old people. The amount involved could be as high as 2 to 4 percentage points of GDP over the next 50 years (Organisation for Economic Co-operation and Development (OECD), 2000). Care by family will become increasingly difficult, as average household size is bound to decrease; and women, who generally provide these services, will be more and more integrated into the labour force.

However, the effects of ageing on health care are not easy to predict, because they are also influenced by non-demographic factors such as real benefits per inhabitant, cost of health care, future trends in morbidity for people at the top of the age pyramid etc.

Furthermore, the demographic impact depends on the old age threshold which in this field is much more flexible[8] than in others (for example, pension system), being mainly determined by the incidence of disability and other chronic conditions. In this regard, the recent results provided by ISTAT are heartening indeed; according to them about 90 per cent of life expectancy of men aged 65 (87 per cent of life expectancy of women aged 65) would be lived without disability (Cappellini and Cavicchia, 1999).

The measure of the future impact of the growing health expenditures on public finance very much depends on technological advances which will play a crucial but uncertain role in terms of costs and benefits.

The increase in expenditures for pensions and health care will be only partially offset by the fall of public spending on education, because in this sector the reduction is expected to be modest. This is because overall expenditure on education is much less than that on pensions and health care, and the decrease in the size of student population will be much less than the increase in the elderly population: according to the medium-variant projections of the United Nations (1999), the proportion of persons in school aged 6-14 will go from 9 to 7.5 per cent in the next 50 years, while the proportion of persons aged 65 years or over will double from 17 to 35 per cent in the same period. In addition, average cost per unit education may increase in the attempt to improve quality and to promote lifetime training which would enable elderly workers to remain in the labour forces.

(b) Fiscal policy and intergenerational fairness

Demographic ageing will greatly impact on the intergenerational sustainability and equity of current fiscal policy.

Although the high public debt poses enormous obstacles to achieving an intergenerational equilibrium, the ageing population distorts even more the generational balance.

In a recent study, Franco and Sartor (1999) assess, in the light of the results of "generational accounting",[9] that the demographic transition, more than the large outstanding government debt, will be responsible for the generational imbalance in the current fiscal policy which, if no changes are introduced, will lead to a redistribution to the disadvantage of future generations.

To obtain an idea of the financial burden of ageing, we should think that if we maintained the population scenario existing in 1995, the public debt sustainability would be consistent with a cut of about 7 per cent in taxes to be paid by all generations. On the contrary, under the baseline scenario (main variant[10]) of population projections provided by ISTAT (1997), the long-term sustainability of the 1995 fiscal policy would require future generations to face a 53 per cent increase in all taxes aimed at balancing the intertemporal budget constraints. Alternatively, an increase of about 10 per cent in taxes to be paid by all generations, future as well as current generations of living Italians, would be necessary to restore intergenerational balance and to ensure government debt sustainability (Franco and Sartor, 1999).

Within the European context, Italy is marked by the highest taxes to be paid by young persons; the highest generosity of old-age payments; and a positive value of net tax payments for a newborn.

3.   Other implications of population ageing and population decline

Space constraints prevent me from exploring in detail all the consequences of an ageing population and declining population, such as those concerning

179

the military sector; transfers of property by succession, with a potential effect of the concentration thereof; and modification of consumption structure. Above all, two main aspects should be highlighted: the changes of households structures and typologies; and the modification of the electorate.

Ageing will reduce the average size of households, and will impact on families' economy since the network of relatives plays a very important role in Italy in respect of providing childcare services. Since private childcare centres are rare and expensive, families with working mothers and young children rely heavily on the helping network of relatives, especially for childcare and income transfers.

Ageing will clearly influence the structure of the electorate in favour of elderly voters, who could be tempted to support a greater share of public expenditures for elderly people at the expense of schools and childcare. Tension between generations may arise as a result.

C. COPING WITH THE CONSEQUENCES OF AGEING: WHAT POLICY MAKERS SHOULD THINK ABOUT FOR AN "OLD SOCIETY"

1. *Getting out of the predicament: the pension system reforms*

(a) *Increasing active lifespan in the labour market*

Since the activity rates of older Italian workers are particularly low, a particularly effective response to the challenge posed by an ageing society would be an increase in the actual age of retirement. This solution would have the double advantage of reducing the number of retirees and, at the same time, increasing the number of workers. Therefore, the challenge is to find suitable means to encourage people to work longer, taking for granted the fact that it is inconceivable they could be forced to do so.

The Amato and Dini reforms have taken initial steps along these lines, increasing the length of the contribution period for full benefits and linking lifetime benefits and contributions for junior workers and newcomers. However, the new regime will be fully phased in only in several decades (2035)[11] and through most of the transition period there will be strong incentives to retire early, as the increase in benefits for an additional year of work, after having fulfilled seniority pension requirements, does not seem to counter the financial costs stemming from additional contributions and shorter expected retirement (Ferraresi and Fornero, 2000).

In order to increase the incentives to remain longer in the labour market, raising the participation rates of older males, the following measures seem to be particularly suitable: the transition to a more actuarially neutral pension system,[12] the introduction of an actuarial fairness (taking into account life expectancy at retirement) also for seniority pensions, and the speeding up of the transition process towards the new regime[13] (for example, applying the pro rata mechanism to all existing workers), even if, in this case, many workers could consider it more profitable to retire immediately, in order not to lose their "entitlements".

However, no public intervention could be effective if the behaviour of firms remains unchanged, and therefore policies aimed at preventing the dismissal of older workers in the context of industrial restructuring are also needed.

If the average age of retirement is largely determined by the minimum statutory retirement age (57 years in the new system), as it seems to be, the age of retirement will be still low in the future. In 1998, it was 57 years for men and 56 years for women (Bank of Italy, 2000). Therefore, the policy response should be the most comprehensive one: it should eliminate all features distorting the choice between continued working and retirement in favour of the latter.

Gradual retirement policies would be indirectly aimed at increasing the age of retirement, as a further rise in the statutory retirement age cannot be proposed to certain segments of the population (for example, those less educated who, presumably, started working earlier).

On the other hand, several changes affecting the labour market will keep pace with a natural postponement of retirement. Individuals with discontinuous careers, high educational level, late entry into the labour market and unemployment spells, tend to postpone their retirement, other things being equal. In this regard, it would be interesting to investigate how the future demographic changes (for example, household structures and typologies) will impact on the retirement decisions, as retirement choices are not the result merely of an economic strategy, and are strongly influenced by demographic factors, such as a presence of a spouse already retired etc. (Testa, 1999).

The late transition to retirement gives rise to the issue of the productivity of older workers, a subject where unanimous opinions have not yet been reached. There are not many reasons for believing that an elderly worker should be less productive than a young one in the new knowledge-based economy. Perhaps only the introduction of an entirely new class of technology (such as digital technology) requiring a new mode of thought could be a real threat for older workers (MacKellar, 2000). Nonetheless, a postponement of withdrawal from the labour force calls for a re-examination of labour and social policies towards old workers, aimed at retraining them, mainly in terms of flexibility and mobility, and solving any problems related to poor health.

(b) *Diversifying the structure of retirement income:*
    towards a mixed pension system

Another way to cope with the future population ageing is to switch partially from a pay-as-you-go system to a funded system, one theoretically less sensitive to demographic changes.

The transition implies a lot of problems that are not easy to solve, among which is the necessity of finding financial resources to implement it while maintaining intergenerational equity, as current workers would pay twice: once for the pensions of current workers and again for their own pension fund.

Some authors (Castellino and Fornero, 1999) claim that to move gradually towards a mixed system (*partially funded*, consisting of a pay-as-you-go component and complementary fully funded plans) would be both feasible and wise: a supplementary funded component may be introduced in Italy through the switching of other savings, such as the flows to severance pay funds (*trattamento di fine rapporto*). The process should be very slow, but the burdens would be offset by considerable advantages for future generations, stemming from larger expected returns on the funded component, more savings and accumulation, and a diversified pension portfolio involving a better risk-return combination. A so-called multi-pillar system would diversify the structure of retirement income, lowering the risks of future income loss. It could ensure an adequate retirement income provision limiting the burden of taxation on the active population—taxation that, in Italy, is one of the highest among the Organisation for Economic Co-operation and Development (OECD) countries.

The transition should be accompanied by a strengthening of financial market infrastructure, in particular the development of an effective regulatory and supervisory framework for pension schemes, while paying attention to the growing diversity among older people in terms of income, housing and health.

Today pensioners are quite well off and there is no evidence that they are one of the poorest segments of the population (Brugiavini and Fornero, 1998). The incidence of poverty is greater (and increasing) among young families with three or more children, particularly if they live in the south, while among the elderly, only single women living in the south are exposed to a high risk of social and economic exclusion (Baldacci, Inglese and Nazzaro, 1999).

Nevertheless, three aspects should be kept in mind:

(*a*) The public pension system plays a crucial role in providing retirement income: over 70 per cent of the income of the retired comes from public benefits (60 per cent from old age, seniority and survivor pensions; 10 per cent from disability pension or basic pension);

(*b*) The relatively well-off status of old people is often the result of the possibility of relying on income sources of other members living in the same household;

(*c*) The heterogeneity of economic conditions among elderly people is likely to increase in the future, as components with individual risks (for example, market assets) increase in weight compared with components with a common risk for all the elderly (for example, public pensions) (Disney, Mira d'Ercole and Scherer, 1998).

The ageing population will reduce the size of households and the reform of the pension system will cut the benefits of new generations of retired people. Therefore, poverty could be on the increase among the old population in future decades. A recent report on economic conditions among the elderly (Pace and Pisani, 1998) highlights the growth of poverty diffusion and intensity among persons aged 65 years or over compared with the rest of the population. Therefore, we should not ignore the risk of social exclusion and poverty in old age.

2. *Changing the demographic forces: a window of opportunity?*

(*a*) *A recovery of fertility*

Measures to improve activity rates would not be sufficient to prevent the labour force from declining in the long run, if fertility rate remained as low as it is at present. Thus, one of the most important policy measures aimed at countering the future population decline and ageing, in the long term, is to raise fertility rates so as to bring them (close) to the replacement level. The range of action is largely dependent on the various determinants of low fertility. First, we should consider that, in Italy, there seems to be a gap between the expected number of children at the end of the reproductive age span, which is close to the replacement level, and the number of children that cohorts are actually likely to have (table 5). This fertility gap highlights the existing obstacles to the fulfilment of expectations, and a "latent demand for family support" (Chesnais, 1998).

But what kind of support? Institutional rigidities (for example, inadequate opening hours for childcare centres, insufficient private services, high youth unemployment, expensive loans) and the duality of the Italian labour market—that is to say, overprotectiveness towards those who already have an occupation (mostly people in their thirties or older) but extreme demandingness towards young job-seekers (younger persons)—call for deregulation in the labour market, and for specific policies aimed at improving the effectiveness of childcare centres, particularly services for children under age 3, which are scarce and irregularly distributed on the territory.

It is less easy to find immediate prescriptions for other factors in fertility decline, such as: disproportionate sharing of household tasks between the two spouses (to the disadvantage of women); uncertainty, lack of points of reference, fear that things may change abruptly; hedonism, post-materialism and secularization, with their new philosophy of life; late transition to adulthood; familism (typical of the Italian society), which induces parents to invest in children enormous quantities of energy, time and resources.

What is pivotal in these cases is an attitude that, at best, can be changed only with considerable time and energy.

Economic determinants of low fertility offer more intervention options: for instance, an effective system of childcare and family services, which will free at least part of the mother's time,[14] could counter the increased opportunity costs of motherhood.[15]

TABLE 5. AVERAGE EXPECTED AND CURRENT NUMBER OF CHILDREN, BY AGE OF MOTHER AND AREA, 1996

Age	Cohort	North Expected	North Current	Centre Expected	Centre Current	South Expected	South Current	Italy Expected	Italy Current
20-24	1971-1975	2.0	..	2.0	..	2.2	..	2.1	..
25-29	1966-1970	1.9	1.2[a]	2.2	1.3[a]	2.3	1.7[a]	2.1	1.4[a]
30-34	1961-1965	1.9	1.3	2.0	1.4	2.3	1.9	2.1	1.6
35-39	1956-1960	1.8	1.5	1.8	1.6	2.3	2.1	2.0	1.7
40-44	1951-1955	1.7	1.6	1.9	1.7	2.5	2.2	2.0	1.9
45-49	1946-1950	1.9	1.7	1.8	1.8	2.6	2.4	2.1	2.0
Total		1.9	1.5[b]	2.0	1.6[b]	2.3	2.1[b]	2.1	1.8[b]

Source: De Santis and Testa (2000).
[a]Cohort born in 1966.
[b]Cohorts born in 1946-1966.

Beyond the opportunity costs, children-related costs appear to be high (Ekert, 1994), and they are on the increase, as several public actions (for example, the introduction of compulsory education and pension systems) unintentionally make children even more expensive. Generous old-age government transfers substitute for the redistribution from (middle-aged) children to elderly parents, so that children do not bear fruit any more but still generate costs, and the balance between costs and benefits may become heavily negative (De Sandre, 1994; Cigno, 1991). In addition, since family allowances play a minor role if compared with pensions in the Italian welfare system, large and young families may be exposed to higher risks of economic vulnerability.[16]

In this case, if a society thinks that children are, at least partly, a public good (because they perpetuate culture, because they are essential for a pay-as-you-go public pension system etc.), it must be prepared to pay more for them than it customarily does. Many possible ways of doing this have been suggested: lump sums or monthly instalments, cash or payments in goods and services, subject to means testing or not, of fixed or varying amount (depending, for instance, on the economic status of the household, on birth order etc.) and so forth.

What should be stressed is that each response to fertility decline advocates financial support. It may be familism, and by giving families enough resources per child, one may hope to induce them to have not only high-quality children (which they do anyway), but also more children (which they would not do otherwise). It may be a matter of social recognition, and by attaching a formal payment to the very fact of bearing and rearing children, one automatically upgrades these to the dignity of an officially recognized, and socially valued, activity. It may be uncertainty about the future, and this solution would be tantamount to firmly stating that investing in children is part of the society's commitments for the foreseeable future. And so on.

This financial effort can be effective only if one is prepared to invest a considerable amount of resources in it. In Italy, which has a high public debt inherited from the past (roughly as large as GDP itself), and is subject to strict fiscal controls pursuant to its entry into the European Union,[17] no large reform is going to be possible, and no relevant investment is going to be made in future generations, unless such a legislative change goes along with other major fiscal reforms.

Another possibility exists, though. Further adjustments of the pension system (foreseen in 2001) could be exploited to reform the intergenerational transfer system more thoroughly, taking explicitly into account also the youngest generations, which will have to support the main burden of the last pension adjustments and are penalized also in a generational accounting perspective. In this regard, some proposals have already been put forward among demographers (De Santis, 1997a, 1997b), with the double advantage of encouraging fertility and stabilizing the financial flows of the transfer system itself, even in case of future fertility fluctuations.

One could object to this reasoning that "pronatalist" interventions, where implemented, have not generated the desired effects. This is due to the fact that the determinants of reproductive behaviours are manifold, complex, tied to each other, and not yet well known.[18]

Nevertheless, it is significant that over the last 30 years, along with the fertility decline, the proportion of social expenditure devoted to family allowances was nearly cancelled out (going from 40 per cent in 1960 to 5 per cent in 1990), while, in the same period, the proportion of social expenditures committed to pension benefits doubled from 40 to 80 per cent.

Furthermore, it should be kept in mind that in a country with the lowest fertility levels, such as Italy, there is no housing policy, surely not in any possible pronatalist sense; the labour policy for working mothers is scarcely developed;[19] and the fiscal burden is largely independent of family size, acting presumably as an implicit antinatalist measure (Rossi, 1997).

(b) Replacement migration

Migration could offer another option to offset population ageing and decline, considering that the rise of mortality rates (for example, through the non-expenditure of some health benefits) is an absolutely inconceivable hypothesis for all civilized countries.

Migration has an immediate and relatively strong impact on the working-age population, owing to the young age structure of immigrants. In addition, since fertility rates among immigrant women are often relatively high, this can also raise fertility level in the medium term.

In Italy, migration is particularly beneficial for the labour demand in two sectors: industry and personal services. Indeed, the relative scarcity of labour, particularly of blue-collar workers, has already induced some firms in northern Italy to recruit foreign workers,[20] as the southern Italians do not go to the north, despite the high unemployment rate (22 per cent) of the south, for different reasons, such as: the higher cost of living, the low-skilled jobs allegedly available and their own way of life which prevents them from making sacrifices and being get-ahead-type persons, because of the highly protective family environment in which they were brought up.[21] The foreign labour force also meets the labour demand in the housework sector and personal services, which the local labour supply cannot meet, both because it is shrinking and because its expectations are higher.

Moreover, relevant migration flows would reduce significantly the degree of generational imbalance, lowering the absolute difference in generational accounts between a newborn and an unborn person (Franco and Sartor, 1999).

These circumstances, coupled with the enormous quantitative and qualitative population imbalances between the two sides of the Mediterranean Sea, make the "zero immigration policy" scarcely conceivable for the future.

Nonetheless, migration can be regarded neither as a mere instrument to achieve demographic or economic targets nor, which would be worse, as a panacea for socio-economic problems arising in an ageing society.

On the one hand, migration flows that could partially compensate Italian population decline should be very large to counter Italian population ageing (figure III and United Nations, 2001) and, in any case, migration policy could not easily reach precise demographic objectives owing to the difficulties in controlling volume and composition of net migration. On the other hand, such

Figure III. Average annual migration necessary to achieve different population objectives
(Thousands)

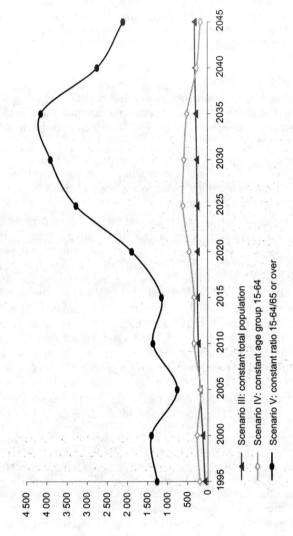

- Scenario III: constant total population
- Scenario IV: constant age group 15-64
- Scenario V: constant ratio 15-64/65 or over

Source: United Nations (2001).

NOTE: The replacement migration study considers five different scenarios, building upon the medium variant of the United Nations *World Population Prospects: The 1998 Revision*. Scenario I is the medium variant of the 1998 Revision. Scenario II is the medium variant of the 1998 Revision, amended by assuming zero migration after 1995.

large flows would create more problems than they would solve. Migration is a long process including many stages: individual presence; family reunification; second-generation arrival; and integration in the labour market and in the whole society. All these phases have to be considered in order to work out an adequate integration policy.

The contradiction between the tendency to reduce flows, toughening criteria for the legal entry of migrants, and the large incentives to migrate in the origin countries will accentuate, in the next decades, the problem of illegal immigration, whose elimination is one of the first measures to enhance foreign human resources and to secure a peaceful cohabitation between the local and the foreign population.

D. Conclusion

The implications of an ageing population go beyond the impacts considered in this work. They are multifaceted and therefore they will require a comprehensive package of reforms.

In the short run, policies aimed at tackling the consequences of population ageing, for example, the pension system reforms, seem more necessary and urgent. They should attain two main objectives: an increase in the active life spent in the labour market and the diversification of retirement income sources. In the long run, to ensure a long-term equilibrium, a policy counterbalancing the determinants of population ageing and decline, for example, the fertility decline, should be carried out, too.

Probably, economic development based on new technologies and globalization would offer the best hope for solving many of the socio-economic challenges posed by the large demographic changes. The rate of productivity growth is one of the most important variables over a timescale of decades, but one that is practically impossible to project.

The cost of ageing will very much depend on the elasticity of the old-age threshold and on the rapidity and magnitude of the reform package to be implemented: the wider the range of the government interventions and the faster their implementation, the more effective their impact will be. The expenses of this financial effort will probably be enormous; nevertheless, they are worth undertaking: they should be considered a "huge plan for investment in equilibrium", aimed at guaranteeing a fair intergenerational contract, on which the future welfare of society—and, more generally, a non-painful management of the problems arising from the post-transitional demography—will depend.

Notes

[1]The disincentives for older workers to remain active in the labour market after the earliest age at which pensions become available have risen over the last 30 years. A 55-year-old male working for 10 more years would have increased the pension replacement rate by 24 percentage points in 1967, compared with only 10 percentage points in 1995. The so-called "implicit" tax on continued work for the 55-70 age span was close to 80 per cent in Italy in 1995: this was the

187

highest level among OECD countries (Visco, 2000). Moreover, there exist disincentives to remain active in the labour market once the standard age of retirement is reached: in most cases (apart from self-employed and farm employees) the law forbids combining work and receipt of an old-age pension.

[2]Policies to increase labour-force participation also need to embrace skill development, since there is a strong mismatch between courses taught in high schools and requirements of the business sector in Italy. A long-term plan called *Masterplan* is currently being designed with the aim of responding to this weakness (Organisation for Economic Co-operation and Development (OECD), 2000).

[3]The remaining 27 per cent of the social expenditures is shared among health-care spending (21.5 per cent), maternity-family-children (3.6 per cent) and unemployment (1.9 per cent), while nothing is provided for housing (Eurostat, 1999).

[4]Decree-Law No. 421 and Decree-Law No. 503, 30 December 1992.

[5]Law No. 335, 1995, 8 August 1995. This second law was adjusted with further measures adopted under the Prodi Government (Law No. 449, 27 November 1997).

[6]The benefits are linked to a "virtual capital" accrued by each individual during his working life.

[7]The Dini reform refers to the life table of 1990.

[8]Indeed, some have proposed defining as "old" those whose remaining life expectancy is about 10 years (Ryder, 1975).

[9]The method was originally developed by Auerbach, Gokhale and Kotlikoff (1992). It is aimed at reconstructing the net financial position of all citizens, by sex and age, with respect to the public sector.

[10]The main variant of ISTAT population projections assumes that: (*a*) cohorts' fertility will continue its downward trend until it reaches a stationary value (1.45) for women born in 1975; (*b*) a 1.3-year increase in life expectancy at birth in 1995-2005, and another 1.6-year increase in 2005-2015; (*c*) a net immigration of 50,000 per year.

[11]Until 2035 the new rules will be entirely applied only to newcomers, while they will partially affect the persons already working (for less than 18 years) when the reforms came into effect, on the basis of a pro rata mechanism. According to it, pension benefits are determined on the basis of the length of time workers have spent under each programme. This means that about 45 per cent of the employed people will continue to benefit from the generosity of the pre-reform system.

[12]Blöndal and Scarpetta (1998) estimated that moving towards an actuarially neutral pension system (a system where pension arrangements neither penalize nor unduly benefit those who retire earlier or later than the standard retirement age) would have the effect of raising the activity rates of males aged 55-65 by over 20 percentage points.

[13]This speeding up would also reduce future government expenditures and the degree of intergenerational imbalances (Franco and Sartor, 1999).

[14]This is partly already done, since in Italy fathers, instead of mothers, can take a leave of six months (paid at 30 per cent of salary) during their child's first year. Afterwards, if children under the age of 8 get sick, one of the two parents (indifferently) can take a sick leave that is unpaid.

[15]Any hour that women do not spend working (for instance, because they are looking after their baby) brings about an opportunity cost (= unearned wage) which may be very high, given their higher female educational levels.

[16]Since family plays a very important role as welfare provider, there is an increasing dependency of the youth on the older people (one might speak of family dependency instead of welfare dependency). Under these circumstances, we should not be surprised if Italy has one of the most extended systems of family obligations and one of the lowest fertility levels in the world.

[17]The future Italian budgetary policy framework is defined by the Stability and Growth Pact (for example, the objective of a "close to balance" budget deficit).

[18]Future progress in the search for the causes of new reproduction behaviour and fertility decline will probably be achieved by the Observatory on the reproductive intentions of Italian women launched by the National Institute for Population Research (IRP) (Gesano and others, 2000).

[19]Mention should be made of the circumstance that women can benefit from four months of virtual pension contributions for each child they have, up to a maximum of one year (= three children). This measure allows them to retire up to one year earlier than would otherwise be possible.

[20]According to the results of a recent survey conducted by Unione Italiana delle Camere del Commercio (Unioncamere) on "manpower needs of the Italian firms", the Italian companies would need approximately over 200,000 immigrant workers for the period 1999-2000. The structural requirements of the foreign workforce, despite the high unemployment rates of several Italian regions, are due, in addition to demographic factors, to the mismatch between labour demand and supply mainly in low-skilled jobs, but also in high-skilled ones (Gagliardi, 2000).

[21]"Why Italy's southerners stay put", *The Economist*, 22 July 2000.

REFERENCES

Auerbach, A., J. Gokhale and L. Kotlikoff (1992). Generational accounting: a new approach to understanding the effects of fiscal policy on saving. *Scandinavian Journal of Economics*, vol. 94, pp. 303-318.

Baldacci, E., L. Inglese and O. Nazzaro (1999). Le caratteristiche socio-economiche dei percettori delle prestazioni pensionistiche. Paper presented at the Conference: Giornate di studio sulla popolazione. Florence, 7-9 January.

Baldini, M., and C. Mazzaferro (2000). Demographic transition and household saving in Italy (http://www.cerp.unito.it). Center for Research on Pensions and Welfare Policies (CERP) Working Papers. Accessed on 10 June 2000.

Bank of Italy (2000). *Survey of Household Income and Wealth: Year 1998*, vol. 10, No. 22. Rome.

Blöndal, S., and S. Scarpetta (1998). The retirement decision in OECD countries (http://www.oecd. org). OECD Economics Department Working Paper, No. 202. Accessed on October 1998.

Brugiavini, A., and E. Fornero (1998). A pension system in transition: the case of Italy (http:// www.cerp.unito.it). CERP Working Papers. Accessed on 10 June 2000.

Cappellini, G., and A. Cavicchia (1999). Invecchiamento della popolazione e strategie per affrontarlo: sintesi della XXXVI riunione scientifica della SIEDS. *Rivista italiana di Economia, Demografia e Statistica*, vol. 53, No. 3, pp. 261-277.

Castellino, O., and E. Fornero (1998). From PAYG to funding in Italy: a feasible transition? (http:// www.cerp.unito.it). CERP Working Papers. Accessed on 7 August 2000.

Chesnais, J. C. (1998). Below-replacement fertility in the European Union (EU-15): facts and policies, 1960-1997, *Review of Population and Social Policy*, No. 7, pp. 63-81.

Cigno, A. (1991). *Economics of the Family*. Oxford, United Kingdom: Clarendon Press.

De Sandre, P. (1994). Demografia e politiche di popolazione. In *Politiche per la popolazione in Italia*. Turin, Italy: Ed. della Fondazione Giovanni Agnelli, pp. 59-71.

De Santis, G. (1997a). *Demografia ed economia*. Bologna, Italy: Il Mulino.

_____ (1997b). Welfare and ageing: how to achieve equity between and within the generations. *International Population Conference/Congrès International de la Population*, Beijing, vol. 1, pp. 185-201. Liège, Belgium: International Union for the Scientific Study of Population.

_____, and M. R. Testa (2000). Fertility trends and family policy in Italy. Mimeograph.

De Vincenti, Claudio, ed. (2000). *Gli anziani in Europa: sistemi sociali e modelli di welfare a confronto*. IX Rapporto Centro Europa Ricerche-Sindacato Pensionati Italiani (CER-SPI). Rome: Laterza.

Disney, R., M. Mira d'Ercole and P. Scherer (1998). Resources during retirement (http://www. oecd.org). OECD Working Paper. Accessed in October 1998.

Ekert, G. (1994). Chiffrer une évolution du coût de l'enfant? *Population*, vol. 49, No. 6, pp. 1389-1418.

Eurostat (1999). Dépenses et recettes de protection sociale, 1980-1996: Methodologie Sespros 1996. Luxembourg.

189

Ferraresi, P. M., and E. Fornero (2000). Social security transition in Italy: costs, distortions and (some) possible corrections (http://www.cerp.unito.it). CERP Working Papers. Accessed on 7 August 2000.

Franco, D., and N. Sartor (1999). Italy: high public debt and population ageing. In *Generational Accounting in Europe*, European Economy, No. 6. Brussels: European Commission, pp. 117-132.

Gagliardi, C. (2000). La domanda di lavoro immigrato delle imprese italiane: aspetti quantitativi e qualitativi. Paper presented at the Conference: Migrations, Labour Market and Economic Development. Milan, 23 and 24 November.

Gesano, G., and others (2000). Le intenzioni, i desideri e le scelte delle donne italiane in tema di fecondità. IRP Working Paper, No. 1, Rome.

Istituto Nazionale di Statistica (ISTAT) (1997). Population Projections by Sex, Age and Region. Base 1.1.1996, Informazioni, No. 1, Rome.

MacKellar, F. L. (2000). The predicament of population aging: a review essay. *Population and Development Review*, vol. 26, No. 2, pp. 365-397.

Ministero del Tesoro (1998). *Gli effetti economici e finanziari dell'invecchiamento della popolazione*. Rome.

_____ (1999). *Aggiornamento del modello di previsione del sistema pensionistico della RGS: le previsioni '99*. Rome.

Organisation for Economic Co-operation and Development (OECD) (2000). Economic surveys of Italy: assessment and recommendations (http://www.oecd.org). OECD, Paris. Accessed in October 2000.

Pace, D., and S. Pisani, eds. (1998). *Le condizioni economiche degli anziani*. VII Rapporto CER-SPI. Rome: Laterza.

Padoa Schioppa Kostoris, F., ed. (1996). *Pensioni e risanamento della finanza pubblica*. Bologna, Italy: Il Mulino.

Rossi, N. (1997). Il trattamento fiscale delle famiglie. In *Lo stato delle famiglie in Italia*, M. Barbagli and C. Saraceno, eds., Bologna, Italy: Il Mulino, pp. 321-327.

Ryder, N. (1975). Notes on stationary populations. *Population Index*, vol. 41, No. 1.

Testa, M. R. (1999). The transition from work to retirement in Italy. Ph.D. dissertation, Department of Statistics, University of Florence, Florence, Italy.

Turner, D., and others (1998). The macro economic implications of ageing in a global context (http://www.oecd.org). OECD Working Paper, No. 193. Accessed in October 1998.

United Nations (1999). *World Population Prospects: The 1998 Revision*, vol. I, *Comprehensive Tables*. Sales No. E.99.XIII.9.

_____ (2001). *Replacement Migration: Is It a Solution to Declining and Ageing Populations?* Sales No. E.01.XIII.19.

Visco, I. (2000). Welfare systems, ageing, and work: an OECD perspective. *BNL Quarterly Review*, No. 212, pp. 3-29.

POPULATION POLICIES AND THE COMING OF A HYPER-AGED AND DEPOPULATING SOCIETY: THE CASE OF JAPAN

*Makoto Atoh**

A. PROSPECTS OF THE JAPANESE POPULATION

1. *Longer lifespan and declining fertility*

Japan completed its "vital revolution" around 1960. Mortality had already gradually declined before the Second World War, but in the 15 years after the war, infant and child mortality and youth mortality were dramatically reduced owing to the control of major infectious diseases, such as pneumonia, dysentery and tuberculosis. Life expectancy at birth reached 65 years for males and 70 years for females in 1960, catching up with the mortality levels of the contemporary developed countries. Fertility had also declined gradually before the war, but it rose sharply, just after the three-year post-war baby boom, to the replacement level at the end of the 1950s.

Until around the beginning of the 1970s, fertility maintained the replacement level attained starting at the end of the 1950s. Then, fertility dropped below this level in 1974, and continued to decline thereafter; and a total fertility rate (TFR) of 1.34 was recorded in 1999. The main demographic cause of such a quarter-century-long fertility decline was analysed as being the conspicuous rise in the proportion never married among women in their twenties and early thirties, and also the decline in marital fertility since the middle of the 1980s (Atoh, 1984; Kaneko, 2000). Cohabitation and extramarital fertility have been negligible in Japan during the period of fertility decline, in contrast with many European countries, so that the rise in the proportion never married has directly contributed to fertility decline. It is true that cohort-completed fertility remained just below the replacement level between the birth cohorts of the early 1930s and those of the middle of the 1950s. However, the comparisons of cumulative fertility at the same age levels for the subsequent birth cohorts following them revealed its gradual declining trend (National Institute of Population and Social Security Research (NIPSSR), 1999).

2. *The comparison of official population projections undertaken since the middle of the 1970s*

The National Institute of Population and Social Security Research (formerly the Institute of Population Problems), a government institute belonging

*National Institute of Population and Social Security Research, Tokyo, Japan.

to the Japanese Ministry of Health and Welfare, has undertaken five official population projections (in 1976, 1981, 1986, 1992 and 1997) since the middle of the 1970s (IPP, 1976, 1982, 1987, 1992; National Institute of Population and Social Security Research (NIPSSR), 1997). The comparison of the assumptions and outcomes of these projections would reveal how population prospects in the twenty-first century have changed in accordance with the ongoing fertility decline during the last quarter of the twentieth century.

Changes in the assumptions of vital rates

Assumptions of mortality were set up for the 1976 and 1981 projections by the construction of future life tables based on the lowest age- and sex-specific mortality rates observed at prefectural levels, and for the 1986, 1992 and 1997 projections that were based on future life tables which were built up by extrapolating the trend curves applied for age-, sex- and cause of death–specific mortality rates. It turned out that assumptions of mortality decline were always conservative and thus observed gains of longevity always surpassed the assumptions (see figure I (*a*) and (*b*)). As a result, the more recent projections have assumed the larger gains in life expectancy at birth in the future: the life expectancy at birth for 2050 was assumed to be 79.4 years for males and 86.5 years for females in the latest projections.[1]

As for fertility assumptions, the method of transformation of the future cohort fertility rates into future TFRs has been used for all the projections. Then, how have cohort fertility rates been assumed for the future? The basic idea behind the constructing of fertility assumptions has been that the rise in the proportion never married among women in their twenties would decelerate gradually and women in their thirties would recuperate their delayed births (Atoh, 1984; Kaneko, 1993). It has been assumed, therefore, that the cohort-completed fertility would never drop to the level of the TFR at the time of each projection or, in other words, that the TFR would rebound eventually to the assumed level of future cohort-completed fertility.

Since the proportion never married has risen among women in their twenties and even in their thirties much more than expected, the observed trend of the TFR has always betrayed its assumptions (see figure II). In the 1976, 1981 and 1986 projections, it was assumed that cohort-completed fertility could stay around the replacement level in the future because the TFR decline was assumed to be caused primarily by short-term changes in marriage and birth timing, not by the changes in "quantum" factors.[2] In the latest two projections, however, it was assumed that the more recent female cohorts could not recuperate the delayed births during their thirties because of the astounding rise in the proportion never married observed among women in their thirties, up to about 20 per cent for women in their early thirties in 1995, and thus that cohort-completed fertility would gradually decline from 2.00 for the 1955 birth cohort to 1.61 for the 1980 birth cohort in the case of the medium variant of the 1997 projections.[3]

As for assumptions on international migration, the annual average age- and sex-specific net migration rates observed at the time of each projection were assumed to be constant in the future. Since the observed annual net mi-

Figure I (a). Comparison of assumptions of female life expectancy at birth in five official population projections: Japan

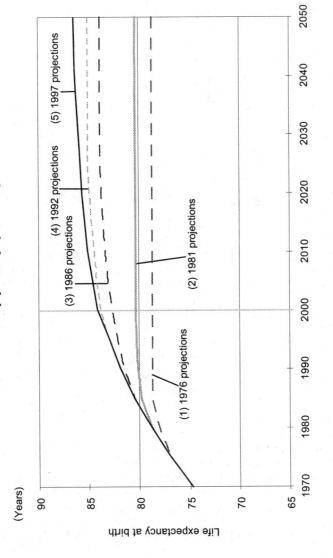

Sources: IPP (1976, 1982, 1987, 1992); NIPSSR (1997).

193

**Figure I (*b*).   Comparison of assumptions of male life expectancy at birth
in five official population projections: Japan**

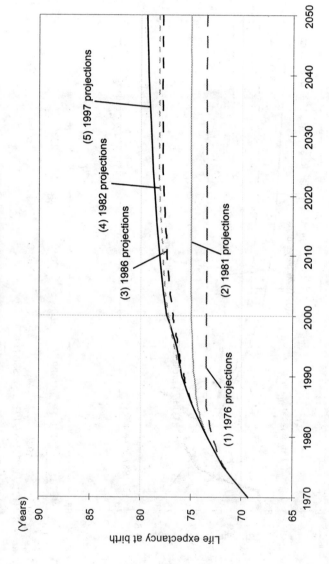

(Years)

Life expectancy at birth

(5) 1997 projections

(4) 1982 projections

(3) 1986 projections

(2) 1981 projections

(1) 1976 projections

Sources: IPP (1976, 1982, 1987, 1992); NIPSSR (1997).

**Figure II. Comparison of assumptions of the total fertility rate
in five official population projections: Japan**

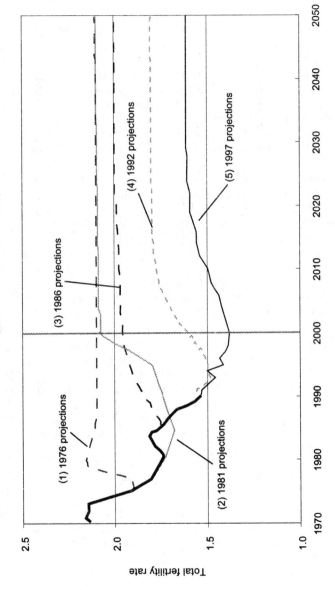

Sources: IPP (1976, 1982, 1987, 1992); NIPSSR (1997).

gration rate for the whole population has been extremely low, as is shown by a figure of –0.1 per million for the period 1990-1995, the effect of international migration on the outcome of population projections has been negligible.

Changes in the outcome of projections

According to the medium variant of the 1976 projections, for which gains in longevity in the future were assumed to be very modest but the TFR was assumed to bounce back immediately to the replacement level, the size of the total population was projected gradually to approach a stationary population of about 140 million after the 2020s (see figure III). In the more recent projections, since the final levels of the TFR were assumed to be lower than the previous ones under the replacement level, the total population was projected to reach a peak in around 2010 and start to decrease continuously thereafter. The medium variant of the latest 1997 projections showed that the Japanese total population would increase from 126 million in 1995, reach a peak at 128 million in 2007 and decline thereafter to 100 million in 2050: the annual population growth rate was expected to be –0.8 per cent during the 2040s.[4]

As for changes in age structure, the medium variant of the 1976 projections in which the TFR was assumed to rebound immediately to the replacement level showed that the proportion of elderly people aged 65 years or over would continue to increase from 7.9 per cent in 1975 to about 18 per cent in the 2020s and stabilize thereafter. The prospect of the proportion of the elderly increased gradually for the subsequent projections (see figure IV). The medium variant of the latest 1997 projections showed that the proportion of the elderly would increase from 14.5 per cent in 1995, through 25 per cent in 2015, to over 30 per cent at the end of the 2030s.

Similarly, the medium variant of the 1976 projections showed that the aged dependency ratio, the ratio of the elderly population aged 65 years or over to the working-age population aged 15-64, would increase from 11.7 per cent in 1975 but would stabilize at the level of just less than 30 per cent in 2050 (see figure V). The medium variant of the 1997 projections revealed that the aged dependency ratio would increase from 20.9 per cent in 1995 to 59.1 per cent in 2050.[5] The aged dependency ratio in 2050 for the latest projections was projected to become about twice as great as in the outcome of the 1976 projections.

Comparison of the 1997 projections of the Japanese Government and the 1998 projections of the United Nations

The assumptions of vital rates and the outcome of the 1997 projections for Japan undertaken by the Japanese Government are compared with those of the latest projections by the United Nations (United Nations, 1999), as is shown in the table.

The latest projections of the United Nations assumed somewhat longer life expectancy at birth, longer by 1.2 years for males and by 0.2 years for females in 2050, and a somewhat higher TFR, higher by 0.12 in 2050 than that of the latest official Japanese projections. (The difference in the assumptions

196

Figure III. Comparison of the outcomes of the total population size in five official population projections: Japan

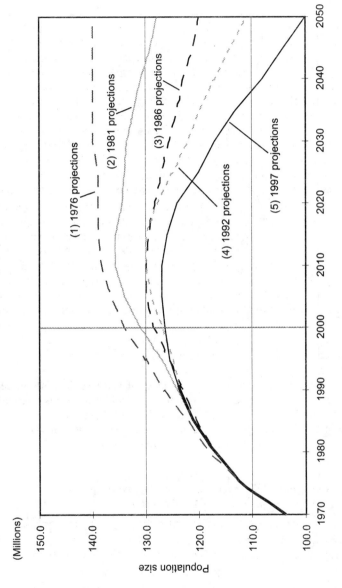

Sources: IPP (1976, 1982, 1987, 1992); NIPSSR (1997).

Figure IV. Comparison of the outcomes of the proportion of the elderly aged 65 years or over in the total population in five official population projections: Japan

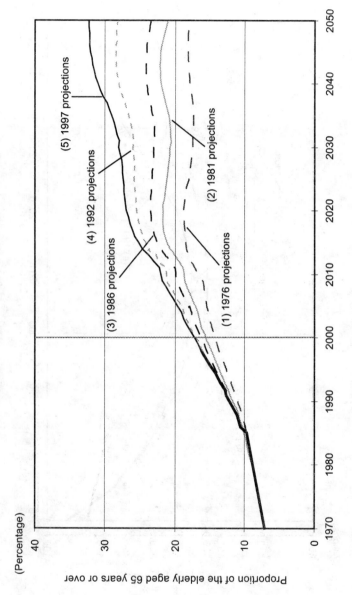

(Percentage)

Proportion of the elderly aged 65 years or over

(5) 1997 projections

(4) 1992 projections

(3) 1986 projections

(2) 1981 projections

(1) 1976 projections

Sources: IPP (1976, 1982, 1987, 1992); NIPSSR (1997).

Figure V. Comparison of the outcomes of the aged dependency ratio in five population projections: Japan

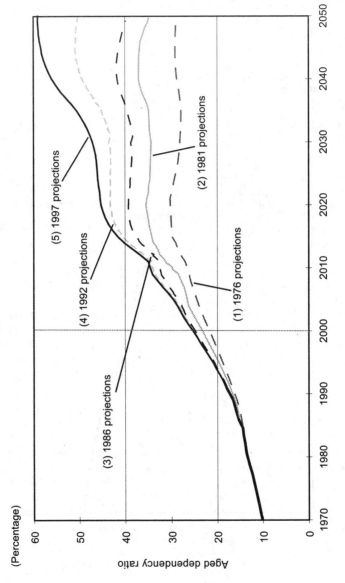

(Percentage)

Sources: IPP (1976, 1982, 1987, 1992); NIPSSR (1997).

COMPARISON OF THE POPULATION PROJECTIONS OF JAPAN UNDERTAKEN BY THE JAPANESE
GOVERNMENT AND THOSE UNDERTAKEN BY THE UNITED NATIONS

		2025		2050	
Demographic indicators	1995	Japanese Government (1997)	United Nations (1998)	Japanese Government (1997)	United Nations (1998)
Life expectancy at birth (male)....	76.36	78.80	78.80	79.40	80.60
(female) ..	82.84	85.83	84.90	86.50	86.70
TFR	1.42	1.61	1.73	1.61	1.75
Annual average net migration rate (per thousand population)...	-0.1	-0.1	0.0	-0.1	0.0
Total population (thousands)	125 570	120 913	121 150	100 496	104 921
Proportion of the elderly (percentage).................	14.5	27.4	26.7	32.3	31.8
Aged dependency ratio (percentage)................	20.9	46.0	44.7	59.1	58.4
Potential support ratio (percentage)................	4.77	2.17	2.24	1.69	1.71

Sources: National Institute of Population and Social Security Research (1997); and United Nations (1999).

NOTE: Vital rates of the United Nations projections are for 2020-2025 and for 2040-2050. Vital rates of the Japanese government projections are for the single year indicated, except annual average net migration rates which are based on figures for the five years before the year indicated.

on international migration was negligible.) Because of this, the United Nations projections resulted in a somewhat larger and less aged population in 2050 than that projected by the Japanese Government, but the difference was modest, that is to say, the total population of the United Nations projections was only 0.2 per cent (240,000) larger for 2025 and 4 per cent (4.4 million) larger for 2050 than the Japanese official projections. Also, the difference between them in the potential support ratio, that is to say, the ratio of the working-age population to the elderly population, was only 0.07 for 2025 and 0.02 for 2050.

B. POLICY RESPONSES TO DECLINING FERTILITY

As was shown in several revisions of Japanese official population projections and the latest United Nations projections, there is a greater probability that Japan would become a hyper-aged society with ever-decreasing population at least during the first half of the twenty-first century. This is partly due to large gains in life expectancy at old ages and mainly due to a large decline in fertility below the replacement level. Such population prospects seem to overshadow Japanese society in terms of such broad areas as labour, saving, consumption, economic growth, the social security system, including social insurance such as old-age pensions, medical insurance and long-term care insurance, and families and communities.

In the 1970s and the 1980s, the Japanese Government strengthened social security programmes in respect of providing elderly people with benevolent medical care services and benevolent old-age pensions on the premise that

Japan could have enough of a working population to support an increasing number of the elderly population as long as fertility did not undergo an extreme decline below the replacement level. However, in the 1990s, faced with the prospect of the coming of a hyper-aged society in the first half of the twenty-first century, the Japanese Government proposed and implemented various plans for restructuring the social security system (Ministry of Health and Welfare, 2000),[6] on the one hand, but also took action, though indirectly, for influencing demographic trends, on the other. In the present paper, only policy responses to demographic factors, namely fertility and international migration, will be discussed in detail.

"1.57 shock" and the beginning of policy responses

Japanese fertility has continued to decline below the replacement level since the middle of the 1970s, but it was only in 1990 that, being concerned about declining fertility, the Japanese Government began to examine policy options. In that year, it was announced that the TFR in 1989 had been 1.57, the lowest in the history of vital statistics in Japan; and "1.57 shock" became a trendy phrase among the public. In 1990, the Government established an interministerial liaison committee for "creating an environment where people can bear and rear healthy children" in the Office of the Cabinet Council on Internal Affairs. This committee delivered a brief policy guideline on declining fertility in 1991 (Office of the Cabinet Council on Internal Affairs, 1991). With the basic recognition that the issue of declining fertility was deeply related to the individual person's human right to decide on marriage and childbearing, it expressed its view that the Government should promote only the creation of a social environment to support young people who desire to marry and raise children, and it set forth three basic policy guidelines: (*a*) to maintain harmony between family life and occupational life, (*b*) to improve living conditions (such as housing) and (*c*) to support child-rearing economically and psychologically.

In line with the guideline, a bill to raise child allowances partially and a bill for parental leave were passed in the Parliament in 1991. The latter had employers recognize that their full-time employees had a right to take a one-year parental leave to raise a child under one year of age. Later (in 1994), it was decided that parental leave-takers would be given 25 per cent of their wage before taking the leave, while being exempted from paying premiums of the employees' pensions and health insurance while on leave. In the same year, the basic policy direction for supporting childcare (nicknamed the "Angel Plan") was formulated. Under the five-year urgent childcare programme (1995-1999) related to the Angel Plan, the Government increased authorized nursery schools to accommodate children in urban sectors on waiting lists, expanded their provision of services, such as infant care, extended hours of childcare and counselling on childcare, encouraged kindergartens to render extended childcare services, expanded after-school care for elementary school children, and promoted the establishment of family support centres (babysitter networks organized by local governments) in urban areas (Ministry of Health and Welfare, 1996, 1998).

Report by the Advisory Council on Population Problems

In 1997, the Advisory Council on Population Problems, belonging to the Ministry of Health and Welfare, published its report after 10 months of intensive deliberations on the background and consequences of declining fertility (Policy Planning and Evaluation Division of the Minister's Secretariat, Ministry of Health and Welfare, 1998). Elaborating on this report, the White Paper on Health and Welfare for 1998 was published by the Ministry of Health and Welfare in 1998 (Ministry of Health and Welfare, 1998). Both documents made it clear that the major cause for declining fertility was the increasing proportion never married among the youth. They emphasized that behind this phenomenon had been a heightened sense of the burden felt by working women of making child-rearing and working outside compatible. They analysed the fact that, even when women's participation in the labour market and other social activities had been expanding, the fixed employment practices and corporate culture—such as long daily work-hours, the difficulties of taking leave from work and the difficulties of finding full-time jobs again experienced by women who had quit their jobs at the time of their marriage or their first birth as well as the fixed gender role division, namely, the system of husbands as breadwinners and wives as homemakers—had not changed enough in Japan. In addition to the promotion of the Angel Plan to support families with small children, therefore, both papers suggested as the main policy goal the rectification of the stereotyped gender role division and the work-centred employment practices neglecting employees' family life.

Based on the proposal in the two papers, an ad hoc committee of experts to consider policy responses to declining fertility in the Prime Minister's Office was set up in 1998 and the Cabinet Ministers' conference on declining fertility was set up. Through the latter, the Government announced "Basic policies to promote programmes related to declining fertility" in 1999, based on which a new Angel Plan for 1999-2004 was formulated to expand facilities and services for childcare. Furthermore, in 2000, a bill to raise the rate of the parental leave benefit to 40 per cent of the salary received before taking the leave and a bill extending the age of the recipients of child allowances from under three to under six years were enacted (Ministry of Health and Welfare, 2000; Ministry of Labour, 2000).

Evaluation of policy responses to declining fertility

In what ways are the policy responses to declining fertility that the Japanese Government has undertaken for the last decade being evaluated?

First, are Japanese policies on this issue characterized as pronatalist? To the inquiry sent to all United Nations Member countries on their population policies by the Population Division of the United Nations Secretariat, the Japanese Government responded by stating publicly that it recognized its fertility was "too low" but had not taken any intervention to "raise fertility" (United Nations, 1998). Moreover, the Japanese Government has never mentioned the goal of raising fertility or a specific desired fertility level in any official documents, and has not undertaken any media campaign to encourage fertility, raised child allowances to a level comparable with that of many Western European countries or limited any effective means for fertility control. Therefore, Japanese policies related to declining fertility can be said to be not pronatalist policies but rather family policies, the main goal of which is to improve the childcare environment for families.[7]

Second, the ideal of Japanese family policies seems to have changed from a pro-traditional (family) model based on a division of gender roles to a pro-egalitarian model that characterizes family policies in Nordic countries;[8] but the reality is that about 70 per cent of working women still quit their job either at their time of marriage or at their first birth, and so the labour-force participation rates among women in their thirties in Japan are much lower than those in Nordic countries. This may be due to the robustness of traditional family norms based on the division of gender roles as well as to the difficulties of converting the employment practices of private companies into family-friendly ones.

Third, it can be said that the family policies of the Japanese Government, despite its decade-long efforts, have not been effective so far in raising fertility, since Japanese fertility has continued to decline in this decade. It is not clear yet whether the ineffectiveness of those efforts has been due to its piecemeal approach, to the deficiency of the budget in respect of realizing the goals of various programmes[9] or to the fact that family policies focusing on married couples are not effective with respect to changing the trend of delaying marriage among young people.

C. POLICIES RELATED TO INTERNATIONAL MIGRATION

From emigration policies to immigration policies

Japan was a country of emigration rather than one of immigration for a long time after it opened its feudal society to the outside world at the end of the 1860s. While population growth accelerated owing to gradual mortality decline, the expansion of labour opportunities accompanying modern economic growth was not sufficient before the Second World War. This was the basic source of emigration pressure in pre-war Japan. Outmigration to colonial regions and emigration to China, South-East Asian regions, the United States of America, and Latin American countries such as Brazil and Peru were popular in the pre-war years, and the Japanese Government was implicated, directly or indirectly, in this stream of emigration. Emigration pressure gradually weakened in the post-war years because of the fertility transition in the 1950s as well as the high economic growth of the subsequent period, and government efforts to send out emigrants for permanent settlement in Latin American countries almost ended in the 1960s (Policy Planning and Evaluation Division of the Minister's Secretariat, Ministry of Health and Welfare, 1993).

In the mid-1980s, Japan plunged into a "bubble economy", which, all of a sudden, gave rise to a severe labour shortage. The situation was aggravated by the fact that Japanese young people were inclined to be hesitant about taking the so-called 3D jobs, namely, those that were difficult, dirty and dangerous, because they had grown up in more affluent families and were enrolled in higher levels of education than their parents. Furthermore, the Japanese labour market became very attractive for would-be immigrants in developing countries because of the rapid appreciation of the Japanese yen which had been produced by the Plaza Agreement in 1985. As a result, Japan was transformed into a country of immigration rather than one of emigration.

While the net inflow of foreign people had been much less than 10,000 per year up until the mid-1970s, it continued to increase, reaching a peak of 260,000, 0.2 per cent of the total population, in 1992. Whereas the proportion of foreign residents in Japan, mostly composed of persons from the Republic of Korea with a permanent residence visa, had been about 0.6 per cent of the total population in post-war years, owing to the rapid inflow of foreign people at the time of the "bubble economy", even the proportion of registered foreign residents overshot the level of 1 per cent of the total population in the early 1990s, with the major share of those having come from Latin American countries and Asian countries other than the Republic of Korea (National Institute of Population and Social Security Research, 1999). The latest estimate of this proportion is 1.44 per cent in 1999, including illegal stayers estimated to be about 270,000.

At the moment when Japan faced an increasing number of illegal stayers (supposed also to be illegal workers), there was fierce debate among opinion leaders on whether Japan should open the door of its labour market to foreign workers, especially unskilled or semi-skilled workers (Nishio, 1988; Hanami and Kuwabara, 1989; Miyajima, 1989). The response to this issue by the Japanese Government was the overall revision in 1989 of the Law on the Regulation of Emigration and Immigration and Refugee Recognition, which clarified and expanded the requirements needed for foreign people to stay and/or work in Japan. The thrust of this revision was that (*a*) unskilled workers were not permitted to stay, (*b*) descendants of Japanese were permitted to stay and work and (*c*) employers of illegal workers and their families were punished (Tanaka and Ebashi, 1997). Because of this revision, the number of foreign workers who were descendants of Japanese in Latin American countries, such as Brazil and Peru, increased dramatically, but the number of illegal stayers has not been affected much.

Immigration policy in a hyper-aged and
depopulating society: replacement migration?

The "bubble economy" collapsed in the early 1990s and the Japanese economy has stagnated since then, with rising unemployment rates. Because of this economic change, the current policy debate on immigration policies is not so hot as in the 1980s. Although the net inflow of foreign people dropped dramatically in the first half of the 1990s, it has been increasing again since the latter half of the 1990s, and the proportion of foreign residents has also been increasing. This trend suggests that the Japanese economy has come to depend necessarily upon foreign workers, at least in some types of jobs or industries.

The Population Division of the United Nations Secretariat published a report showing to what extent a country or a region needed "replacement migration" in order to maintain (*a*) the current size of the total population, (*b*) the current size of the working-age population or (*c*) the current potential support ratio up to 2050 (United Nations, 2001). According to this, Japan needs (*a*) 300,000 immigrants on average every year, (*b*) 600,000 immigrants on average every year or (*c*) 10 million immigrants on average every year.

Such a calculation of replacement migration is demographically valid but seems to be economically unrealistic and socially and politically unacceptable as policy options for the Japanese Government.

First, there is no economically clear evidence for the necessity to keep the current level of the size of the working-age population or of the potential support ratio, let alone the current size of the total population. It goes without saying that, from the economic point of view, it is not the size of the working-age population but rather the size of the labour force that is important. While labour demand in the future can be reduced by gains in labour productivity due to technological innovation, such as the revolution of information technology (IT), the labour supply can be expanded considerably by the involvement of more women and/or more elderly people in the labour market. If more elderly people take a role supporting other elderly people economically and socially, the economic and social support ratio can be raised substantially.

Second, Japan is a country where there have been only about 100,000 net immigrants annually on average in the recent past and foreign residents occupy the level of only 1 per cent of the total population. In such a society, it would be socially and politically infeasible to accept a number of immigrants as large as from several hundred thousand to several million people annually, as is suggested by the replacement migration calculated for Japan by the Population Division of the United Nations Secretariat.

Replacement migration does not seem to be a realistic policy option for Japan. However, it is certain that fewer young people will dare to take 3D jobs owing to declining fertility and rising educational aspirations, labour demand for workers for long-term care will surely rise because of an increasing old-old population, and more professional and technical workers will be needed in such areas as information technology in this era of global competition. If so, then in a hyper-aged and depopulating country like Japan, more foreign workers will be needed in the decades ahead than in the past decades, though their numbers may not be as great as those contained in the estimates of the Population Division.

NOTES

[1] Only one scenario has been prepared for mortality assumptions in all the official population projections in Japan.

[2] The setting up of fertility assumption of these official projections seems to have been implicitly influenced by the demographic transition theories which had suggested the continuation of replacement-level fertility in the post-transitional stage.

[3] The idea behind the setting up of the fertility assumption of the two latest official projections seems to be in accordance with the second demographic transition theory that has been asserted by D. Van de Kaa and R. Lesthaeghe (Van de Kaa, 1987, 1999; Lesthaeghe and others, 1999). Three scenarios have been prepared for fertility assumptions in all the official population projections in Japan: for the 1997 projections, the high variant of the completed fertility of the 1980 birth cohort was assumed to be 1.85 and the low variant thereof was assumed to be 1.38.

[4]Three variants have been prepared in all the official population projections in Japan, in accordance with three assumptions on fertility: for the 1997 projections, the total population projected for 2050 was 110 million for the high variant and 92 million for the low variant.

[5]The aged dependency ratio projected for 2050 was 52.8 per cent for the high variant and 65.2 per cent for the low variant.

[6]Since the Japanese national pension scheme has been characterized by the pay-as-you-go system, it has been destined to be severely influenced by changes in the prospects of population ageing. Thus, every time new official population projections were undertaken since the middle of the 1980s, the national pension scheme had to be revised in such a way as to raise pension premiums and to cut pension benefits.

[7]At the municipal level, local governments of many towns and villages suffering from the effects of their decreasing and ageing populations have taken a more explicit pronatalist position.

[8]A. Gauthier classified family policies of the developed countries into four types, namely, (a) pronatalist (such as those of France), (b) pro-traditional (such as those of Germany), (c) pro-egalitarian (such as those of the Nordic countries) and (d) non-interventionist (such as those of the Anglo-Saxon countries) (Gauthier, 1996). Japanese family policies seem to move from (b) to (c), at least at the Government's statement level, as well as in some policy programmes.

[9]For the past 30 years, the increase of social expenditures for children has been only just over 20 per cent of that of social expenditures for the elderly in Japan (Fukuda, 1999).

REFERENCES

Atoh, Makoto (1984). Causes of declining fertility and its prospects. *Journal of Population Problems*, No. 171, pp. 22-35.

Fukuda, Motoo (1999). *Restructuring of the Social Security System: Its Transition to the System Giving Importance to Child Support*. Tokyo: Chuo-Hoki.

Gauthier, Anne H. (1996). *The State and the Family: A Comparative Analysis of Family Policies in Industrialized Countries*. New York: Clarendon Press.

Hanami, Tadashi, and Yasuo Kuwabara (1989). *Tomorrow's Neighbours: Foreign Workers*. Tokyo: Toyokeizai.

Institute of Population Problems (IPP) (1976). *Future Population Projections for Japan as of November 1976*. IPP Research Series No. 213. Tokyo.

_____ (1982). *Future Population Projections for Japan as of November 1981*. IPP Research Series No. 227. Tokyo.

_____ (1987). *Population Projections for Japan as of December 1986*. IPP Research Series No. 244. Tokyo.

_____ (1992). *Population Projections for Japan as of December 1986*. IPP Research Series No. 274. Tokyo.

Kaneko, Ryuichi (1993). A projection system for future age-specific fertility rates. *Journal of Population Problems*, vol. 49, No. 1, pp. 17-38.

_____ (2000). Below-replacement fertility in Japan: trends, determinants and prospects. In *Population Bulletin of the United Nations: Below Replacement Fertility*, Special Issue, Nos. 40/41 (1999). Sales No. E.99.XIII.13, pp. 266-291. New York: United Nations.

Lesthaeghe, Ron, and others. (1999). Is low fertility a temporary phenomenon in the European Union? *Population and Development Review*, vol. 25, No. 2, pp. 211-228.

Ministry of Health and Welfare (1996). *White Paper on Health and Welfare for 1996: Families and the Social Security System—Social Support to Families*. Tokyo.

_____ (1998). *White Paper on Health and Welfare for 1998: Reflecting a Society with Fewer Children: To Build a Society Where People Can Have Dreams to Bear and Rear Children*. Tokyo.

_____ (2000). *White Paper on Health and Welfare for 2000: Seeking a New Image of Elderly People*. Tokyo.

Ministry of Labour (2000). *White Paper on Women's Labour*. Tokyo.

Miyajima, Takashi (1989). *The Logic for Accepting Foreign Workers*. Tokyo: Akashi-shoten.

National Institute of Population and Social Security Research (NIPSSR) (1997). *Population Projections for Japan as of January 1997*, NIPSSR Research Series, No. 291. Tokyo.

_____ (1999). *Latest Demographic Statistics 1999*, Research Series, No. 297. Tokyo.

Nishio, Kanji (1988). *Strategic Closing-the-Door Policy*. Tokyo: Kodansha.

Office of the Cabinet Council on Internal Affairs (1991). *On the Creation of an Environment Where People Can Bear and Rear Healthy Children*. Tokyo.

Olshansky, S. Jay, and A. Brian Ault (1986). The fourth stage of the epidemiological transition: the age of delayed degenerative diseases. *The Milbank Memorial Fund Quarterly*, vol. 64, No. 3, pp. 355-391.

Omran, Abdel R. (1971). The epidemiologic transition: a theory of the epidemiology of population change. *The Milbank Memorial Fund Quarterly*, vol. 49, No. 4, pp. 509-538.

Policy Planning and Evaluation Division of the Minister's Secretariat, Ministry of Health and Welfare, ed. (1993). *The Current State of International Migration: Japan and the World*. Tokyo: Toyokeizai.

_____ (1998). *A Society with a Decreasing Population: Responsibilities and Choices for the Future*. Tokyo: Gyosei.

Tanaka, Hiroshi, and Takeshi Ebashi, eds. (1997). *White Paper on Human Rights of Foreign Residents in Japan*. Tokyo: Akashi-shoten.

United Nations (1998). *National Population Policies* and addendum. Sales No. E.99.XIII.3.

_____ (1999). *World Population Prospects: The 1998 Revision*, vol. I, *Comprehensive Tables*. Sales No. E.99.XIII.9.

_____ (2001). *Replacement Migration: Is It a Solution to Declining and Ageing Populations?* Sales No. E.01.XIII.19.

Van de Kaa, Dirk J. (1987). Europe's second demographic transition. *Population Bulletin* (Population Reference Bureau), vol. 42, No. 1.

_____ (1999). Europe and its population: the long view. In European Population Conference, *European Populations: Unity in Diversity*. Dordrecht, Netherlands: Kluwer Academic Publishers, pp. 1-50.

THE IMPACT OF POPULATION DECLINE AND POPU-LATION AGEING IN JAPAN FROM THE PERSPEC-TIVES OF SOCIAL AND LABOUR POLICY

*Yukiko Katsumata**

A. THE IMPACTS OF POPULATION DECLINE AND POPULATION AGEING IN JAPAN: DOMESTIC DISCUSSIONS

The socio-economic consequence of population ageing and declining fertility has been a change in the role of "those who support" and "those who are supported". This is illustrated by the change in the dependency ratio of the working-age population to the retired-age population (the population of those aged 65 years or over divided by the population of those aged 15-64). The dependency ratio was relatively high before the Second World War, but began to decline after the war and reached its lowest point (43.5) in 1990. Then the ratio began to increase again and has continued to do so up until the present day. Before 1990, the ratio increased as a result of the decreasing child population (those under age 15); however, after 1990, it began to increase as a result of the increasing elderly population (those over age 65) (see figure I). In 1950, shortly after the war, the ratio was recorded as 67.5. Population projections estimate that the ratio will reach the same level again between 2015 and 2020. Even if the ratio is shown to be the same during the two periods, the social phenomena are quite different. The differences—that the vast majority of "those who are being supported" have become elderly and that the number of "those who support" is no longer increasing but decreasing—are the key issues of domestic discussions. Important issues to be discussed are the socio-economic consequences of the declining working-age population and how to cope with the changes by reforming social schemes.

1. *Various projections for declining labour-force participation rates in Japan*

Projections for labour-force participation rates have been reported both by the Government and by a private think tank. The major results are collected in table 1. At present, Japan's labour-force participation rate is 62.9 per cent, based on the average between male and female labour-force participation rates for 1999. However, the labour-force participation rates for men and women should be analysed separately owing to the great differences in their characteristics. Therefore, separate data are examined in the following sections.

---

*National Institute of Population and Social Security Research, Tokyo, Japan.

Figure I. Japan's age dependency ratio: long-term trends

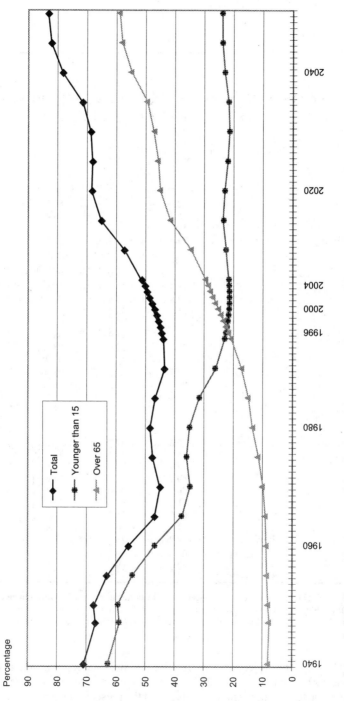

Sources: Statistics Bureau, Management and Coordination Agency, Population Census of Japan, various years (1940-1996); and National Institute of Population and Social Security Research, population estimates, 1997-2050 (1997).

TABLE 1.   JAPAN'S LABOUR-FORCE PARTICIPATION RATE: PRESENT STATUS
AND VARIOUS PROJECTIONS
(*Percentage*)

	1999	2025		
	(1)	(2)	(3)	(4)
Men and women				
Total (15 and over)............	62.9	59.1	58.5	60.2
15-19	17.7	17.8	18.8	
20-24	72.7	74.1	75.1	
25-29	83.0	85.2	84.4	69.9
30-34	77.3	81.6	78.7	
35-39	79.8	82.9	81.7	
40-44	83.8	86.7	85.4	
45-49	84.7	87.2	86.4	
50-54	82.4	85.2	84.2	87.2
55-59	76.3	79.8	78.6	
60-64	56.3	71.3	65.3	
65 and over	23.4	21.4	22.5	14.1
Men				
Total (15 and over)............	76.9	71.4	72.1	70.5
15-19	18.5	20.0	20.6	19.6
20-24	72.8	75.8	76.4	77.2
25-29	95.6	96.3	96.6	99.4
30-34	97.5	97.6	98.0	99.7
35-39	97.7	97.9	98.1	98.5
40-44	97.7	97.9	98.1	98.7
45-49	97.5	97.6	97.9	98.6
50-54	97.1	96.8	97.9	98.6
55-59	94.7	93.3	94.8	95.7
60-64	74.1	82.4	83.4	95.4
65 and over.................	32.5	31.0	31.9	21.3
Women				
Total (15 and over)............	49.6	47.7	45.9	50.6
15-19	16.8	15.4	17.0	18.6
20-24	72.4	72.2	73.6	77.0
25-29	69.7	73.4	71.6	
30-34	56.7	65.0	58.4	83.7
35-39	61.5	67.3	64.5	
40-44	69.5	75.0	72.1	83.2
45-49	71.8	76.5	74.4	89.7
50-54	67.9	73.4	70.8	68.4
55-59	58.7	66.5	62.6	44.2
60-64	39.7	60.7	47.9	23.7
65 and over	14.9	14.4	15.6	8.8

Sources: (1) Statistics Bureau Management and Coordination Agency, Government of Japan
(2000); (2) Study Group on Labour Policy, June 1999; (3) Ministry of Labour, White Paper on
Labour, 2000; (4) Japan Center for Economic Research, *A New Start for Japan's Economy, 2000.*
Tokyo.

Government projections reported by the Study Group on Labour Policy
in June 1999 estimate that by 2025 the labour-force participation rate of men
will decline to 71.4 per cent (compared with the present 76.9 per cent) and that

of women will decline to 47.7 per cent (compared with the present 49.6 per cent). A private think tank (Japan Center for Economic Research) estimates a further decline in the male participation rate to 70.5 per cent. On the other hand, it estimates that the female participation rate will increase above the present rate to 50.6 per cent. Both institutions used the population projections of the National Institute of Population and Social Security Research presented in January 1997; therefore, the different results were due to the different socio-economic conditions they projected for 2025. The economic growth rate and the supply-and-demand conditions of Japan's labour market were predicted differently. The government projection was based on conditions of average future annual economic growth of 2 per cent and an unemployment rate of 4.2 per cent by 2025, whereas the private think-tank projection set the annual economic growth rate at 1.7 per cent and the unemployment rate at 5.3 per cent. Also, the images of Japan's future industrial structure and goals of social measures for dealing with a society that is ageing and declining in fertility are not the same in the two projections. The assumption that information technology (IT) and globalization will play major roles in Japan's future industrial structural change was shared by both projections; but the images of goals regarding elderly (aged 60-65) participation in the labour force and women's participation in the labour force during their child-rearing years were different. The government projections are somewhat optimistic about the extension of retirement age to 65 years. On the other hand, the private think tank's projections are more optimistic regarding women's participation in the labour force during child-rearing periods. On the whole, both projections show that, in the future, overall labour-force participation rates will decrease but the lifetime female labour-force participation rate will increase.

2. Macroeconomic impacts of ageing and declining fertility rates

The impact of the declining labour-force participation rate is a major concern among Japanese people. Both government organizations and private groups have expressed concern about possible negative effects on Japan's future economic growth and a loss of vitality in Japanese society. However, concerns have abated in the past few years owing to the fact that the so-called IT revolution is taking place in Japanese industry and productivity has improved dramatically. The Ministry of Labour presented its rather optimistic views of the future in the *White Paper on Labour, 2000*, published in June 2000. It referred to a study among Organisation for Economic Co-operation and Development (OECD) countries that had found that people made efforts to improve labour-saving technology in order to cope with declines in the growth rate of labour-force participation. The report stated: "In recent years, IT has become a powerful measure for future economic development in Japanese society and it is being actively promoted by various organizations both in the public and in the private sectors. We expect that further active investments in IT markets will contribute greatly to technological developments." The paper then presented optimistic projections for Japan's economic growth rate by quoting a report from the Industrial Structure Council: "Approximately 2 per cent annual economic growth is quite a realistic goal if people keep investing in research and development of IT under the projection of declining in labour-force participation and slowing down the rate of increase in accumulation of capital compared with increasing rate of gross domestic product (GDP)." The previously mentioned private think tank also presented its long-term economic forecast that the annual increase of net GDP between 2015 and 2025 would be approximately 1.8 per cent. However, concerns remain about the impact of an ageing society on Japan's future. Various socio-economic measures are being proposed and implemented under the slogan of "A vigorous ageing society in the twenty-first century".

3. *Japan's labour policy concerning ageing and declining fertility rates*

Even if the optimistic views presented above become true, shortage of labour will remain a major concern. An imbalance between labour supply and labour demand, called "labour-market mismatching", will most likely occur in the future. For instance, imbalanced labour supply and demand among first, second and third industries negatively affects the labour market for new graduates; and we all know that the present low fertility rate will cause the population to begin decreasing in 2008.

(*a*) *Foreign immigrant workers*

In the late 1980s, the labour shortage in the manufacturing industry became an apparent problem for Japanese society. An amendment to Japanese immigration law in 1990 allowed immigrant workers of Japanese descent from South America to work in Japan. In the 1990s, a new on-the-job training scheme for foreign workers was implemented and a number of workers from Asia began working in Japan. The introduction of foreign immigrant workers has been hotly debated in Japan. Various interest groups, such as enterprises and trade unions, hold different opinions, and, since the war, the Japanese Government has had rather strict regulations concerning foreign immigrant workers.

The debate on foreign immigrant workers became extremely active in 1999 when opposing proposals were presented by two governmental organizations. First, the Economic Strategy Council, an advisory group to then Prime Minister Obuchi, submitted a report entitled "Strategies for Reviving the Japanese Economy" in February 1999, where it proposed the introduction of foreign immigrant workers. The report stated: "Furthermore, a necessary legal framework will be positively discussed to accommodate foreign workers, including extension of permit of stay for skilled trainees. Third, considering measures taken in other countries to cope with the declining number of births and increases in foreign immigrants, the nationality laws need to be reviewed."[1]

An advisory group for the Ministry of Labour also submitted a report entitled "Projection of Supply and Demand in Japan's Labour Force". This report also emphasized the importance of investigating the accommodation of foreign immigrant workers in specialized and technical fields, but cautioned against the introduction of unskilled foreign workers. Its position against the introduction of foreign workers was stated as follows: "It is not an agreeable or appropriate measure to introduce immigrant workers as a solution to the labour shortage in a society that is ageing and declining in fertility. We must be aware of its massive socio-economic effects."[2]

We must understand the background of such debate. The year 1999 was the year before long-term care insurance was implemented in Japan. A number of new businesses were making preparations to offer care services, and people were concerned about a possible shortage of care workers. However, when the long-term care insurance scheme was introduced in April 2000, a shortage of care workers did not occur owing to an overestimation in demands for care services. Today, the debate on foreign immigrant workers continues to be discussed vigorously. However, there is a consensus at policy discussion on the exclusion of low-skilled labour. The Government has been promoting certified skilled workers in the long-term care field. Care workers are not considered to be unskilled. It may be too early to discuss the possibility of introducing foreign workers into the welfare field owing to the fact that communication ability in Japanese and training are essential.

(b) Employment of the elderly

Up until very recently, Japan maintained one of the lowest unemployment rates among OECD countries. People were generally not very interested in unemployment issues. However, the employment and unemployment of the elderly have always been important issues—they were even in those days—because they are closely related to the issue of public pension reform.

In 1985, major public pension reforms were implemented, which established the present two-tiered public pension structure.[3] Since that time, pension administrative officials and scholars have discussed extending the pensionable age from 60 to 65, based on financial forecasts for public pension schemes in an ageing society. A law for stabilizing and promoting elderly employment opportunities was approved in the Diet almost unanimously in 1986. In June 1990, the law was amended to include security and promotion of employment opportunities for those in their early sixties. In 1994, a gradual raising of the pensionable age for the first tier to 65 was approved in the Diet, and in April 2000, the most recent pension reform act was approved, which raised the second tier of pensionable age to 65 between 2013 and 2025. (The relationship between public pension schemes and labour policy will be discussed in section B below.)

The high labour-force participation rate among the Japanese elderly is well known (see figure II). In 1998, the labour-force participation rate among Japanese elderly aged 65 years or over was 35.9 per cent, far higher than that of other OECD countries. The labour-force participation rate is usually affected by industrial structures: if there is a relatively high rate of self-employment, then the elderly labour-force participation rate tends to be high. However, this is not the case in Japan. The level of retirement age is another factor that raises the elderly labour-force participation rate. In 1999, over 99 per cent of companies that facilitate retirement set the retirement age at 60 (see figure III). Therefore, retirement age does not affect those over age 65. The high rate of labour-force participation by the elderly is not a recent phenomenon in Japan. It was once very high, but has been gradually declining (see figure IV).

Figure II. Labour-force participation rate of the elderly (aged 65 years or over), 1998

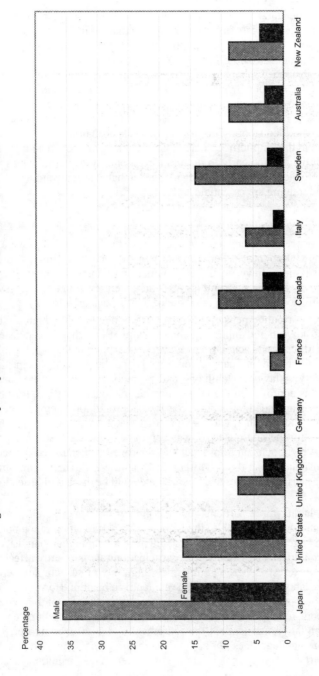

Source: OECD (1999).

Figure III. Retirement age transitions of private companies

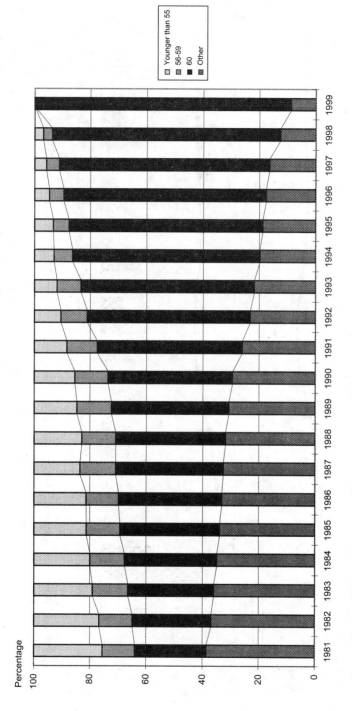

Source: Ministry of Labour, Government of Japan, Employment Survey.

215

Figure IV.   Trends in the labour-force participation rate among the Japanese elderly

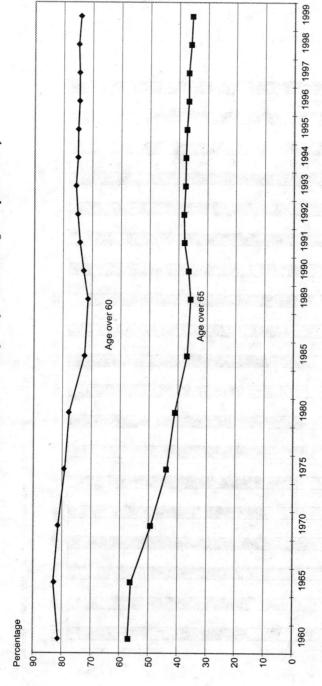

Source: Statistics Bureau, Management and Coordination Agency, Government of Japan, Annual Report on the Labour-force Survey.

A study involving Japan and four other countries illustrated the relatively enthusiastic attitude of the Japanese elderly towards working. The study asked elderly individuals aged 60 years or over who were currently engaged in paid employment, "Do you want to continue paid employment in the future?" Of Japanese respondents, 89.4 per cent answered yes, compared with 90 per cent of United States respondents, 82.8 per cent of Thai respondents, 79.9 per cent of Republic of Korea respondents and 69.4 per cent of German respondents. These results do not indicate that Japanese elderly are particularly enthusiastic about working compared with other nationalities. The following question to the same group concerned the reasons for working. The largest number of people of every nationality answered, "Because of the income". However, in the United States and Germany, most people chose as their second reason, "Because I enjoy working"; but in Japan and the Republic of Korea, people chose "Because working is good for my health" as their second reason.

It is not easy to analyse the reason for the high labour-force participation rate among the Japanese elderly. Various empirical studies have indicated the strong correlation between income level and labour-force participation (see figure V). The group of elderly individuals between the ages of 65 and 69 are the most likely pension beneficiaries. Among men, those receiving smaller pension benefits have a higher tendency to work. Another study proves the correlation between health and labour-force participation.[4] I conducted such a study with a colleague and found that health conditions are a strong determining factor in employment (Kimura and Katsumata, 2000).

(c) *Employment of young people*

The high unemployment rate among the younger generation is an important issue among OECD countries, but it was not given serious consideration in Japan until very recently. However, this fact does not necessarily indicate a lower rate of unemployment among Japanese youth. Rather, the unemployment rate of Japanese young people is relatively high, almost as high as that of the elderly (see figure VI). The reason that the high unemployment rate among the elderly receives more attention is not that people are uninterested in the high youth unemployment rate but rather that elderly unemployment issues are discussed in the context of public pension schemes. In 1999, the average unemployment rate was 4.7 per cent, the highest annual unemployment rate since the Second World War. Among age groups, the highest unemployment rate was 15.1 per cent for males between the ages of 15 and 19, followed by 10.2 per cent for those males between the ages of 60 and 64.

The White Paper on Labour, 2000, devoted one chapter to discussing youth unemployment and new trends in youth employment such as the existence of the so-called *furita*. Generally speaking, *furita* are young people who neither go on to higher education nor become full-time employees. They are most likely to work as part-time employees under short or temporary employment contracts. According to the estimates by the Ministry of Labour, approximately 1,510,000 people (610,000 male, 910,000 female) between the ages of 15 and 34 were considered *furita* in 1997, approximately 4.3 per cent of the total population of the same age group.

Figure V. Proportion of elderly people in the labour force (according to pension benefits bracket)

(*Aged between 65 and 69*)

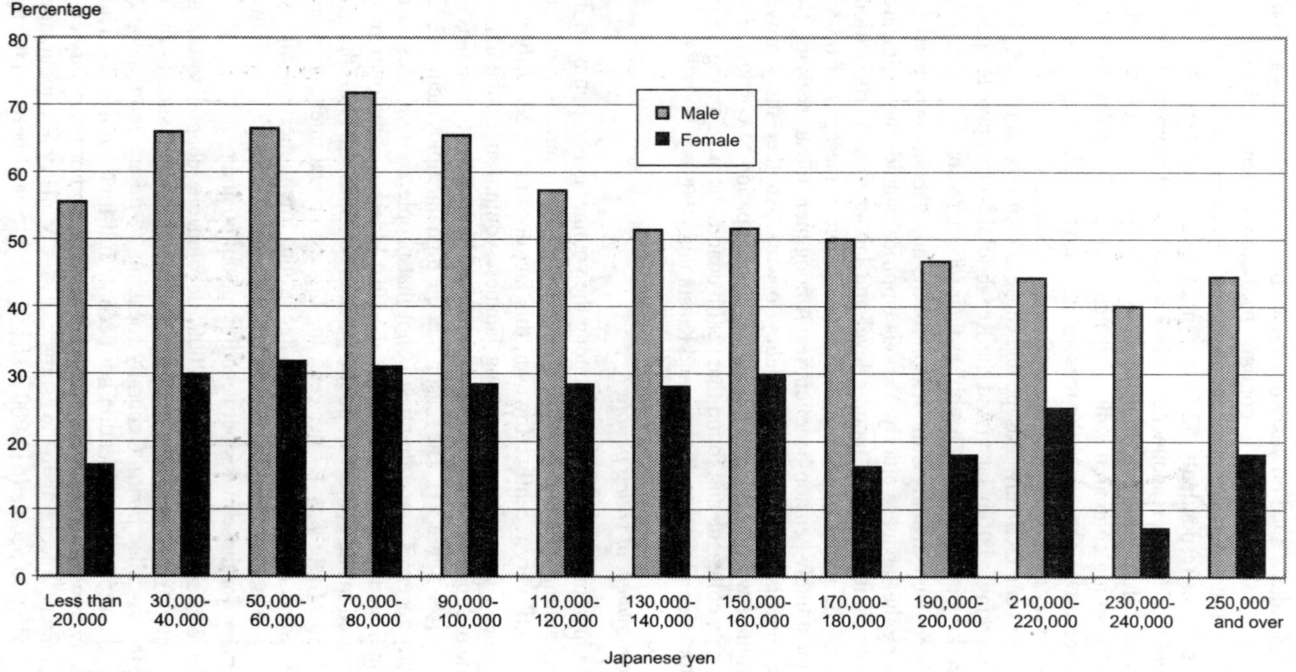

Percentage
80
70
60
50
40
30
20
10
0
Male
Female
Less than 20,000
30,000-40,000
50,000-60,000
70,000-80,000
90,000-100,000
110,000-120,000
130,000-140,000
150,000-160,000
170,000-180,000
190,000-200,000
210,000-220,000
230,000-240,000
250,000 and over
Japanese yen

Source: Ministry of Labour, survey on elderly employees in 1997.

Percentage

Figure VI. Trends in the unemployment rate, by age group

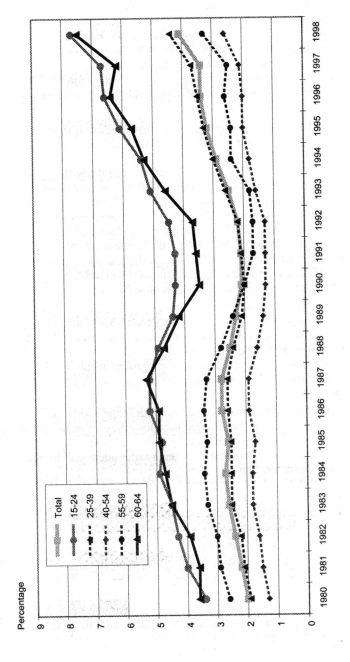

Total
15-24
25-39
40-54
55-59
60-64

Source: Annual Report on the Labour-force Survey.

It is thought that, in the near future, the labour force in the younger generation will shrink, but one must bear in mind that some young people choose to be *furita* and do not enter the regular employment system. Therefore, the concept and definition of unemployment among youth must be reconsidered. *Furita* tend to change jobs frequently. They can afford to do so because they are often living with their parents, enjoying the single life without paying their own living expenses. A Japanese sociologist has coined the term "parasite singles" to refer to these young people who depend on their parents economically. This can be considered one of the consequences of lower fertility and fewer children.

4. Future perspectives on the benefits and burdens for social security in Japan

As part of the "Vigorous ageing society in the twenty-first century", the Japanese Government announced that the national burden (taxes and social security contributions) should be kept to less than 50 per cent of national income.[5] It is believed that big government is harmful to society and that public spending should be kept to a certain level. Public spending includes not only social security benefits and social services for Japanese citizens but also capital investments as well as national defence expenditures etc. Therefore, the Ministry of Health and Welfare also estimated a probable level for the benefits and burdens of social security in the future (see table 2).

The numbers in parentheses in table 2 in the row entitled "Long-term care included in the upper column" indicate that certain costs for elderly care are taken from present medical care and social welfare expenditures. Although this table was made before long-term care insurance was implemented, the amount was estimated because long-term care insurance was proposed to reduce medical expenditures for the elderly. (This is described in more detail in the following section.)

This table lists three possible conditions for future economic growth. According to case B, which is most often used for official discussions, the level of benefits and burdens of social security will be 33.5 per cent in 2025. This means that the size of social security benefits and burdens will be nearly doubled compared with 1995 levels.

B. STRUCTURAL REFORM AND NEW MEASURES FOR SOCIAL SECURITY

1. Japanese social security measures to support the retiring elderly: from employment to public pension

(a) Employment policy

In 1994, the pensionable age for the first tier was raised. At the same time, various employment measures were implemented in order to promote elderly participation in the labour force. First, the Ministry of Labour determined that all companies should raise the retirement age to 60, compared with the situation in 1990 where only 64.1 per cent of Japanese companies set their

TABLE 2.   FUTURE PERSPECTIVES ON THE BENEFITS AND BURDENS FOR SOCIAL SECURITY
(*Compared with national income (NI)*)

A: Growth of nominal national income: 3.5 per cent for fiscal year 2000 and before; 3.0 per cent for fiscal year 2001 and beyond

B: Growth of nominal national income: 1.75 per cent for fiscal year 2000 and before; 2.0 per cent for fiscal year 2001 and beyond

C: Growth of nominal national income: 1.75 per cent for fiscal year 2000 and before; 1.5 per cent for fiscal year 2001 and beyond

| | Fiscal year 1995 | | Fiscal year 2025 | | | | | |
| | | | A | | B | | C | |
	Trillions of yen	*Compared with NI (percentage)*	*Trillions of yen*	*Compared with NI (percentage)*	*Trillions of yen*	*Compared with NI (percentage)*	*Trillions of yen*	*Compared with NI (percentage)*
Social security benefits	65	17	274	29.5	230	33.5	216	35.5
Pension	34	9	142	15.5	109	16	98	16
Medical care	24	6	90	10	90	13	90	15
Welfare	7	2	41	4.5	31	4.5	27	4.5
Long-term care included in the upper column ...	(-)	(-)	(21)	(2.5)	(16)	(2.5)	(14)	(2.5)
Burdens related to social security	70	18.5	272	29.5	230	33.5	216	35.5

Source: National Institute of Population and Social Security Research, "Population projection for Japan (estimated January 1997)", estimate based on medium estimates by the Ministry of Health and Welfare as of September 1997.

NOTE: Estimates in case long-term care insurance is introduced.

retirement age at 60. Additionally, various subsidies were introduced for the promotion of elderly participation in the workforce. In 1990, a subsidy for employers who implemented a continuous employment scheme, as well as a grant for employers who hired elderly workers over age 60, was initiated. In 1996, in order to promote continued employment of those between the ages of 60 and 65, a subsidy was introduced that provides 25 per cent of the wages earned by people over 60 years of age to elderly people under age 65 who are continuing to work but whose wage has dropped considerably since turning 60. In February 2000, the employment insurance scheme was amended and the definition of applicable "elderly" was extended to the age groups between 45 and 55. These benefits can be more efficiently provided to elderly job-seekers for a longer period of time.

(*b*)   *Income security (public pension)*

In 1994, partial pension benefits for elderly employees aged 60-65 were reformed. Before the reform, the partial pension scheme had been criticized for its lack of promotion of the employment of elderly workers. This new measure was called the "American system" and encourages elderly pensioners to rejoin the labour market. According to the pension reform act, in 2000, elderly pensioners can earn a monthly income of up to 220,000 yen, and only incur deductions of 20 per cent from their pension benefits. However, all partial pension benefits are cut if monthly income exceeds 370,000 yen. Figures VII and VIII describe the manner in which partial pension benefits are deducted according to one's earnings. Figure VII offers an example involving a person who receives partial pension benefits of 100,000 yen and figure VIII offers an example involving a person who receives partial pension benefits of 250,000 yen. Takada (1994) expressed reservations about this reform, indicating the fact that only highly paid skilled workers benefit from the new pension scheme. It may be true that unskilled, low-paid workers are less likely to secure the opportunity to earn relatively high wages. The average amount of pension benefits per capita for retired pensioners with regular full pension and for pensioners with partial pension changed between 1995 and 1996. The monthly average benefit received by a male retired full pensioner was 206,800 yen in 1994 and that of a partial pensioner was 184,667 yen. Then, in 1995, the full pensioner's amount was reduced to 197,049 and the partial pensioner's amount was increased to 206,391. The numbers of partial pension beneficiaries increased substantially between 1995 and 1996 (see figure IX).

2.   *Introducing long-term care insurance and improving efficiency in the Japanese health-care system*

Social expenditures for the elderly increased much faster than those for the rest of the population. Up until 1980, the rate of increase in medical care expenditures was higher than the rate of increase of expenditures for pension and other sectors. This was due to the fact that medical expenditures for the elderly boomed after 1973. The year 1973 was an epoch-making year for medical expenditures due to the fact that, in 1973, co-payment of medical care insurance

Figure VII. Partial employee's pension by monthly earned income
(case of monthly pension in the amount of 100,000 yen)

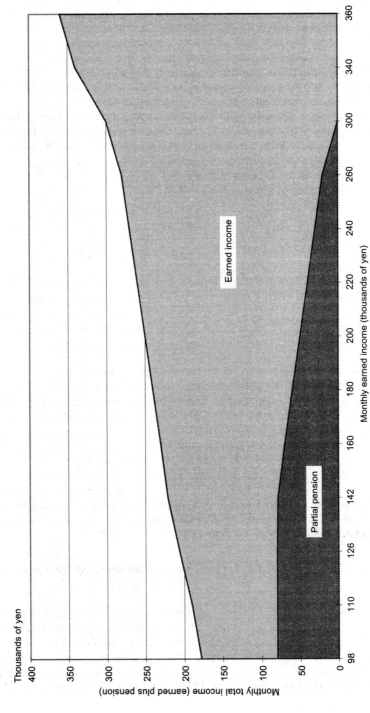

Figure VIII. Partial employee's pension by monthly earned income
(case of monthly pension in the amount of 250,000 yen)

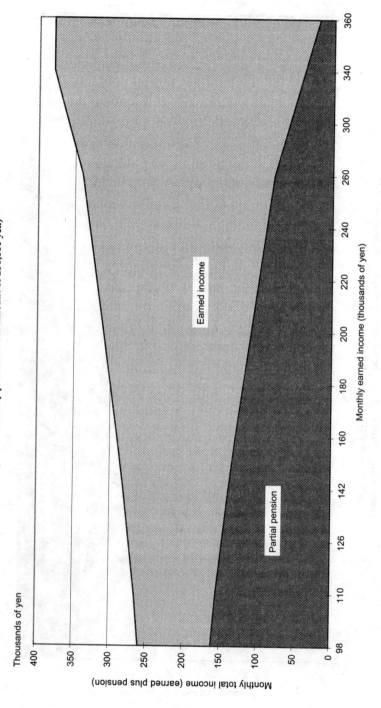

Figure IX. Trends in number of new beneficiaries: full pension vs. partial pension

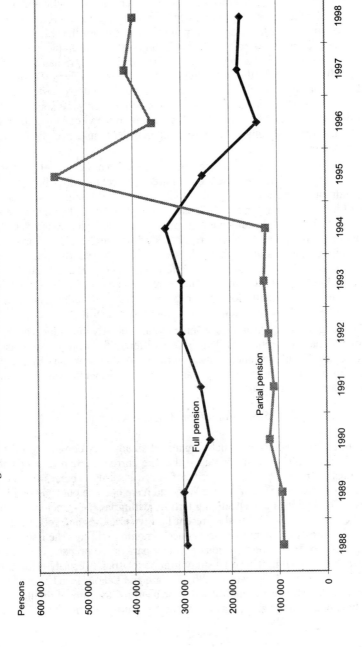

Source: Social Security Agency, Government of Japan.

for the elderly was abolished and it began to be subsidized by the national budget. Subsequently, demand for elderly medical services increased rapidly and, during the next 10 years, the national medical insurance scheme accumulated substantial debts. In 1978, a cross-subsidized system called Health and Medical Services for the Elderly was introduced. This system functions on the principle of equality of burden-sharing of medical care costs for the elderly among full Japanese nationals. After introduction of this system, the employees' medical insurance systems including Society-Managed Health Care had its burden significantly enlarged. In the following years, a series of reform measures to slow the expansion of medical care expenditures for the elderly were initiated. For example, elderly patients no longer receive co-payment waivers; however, they still pay a reduced fixed amount. Also, a new method of lump-sum payment for hospitals and clinics was introduced in order to improve efficiency in health-care facilities.

Before long-term care insurance was introduced, a number of elderly people were hospitalized not because they required medical treatment but because their conditions demanded an assisted-living residential facility. The average length of hospitalization for elderly Japanese is much higher than that of other countries. We call this phenomenon "hospitalization for social reasons". Other reasons for the high hospitalization rate of elderly persons are the shortage of social welfare facilities and home-help services for the elderly, and the fact that the cost-sharing system for social welfare services places a high burden on middle-income elderly individuals, who therefore choose to stay in hospitals owing to their substantially lower cost. No cooperation or adjustments were made between medical care facilities and elderly care facilities.

The long-term care insurance scheme requires elderly individuals to share the cost and make contributions. This is very different from other social insurance schemes. Even pensioners must contribute to long-term care insurance. Those who are receiving welfare assistance can have the welfare system make contributions on their behalf.

3. Structural reform in social security

Former Prime Minister Obuchi organized an advisory committee for social security in 2000, which concluded that the current system of social security must be reformed. The majority of social security schemes had been implemented after the Second World War, and have become outdated and impractical. The ageing and the declining fertility within Japanese society require new schemes to correspond to the present family structures and social conditions. Therefore, this committee meets once a month to discuss the issues and goals of reform. In addition, various political parties are preparing effective strategies by organizing their own study groups for social security reform. In April 2001, the new Ministry of Health, Welfare and Labour is to begin its administrative duties. The reorganization of the central Government should have a positive impact on the present status of social security reform.

C. CONCLUSION AND REMARKS

Actual reform of the Japanese social security system will take place in the near future. A series of reports will be published by various committees in the next few years, and a scholar in one of the committees has proposed that the reform measures be free from demographic changes. I wonder if this is a pragmatic attitude. Every nation has its own unique process of social development. I have no idea what he meant by measures being "free from demographic changes", but we must learn from our previous new schemes, which did not carefully consider the impact of demography. I believe that we should invent new measures while paying close attention to demographic changes.

NOTES

[1] "Strategies for Reviving the Japanese Economy" is available in English at the official web site for the Prime Minister's Office (http://www.kantei.go.jp/foreign/senryaku/990317report. html).

[2] The Study Team on Labour Policy, an advisory group for the Ministry of Labour, submitted its report in May 1999.

[3] Further detailed information on Japanese public pension schemes is available at the web site of the National Institute of Population and Social Security Research (http://www.ipss.go.jp/).

[4] According to the Ministry of Labour's "Survey on Elderly Employees" in 1997, 83.7 per cent of males 60 years of age in the workforce consider themselves in good health, whereas only 68.3 per cent of males 60 years of age not in the workforce consider themselves in good health.

[5] Historically, the Japanese Government has used the term "national income" rather than GDP. National income used in government data is calculated by the following formula: net national product minus indirect tax plus subsidies.

REFERENCES

Katsumata, Yukiko (2000). Japanese social security measures to support the retiring aged: from employment insurance and public pension. Paper presented at the Year 2000 International Research Conference on Social Security, International Social Security Association, Helsinki, 25-27 September.

Kimura, Yoko, and Yukiko Katsumata (2000). Household of elderly, structure of income and consumption. In *Changing Household and Social Security*, Yoshio Matsuda, ed. Tokyo: Tokyo University Press, pp. 179-197.

Ministry of Labour (1997). Status of Elderly Workers: Result of Survey for 1996. Tokyo.

_____ (2000). White Paper on Labour, 2000. Tokyo.

OECD (1995). *The Transition from Work to Retirement*. Paris.

_____ (1999). *Labour Force Statistics*. Paris.

Statistics Bureau, Management and Coordination Agency, Government of Japan (2000). Annual Report on the Labour-force Survey, 1999.

Takada, Kazuo (1994). Recent tax reform and elderly employment. *Roudojiho*, No. 555 (October 1994), pp. 16-31.

POLICY RESPONSES TO POPULATION AGEING AND POPULATION DECLINE IN THE REPUBLIC OF KOREA

*Namhoon Cho**

A. INTRODUCTION

The Republic of Korea has undergone demographic changes at a pace that has dazzled many population scientists. Fertility has declined to a level far below the replacement level within a short span of two and a half decades. Concerted government policies and family planning programmes played a major role in achieving this momentous transition. The total fertility rate in the Republic of Korea rapidly decreased from 6.0 in 1960 to 1.6 in 1987. Thereafter, the total fertility rate (TFR) fluctuated between 1.7 and 1.8, but has recently decreased further to 1.48 in 1998 and 1.42 in 1999 (see table 1). It is estimated that if the current low fertility continues, the population in Korea will stabilize at around 52.8 million people by the year 2028, and will begin to decrease thereafter.

Socio-economic development factors that have resulted in the decline in fertility include rapid urbanization, increase in educational and economic participation of females, increase in educational attainment of both males and females, and reduction in infant and child mortality rates. Other, equally important factors that have affected fertility in the Republic of Korea include changes in the value of or preference for the number of children, family structure, marriage behaviour, and role and function of the family, especially in respect of support for the elderly. In addition, improvement in nutrition, improvement in health status, change in lifestyle etc., which are often concomitant with socio-economic development, have played a role in reducing mortality, including infant and maternal mortality rates, thereby resulting in a considerable rise in life expectancy. The infant mortality decreased from 45 per 1,000 live births in 1970 to 7.7 in 1998, while the life expectancy at birth had been 52.4 years for both sexes in 1960 but increased to 74.4 years in 1997 (National Statistical Office, 1999).

The fertility decline in the Republic of Korea has been attributed to the increase in proportion of single women and the attitude among women that it is necessary to decrease the number of children. The proportion of women in age group 20-24 who have never married increased from 57.3 per cent in 1970 to 83.3 per cent in 1995. There has also been an increase in the proportion of women who have never married for age groups 25-29 and 30-34. The

*Korea Institute for Health and Social Affairs, Seoul, Republic of Korea.

TABLE 1. TRENDS IN TOTAL FERTILITY RATE (TFR) IN
THE REPUBLIC OF KOREA, 1960-1999

Year	1960[a]	1974[b]	1984[b]	1987[b]	1993[b]	1996[b]	1998[a]	1999[a]
TFR	6.0	3.6	2.1	1.6	1.8	1.7	1.48	1.42

[a]National Statistical Office, *Report on Vital Statistics Based on Vital Registration*, each year.

[b]Korea Institute for Health and Social Affairs, *National Fertility and Family Health Survey*, each year.

proportion for age group 25-29 was only 9.7 per cent in 1970 but 29.6 per cent in 1995, and the proportion for age group 30-34 increased from 1.4 to 6.7 per cent during the same period (see table 2). Accordingly, the age at first marriage of females increased from 21.6 years in 1960 to 24.1 years in 1980 and 26.2 years in 1998. The proportion of single women and the age at first marriage of females are expected to increase continuously in the immediate future (Cho and Lee, 1999).

Although achievements have exceeded expectations in terms of the population goals in the Republic of Korea, several new population problems have emerged. These new problems must be faced with the same determination and imagination that were used to solve the population problems in the past. Major consequences resulting from the rapid fertility decline include the shrinking of the labour force and the growth of the elderly population. There is a range of policy options available and measures that can be taken in response to labour-supply problems. Concentration on capital-intensive production, raising retirement ages and greater labour-force participation by women are among the obvious choices.

The growth in the number of elderly people poses the single most difficult challenge. Moreover, elderly people are living longer, which means that they are more susceptible to chronic health problems which may demand long-term treatment and nursing care. The implications of the decline in fertility and changes in population structure are serious and crucially important matters in terms of health and pension expenditures in the immediate future.

The Republic of Korea shifted its role to accommodate these dimensions in the future population policy directions. Under these circumstances, the Government adopted new directions and strategies for the population policy in June 1996, which focused primarily on population quality and welfare rather than on demographic arenas. The major goals of the new population policy were: (*a*) to maintain the replacement level of fertility and to improve morbidity and mortality levels as part of the process of achieving sustainable socio-economic development; (*b*) to enhance family health and welfare; (*c*) to prevent the imbalance of sex ratio at birth and to reduce the incidence of induced abortions; (*d*) to tackle sex-related problems of youths and adolescents; (*e*) to empower women by expanding their employment opportunities and welfare services; and (*f*) to improve work opportunities and provide adequate health-care and welfare services for the elderly (Cho, 1996).

229

TABLE 2.   TRENDS IN SOCIO-ECONOMIC FACTORS AFFECTING
DECLINE IN FERTILITY, 1960-1998

	1960	1970	1980	1990	1995	1998
Female education[a] (percentage)	13.0	23.5	45.0	88.2	95.8	..
Female LFPR[b] (percentage)	36.3[c]	39.3	42.8	47.0	48.3	47.0
Age at first marriage for females (years)	21.6	23.3	24.1	24.9	25.4	26.2
Proportion of single females (percentage)						
20-24	..	57.3	66.1	80.4	83.3	..
25-29	..	9.7	14.1	22.1	29.6	..
30-34	..	1.4	2.7	5.3	6.7	..
Urbanization (percentage)	28	41	57	74	78	..
Infant mortality rate	..	45	17 (1981)	13 (1987)	9.9 (1993)	7.7 (1996)

Sources: National Statistical Office, *Population and Housing Census Report*, each year, and *Annual Report on the Economically Active Population Survey*, each year; Korea Institute for Health and Social Affairs, *1998 Health and Welfare Indicators in Korea*, 1998; and Ministry of Health and Welfare and Korea Institute for Health and Social Affairs, *1996 Infant and Neo-natal Mortality and Causes of Death in Korea*, 1998.

[a] Proportion of females aged 20-24 who have attended secondary school or above.
[b] Labour-force participation rate.
[c] Survey conducted in 1963, among persons 14 years of age or over.

However, despite the transition of the population policy in the Republic of Korea, the TFR continuously declined as shown in table 1. This phenomenon is expected to accelerate with continuous increase in age at first marriage and the proportion of single women, which may make the recovery of fertility to its earlier level difficult. Thus, the present paper explains: (*a*) the demographic prospects in the Republic of Korea during the next half-century, in comparison with the United Nations estimates; (*b*) the possible consequences of population decline and population ageing; and (*c*) the various policy options.

B. POPULATION PROSPECTS FOR THE NEXT HALF-CENTURY

In 1996, the National Statistical Office projected the population of the Republic of Korea, based on the result of the 1995 Population and Housing Census. The assumptions for the 1996 population projection, which is the most recent study available, reflected the past trends in the components of population change, namely, fertility, mortality and migration. The national population projection (National Statistical Office, 1996) assumed that the TFR would remain 1.7 until 2015 and increase thereafter to 1.8, which figure would be maintained onward under the medium variant. As a mortality assumption, the 1996 projection assumed the life expectancy at birth for 2000 as 71.02 years for males and 78.64 years for females, and that these figures would increase to 75.4 years and 82.5 years, respectively, in 2030 (see table 3).

As for the international migration assumption, the number of emigrants increased owing to the increasing number of students and employed who went abroad for the purposes of study and employment, and was offset by the increasing number of foreign worker migrants in the Republic of Korea; thus, the 1996 population projection assumed the total net migration to be minus 30,000 for the future migrants, which was the average of net migration during 1990-1995. This study makes an attempt to project the future population, adopting

TABLE 3.   ASSUMPTIONS FOR THE NATIONAL POPULATION
PROJECTION FOR 2000-2050

| Year | TFR (medium) | Life expectancy at birth (years) | | Net migration (persons) | Sex ratio (males per 100 female live births) |
		Male	Female		
2000.	1.71	71.02	78.64	-30,000	112.7
2005.	1.71	72.27	79.74	-30,000	110.7
2010.	1.74	73.27	80.69	-30,000	108.9
2015.	1.80	73.87	81.19	-30,000	107.0
2020.	1.80	74.47	81.68	-30,000	107.0
2025.	1.80	74.97	82.09	-30,000	107.0
2030.	1.80	75.42	82.45	-30,000	107.0
2035.	1.80	76.67	83.70	-30,000	107.0
2040.	1.80	77.92	84.95	-30,000	107.0
2045.	1.80	79.17	86.20	-30,000	107.0
2050.	1.80	80.47	87.45	-30,000	107.0

Source: National Statistical Office, *Future Population Projection*, December 1996.

the same assumptions as those used by the 1996 projection which included the mortality change only from 2000 to 2050. It is extended from the 1996 projection by the National Statistical Office (at the medium variant), which projected the population up to 2030.

According to the 1996 projection and the extended projection by this study, a zero population growth rate will be reached in 2028 with a population size of 52.8 million, and thereafter the population of the Republic of Korea will decrease to 51.5 million in 2050. The absolute size of the working-age population will start to decrease after reaching its peak (36.5 million) in 2018 as the declining youth population enters working age. With the increase in life expectancy, the aged population 65 years of age or over has increased and will continue to increase with a high growth rate of approximately 4 per cent per annum. The proportion of the elderly reached 7 per cent in 2000 and will double (to 14.3 per cent) in 2022, indicating that the Republic of Korea has become an ageing society. The potential support ratio will decrease from 10.0 in 2000 to 4.1 in 2025 and to 2.2 in 2050 (see table 4).

Here, the national projection was compared with the United Nations projection, made by the Population Division of the United Nations Secretariat (United Nations, 2001). Although the United Nations projections were made with various scenarios from I to V, the national projection can be compared with the United Nations projection of scenario I, at least in terms of the migration assumption; the national projection assumed an annual net migration of 30,000 to 2030 and the United Nations projection of scenario I assumed a total net migration of 450,000 from 1995 to 2020 and zero thereafter. The other United Nations scenarios assumed no migration. The national projection shows that the total population will achieve a peak in 2028 with a size of 52.8 million, whereas the United Nations projection shows a peak point in 2035 with a maximum size of 53.0 million. The absolute size of the working-age population will reach a peak in 2018 with a size of 36.5 million in the national projection, compared with a peak of 36.3 million in the year 2020 in the United Nations projection (see table 5).

A main feature of the comparison between two projections is that the youth population and the working-age population will decrease faster in the national projection than in the United Nations projection; and the aged population will increase more speedily in the national projection than in the United Nations projection. Influenced by an increase in an old population rather than a decrease in a young population, the total population will decrease faster in the United Nations projection than in the national projection. As a result, the potential support ratio will decline faster in the United Nations projection than in the national projection.

As for net migration, both the average annual number and the total number of migrants are bigger in the national projection than in the United Nations projection; such a difference is simply a result of the difference in the assumptions adopted by the projections. Although there are some differences in the main results between two projections, it is evident that the population of the Republic of Korea will be rapidly ageing with both youth and working-age populations declining after certain years.

TABLE 4. NATIONAL POPULATION ESTIMATES IN THE REPUBLIC OF KOREA,
2000-2050: MEDIUM VARIANT

Year	Total population		0-14			15-64[a]		65 or over[b]		
	Thousands	Percentage	Thousands	Percentage		Thousands	Percentage	Thousands	Percentage	Ratio[c]
2000........	47 275	100.0	10 233	21.7		33 671	71.2	3 371	7.1	10.01
2005........	49 123	100.0	10 421	21.2		34 450	70.1	4 253	8.7	8.10
2010........	50 618	100.0	10 080	19.9		35 506	70.1	5 032	10.0	7.06
2015........	51 677	100.0	9 515	18.4		36 316	70.3	5 846	11.3	6.21
2020........	52 358	100.0	9 013	17.1		36 446	69.7	6 899	13.2	5.29
2025........	52 712	100.0	8 633	16.4		35 465	67.3	8 613	16.3	4.12
2030........	52 744	100.0	8 448	16.0		34 130	64.7	10 165	19.3	3.36
2035........	52 896	100.0	8 338	15.8		32 877	62.2	11 681	22.1	2.81
2040........	52 810	100.0	8 175	15.5		31 584	59.8	13 051	24.7	2.42
2045........	52 327	100.0	7 922	15.1		30 764	58.8	13 641	26.1	2.26
2050........	51 546	100.0	7 687	14.9		29 935	58.1	13 924	27.0	2.15

Sources: United Nations (2001); and National Statistical Office (1996).

[a]Year of peak reached in the absolute size of working population: 2018 with 36.5 million.

[b]Proportion of the elderly population aged 65 years or over: 7.1 per cent in 2000 and 14.3 per cent in 2022.

[c]Potential support ratio: persons of working age per person aged 65 years or older.

TABLE 5. POPULATION ESTIMATES FOR THE REPUBLIC OF KOREA: COMPARISON OF NATIONAL MEDIAN VARIANT WITH UNITED NATIONS SCENARIO I

	National projection			United Nations projection		
	2000	2025	2050	2000	2025	2050
			Thousands			
Total population............	47 275	52 712	51 546	46 844	52 533	51 275
0-14.................	10 233	8 633	7 687	10 068	8 956	8 209
15-64................	33 671	35 465	29 935	33 623	35 557	30 401
65+.................	3 371	8 613	13 924	3 152	8 020	12 665
Average annual number of migrants..........	-	-30	-30	-	-14	0
Total number of migrants........	-	-750	-750	-	-350	0
			Potential support ratio			
	9.99	4.12	2.15	10.67	4.43	2.40

Sources: United Nations (2001); and National Statistical Office (1996).

C. Socio-economic consequences of demographic transition

1. *Labour shortage and ageing*

The population ageing and the decline in the growth rate have already led to a labour shortage in some sectors. The labour shortage, as measured by the vacancy rate (the ratio of unfilled vacancies to current employees), has been serious, specifically for the production workers (mostly unskilled workers), causing the small and medium-sized manufacturing firms to suffer. The labour shortage rate has been maintained at 2-5 per cent during the last 10 years and that for the unskilled has increased to more than 10 per cent (see table 6).

This labour shortage might be attributable to the accelerated growth of gross domestic product (GDP), which led to an excessive demand for labour in the manufacturing sector, and an increase in the labour force with higher educational attainment (in 1996, about 62 per cent of the labour force had received higher education and about 20 per cent had graduated from college or university); but it seems to be related to the change in the age structure of the population, which implies that this phenomenon will be structural and long-term.

There has been an increasing trend in respect of the number of foreign workers who moved to the Republic of Korea in the 1990s; this phenomenon is a result of the high growth of the economy of the Republic of Korea during the 1990s which has caused a rise in wages and, subsequently, level of income, so that domestic labourers have developed a tendency to avoid difficult, dirty and dangerous work. As a result, there has been a shortage of labour in small and medium-sized manufacturer establishments. Foreign labour is inclined to work in the Republic of Korea owing to the high wages and also because small and medium-sized manufacturing establishments prefer foreign workers who are not reluctant to undertake hard and dangerous work for cheap wages.

As can be seen from table 7, the total number of foreign workers, legal and illegal, was estimated at 81,824 in 1994 and at 210,494 in 1996, showing an increase of 157.3 per cent over two years. In 1996, approximately 61 per cent of all foreign workers were illegally employed, in comparison with 58.9 per cent in 1994. However, the economic crisis that began in 1997 has had an impact on the movement of foreign workers; the number of foreign workers working in the Republic of Korea was 157,689 in 1998, which is a decrease of 25.1 per cent from 1996. The decrease may be a result of the rise in the exchange rate and lack of jobs during the economic crisis in the Republic of Korea. However, the ratio of illegal foreign workers to total foreign workers is still high.

In the Republic of Korea, the ageing of the labour force has accelerated. The proportion of the economically active population of ages 45 or over increased from 39.1 per cent in 1990 to 40.9 per cent in 1999. Accordingly, the average age of the total economically active population increased from 32.2 years in 1990 to 34.3 years in 1999 (see table 8). This labour-ageing phenomenon is expected to accelerate, as the total population ageing rises. On the other hand, it was attributable to the fact that aged workers want to work longer simply because they expect to live longer and are healthy enough to work even in relatively unpleasant workplaces. However, most aged workers are non-wage

TABLE 6. VACANCY RATE[a] IN THE REPUBLIC OF KOREA, 1984-1997
(Percentage)

Year	All establishments	Production workers	Unskilled workers	Year	All establishments	Production workers	Unskilled workers
1984.	2.98	3.95	8.02	1991.	5.48	9.07	20.13
1985.	1.75	2.35	4.90	1992.	4.26	6.76	10.86
1986.	2.30	3.20	8.34	1993.	3.62	6.04	14.74
1987.	3.29	4.79	11.12	1994.	3.57	5.64	12.90
1988.	3.54	5.24	12.29	1995.	3.71	5.80	11.41
1989.	3.21	4.92	11.82	1996.	2.98	4.80	16.24
1990.	4.34	6.85	16.23	1997.	2.44	3.88	12.58

Source: Ministry of Labour, Labour Demand Trend Survey Report, each year.

[a] Ratio of unfilled vacancies to current employees.

TABLE 7. TRENDS IN THE NUMBER OF FOREIGN LABOURERS, BY LEGAL STATUS, 1994-1998

Year	Total	Legal workers	Trainees	Illegal workers
1994.........	81 824 (100.0)	5 265 (6.4)	28 328 (34.6)	48 231 (58.9)
1996.........	210 494 (100.0)	13 420 (6.4)	68 020 (32.3)	129 054 (61.3)
1998.........	157 689 (100.0)	11 143 (7.1)	47 009 (29.8)	99 537 (63.1)

Source: Ministry of Labour, *Labour White Paper*, each year.
NOTE: Figure as percentage of total in parentheses.

workers, such as self-employed and family workers, and they are mostly employed in the agricultural or service sectors.

2. Increase in medical costs

The increase in the elderly population has resulted in the rise of medical costs in the Republic Korea. At present, health insurance or medical assistance programmes (for those who are supported by the Livelihood Protection Law) cover all persons in the Republic of Korea. As of 1995, 96.7 per cent of those aged 65 years or over were covered by health insurance and the rest of the elderly were covered by medical assistance. Despite the high coverage of health insurance, there was an increase in medical expenditures owing to the population ageing in the Republic of Korea. The health insurance cost for elderly persons shows a speedier increase than the total population; the cost for older persons shows an increase rate of 27.7 per cent, compared with 18.7 per cent for the total population between 1995 and 1998. The amount of the medical insurance cost for the elderly accounted for 12.8 per cent of the total cost in 1985 and increased to 15.9 per cent in 1998 (see table 9). The medical costs per elderly person are over two times those for each person under age 65.

TABLE 8. PROPORTION OF ECONOMICALLY ACTIVE POPULATION OF AGES 45 OR OVER AND AVERAGE AGE OF ECONOMICALLY ACTIVE POPULATION IN THE REPUBLIC OF KOREA, 1990-1999

Year	Total Percentage[a]	Total Average age[b] (years)	Male Percentage[a]	Male Average age[b] (years)	Female Percentage[a]	Female Average age[b] (years)
1990.........	39.1	32.2	39.5	32.0	38.4	32.5
1991.........	39.1	32.1	39.6	32.1	38.4	32.2
1992.........	39.4	32.8	39.9	32.7	38.8	33.0
1993.........	39.3	31.5	39.7	31.5	38.6	31.7
1994.........	39.5	32.1	39.9	32.1	38.9	32.2
1995.........	39.7	32.3	40.1	32.2	39.1	32.3
1996.........	40.0	32.8	40.4	32.9	39.4	32.6
1997.........	40.3	33.7	40.8	34.1	39.7	33.3
1998.........	40.6	33.6	41.0	33.9	40.0	33.2
1999.........	40.9	34.3	41.2	34.3	40.4	34.4

Source: National Statistical Office, *Annual Report on the Economically Active Population Survey*, each year.
[a]Proportion of economically active population of ages 45 or over.
[b]Average age of economically active population.

3. Growing burden on the national pension scheme

Since the process of population ageing will continue to accelerate in the future, the financial crisis of the national pension is anticipated. According to an actuarial estimate, the total number of beneficiaries of the old-age pension will increase rapidly although the number of insurants who pay contributions to the pension will decrease. The number of pensioners will increase up to about 45 per cent of the total number of the pension insurants, implying that the burden of the working-age population will sharply increase. By 2034, the total pension expenditure will exceed the total revenue. As a result, the accumulated pension reserve is expected to be exhausted in 2048 (see table 10). Thus, population ageing in the Republic of Korea will be a serious burden on the pension system, and the future young generations will have to pay heavy contributions in order to sustain the system.

To cope with the anticipated financial insustainability of the old-age pension in the Republic of Korea, the Government took action in order to revise the National Pension Act in December 1998. The most notable change is the target replacement rate for the average wage workers of 40 years with contribution histories being reduced from 70 to 60 per cent. Also, the retirement age will be increased from 60 to 61 in 2013 and will rise 1 year every 5 years thereafter until reaching the age of 65 in 2033.

TABLE 9.   MEDICAL EXPENDITURE BY AGE IN THE
REPUBLIC OF KOREA, 1995 AND 1998

Age	1995	1998	Annual growth rate (percentage)
	(Billions of won)		
0.	1 122	1 582	12.15
1-4.	2 756	4 353	16.46
5-9.	1 875	3 263	20.29
10-14.	1 217	1 740	12.66
15-19.	1 397	2 252	17.25
20-24.	2 129	2 788	9.41
25-29.	3 275	4 880	14.22
30-34.	3 033	4 365	12.91
35-39.	2 936	4 793	17.74
40-44.	2 469	4 450	21.71
45-49.	2 482	4 142	18.61
50-54.	2 958	4 387	14.03
55-59.	3 144	5 624	21.38
60-64.	2 668	5 276	25.51
65-69.	2 085	4 140	25.68
70-74.	1 505	3 029	26.24
75+	1 301	3 018	32.38
Total (A)	38 353	64 080	18.66
65 + (B).	4 892	10 187	27.70
(B)/(A) (percentage)	12.75	15.90	

Source: Korea Health Insurance Cooperation, *Health Insurance Expenditure*, 2000.

TABLE 10. ESTIMATE OF PENSION FINANCING IN THE REPUBLIC OF KOREA, 2000-2050

Year	Reserve	Total revenue	Total expenditure[a]	Balance (B - C)	Insurants	Beneficiaries of old-age pension	Maturity ratio (F/E) (percentage)	Funded ratio (A/C)
	(A)	(B)	(C)	(D)	(E)	(F)	(G)	(H)
		(Hundreds of millions of won)[a]			(Thousands of persons)			
2000	565 846	141 131	45 207	95 923	16 425	363	2.2	12.5
2005	1 338 037	268 783	46 547	222 236	17 470	1 101	6.3	28.7
2010	2 489 249	414 791	90 782	324 008	18 199	1 780	9.8	27.4
2015	3 813 478	524 016	152 704	371 312	18 141	2 392	13.2	25.0
2020	5 166 792	655 605	260 537	395 068	17 674	3 545	20.1	19.8
2025	6 025 718	704 601	424 010	280 590	17 036	4 969	29.2	14.2
2030	6 309 898	768 113	603 656	164 458	16 318	6 094	37.3	10.5
2034	5 906 253	752 760	753 661	-901	15 636	6 912	44.2	7.8
2035	5 724 852	752 460	789 806	-37 346	15 500	7 067	45.6	7.2
2040	4 256 564	726 316	984 919	-258 603	14 891	7 704	51.7	4.3
2045	1 725 581	644 793	1 183 965	-539 173	14 315	8 076	56.4	1.5
2048	-348 146	554 185	1 293 768	-739 583	14 192	8 090	57.0	-0.3
2050	-1 852 905	576 343	1 355 556	-779 212	14 092	7 993	56.7	-1.4

Source: National Pension Research Centre, *Actuarial Estimation of the National Pension*, 2000.

[a] At constant prices of 2000.

D. POLICY OPTIONS

1. *Policies related to population ageing and decline*

Despite the Government's action to shift the directions of population policy from population control to population quality and welfare in 1996, so as to overcome the many challenges stemming from low fertility, the decline in fertility has continued. Except for these policy measures, there have been no direct population policies, established and implemented, to address the determinants of expected population ageing and decline. However, it can be said that some indirect policies were used to check the rapid decline in fertility which focused mainly on support for the compatibility of work and child-rearing for women. These programmes included expansion of childcare institutions including those at the workplace, extension of maternity leave, adoption of paternity leave (in the government sector), payment of family allowance etc.

The current Immigration Law in the Republic of Korea prohibits the migration of non-professional workers to the Republic of Korea, and any policy has taken into consideration the influx of migrants to compensate for the expected decline of the working-age population in the Republic of Korea. Since the 1990s, the number of foreign workers in the Republic of Korea, most of them illegal, has considerably increased. However, the Government contends that approximately 200,000 foreign workers, which is 1 per cent of the total economically active population of the Republic of Korea, is the optimum size for the foreign worker force within the country. Nowadays, the Government is attempting to promulgate the Foreign Worker Permission Act, which will allow a certain number of foreign workers (about 1 per cent of the total economically active population) to work, for less than three years, in the Republic of Korea. The main aim of such legal reform is to prevent the illegalization of foreign trainees, who are allowed to train for two years under the Industry Trainee System, which started in the early 1990s.

An expert meeting, which was held at the Korea Institute for Health and Social Affairs in July 2000, suggested that preparations for the expected population ageing and decline be taken into consideration. This meeting concluded that, although policy will inevitably have a difficult time returning to the current trend in fertility, some policies, such as the extension of childcare leave, payment of child allowance, increase in compatibility between child-rearing and work of women, need to be established in order to encourage women to marry and have the number of children they want.

2. *Polices related to the consequences of the demographic transition*

(a) *Policies on the elderly*

In response to the rapid increase of the elderly population, the Government has carried out various policy measures with respect to the elderly to keep them healthy and active during their old age. Among these policy measures, income maintenance programmes, health maintenance programmes and residential programmes are important.

Public pension programmes, public assistance based on the Livelihood Protection Law, and the non-contributory old-age pension are three components of public policy that aim at enhancing the economic security of the elderly in the Republic of Korea. The main source of income for the majority of the retired old people is the savings or assets that they accrued during their lifetime or support from their children. For the aged who are not covered by the National Pension Scheme which was started in 1988, a non-contributory old-age pension programme was introduced in 1998 for the elderly in low income brackets. Along with this, public assistance allowance is provided for the elderly aged 65 years or over who are covered by the public assistance programme. The Government also provides various measures, for example, tax exemption, to enhance income security for the aged.

There are three programmes to enhance employment of the elderly, including the Elderly Job Placement Centre, the Elderly Workplace and Elderly Employment Promotion. According to the Act that created these programmes, based on the Elderly Employment Promotion Programme enacted in 1991, establishments with 300 employees are to employ a proportion of aged workers greater than 3 per cent of the total employees. The Act also recommends that the Government provide more training facilities and more job information for the aged workers. Although the Act lacks compulsory enforcement, its effects seem great. The public enterprises extended the mandatory retirement age up to 60 and leading private enterprises followed the practices of the public sector.

To improve the health of the elderly through diagnosing geriatric diseases at an early stage and providing health education, the Government has given subsidies to local health centres or hospitals for medical check-ups of the low-income elderly. The elderly who are suspected to have some diseases through the first screening test should be given further examinations. Further, the proportion of senile dementia among the old-age population is estimated to be 8.3 per cent and the actual number is estimated to be about 240,000 persons in the Republic of Korea. To care for the aged with senile dementia, the Government has started a "10-year plan for senile dementia" extending from 1996 to 2005, which includes construction of nursing facilities and hospitals.

As society transforms and traditional family support has weakened, and the number of the elderly living alone or as couples without children has increased, the need for social welfare services for the elderly who continue living in their own home has grown. To encourage living in the community, home help services, day-care centres for the elderly, and short-term care centres are available for the elderly in need. In addition, the number of persons at risk of being admitted for some forms of institutional care has increased. At present, welfare facilities for the aged are classified into three groups, including residential homes, nursing homes for the severely disabled elderly and geriatric hospitals. These facilities are divided into three categories—free-of-charge facilities, low-price facilities and pay facilities—depending on the individual ability to pay. The eligibility for free-of-charge or low-price facilities is confined to the low-income group. The Government has recently increased the amount of subsidies to free-of-charge or low-price nursing homes, and developed the policy of long-term care service for the elderly to respond to the rapid increase in the number of frail elderly.

(b) Policies on women

In the Republic of Korea, there have been great efforts to improve women's status, socially and economically. The Government has prioritized policy regarding promotion of women rights and gender equality and equity. In 1998, the Government established the Presidential Commission on Women's Affairs (PCWA) at the ministerial level, aimed at planning, implementing, monitoring and evaluating policies related to women's empowerment and gender equality, in an integrated and effective manner. This Commission is to be renamed the Ministry of Women, in order to intensify its status and function. As for the employment status of women, the participation of women in the labour force gradually increased from 40.5 per cent in 1981 to 59.8 per cent in 1998 for married women, while the labour-force participation rate remained at 46 per cent for unmarried females (see table 11). However, the rates of the Republic of Korea are still low, in comparison with those of some developed countries.

To encourage women's economic participation, the Government of the Republic of Korea has made efforts to increase the proportion of women in governmental committees, and plans to increase the proportion to 30 per cent by 2002. A female public employee target system has been implemented to facilitate the recruitment of a target number of women into the public sector each year; the proportion of women employed in the public sector was 10 per cent and was planned to reach 20 per cent by 1999. Also, the Government of the Republic of Korea has been trying to provide married women with more job opportunities by increasing the number of nurseries substantially by providing tax incentives for companies operating nurseries.

Specifically, in order to support women's employment, the Government introduced the Equal Employment Act in 1988, which prohibits discrimination against women in such areas as recruitment, promotion, training and job arrangements. Following the recent economic crisis, female workers were laid off owing to gender in the process of corporate restructuring. Hence, the Government revised the Labour Standard Act in 1998, prohibiting the discharge based on sex discrimination. The Government has also been expanding job-training opportunities for women. In the Republic of Korea, the policies for increasing the female labour-force participation rate are a response to solving the expected labour shortage in the Republic of Korea.

(c) Policies on labour supply

In response to the expected labour shortage, the mismatch problem in youth labour markets, which currently leads to the high unemployment rate for

TABLE 11. ECONOMIC PARTICIPATION RATES OF FEMALES,BY MARITAL STATUS, 1981-1998

(Percentage)

	1981	1985	1990	1996	1998
Total females	42.3	41.9	47.0	48.7	47.0
Unmarried	47.7	39.5	45.6	46.0	46.0
Married	40.5	41.9	46.8	50.5	59.8

Source: National Statistical Office, *Report on Economically Active Population*, 1981-1998.

242

the younger ages, needs to be solved, although the solution cannot be a solution for the problems inherited from the change in the age structure. Vocational training needs to be modified and flexible enough to meet the needs that will be created by the expected labour shortage as well as changes in the other social and economic circumstances, such as industrial structure, employment structure, production process, technology and the education system. In addition, vocational training needs to be provided not only for youth but also for the female, the aged and the disabled.

The Government is very cautious about inviting foreign workers, fearing possible undesirable social tensions and repercussions. Economic cooperation with the Democratic People's Republic of Korea could be a positive solution for solving labour shortage problems, since workers in the Democratic People's Republic of Korea have the technical know-how as well as the disciplined spirit required for employment in labour-intensive industries. At the same time, the Government is trying to encourage investments in labour-saving technology in the hope that we can utilize the saved labour force in labour-intensive industries.

Foreign direct investment in developing countries as well as increased investment in on-the-job training of unskilled domestic workers could solve the problem of labour shortage in production workers. Therefore, the Government has adopted a system of industrial training for foreigners as a means of mitigating the lack of labour, which allows a certain number of trainees and allots them to medium-sized establishments suffering from lack of labour. The annual number of trainees has been between 10,000 and 30,000 since 1992 and there are plans to have a total number of 93,800 foreign trainees by 1998. They have been allocated to manufacturers, construction, fishery etc. (Ministry of Labour, 1999).

E. CONCLUSION

There is no doubt that the number of the elderly will increase and the absolute size of the total population will decline in the future. Although the United Nations projected the size of net immigration in the Republic of Korea assuming that the maximum size of total population in 2030 and the maximum size of working-age population in 2020 would remain constant in the future, it cannot be ensured that such maximum sizes are the most optimum in terms of the socio-economic, environmental and other factors. In other words, the criteria for projection of the numbers of net immigration should be determined taking into account all the factors to be included in addition to demographic factors.

However, experts agree that the change in population size and structure, specifically population ageing, will require an influx of foreign labour migrants to keep the national productivity that will help accommodate the promotion of quality of life for the whole population. In this context, it is worthwhile to thank the United Nations for its projection effort and suggest that the Republic of Korea pay full attention to preparations for the expected population ageing and decline. Specifically, the present occasion provides an opportunity to emphasize to policy makers that the future population policies need to be integrated with health, welfare and social security–related policies.

Since female participation in economic activity is still low in comparison with that in Western countries, the policy for increasing women's economic participation will play an important role in compensating for the expected shortage of labour, through which support for the increasing number of old persons can be facilitated. As a matter of fact, the Government of the Republic of Korea has made efforts to improve conditions for encouraging female employment; they include improvement in the area of gender discrimination in employment and increasing compatibility of women's work with child-rearing.

We should also consider the need of the Government of the Republic of Korea to adopt policies to maximize the capability of older persons to work, since the number of old persons who are healthy will continue to increase. In addition, reunification of the Republic of Korea and the Democratic People's Republic of Korea will attenuate population ageing and decline because of the decline of the working-age population. Finally, faced with the increase in a healthy old population combined with the rise in life expectancy, the Government needs to gradually effect an increase in the retirement age, which will contribute to stabilization of future health insurance and pension financing in the Republic of Korea in the long run. To reiterate, in order for the Republic of Korea to maintain and/or increase the total fertility rate, future population policy should be implemented in a manner that encompasses integration with socio-economic and welfare policies. The new population policy as adopted in 1996 was a step in the right direction. However, in order to achieve any future successes, further strengthening, as elaborated above, of the existing social security, social welfare, employment, human resource development and health promotion–related policies is essential. In addition, research studies on policy responses to population decline and population ageing should be continuously conducted, and further efforts should be directed towards making policy makers understand the importance of population policy for their success.

REFERENCES

Cho, Namhoon (1996). *Achievements and Challenges of the Population Policy Development in the Republic of Korea*. Seoul: Korea Institute for Health and Social Affairs, pp. 34-36.

_____, and Samsik Lee (1999). *Population and Development in the Republic of Korea: Focus on the ICPD Programme of Action*. Seoul: Korea Institute for Health and Social Affairs, pp. 13-30.

Ministry of Health and Welfare and Korea Institute for Health and Social Affairs (1998). *1996 Infant and Neonatal Mortality and Causes of Death*. Seoul, pp. 62-69.

Ministry of Labour (1999). *Labour White Paper*. Seoul, pp. 99-102.

National Statistical Office (1996). *Future Population Projection*. Seoul, pp. 34-52 and 61-107.

_____ (1999). *1971-1997 Life Tables for Korea*. Seoul, p. 11.

United Nations (2000). *Population Bulletin of the United Nations: Below Replacement Fertility*, Special Issue Nos. 40/41 (1999). Sales No. E.99.XIII.13.

United Nations (2001). *Replacement Migration: Is It a Solution to Declining and Ageing Populations?* Sales No. E.01.XIII.19, chap. IV, sect. B.5.

POLICY RESPONSES TO LOW FERTILITY AND POPULATION AGEING IN THE REPUBLIC OF KOREA

*Ik Ki Kim**

A. INTRODUCTION

Demographic transition in the Republic of Korea started at the beginning of the 1960s mainly owing to the interaction of rapid socio-economic development and full-scale adoption of family planning programmes (Kim, 1987). During the period of the first five-year economic development plan, 1962-1967, the gross national product (GNP) grew at an annual rate of 7.0 per cent. Since then, the economy of the Republic of Korea has consistently grown at a record high speed. The national family planning programme has been very successful since its initiation in 1962.

The crude death rate in the Republic of Korea showed a tremendously high level of 33 per thousand in 1955. Since then, the mortality level has drastically declined. The crude death rate decreased to 16 per thousand in 1960 and then to 5.3 per thousand in 1996 (Kim, 1999). In accordance with the continuous decline of the crude death rate, life expectancy at birth has consistently increased over time (Korea National Statistical Office, 1997). Life expectancy at birth in 1960 was 51.1 years for males and 57.3 years for females. Life expectancy for males increased from 57.2 years in 1970 to 69.5 years in 1996. Life expectancy for females increased from 64.1 years in 1970 to 77.4 years in 1996.

Decrease of the fertility level has also affected population ageing in the Republic of Korea. The crude birth rate in 1960 was as high as 45 per thousand. The crude birth rate declined to 23.4 in 1980 and then to 15.2 per thousand in 1996 (Kim, 1999). The total fertility rate also decreased from 6.0 in 1960 to 4.5 in 1970 and then to 2.7 in 1980. The total fertility rate in the Republic of Korea decreased to the replacement level in 1984 and has remained below the replacement level since then (Cho and Byun, 1998). The total fertility level in 1995 indicates a figure of 1.74.

The rapid process of demographic transition in the Republic of Korea has brought about an increase of both the absolute number and the proportion of the elderly. The proportion of the elderly aged 65 years or over was only 3.3 per cent in 1966; but it increased to 5.9 per cent in 1995 and is projected to increase to 19.3 per cent in 2030 (Korea National Statistical Office, 1996). According to Chung (1998), the speed of ageing of the population of the Republic of Korea is apparently faster than that of developed countries. The Republic of

---

*Dongguk University, Department of Sociology, Seoul, the Republic of Korea.

Korea, which has already experienced large declines in fertility and mortality, has a tremendous momentum for further population ageing (Kim, 1999). The projected declines in fertility and mortality will add to the momentum for even further population ageing in the Republic of Korea (Kim and others, 1996). Low fertility would eventually bring about declines in the size of population, and declines in the population of working age as well as various socio-economic problems.

The present paper investigates the demographic prospects of the Republic of Korea, in comparison with the results presented by the Population Division of the United Nations Secretariat. Then, the paper examines the possible consequences of low fertility and population ageing. Finally, the paper deals with the various policy options that the Government of the Republic of Korea could adopt to cope with the low fertility and population ageing. Different from populations of other developed countries, the population of the Republic of Korea is projected to decline after its peak in 2030. Thus, in this paper it may be more appropriate to use the term "low fertility" instead of "population decline" in figuring out the consequences and policy options of population decline and population ageing.

B. DEMOGRAPHIC PROSPECTS IN THE REPUBLIC OF KOREA, 1995-2050

Building upon the medium variant of the 1998 Revision of *World Population Prospects* (United Nations, 1999), the project of the Population Division of the United Nations Secretariat on replacement migration considers five different scenarios (United Nations, 2001). According to scenario I, the population in the Republic of Korea would increase from 44.9 million in 1995 to 53.0 million in 2030, and then decline to 51.3 million in 2050 (United Nations, 2001, table A.9). The working-age population in the Republic of Korea is projected to increase from 31.9 million in 1995 to 36.3 million in 2020, and then decrease to 30.4 million in 2050 (ibid., table A.10) The population aged 65 years or over would increase from 2.5 million in 1995 to 12.7 million in 2050. As a result of these changes, the potential support ratio, which is defined as the ratio of the population aged 15-64 years to the population aged 65 years or over, would drop from 12.6 in 1995 to 5.7 in 2020, and then to 2.4 in 2050.

Scenario II is based on the same assumptions of scenario I, but with net zero migration from 1995 through 2050. This scenario shows results similar to those of scenario I. According to scenario III, which keeps the size of the total population at the maximum level of 53.5 million in 2035, it would be necessary to have 1.5 million net immigrants between 2035 and 2050. Then, 3.2 per cent of the population in the Republic of Korea would be immigrants and their descendants in 2050. Scenario IV predicts that the Republic of Korea would need a total of 6.4 million immigrants between 2020 and 2050 in order to keep the size of the working-age population constant at its maximum of 36.6 million in 2020. Then, 13.9 per cent of the population in the Republic of Korea would be immigrants and their descendants in 2050.

Finally, scenario V predicts that it would be necessary to have a total of 5.1 billion immigrants from 1995 to 2050 in order to keep the potential support ratio at the level of 12.6 in 1995. Under this scenario, the total population in the Republic of Korea is projected to be 6.2 billion in 2050, of which 99 per cent of the population would be immigrants and their descendants. This extreme result indicates that scenario V is not realistic and thus the 1995 level of the potential support ratio would drastically change in the future.

Then, let us compare the results of the population project carried out by the Population Division with those of the Korea National Statistical Office. Table 1 illustrates major indicators of two projections on the population of the Republic of Korea. The Population Division projection is based on the assumption that the population in the Republic of Korea would change according to the levels of fertility and mortality of the medium variant of the United Nations 1998 Revision (United Nations, 2001). The Korea National Statistical Office projection uses the "cohort component method", employing the 1995 census population to set up the base population (Tae Hun Kim, 1997). The Korea National Statistical Office projection used the populations of three consecutive years (1994, 1995, 1996) for the weighted average population and then finally calculated the midyear population for the base population because the date for the census was the first of November.

The most important differences between the Population Division projection and the Korea National Statistical Office projection are in the levels of total fertility rate and net migration rate. The assumption on fertility of the Population Division projection is to keep the total fertility rate at 1.90 from 2020, whereas that of the Korea National Statistical Office is to keep the total fertility rate at 1.80 from 2020. In terms of the assumption on migration, the Population Division projection assumes no net migration after 2020. However, the Korea National Statistical Office projection predicts that the net migration rate would remain at the level of 0.5-0.6 from 1995 to 2030.

Based on the medium-variant projection, the Population Division predicts that the population in the Republic of Korea would increase from 44.9 million in 1995 to the maximum of 52.9 million in 2030, and then decrease to 51.3 million in 2050. According to the Korea National Statistical Office projection, the population in the Republic of Korea is projected to increase from 45.1 million in 1995 to 52.7 million in 2030. Using the same assumption of the Korea National Statistical Office projection, Tae Hun Kim (1997) predicts that the population in the Republic of Korea would decrease from 52.7 million in 2030 to 48.5 million in 2050.

Table 1 indicates that there are some discrepancies between the results of the Population Division projection and those of the Korea National Statistical Office projection. Let us examine the discrepancy more specifically. Table 2 shows the differences of some indicators between these two projections. First of all, total fertility rates assumed by the Population Division are higher than those of the Korea National Statistical Office from 2010. On the other hand, net migration rates predicted by the Population Division are lower than those of the Korea National Statistical Office from 2000. Based on the differences of the assumptions in respect of total fertility rate and net migration rate, the results of the two projected populations turned out to be different.

TABLE 1. MAJOR INDICATORS OF POPULATION PROJECTIONS IN THE REPUBLIC OF KOREA, 1995-2050

Indicator	Population Division of the United Nations Secretariat projection[a]							Korea National Statistical Office projection[b]						
	1995	2000	2010	2020	2030	2040	2050	1995	2000	2010	2020	2030	2040[c]	2050[c]
Total population (thousands)	44 949	46 844	49 976	51 893	52 898	52 700	51 275	45 093	47 275	50,618	52 358	52 744	51 412	48 508
Male (thousands)	22 646	23 624	25 183	26 053	26 438	26 250	25 496	22 705	23 831	25 536	26 384	26 492	..	..
Female (thousands)	22 303	23 220	24 793	25 840	26 460	26 450	25 779	22 388	23 443	25 081	25 974	26 252	..	..
Sex ratio	101.5	101.7	101.6	100.8	99.9	99.2	98.9	101.4	101.7	101.8	101.6	100.9	..	..
Potential support ratio	12.6	10.6	7.6	5.6	3.6	2.6	2.4	11.9	10.0	7.0	5.2	3.3	2.5	2.4
Age composition														
(0-14)	23.5	21.5	19.7	17.7	16.7	16.3	16.0	23.4	21.7	19.9	17.2	16.0	15.8	15.4
(15-64)	70.9	71.8	71.0	70.0	65.2	60.9	59.3	70.7	71.2	70.1	69.6	64.7	60.7	60.0
(65+)	5.6	6.7	9.3	12.3	18.1	22.8	24.7	5.9	7.1	10.0	13.2	19.3	23.5	24.6
Mean age	29.2	31.4	36.0	39.7	42.3	43.6	44.4	29.5	32.9	36.3	39.5	42.2	..	..
		1995-2000	2005-2010	2015-2020	2025-2030	2030-2040	2040-2050	1995	2000	2010	2020	2030	2040	2050
Crude birth rate		14.9	13.2	11.6	11.2	10.8	10.5	15.6	14.2	11.8	10.8	10.6	..	..
Crude death rate		6.2	7.0	8.2	9.8	11.2	13.2	5.5	5.9	7.1	8.9	10.4	..	..
Population growth rate		0.8	0.6	0.3	0.1	-0.0	-0.2	0.9	0.7	0.4	0.1	-0.0	-0.5	-0.6
Net migration rate		-0.4	-0.4	-0.2	0.0	0.0	0.0	0.6	0.6	0.5	0.6	0.6	..	..
Total fertility rate		1.7	1.8	1.9	1.9	1.9	1.9	1.7	1.7	1.7	1.8	1.8	..	..
Life expectancy at birth (both sexes)		72.4	74.5	76.3	77.8	78.7	79.6	73.5	74.9	77.0	78.1	79.0	..	..

[a]United Nations (2001), table A.9.
[b]Korea National Statistical Office (1996).
[c]Tae Hun Kim (1997), p. 173.

248

TABLE 2. DISCREPANCY OF MAJOR INDICATORS BETWEEN THE PROJECTION OF THE POPU-
LATION DIVISION OF THE UNITED NATIONS SECRETARIAT AND THE KOREA NATIONAL
STATISTICAL OFFICE PROJECTION IN THE REPUBLIC OF KOREA, 1995-2050

Indicator	1995	2000	2010	2020	2030	2040	2050
Total population (thousands)	-144	-431	-642	-465	154	1 288	2 767
Sex ratio	0.1	0.0	-0.2	-0.8	-1.0	..	..
Proportion of the elderly aged 65+	-0.3	-0.4	-0.7	-0.9	-1.2	-0.7	0.1
Potential support ratio . . .	0.68	0.69	0.62	0.42	0.25	0.09	-0.04
Population growth rate . .	..	-0.12	-0.19	-0.09	0.01	0.00	0.31
Net migration rate	..	-1.0	-1.0	-0.7	-0.6	-0.6	..
Total fertility rate	..	-0.09	0.05	0.15	0.1	0.1	..

Sources: United Nations, 2001; Korea National Statistical Office (1996); and Tae Hun Kim (1997).

NOTE: Discrepancy for each indicator is calculated on the basis of table 1 (Population Division of the United Nations Secretariat and Korea National Statistical Office).

The total populations predicted by the Population Division are lower than those predicted by the Korea National Statistical Office until 2020. Starting with 2030, however, the total populations projected by the Population Division are much higher than those predicted by the Korea National Statistical Office. The projected population in 2050 would be 51.3 million for the Population Division projection but 48.5 million for the Korea National Statistical Office (actually Kim's projection). The Korea National Statistical Office projection indicates that population decline in the Republic of Korea would be more drastic than was predicted by the Population Division.

C. CONSEQUENCES OF LOW FERTILITY AND POPULATION AGEING

The rapid process of fertility decline and population ageing due to the rapid demographic transition has substantially affected the society of the Republic of Korea. The effects of these changes, however, would be even more enormous and serious in the future. Let us examine the consequences of low fertility and population ageing in some detail. First of all, increase of the proportion of the elderly has affected both the dependency ratio and the ageing index. The dependency ratio of the population aged 65 years or over was 8.3 in 1995 and is projected to be 25.2 in 2030. The ageing index was only 29.8 in 1995 but is projected to increase to 120.6 in 2030. The ageing index indicates that in 2030 the population aged 65 years or over would be larger by 21 per cent than the population aged 0-14 (Kim, 1999).

Low fertility and population ageing have affected the size and proportion of the working-age population (15-64 years). The size of the working-age population in the Republic of Korea has consistently increased up to now and is projected to increase until 2020, and then decrease (Chang and others, 1996).

The proportion of the working-age population increased until 2000, but is projected to decrease consistently from then on. The Population Division (2001) predicts that the population of working age in the Republic of Korea would decline by 6.4 million from 1995 to 2050. Low fertility would also bring about the decline of the size of the population newly entering working age. Thus, the working-age population would be ageing accordingly.

Low fertility in the Republic of Korea has brought about the increasing imbalance in the sex ratio (Kim, 1999). Society in the Republic of Korea has a long tradition of a strong preference for boys (Kim, 1987). The tradition of son preference has become even stronger as the fertility level has declined. The sex ratio at birth increased from 105.3 in 1980 to 116.6 in 1990 (Chang and others, 1996). In 1990, the sex ratio for the fourth birth was as high as 214.1. In 2010, the sex ratio for the marriage mate is predicted to be 123.4 (Tae Hun Kim, 1997).

For the past three decades, the educational attainment of the elderly in the Republic of Korea has consistently increased. However, improvement in the educational attainment is projected to be greater for the female elderly than for the male elderly (Kim and others, 1996). The literacy rate for the female elderly in the Republic of Korea was 20 per cent in 1980 but it would increase to over 95 per cent by 2020 (Hermalin and Christenson, 1991). This change will significantly affect the role of the elderly both in the family and in the society, and will also influence the pattern of support for the elderly.

Low fertility and population ageing have affected the living arrangements of the elderly. In recent years, the proportions of the elderly of the Republic of Korea living alone or living with spouse only have greatly increased while the proportion of those living with family members has decreased (Kim and Choe, 1992). The elderly living alone suffer from serious economic problems. The fact that an increasing proportion of the elderly are living alone indicates that the tradition of strong family support is weakening. Economic difficulties are not confined only to the elderly living alone. A 1984 Republic of Korea Elderly Survey revealed that about half of the elderly aged 60 years or over had financial difficulties (Lim and others, 1985). According to a 1988 survey (Korea Gallup, 1990), the proportion of elderly respondents who reported financial difficulties was almost two thirds. The most recent survey (Chung and others, 1998) indicates that 50 per cent of the elderly of the Republic of Korea feel poor in their financial status.

Financial difficulty is a serious problem to the elderly in general. In the Republic of Korea, however, this problem is much more severe among the rural elderly because of the massive outmigration of young people from rural areas. Massive outmigration of young people from rural areas has brought about different patterns of living arrangements of the elderly in urban and rural areas (Kim, 2000). The most salient finding here is that more than half of the rural elderly live alone or live only with spouse (Kim, 2000). This is clearly related to the labour shortage due to the lack of young people in rural areas. Accordingly, the problem of labour shortage is much more serious in rural areas than in urban areas. As population ageing proceeds, this problem will even worsen.

Population ageing requires adaptation to the problem of long-term care of the elderly. As in the United States of America, the population of the elderly aged 75 years or over in the Republic of Korea has increased faster than the total population of those 65 years or over (Eustis, Greenberg and Pattern, 1984; Kim, 1999). The significance of the disproportionate increase in "old old" (as opposed to "young old") for long-term care lies in the greater prevalence of functional impairment and chronic disease among the very old. Functional impairment and the need for help can have enormous impact on the elderly and their families (Kim and Maeda, 2001).

According to a 1995 survey in the Republic of Korea (Park, 1999), the proportion of the elderly who needed long-term care owing to the impairment in ADL (activities of daily living) or IADL (instrumental activities of daily living) was 46.3 per cent. In addition, the proportion of the elderly who could not live by themselves owing to functional impairment was 5.6 per cent among the whole elderly population. Thus, in accordance with population ageing, the medical expenses for the elderly have drastically increased. From 1985 to 1996, the medical expenses for the total population increased 12.7 times, whereas those for the elderly population increased 35.5 times (Park, 1999).

Despite the fact that the absolute number and proportion of the elderly have increased, the proportion of the welfare services for the elderly in the Republic of Korea has rather decreased in recent years (Kim, 1999). The role of the Government in the provision of welfare services for the elderly will be more limited as the elderly population continuously increases. In this situation, the family should continuously take part in the care of the elderly. Most people in the Republic of Korea take it for granted that they will receive support from their own children. Contrary to their expectations, however, there are many circumstances under which such support is not available from their children owing to the recent socio-economic changes (Kim, 1999). It is really a dilemma whether the elderly should be taken care of by the family or by the Government.

Pension is another serious issue as a consequence of population ageing. A population projection suggests that the pension system in the Republic of Korea would encounter operating deficits soon after it became fully functional, requiring an increase in contribution rates, government support from tax revenues, or both (Westley, 1998). Chung (1998) predicts that if the national pension system in the Republic of Korea continues to be operated the way it is currently, the reserve fund would be exhausted by the year 2033.

D.   POLICY OPTIONS WITH LOW FERTILITY AND POPULATION AGEING

In section C, this paper examined various consequences of low fertility and population ageing in the Republic of Korea. As the Population Division (2001) argued, fertility would not recover sufficiently to reach the replacement level and thus population ageing would be a continuous phenomenon in the foreseeable future. In accordance with this argument, the Population Division (2000, chap. I, thirteenth para.) suggests that, among the demographic variables, only international migration could be instrumental in addressing population decline and population ageing in the short to medium term.

According to scenario IV of the Population Division (2001), which involves keeping the working-age group (15-64 years) constant, the Republic of Korea would need 6.4 million immigrants from 1995 to 2050. Then, would replacement migration be the only possible and acceptable policy in coping with the population decline and population ageing in the Republic of Korea? If not, what would be other policy options available to solve these problems? The present section examines the acceptability of adopting a new immigration policy in the Republic of Korea and explores some policy options that the Government of the Republic of Korea has adopted or will adopt in coping with low fertility and population ageing.

First and foremost, large volumes of immigrants (for instance, 6.4 million) would confront serious social and political objections in the Republic of Korea. The Republic of Korea has traditionally been a uniracial country for the past 5,000 years. In terms of the immigration policy, the Republic of Korea has been a sending, not a receiving, country. Thus, adopting a new immigration policy would entail facing many difficulties. Up to now, the immigration law of the Republic of Korea has continuously restricted the admission of new foreign workers to even a few categories. Legal status was offered only to those who would be employed in reporting, technology transfer, business, capital investment, education and research, or entertainment, or for employment that had been recommended by a government minister (Abella and Park, 1995). Unskilled foreign labour was not allowed to enter, but trainees were allowed to enter the Republic of Korea.

Over the last few years, however, a large number of unskilled foreign workers have entered the Republic of Korea for the purpose of employment because of the shortage of labour in certain occupations. They have grown from a few thousand in the early 1980s to current estimates of 168,000 in 1999 (Korea Bureau of Medium-sized Industries, 1999). Of that number, 65 per cent of workers are working illegally. Because of their illegal status, most of the illegal workers (overstayers) receive smaller wages and worse benefits than workers of the Republic of Korea and they also face many problems of human rights. The problems caused by immigration would be much more complicated than those of foreign workers who temporarily stay in the Republic of Korea. Immigration in sufficient numbers to fill up the labour shortage due to low fertility and population ageing would also arouse fears of loss of national identity (United Nations, 2001). Thus, the adoption of a new immigration policy in the Republic of Korea may not be the best policy option for coping with the labour shortage in the short run.

The Government of the Republic of Korea launched a full-scale national family planning programme in 1962. Since then, the national family planning programmes in accordance with the rapid socio-economic development have been very effective in controlling the record high fertility (Kim, 1987). The Republic of Korea has been known to be one of the most successful countries in regard to adopting national family planning programmes. The total fertility rate in the Republic of Korea reached the replacement level in 1984. Since then, the total fertility rate in the Republic of Korea has remained at the below-replacement level.

The low fertility has brought about many problems, such as population ageing, a labour shortage and imbalance of the sex ratio. Confronted with new population problems, the Government of the Republic of Korea changed the direction of the family planning programme from the quantitative control of population to the qualitative consideration of population. In 1966, the Government of the Republic of Korea officially announced the adoption of "the new population policy", which focuses on the quality of life and welfare for the population of the Republic of Korea (Chang and others, 1996).

Cho and Byun (1988, p. 8) identified the goals of the new population policy as follows: (a) to maintain the below-replacement level of fertility and to improve morbidity and mortality levels as part of the process of achieving sustainable socio-economic development; (b) to enhance family health and welfare; (c) to prevent the imbalance of sex ratios at birth and to reduce the incidence of induced abortions; (d) to tackle the sex-related problems of the youth and adolescents; (e) to empower women by expanding employment opportunities and welfare services for them; and (f) to improve work opportunities and provide adequate health care and welfare services for the elderly.

Among the goals of the new population policy, the first and the most important policy is to keep the below-replacement level of fertility. Actually, return to the high fertility of the 1960s is not desirable and most unlikely. However, population ageing due to a below-replacement level of fertility causes rapid changes in age structure and brings about new perspectives concerning the welfare of the whole population. Thus, in the Republic of Korea the challenge for policy development is to put in place adaptive mechanisms that will allow the society of the Republic of Korea to prosper over the long run (Teitelbaum, 2000).

As mentioned above, the actual goals of the new population policy in the Republic of Korea are related to the adaptive mechanisms. Among the adaptive mechanisms, improving work opportunities is one of the important goals of the new population policy. The Republic of Korea Ministry of Health and Welfare announced the adoption of the general policy for the welfare of the elderly in 1995 and suggested five measures in terms of the enlargement of the work opportunities for the elderly (Park, 1999, pp. 45-46).

The five measures for improving work opportunities are as follows: (a) to develop and enlarge the appropriate work opportunities for the elderly; (b) to prolong the retirement age and to abolish the age limitation for newly employed workers; (c) to make public the necessity of providing job activities for the elderly; (d) to activate the support system for the organizations introducing work opportunities to the elderly; and (e) to establish and enlarge the joint workplace for the elderly.

The retirement system is important not only for ensuring the stable lives of the elderly but also for controlling the problems of labour shortage. The Government of the Republic of Korea introduced the compulsory retirement system for government officers in 1963 (Yoo, 1999). Under the current system, most government workers are to retire as early as 60 years of age, with the exception of professional government workers like teachers (62 years of age) and professors (65 years of age). The situation of workers in the private sector is even worse than that of government workers. About 65 per cent of the employees working in the private industries retire at age 55 (Yoo, 1999). According to a national survey (Rhee and others, 1994), most of the elderly of the Republic of Korea (79.9 per cent) want to remain in the workplace as long as possible. Prolongation of the retirement age may thus be indispensable not only for the welfare of the elderly but also as a supplement for the labour shortage due to population decline.

Then, what is the most appropriate retirement age in the Republic of Korea? According to the project on replacement migration by the Population Division (2001), the upper limit of the working age needed in order to obtain in 2050 the potential support ratio observed in 1995 would be 82.2 years in the absence of migration. This number, however, seems to be unrealistic. According to a national survey (Rhee and others, 1994), 24.8 per cent of the elderly respondents believed that the existing compulsory retirement system should be abolished. At this point, it may be difficult to set a certain age as the appropriate age. Instead, the retirement age should be flexible depending upon the health condition and ability of the elderly.

In order to fill up the labour shortage in the future, the Government of the Republic of Korea should provide more opportunities for female participation in the labour force. Although the employment of women has grown much faster than the growth of employment of men since 1985, the proportion of women who are currently working is still much smaller than that of men (Abella and Park, 1995). According to the 1998 the *Korea Statistical Yearbook* (Korea National Statistical Office, 1998), the labour-force participation rate for males who are aged 15 years or over was 75.6 in 1997. On the other hand, the labour-force participation rate for females who were aged 15 years or over was only 49.5 per cent.

To facilitate female labour-force participation, the society of the Republic of Korea should establish better infrastructure and environment for female workers. Infrastructure and environment for female workers should include not only institutional reform such as equal opportunities for both sexes but also provision of hardware such as childcare facilities at work. In the Republic of Korea, there has traditionally been severe sex discrimination both in society and at home. Especially at the workplace, there has been sex discrimination in recruiting new employees, providing benefits and salary, and discharging from work etc. Sex discrimination in all these areas should be abolished.

In addition, firms should assume some roles that allow them to cope with the labour shortage in the future. Abella and Park (1995) suggest that firms take short-run adjustments and long-run adjustments. Specific measures for these adjustments are as follows. For the short-run adjustments: (*a*) make more intensive use of the regular workforce through overtime; (*b*) employ part-time workers, labour contractors or foreign workers; and (*c*) cut down on operations and reduce output. For the long-run adjustments: (*a*) raise wages/offer other incentives for workers to stay; (*b*) improve working environment and conditions; (*c*) adopt labour-saving technology/automate operations; (*d*) shift to less labour-intensive product lines; and (e) relocate factories to places/countries where labour is more abundant.

Finally, policy options in relation to low fertility and population ageing should centre on the welfare of the elderly. In the Republic of Korea, women—specifically the wife of the first son—have traditionally taken care of the elderly. However, the increase in the labour-force participation of women has diminished the role of women in the support of the elderly. A greater increase in women's labour-force participation in the future for the purpose of reducing the labour shortage would seriously affect the support system for the elderly.

Furthermore, long-term care has emerged as a salient issue because of a rapidly growing population in need, dramatically increasing health-care costs for the impaired elderly, and the progressively smaller ability to pay for long-term care on an individual basis because of rising medical costs (Kim and Maeda, 2000). Thus, it is expected that the majority of the elderly would have increasing difficulties in obtaining care services at home. A significant policy issue is whether the supply of medical personnel and facilities—more importantly, expenditures in the future—would be sufficient to care for the frail elderly and whether alternatives to institutionalization would assist in meeting their needs.

The emergence of this problem is reflected in the rising demand for social welfare for the elderly and increasing the Government's responsibility to support the elderly. It is a challenge for the Government to develop appropriate and effective programmes to provide needed services for the elderly. As mentioned above, however, the role of the Government of the Republic of Korea must be limited in providing full services for the elderly. Thus, the Republic of Korea should mobilize all the resources of government, industries, communities and families to meet this challenge.

E. CONCLUDING REMARKS

The Republic of Korea has experienced a very rapid process of declining fertility and thus population ageing since the beginning of the 1960s. Because of this trend, both the Population Division and the Korea National Statistical Office predict that the population of working age in the Republic of Korea will drastically decrease from 1995 to 2050. In connection with the drastic decline of the labour force, the Population Division suggests that accepting immigrants would be the only acceptable policy to cope with the labour shortage due to the low fertility. The Republic of Korea entered the stage of a below-replacement level of fertility in 1984. Since then, the total fertility rate has remained at the below-replacement level. So far, the rapid process of fertility decline and population ageing has substantially affected the society of the Republic of Korea and will affect the society of the Republic of Korea to a great extent in the future.

Low fertility has brought about various new population problems. Thus, in 1966 the Government of the Republic of Korea officially adopted the new population policy, which focuses on the quality of life rather than population control. One of the most important goals of the new population policy is to maintain the below-replacement level of fertility. However, keeping the below-replacement level of fertility would accelerate the process of population ageing. In conjunction with low fertility and population ageing, various adaptive mechanisms would be necessary, especially to reduce the labour shortage. Adopting a new immigration policy that entailed accepting a significant number of immigrants into the Republic of Korea may not be indicated for the time being. In the long run, however, a new immigration policy would be indispensable if the below-replacement level of fertility continued without limit.

REFERENCES

Abella, Manolo I., and Young-bum Park (1995). Labour shortages and foreign workers in small firms of the Republic of Korea. In *Adjustments to Labour Shortages and Foreign Workers in the Republic of Korea*, Manolo I. Abella, Young-bum Park and W. R. Bohning, eds. Geneva: International Labour Office, pp. 1-18.

Chang, Young Sik, and others (1996). *Population Size, Structural Change and Policy Questions Depending on the New Population Projection* (in Korean). Seoul: Korea Institute for Health and Social Affairs.

Cho, Nam-Hoon, and Young-Chan Byun (1998). New challenges of population policy development in Korea. Paper presented at the International Symposium on Population and Development Policies in Low-fertility Countries. Korea Institute for Health and Social Affairs, Seoul.

Chung, Kyunghee (1998). Ageing and social welfare policies: health-care and income maintenance programmes. Paper presented at the International Symposium on Population and Development Policies in Low-fertility Countries. Korea Institute for Health and Social Affairs.

_____, and others (1998). *National Survey of Living Conditions and Welfare Needs of Older Persons*. Seoul: Korea Institute for Health and Social Affairs.

Eustis, N., J. Greenberg and S. Pattern (1984). *Long-term Care for Older Persons: A Policy Perspective*. Monterey, California: Brooks/Cole Publishing Co.

Hermalin, Albert I., and B. A. Christenson (1991). Comparative analysis of the changing educational composition of the elderly population in five Asian countries: a preliminary report. Population Studies Center Research Report, No. 91-11. Ann Arbor: University of Michigan Population Studies Center.

Kim, Ik Ki (1987). *Socioeconomic Development and Fertility Behavior in Korea*. Seoul: Population and Development Studies Center, Seoul National University.

_____ (1999). Population aging in Korea: social problems and solutions. *Journal of Sociology and Social Welfare* (Kalamazoo, Michigan), vol. 24, No. 1, pp. 107-123.

_____ (2000). Different patterns of the living arrangements of the elderly in urban and rural Korea. Paper presented at the annual meeting of the Population Association of Japan, Tokyo, Waseda University, 2 and 3 June.

_____, and Ehn H. Choe (1992). Support exchange patterns of the elderly in Korea. *Asia-Pacific Population Journal* (Bangkok), vol. 7, No. 3, pp. 89-104.

_____, and others (1996). Population aging in Korea: changes since the 1960s. *Journal of Cross-Cultural Gerontology* (Boston, Massachusetts), vol. 11, pp. 369-388.

_____, and Daisaku Maeda (2001). A comparative study on sociodemographic changes and long-term care needs of the elderly in Japan and South Korea. *Journal of Cross-Cultural Gerontology* (Boston, Massachusetts), vol. 16, No. 3, pp. 237-255.

Kim, Tae Hun (1997). Population prospects and social effects. In *Understanding of Fertility Transition in Korea* (in Korean), Tae Hwan Kwon and others, eds. Seoul: Ilsin Publishing Company.

Korea Bureau of Medium-sized Industries (1999). Report to the Korean National Assembly (in Korean). March.

Korea Gallup (1990). *Lifestyle and Value of the Aged in Korea* (in Korean). Seoul: Korea Gallup.

Korea National Statistical Office (1996). *Population Projection* (in Korean). Daejeon, Republic of Korea.

_____ (1997). *Korea Statistical Yearbook*. Daejeon, Republic of Korea.

_____ (1998). *Korea Statistical Yearbook*. Daejeon, Republic of Korea.

Lim, Jong Kwon, and others (1985). *A Study on the Aged Population in Korea* (in Korean). Seoul: Korea Institute for Population and Health.

Park, Kwang Jun (1999). Ageing society and social policy. In *Ageing Society and Welfare for the Elderly* (in Korean), Kwang Jun Park and others, eds. Seoul: Sejong Publishing Company, pp. 25-47.

Rhee, Ka Oak, and others (1994). *Analysis of Life Conditions of the Elderly and Policy Questions* (in Korean). Seoul: Korea Institute for Health and Social Affairs.

Teitelbaum, Michael (2000). Sustained below-replacement fertility: realities and responses. *Population Bulletin of the United Nations: Below Replacement Fertility*, Special Issue Nos. 40/41 (1999), pp. 161-182. Sales No. E.99.XIII.13. New York: United Nations.

United Nations (1999). *World Population Prospects: The 1998 Revision*, vol. I, *Comprehensive Tables*. Sales No. E.99.XIII.9.

_____ (2001). *Below Replacement Fertility*. Population Bulletin of the United Nations.

_____ (2001). *Replacement Migration: Is It a Solution to Declining and Ageing Populations?* Sales No. E.01.XIII.19.

Westley, Sidney B. (1998). Asia's next challenge: caring for the elderly. *Asia-Pacific Population and Policy* (Honolulu, Hawaii), No. 45 (April).

Yoo, Seong-Ho (1999). The economic status of the aged and income security programmes for the aged in Korea. *Ageing in Korea: Today and Tomorrow* (Seoul), pp. 67-82.

POPULATION DECLINE AND POPULATION AGEING IN THE RUSSIAN FEDERATION

*Svetlana V. Nikitina**

During recent years, the demographic situation in the Russian Federation has become a topic of great concern on the part both of the government authorities of the Russian Federation and of the mass media. The parliamentary hearings "On the demographic situation in the Russian Federation and the measures of the Government of the Russian Federation with respect to its optimization" were held in the State Duma in 2000. The President of the Russian Federation, Vladimir Putin, began his first message to the Federal Assembly with the evaluation of the demographic situation. The Internet panel on the demographic problems of the Russian Federation was held in the Press Centre of the Russian Government in July 2000. The leading Russian demographers took part in the meeting. The individual questions sent via the Internet demonstrated the growing public interest in the demographic problems of the Russian Federation.

The increasing crisis phenomena within the demographic development of the Russian Federation have forced the Russian Government to take into account the estimations and projections of experts and scientists and, when developing the main directions of the long-term socio-economic policy of the Government of the Russian Federation, to take into consideration the fact that these are the demographic processes underlying many long-term tendencies within the socio-economic development of the country.

A. DEMOGRAPHIC SITUATION IN THE RUSSIAN FEDERATION AND ITS POSSIBLE FURTHER DEVELOPMENT

By early 2000, the resident population of the Russian Federation was 145.6 million people (see figure I). During 1999, the number of Russians was reduced by 768,400 people or by 0.5 per cent. It is the most considerable figure of the annual decrease during the whole depopulation period which started in 1992. During the past eight years, the population of the Russian Federation decreased by 2.8 million or by 2 per cent.

Natural population loss is the main depopulation factor; it is stable and long-term by nature. In 1999, the number of deaths exceeded the number of births by 929,600 people or by a factor of 1.8. The total natural loss for the past eight years reached 5.9 million people.

---

*State Committee of the Russian Federation on Statistics.

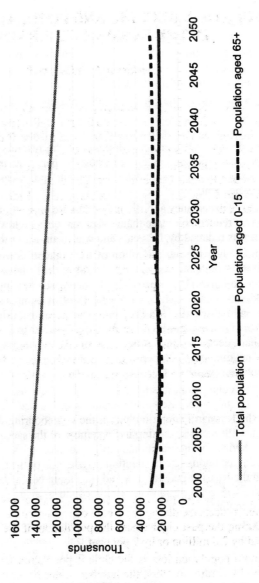

Figure I. Population of the Russian Federation
(Goskomstat of the Russian Federation: projections)

Total population ——— Population aged 0-15 ——— ----- Population aged 65+

The most dramatic problem of the contemporary demographic development of the Russian Federation is the high level of mortality. Some easing of the negative aspects within the mortality situation development in 1995-1998 was short-term. In many respects, it was caused by the age changes in the population structure, and the decrease in the number of deaths due to accidents, poisonings and injuries, and also to diseases of the circulatory system, that is to say, the causes of the excessive rise of mortality observed in the early 1990s.

In 1999, the number of deaths increased by 8 per cent as compared with 1998. Thus, the crude death rate for the population of the Russian Federation (the number of deaths per 1,000 persons) increased from 13.6 to 14.7 (it was higher only in 1994 and 1995, at 15.7 and 15.0, respectively).

This increase is due equally to all main causes of death and is observed in all locations.

The largest increase in mortality in 1999 was caused by infectious and parasitic diseases: 29 per cent; diseases of the respiratory system: 13.5 per cent; accidents, poisonings and injuries: 10 per cent; transport injuries and homicides: 14 per cent; suicides: 11 per cent; and diseases of the circulatory system: 9 per cent.

The life expectancy at birth in 1999 for the population of the Russian Federation was reduced by more than 1 year and became lower than 66 years (for males, it was reduced by 1.5 years and was again lower than 60 years).

Since 1992, the net migration of the population from foreign countries (mainly from the Commonwealth of Independent States (CIS) countries and the Baltic countries) has constrained the decrease of the population of the Russian Federation. As a whole, for 1992-1999, it compensated for the natural population loss by half. However, in the past year, net migration decreased almost by half as compared with 1998 (from 284,700 to 154,600 people) owing to the sharp decline in the number of persons arriving in the Russian Federation and net migration compensated for only 16.7 per cent of the natural loss of the population (in 1998, 41 per cent; in 1994, 93 per cent) (see figure II).

In this connection, it is necessary to note the sensitive and rapid reaction of the migration processes to the changes in the socio-economic conditions both in the Russian Federation and in the neighbouring countries. Following the August 1998 crisis, starting in September of the same year, the number of persons leaving for the traditional emigration countries began to increase to a marked degree (alongside the continued reduction of the number of persons arriving in the Russian Federation), and starting in November, the number leaving for the CIS countries and the Baltic countries also began to increase. This tendency continued till June 1999.

In 1999, 85,000 inhabitants of the Russian Federation left to go far abroad (foreign countries excluding CIS and the Baltic countries). In 1998, the figure was 80,000 people. As previously, about 90 per cent of the emigrants departed for Germany, Israel and the United States of America. The most considerable increase was in the number of Russian citizens leaving for Israel (from 12,800 to 20,000 people). At the same time, the number of immigrants to the Russian Federation from far abroad was reduced from 18,700 to 13,100 people. More than 50 per cent of the immigrants were former inhabitants of China (3,900

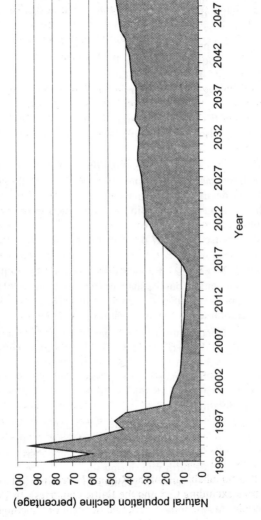

Figure II. Replacement migration
(Goskomstat of the Russian Federation: projections)

people or 39.8 per cent), Germany (1,900 or 14.5 per cent) or Israel (1,400 or 10.7 per cent).

The largest migration exchange is still observed between Russia and the successor States of the Union of Soviet Socialist Republics. Annually, about 95 per cent of persons arriving and 60 per cent of persons leaving come from these countries.

The demographic indicators for 2000 fix the continuation of the negative tendencies. During the first eight months of 2000, the number of inhabitants of the Russian Federation decreased by 507,400 people or by 0.3 per cent (for the same period of 1999, by 0.4 per cent).

According to the projection of the State Committee of the Russian Federation on Statistics (Goskomstat of the Russian Federation) produced for the period extending until 2016, the population of the Russian Federation will continue to decrease during all of the forecast period. The positive net migration will not compensate for the natural decline of the population. By 2016, the size of the resident population of the Russian Federation will be 134 million people, having decreased by 11.6 million people or by 8 per cent as compared with the beginning of 2000.

The share of the working-age population (males, 16-59 years; females, 16-54 years) will increase slightly from 59.3 per cent in 2000 to 63.6 per cent in 2007, and then decline to 59.7 per cent by 2016. At the same time, the structure of the working-age population will undergo significant changes. The share of the population aged 45 years or over within the total working-age population will increase from 25.7 per cent at the beginning of 2000 to 30 per cent in 2016.

Not only will the process of population ageing influence the structure of the working-age population, but the share of the population of older age groups within the total population will also increase. By 2016, each fifth inhabitant of the Russian Federation will be aged 60 years or over.

The potential support ratio (the number of persons of working age per person past working age) will decline from 3 at the beginning of 2000 to 2.3 by 2016. However, the cumulative potential support ratio (the number of persons of working age per children and persons past working age) by 2016 would not exceed the level of 2000 (1.5), owing to the decline of the share of children within the total population.

Thus, the expected tendencies of the demographic development of the Russian Federation forecast by the Goskomstat of the Russian Federation—decline in the population, decrease in net migration, some increase in the number of births and in the crude birth rate during the first 10 years of the forecast period (owing to the increase in the number of women aged 20-29 with the highest level of childbearing till 2008), decline in the infant mortality rate and increase in life expectancy at birth—correspond as a whole to the projection of the Population Division of the United Nations Secretariat (see table). However, owing to the recent tendencies within the demographic development of the Russian Federation, the projection of the Population Division of the United Nations Secretariat is likely to be too optimistic.

MEDIUM-VARIANT PROJECTIONS BY THE GOSKOMSTAT OF THE RUSSIAN FEDERATION AS COMPARED WITH
THE PROJECTION BY THE POPULATION DIVISION OF THE UNITED NATIONS SECRETARIAT

	Population Division of the United Nations Secretariat: projections			Goskomstat of the Russian Federation: projections		
	2000-2005	2005-2010	2010-2015	2000-2005	2005-2010	2010-2015
Births per year (thousands)	1 522	1 610	1 533	1 280	1 309	1 202
Deaths per year (thousands)	2 098	2 041	1 982	2 079	2 066	2 039
Net migration per year (thousands)	299	204	154	105	73	65
Crude birth rate (per 1,000 population)	10.4	11.1	10.7	9.0	9.3	8.8
Crude death rate (per 1,000 population)	14.3	14.1	13.8	14.5	14.8	15.0
Total fertility rate (per woman)	1.38	1.45	1.52	1.19	1.17	1.16
Infant mortality rate (per 1,000 births)	18	16	15	18.3	16.8	15.4
Life expectancy at birth (years)						
Males	61.3	63.3	65.3	61.3	62.3	63.4
Females	73.2	74.2	75.2	73.2	74.2	75.1
Both sexes combined	67.1	68.7	70.3	67.1	68.1	69.1

Sources: World Population Prospects: The 1998 Revision, vol. I, Comprehensive Tables (United Nations publication, Sales No. E.99.XIII.9); and Goskomstat of the Russian Federation, Population of the Russian Federation till 2016 (Moscow, 1999).

The assumptions concerning the probable future trends in fertility, mortality and migration were developed by the Goskomstat of the Russian Federation based on the present demographic tendencies, prospects of the socio-economic development of the Russian Federation and the health status of the population.

Some years into the future, the consequences of the socio-economic crisis along with the changes in the reproductive behaviour of the population will have an effect on the level of fertility in the Russian Federation. According to sociological surveys, the uncertain future is one of the reasons for the child-birth delay.

Also, during recent years, a deterioration of the reproductive health of women has been observed. During the last 10 years, the prevalence of anaemia among pregnant women has grown more than six times, the number of late toxicoses has increased by 40 per cent, and the number of normal childbirths has been sharply reduced to 32 per cent (in some territories of the Russian Federation, to 25 per cent). Approximately 15 per cent of married couples in Russia are sterile, and 50-60 per cent of these cases are the result of female sterility.

The health status of girls reaching the childbearing age is also unfavourable. The frequency of gynaecologic diseases among female teenagers negatively impacting on the reproductive functions has increased sharply during the last five years.

The Russian fertility model will resemble more and more the Western European one. Currently, the relative proximity of the values of the total fertility rate in the Russian Federation and in the Western countries is combined with considerable differences in the age-specific birth rate, mean age of women at childbearing and other special indicators of fertility.

The future dynamics of mortality depend on the quality of life, the health status of the population and health services. The assumptions of mortality up to 2016 were based on the considerable worsening of the health of the population of the Russian Federation, first of all that of children. The general sick rate among children under age 14 has increased by almost 10 per cent during the last five years. Approximately 50 per cent of teenagers aged 15-17 suffer from chronic diseases.

According to sociological research, more than 2.5 million Russian citizens use drugs on a regular basis, 76 per cent of whom are young people under age 30.

Based on the above, the Goskomstat of the Russian Federation forecasts a slower increase of life expectancy at birth than does the Population Division of the United Nations Secretariat. The process of ageing of the population of the Russian Federation will cause an increase of the crude death rate during the forecast period.

The projection of the migration to the Russian Federation from the CIS countries and the Baltic countries developed by the Goskomstat of the Russian Federation is based on the combined assumption of "the stable Russian-speaking diaspora" for Belarus, Ukraine, the Baltic countries and the Republic of Moldova and of "the slow repatriation" for the remaining CIS countries.

It is supposed that migration far abroad will continue to be an ethnic one. Its dynamics are connected with the decline in the number of ethnic Germans and Jews living in the Russian Federation. The volumes of illegal migration were not taken into consideration owing to the fact that for most of the immigrants concerned, the Russian Federation is attractive only as a country where one can legalize one's status and make ready for departure to the economically developed Western countries (the estimated number of such immigrants is 700,000–1.5 million).

The decrease in net migration during the projection period has several causes, inter alia, the decline of the migration potential in both the CIS countries and the Baltic countries, owing to the decline and ageing of the Russian-speaking diaspora and the unattractiveness of the Russian Federation for potential migrants owing to the material difficulties of settling in this country.

In the long term, the role of migration will increase. Despite some forecast increase in the level of fertility in the Russian Federation (total fertility rate (TFR) in 2050, 1.7) and the decrease in the mortality of the population, especially in working age (the life expectancy at birth in 2050 would be, for males, 68 years, and for females, 77 years), international migration will continue to be the main factor constraining the depopulation process. By the middle of the next century, the population of the Russian Federation, according to the projection by the Goskomstat of Russia, will be 114 million people. The forecast total number of net immigrants will be 12 million people between 2000 and 2050.

B. SOCIO-ECONOMIC CONSEQUENCES OF POPULATION DECLINE AND POPULATION AGEING IN THE RUSSIAN FEDERATION

One of the main problems connected with depopulation for the Russian Federation with its huge territory and low density of population is the decline of its geopolitical position in the world. During the next few decades, population decline in the Russian Federation will take place in parallel with the growth of the population of most neighbouring countries. This could exert very strong migration pressure on the Russian Federation and probably cause attempts at territorial expansion.

The most urgent problem for the economy of the Russian Federation caused by population ageing will be the rising pressure on the government budget and the more urgent necessity of financing the pension and social security systems.

In the Russian Federation, the government pension system fails to provide a somewhat normal standard of living for elderly people. Despite the measures intended to increase pensions, the mean size of the pensions provided is still below the cost of living of pensioners. Even the improvement of the economic situation would not necessarily increase the pension fund contributions to a marked degree because, according to the Goskomstat projection, the number of working-age persons who are the main tax bearers will start to decrease beginning in 2006. The absence of integrated reforms will cause in the long-term perspective a dangerous aggravation of the financial status of the pension system which will take place under the influence of the gradual ageing of the population of the Russian Federation.

The increase of the number of old persons will create a demand for the development of social support services for lonely elderly people and expansion of the network of old people's homes and boarding houses. Currently, these institutions in the Russian Federation experience serious problems with respect to material and personnel maintenance.

The changes in the age structure of the population will also create problems for the public-health system. The increase of the share of elderly persons with greater needs in respect of medical treatment will place a heavier load on the medical establishments. The latter will require the reorganization of the public-health system for the purpose of improving geriatric help. For all age groups, it is necessary to improve information on health, including reproductive health and nutrition, because the health of old persons depends both on the quality of the rendered medical services and living conditions and on the status of health during the young years.

The process of population ageing will influence the economy through the pressure on the government budget but it can also entail changes in the economic behaviour of the labour force. The increase in the share of the older age groups in the working-age population can influence the capability of the labour force to perceive innovations in the world of high technologies.

C. Measures that the Government can undertake in order to improve the existing situation

The topic of conducting demographic policy with specific targets causes serious disputes during discussions of the demographic situation.

1. *Fertility*

Most Russian demographers think that fertility in the Russian Federation cannot be increased by any government measures and that the model of a family with one or two children is the final choice for the population of the Russian Federation. They usually argue that the total fertility rate in the developed European countries is below the replacement level despite the high standard of living of the population and the efforts of the Governments of these countries.

In fact, the demographic development of the Russian Federation is similar to that of the Western European countries. However, while the decrease of the fertility in the developed countries is the objective result of the demographic transition, the changes in the reproductive behaviour of the population of the Russian Federation were considerably speeded up and stimulated by the interference of the State. The rapid industrialization of the Soviet era with its total involvement of all working-age women in public production and the liquidation of the social class of housewives, and the prevalence of the two-income family, naturally contributed to the decline of fertility and to the unstable family. In the late 1990s, the decline of the family lifestyle under the conditions of the long-term economic crisis resulted in the opinion that the birth of children was an obstacle to achieving an acceptable standard of well-being. According to a number of sociodemographic surveys, the typical orientation of the majority of the population with their one-child families towards the material side of well-being made them even consider all living conditions insufficient for bringing a second child into the family. The mass psychology of following the normative model of a family with one or two children makes people condemn any other behaviour as interfering with the quality of the generally accepted, mainly material requirements for bringing up and supporting children in a family.

Besides the conscious refusal of the birth of children, approximately 20 per cent of Russian families are really compelled to put aside the birth of a child owing to difficult living conditions.

As a result of all these processes, the Russian Federation is characterized by an extremely low level of fertility even by the standards of the developed countries.

The draft concept of the demographic policy developed by the Ministry of Labour and Social Development of the Russian Federation points out each family's right to define for itself the desirable number of children along with the right of the State to stimulate those types of family that correspond to the targets of the demographic policy of the Russian Federation.

The above-mentioned draft concept notes that in order to increase the level of fertility, it is necessary to provide families with a standard of living enabling them to bring up several children. In the new economic situation, the systems of privileges and compensations in the field of taxation, credit etc. should create the most favourable conditions for the normal life of a family with several children. It is necessary also to assist the family in the realization of its own potential. Moreover, it is necessary to create an information system for the promotion of family values.

Thus, a special family policy aimed at the revival and strengthening of the family as a social institution will promote the increase of fertility. Even if the replacement level is not attained, at all events, family policy should raise fertility up to the level of the developed countries with the highest birth rates. This scenario for fertility was incorporated in the high-variant projection by the Goskomstat of the Russian Federation and it corresponds to the basis for fertility designed for the medium-variant projection for the Russian Federation by the Population Division of the United Nations Secretariat.

2. *Mortality*

Another source of decrease of the depopulation rate in the Russian Federation is the preservation of the life of the generations already living.

In the Russian Federation, the most vital problem is the high level of premature mortality of the population. In 1999, 580,000 Russians of working age died, constituting 27 per cent of all deaths. The main causes of the mortality of the working-age population are accidents, poisonings and injuries.

There is still a high level of maternal mortality which in the Russian Federation is several times as high as in the economically developed European countries.

The low level of reproductive health of women constrains to some extent the decrease of infant mortality because the main causes of infant mortality are closely connected with the health of the mother, and each third child is born with a pathology.

In the Russian Federation, as well as in the other republics of the former Union of Soviet Socialist Republics, after the progress achieved in resisting infectious diseases, since the mid-1960s the centralized State system of public-health services has failed to counter effectively the predominance of the diseases of endogenous character more typical of people of older ages, namely, the diseases of the blood and circulatory system and the endocrine system, neoplasms etc. Only by itself, the improvement of the coverage of the population with medical care, without the radical improvement of its quality and without the broad introduction into practice of new medical technologies, could not generate further progress in resisting mortality.

The transition to a market economy has demonstrated the existing problems still more. The accumulation of the unfavourable changes in public health during the previous decades, combined with the decline in the standard of living of the population under the unsatisfactory conditions of the social sphere and basic medicine, the inaccessibility of highly effective means of medical treatment for the majority of the population, ecological troubles and the rise in crime, has aggravated the mortality situation in the Russian Federation.

The problems listed in the concept of the development of public-health services and medical science in the Russian Federation should be among the priority ones addressed when implementing government measures aimed at improving the health of the nation.

The main target can be achieved by solving a number of problems. This would include changes in the approaches to the formation of public-health policy, and to the evaluation of the contribution of public-health services to the national economy; the improvement of the public-health services management system; the creation of an effective economic basis for public-health services and for stimulating the maintenance of personal health; the improvement of the organization of the system of the differentiated provision of medical and pharmaceutical services; State support of the domestic medical industry; the development of the sciences in every possible way as a guarantor of the success of the intended transformations; the solution of personnel problems taking into account the contemporary needs of industry; and the maximum extension of the social basis of public-health services.

Now, it is clear that the State cannot immediately invest considerable financial resources in the health of the nation even in the event of economic growth. If the financing of the public-health system is not adequate, the effective measures can be the ones aimed at changes in the behaviour of people concerning their health: training, informing through the mass media about risk factors, a specific fiscal policy within the alcohol and tobacco markets along with simultaneous stricter control of product quality.

One can expect a decrease in the mortality of the population in the event of an improvement in living conditions, the active formation of healthy life-styles of the general public and maintenance of the psycho-emotional and material well-being over a long period of time.

According to the high-level version of the population projection by the Goskomstat of the Russian Federation, such a policy could allow saving the lives of 200,000-250,000 people annually.

3. External migration

Currently, migration is the only real source of population increase in this country. By the estimate of the Population Division of the United Nations Secretariat, the Russian Federation needs about 500,000 immigrants annually in order to preserve an invariable population size during the next 50 years. The total volume of net migration between 2000 and 2050 will be approximately 25 million people (by the estimate of the Goskomstat of the Russian Federation, 45 million people). The publication on replacement migration issued by the Population Division of the United Nations Secretariat (United Nations, 2001) is highly interesting, as noted by the Russian delegation to the thirty-third session of the Commission on Population and Development. Such calculations would help in the development of national projections of the movement of population, and in the simulation of possible ways for the country to develop demographically. In migration policy decision-making, one should consider the problem of substituting for the natural population loss by migration in connection with the geopolitical situation, tendencies and prospects of economic development, capacity of the labour market, availability and development of the social infrastructure etc.

The experts from the Ministry of Labour and Social Development of the Russian Federation think that the national labour market cannot manage the large-scale inflow of the labour force into the Russian Federation given that the number of the unemployed exceeds 8 million people and the latent unemployment is rather high. The forecast growth of production following the creation of new jobs will hardly reduce the tension in the labour market, as the working-age population will grow too. Also, the inflow of immigrants contributes to the rejuvenation of the labour force but, under the conditions of unemployment, it will contribute also to a forcing out of older people from employment. So, engaging the immigrants can contribute to the growth of social tension, to the development of inter-ethnic conflicts and to the creation of an intolerant atmosphere towards the immigrants in the society.

Also, there can be problems connected with settling the immigrants. When addressing this topic, one should take into account the possible threat to the territorial integrity of the Russian Federation, the guarantee of the right of the indigenous small populations of the extreme north, Siberia and the far east of the Russian Federation to the defence of their native land, and the right of the immigrants themselves to freedom of movement.

Even the proposals of some scientists to direct the immigrants' flow towards the agriculture of the European part of the Russian Federation cannot solve the problem.

Many rural areas of the central Russian Federation have been really deprived of their population but the urbanization process is not the only reason. Collectivization, dispossession by big farmers, liquidation of the villages without a prosperous future, and also the too low procurement prices for agricultural production have resulted in the very large scale migration outflow of the rural population. However, one could observe the reverse process in the early 1990s during the development of the private farms movement. The problems of Russian agriculture go much deeper than the lack of a young working-age population.

Today, the Russian Federation especially needs a reasonable migration policy corresponding to the interests of its socio-economic development. Now, it is clear that the Russian Federation needs the migration increase; however, the experts from the Ministry of Economics of the Russian Federation think that one should evaluate both from the demographic and from the economic point of view the extent to which the Russian Federation would benefit from engaging the immigrants, including the number of them, countries of origin, sex and age structure, educational level etc.

The report on replacement migration of the Population Division of the United Nations Secretariat notes that the main share of contemporary immigration to the Russian Federation is the result of the return migration of ethnic Russians from the other republics of the former Union of Soviet Socialist Republics. According to the expert estimates, the present real potential Russian repatriation to the Russian Federation is approximately 3 million–3.5 million people. Together with the potential migrants belonging to other indigenous ethnic groups of the Russian Federation and also mixed families, this figure may be about 10 million people. For the most part, these are highly skilled specialists. Also, not taking into consideration the refugees and enforced settlers, these are the persons with some initial capital, the latter factor being especially important under existing conditions where, as a rule, there are no budgetary funds even for the solution of the problems of the enforced migration to the Russian Federation. Therefore, the migration policy should be focused on enticing this group of potential immigrants to the Russian Federation. The necessity of stimulating migration from the CIS and Baltic countries is pointed out in the draft concept of the demographic policy of the Russian Federation, in the draft concept of the migration policy of the Russian Federation and also in the draft main directions of the long-term socio-economic policy of the Government of the Russian Federation.

In the Russian Federation, owing to its diverse ethnic structure, cultural and ethnic traditions and religious beliefs are diverse too. In this connection, the experts from the Ministry for Federal Affairs, Nationalities and Migration Policy of the Russian Federation think that one should take into account the ethnic component of migration and create immigration programmes aimed at immigrants from specific countries, the number of whom should be regulated by means of quotas for the admitted immigrants.

Also, one should develop temporary labour migration. Almost 70 per cent of the territory of the Russian Federation is in the extreme north and related areas with severe climatic conditions. A considerable share of the natural resources of the Russian Federation is concentrated within these areas and a decrease in the number of members of the able-bodied population will be negatively reflected in the position of the mining industries. However, this problem can be solved by the use of the temporary labour migration (long-term shifts method of labour organization).

D. GOVERNMENT MEASURES CONCERNING THE CONSEQUENCES OF DEMOGRAPHIC CHANGES

It is clear that the measures that can be undertaken by the Government of the Russian Federation in order to increase fertility or to cause a decline in mortality will not result in instantaneous outcome. To induce migration, one also needs a number of socio-economic conditions. Therefore, owing to the unfavourable age structure of the population, the Government of the Russian Federation is going to update social policy to some extent. First of all, this entails reforming the pension system. The pension reforms should be aimed at the solution of two interconnected problems. They should preserve the current financial stability of the pension system and increase the real level of pensions in order to overcome the negative consequences of the 1998 financial crisis. In the long term, they should prevent a crisis of the pension system owing to the ageing of the population of the Russian Federation. For the solution of the latter problem, the Government of the Russian Federation is going to introduce the accumulative financing of pensions for the working population. For the purpose of accumulation, a part of the social tax directed to the pension fund will be used. During the coming years, these contributions will be increased up to 9-10 percentage points. The contributions of the social tax to the distributive pension system will be followed by the reduced value of the contributions to the accumulation system.

The personal accumulative pension accounts are very likely to be opened in early 2002. Also, the development of a system of voluntary pensions is planned. Whether such a reorganization of the pension system will help us to solve the problem will become clear some time later. The creation of the accumulative pensions requires some specific conditions: first, constant income during all of the economically active life of a birth cohort; and second, a long-term period of economic stability permitting the standby capital to accumulate. A separate problem will involve the necessity of exercising control over non-State pension funds.

As regards the necessity of raising the retirement age, this subject has been discussed for a long time. However, the Minister of Labour and Social Development of the Russian Federation says that the subject has ceased to be debated in the Government. The health status of Russians, which is adequately reflected by the indicator of life expectancy at birth, is so depressing that any rise in the official pension age can result in a considerable increase in population mortality and in the growth of the number of the persons retiring ahead of time owing to disability.

One can expect that a future increase in the standard of living of the population and the reform of the public-health system in accordance with the main directions of the long-term socio-economic policy of the Government of the Russian Federation would allow the lives of the active population to be extended and the revision of the generally adopted retirement age to begin.

REFERENCES

Antonov, A. *A Russian Family and the Potential of the Home Economy: Crisis of the Social Policy.* Moscow.

Centre for Strategic Research (2000). Draft of the main directions of the long-term socio-economic policy of the Government of the Russian Federation.

Committee for Health Protection and Sports of the State Duma (2000). Recommendations of the Parliamentary Hearings "On the demographic situation in the Russian Federation and the measures of the Government of the Russian Federation with respect to its optimization". 30 May.

Federal Migration Agency (1999). Draft concept of the migration policy of the Russian Federation. Moscow.

Ministry of Labour and Social Development of the Russian Federation (2000). Draft concept of the demographic policy of the Russian Federation. Moscow.

Ministry of Public Health of the Russian Federation (1999). *Health Status of the Population of the Russian Federation in 1998.* Moscow.

Moscovsky Komsomolets (2000). Interview with the Minister of Labour and Social Development of the Russian Federation. 19 June.

REPLACEMENT MIGRATION: IS IT A SOLUTION FOR THE RUSSIAN FEDERATION?

*Anatoly Vishnevsky**

INTRODUCTION

The main assumptions and certain results of the population projection for the Russian Federation for the years 2000-2050 are summarized in the table that accompanies the present report. This projection was elaborated by the author in collaboration with Dr. Evgeny Andreev. The purpose was not to predict, with the maximum possible confidence, how the country's population size and age composition would actually vary in the next 50 years, but rather to examine the paths of such changes in accordance with certain more or less feasible scenarios of demographic development.

1. *Three groups of scenarios*

The 12 proposed scenarios are divided into three groups:

Group I: Scenarios with a zero net migration. This set of scenarios permits the estimation of the possibilities of population increase and potential changes in the age composition of population entirely as a result of an interaction between fertility and mortality. The Group I scenarios show that, under any somewhat realistic assumptions with regard to these two processes, the natural increase in the population of the Russian Federation will be negative during the next 50 years, while population size will steadily decrease.

Group II: Scenarios with a constant population size across the whole period 2000-2050. These indicate the net migration to the Russian Federation required to compensate the consequences of a negative natural increase and to assure a constant population size up to 2050.

Group III: Scenarios with a rising population size. Scenarios in this group permit the estimation of the annual net migration to the Russian Federation required to assure an annual 0.5 per cent increase in population size during the next 50 years.

In all scenarios, the fertility and mortality indicators are considered independent variables, primarily determining population dynamics. Therefore, the choice of employed fertility and mortality assumptions needs to be substantiated from the very beginning. As for migration (wherever it exists, that is to say, in

*Russian Academy of Sciences, Center for Demography and Human Ecology, Moscow, Russian Federation.

the second and third sets of scenarios), it is a possible exogenous response to a course of events predetermined by an endogenous demographic development, and its value should be determined as a result of projection calculations.

2. Fertility assumptions

The fertility rate in the Russian Federation was decreasing during the whole twentieth century. In the mid-1960s, it plummeted, for the first time, below the replacement level and continued to decrease. In the 1990s, this decrease accelerated. By the end of the century, the total fertility rate in the Russian Federation, as in some other European countries, dropped below the 1.3 and even below the 1.2 mark.

The reasons for such a deep drop have not been completely understood. There are different factors that are usually mentioned by researchers to explain the decline of fertility in developed countries; but these factors are so manifold and interchangeable that it calls into question the very possibility of finding an adequate explanation with such a "factorist" approach. More probably, the influence of different factors on fertility behaviour and thus on fertility level is only an intermediary mechanism, and through the actions of concrete factors, the more general systemic, homeostatic reactions are realized.

The most important and most threatening element of the actual global demographic situation is the rapid growth of the world population. According to all projections, this growth will stop in the twenty-first century; but simple stabilization of the world population at the level of 10 billion to 12 billion is not sufficient to reduce the growing population pressure on global resources. From the standpoint of self-protection of human civilization, it would be much better to arrive at a stage of population decline. Rising mortality being excluded as an option, achieving fertility below replacement level is the only mechanism that can lead to such an evolution. Sooner or later this mechanism will be adopted by all nations, but initially it must be created—"invented"—somewhere. It is not surprising that the "inventors" are also those that "invented" low mortality, that is to say, the industrially advanced nations. Even if such an "invention" can be detrimental to many of them, the implicit objective logic of global survival proves to be more important than an egoistic logic of individual nations. If this hypothesis is correct, the main determinants of the fertility decline below replacement level in all industrialized countries do not have their most profound roots in the specific life conditions of those countries. Such a decline is a part of a global demographic process that is being driven by its own inherent forces.

One cannot therefore expect the Russian Federation to find itself outside this trend, common for countries with roughly the same level of economic and social development.

It is unlikely that all these countries would experience, during the next 50 years, a turnaround in fertility rates; rather the opposite may be expected: the continuation of the present low fertility rate up to 2050. Moreover, its further decrease is not improbable. However, in view of the insufficient current knowledge of the fertility dynamics mechanisms, its future rise cannot be entirely excluded.

The present projection assumes total fertility rates of 1.3 and 2.0 as the lower and upper bounds, correspondingly, of the probable fertility changes. The first value will remain unchanged over the whole period up to 2050, while the second one will gradually rise from 1.3 in 2000 to 2.0 in 2050.

3. *Mortality assumptions*

While fertility dynamics in the Russian Federation are quite similar to those in most industrialized countries, the mortality dynamics are significantly different, because a steady mortality decrease, typical of those countries, ceased in the Russian Federation a few decades ago. However, the global experience clearly shows that such a decrease is possible in principle, so a decrease in mortality in the Russian Federation before 2050 seems much more likely than a rise in fertility.

The Russian Federation's current lagging behind most Western countries may be explained primarily by an excessive premature mortality, compared with the West, due to external causes and circulatory diseases. In 1995, these two groups of causes of death were responsible for 85 per cent of the excessive mortality in the age groups below 70 years. Among them, external causes were responsible for 46 per cent of excessive deaths of men and for 25 per cent of deaths of women (Vishnevsky and Shkolnikov, 1997, pp. 80-81). The Western experience suggests that a successful struggle against mortality owing to such causes is much more directly and obviously connected (as compared with the fertility trends) to the general socio-economic climate. The changes in this climate that are being prepared by the current reforms will result, sooner or later, in a mortality trend turnabout in the Russian Federation; it will start to gradually decrease down to the level observed in Western countries.

As in the case of fertility assumptions, the projection determines the lower and upper bounds of probable changes in life expectancy (e_0). The first values of the parameter e_0 are equal to 59.9 years for men and 72.5 years for women, recorded at the end of the century and remaining constant over the whole projection period. The second values of the parameter e_0 are equal to 77.0 years for men and 83.0 years for women by 2050 (while gradually reaching these values over the whole period).

Even if the actual fertility and mortality dynamics differ from those assumed in the current projection, the assumptions made therein allow for covering a very wide range of more or less probable prognostic scenarios, while the computational results offer a clear estimation of trends and extents of the population size and composition under various assumptions as regards future fertility and mortality developments.

A. THE ANALYTICAL POPULATION PROJECTION FOR THE RUSSIAN FEDERATION 2000-2050: MAIN RESULTS

1. *Changes in population size*

The population size of the Russian Federation in 2025 and 2050 by projection scenario is presented in the table, section F, and in the figure.

POPULATION PROJECTION FOR THE RUSSIAN FEDERATION, 2000-2050: MAIN ASSUMPTIONS AND RESULTS

Year or period	Scenarios with zero migration				Scenarios with zero population growth				Scenarios with 0.5 per cent annual population growth			
	Scenario I A $TFR=1.3$ const. e_0	Scenario I B $TFR=1.3$ incr. e_0	Scenario I C $TFR=2.0$ const. e_0	Scenario I D $TFR=2.0$ incr. e_0	Scenario II A $TFR=1.3$ const. e_0	Scenario II B $TFR=1.3$ incr. e_0	Scenario II C $TFR=2.0$ const. e_0	Scenario II D $TFR=2.0$ incr. e_0	Scenario III A $TFR=1.3$ const. e_0	Scenario III B $TFR=1.3$ incr. e_0	Scenario III C $TFR=2.0$ const. e_0	Scenario III D $TFR=2.0$ incr. e_0
A. Total fertility rate (TFR)												
1959	2.60	2.60	2.60	2.60	2.60	2.60	2.60	2.60	2.60	2.60	2.60	2.60
1975	1.98	1.98	1.98	1.98	1.98	1.98	1.98	1.98	1.98	1.98	1.98	1.98
2000	1.30	1.30	1.30	1.30	1.30	1.30	1.30	1.30	1.30	1.30	1.30	1.30
2025	1.30	1.30	1.50	1.50	1.30	1.30	1.50	1.50	1.30	1.30	1.50	1.50
2050	1.30	1.30	2.00	2.00	1.30	1.30	2.00	2.00	1.30	1.30	2.00	2.00
B. Male life expectancy												
1959	63.2	63.2	63.2	63.2	63.2	63.2	63.2	63.2	63.2	63.2	63.2	63.2
1975	62.6	62.6	62.6	62.6	62.6	62.6	62.6	62.6	62.6	62.6	62.6	62.6
2000	59.9	59.9	59.9	59.9	59.9	59.9	59.9	59.9	59.9	59.9	59.9	59.9
2025	59.9	68.6	59.9	68.6	59.9	68.6	59.9	68.6	59.9	68.6	59.9	68.6
2050	59.9	77.0	59.9	77.0	59.9	77.0	59.9	77.0	59.9	77.0	59.9	77.0
C. Female life expectancy												
1959	71.7	71.7	71.7	71.7	71.7	71.7	71.7	71.7	71.7	71.7	71.7	71.7
1975	73.2	73.2	73.2	73.2	73.2	73.2	73.2	73.2	73.2	73.2	73.2	73.2
2000	72.5	72.5	72.5	72.5	72.5	72.5	72.5	72.5	72.5	72.5	72.5	72.5
2025	72.5	77.9	72.5	77.9	72.5	77.9	72.5	77.9	72.5	77.9	72.5	77.9
2050	72.5	83.0	72.5	83.0	72.5	83.0	72.5	83.0	72.5	83.0	72.5	83.0
D. Average annual net migration (thousands)												
1950-1975	-94	-94	-94	-94	-94	-94	-94	-94	-94	-94	-94	-94
1975-2000	232	232	232	232	232	232	232	232	232	232	232	232
2000-2025	0	0	0	0	1 040	738	1 002	702	1 878	1 550	1 836	1 510
2025-2050	0	0	0	0	1 712	1 066	1 263	677	2 825	2 028	2 268	1 542

	69	69	69	69	69	69	69	69	69	69	69	69
	1 526	2 052	1 789	2 352	689	1 133	902	1 376	0	0	0	0
1950-2000												
2000-2050												

E. Total net migration (thousands)

	69	69	69	69	69	69	69	69	69	69	69	69
	1 526	2 052	1 789	2 352	689	1 133	902	1 376	0	0	0	0
1950-1975	-2 358	-2 358	-2 358	-2 358	-2 358	-2 358	-2 358	-2 358	-2 358	-2 358	-2 358	-2 358
1975-2000	5 800	5 800	5 800	5 800	5 800	5 800	5 800	5 800	5 800	5 800	5 800	5 800
2000-2025	37 750	45 912	38 760	46 962	17 544	25 057	18 438	25 989	0	0	0	0
2025-2050	38 550	56 693	50 688	70 626	16 926	31 583	26 639	42 800	0	0	0	0
1950-2000	3 442	3 442	3 442	3 442	3 442	3 442	3 442	3 442	0	0	0	0
2000-2050	76 300	102 605	89 448	117 588	34 470	56 640	45 077	68 789	0	0	0	0

F. Total population (millions)

	69	69	69	69	69	69	69	69	69	69	69	69
	1 526	2 052	1 789	2 352	689	1 133	902	1 376	0	0	0	0
1950	102.2	102.2	102.2	102.2	102.2	102.2	102.2	102.2	102.2	102.2	102.2	102.2
1975	134.2	134.2	134.2	134.2	134.2	134.2	134.2	134.2	134.2	134.2	134.2	134.2
2000	145.6	145.6	145.6	145.6	145.6	145.6	145.6	145.6	145.6	145.6	145.6	145.6
2025	164.9	164.9	164.9	164.9	145.6	145.6	145.6	145.6	128.8	122.2	128.0	121.4
2050	186.8	186.8	186.8	186.8	145.6	145.6	145.6	145.6	111.7	94.5	103.3	86.5

G. Old-age dependency ratio ((65+)/(15-64), per 100)

	69	69	69	69	69	69	69	69	69	69	69	69
	1 526	2 052	1 789	2 352	689	1 133	902	1 376	0	0	0	0
1939	7	7	7	7	7	7	7	7	7	7	7	7
1959	9	9	9	9	9	9	9	9	9	9	9	9
1975	13	13	13	13	13	13	13	13	13	13	13	13
2000	18	18	18	18	18	18	18	18	18	18	18	18
2025	27	25	27	25	28	26	24	26	29	27	25	27
2050	41	31	40	31	45	33	36	33	50	39	41	41

H. Total dependency ratio ([(0-15)+(65+)]/(15-64), per 100)

	69	69	69	69	69	69	69	69	69	69	69	69
	1 526	2 052	1 789	2 352	689	1 133	902	1 376	0	0	0	0
1939	69	69	69	69	69	69	69	69	69	69	69	69
1959	54	54	54	54	54	54	54	54	54	54	54	54
1975	49	49	49	49	49	49	49	49	49	49	49	49
2000	43	43	43	43	43	43	43	43	43	43	43	43
2025	48	47	48	46	49	47	44	46	50	48	45	47
2050	69	60	61	52	71	61	54	53	75	66	58	60

Population of the Russian Federation, 1950-2050

(2000-2050: by projection variants)

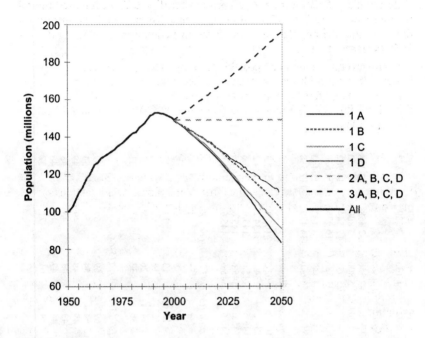

(a) *Scenarios with a zero net migration*

Even a simultaneous and quite significant rise of both fertility and life expectancy would be unable to break the downward trend in population size and its gradual approach to the 1950 level. It should be noted that by 1950 the Russian Federation still had not restored its population size of 110 million that had been recorded in 1940.

In the worst case under accepted assumptions, that is to say, at the constant current low fertility and high mortality (scenario I A), 86.5 million is all that can be expected as a population size in the Russian Federation by 2050.

A fertility increase of up to 2 children per woman by 2050, with an unchanged mortality (scenario I C), would allow this size to rise by about 8 million, up to 94.5 million; however, such a rise has been noted as unlikely.

The effect of mortality decrease seems more probable and in addition it could be much more significant. The Russian Federation is currently suffering enormous demographic losses due to high mortality. Had the age-specific mortality rates in the 1980s and 1990s been the same as in Western countries, the annual number of deaths would have been reduced by 500,000-700,000; this could have notably changed the current balance of births and deaths and delayed the emergence of a negative natural increase.

278

Also in the future, the mere ability to avert population losses, already attained in many countries, would slow down the decrease in the Russian Federation's population size. At a constant fertility rate, a decreased mortality rate would result in 17 million additional Russian Federation citizens, thus bringing the population of the Russian Federation to 103.3 million by 2050 (scenario I B).

However, it would be impossible to completely avert a decrease in population size, even with the most favourable (within the framework of the assumptions made) fertility and mortality evolution. In the best case, the population of the Russian Federation would amount, by 2050, to about 112 million (scenario I D).

(b)   Scenarios with a non-zero net migration

An apparent inability to maintain even a constant population size in the Russian Federation solely due to the fertility and mortality interaction compels one to resort to the third main factor of population dynamics, namely, migration.

Under the above-mentioned assumptions, in order to maintain an unchanged population size over 50 years, the total net migration to the Russian Federation should range from 35 million (about 690,000 per year), in the case of the most favourable fertility and mortality evolution, to 69 million (about 1.4 million per year), in the case of the least favourable fertility and mortality evolution.

For the population size of the Russian Federation to increase by 0.5 per cent annually between 2000 and 2050 (in the 1970s and 1980s, the population of the Russian Federation increased by 0.6-0.75 per cent per year), total net migration to the Russian Federation should range, according to the various fertility and mortality scenarios, from 76 million to 118 million (1.5-2.4 million per year) (see table, sects. D and E).

2.   *Changes in age composition*

The main trend in the age composition changes, according to all scenarios of the projection, is the ageing of the population. It should be noted that the series D scenarios, which are the most favourable with regard to population size increase, are at the same time the least favourable with regard to ageing.

(a)   Scenarios with a zero net migration

On the assumption that the low fertility and high mortality remain unchanged in the course of the next 50 years (scenario I A), the proportion of elderly people (those over age 65) in the Russian Federation population would exceed 26 per cent by 2050, while that proportion was below 6 per cent as recently as 1959, and 12.5 per cent in 1999. At the same time, the proportion of children under age 15 would drop to 12 per cent (compared with 29 per cent in 1959 and 19 per cent in 1999).

Should the scenarios that assume fertility increase and mortality decline become true, two conflicting trends would collide: the fertility rise would, to a certain degree, counterbalance ageing, while the mortality decrease would contribute to it. Therefore, scenario I C (a rising fertility with an unchanged mortality) turns out to be the "youngest" one, while scenario I B (a decreasing mortality at an unchanged low fertility) turns out to be the "oldest" one.

Such changes in age composition also determine the dynamics of the age dependency ratio.

The ratio of the elderly to the adult population will significantly rise in any event. While it was just 9 elderly persons per 100 adults (aged 15-65) in 1959 and 18 per 100 in 1999, it will rise, by 2050, to 41-50 elderly persons per 100 adults, according to the scenario used (table, sect. G).

However, the rise of the *total* dependency ratio (due to both the elderly and children) will be much less impressive. Owing to the peculiarities of the Russian Federation population pyramid, it is not unlikely that this ratio is at its lowest level of the last 50 years, so that its future increase is unavoidable in any case. Yet even by 2035 it will not exceed (and according to most scenarios will even stay below) the ratio observed in 1975, which was already low.

Only after 2035, and then not simultaneously under all scenarios, the total dependency ratio will exceed 50 per 100 adults, increasing gradually towards the year 2050. However even in 2050 it will not reach, at least in scenarios I A, B and C (table, sect. H), the level observed in 1939, when the Russian Federation's population was very young (about 40 children under age 15 per 100 adults). Only scenario I D, which is most optimistic from the viewpoint of population size, augurs an increase in the total dependency ratio of up to 75 per 100 adults; however, it is unlikely that such a scenario reflects the future.

(b) Scenarios with a non-zero net migration

The age composition of migrants is usually notably different from that of the national population, resulting therefore in either washing out—in the case of emigration—or washing up (expansion)—in the case of immigration—of certain age groups.

As a rule, the age composition of migrants is younger. Until the 1980s, three quarters of all the Russian Federation migrants were younger than age 30. By the end of the 1990s, migration flows had "aged" and less than 60 per cent of the total migration flows are below age 30 (Zayonchkovskaya, 1999, pp. 122-124). However, such a change in the age composition of migration flows is, most likely, of a temporary nature. If the Russian Federation actually absorbs, during the period 2000-2050, significant migration flows, they will originate in countries with a young age composition and hence will also be quite young. This will definitely cause a rejuvenating effect upon the age composition of the whole population. The question is, to what extent?

The calculations show that, while migration is incapable of radically changing the main trends in the age composition, its impact may still be quite significant and, at the same time, contradictory. Although in most cases it contributes to the reduction of the dependency ratios (either old age or total), it also produces an unexpected effect in the case of constant low fertility and decreasing mortality (scenarios B). In this case, increases in migration result initially in the reduction of the total dependency ratio, but after a while, the ratio also increases (see table, sect. H).

B.   CONSEQUENCES

1.   *Consequences of population decrease*

Population decline is one of the serious challenges facing the Russian Federation on the verge of the twenty-first century.

Of course, there are no indisputable arguments in favour of population increase at any time and in any place. Besides, population dynamics cannot be viewed separately from other changing demographic realities. Among other things, a decline in population increase, or even a population decrease, is to a larger or lesser degree compensated by a simultaneous rise in the total number of man-years lived, caused by mortality reduction and by an increased life expectancy.

In moving from $e_0 = 50$ years to $e_0 = 75$ years for men and to $e_0 = 80$ for women (which is the route of many industrialized countries in the twentieth century), the total number of years lived by a cohort increases by a factor of 1.5 for men and 1.6 for women. Therefore, in certain respects, the current 725 million Europeans occupy more space on Earth than the 1 billion people at the end of the nineteenth century. Similarly, the current Russian population of 145 million, even with its relatively low life expectancy (67), is equivalent to a population of about 280 million Russians at the beginning of the twentieth century, when life expectancy was less than 35 years.

As to the future, should an optimistic mortality decrease scenario be realized in the Russian Federation even in the case of a constant low fertility (scenario I B), its projected population of 103 million would be equivalent to about 125 million in 1950. If, however, it could be possible to maintain the present population size (scenario II B), it would in 2050 be equivalent, in terms of the total number of years lived, to more than 175 million in 1950.

However, as far as the Russian Federation is concerned, all such considerations should play a limited role owing to a well-known (and long-known) discrepancy between the population and the territorial size of the country. The Russian Federation has always been underpopulated, and this underpopulation became especially apparent after the disintegration of the Union of Soviet Socialist Republics (USSR), from which the Russian Federation has inherited three quarters of the territory but just one half of the population.

Even the more populated European part of the Russian Federation is comparable, with respect to population density, with the territory of the United States of America (27 persons per square kilometre in the European Russian Federation against 29 persons per square kilometre in the United States). When compared with Western Europe, even the historical centre of the Russian Federation does not seem too well populated. One fifth of the country's population is concentrated in the central economic region occupying less than 3 per cent of its territory. However, even in that region, the population density of 62 persons per square kilometre is just above a half of that in the European Union (EU) as a whole (119 persons per square kilometre).

As to the Asian part of the country, its problem of an adequate population has never been solved. The Asian Russian Federation occupies 75 per cent of the whole country's territory but accommodates only 22 per cent of its population, at an average population density of 2.5 persons per square kilometre. The demographic potential of Siberia and the Russian far east is clearly insufficient for exploiting their rich natural resources and for creating a developed and more or less continuous economic and settlement structure.

Moreover, being already unsatisfied with its present population size, the Russian Federation would experience difficulties caused by the decrease of that population, even if partly compensated by an increased life expectancy. In a world suffering from overpopulation, the Russian Federation is still an underpopulated country, which makes it especially sensitive to the population decrease and compels it to seek ways to overcome its struggle against depopulation.

2. Consequences of population ageing

Unfavourable consequences of population ageing are less apparent. In general, it should be noted that a certain mythology exists in the demographic and economic literature which, on the one hand, exaggerates negative consequences of population ageing and, on the other hand, hampers the search for remedies for the real problems caused by ageing.

(a) Years lived by a cohort: the new structure of a lifetime

Fundamental processes, leading to irreversible changes in the population pyramid, are taking place at one generation level. As a result of the mortality decrease and the rectangularization of the curve of survivorship, a general increase in the number of years lived by a cohort is accompanied by an even faster-increasing number of years lived in the adult—and especially the old—ages. As a result of this evolution, the upper part of the pyramid of the time lived by a generation is continuously gaining weight. Hence the anxieties regarding a heavy burden upon the ageing nations' economies caused by an increase in the time lived by citizens of pension age, who are consumers without being producers.

Should one forget, however, that a person who has lived up to old age was once young as well? As mortality decreases, the total number of man-years rises, including productive years, not only consumption-prevalent ones.

As mentioned above, upon moving from $e_0 = 50$ years to $e_0 = 75$ years for men and to $e_0 = 80$ years for women, the total number of years lived by a cohort (and therefore the consumption time) increases by a factor of 1.5 for men and 1.6 for women. However, the number of years lived in the adult age (the "productive period") rises almost by the same factor. For example, according to the Coale and Demeny model life tables (model "West"), it rises by 1.44 for men and 1.47 for women for ages 15-65, and by 1.51 for men and 1.54 for women for ages 20-65. As to the ratio between the years lived in the "dependency period" and the years lived in the "productive period", it remains practically unchanged.

From the economic point of view, the issues of age profiles of consumption or needs and the differentials between levels of per capita expenditures in the young and old dependency periods are crucial. If they are about the same, then the introduction of this economic variable has no effect upon the conclusions from a purely demographic analysis. If, however, the per-head expenditures of elderly dependants are much greater than those of children, then an increased burden of the second "dependency period" is not compensated, in the economic sense, by a decreased burden of the first period.

This issue must be recognized as insufficiently studied, with opposing views appearing in the literature and with greatly varying estimates made by different authors.

For example, one can find the categorical affirmation that "a child absorbs more resources than an old person, on the average. At current mortality and current standards of consumption, educational performance, and social security in the Federal Republic of Germany, it costs society about one fourth to one third more to bring up an average child from birth to age 20 than to support an average person of 60 years of age over the rest of his or her life. This estimate is based on national accounts statistics of the Federal Republic of Germany of 1973 and refers to final private and public consumption expenditure as well to fixed capital formation for internal use" (Wander, 1978, pp. 57-58).

Some other studies, on the contrary, "have estimated that for an industrialized country, on average the cost to support a person aged 65 years or over is substantially greater (roughly two and a half times greater) than the cost to support a young person less than 20 years old" (United Nations, 2001, chap. V, fourth paragraph). Contrary to these extreme statements, the authors of a relatively recent study of economic consequences of population ageing in industrialized societies concluded that, even if the difference in per capita consumption at the opposite end of the age spectrum exists, it is not very important and its "impact on overall needs or consumption expenditures [is] relatively limited" (United Nations, Economic Commission for Europe, 1992, p. 197; see also United Nations, Economic Commission for Europe, 1983).

The same idea was formulated by Richard Easterlin, who clearly underlined a difference between the demographic and the political approach to the same issue:

"The amount of empirical work that has actually been done on relative costs of the two groups is small, but what has been done suggests that economic costs per dependant (private plus public) are, in fact, not much different for older and younger dependants (Easterlin, 1991). If this is so, then the economic burden of dependency on the working-age population is unlikely to be noticeably higher in the first half of the twenty-first century than in the twentieth century, since the increased cost of supporting a larger proportion of older dependants will be offset by the decreased cost of supporting a smaller proportion of younger dependants.

283

"This implies that the real issue to be faced is largely political, namely, how to capture via taxation the savings of households from supporting fewer younger dependants, so that these funds can be used to meet the rise in public expenditures needed to support older dependants. The question of political feasibility is a serious one, but it does not seem insurmountable, given that the workers to be taxed would themselves eventually be beneficiaries of such taxation" (Easterlin, 1994, p. 22).

It should be emphasized also that the ageing of population takes place simultaneously with other economic and social modifications that can neutralize the negative consequences of changing age structure. As summed up in the proceedings of an international symposium on population structure and development in the late 1980s:

"The Symposium recognized that in order to calculate the extra demands placed on the economically active population as a result of population ageing, it would be necessary to consider the reduced burden of support for children and youth along with the increased burden of support for the elderly. Thus the ageing of populations need not lead to reductions in public expenditures per elderly person. Though the share of total income going to the elderly was likely to increase, the absolute level of after-tax income per worker would continue to rise as a result of increased productivity and a reduced burden of youth dependency . . . The effect of population ageing on the capacity to finance public services would depend on the link between population ageing and economic performance. The current assumption that the impact was negative was not well documented. Ageing that occurred as a consequence of low population growth might actually increase per capita income by permitting a greater labour-force participation of women and by increasing the per capita availability of capital" (United Nations, 1988, p. 135).

In any case, private (individual, family) expenditures should be distinguished from public (governmental and other) ones. Childbearing and child-rearing largely remain, in all modern societies, a family matter (even with a significant participation of the public institutions), while the elderly are mainly supported by means of pension systems. Therefore, if the first and second dependency periods are compared with regard to the *public* per-head expenditures only, the second period might in fact turn out to be more expensive. (By the way, this may explain the obvious dramatization of the ageing problem: the Governments are concerned about their increasing share of the economic responsibility for the welfare of the population.) However, the part of the population that lives in the "productive period" provides for both dependency periods, regardless of the channels used for distributing the resources produced.

While remaining within the "generation logic", one should take into account that a person enters his/her second "dependency period" 40-50 years after leaving the first one, during which time the society's wealth has grown. Other conditions being equal, the society now becomes capable of supporting, without excessive strain, the expenditure of the elderly at a level much higher than that existing during their childhood, when their needs were largely formed.

Like any changes, the transition to a new structure of the generation lifetime creates problems related to the adaptation of the social institutions to new demographic realities. The creation of pension systems is one of the prominent responses to this challenge of the twentieth century. However, the demographic changes themselves have predetermined the economic possibility of such a response, particularly by permitting, other things being equal, the increase, almost by the factor of 1.5, of the generation's potential fund of working time. This fact undermines an excessive dramatization of ageing as a *demographic* problem.

(b) Age composition of real populations

Should populations live for a long time under stable demographic conditions (namely, constant fertility and mortality rates), the cohort-related analysis could be also applied to the real population. However, the twentieth century was not a period of stability, but just the contrary: a time of huge changes in fertility and mortality and of the quest for their new equilibrium. The populations, one by one, moved to a new type of intragenerational solidarity. A new, if never explicitly proclaimed, principle was pursued: let each new generation live the same number of years as the preceding one had lived. However, this should not be achieved through a longevity privilege for a few, paid for by premature deaths of the majority, but rather through protection and prolongation of life for as many newborns as possible. Naturally enough, this led to a redistribution of economic resources within the whole time-space occupied by a generation, and particularly by the elderly, and to a fertility decline.

As a result of this decline, each generation was less numerous than the preceding one, and this was the main immediate cause of the ageing observed in most countries in the twentieth century. The population pyramid changes its form owing not to the widening of its upper part but to the narrowing of the lower one. Under such circumstances (which are a priori transitional and temporary), the elderly dependants belong to more populous generations than the adults filling the middle part of the age pyramid, and here a certain discrepancy may really appear.

However, one should not exaggerate the extent and significance of this discrepancy. The changes are occurring more or less gradually and the dependency ratio of the elderly is rising progressively, so this evolution cannot produce any abrupt perturbations and the economy may well adapt to such changes. In any case, the wealthy industrialized nations with an "old" age composition must bear the dependency burden of the elderly *after* their having already contributed to the economic growth. The situation is worse in the developing countries, where the main economic burden is produced by children who have not yet participated in the production of the total wealth, which is modest by itself.

It should be added here that in the twentieth century in the Russian Federation, as in some other European countries, the gradual shifts in the age composition caused by evolutionary demographic changes were accompanied by sharp fluctuations (caused by reasons that were far from demographic ones) of the age composition and, correspondingly, of the economic burden upon the adult population. In the second half of the 1960s, the total age dependency ratio in the Russian Federation was 55-57 per 100 adults. Such a high value will not be reached again until 2035 (and according to only some of the considered scenarios). Society should certainly be prepared for this event, but it should certainly not be overdramatized. If the Russian Federation was able to confront the phenomenon in 1965, why should it be so dangerous 70 years later?

C. CONCLUSIONS

In the Russian Federation, as in most industrialized countries, the balance of births and deaths will most likely be such in the first half of the twenty-first century that the natural population increase will be negative. If the country's population continues to depend largely on natural reproduction, it will unavoidably decrease in size and will age rapidly. These two trends might be counteracted only by an inflow of immigrants, to a larger or smaller extent, depending on the volume and composition of immigration flows.

Within the frameworks of the considered scenarios, this volume ranges from 34.5 million (scenario II D) to 117.6 million (scenario III A) over 50 years (689,000-2,352,000 per year). In order to estimate the feasibility of such parameters, it would be useful to compare them with the actual volumes of net migration to the Russian Federation in 1950-2000. It amounted to 3.4 million (69,000 per year) over 50 years, to 5.8 million (232,000 per year) over the last 25 years, and to 4.5 million (300,000 per year) over the 15-year period when it was highest (1984-1998).

Against such a background, even a minimal annual net migration on the order of 700,000 during the next 25 years (scenarios II B and II D) seems too large and therefore not very likely. Therefore, the migration volumes necessary for the realization of the series D scenarios (an annual population increase of 0.5 per cent), that is to say, 1.5 million to 1.9 million per year in 2000-2025 and 1.5 million to 2.8 million per year in 2025-2050, are even less likely.

Nevertheless, the Russian Federation will not be able to avoid the arrival of large immigration inflows. On the one hand, their inevitability is dictated by the internal demographic situation in the Russian Federation. While unfavourable consequences of population ageing are not so dramatic as sometimes imagined, and those actually present may be largely neutralized by economic and social policy measures, the population decrease will present the Russian Federation with a very hard choice. It should either succumb to a continuous aggravation of the already meagre population/territory ratio, or open wide its doors to immigration. Both solutions bear unwelcome consequences, so the lesser of two evils should be chosen.

On the other hand, future developments cannot be predicted without taking into account the demographic situation outside the Russian Federation, particularly the overpopulation beyond its southern frontiers. This overpopulation together with the increasing mobility of the populations in the neighbouring countries will unavoidably produce a growing migration pressure, at least in the form of illegal migration, which will become more and more difficult to hold in check and which will compel the Russian Federation to respond by expanding the legal immigration possibilities.

Eventually a certain equilibrium of push-and-pull factors will probably be achieved, along with a corresponding annual rate of net migration into the Russian Federation. It will most likely be greater than the current rate. However, one can hardly rely on its ability to neutralize the unfavourable consequences of the present demographic trends, in particular the fertility decline much below the replacement level.

REFERENCES

Easterlin, Richard A. (1991). The economic impact of prospective population changes in advanced industrial countries: an historical perspective. *Journal of Gerontology: Social Sciences* (Saint Louis, Missouri), vol. 46, No. 6, pp. 299-309.

_____ (1994). The birth dearth, ageing, and the economy. In *Human Capital and Economic Development*, Sisay Asefa and Wei-Chiao Huang, eds. Kalamazoo, Michigan: W. E. Upjohn Institute for Employment Research, p. 22.

United Nations (1988). Introduction. In *Economic and Social Implications of Population Ageing: Proceedings of the International Symposium on Population Structure and Development, Tokyo, 10-12 September 1987.* ST/ESA/SER.R/85.

_____ (2001). *Replacement Migration: Is It a Solution to Declining and Ageing Populations?* Sales No. E.01.XIII.19.

_____, Economic Commission for Europe (ECE) (1983). Economic implications of ageing in the ECE region: some selected aspects. In *Economic Bulletin for Europe* (Geneva, Switzerland), vol. 35, No. 3.

_____ (1992). Economic implications of ageing in the ECE region: some selected aspects. In *Demographic Causes and Economic Consequences of Population Ageing. Europe and North America*, George J. Stolnitz, ed. Economic Commission for Europe, Economic Studies, No. 3. Sales No. GV.E.92.0.4.

Vishnevsky, Anatoly, and Vladimir Shkolnikov (1997). *Mortality in the Russian Federation: Main Groups of Risk and Action Priorities.* Proceedings of the Moscow Carnegie Center, vol. 19 (in Russian). Moscow.

Wander, Hilde (1978). Zero population growth now: the lesson from Europe. In *The Economic Consequences of Slowing Population Growth*, Thomas J. Espenshade and William J. Serow, eds. New York: Academic Press.

Zayonchkovskaya, Zhanna (1999). Migration. In *Population of Russia 1999* (in Russian), Anatoly Vishnevsky, ed. Moscow: Knizhny Dom Universitet.

WHO'S AFRAID OF LOW SUPPORT RATIOS? AN UNOFFICIAL RESPONSE FROM THE UNITED KINGDOM TO THE REPORT OF THE POPULATION DIVISION OF THE UNITED NATIONS SECRETARIAT ON REPLACEMENT MIGRATION

*David Coleman**

A. INTRODUCTION

1. *Purpose of the present paper*

In March 2000 the Population Division of the United Nations Secretariat presented a comprehensive analysis of the levels of net immigration that would be technically "required" if an attempt was made to check the eventual population decline, fall in size of workforce and population ageing envisaged in some population projections, up to 2050 (United Nations, 2001). This comprehensive analysis, the first to be made on a common methodology on a fully international basis to address this otherwise familiar issue, has attracted unusual attention and provoked much comment in the media.

The present paper is a response to the Population Division report from the viewpoint of the United Kingdom of Great Britain and Northern Ireland. It begins by reviewing the demographic prospects for the United Kingdom during the half-century 2000-2050 using projections made by the Government Actuary's Department (GAD) of the United Kingdom, in comparison with the results presented by the Population Division of the United Nations Secretariat. Variant GAD projections are presented to explore further the implications of possible future United Kingdom demographic trends, and also to test the migration and fertility levels "required" to achieve various demographic targets.

It then considers the ability of economies and societies, especially those of the United Kingdom, to respond to population ageing and to the possibility of a reduction in population size. The variety of options available, through workforce, productivity, pensions reform and other means, as well as demographic responses, and the likely outcome of events are discussed. It is concluded that in the relatively benign demographic regime of the United Kingdom, future population ageing, in any case mostly unavoidable, can be managed without serious difficulty, given suitable, albeit somewhat painful, adjustments to workforce participation, retirement age and pensions funding. By itself, population

---

*University of Oxford, Oxford, United Kingdom of Great Britain and Northern Ireland.

stabilization, or even mild reduction, is probably to be welcomed in the United Kingdom, while current levels of immigration are judged to be too high.

2. General comments on the report of the Population Division of the United Nations Secretariat

Before comparing details, a general comment about the United Nations report and its ramifications may be appropriate. The report represents an imaginative systematic exploration of one aspect of a fundamental problem that affects, to varying degrees, all developed societies. Its uniform technical treatment of the migration aspect of population ageing is welcome. Because of this systematic approach, and because of the prestige attaching to the Population Division, the report has been widely read and cited. Its statistics will be a definitive benchmark for years to come. In the United Kingdom, it has featured in almost every major national newspaper and journal, and is cited on radio and television whenever issues of migration, ageing or labour shortage are discussed. Along with the asylum crisis and the wish of the United Kingdom Government to rethink immigration policy, the report may claim to have raised consciousness about the whole issue.

This massive publicity, however gratifying it may be to the authors of the report, may have had some unfortunate and doubtless unintended consequences. In the United Kingdom media at any rate, the almost universal impression conveyed to the public is that the United Nations has stated the following: (a) that population, workforce numbers and support ratios must be kept at their present levels and therefore (b) that the projected levels of immigration must be encouraged by the countries concerned. This interpretation of the report has provoked the most comprehensive public misinformation on any demographic-related topic that this author can recall. Some of this is due to the familiar problems of communicating technical information to the media. In the United Kingdom, various pressure groups and some official bodies such as the Commission for Racial Equality have added these arguments to their repertoire of propositions to support immigration and oppose its restriction. For these purposes the United Nations report has been timely, as in recent years the United Kingdom has experienced a crisis of asylum-claiming which has made it, in terms of absolute numbers, the most favoured destination in Europe. In several recent months, claims exceeded even the number made to Germany. United Kingdom pressure groups and commentators in the media are now able to cite the report as evidence that asylum-claimants and illegal immigrants should be welcomed irrespective of the merit of their claims, as they now represent demographic salvation. Despite widespread public anxiety on immigration (British Social Trends, 2000), there are no pressure groups in the United Kingdom devoted to its critical evaluation, an asymmetry apparently general in the Western world (Freeman, 1994).

The strategy and some of the phrasing of the report and of its press release may have contributed, unintentionally, to misunderstandings on this politically sensitive issue. Its concentration on immigration as the "solution", one already well known in demographic circles to be impractical at least in respect of the support ratio, gave the impression that other approaches, possibly more promising, were of little consequence. Alternatives (pensions, retirement and work-force reform, productivity, more substantial changes in fertility) were noted but not evaluated in detail. The political, social and economic costs of large-scale immigration received no mention. The report's concentration on the demographic abstraction of the "potential support ratio", without considering equally or more important non-demographic components of real dependency levels in real societies, has been criticized as "demographism" (Tarmann, 2000).

Further, the repetition of imperative terms such as "needed" and "required" has given the impression to the unreflective that the avoidance of population stability or decline was absolutely necessary and that population ageing was not only intolerable but also avoidable. The demographic targets, parameters in a hypothetical scenario, have been widely interpreted by the media as policy prescriptions. Readers were presented with unqualified statements such as "some immigration is needed to prevent population decline in all countries and regions examined in the report" and "population decline is inevitable in the absence of replacement migration" and would "force Governments to reassess many . . . policies", as though none had already done so.

The notions that population decline is unacceptable and that population ageing is avoidable reflect transatlantic rather than universal Western concerns. Population reduction may be contrary to the American dream but regarded with equanimity elsewhere. While the possibility is strongly opposed by most French opinion (Chesnais, 1995), official reports in the United Kingdom (Population Panel, 1973) have welcomed the prospect of an end to growth. Official responses in Germany (Höhn, 1990) have discussed the management of population decline, and the Netherlands has in the past defined it as a policy aim in the long run, for example, in the 1983 government response to the Dutch Royal Commission on Population, 1977.

Population projections, always wrong in detail, are unusually frail when made over the adventurous time-span of 50 years, which allows many components of potential error to accumulate; and yet health warnings about the uncertainty of speculative pronouncements at this range, discussed, inter alia, by Lee (2000), were effectively absent, and no mention was made of their past record. This is not to say that the general outlines of the United Nations projections are wrong. Overall totals have often been quite well projected (although over much shorter time-spans than 50 years) and the record has improved. However, past United Nations projections for Europe and North America have "relatively large" errors in the age structure at young and old ages even at the modest range of 10 years (Keilman, 1997; 1998, p. 31). Probably all demographers would agree that fertility is unlikely to return to levels above a two-child average, that mortality will continue to fall, that substantial population ageing is inevitable and that the demographic component of the workforce will cease to grow in most countries. Beyond that, there is no reason to suppose that the coming century will not bring at least as many unexpected surprises as the last.

Neither was any mention made of the well-known tendency of synthetic cohort measures such as the total fertility rate (TFR) to understate contemporary fertility levels, or the possibility of feedbacks from public policy affecting the very low level of fertility in some countries. Feedbacks and limiting factors in population projection have already been suggested (mostly in the context of growth, not decline) as a way of making "intelligent" population projections which avoid extreme conclusions (Cohen, 1998; Sanderson, 1998; Ahlburg, Lutz and Vaupel, 1998). However, the Population Division may have implicitly allowed for this in marking up fertility over time in its projections.

In the nature of things, journalists will concentrate on press releases and headlines rather than strain their limited attention span by consulting in detail the scientific comments in the body of reports. It was unfortunate that the press release was presented before the report was available. In the natural sciences, this practice is condemned. It should be avoided in the social sciences as well.

B. DIFFERENCES BETWEEN THE UNITED NATIONS AND THE OFFICIAL UNITED KINGDOM PROJECTIONS

The United Kingdom Government Actuary's Department (GAD) makes regular long-range projections in order to evaluate the financial and demographic prospects of the United Kingdom State pension scheme (Government Actuary, 1999). Along with the United States of America, the United Kingdom is one of the few Governments to require such projections (Lee, 2000). In response to the United Nations report, GAD has undertaken additional long-range projections (Shaw, 2001), on a wide variety of assumptions. Some are presented here by courtesy of GAD (tables 1 and 2).

The United Nations and GAD projections differ in important ways. The GAD starting population is higher, primarily because the United Nations underestimated net immigration to the United Kingdom in the late 1990s. Different assumptions about fertility, mortality and migration lead to further divergence. The final United Nations TFR in 2050 is 5 per cent higher than that of GAD: 1.9 instead of 1.8. Expectation of life at birth by the end of the United Nations projection is lower for men by 0.5 years, and higher for women by 0.5 years even though it begins somewhat lower for both sexes. Either fertility estimate is defensible. Both mortality projections, however, seem too low. The pace of reduction of mortality, especially that of the oldest old (Kannisto and others, 1994), suggests that much greater progress may be made, although this is not universally agreed (Olshansky and Carnes, 1996).

The most striking divergence is in the migration assumptions. The United Nations assumes net immigration of 40,000 per year declining to zero between 2020 and 2025 (United Nations, 2001), compared with a GAD projection of 185,000 between 1998 and 2000 dropping to a permanent 95,000 per year thereafter (Government Actuary, 1998). The United Nations projection is behind the times. It resembles the level and trend of official United Kingdom estimates and projection typical of the early 1990s (Office of Population Censuses and Surveys (OPCS), 1993), when it was set at 50,000 per year declining to zero by 2015-2016. Since then, the reality of growing net immigration has obliged successive GAD revisions to set immigration at 65,000 per year, no longer declining to zero (Government Actuary, 1998), followed by the most recent elevation to a permanent 95,000 in the 1998 projections (Government Actuary, 2000).

TABLE 1. SUMMARY OF VARIANT GAD PROJECTIONS TO 2050

Values 2050 Variable	Projection											
	1 Zero net migration	2 185,000 annual migration	3 TFR= 2.07	4 TFR= 2.00	5 TFR= 1.70	5b Zero net migration; TFR=2.0	5c Zero net migration; TFR=2.075	6 High e0	7 TFR=2.07; high e0	8 TFR=2.0; high e0	11 Constant 1998 fertility, mortality and immigration	GAD 1998 Principal Projection
Population (thousands)	56 108	70 630	71 796	69 527	61 733	60 976	63 059	65 028	72 649	70 378	64 187	64 181
Median age	45.8	43.4	40.4	41.3	45.5	42.7	41.6	44.6	40.9	41.8	42.7	44.1
Population aged 65+ (thousands)	14 608	16 413	15 556	15 556	15 556	14 608	14 608	16 296	16 296	16 296	13 121	15 556
15-64 (percentage)	58.7	60.7	59.7	59.7	60.0	58.6	58.7	59.3	59.1	59.2	63.7	59.9
65+ (percentage)	26.0	23.2	21.7	22.4	25.2	24	23.2	25.1	22.4	23.2	20.4	24.2
Support ratio	2.25	2.61	2.75	2.67	2.38	2.45	2.53	2.37	2.64	2.56	3.12	2.47
Annual population change (thousands)	-240	81	147	91	-133	-103	-54	-11	209	144	-53	0.64
Population growth rate (percentage)	-0.42	0.12	0.20	0.13	-0.21	-0.17	-0.09	-0.02	0.29	0.21	-0.08	-0.10
Net annual migration (thousands)	0	185	95	95	95	0	0	95	95	95	185	95
TFR	1.8	1.8	2.1	2.0	1.7	2.0	2.1	1.8	2.1	2.0	1.7	1.8
e0m	79.7	79.7	79.7	79.7	79.7	79.7	79.7	81.1	81.1	81.1	74.9	79.7
e0f	83.9	83.9	83.9	83.9	83.9	83.9	83.9	85.2	85.2	85.2	79.7	83.9
Support ratio	Upper limit of working age needed to obtain given potential support ratios											
4.09 (1995)	73.6	71.1	70.6	71.1	72.6	72.5	72.1	72.8	71.5	71.9	68.3	72.0
3.5	71.3	69.1	68.4	69.0	70.4	70.3	69.9	70.6	69.3	69.7	66.4	69.9
3.0	69.2	67.0	66.1	66.7	68.3	68.1	67.6	68.5	67.0	67.4	64.5	67.8
	Difference at 2050 between GAD Principal Projection and successive projections											
Population total (thousands)	-8 073	6 449	7 615	5 346	-2 448	-3 205	-1 122	847	8 468	6 197	6	0
Population total (percentage)	-12.58	10.05	11.86	8.33	-3.81	-4.99	-1.75	1.32	13.19	9.66	0.01	0.00
65+ (percentage)	1.80	-1.00	-2.50	-1.80	1.00	-0.20	-1.00	0.90	-1.80	-1.00	-3.80	0.00
Support ratio	-0.22	0.14	0.28	0.20	-0.09	-0.02	0.06	-0.10	0.17	0.09	0.65	0.00

Source: Unpublished calculations by United Kingdom Government Actuary's Department, 8 and 31 August 2000.

NOTE: United Kingdom variant projections based on 1998 GAD Principal Projection to 2050: United Kingdom population (thousands) at 2050. Projection Nos. 9 and 10 are deleted to save space.

TABLE 2. SUMMARY OF VARIANT GAD PROJECTIONS TO 2100

Values 2100					Projection							GAD 1998
	1	2	3	4	5	5b	5c	6	7	8	11	
	Zero net migration	185,000 annual migration	TFR= 2.07	TFR= 2.00	TFR= 1.70	Zero net migration; TFR=2.0	Zero net migration; TFR=2.075	High e0	TFR=2.07; high e0	TFR=2.0; high e0	Constant 1998 fertility, mortality and immigration	Principal Projection
Variable												
Population (thousands)	44 257	72 625	81 808	75 130	53 624	57 204	62 994	64 519	86 956	80 080	61 004	60 052
Median age	45.7	43.5	40.1	41.2	45.4	42.3	41.1	46.8	42.6	43.7	42.6	44.0
Population aged 65+ (thousands)	11 702	17 173	17 219	16 461	13 815	13 354	14 055	18 704	21 784	20 873	12 671	14 660
15-64 (percentage)	58.2	60.3	60.2	60.2	59.4	59.1	59.3	56.2	57.3	57.1	63.3	59.7
65+ (percentage)	26.4	23.6	21.0	21.9	25.8	23.3	22.3	29.0	26.1	26.1	20.8	24.4
Support ratio	2.20	2.55	2.86	2.75	2.31	2.53	2.66	1.94	2.29	2.19	3.05	2.45
Annual population change (thousands)	-212	39	219	124	-144	-60	16	4	327	223	-54	-71
Population growth rate (percentage)	-0.47	0.05	0.27	0.17	-0.26	-0.10	0.03	0.01	0.38	0.28	-0.09	-0.12
Net annual migration (thousands)	0	185	95	95	95	0	0	95	95	95	185	
TFR	1.8	1.8	2.1	2.0	1.7	2.0	2.1	1.8	2.1	2.0	1.7	
e0m	80.1	80.1	80.1	80.1	80.1	80.1	80.1	86.5	86.5	86.5	74.9	
e0f	84.2	84.2	84.2	84.2	84.2	84.2	84.2	90.4	90.4	90.4	79.7	
Upper limit of working age needed to obtain given potential support ratios												
Support ratio												
4.09 (1995)	73.6	71.1	70.6	71.1	72.6				71.5	71.9	68.3	72.0
3.5	71.3	69.1	68.4	69.0	70.4				69.3	69.7	66.4	69.9
3.0	69.2	67.0	66.1	66.7	68.3				67.0	67.4	64.5	67.3
Difference at 2100 between GAD Principal Projection and successive projections												
Population total (thousands)	-15 795	12 573	21 756	15 078	-6 428	-2 848	2 942	4 467	26 904	20 028	952	0
Population total (percentage)	-26.30	20.94	36.23	25.11	-10.70	-4.74	4.90	7.44	44.80	33.35	1.59	0.00
65+ (percentage)	2.00	-0.80	-3.40	-2.50	1.40	-1.10	-2.10	4.60	1.70	1.70	-3.60	0.00
Support ratio	-0.25	0.10	0.41	0.30	-0.14	0.08	0.21	-0.51	-0.16	-0.26	0.60	0.00

Source: Unpublished calculations by United Kingdom Government Actuary's Department, 8 and 31 August 2000.

NOTE: Variant projections based on 1998 GAD Principal Projection: United Kingdom population (thousands) at 2100.

293

Even the recent GAD projection beyond 2000 considerably understates the current flow of 185,000 (Office of National Statistics (ONS), 2000a). The projection invites us to accept a large drop in immigration, to net 95,000 per year, on grounds that may be questionable. The evidence suggests a weakening effectiveness of the traditional United Kingdom policy aim of minimizing immigration (Coleman, 1997). Furthermore, the new Government since 1997 has relaxed some controls, permitting an acceleration of flows for purposes of marriage, and expanded entitlements to entry. It is considering increasing immigration further as a matter of policy, on labour-force and demographic pretexts (Roche, 2000). Its measures to curb asylum flows have been rewarded with record inflows: the United Kingdom became the favoured European asylum destination in 2000. There seem to be no grounds for supposing a halving of net inflows to 95,000. Further increases over the current 185,000 are more likely once cyclical downturns are taken into account.

The total population in 2050 projected by GAD is 7 million—13 per cent—higher than the United Nations medium-variant projection, mostly because of the difference in migration assumptions. The projected population aged 65 years or over is 11 per cent higher. The age burden of the population projected by GAD is accordingly slightly lower, with a slightly higher potential support ratio.

This substantial increase in population arising from the difference in migration assumptions does not generate commensurate changes in age structure, however. The potential support ratio improves by 0.15 (6.5 per cent). The upper limit of working age required in 2050 to maintain the 1995 support ratio of 4.09 falls by 0.3 years, a small advantage for an extra 7 million people. This illustrates the familiar general proposition that even substantial increases in immigration do not have a commensurate impact on population ageing.

C. VARIANT RUNS BASED ON THE 1998 GAD PRINCIPAL PROJECTION

We now turn to investigate a range of projections based on various different plausible assumptions imposed on the 1998 GAD Principal Projection. The projections have all been continued to 2100 (table 2). While even more precarious than a 50-year projection, this shows the long-term stable or quasi-stable distributions to which the assumptions would give rise, including the effects of continued improvement in survival, and long-term implications for population size. The projections to 2100 also show the mildly favourable effects on age structure and dependency of the final disappearance of the baby-boom cohorts which causes a once-for-all worsening of dependency from the 2020s.

1. *Zero net migration*

This projection assumes zero net migration at all ages, not just net migration overall (the United Nations zero migration variant does the same). This is quite a strong assumption. It produces the lowest final population total of all (by 2050, 8.01 million—12.6 per cent—less than the GAD 1998 Principal Projection, 3 million less than the 2000 figure, and 44.3 million total population in 2100). The proportions aged 65 years or over and the support ratio are the least "favourable" of any of the projections considered so far, with the "required" limit of working age at the highest level. These results resemble those of previous United Kingdom projections made by GAD in 1994 and 1996 which assumed lower migration declining eventually to zero.

2. Constant migration at 185,000

This assumes that migration will continue at the 1998 level of 185,000 net intake per year, that is to say, 9.25 million net immigrants over the next 50 years. Equal numbers of male and female immigrants are assumed. Not surprisingly, this projection generates substantial population growth to 70.6 million in 2050 (72.6 million in 2100), 6.45 million (10.1 per cent) more than in the GAD 1998 Principal Projection. The migration effect increases the United Kingdom population by 14.5 million people (25.9 per cent) compared with the zero migration projection in 2050 and by 11.4 million over the actual 1998 population of 59.2 million (19.2 per cent). Like all the other projections, this assumes, unrealistically, that immigrants immediately acquire the fertility and mortality patterns of the host population.

This considerable increase in population does not have commensurate effects upon the age structure (tables 1 and 2). Median age falls to 43.4 by 2050 compared with 44.1 in the GAD 1998 and with 45.8 in the zero migration projection. The potential support ratio rises to 2.61 and the "required" upper limit of working age falls to 71.1. This level of migration not only exceeds the United Nations scenario "requirements" for constant total population (on average 48,000 net immigrants per year) but is also comfortably ahead of the numbers calculated by the United Nations to provide a constant age group 15-64 (on average, 114,000 per year) (United Nations, 2001, table 24).

3. Replacement fertility (TFR = 2.075)

In this projection, fertility is raised by 22 per cent to 2.075, the "replacement" TFR, while net immigration and expectation of life remain at the GAD Principal Projection levels. Total population increases to 1.2 million more than the high-immigration variant (to 71.8 million by 2050) and to considerably more (81.8 million) by 2100. By 2050, this projection produces the lowest proportion of population aged 65 years or over (21.7 per cent), the lowest median age (40.4) and the highest potential support ratio (2.75 and rising) of any of the variant projections other than the "constant values" projection noted below.

4. High fertility (TFR = 2.0)

This scenario is the same as the official GAD-based high-fertility variant, representing an increase in TFR over the GAD Principal Projection of 0.2 or 11 per cent. Its effects approach those of the previous scenario.

5. Low fertility (TFR = 1.7)

This scenario assumes that fertility remains at its present level of 1.7 instead of increasing to 1.8 as expected in the GAD Principal Projection, remaining therefore 0.1 or 5.6 per cent less. By 2050, population declines by 2.45 million (-3.8 per cent) with the potential support ratio down to 2.38. Proportion of population aged 65 years or over rises to 25.2 per cent.

5b.   *Zero net migration with TFR = 2.0;*
5c.   *Zero net migration and TFR = 2.075*

Identical to projections Nos. 4 and 3, respectively, but with zero migration. In 5c, the increase of fertility to replacement rate (2.075) adds 3 million to population growth, which reaches a peak of 63 million in 2050 despite the absence of net migration—about the same as the GAD Principal Projection. However, median age is reduced considerably to 41.6 and the potential support ratio is slightly more favourable (2.53). This projection ends the century with a population of 63 million growing at a negligible rate (mortality ceases to improve in 2060).

6.   *Lower mortality (e0m = 81.1, e0f = 85.2)*

Here the expectation of life at birth for males ($e0m$) is allowed to rise from the official GAD figure of 79.7 and the expectation of life at birth for females ($e0f$) from the official GAD figure of 83.9 by 2050 (very pessimistic, in this author's view) to the slightly higher figures of 81.1 and 85.2, respectively (only slightly less pessimistic). TFR remains at 1.8 and net immigration at 95,000. This amelioration of mortality is at the rate projected by Tuljapurkar, Li and Boe (2000). Population increases by 0.85 million. Because the benefit in survival accrues to the older population, the potential support ratio falls slightly to 2.37 compared with 2.47 for the GAD 1998 Principal Projection. By 2100, the application of this conservative assumption leads to the arresting conclusion that $e0m$ will reach 86.5 and $e0f$, 90.4 years. Twenty-nine per cent of the population of 64.5 million would be aged 65 years or over with a support ratio of 1.9, and population growth would be almost exactly zero.

7.   *Replacement fertility (TFR = 2.075) and high life expectancy*

This projection combines the replacement fertility of projection 3 with the increased survival of projection 6. This produces the most substantial population growth of any scenario (72.6 million by 2050, 87.0 million by 2100). By 2050, it yields a low median age (40.9) and a high potential support ratio (2.64), comparable with the replacement fertility projection. By 2100, the population is older and bigger.

8.   *TFR = 2.0 with high life expectancy*

This simulation represents a more moderate version of the previous one, with a less favourable potential support ratio, and a surprisingly large fall in the projected 2100 population (down by 7 million to 80 million). In the opinion of this author, an outcome of the kind represented by projection 7 or 8, apart from the migration assumption, may be the most realistic in the long run.

11. *Constant fertility, mortality and immigration*

Here vital rates are left exactly as they are in 1998, as a kind of benchmark. This generates almost exactly the same population total as the GAD 1998 Principal Projection by 2050, but with a somewhat different age structure. TFR, immigration and expectation of life at birth for both sexes remains at today's level, that is to say, for the last-mentioned, about six years below the eventual figure projected for 2050. This depresses population growth. However, through its prevention of an important component of growth in the older population, combined with the effects of high immigration, this projection keeps the proportion aged 65 years or over the lowest of any scenario (20.4 per cent). The support ratio is kept to its highest level (3.12), with an upper limit of "required" working age at 68.3, almost three years below that in any other projection. This underlines the important effects of mortality upon age structures in the twenty-first century (Calot and Sardon, 1999).

Finally, it is instructive to look at some projections where the fertility assumptions go beyond the realm of credibility (not shown here in detail; see Shaw (2001), figure 8). For example, with TFR = 2.5 (the level in 1970), the support ratio recovers to about 3.7, although at the cost of continuing population growth, while even 1 million net immigrants per year cannot prevent its declining constantly to 3 and below.

D. IMMIGRATION/FERTILITY "REQUIREMENTS"

The alternative method (as in the report of the Population Division) is to approach the question from the other direction: to determine the levels of migration or fertility (or other changes) required to achieve certain demographic targets. However, the Population Division determined these annual "requirements" by averaging the 50-year total. Very different results are obtained if this requirement is calculated on a year-to-year basis. The annual required inflow then becomes very volatile (table 3), as earlier demographers have shown.

In order to maintain the potential support ratio at 4.22, the necessary annual net inflow calculated on this basis reaches 1.5 million per year by 2025, falls to nearly half a million per year by 2040 and rises to over 5 million per year at the end of the century. To maintain a constant workforce size requires annual net immigration peaking at 330,000 around 2025. The inflows "required" are very much at the mercy of the size of successive birth cohorts; past fluctuations in fertility determine annual "requirements" for immigrants. It would be impossible to control immigration in such a fine-tuned manner, and these figures take no account of economic trends and workforce participation, which determine the real support ratio and labour demand. Most immigration is non-economic anyway, just as much in the United States and Canada as in Europe, if not more; "planned" migration envisaged here would have to

297

compete with unplanned family and asylum migration. Migration while easy to start is particularly difficult to stop if coming from a poor country. The difficulty of stop-go immigration required to this end was first demonstrated over a decade ago (Blanchet, 1989; Wattelaar and Roumans, 1990), and those conclusions have stood the test of time.

The most exciting projection is, of course, the incredible in pursuit of the implausible; that is to say, the population size implied by the migration "required" to maintain the potential support ratio (table 4). On this requirement, the United Kingdom population would exceed 100 million even by 2040, 200 million by 2070 and 300 million by 2090. Population size required to meet the workforce criterion is much more modest, as the United Nations report itself notes. By 2050, the population size implied by the "required" migration to keep workforce constant at 1998 levels is only 63 million and remains at about that level until the end of the century—lower than in the GAD 1998 Principal Projection. This is because the United Kingdom is already experiencing a high level of migration, considerably more than it "needs". The United Kingdom also enjoys a relatively benign fertility regime, which ensures that projected declines in any sector of the population are small. Maintaining the workforce achieved by later years requires somewhat larger population size, but never one exceeding 68 million.

E. EVALUATING RESULTS

The first conclusion is that, short of the impossibly high levels of immigration "required" to maintain the potential support ratio, no reasonable assumption of future demographic change makes a very radical difference to any of the indicators by 2050 (table 5 and figure). Furthermore, because of the momentum of the present age structure, changes in vital rates may take a long time to have significant effects; stable population structures take time. The values of the potential support ratio, for example, range from 2.25 to 3.12, all very far from the current 4.1. Excluding the figure of 3.12, derived from an impossible "no change" scenario, the effective range is from 2.25 to 2.75. National retirement age to conserve the existing potential support ratio varies from 70 to 74. The demographic aspects of population ageing and the decline of potential support ratios are inevitable: it is impossible for modern vital rates to preserve the age structure created by former vital rates now irrevocably extinct. This situation will have to be lived with for as long as the species survives. While the numbers of contributors will remain almost constant from 2000 to 2061, the numbers of pensioners increase rapidly after 2020. Their numbers then cease to increase and even decline after 2040 to establish a new equilibrium (Government Actuary, 1999, figure 4.2) as the baby-boom queue at last moves on from the benefit office to the pearly gates. But in the case of the United Kingdom, compared with many other countries, the demographic problems of ageing are relatively benign. Amelioration and management must come primarily from non-demographic channels, as noted below. The figure plots population size against potential support ratio for the various simulations described above by the year 2050.

TABLE 3. ANNUAL NET MIGRATION "REQUIRED" TO ACHIEVE GIVEN POPULATION, WORKFORCE AND POTENTIAL SUPPORT RATIO TARGETS, UNITED KINGDOM, 1998-2100

(Thousands)

Target	1998	2000	2010	2020	2025	2030	2040	2050	2060	2070	2080	2100
Potential support ratio												
3.0	175	99	95	95	932	629	-66	221	671	1 232	-653	-32
3.5	175	99	95	939	1 346	661	-74	679	2 013	1 206	-1 260	1 536
4.22	175	99	1 195	1 063	1 523	833	578	2 651	2 304	1 331	974	5 854
Workforce absolute size												
15-64 as in 1998	-115	-121	134	222	329	173	-11	172	226	120	38	170
Population absolute size 1998 population	-75	-60	-27	14	67	134	170	162	120	107	116	123

Source: Unpublished calculations by United Kingdom Government Actuary's Department.

TABLE 4. POPULATION SIZE "REQUIRED" TO MAINTAIN POPULATION AND WORKFORCE TARGETS, UNITED KINGDOM, 1998-2100

(Thousands)

Target	1998	2000	2010	2020	2025	2030	2050	2060	2080	2100
Potential support ratio										
3.0	59 237	59 750	61 587	63 470	64 235	69 139	77 026	77 957	100 612	90 799
3.5	59 237	59 750	61 587	64 948	70 507	78 761	89 983	97 276	142 625	143 923
4.22	59 237	59 750	63 371	76 637	84 383	94 716	118 902	152 648	213 207	303 371
Workforce absolute size										
15-64 as in 1998	59 237	59 155	58 578	60 145	61 492	63 273	63 093	63 125	64 723	63 481

Source: Unpublished calculations by United Kingdom Government Actuary's Department.

		Population values in 2050				
No.	Projection	Total population	Median age	Percentage aged 65+	Support ratio	Working-age limit
13	1998 actual	59 237	36.9	15.7	4.15	62.5
11	Constant 1998	64 187	42.7	20.4	3.12	68.3
3	GAD TFR = 2.07	71 796	40.4	21.7	2.75	70.6
4	GAD TFR = 2.0	69 527	41.3	22.4	2.67	71.1
7	TFR = 2.07, high e0	72 649	40.9	22.4	2.64	71.5
2	GAD 185,000 annual migration	70 630	43.4	23.2	2.61	71.1
8	TFR 2.0, high e0	70 378	41.8	23.2	2.56	71.9
5c	GAD TFR = 2.07, 0 migration	63 059	41.6	23.2	2.53	72.1
21	TFR = 2.075, 0 migration	63 100	41.6	23.2	2.53	72.1
12	GAD 1998 Principal Projection	64 181	44.1	24.2	2.47	72.0
5b	GAD TFR = 2.0, 0 migration	60 976	42.7	24.0	2.45	75.5
20	TFR = 2.0, 0 migration	61 000	42.7	24.0	2.45	75.5
9	TFR 2.07, high e0, 0 migration	63 874	42.2	24.0	2.42	73.0
5	GAD TFR = 1.7	61 733	45.5	25.2	2.38	72.6
6	GAD high e0	65 028	44.6	25.1	2.37	72.8
10	TFR = 2.0, high e0, 0 migration	61 790	43.2	24.8	2.34	73.4
1	GAD 0 migration	56 108	45.8	26.0	2.25	73.6

Source: Unpublished calculations by United Kingdom Government Actuary's Department.

The "constant support ratio" projection with very high (1 million plus) annual immigration dictates the scale of the upper graph in the figure, with double the population of every other projection. The next "best buy" in terms of potential support ratio is No. 11 (3.12), where vital rates and immigration are left at their current 1998 level (table 5). The distance between that projection and the current potential support ratio (4.1) shows how much of today's potential support ratio is owed to the inheritance of the vital rates of the past, preserved in today's age structure but lost forever by 2050. Most of the additional 5 million population in that scenario is the result of the continuation of immigration at today's high annual level of 185,000.

That constant-values scenario is hardly an option unless Governments act to suppress the improvement of survival and birth rates. The lower graph in the figure shows the range of scenarios based on the more "reasonable" assumptions. These occupy a small elliptical demographic space in the upper graph, but a change of scale in the lower graph shows that this space is actually substantial: a range of total population from 56 million to 73 million (a range of 17 million or 30 per cent of the lower figure), and a smaller range of support ratio, from 2.25 to 2.75 or 22 per cent. The projections fall naturally into three loose clusters along this narrow range of potential support ratio. The first, with the lowest population growth (down to about 56 million) and lowest support ratios between 2.25 and 2.35, include the two zero migration scenarios. The United Nations medium variant for the United Kingdom is close in population size to the United Nations zero migration variant because the assumed level of migration in the medium variant is so low. Higher replacement fertility, and lower mortality, lift the zero migration projections to a higher level of

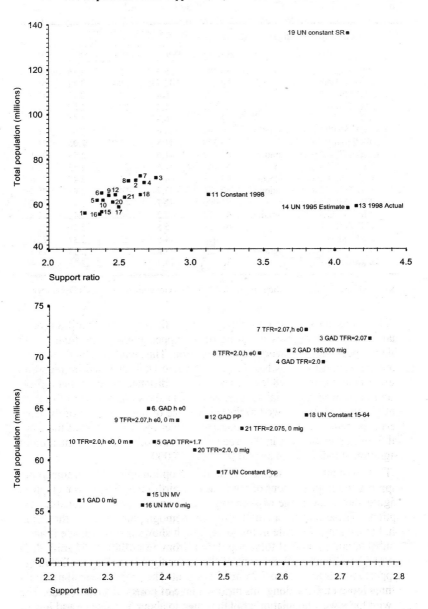

Population versus support ratio, GAD and United Nations

NOTE: The lower graph is an enlargement of the left part of the upper graph.

population (between 60 million and 65 million) and potential support ratios from about 2.35 to 2.55 (GAD 9) in a middle cluster, all close to the GAD 12 Principal Projection. Increased survival combined with 95,000 annual migration (GAD 6) predictably slightly worsens the support ratio.

A third cluster of variants generates considerably higher population growth, by 4-8 million people more than the GAD Principal Projection, to between 70 million and 74 million (see table 6). These are all the higher TFR variants (TFR = 2.0 or 2.07), some in combination with higher survival, all with standard 95,000 immigration, plus the standard GAD variant with the high current migration level of 185,000. The GAD 3 projection with replacement fertility (and standard 95,000 immigration) gives the highest potential support ratio (2.75).

TABLE 6. COMPARISON OF DIFFERENT SCENARIOS WITH
GAD PRINCIPAL PROJECTION (PP)

	Total population (thousands)	Median age	Percentage aged 65+	Support ratio	Working-age limit
GAD 1998 PP	64 181	44.1	24.2	2.47	72.0
Fertility effect					
2.07	7 615	-3.7	-2.5	0.28	-1.4
2.00	5 346	-2.8	-1.8	0.20	-0.9
1.70	-2 448	1.4	1.0	-0.09	0.6
As GAD 1998 = 100					
Fertility effect (GAD 95,000 annual migration)					
2.07	111.9	91.6	89.7	111.3	98.1
2.00	108.3	93.7	92.6	108.1	98.8
1.70	96.2	103.2	104.1	96.4	100.8
Fertility effect (zero migration)					
2.07	98.3	94.3	95.9	102.4	100.1
2.00	95.0	96.8	99.2	99.2	104.9
1.70	..	..	..	..	..
Migration effect (GAD fertility trends)					
Zero	87.4	103.9	107.4	91.1	102.2
185,000	110.0	98.4	95.9	105.7	98.8
Ageing effect (GAD fertility and migration)					
No change	92.3	96.8	84.3	126.3	94.9
Higher e0	101.3	101.1	103.7	96.0	101.1

Source: Unpublished calculations by United Kingdom Government Actuary's Department.

The effects of changes in fertility, immigration and survival respectively upon the potential support ratio, holding the other two variables constant, are presented in table 7. The first shows the effects on percentage change of the support ratio, of given percentage changes in each variable. It may not be intuitively obvious what the equivalence is between a given percentage increase in fertility and the same percentage increase in immigration etc. So the effects are also compared through the change in support ratio generated per million in-

TABLE 7. VARIATIONS OF THE POTENTIAL SUPPORT RATIO

Change in potential support ratio per million increase in population generated by:		
Fertility	Immigration	Expectation of life
0.037	0.025	-0.119

Percentage change in potential support ratio per million increase in population:		
Fertility	Immigration	Expectation of life
1.545	1.102	-4.689

Percentage change in potential support ratio from 10 per cent increase in each variable:		
Fertility	Immigration	Expectation of life
7.075	0.597	-2.424

Source: Unpublished calculations by United Kingdom Government Actuary's Department.

crease in population size caused by change in each variable. The most efficient process yields the biggest increase in support ratio for the smallest percentage increase in population, or increase produced in population size.

In the lower graph of the figure, the diagonal from GAD 1 through GAD 12 to GAD 2 shows the effect given constant fertility of net annual immigration increasing from 0 to 95,000 to 185,000. From lowest to highest, this gives an additional population of 14.5 million with an improvement in potential support ratio of 0.36, or 0.025 per million population.

The effect of increased fertility with constant 95,000 net immigration is shown in the more favourable slope from GAD 5 through GAD 12 to GAD 4 and GAD 3, and also from GAD 20 to GAD 21: a population increase of 10 million for an increase in support ratio of 0.37. This represents a "rate of improvement" of support ratio of 0.037 per million population, about 50 per cent more efficient than that attained by the migration route (0.025). However, any increase in fertility brings an increase in child support costs. Even replacement TFR, of course, cannot restore a potential support ratio of 4.1. A similar slope is given by the line with constant zero migration but increasing fertility, from GAD 1 with zero migration (TFR = 1.8) through GAD 20 with TFR = 2.0 and finally GAD 21 with TFR = 2.075. In projection 21, the population is not quite stable but there is hardly any future population growth to 2100. The potential support ratio is just over 2.5 and the externalities of the high migration streams in other projections are permanently avoided.

Finally, the effects of increased survival, at constant levels of fertility and migration, move the potential support ratio sharply backwards with small increases in population size. Examples are the transition from No. 3 to No. 7 and the parallel transition from No. 4 to No. 8 and from No. 6 to No. 12. The effect is to worsen the potential support ratio by 0.119 for every million increase in population arising solely from longer survival.

These coefficients are derived from the actual data in the scenarios. Equivalent comparisons do not produce exactly the same results. Somewhat different values would be obtained if truly stable populations were being compared. This being said, as expected from demographic theory, fertility emerges as by far the most efficient factor affecting potential support ratio. This is particularly marked in the comparison based upon the effect of a given percentage increase in the value of each independent variable.

How impressive this is depends upon the degree to which it is feasible to envisage changes in each variable. From 1964 to 2000, the TFR of the United Kingdom varied from 2.94 to 1.66, the higher figure representing an increase of 77 per cent over the lower figure. In the last 20 years, it has varied between 1.7 and 1.84. Net annual immigration has varied from −87,000 in the 1960s to +185,000 in the latest year, 1998. During the 1980s and 1990s, the figure only exceeded 100,000 in the last few, highly exceptional years (which may, of course, become the norm).

So far the effective demographic effects of actual immigration have been more modest than those of fertility. The effects measured in terms of population growth need to be interpreted in terms of the ease with which each variable can influence growth. Further increases in survival have substantial effects on age structure but more modest effects on population size. Astonishing improvements in survival would be needed for a United Kingdom population increase of more than 2-3 million, while this would be easy to obtain with feasible changes in fertility or immigration.

F. POSSIBLE POLICY RESPONSES

The actual policies proposed in response to population ageing by the Government of the United Kingdom are authoritatively presented elsewhere in Karen Dunnell's paper and need no review here. A few general alternatives will briefly be listed. No complete policy solution is possible; any amelioration of the situation must depend on a multiple response, which falls into four broad categories.

1. *Microeconomics and social policy*

In respect of financial and fiscal arrangements for pensions, savings and old-age health care, population ageing has undermined the original demographic underpinnings of public sector pay-as-you-go (PAYG) schemes. These are unfunded pensions whereby money is removed from workers by taxation and given to retired persons as pensions, with (usually) defined benefits. The United Kingdom National Insurance "Fund", for example, is not a fund in the form of an investment of cumulated contributions, as in funded pensions, but merely a header tank, into which workers' National Insurance (tax) contributions flow and from which pensions are drained off continuously. Such schemes were conceived in a world when support ratios were 10 or more and must now survive when such ratios are falling to 3 or less. Either pension promises must be denied or taxation substantially increased, from about 15 to about 40-50 per cent of pay according to various projections.

This problem could have been seen coming a long way off. Far-sighted Governments had already begun to revise, or encourage alternatives to, the more baroque PAYG commitments before liability became too great, although not always very successfully. For example, the United Kingdom's unfunded State Earnings Related Pension Scheme (SERPS) introduced in 1978 promised greatly to increase public liability for pensions (Kay, 1988). The then Government, committed to private sector alternatives and deregulation, wished to eliminate SERPS altogether. This proved impossible, although tempting tax reliefs were offered to encourage contracting out in favour of privately funded pensions. In the event, this proved expensive and provoked an over-hasty expansion into private sector alternatives, some of which were mis-sold or mismanaged. SERPS is to be discontinued in 2002 and replaced by the new State Second Pension (SSP) intended for low to moderate earners. The general aim of the present Government, however, is to increase the proportion of pensions provided by the State from today's 60 to 40 per cent. From April 2001, "stakeholder" pensions will open, intended to give additional funded pensions entitlement even to the poorest, through a change in the rules to make it much easier for all those in employment to contribute to an independent pension.

The adoption by the Government of the United Kingdom of the linkage of State flat-rate pensions to prices, not earnings, through the Social Security Administration Act 1992 has had a powerful downward effect upon pension costs (table 8). This reduction in the rate of increase in the real value of State pensions has attracted much criticism and pressure from trade unions and pensioners groups for restoration of the earnings link; but what it means is that the United Kingdom is the only major country whose working population is not expected to bear a substantial increase in the burden of State contributions on the working-age population over the next several decades (Eatwell, 1999, p. 57).

Authoritative reviews (for example, Organisation for Economic Co-operation and Development (OECD), 1988; UNECE, 1999a; Daykin and Lewis, 1999) point out that any amelioration of the problem should be found within the parameters of the existing system. None even mentioned immigration. No specific pension reform provided a panacea: a multiple response was needed. Although the impact of population ageing may be less evident in a funded system, payment of any pensions to the elderly inevitably involves a transfer of resources from the wealth-creating part of the economy. The value of investments must be affected by changes in the balance of buyers and sellers.

A move to funded schemes is assumed, however, to benefit the economy by generating new productive investment, if it does not replace other investment. That may encourage faster sustainable growth, low inflation and low unemployment, all of which will make pensions more affordable, although the reality of this response has been questioned (Chand and Jaeger, 1996; Eatwell, 1999). The World Bank (1994) has suggested a three-pillar system: continuing flat rate social security blanket pensions to protect the poorest, a funded second pillar of occupational pensions and a third funded private pension system—a view that enjoys widespread support but with different views as to the appropriate relative size of each pillar.

Among European countries, the United Kingdom is far ahead in reform, having a much higher ratio of funded occupation and private schemes invested in the stock exchange and government securities compared with its European

TABLE 8. PROPORTION OF GDP TAKEN BY STATE PENSIONS, WITH CORRESPONDING
INCREASES IN CONTRIBUTIONS PAID BY WORKERS, 1984-2040, SELECTED COUNTRIES

	1984	2000	2020	2040
Germany				
Pensions as per cent of GDP . .	13.7	16.4	21.6	31.1
Burden (1980 = 100)	100	106	124	154
Japan				
Pensions as per cent of GDP . .	6.0	9.4	14.0	15.7
Burden (1980 = 100)	100	115	142	154
Netherlands				
Pensions as per cent of GDP . .	12.1	13.4	19.6	28.5
Burden (1980 = 100)	100	100	114	139
United Kingdom				
Pensions as per cent of GDP . .	7.7	7.5	8.6	11.2
Burden (1980 = 100)	100	93	101	111
United States				
Pensions as per cent of GDP . .	8.1	8.2	11.3	14.6
Burden (1980 = 100)	100	96	117	131

Source: Organisation for Economic Co-operation and Development (OECD) (1988); and
Eatwell (1999).

NOTE: "Burden" is the real value of pensions per head of the working-age population 15-64,
that is to say, an estimate of the increase in transfer costs that the average worker can expect.

neighbours, where PAYG earnings-related State pensions are the norm. The
implied debt of these schemes exceeds the gross domestic product (GDP) of
many European countries (Social Security Committee, 1996). However, the
United Kingdom's advantage may be lost if such indebtedness is pooled on any
future junction with the euro (Stein, 1997).

2. *Macroeconomic responses*

Higher productivity (output per worker), competitiveness and economic
growth would go a long way towards resolving the higher costs of an economy
with an ageing population, with its relatively higher levels of additional consumption by the elderly. To begin with, lower labour-force growth reduces
the burden of providing capital for new workers and raises the consumption
(standard of living) level associated with any given capital stock. The positive
effect is more powerful than the costs of ageing, up to a workforce decline
rate of 0.5 per cent per year, according to Weil (1997, pp. 984-985). Most
calculations assume that population ageing will increase consumption adjusted
for needs (taking into account reduced child dependency) by an extra 0.5 per
cent of GDP per year, thus trimming one quarter from a (modest) assumed
economic growth rate of 2 per cent (Weil, 1997). Properly managed through
reform of work practices and higher capital investment, population ageing and
its supposed relative worker shortages may provide a needed stimulus to higher
productivity in Europe, where the position is weak compared with that of its
competitors (the United States, Japan and some Asian industrialized economies). However, if this requires a higher capital/labour ratio than previously,

one of the advantages noted above is lost. A relative shortage of workers could force entrepreneurs into the unwelcome task of reforming work practices and investing in more modern processes, which would raise real wages for a non-growing or smaller but more productive workforce.

Enterprises that cannot do this, or cannot afford to pay market-clearing rates for the work in question—garment trades, ancient foundries, fruit-picking and other low-skill activities—can be abandoned or their activities moved off-shore and third world imports substituted for them. It is a temptation to use "cheap immigrant labour" to permit undercapitalized, low-productivity enter-prises to survive beyond their sell-by date, preserving an obsolete economy and reducing national competitiveness (United States Department of Labor, 1989). The situation may be reached where unprofitable industries with permanently resident immigrant workforces could survive only with a public subsidy, as is the case with coal mines in Germany. The enhancement of international com-petitiveness, quite apart from any response to supposed labour shortages and the costs of an ageing population, requires capital investment to increase pro-ductivity. This will move developed economies further from labour-intensive to capital-intensive activities. In various European countries, additional annual productivity growth peaking at 0.5-0.8 per cent would be adequate by itself to cope with the extra burden of old-age dependency (European Commission, 1996). This is similar to the estimate by Weil (1997).

3. Workforce measures

Other major adjustments within the demographic system are possible to increase the size of the active population: first, mobilizing the inactive popula-tion of existing working age (that is to say, increasing workforce participation rates), which increases the numerator of the support ratio; second, expanding the boundaries of working age itself by encouraging later retirement, which takes into account the prolongation of expectation of life. If the latter can be achieved, it would be a particularly effective move, as it simultaneously in-creases the numerator of the support ratio and reduces its denominator.

Workforce participation rates cannot increase forever, of course, and by themselves provide a once-for-all, but potentially enduring advantage up to around 2020 (Lesthaeghe, 2000). In Europe since the Second World War, changes in workforce participation, particularly by women, have often had a more powerful effect on the labour force than has demographic change, includ-ing immigration (Eurostat, 1988). Europe has considerable unused reserves of population of working age (European Commission, 1991). Unemployment is high, hidden unemployment is often equivalent in magnitude, workforce participation rates low. In some Southern countries, employment is too much concentrated in protected public sector bureaucratic activities which impede, rather than promote, economic growth. Many of these problems are linked to an excessively high level of "social protection", including State-funded pen-sions, which raises labour costs and thus unemployment, at present about 9 per cent in continental Europe.

In the United Kingdom, growth in the workforce has been projected officially only to 2011 (Armitage and Scott, 1998), so it is not possible to incorporate official workforce projections into the population scenarios beyond 2011. By that year, the labour force in Great Britain (excluding Northern Ireland) is expected to have grown from 28.0 million to 28.6 million. Demographic growth accounts for 55 per cent of the increase; the rest is the result of contrasting trends in male and female economic activity. In recent decades, as elsewhere in Europe, male activity rates have fallen through early retirement, and those of women have increased. Activity rates as a proportion of males aged 16-64 are projected to fall from 84.4 to 81.7 per cent and those of women aged 16-59 to rise from 73.1 to 75.4 per cent. Early retirement of men has had a powerful erosive effect on the United Kingdom workforce. In the 1980s, it was encouraged to make way for young workers in the baby-boom cohorts then suffering high unemployment. More recently, the rise of "incapacity" early retirement in the United Kingdom has provided a convenient way of removing older workers on dubious medical grounds, whose redundancy is then paid for at public expense. By the early 1990s, this became the fastest-growing form of welfare transfer in the United Kingdom, increasing from 4.6 billion pounds (£) in 1990-1991 to £7.4 billion in 1997-1998 (peaking at £8 billion in 1994-1995 (Government Actuary, 1999, table 12.2)), a rate of increase of disability hitherto unknown to medical science.

The Government Actuary (1999), in his projections of active population in relation to pension entitlement, assumes that the activity rates achieved by 2011 will remain constant to 2051. They include about a million further individuals who continue working beyond retirement age. Their addition increases the workforce total from 28.96 million in 2001 to 29.77 million by 2011. Projecting United Kingdom workforce beyond 2011 is complicated by the switch of female pension entitlement from age 60 to age 65 by 2021. It is not clear how female economic activity will respond. Nonetheless, preservation of the 2011 rate for 40 years is quite a conservative assumption. The decline in male activity rates has slowed in the United Kingdom and current United Kingdom government policy, described in Karen Dunnell's paper, aims to reverse this decline. Female participation rates have been increasing for some time and there is no reason to suppose that they will cease to rise after 2011, quite apart from the imponderable effects of the increase in formal retirement age. United Kingdom rates, although relatively high by European Union (EU) standards, still have some way to go before they match those of some rich European countries. What is the realistic scope for further increase? For example, in terms of the population of nominal working age from 16 to 64, the United Kingdom ranked eighth overall in OECD economies in 1999. These comparisons are not altogether straightforward, not least because the proportions of women working part-time differ internationally (these are high in the United Kingdom), and these data do not include persons aged 65 years or over who are in the workforce. Table 9 suggests that there is some scope for further increase in United Kingdom workforce participation rates, which could rise by about another 7 percentage points before they reach the level of Switzerland. Norway or Denmark might be a more realistic "target", and here the United Kingdom male workforce participation rates are already their equal. There is more scope for an increase in female workforce participation rates, however. By 2051, the potential support ratio will have fallen from 4.1 to 2.47, as noted above. If the 1998 United Kingdom workforce participation rates still apply in 2051, the proportion of population aged 15-64 that is economically active will fall to 75.1.

What really matters, however, is the support ratio between those receiving benefits and those working and paying taxes. Table 10 presents two ways of calculating this, under various hypotheses for the future. Column 2 shows the ratio of actual workforce on these hypotheses to formally defined old-age dependants in receipt of retirement pensions assuming a uniform retirement age of 65. Column 3 shows the ratio of the actual workforce to all dependants over age 15, that is to say, the population over age 15 that is not economically active, not just that aged 65 years or over. Naturally, the ratios in column 3 are even less favourable than those in column 2. However, with different hypotheses about workforce participation, they "improve" much more. In column 2, the number of dependants is fixed, determined demographically by the population aged 65 years or over. In column 3, as the workforce increases, the dependent population, although always larger, decreases in proportion. This latter dependent population gives a better idea of the dependency burden. A large part of the under-65 dependent population is, of course, those who have retired early, before age 65. However, it also includes those who never work at all ages, and young people who have not yet entered the workforce.

In 1998 the support ratio for old-age pensioners was 3.19 and at constant workforce participation rates will fall to 1.86 in 2051. The "actual" support ratio for all non-working dependants over age 15 begins at an even lower level, namely, 1.67, and falls to just 1.19 at constant participation rates by 2051. Can any plausible increases in workforce participation, within the framework of a retirement age of 65, restore the balance to any figure comparable to the starting point of 1.67? This is the only important goal, because it determines the

TABLE 9. LABOUR-FORCE ACTIVITY RATES: THE TOP 10 IN 1999 OF THE ORGANISATION FOR ECONOMIC CO-OPERATION AND DEVELOPMENT

(Percentage)

Country	Overall activity rate	Male activity rate	Female activity rate	Females in workforce (percentage)
Iceland	89.8	94.3	85.2	38.4
Switzerland	84.9	92.2	77.3	39.7
Norway.	82.0	86.5	77.3	45.7
Denmark.	81.1	85.6	76.5	40.2
Sweden.	79.5	82.5	76.4	47.8
United States	79.5	86.7	72.6	45.7
Japan	78.1	92.4	63.7	..
United Kingdom.	77.6	85.7	69.4	43.3
Canada	76.4	83.4	70.4	45.0
Netherlands[a]	73.5	83.7	63.1	39.7

Sources: Organisation for Economic Co-operation and Development (OECD) (1999); United Nations, Economic Commission for Europe (1997), p. 94, table 4.1.

NOTE: These activity rates are relative to the population aged 16-64. Activity rates include persons in employment plus the unemployed seeking work.

[a]Netherlands data refer to 1998; percentage of females in workforce refers to 1996.

TABLE 10. FUTURE SUPPORT RATIOS AND PERCENTAGE OF POPULATION OF WORKING AGE
ECONOMICALLY ACTIVE, ON VARIOUS HYPOTHESES, UNITED KINGDOM

Year	Scenario	Potential SR (1)	Actual SR to 65+ (2)	Actual SR to non-workers (3)	Percentage population aged 15-64 economically active (4)
1998	1998 wpr	4.15	3.19	1.67	76.9
2051	1998 wpr	2.47	1.86	1.19	75.1
2051	D99m + D99f	2.47	1.94	1.27	78.7
2051	J99m + D99f	2.47	2.00	1.36	80.9
2051	J99m + UK21f	2.47	2.03	1.49	82.1
2051	GB71m + GB21f	2.47	2.09	1.54	84.2
2051	100 per cent working	2.47	2.47	2.47	100.0

Source: Unpublished calculations by United Kingdom Government Actuary's Department.
NOTE:
Potential SR = potential support ratio (population 15-64/population 65+)
Actual SR to 65+ = actual support ratio of actual working population/population 65+
Actual SR to non-workers = actual support ratio of actual working population/non-working
    population aged 15 years or over
1998 wpr = actual workforce participation rates for males and females in 1998
D99m, D99f = workforce participation rates for Danish males and females, 1999
J99m = workforce participation rates for Japanese males, 1999
UK21f = hypothetical workforce participation rates, United Kingdom females after equalization
    of statutory retirement age to 65; assumes participation rates in same proportion to those
    of men in 1998 among women aged 55-59 or over
GB71m = actual workforce participation rates of men in Great Britain, 1971
Because of differences in age-group boundaries etc., these calculations are only approximate.

balance between production and consumption. Here, "plausible" is taken to
refer to rates actually achieved in developed societies.

For Europe in general, a calculation made in 1990 showed that, if the
whole EU developed employment participation rates equivalent to those of
Denmark, then over 30 million persons would be added to the labour force
(Coleman, 1992). That is considerably more than the shortfall in labour force
projected for the next 20 years. What would Danish labour-force participation
rates of 1999 do for the United Kingdom workforce in 2051? A modest improvement is evident, arising from improvements in female rates only; those
of men are about the same, and at some ages are actually lower in Denmark.
Given the social similarities between the United Kingdom and Denmark, and
the current drift of government policy, that does not seem at all far-fetched.
Would it be possible to go a stage further, and imagine British men with Japanese rates (up to age 64 only)? Japanese male workforce participation is much
lower than in the United Kingdom at the youngest ages, but higher in older
ages. This, combined with Danish female rates, brings the support ratios up
to 2.00 and 1.36. Even the high Scandinavian rates may well increase further.
The low variant of the Swedish labour-force projections to age 64 from 1998 to
2015, for example, shows a fall of 0.3 per cent, while the high variant indicates
an increase of 6.9 per cent (Hultin, 1999).

It must not be forgotten that between 2011 and 2021 United Kingdom "official" female retirement age increases from 60 to 65. The effect of this is assumed here to bring female workforce participation rates in age groups over age 55 (based on the official projection to 2011) up to the same proportion as the male rates that obtained at ages 55-59 in 1998. Finally, the projected female rate is combined with the actual male rates that obtained in Great Britain in 1971, before the really substantial increase of early retirement. This restores the actual support ratios to 2.09 and 1.54. The latter figure is 92 per cent of the actual support ratio on which we are surviving at present. It must, of course, be unrealistic to imagine the exact reinvention of 1971 male rates, not least because of the rise of tertiary education, presumably irreversible, also necessary to maintain a productive workforce; but these scenarios, however crude, do suggest that considerable amelioration of the changes from today's real (as opposed to potential) situation may be achieved within the workforce even within the retirement age of 65.

Note that these ratios are computed on a different basis from the less favourable ratios in column 4 of table 11. The less favourable ratios exclude the unemployed and persons working whose pay is too low for them to make National Insurance contributions. The relative change is more important here than the absolute values. The bottom line reminds us that even with 100 per cent of the population of working age in work, the actual 2051 support ratios cannot be better than the 2051 potential support ratio of 2.47. These cannot equal the actual 1998 support ratio of contributors to pensioners of 3.19 without workforce participation rates of up to 120 per cent, an idea for which British workers may as yet be unprepared.

It is also important to remember that the reversal of early retirement trends, and the increase of female participation rates envisaged above may require important improvements in conditions of work. While working hours for manual workers may have declined, those of many in business and the professions have increased and, in some cases, become more stressful. This needs to be countered if some causes of early retirement are to be addressed, combined perhaps with schemes for gradual withdrawal from work rather than abrupt total retirement. Further increases in female workforce participation, including return to work after children, would be greatly assisted by a more flexible work regime, even though this would impose costs on employers. Underused options, some already facilitated by the United Kingdom tax system, include childcare vouchers as an employee benefit, workplace nurseries, career breaks, flexible working and teleworking (Jenkins, 2000). These measures are already commonplace as reflected in Scandinavian workforce participation rates and higher fertility. The working of mothers, contrary to some suppositions, does not appear to damage the well-being of children, any more than it depresses fertility (Bianchi, 2000).

4. Reserves of labour and "hidden unemployment"

Where are the reserves of economically inactive or unemployed labour to be found, who may join the active workforce? Over and above the total of registered unemployed is a substantial population of "hidden unemployed":

311

TABLE 11. PENSIONER SUPPORT RATIOS, UNITED KINGDOM, 2000-2060

	(2)		(3)		(4)		(5)		(6)
	Demographic support ratio: population 15-64 to 65 or over		Pensioner support ratio (female pension age rising 2010-2020 to 65)		Support ratio of employed contributors to pension recipients		Total demographic support ratio: population 15-64 to 65+ and 0-14		(5) weighted for support needs: 2000 as 100
Year		2000 as 100		2000 as 100		2000 as 100		2000 as 100	
2000........	4.2	100	3.4	100	1.8	100	1.89	100	100
2010........	4.1	97	3.2	94	1.7	94	1.99	105	108
2020........	3.4	81	3.3	97	1.8	100	1.80	95	101
2030........	2.7	65	2.7	79	1.4	78	1.58	83	91
2040........	2.4	58	2.4	71	1.3	72	1.48	78	87
2050........	2.5	59	2.5	74	1.4	78	1.50	79	88
2060........	2.4	57	2.4	71	1.3	72	1.30	69	74

Sources: Office of National Statistics (2000); Government Actuary (1999) tables 4.3 and 4.4, and GAD unpublished tables.

NOTE:

Column 2: GAD 1998-based Principal Projection.

Column 3: takes into account change in pension entitlement age for females to 65 from 2010 to 2020.

Column 4: takes into account workforce participation rates, the earnings threshold below which contributions are not made, and pension recipients overseas. Earnings thresholds for National Insurance contributions are assumed to rise with prices, not earnings.

Weighted total support ratio computed by weighting youth burden by 0.33 and aged burden by 0.67.

discouraged workers who are not seeking work, people taking extra courses of study, people on makeweight State employment schemes, people who have taken early retirement. In Germany, this was estimated to comprise 2.6 million people in 1998, compared with 4.3 million registered unemployed. An equivalent estimate for the United Kingdom for 1996 was 7.2 per cent of the potential labour force. Added to registered unemployment, this yielded a "broad unemployment" figure of 12.9 per cent for the United Kingdom in 1996, 15.6 per cent for the Netherlands and 15.0 per cent for Germany (Fuchs and Schmidt, 2000, table 2). This does not include persons outside the labour force altogether but who are of working age.

In most European countries, unemployment rates among foreigners are between 50 and 100 per cent higher than in the native population, and workforce participation rates in the population of working age are generally lower. In some, but not all, European countries, this dismal situation applies to the children of immigrants as well as to the immigrants themselves (Organisation for Economic Co-operation and Development, 1999). In the United Kingdom in 1998, for example, the unemployment rate of Pakistani/Bangladeshi men was 18 per cent, three times that of white men (6 per cent), and 14 per cent for men from all ethnic minority groups. These "ethnic minority" populations of non-European origin are by no means all immigrants: the population embraces the descendants of post-war immigrants (this is also true of many foreigners in European countries, especially Germany). Perhaps two thirds of the ethnic minority population of working age is immigrant. Workforce participation rates are also low: 76 per cent of men aged 16-64 are economically active compared with 80 per cent of the white population in that age group. Among women, only 30 per cent of Pakistani and 20 per cent of Bangladeshi women are economically active compared with 74 per cent of white women (Sly, Thair and Risdon, 1999, table 1). These unfavourable unemployment and activity rates, arising from the non-economic nature of most mass migration after the 1970s, and from weak workforce skills, make the suggestion that mass migration should resume to cure the labour shortage look a little eccentric; but in theory migrants constitute a substantial reserve of labour, the mobilization of which is a social as well as a labour-market priority. Foreign workers entering under work permit schemes for specified jobs are seldom unemployed, at least to begin with, but form only a relatively small part of the total foreign population in many European countries today.

When projections take into account both demographic change and future workforce participation rate change, both the projected and the potential labour supply situation can look more favourable. Statistical Office of the European Communities (Eurostat) variant projections combined with workforce participation rate projections showed that, except in the case of Italy, the workforce in most Western countries will either remain constant or grow substantially at least until 2020. According to these calculations, aggregate net inflows of labour will not be necessary before then, if at all (Feld, 2000). In the case of the United Kingdom, only a combination of a low total fertility rate (TFR) of 1.5, immigration of +21,000 per year and low workforce participation leads to a decline (about 5 per cent) in the active population by 2020. Other combinations yield workforce growth up to 13 per cent (1.4 million) up to 2020.

5. *Redefining the length of active life and retirement*

Increasingly, population ageing arises from longer life expectation. Can this, in part, bring its own salvation, in that a proportion of the extra years are years of active life, characterized by the ability to engage in work as well as active retirement? Later retirement would simultaneously increase the numerator and decrease the denominator of the support ratio equation. The United Nations and GAD variant projections computed the maximum age of retirement required in order to preserve, without any other changes, the United Kingdom support ratio at the current level of 4.1. These estimates are purely demographic, determining solely the increase from age 65 as the upper boundary of the nominally active population, and the lower boundary of the "aged dependent" population, for the calculation of the potential support ratio. This calculation yields a narrow range of maximum retirement ages around age 70-75, with the average about 72. This is between 5 and 9 years older than the current demographic boundary between active and dependent, which is also the standard age of retirement in most countries (65; 60 in Italy, 66 in Denmark). Is this matched to any degree by the shifting backwards of the onset of real old age?

At face value, this increase in "required" retirement age is of about the same order of magnitude as the increase in expectation of life at birth in the post-war period, when pension entitlement age was the same as it is now. In 1950-1952, expectation of life in England and Wales was 66.4 years for males and 71.5 for females—in the case of males, just under retirement age. There has therefore been a gain of 8.4 years for males and 8.3 years for females by 1997, rather more than the projected increases in retirement age in most scenarios. Much of this improvement in mortality, of course, has arisen from a reduction of infant and child deaths. A fairer picture might be given by comparing expectations of life at age 15. Here the gain is more modest: from 54.4 years for males and 59.0 years for females in 1950-1952 to 60.5 years for males and 65.4 years for females in 1997, that is to say, a gain of over 6 years for each sex.

Healthy life expectation, however, has not increased pro rata with expectation of life. In the United Kingdom, period rates of chronic illness in the population aged 55-64 have not improved in the last decade even though this age group has experienced the biggest fall in mortality in the last decade (Dunnell and Dix, 2000). Since 1981, expectation of life at birth has increased by 3.3 years for males and 2.6 for females. Of these additional years, 2 years in the case of each sex are "healthy" additional years, and 1.3 and 0.6 are unhealthy (Kelly, Baker and Gupta, 2000). Calculations for longer periods of time are difficult to make because surveys did not ask appropriate questions in the past; but if these ratios are applied to the total gains since 1950-1952, we have 6 years of additional healthy life for each sex since 1951.

Of course, the original expectation of life, at any age, would not have consisted entirely of years of healthy life either, but for reasons explained above we do not know if expectation of healthy and expectation of unhealthy life have had parallel tracks over any length of time. These are not bad gains, although different studies give different results. Methods using cohort data, however, appear to capture more substantial advances in expectation of active life. For the United States population, for example, these new methods give almost double the expectation of active life at some ages compared with traditional methods. For males in the 1990s, this amounted to 13.7 years of active life out of a total of 15.7 from the completed-cohort estimates compared with 7.4 active years out of 15.1 for the period estimates (Manton and Land, 2000, table 4).

6. A broader view of dependency

An official, and more refined, projection of dependency on various definitions is given in columns 2, 3 and 4 of table 11. Column 2 shows the conventional potential support ratio on purely demographic grounds, familiar from previous tables. Column 3 gives the potential support ratio corrected for the fact that female pension entitlement age in the United Kingdom, still 60, will rise to 65 from 2010-2020, following the Pensions Act, 1995. That reduces the number of pensioners, other things being equal, by 2.2 million during the 2020s and transfers them, at least nominally, to the active population. Not all women will work until age 65, of course, but State pensions will not be paid out until that age, so the revision benefits the future solvency of the National Insurance Fund. Column 4 is a refinement over previous attempts to construct a more realistic support ratio. It assumes constant 2011 projected workforce participation rates but also takes into account the fact that not all employed workers actually contribute to the support of the elderly through National Insurance contributions. This is because many on low wages are paid less than the earnings threshhold below which contributions are not imposed (in 2000, £66.75 per week; see Government Actuary (1999), appendix, for details). Because of these deductions, the support ratio becomes even less favourable than that based on constant 2011 workforce participation rates. The aged, however, are not the only dependants. The overall dependency ratio in any population, and therefore its reciprocal, the support ratio, always includes youthful dependants, conventionally all those under age 15. It is a demographic commonplace that stationary populations with different age structures have similar overall dependency (support) ratios, which only differ in their composition, with the elderly predominating in those with low fertility. The ratio worsens as population grows or declines. As the proportion of elderly increases with an ageing population, that of the young declines, as column 5 shows. Perfect compensation is not on offer, however, as elderly dependants are generally assumed to cost about three times youthful ones. Column 6 weights the total support ratio accordingly. The net result is a slight amelioration of the future burden (see also table 11).

7. The real retirement age and the real support ratio

The pattern of early retirement noted above means that a realistic assessment of support ratio trends cannot assume a real retirement age of 65: it is already considerably lower. As noted above, the actual "support ratio" of real

315

taxpayers to real pension recipients is thereby already much less favourable than the "demographic" support. The economy has already been dealing with a ratio of 1.81 rather than 4.1 without notable distress. In this respect, we have already seen the future, and it still works. Indeed, it should be noted that the United Kingdom has already managed considerable population ageing and hardly noticed it. In 1901, the potential support ratio in England and Wales was 7.47, with only 4.7 per cent of the population aged 65 years or over. To maintain that potential support ratio today would require the United Kingdom population to have grown to 116 million today and to be growing at an impressive rate.

Comprehensive statistics on the actual age of withdrawal from work do not seem to be available; but a simple calculation based on the unweighted distributions at retirement age of members of 26 occupational pension schemes in 1998 (Incomes Data Services (IDS), 1999, table 2) shows that their mean age at retirement was 56.7 and the median age 54.4. That is almost 10 years before the "official" retirement age. If that figure is representative, then it puts a somewhat different complexion upon the figure of 72 noted above for future retirement age in the "replacement" scenarios. If actual mean age of retirement now is about 56, then a simple calculation suggests that the actual age of retirement needed in future to preserve the present support ratio would be 55.5 + (72 - 65) = 62.5. In other words, preservation of the support ratio, even if solely the "responsibility" of an upward move in retirement age, would require men to retire only 2.5 years before they are officially expected to, instead of 9.5 years earlier as at present. This rough estimate, however, must exaggerate the advantage from this consideration. Men with occupational pension schemes for whom these data are available can afford to retire before men (mostly manual workers) dependent mostly or entirely on the State pension. Furthermore, workforce participation into older life may well not be prolonged at very high rates. However, a very simple calculation of the mean age at retirement based on the distribution of male participation rates for 1998 yields a mean age of retirement of 57.8, which is not far off the previous estimate.

8. Who's afraid of low support ratios?

At the end of the day, the important consideration is not the simple figures of the potential support ratios themselves but what they imply, in a given national demographic, workforce and economic situation, for the relative costs of projected increases in dependency. These can be regarded as the fraction of each year's total national economic activity devoted to supplying the goods and services consumed by the retired, provided both by contributions (from labour) and by returns on assets (from capital (Thompson, 2000, p. 70)). Are these projected costs, on the taxes of workers or on national GDP, sustainable in the light of reasonable expectations of economic growth or can they be made so by reasonable adjustments? That is all that matters. If so, there is no need to worry unduly about demographic abstractions such as support ratios. If not—but only if not—then more radical alternatives may need to be considered. The observations below provide only a very modest answer to the question because

316

they refer only to one component of this cost. Nonetheless, the answer does not seem to be too terrifying.

9. *Effects of income growth on pension costs*

Future prospects are highly sensitive to purely fiscal and economic change. Much depends on economic growth, the prospects for which now seem more favourable than for a long time. With faster economic growth, employment rates and incomes rise, and more people will be drawn into National Insurance contribution or other taxes as their incomes cross the progressive NI thresholds. As a component of economic growth, unemployment or its reverse is particularly important, as higher unemployment raises the burden of old-age pensioners upon those currently employed. Economic growth is another way of describing the real rate of return on investments and therefore on the growth of pension funds. If real returns are just 2 per cent per annum, then payments of 10 per cent of salary over a career of 40 years are needed to fund a pension of 35 per cent of final salary. With returns of 6 per cent, well within previous experience, the same pension could be provided with just 5 per cent of salary (European Federation for Retirement Pensions).

In the 1980s, it was assumed that the non-accelerating inflation rate of unemployment (NAIRU), otherwise known as the "natural level of unemployment", was inexorably increasing to 5 or even 8 per cent as a result of welfare and technical changes (United Nations, Economic Commission for Europe, 1997), thus making the future pensions problem worse. Recent analyses suggest a radical change in macroeconomic relationships which may permit the coexistence, previously thought impossible, of economic growth of between 3 and 4 per cent, continued low inflation (2-3 per cent) and low unemployment (4 per cent). Furthermore, with higher economic growth, the relative cost of State PAYG pensions pegged to prices, not wages, will decline in the United Kingdom, although at the cost of the relative but not the absolute income of recipients.

Looking at the United Kingdom case, the ratios in columns 3 and 4 of table 11 would lead, other things being equal, to a 40 per cent increase in the rate of National Insurance contributions over 50 years (from today's 10 per cent to employees to 14 per cent, at the highest rate of contributions; employers pay 12.5 per cent in addition, which would then become 16.5 per cent). This is a serious but not catastrophic increase in that form of tax (that, of course, is the impact only on State pensions, not on funded ones). It would raise the United Kingdom tax "wedge" from today's 32 per cent to 36 per cent (the current rate for production workers in France is 48 per cent, in Germany 52 per cent). However, the ratios in column 4 assume that earnings limits for NI contributions are increased in line with prices. If earnings limits at which payment of NI is triggered were increased in line with earnings (which, given 1.5 per cent economic growth assumed, would be higher limits), then the number of contributors would be reduced by 2.2 million by 2060 and the position would be correspondingly worse. These considerations apply specifically to State pension funding and only more generally to other aspects of old-age support.

The choice between indexing to prices or earnings has significant consequences (table 12). Assuming 2 per cent economic growth, the overall contribution rate would rise by 2061 to 27.6 per cent from 20 per cent if pensions rose with earnings, but would actually fall to 14 per cent if indexed to prices. By the same token, National Insurance Fund expenditure would rise from 5.5 per cent of GDP to 7.7 per cent, or alternatively fall to 3.7 per cent. Even if pensions were raised in line with earnings, however, thereby taking a higher proportion of workers' incomes, 60 years of economic growth would still yield a substantial increase in real incomes. Even with the modest real growth rate forecast of 1.5 per cent per annum, they would reach 2.4 times current real levels (Government Actuary, 1999, p. 13). SERPS, over and above the State flat-rate pension, complicates the story but in essence it remains the same (see Government Actuary (1999) for more details). Expenditure on SERPS is 9 per cent of NI expenditure at present.

Finally, on the issue of tax, the black economy is a substantial burden on support ratios, as many workers thereby evade contributing to State pensions schemes but will no doubt claim a pension or equivalent welfare. Even in Denmark, 3.6-4.5 per cent of GDP is estimated to be within the black economy in 1994, involving about 26 per cent of the population (Mogensen and others, 1995). These figures are likely to be much higher in other European countries. Any regularization of the black economy could bring substantial benefits to

TABLE 12.   EFFECT ON CONTRIBUTIONS OF EARNINGS VERSUS PRICES INDEXATION, UNITED KINGDOM, 2000 AND 2061

	Earnings	Price
Joint employee/employer contribution rate as percentage of earnings		
1999-2000	20.0	20.0
2060-2061	27.6	14.0
National Insurance fund expenditure as percentage of GDP		
1999-2000	5.5	5.5
2060-2061	7.7	3.7
Pensions as percentage of earnings Basic flat rate		
1999-2000	15	15
2060-2061	15	6
SERPS		
1999-2000	17	17
2060-2061	17	11
GDP per pensioner (1999-2000 = 100)		
1999-2000	100.0	100.0
2060-2061	105.1	50.2

Source: Government Actuary (1999).

NOTE: Figures with no decimals estimated from graph. Projections assume real income growth of 1.5 per cent per year.

real support ratios. Paradoxically, the black economy is encouraged, inter alia, by high social protection costs on regular labour, in part to help pay for State pension schemes.

All of these elements are susceptible to policy changes. The fortuitous intervention of the European Court, for example, obliged the United Kingdom Government to equalize its pension entitlement age for men and women. Welfare considerations suggested equalization at 60. Demographic imperatives argued otherwise (Department of Social Security, 1991). Retirement age for both sexes will be fixed at 65 from 2010-2015, occasioning at least a notional marked improvement in United Kingdom dependency ratio trends, as noted above. Under the United Kingdom's "Foresight" programme launched in 1993 (Department of Trade and Industry, 2000), as Karen Dunnell describes in her paper, steps are also in hand to discourage unjustified disability-based early retirement and to encourage later working. Tax reliefs are being removed from private pensions taken before age 55; the tax system will make working beyond age 65 easier; and legislation is being introduced, on United States lines, to make age alone inadequate grounds for not hiring, or dismissing, labour. Both employers and Government are likely to discourage favourable early retirement terms in occupational pension schemes (for example, through the use of "defined contribution", not "defined benefit", schemes). Access to ill-health early retirement is likely to be subject to more stringent criteria. "Phased retirement" will be encouraged whereby the pensioner continues in part-time work, a response currently discouraged by "final salary" pension schemes where pension is determined by the last level of salary, not the maximum ever reached (Incomes Data Services (IDS), 1999).

Some countries have already started to move their retirement age back from the original fixed limits; to 67 in the United States and to 65 in Italy and Japan. The United Kingdom has not yet considered such action. Costs of ill health among the elderly have not received the same attention as pensions. Some calculations, taking into account the reduction of child dependency costs, come to quite modest conclusions about the additional real expenditure, at least for the United Kingdom (Ermisch, 1990). Sixty per cent of the health expenditure on an individual is concentrated in the 12 months before death. Sixty per cent of health expenditure therefore depends on the annual number of deaths, which is projected to increase by 17.5 per cent in EU by 2025 (European Commission, 1996, p. 43).

10. *A multiphasic response*

No one factor can ameliorate the situation by itself except with considerable discomfort. We therefore need to address simultaneously as many of these contributing factors as possible. Given the powerful effects of economic growth, pensions reform and workforce change on the viability of systems, we may be in danger of missing the point by concentrating too much on the outer demographic structure rather than on the fiscal, economic and workforce structures within it. What matters is whether an affordable system can be developed, not what the potential support ratios are.

The European Commission's Annual Review of the demographic situation in Europe in 1995 (European Commission, 1996) recognized the contribution of migration to further population increase but noted that recent immigration, at that time declining, had not been primarily related to economic needs and that the proportion of foreigners in the workforce had been constant for some time. It dismissed the notion that immigration could be an adequate compensation for population ageing, as it would require between 8 and 14 times even the then current high level of net immigration (7 million per year by 2024). Productivity growth required to meet the additional demands on the economy created from pensions would be between 0.1 and 0.3 per cent annually up to 2005, increasing to 0.5 per cent per year by 2025. Such an additional diversion to pension costs would, for example, reduce a real annual GDP growth rate from, say, 3 to 2.5 per cent. While formal retirement age is 65 in most EU States, actual retirement age is about 60. Preservation of that status quo would require actual retirement age to rise by between 5 and 6 years, to between 65 and 66 depending on which of the EU scenarios was to be chosen. (The United Nations scenarios' "requirement" of retirement deferred to 72 or more assumes, presumably, actual retirement at 65.) On that basis, managing the additional costs of State pensions simply requires people to stop work when they are "expected" to, at some time in the future—a conclusion similar to that reached above in respect of the United Kingdom. For the United Kingdom itself, the scenarios indicate that an annual increase in work productivity rising to 0.8 per cent by 2025 would be needed to cover additional costs of pensions transfers, in the absence of any other measures.

No multivariate model illustrating the simultaneous effects of parallel changes in the support system has yet been developed for the United Kingdom and time has not sufficed to prepare one; but some for other countries may be approximately applicable, given the relatively favourable United Kingdom demographic and pensions position. The scenarios shown below in table 13 do not quite match the approaches taken so far. They incorporate total dependency, including the falling costs due to the fall in the proportion of dependent children, and extend only to 2035. The assumptions on retirement age and participation rates (not unlike the procedure adopted in an earlier section) are that all the countries concerned will eventually adopt retirement ages and participation rates already observed in some other countries today: in Japan (for retirement age) and Norway (for participation rates). A 10 per cent reduction in replacement rates is also assumed.

The incorporation of all dependency (all those not working of all ages, including children) into the equation somewhat ameliorates the expectation of future dependency and future costs, to an increase of 10 percentage points instead of a doubling. A similar conclusion has been reached for the United Kingdom (Ermisch, 1990). However, the weighting of the elderly used in this example is only twice that of a young dependant, not the three times usually assumed. Either option by itself has a substantial and comparable effect on the otherwise expected worsening of dependency and contribution rates (table 13). Both together restore the position to almost the 1995 level and, in the case of France, Germany and Italy, to an even more favourable position, further enhanced by a 10 per cent reduction in replacement rates (Gillion, 1999). Note,

	Japan	France	Germany	Norway	Italy
Total dependency ratio					
1995 base level....................	46.0	55.6	50.8	48.2	59.9
2035 projection					
No change	55.8	63.3	61.5	56.5	69.9
Older retirement for men	55.8	57.3	54.8	52.8	62.0
Increased female participation.......	52.8	59.1	57.4	56.5	60.4
Both	52.8	**53.2**	**50.7**	52.8	**52.5**
Both plus lower replacement rate	52.8	**53.2**	**50.7**	52.8	**52.5**
Contribution rates in 2035 (*percentage*)					
1995 base level....................	33.8	42.9	38.3	35.8	47.2
2035 projection					
No change	43.1	50.8	48.9	43.8	58.2
Older retirement for men	43.1	44.6	42.1	40.2	49.5
Increased female participation.......	40.2	46.5	44.7	43.8	47.8
Both	40.2	**40.5**	**38.2**	40.2	**39.9**
Both plus lower replacement rate	37.7	**38.0**	**35.7**	37.7	**37.4**

Source: Gillion (1999), table 2.A.2.

NOTE:

Retirement age is that of Japan.

Women's workforce participation rates are those of Norway.

Dependency is an *overall* measure here, including non-elderly dependants of all ages.

Contribution rates relate to all age groups needing support.

For dependency ratios and contribution rates, count children as 0.5 adult, pensioner as 0.75 adult.

Figures in bold indicate a more favourable outcome than the 1995 base level.

however, that improvements in workforce participation rates cannot have a further enhancing effect once they have reached their maximum level.

11. *Demographic measures*

The most "strategic" responses involve the number of people themselves. The migration option, the subject of the United Nations report, need not be mentioned further. The much more powerful, if delayed, effects of fertility upon age structure were discussed above and do not need repeating. Turning on immigration, to increase current large flows even further, would be easy. Turning it off again is quite a different matter.

How changeable is the birth rate likely to be? If it does not increase spontaneously, is it susceptible to public policy measures? There is little consensus on either of these points despite an extensive literature. There appear to be no limits to low fertility in the predominantly economic models that attempt to explain its variation (Golini, 1998). Much of the reduction in period measures of fertility, it is well known, is due to the postponement of births; but in most populations, the recovery of fertility rates at older ages has so far been insufficient to compensate for the decline in earlier ages, pointing to a fall in completed cohort fertility to below replacement level (Lesthaeghe, 2000;

Frejka and Calot, 2000). Most researchers seem pessimistic about a return of fertility to replacement rates in European countries. Nonetheless, spontaneous recovery of fertility to levels closer to replacement might arise from a number of processes. The delay in childbearing has not yet ended in any country and we cannot foretell likely responses when it does. There may be general population-level tendencies to equilibrium. Enhanced welfare arrangements or other measures that improve the status of women may remove obstacles to childbearing (Lutz, 2000). Biological and behaviour-genetic models may provide other reasons why fertility should not drop to very low levels (Foster, 2000; Morgan and King, 2001).

The prospect of higher birth rates is underpinned by the consistent finding, after 30 years of surveys, that European women wish on average to have about two children (although seldom many more). Furthermore, like investments, actual birth rates can go up as well as down. Several Scandinavian countries have experienced rising birth rates since the 1980s, although that of Sweden took a sharp downturn in the mid-1990s. The TFR in Denmark is off its peak but in Norway it continues at over 1.8 (1.84 in 1999). In Ireland, the TFR has remained at about 1.9 after falling below replacement level. Of the 15 EU countries plus Norway and Switzerland, 13 out of 17 had a higher TFR in 1999 than in 1998, although the increases were mostly tiny (Eurostat, 2000, table 3). More recent French data suggest a more substantial increase to 1.9 during the first quarter of 2000. Outside Europe, Australia, Canada, New Zealand and the United States, none of which had ever seen low birth rates, increased their fertility above levels of the 1980s. New Zealand and the United States continue at about replacement level. Although ethnic minority fertility is higher than average in those countries, contrary to some views the non-minority population also continue to have higher birth rates than almost any European countries. In the United States (1999), the TFR in all groups increased further from 1998 to 1999, from 2.059 overall to 2.075 (Curtin and Martin, 2000, p. 4). Coincidentally, the latter figure is exactly the replacement rate for the United Kingdom. In some populations, richer and better-educated women now have more children than average; female workforce participation is no longer an impediment to having a third child, at least not in Scandinavia. For whatever reason, most national and international projections, including the GAD Principal Projection and the United Nations medium variant, expect a modest recovery in fertility, although one stopping short of replacement level.

If the birth rate does not increase spontaneously, is it responsive to public policy measures? Opinion here is strongly divided. Public policy effects upon the birth rate can be intended or (more usually in the West) unintended (Gauthier, 1996). Few Western countries explicitly attempt to increase their birth rate although many are concerned that it is too low. Most Governments favour welfare policies for the family (welfare payments, workplace and housing policies etc.) for welfare reasons only. While these might incidentally make it easier for women to have the number of children they say they want, most Governments still shy away from overtly "pronatalist" measures or rhetoric. Evaluations of the effects of welfare policies face great difficulties from the great variety of forms of assistance from which families can benefit, within which direct family allowances may play only a modest role (Hantrais, 1997).

322

However, as modern States spend between 30 and 60 per cent of national income, policy measures of various sorts must affect the rationality of most household decisions. Some studies have found evidence only for a weak effect of welfare and fiscal changes on family size and the pattern of family formation (Gauthier and Hatzius, 1997). Others report somewhat stronger effects. In the early 1980s, French pronatalist measures were estimated to have added about 0.3 to the TFR (Calot and Chesnais, 1983). The Swedish case in particular is claimed to be an example of precise, if temporary, response of marriage and birth rates and intervals to changes in relative financial advantage, including the fertility downturn following more recent retrenchment and raised unemployment (Hoem, 2000).

Family subsidies of various kinds, State childcare, preferential access to housing in the absence of an open housing market and other measures in the former communist countries of Eastern Europe attempted simultaneously to promote female workforce participation and the birth rate. Although their attempts are often dismissed as having had no more than a transient effect in detail, they appear to have maintained Eastern bloc fertility at close to replacement until their withdrawal during the post-1990 transition period (David, 1982; United Nations, Economic Commission for Europe, 1999b). However, these policies operated in a system of universally early marriage, limited access to modern contraception and few social outlets as alternatives to family life. Within Western Europe, the low level of fertility in the (paradoxically) familist Southern European countries, and also in Japan, seems unlikely to be reversed without a broader shift in personal and political culture. Societies with high gender inequality will continue to suffer lower birth rates (McDonald, 2000).

In this situation, the example of the United Kingdom is somewhat anomalous. The United Kingdom has relatively modest family support programmes but nonetheless maintains a relatively high birth rate. Annoyed French colleagues have attributed this to an excess of careless, unplanned early childbearing, encouraged perhaps by specifically (unhelpful) British attitudes towards sex education and perverse incentives in the welfare system. United Kingdom age-specific fertility rates in age group 15-19 are certainly anomalously high, four times the EU average and large enough to distort the United Kingdom age-specific fertility rate profile compared with that of most other European countries (Chandola, Coleman and Hiorns, 1999). Paradoxically, the only United Kingdom policy aimed at fertility is a specific target to reduce the teenage conception rate by half by 2010, on welfare grounds (Social Exclusion Unit, 1999). If this was eventually successful in reducing teenage fertility to the EU average, it would bring the United Kingdom TFR closer to 1.6 than its current 1.7; other things being equal, this would not help with the problem in hand.

G. CONCLUSIONS

There is no "solution" to the problem of population ageing and there cannot be one short of high rates of population growth or mass age-specific euthanasia. The answers to the two questions posed in the subtitle of the United

Nations report (can immigration solve problems of population decline and population ageing) are quite simple. They are respectively:

1. Yes, if you really think you want to.

2. No, except at rates of immigration so high that they would generate economically and environmentally unsustainable population growth rates and permanently and radically change the cultural and ethnic composition of the host population: "replacement migration", indeed.

These answers are already well known to demographers. Older populations and their problems will be a permanent feature of developed societies for the whole future of the species, the very long-term existence of which is henceforth absolutely dependent upon the preservation of a TFR very close to 2.

In the broadest view, to paraphrase Weil (1997, pp. 1009-1010), the costs of population ageing arise largely from the inevitable passing of the transient benefits of reduced fertility that were enjoyed during the twentieth century. In the early years of demographic transition, this falling birth rate created a demographically unstable half-century of favourable dependency ratios. Now that these advantages have passed, resources once needed for dependent children must be transferred to the elderly as a new long-term quasi-stable population system is established. In the United Kingdom and elsewhere, this system has a similar nominal dependency ratio to the previous one but a different, less favourable composition. Change in the real support ratio is proportional to the difference between the average age of consumption (Ac) and the average age of production (Ay). Maximum real support ratio arises when the two averages are the same, assuming an equal weighting of needs. Western populations have moved from a position where Ac was lower than Ay, to the reverse case, where Ay is lower than Ac, perhaps by four years, not a large number because consumption is highest at the beginning and the end of life (Weil, 1997, p. 981). The delivery channels of support will also be different. Families, which made and still make the greatest provision for children, will see the burden of transfers eased. A higher proportion of transfers to the elderly will pass through the State. Hence, those populations that also have a tradition of family care for the elderly will suffer most, as noted above.

Specific technical conclusions need only be restated briefly. The United Nations projections differ from those produced by the United Kingdom Government Actuary's Department in several ways. Estimates for current United Kingdom population, and in particular of net immigration, are well below current United Kingdom levels. Current United Kingdom immigration is today so high (pro rata similar to that to the United States) that it exceeds the UN "requirements" for population growth and workforce growth. GAD future immigration assumptions themselves are also out of line with current trends. The projections made by GAD on a variety of plausible assumptions yield a relatively restricted range of future United Kingdom population and age structures. Potential support ratios are about 2.5, a "required" maximum formal retirement age about 72, median age about 42 (table 5). These results underline the conclusion that substantial population ageing will be impossible to avoid. No plausible demographic change makes a big difference. None of these seem to this author to be obviously catastrophic.

As expected from theory, higher fertility is a more "efficient" way of protecting potential support ratio than is immigration. Increases in fertility with reduction of immigration would tend to minimize future population growth while producing a more favourable potential support ratio. Welfare measures, justified on welfare grounds, might have the effect of encouraging future fertility because they would respond to unmet need for children, helping women to have the number of children that, on average, they say they want. United Kingdom government welfare and workforce policy seems to be moving in this direction, although no doubt without any demographic intent, the rationale being, Look after the interests of women and the population will look after itself. Large-scale migration is an undesirable alternative not just because it is an inefficient means of reducing population ageing but because it is also likely to present the host society with serious and avoidable cultural, social and political difficulties and economic costs (Coleman, 1994, 1997).

In the longer term, longer survival will increasingly determine all future population ageing. Although estimates of gains in active life differ, there are grounds for hoping that increases in active life will make an extension of working life reasonable, as well as to some extent necessary. That aspect of population ageing brings, in part, its own solution, by pushing back the real, as opposed to the nominal, boundaries of old age.

Potential support ratios on fixed boundaries remain a demographic abstraction. What matters is not demographic abstractions but whether the future costs of dependency are sustainable in the economic and social environment of the future. Fiscal and workforce reforms within the demographic system offer much more flexible and promising ways of adapting to population ageing and some of the measures are desirable in their own right. In the view of this writer, although it is not that of Her Majesty's Government, the issue at the moment is how to prevent unwelcome population increase and high immigration, rather than worrying about the consequences of population decline.

In the United Kingdom situation, "demographic time bombs" go off only in the media, not in real life. Labour-market, retirement and pension reforms, some already under way, together with future expectations of even modest economic growth and productivity, together offer the prospect of a reasonably effective and affordable management of this burden, although definitely not a "solution". Consideration of real support ratios needs to take into account the diminution of dependency from the youthful population, the successful negotiation of substantial population ageing already achieved since the beginning of the twentieth century, and the reality of actual retirement ages substantially below "official" retirement age.

It would greatly improve public, and governmental, appreciation of the problems of ageing that confront modern societies if the Population Division of the United Nations Secretariat, as a result of the Expert Group meeting, chose to diversify its approach on population ageing. It should move away from a concentration on what was already known to be an unsuitable demographic and social expedient in the form of mass migration, to address a broader repertoire of more realistic responses.

Acknowledgements

The projections in this paper were entirely the work of Mr. Chris Shaw and Mr. Adam Michaels of the United Kingdom Government Actuary's Department, without whose generous expert help the paper could not have been written. These projections will be developed further for publication in the journal *Population Trends*, No. 103, under their authorship later in 2001. The corrections, data and other help from Dr. Walter Eltis, Ms. Monica Hultin and Mr. Chris Shaw are gratefully acknowledged. The interpretations placed here upon the results, all other opinions and all errors and omissions are the responsibility of the author alone.

REFERENCES

Ahlburg, D. A., W. Lutz and J. W. Vaupel (1998). Ways to improve forecasting: what should be done differently in the future? In *Frontiers of Population Forecasting*, supplement to vol. 24 of *Population and Development Review*, W. Lutz, J. W. Vaupel and D. A. Ahlburg, eds. New York: The Population Council, pp. 191-198.

Armitage, R., and M. Scott (1998). British labour force projections, 1998-2011. *Labour Market Trends* (London), vol. 106, No. 6.

Bianchi, S. M. (2000). Maternal employment and time with children: dramatic change or surprising continuity? *Demography* (Chicago), vol. 37, No. 4, pp. 401-414.

Blanchet, D. (1989). Regulating the age structure of a population through migration. *Population* (Paris), vol. 44 , No. 1, pp. 23-37.

Calot, G., and J.-C. Chesnais (1983). L'efficacité des politiques incitatrices en matière de natalité. In *International Union for the Scientific Study of Population (IUSSP) Colloquium*. Liège, Belgium: IUSSP.

Calot, G., and J.-P. Sardon (1999). Les facteurs du vieillissement démographique. *Population* (Paris), vol. 54, No. 3, pp. 509-552.

Chand, S. K., and A. Jaeger (1996). *Ageing Populations and Public Pension Schemes*. Occasional Paper, No. 147. Washington, D.C.: International Monetary Fund.

Chandola, T., D. A. Coleman and R. W. Hiorns (1999). Recent European fertility patterns: fitting curves to "distorted" distributions. *Population Studies* (Washington, D.C.), vol. 53, No. 3, pp. 317-329.

Chesnais, J.-C. (1995). *Le crépuscule de l'Occident: dénatalité, condition des femmes et immigration*. Paris: Robert Laffont.

Cohen, J. E. (1998). Should population projections consider "limiting factors" and if so, how? In *Frontiers of Population Forecasting*, supplement to vol. 24 of *Population and Development Review* (New York), W. Lutz, J. W. Vaupel and D. A. Ahlburg, eds. New York: The Population Council, pp. 118-138.

Coleman, D. A. (1992). Does Europe need immigrants? Population and workforce projections. *International Migration Review* (New York), vol. 26, No. 2, pp. 413-461.

_____ (1994). Integration and assimilation policies in Europe. In *International Migration and Integration: Regional Pressures and Processes*, Economic Studies, No. 7, M. Macura and D. A. Coleman, eds. Sales No. GV.E.94.0.25. Geneva: Economic Commission for Europe.

_____ (1997). UK immigration policy: "firm but fair", and failing? *Policy Studies* (Lawrence, Kansas), vol. 17, No. 3, pp. 195-213.

Curtin, S. C., and J. A. Martin (2000). Births: preliminary data for 1999. *National Vital Statistics Reports* (Hyattsville, Maryland), vol. 48, No. 14.

David, H. P. (1982). Eastern Europe: pronatalist policies and private behaviour. *Population Bulletin* (Washington, D.C.), vol. 36, No. 6, p. 48.

Daykin, C. D., and D. Lewis (1999). A crisis of longer life: reforming pension systems. *British Actuarial Journal* (Oxford), vol. 5, part 1, No. 21, pp. 55-113.

Department of Social Security (1991). *Options for Equality in State Pension Age*, Cmnd. 1723. London: HM Stationery Office.

Department of Trade and Industry (2000). *The Age Shift: A Consultation Document from the Ageing Population Panel*. London: Department of Trade and Industry.

Dunnell, K., and D. Dix (2000). Are we looking forward to a longer or healthier retirement? *Health Statistics Quarterly* (London), vol. 6, pp. 18-25.

Eatwell, J. (1999). The anatomy of the pensions "crisis". In *Economic Survey of Europe 1999*, No. 3. Sales No. E.99.II.E.4, chap. 2. New York and Geneva: United Nations.

Ermisch, J. (1990). *Fewer Babies, Longer Lives*. York, United Kingdom: Rowntree Foundation.

European Commission (1991). *Employment in Europe 1991*. Luxembourg: European Commission, DG Employment, Industrial Relations and Social Affairs.

_____ (1996). *The Demographic Situation in the European Union 1995*. Luxembourg: Office for Official Publications of the European Unions.

European Federation for Retirement Provision (1999). *European Pensions: The New Challenges*. London: Royal Institute of International Affairs.

Eurostat (1988). *Demographic and Labour Force Analysis based on Eurostat Data Banks*. Luxembourg: Office for the Official Publications of the European Communities.

_____ (2000). First results of the demographic data collection for 1999 in Europe. In *Statistics in Focus—Theme 3—10/2000*. Luxembourg: Office for the Official Publications of the European Communities.

Feld, S. (2000). Active population growth and immigration hypotheses in Western Europe. *European Journal of Population* (Amsterdam), vol. 16, pp. 3-40.

Foster, C. (2000). The limits to low fertility: a biosocial approach. *Population and Development Review* (New York), vol. 26, No. 2, pp. 209-234.

Freeman, G. S. (1994). Can liberal States control unwanted migration? *Annals of the American Association for Political and Social Sciences* (Philadelphia, Pennsylvania), No. 534, pp. 17-30.

Frejka, T., and G. Calot (2000). The cohort fertility story: industrialized countries in the second half of the twentieth and in the early twenty-first century. Presented at Population Association of America Annual Meeting, March 2000, Los Angeles, California, mimeo, p. 67.

Fuchs, J., and D. Schmidt (2000). The hidden labour force in the United Kingdom: a contribution to the quantification of underemployment in international comparisons. *IAB Labour Market Research Topics* (Nuremberg, Germany), No. 39, p. 23.

Gauthier, A. H. (1996). *The State and the Family: A Comparative Analysis of Family Policies in Industrialized Countries*. Oxford: Oxford University Press.

_____, and J. Hatzius (1997). Family benefits and fertility: an econometric analysis. *Population Studies* (New York), vol. 51, No. 3, pp. 295-306.

Gillion, C. (1999). The macroeconomics of pension reform. In *Economic Survey of Europe 1999*, No. 3. Sales No. E.99.II.E.4, discussion 2.A of chap. 2. New York: United Nations.

Golini, A. (1998). How low can fertility get? An empirical investigation. *Population and Development Review* (New York), vol. 24, No. 1, pp. 59-73.

Government Actuary (1998). *National Population Projections: 1996-based*. London: HM Stationery Office, Series PP2, No. 21.

_____ (1999). *National Insurance Fund Long-Term Financial Estimates*, Cmnd. 4406. London: HM Stationery Office.

_____ (2000). *National Population Projections: 1998-based*. London: HM Stationery Office, Series PP2, No. 22.

Hantrais, L. (1997). Exploring relationships between social policy and changing family forms within the European Union. *European Journal of Population* (Amsterdam), vol. 13, No. 4, pp. 339-379.

Hoem, B. (2000). Entry into motherhood in Sweden: the influence of economic factors on the rise and fall in fertility, 1986-1997. *Demographic Research*, vol. 2/4, No. 2, article 4 (http://www.demographicresearch.org). Accessed on 17 April 2000.

Höhn, C. (1990). International transmission of population policy experience in Western Europe. In *International Transmission of Population Policy Experience: Proceedings of the Expert Group Meeting on the International Transmission of Population Policy Experience, New York City, 27-30 June 1988*. Sales No. E.91.XIII.10. New York: United Nations, pp. 145-158.

Home Office (1994). *Immigration and Nationality Department Annual Report 1994*. London: Home Office.

Hultin, M. (1999). Labour force 2015: two different long-term labour force scenarios. In *Information about Education and Labour Market 1999: 2*. Stockholm: Statistics Sweden.

Incomes Data Services (IDS) (1999). Early retirement patterns persist. *IDS Pensions Bulletin* (London), vol. 128, pp. 8-15.

Jenkins, L. (2000). The changing world of work. In *Pensions for Today: Confederation of British Industry Business Guide*. London: Caspian Publishing/Confederation of British Industry, pp. 38-43.

Kannisto, V., and others (1994). Reduction in mortality at advanced ages: several decades of evidence from 27 countries. *Population and Development Review* (New York), vol. 20, No. 4, pp. 793-810.

Kay, J. A. (1988). The welfare crisis in an ageing population. In *The Political Economy of Health and Welfare*, M. Keynes, D. A. Coleman and N. H. Dimsdale, eds. London: Macmillan, pp. 136-145.

Keilman, N. (1997). Ex-post errors in official population forecasts in industrialized countries. *Journal of Official Statistics—Statistics Sweden* (Stockholm), vol. 13, No. 3, pp. 245-277.

_____ (1998). How accurate are the United Nations world population projections? In *Frontiers of Population Forecasting*, supplement to vol. 24 of *Population and Development Review* (New York), W. Lutz, J. W. Vaupel and D. A. Ahlburg, eds. New York: Population Council, pp. 15-41.

Kelly, S., A. Baker and S. Gupta (2000). Healthy life expectancy in Great Britain, 1980-96, and its use as an indicator in United Kingdom government strategies. *Health Statistics Quarterly* (London), No. 7, pp. 32-37.

Lee, R. (2000). Long-term population projections and the US Social Security System. *Population and Development Review* (New York), vol. 26, No. 1, pp. 137-143.

Lesthaeghe, R. (2000). Europe's demographic issues: fertility, household formation and replacement migration. Presented at British Society for Population Studies/Netherlands Demographic Association Annual Conference, 2000. Utrecht, Netherlands, mimeo, p. 27.

Lutz, W. (2000). Determinants of low fertility and ageing prospects for Europe. In *Family Issues between Gender and Generations: Seminar Report from the European Observatory on Family Matters*, S. Trnka, ed. Luxembourg: Office for Official Publications of the European Communities, pp. 49-65.

Manton, K. G., and K. C. Land (2000). Active life expectancy estimates for the US elderly population: a multidimensional continuous-mixture model of functional change applied to completed cohorts, 1982-1996. *Demography* (Chicago), vol. 37, No. 3, pp. 253-265.

McDonald, P. (2000). Gender equity in theories of fertility transition. *Population and Development Review* (New York), vol. 26, No. 1, pp. 427-440.

Mogensen, G. V., and others (1995). *The Shadow Economy in Denmark 1994: Measurement and Results*. Copenhagen: Rockwool Foundation, Research Unit.

Morgan, S. P., and R. B. King (2001). Why have children in the 21st century? Biological predisposition, social coercion, rational choice? *European Journal of Population* (Amsterdam), vol. 17, pp. 3-20.

National Center for Health Statistics (2000). Births: preliminary data for 1999. *National Vital Statistics Reports* (Hyattsville, Maryland), vol. 48, No. 14.

Office of National Statistics (ONS) (2000a). *International Migration 1998 Series*. London: HM Stationery Office, MN No. 25.

_____ (2000b). *UK Population Estimates*. London: HM Stationery Office, first release 1999.

Office of Population, Censuses and Surveys (OPCS) (1993). *National Population Projections: 1991-based Series*. London: HM Stationery Office, PP2, No. 18.

Olshansky, J., and B. A. Carnes (1996). Prospects for extended survival: a critical review of the biological evidence. In *Health and Mortality among Elderly Populations*, G. Caselli and A. D. Lopez, eds. Oxford: Clarendon Press, pp. 39-58.

Organisation for Economic Co-operation and Development (OECD) (1988). *Ageing Populations: The Social Policy Implications*. Paris: OECD.

_____ (1999). *Trends in International Migration*. Paris: OECD Continuous Reporting System on Migration (SOPEMI) ed.

_____ (2000). *Economic Outlook, June 2000*. Paris: OECD.

Roche, B. (2000). UK migration in a global economy. Speech by Barbara Roche, United Kingdom Immigration Minister, at the International Public Policy Foundation, London.

Sanderson, W. C. (1998). Knowledge can improve forecasts: a review of selected socio-economic population projection models. In *Frontiers of Population Forecasting*, supplement to vol. 24 of *Population and Development Review* (New York), W. Lutz, J. W. Vaupel and D. A. Ahlburg, eds. New York: The Population Council, pp. 88-117.

Shaw, C. (2001). United Kingdom population trends in the twenty-first century. *Population Trends* (London), vol. 103, No. 1, pp. 37-46.

Sly, F., T. Thair and A. Risdon (1999). Trends in the labour-market participation of ethnic groups. *Labour Market Trends* (London), pp. 631-639.

Social Exclusion Unit (1999). *Teenage Pregnancy: A Report by the Social Exclusion Unit*. London: HM Stationery Office.

Social Security Committee (1996). *Unfunded Pension Liabilities in the European Union*. London: House of Commons Papers HC23, HM Stationery Office.

Stein, G. (1997). *Mounting Debts: The Coming European Pensions Crisis*. London: Politeia.

Tarmann, A. (2000). The flap over replacement migration. *Population Today* (Washington, D.C.), vol. 28, No. 4, pp. 1-2.

Thompson, L. H. (2000). Forging a new consensus on pensions. In *Economic Survey of Europe 1999*, No. 3. Sales No. E.99.II.E.4, chap. 3. New York: United Nations.

Tuljapurkar, S., N. Li and C. Boe (2000). A universal pattern of mortality decline in the G7 countries. *Nature* (London), vol. 405, pp. 789-792.

United Nations (2001). *Replacement Migration: Is It a Solution to Declining and Ageing Populations?* Sales No. E.01.XIII.19.

_____, Economic Commission for Europe (1991). *Economic Survey of Europe in 1990-1991*. Sales No. E.91.II.E.1, chap. 5.

_____ (1997). *Trends in Europe and North America 1996/1997: Statistical Yearbook of the ECE*. Sales No. E.97.II.E.5.

_____ (1999a). Demographic ageing and the reform of pension systems in the ECE region. In *Economic Survey of Europe 1999*, No. 3. Sales No. E.99.II.E.4, part two.

_____ (1999b). Fertility decline in the transition economies, 1982-1997: political, economic and social factors. In *Economic Survey of Europe 1999*, No. 1. Sales No. E.99.II.E.2, chap. 4.

United States Department of Labor (1989). *The Effects of Immigration on the US Economy and Labor Market*. Washington, D.C.: United States Government Printing Office.

Wattelaar, C., and G. Roumans (1990). Immigration, factor of population equilibrium? Some simulations. In *Migration: Demographic Aspects*. Paris: OECD.

Weil, D. (1997). The economics of population ageing. In *Handbook of Population and Family Economics*, M. R. Rosenzweig and O. Stark, eds. Amsterdam: Elsevier, vol. 1B, pp. 967-1014.

World Bank (1994). *Averting the Old Age Crisis*. Oxford: Oxford University Press.

POLICY RESPONSES TO POPULATION AGEING AND POPULATION DECLINE: UNITED KINGDOM OF GREAT BRITAIN AND NORTHERN IRELAND

*Karen Dunnell**

A. INTRODUCTION

The present paper sets out the demographic prospects for the United Kingdom of Great Britain and Northern Ireland during the next half-century and the possible consequences of the resulting ageing of the population and reduction in the working population. It then aims to summarize the impact that these projections have had on government policy in the United Kingdom.

The paper has been prepared within the Office for National Statistics in the United Kingdom. It therefore draws only on official statistics and reports when describing the demographic situation. In the sections on policy, only those policy statements in the public domain have been accessed.

B. POPULATION PROJECTIONS

1. *Base population*

The most recent population projections for the United Kingdom were published in March 2000 (Shaw, 2000). They are based on the mid-1998 population estimates produced by the Office for National Statistics (ONS) (1999a), the General Register Office for Scotland (General Register Office for Scotland, 1999) and the Northern Ireland Statistics and Research Agency (Registrar General for Northern Ireland, 1999). The projections are produced by the Government Actuary's Department in consultation with the Registrars General of the constituent countries of the United Kingdom. The estimated population in mid-1998 was 59.2 million.

2. *Underlying assumptions for projections*

(a) Fertility

The fertility assumption used is a cohort measure giving the average number of children that women born in particular years will have. This average

---

*Office for National Statistics, London, United Kingdom of Great Britain and Northern Ireland.

completed family size has been falling from a peak of 2.5 children for women born in the mid-1930s. It fell to replacement level for women born around 1950 and is assumed to continue to decline until the 1975 birth cohort and eventually level off at 1.80 children per woman. This level is similar to the total (period) fertility rate observed in the United Kingdom since the mid-1970s.

(b) Mortality

Mortality rates are based on trends in rates in recent years. These rates have been decreasing year after year for every age group except young adults. It has been assumed that the annual reduction in mortality rates will tend towards a reduction of about 0.5 per cent a year at all ages by 2032-2033.

Life expectancy at birth is assumed to rise from 74.9 years in 1998-1999 to 78.5 years in 2020-2021 for males, and from 79.7 to 82.7 years for females. Life expectancy is assumed to continue to increase in the longer term, although the rate of improvement is assumed to diminish. On this basis, life expectancy at birth for males and females in 2051 will be about 80 and 84 years, respectively.

(c) Migration

Net international migration fluctuates considerably from year to year in the United Kingdom. However, the underlying trend has been upward, with annual net migration in the four years leading to mid-1998 averaging over 100,000 persons per year. The estimate for 1998 as a whole is 178,000 (Office for National Statistics (ONS), 1999b), the highest figure on record. These figures have been used for the short-term projections but for 2001-2002 onward an assumption of 95,000 has been used. Analysis of surveys and other sources suggests a levelling off of the recent increase in inward migration. Nevertheless, this value is considerably higher than the previous assumption of 65,000 incorporated in the mid-1996 projections, and more than double the latest United Nations medium-variant assumption.

The trends informing these assumptions and the assumed levels themselves are shown in the figure.

3. Total population projections

The population of the United Kingdom is projected to increase gradually from 59.2 million in 1998 to reach 63.6 million by 2021. This is equivalent to an average annual rate of growth of 0.3 per cent. Just over half the projected 4.4 million increase between 1998 and 2021 is attributable to net inward migration. The remainder is due to projected natural increase (more births than deaths). Longer-term projections suggest the population will peak at nearly 65 million in the year 2036. The population would then gradually start to fall, declining to about 64 million by the middle of the next century.

Assumptions for 1998-based national population projections, United Kingdom

(a) Total fertility rate (TFR) and average completed family size (CFS),[a] 1951-2021

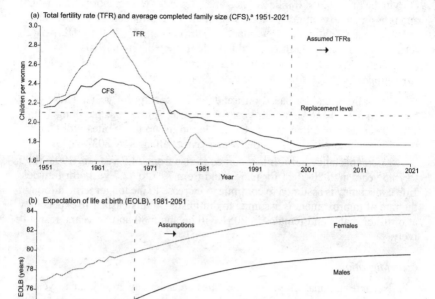

(b) Expectation of life at birth (EOLB), 1981-2051

(c) Total net migration, 1982-1983 to 2020-2021

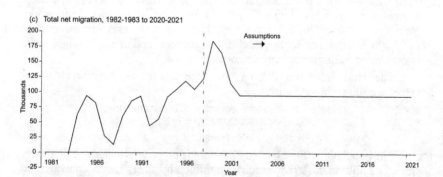

[a]CFS relates to cohort born 28 years earlier, 28 years being roughly the mean age at childbearing. Assumed CFS is given for cohorts that have not yet completed childbearing.

C. DEMOGRAPHIC CONSEQUENCES OF UNITED KINGDOM POPULATION PROJECTIONS

1. *Age distribution*

Table 1 summarizes the projected structure of the population. It will become gradually older with the median age of the population rising from 38 years in 2001 to 44 years in 2041, when it is expected to stabilize.

The number of children under age 16 is projected to fall by 6.5 per cent by 2011 and remain about 11.3 million for a further 20 years. They will represent just 17 per cent of the total population.

The effect of the ageing of the population can also be seen by the increasing proportion of people aged 60 or more. In 2001, this group represents 20 per cent of the total. By 2031, it will be 30 per cent of the total, levelling at 31 per cent by 2051. The proportion in the oldest, 75+ age group is projected to double from 7 to 14 per cent over the 50-year period.

The working-age population will also become much older on average. Little change is projected in the number of adults under age 30. However, as the baby-boom generations of the mid-1960s age, the size of older age groups will change markedly. Age group 30-44 is projected to fall from 13.3 million in 1998 to 12.1 million in 2021, but age group 45-59 is projected to increase by nearly one quarter over the same period, from 10.8 million in 1998 to 13.3 million in 2021.

2. *Dependency ratios*

Currently in Great Britain, only about 55 per cent of men and 30 per cent of women in age group 60-64 are economically active (Armitage and Scott, 1998). Current eligibility for State pensions begins at age 60 for women and age 65 for men. Between 2010 and 2020, State retirement age will gradually

TABLE 1. PROJECTED POPULATION, AGE DISTRIBUTION,
UNITED KINGDOM, 2001-2051

(*Percentage*)

	2001	2011	2021	2031	2041	2051
0-15	20	18	18	17	17	17
16-29	18	18	17	16	16	16
30-44	23	20	19	19	18	18
45-59	19	21	21	18	19	18
60-74	13	15	17	19	17	17
75+	7	8	9	11	13	14
Median age	38	41	42	43	44	44
Thousands of persons . . .	59 954	61 773	63 642	64 768	64 781	64 089

Source: Shaw (2000).

be equalized at age 65 for both men and women. This makes calculation and interpretation of dependency rates based on State pension ages more complex than usual.

Table 2 shows that the overall dependency ratio will continue its current downward trend to 586 dependants per 1,000 persons of working age in 2021 when the increase in women's retirement age is complete. It will then rise rapidly, with the longer-term projections suggesting a levelling off at about 700 per 1,000 from the mid-2030s. This is a level similar to that in the United Kingdom in the 1970s, when children, rather than the elderly, constituted the majority of dependants.

3. *Labour-force projections*

Because not all persons of working age are economically active, short-term projections of the size and composition of the labour force are an important addition to our information about future populations. The latest published projections for Great Britain are for the years 1998-2011 (Armitage and Scott, 1998).

As can be seen from table 3, the labour force is expected to increase slowly during the first decade of the century. Fifty-five per cent of the increase is attributable to demographic projections. Activity rates for men in all age groups except the youngest have been decreasing over the last 20 years. This trend is projected to continue. In contrast, the rates for women are increasing and projected to continue. The result, as can be seen in the table, is very little change in economic activity rates overall.

4. *Trends in health*

A recent analysis of trends in health indicators for people aged 55-64 (Dunnell and Dix, 2000) raised many questions about whether health in this age group was improving in the way that mortality rate reduction suggests. There were signs of increasing or unchanging health problems in relation to some cancers, obesity, common chronic illnesses, self-reported health and

TABLE 2.   DEPENDENCY RATES, UNITED KINGDOM, 2001-2051

Dependants per 1,000 persons of working age	2001	2011	2021	2031	2041	2051
Under age 16	325	294	282	291	288	287
Pensioners	291	309	304	381	417	412
TOTAL	616	603	586	672	705	700

Source: Shaw (2000).
NOTE: Working-age and pensionable age populations based on State retirement age for given year. Between 2010 and 2020, State retirement age will change from 65 years for men and 60 years for women, to 65 years for both sexes.

TABLE 3.   SIZE OF THE LABOUR FORCE, GREAT BRITAIN, 2001 AND 2011

TABLE 3.   SIZE OF THE LABOUR FORCE, GREAT BRITAIN, 2001 AND 2011
(*Thousands*)

	2001	2011
Men aged 16-64	15 686	15 752
Women aged 16-59	12 346	12 852
All	28 031	28 604
All including those over retirement age	28 963	29 768
Activity rates[a]		
Men	84.4	81.7
Women	73.1	75.4
All	79.0	78.8

Source: Armitage and Scott (1998).
[a]As a percentage of men aged 16-64 and women aged 16-59.

blood pressure levels. Improvements were found in smoking levels, lung cancer and dental health. Healthy life expectancy may be increasing, but not by as much as life expectancy. This conclusion was confirmed by a cohort analysis of some of the same health survey data (Evandrou and Falkingham, 2000): "In short, the evidence on the health of future elders is somewhat mixed. Thus, it is premature to assume that tomorrow's elderly will be healthier than today's."

5.   *Household projections*

There are several significant trends in family formation and dissolution patterns in the United Kingdom that affect projections of households. Projections for England are prepared by the government department responsible for housing (King and others, 2000). In the United Kingdom, people are marrying later and divorcing more. These patterns are also reflected in increasing common informal unions—cohabitation. Thus, significant increases in single-person households are expected among both younger and older groups in the population. Whereas the total population of England is expected to increase by 7 per cent, the number of households is expected to rise by 14 per cent, from 21 million to 24 million, by 2021.

D.   GOVERNMENT RESPONSES TO THE AGEING OF THE POPULATION

The Government of the United Kingdom has been aware of the ageing of the population for many years. The increasing importance of older people for the economy and government services has led to several initiatives designed to improve awareness of, and thus services for, older people. For example, the Government of the United Kingdom has a ministerial group on ageing, has published the findings of a Royal Commission on Long-term Care and has a central group working on "Active Ageing" which has produced several reports; but foremost in respect of the look into the future, in terms of the identification of policy options for the public, private and voluntary sectors and individuals, is the Government's Foresight Programme.

1. *Foresight Programme*

The Foresight Programme was launched in 1993. It is driven by the goals of increasing wealth creation and improving quality of life. The programme brings together business, government, the science base and others to identify the threats and opportunities that we are likely to face over the next 10 or 20 years. It has a panel-based structure and operates on a five-year cycle. The new round began in 1999. Each panel is carrying out a wide consultation looking at the future for a particular area. One of the three high-level thematic panels is the Ageing Population Panel. Its consultation document (Department of Trade and Industry, 2000) was launched in May 2000. A report on the results was issued in December 2000.

The consultation document sets out the demographic situation and then explores issues, opportunities and challenges in five priority areas: labour, leisure and learning; finance; health care; design for living; and information and communication technology (ICT).

This paper now draws together the kinds of policy options that the Foresight panel has identified for consultation:

(a) *Labour, leisure and learning*:

- Age should become irrelevant in the labour market; value should be based on skills and competencies;

- Removal of set retirement ages;

- Reducing numbers of older employees will cease to be an option;

- Employers will need to develop schemes to retain older workers and maintain their skills;

- Respond to increased demand for learning and new methods, for example, information technology–based;

- Learning will be required for labour and leisure purposes;

(b) *Finance*:

- Government to have a key role in highlighting need for higher savings to pay for extended retirement with less State provision;

- Public/private partnership to ensure support for all;

- Greater use of capital tied up in housing would require a regulatory framework;

- Government to introduce "staged pensions" whereby the State pension would rise at higher ages to compensate for the lengthening of retirement;

(c) *Health care*:

- Need to cope with growing demand for health care and new treatments;

336

- Need to cope with increasing social polarization and diversity among future cohorts of older people;
- Increased demand for public caregivers and social changes are likely to limit informal caring;
- Implications for training of health professionals;
- Increased expectation that older people will take charge of their health;

(d) *Design for living*:
- Impact on regulations etc. for local planning, housing and transport;

(e) *ICT*:
- Need to avoid emergence of electronic disenfranchisement. This is important for the Government as it seeks to use electronic means to deliver services and information to citizens.

This Foresight Programme consultation document identifies the wide variety of directions that policy could take in future years. Much but not all of United Kingdom government policy works within a three-year planning and finance cycle which tends to constrain longer-term policy-making. There is also a strong and increasing devolution of policy-making and service provision away from central government. The paper now goes on to look at some of the policy responses to the ageing population so far.

2. *Employment and training*

Key aspects of the Government's labour-market policies include promoting job creation and helping people to overcome the barriers preventing their moving from welfare into work. The policy emphasis is partly driven by the high levels of unemployment experienced in the 1980s and early 1990s and heavy dependency of young families on State benefits. However, the rapidly changing world economy has made education and training among the Government's top priorities to ensure that the United Kingdom workforce has the necessary skills to meet the challenges. There are now many national and local organizations supported by government that aim to increase skills and competencies at all levels.

The United Kingdom is also an important supporter of the European Union (EU) "Employability Initiative". This stresses skills and adaptability as essential in the developing economy. Equal opportunity is also a strong element of this initiative. Moves towards more flexible working arrangements not only improve equality but attract more and more women—and possibly, in future, older workers—into the labour force.

The equality imperative was the driver behind the United Kingdom's recent planned increase in the State retirement age for women. The current ages of 65 for men and 60 for women were unacceptable. It was the foreseen demographic trends that led to the common age of retirement at 65 rather than at 60. This transition will take place between 2010 and 2020. There are no current moves to increase this age—indeed, the current trend in the United Kingdom is towards earlier retirement.

The Government is aware of the potential problems of this trend continuing. It has commissioned a report and accepted the recommendations made (Cabinet Office, 2000). These fall under four headings:

- Changing the culture to raise expectations of older people and stop making judgements based on their age range rather than on their true value and potential;

- Enabling and encouraging over-fifties to stay in work;

- Helping and encouraging displaced workers to re-enter work;

- Helping older people to make use of their skills and experience for the benefit of the wider community.

These initiatives build on the ideas set out in the Foresight Programme and will be driven forward by the central Active Ageing team.

Some public bodies are already responding to current and predicted future shortages of skilled staff. For example, in 1999, the Department of Health issued a consultation booklet (Department of Health, 1999a) on improving working lives in the National Health Service (NHS). It noted that "women make up the majority of the NHS workforce. More flexible and part-time training and working patterns are essential if we want to maximize their contribution throughout their careers." One aspect of flexibility is retirement and a circular on flexible retirement was issued to NHS in July 2000 (Department of Health, 2000). It announced the availability of guidance booklets and summarized its proposals:

- An increasing number of NHS staff are over age 50. Extending the contribution of staff pre- and post-retirement is an essential part of a Trust strategy to expand the workforce and tackle vacancies. The guidance booklets enclosed with this circular give information to employers and staff on the benefits of offering flexible working patterns to those nearing retirement, or who have recently retired. It also includes information about the pension implications;

- Additional funding was available to Trusts encouraging staff planning to retire shortly to defer their retirement until spring 2001;

- A letter would be sent to recently retired nurses under age 65 drawing their attention to this initiative and to ways through which they can come back to work in NHS, especially over the winter months.

This policy initiative on the part of NHS is very important in the United Kingdom. NHS is one of the largest employers in the world, the largest in the United Kingdom, with a workforce of nearly 1 million people.

3. *Health and care*

Older people are the heaviest users of health and care services, with utilization increasing with age. The ageing of the population has always therefore to be taken into account in government resource allocation, because most health services in the United Kingdom are publicly funded. Real increases of 6.3 per cent annually have recently been announced with an acknowledgement that older people will be among the principle beneficiaries. The large number of health and care initiatives relevant to the older population focus on improving the quality and coherence of services in the next few years.

However, there has been a major policy development on the public-health front. This strategy was set out for England in 1999 (Department of Health, 1999b) with similar strategies for the other United Kingdom countries. The two main aims are:

- To improve the health of the population by increasing the length of people's lives and the numbers of years people spend free from illness;

- To improve the health of the least well-off people in society.

The strategy recommends actions to combat the four major causes of premature death and avoidable ill health: cancer, coronary heart disease and stroke, accidental injury and mental illness. While many of the policy recommendations address the underlying causes of ill health and inequality, most of the targets for 2010 are expressed in terms of reducing mortality.

4. Pensions

Over the next 50 years, the number of people over State pension age in the United Kingdom is forecast to increase by 44 per cent. The new United Kingdom framework for pensions (Department of Social Security, 1998) has been developed with a long-term view and also reflecting the growing role of private pension provision. However, the Government does recognize the significant problems of pensioners who are entirely dependent on State pensions and benefits. Since 1981, the gap between the richest and poorest pensioners has grown. Women tend to fare worse than men. This is because of their different working patterns resulting in a lower likelihood of an occupational pension and greater life expectancy. It is estimated that if current policies are not changed, by 2025 one in three of the retired could have to rely on income-related State benefits in their retirement. Strategies to improve this situation that are being embodied in new legislation include:

- The basic State pension's remaining the key building block of the system and continuing to be increased at least in line with price indexes;

- A new second-tier State pension for employees which is more generous for low earners;

- A new framework for flexible, secure, value-for-money pension schemes;

- Improved pensions education and the provision of an annual pension statement to every adult;

- A means-tested guaranteed minimum income.

These improvements are expected to lead to changes that will allow the Government to meet the demographic challenge while delivering a decent income in retirement for everyone and maintaining public expenditure at prudent levels. State spending is expected to increase but income from private pensions will increase even more. Currently, about 60 per cent of pension income is accounted for by the State and 40 per cent by the private sector. With the reforms, the State's share is expected to fall to about 40 per cent by 2050. On current projections, State spending on pensions is not expected to increase as a proportion of gross domestic product (GDP).

5. *Immigration*

As can be seen from the section on population projections, net migration is the most difficult area on which to make assumptions. In the United Kingdom, immigration is greater than emigration, with the projected net migration at 95,000 per year. There is a large body of legislation determining the right to reside in the United Kingdom and controls have generally tightened over the last 30 years, easing somewhat since 1997. At the same time there has been increased freedom to live and work in the United Kingdom for members of the European Economic Area. The United Kingdom also has a tradition of receiving asylum-seekers; these have increased in number in the last few years, although less than one in five are granted asylum.

One of the suggestions in the United Nations work is that immigration could partly help solve the problem of a declining workforce and increasing dependency ratio. The Government of the United Kingdom is currently rethinking its policy in this area, the demographic situation being one of the drivers. There is recognition that some of the country's skill gaps could, to some extent, be filled with workers from abroad. This was the case after the Second World War when large numbers of people moved to Great Britain from Commonwealth countries to fill gaps in particular industries. This was mainly in response to recruitment campaigns by various large employers rather than to a central government initiative.

NHS is a major public sector employer. It has always depended to a significant extent on workers from abroad. Again, it is recognizing the value of recruiting from abroad and has issued guidance to NHS organizations (Department of Health, 1999c). This focuses on the area of nurses and midwives, where needs are most acute, but is also applicable across the range of non-medical professions.

6. *Population policy*

The United Kingdom policy on population was presented to the International Conference on Population, held in Mexico in 1984, and the International Conference on Population and Development, held in Cairo in 1994. The following statement was presented and remains the official United Kingdom policy (Office for National Statistics (ONS), 1993).

"The United Kingdom Government does not pursue a population policy in the sense of actively trying to influence the overall size of the population, its age structure, or the components of change, except in the field of immigration. Nor has it expressed a view about the size of population, or the age structure, that would be desirable for the United Kingdom. Its primary concern is for the well-being of the population, although it continually monitors demographic trends and developments. The current level of births has not been the cause of general anxiety. The prevailing view is that decisions about fertility and childbearing are for people themselves to make, but that it is proper for government to provide individuals with the information and the means necessary to make their decisions effective. To this end, the Government provides assistance with family planning as part of the National Health Service. The 'ageing' of the population does raise social and economic issues. However, it is believed that these will prove manageable; and also, to a degree, that society will adapt.

"The Government takes population matters into account in formulating economic and social policy. Many aspects of economic and social policy will, of course, influence population change."

As we have seen from this brief summary of United Kingdom policy responses to long-term demographic change, few policy areas are significantly driven by the long-term prospects. This reflects a policy where the changes are perceived as being manageable and society adaptable. The central Active Ageing initiative and the Foresight Programme aim to encourage a longer perspective, particularly in the areas of science, technology and employment.

REFERENCES

Armitage, Bob, and Mark Scott (1998). British labour force projections: 1998-2011. *Labour Market Trends* (London), vol. 106, No. 6.

Cabinet Office (2000). *Winning the Generation Game: Improving Opportunities for People Aged 50-65 in Work and Community Activity*. London: Cabinet Office.

Department of Health (1999a). *Improving Working Lives in the National Health Service (NHS)*. London: Department of Health.

_____ (1999b). *Saving Lives: Our Healthier Nation*. London: Department of Health.

_____ (1999c). *Guidance on International Nursing Recruitment*. London: Department of Health.

_____ (2000). Flexible retirement. Circular HSC 2000/022. London: Department of Health.

Department of Social Security (1998). *A New Contract for Welfare: Partnership in Pensions*. London: Department of Social Security.

Department of Trade and Industry (2000). *The Age Shift—A Consultative Document*. London: Department of Trade and Industry.

Dunnell, Karen, and David Dix (2000). Are we looking forward to a longer and healthier retirement?, *Health Statistics Quarterly* (London), vol. 6, pp. 18-24.

Evandrou, Maria, and Jane Falkingham (2000). Looking back to look forward: lessons from four birth cohorts for ageing in the 21st century. *Population Trends* (London), vol. 99 (spring), pp. 27-36.

General Register Office for Scotland (GROS) (1999). *Mid-1998 Population Estimates: Scotland*. Edinburgh: GROS.

King, Dave, and others (2000). Population of households in England to 2021. *Population Trends* (London), vol. 99.

Office for National Statistics (ONS) (1993). Editorial. *Population Trends* (London), vol. 72.

_____ (1999a). *Mid-1998 Population Estimates: England and Wales*, Series PE, No. 1. London: ONS.

_____ (1999b). *International Migration 1998*, vol. 99, No. 383. London: ONS.

Registrar General for Northern Ireland (1999). *Annual Report: 1998*. London: HM Stationery Office.

Shaw, Chris (2000). 1998-based national population projections for the United Kingdom and constituent countries. *Population Trends* (London), vol. 99.

LONG-RANGE DEMOGRAPHIC PROJECTIONS AND THEIR IMPLICATIONS FOR THE UNITED STATES OF AMERICA

*Michael S. Teitelbaum**

A. OFFICIAL PROJECTIONS OF THE UNITED STATES POPULATION

The United States Census Bureau released its most recent long-range demographic projections in January 2000 (United States Census Bureau, 2000). The new series is similar to earlier Census Bureau projections, but extends the projection horizon 20 years further out than previously issued series, to the year 2100. In addition, the new projection series allows both fertility and international migration to vary over time, versus the more typical assumptions of constant values incorporated in earlier projections.

1. *Assumptions*

(*a*) *Fertility*: The period total fertility rate (TFR) of the United States of America has been relatively high by the standards of industrialized countries. In 1997, the reported rate was 2.0325, and this period measure has remained relatively constant since 1989.

For the "short-term" period of the Census projections, defined as 1999-2025, "target total fertility rates" were set on the basis of both demographic theory and adjusted data on birth expectations (adjusted following the method suggested by van Hoorn and Keilman (1997)). These "targets" were set separately for five race/Hispanic or non-Hispanic origin groupings (United States Census Bureau, 2000, pp. 8-9).

For the "long-term" period, 2025-2100, the Census projections adopted two key assumptions: that the period total rate would slowly stabilize, and that current and prospective substantial fertility differentials among the five race/Hispanic origin categories would slowly converge.

The central impacts of these assumptions need to be clearly understood. As may be seen in table 1, the middle-variant projections assume that the total fertility rate of white/non-Hispanic women, reported to be 1.833 in 1999, would rise to 2.0433 by 2050, while that for black/non-Hispanic women would increase from 2.0784 in 1999 to 2.1133 in 2050. Over this same period, the fertility rates of Hispanic women are projected to decline from 2.9205 in 1999 to 2.5628 in 2050. The low- and high-variant projections also include a clear

---

* Alfred P. Sloan Foundation, New York, United States of America.

TABLE 1. PROJECTED TOTAL FERTILITY RATES BY RACE AND HISPANIC OR NON-HISPANIC ORIGIN, 1999-2100

(Rates per 1,000 women as of 1 July; resident population)

Race and Hispanic origin	Lowest series				Middle series				Highest series			
	1999	2025	2050	2100	1999	2025	2050	2100	1999	2025	2050	2100
Total	2 035.8	1 865.5	1 799.7	1 632.1	2 047.5	2 206.8	2 219.0	2 182.9	2 059.2	2 557.5	2 646.8	2 737.4
White, non-Hispanic	1 822.9	1 725.5	1 668.8	1 552.5	1 833.0	2 030.0	2 043.3	2 070.0	1 843.2	2 334.5	2 417.9	2 587.5
Black, non-Hispanic	2 066.9	1 802.0	1 725.9	1 575.0	2 078.4	2 120.0	2 113.3	2 100.0	2 090.0	2 438.0	2 500.8	2 625.0
American Indian, non-Hispanic[a]	2 407.2	1 929.5	1 823.9	1 620.1	2 420.6	2 270.0	2 233.3	2 160.0	2 420.6	2 270.0	2 233.3	2 160.0
Asian, non-Hispanic[b]	2 216.6	1 845.5	1 759.5	1 590.9	2 229.0	2 171.2	2 154.5	2 121.2	2 241.4	2 496.9	2 549.5	2 651.4
Hispanic origin[c]	2 904.3	2 275.7	2 092.9	1 750.4	2 920.5	2 677.3	2 562.8	2 333.8	2 936.7	3 078.9	3 032.6	2 917.2
White	1 998.0	1 867.4	1 806.5	1 640.3	2 009.5	2 210.2	2 230.1	2 198.0	2 021.0	2 563.9	2 667.5	2 764.5
Black	2 110.1	1 836.7	1 760.4	1 598.8	2 121.9	2 164.1	2 159.1	2 131.0	2 133.8	2 493.5	2 558.6	2 663.6
American Indian[a]	2 492.5	2 003.9	1 893.5	1 663.9	2 506.6	2 366.3	2 329.4	2 224.3	2 520.8	2 736.1	2 774.9	2 791.3
Asian[b]	2 264.9	1 877.8	1 785.5	1 603.8	2 277.4	2 205.8	2 180.8	2 134.7	2 289.9	2 531.4	2 573.8	2 664.6

Source: United States Census Bureau, Internet release date: 13 January 2000, table B.

[a] "American Indian" is used to describe the American Indian, Eskimo and Aleut populations.

[b] "Asian" is used to describe the Asian and Pacific islander population.

[c] A person of Hispanic origin may be of any race.

pattern of convergence over this period in the fertility behaviour of these three groups. Should the assumed convergence pattern not occur, in other words, if fertility rates of the white and black non-Hispanic groups over the coming half-century prove to be lower than projected and/or that of the Hispanic group prove to be higher than projected, the proportionate contribution of these groups to demographic change would depart from those calculated in the projections.

High- and low-fertility assumptions were incorporated in projection variants. These were calculated by inflating and deflating the middle series by specified proportions. These inflation/deflation proportions were calculated as linear interpolations rising from zero in 1998 to 15 per cent in 2025. From 2025 to 2100, the inflation/deflation proportions were linearly interpolated to increase from 15 to 25 per cent (United States Census Bureau, p. 11).

(*b*) *Mortality*: Current United States mortality data show substantial disparities between males and females, and among race and ethnic groups. The male/female and white/black mortality differentials have not demonstrated a consistent trend during the twentieth century, increasing during some periods but decreasing during others.

For the purposes of its long-range projections, the Census Bureau assumed a small convergence between male and female mortality, and more substantial narrowing of mortality disparities among race/Hispanic or non-Hispanic origin groups.

Low- and high-mortality variants were based on the 95 per cent confidence interval reported by Lee and Tuljapurkar (1998). The quantitative outcomes of these assumptions may be seen in table 2.

(*c*) *International migration*: The new Census Bureau projections include a departure from the Bureau's previous practice, in which a constant numerical value and a constant set of demographic characteristics were assumed. Instead, the new projection series constructively allows the level and characteristics of international migration flows to change over the projection period. It also incorporates some limited feedback on assumed future migration from the characteristics of the projected basis population (for example, immigration is increased as the projected growth in the size of the United States population of working age declines).

However, while there is some limited feedback of this type allowed, the Census Bureau notes that it was "not able to develop a dynamic model for future international migration that reflects adequately the current base series information, yet conforms to any unifying theory of future change" (United States Census Bureau, p. 16).

For the short term to 2020, the new assumptions are that the rapid rise in legal immigration during the 1990s is a consequence primarily of the large-scale legalization of more than 3 million illegal immigrants during the 1980s, many of whom were able to become United States citizens and then to sponsor the legal immigration of immediate relatives with no numerical limitations. The Bureau assumes that this is a time-limited phenomenon which will peak shortly after 2000, and then decline gradually to zero.[1]

Additional important assumptions are also adopted. Interestingly, these operate in the same direction of producing immigration flows that rise during the early years of the projection period, but then stabilize or decline. In particular:

(*a*)   It is assumed there will be "no change in immigration policy that would result in any change in the quantity of immigrant visas available in numerically limited legal categories between 1998 and 2020" (United States Census Bureau, p. 17);

(*b*)   The flow of refugees to permanent residence is assumed to increase until 2000 and then decline to 2020;

(*c*)   The level of undocumented migration from Mexico and Central America is assumed not to change.

For the first decade of the longer-term projections, from 2020 to 2030, the Bureau assumes that migration to the United States would increase by nearly one third, from about 1.09 million to 1.45 million per year. This assumed increase is posited as a kind of balancing response to the projections' own projected increases in the United States "dependency ratio" during that period, as the large post-war baby-boom cohorts pass age 65 (see discussion of this age boundary elsewhere in the present paper). Following 2030, the assumed level of net immigration is assumed to remain numerically constant (and hence to constitute a declining fraction of a growing population base) for the middle series.

As to "high" and "low" variants, the Bureau emphasizes that its goal is:

" . . . to establish a candid view of the uncertainty surrounding the middle series projection . . . The margin of uncertainty around the middle-level assumption is, of necessity, relatively wider for international migration than for births and deaths. The exogenous character of this component, and its reliance on unpredictable external factors such as the internal policy environment and world events, as well as the lack of demographic determinism in its projection, ensure a comparatively high level of uncertainty for this component" (United States Census Bureau, p. 19).

To be specific, the "high" immigration assumption exceeds the middle series by zero in the base year of 1998, by 75 per cent in 2010 and by 150 per cent in 2100. The "low" variant deviates below the middle series by the reciprocal of these same multipliers, that is to say, 1.0 for 1998, 0.57 for 2010 and 0.40 for 2100 (United States Census Bureau, p. 20). The numerical levels of net international migration that result under the middle assumption appear in table 3.

2.   *Projected population size under projection variants*

Under all three of the above variants, the Census Bureau projections show the United States population continuing to grow in size up to the year 2050, the end of the period under discussion here (see table 4). From the base population of about 270 million in 1998, the middle series projects an increase of nearly 50 per cent, to nearly 404 million. The projected increase for the low series is 16 per cent, to 314 million, and for the high series the comparable projection is an increase of over 100 per cent, to 553 million.

TABLE 2. PROJECTED LIFE EXPECTANCY AT BIRTH, 1999-2100

(*In years; as of 1 July; resident population*)

	Lowest series				Middle series				Highest series			
	1999	*2025*	*2050*	*2100*	*1999*	*2025*	*2050*	*2100*	*1999*	*2025*	*2050*	*2100*
Total population (male)	74.0	76.5	79.5	85.0	74.1	77.6	81.2	88.0	74.1	79.1	83.8	92.3
Total population (female).......	79.7	82.6	84.9	89.3	79.8	83.6	86.7	92.3	79.8	84.6	88.4	95.2

Source: United States Census Bureau, Internet release date: 13 January 2000, table C.

TABLE 3. NET MIGRATION ASSUMPTIONS, 1995-2050,
UNITED STATES CENSUS MIDDLE SERIES

(*In thousands*)

	Per year	*Sum*
1995-2000	915	4 575
2000-2005	951	4 755
2005-2010	872	4 360
2010-2015	713	3 565
2015-2020	734	3 670
2020-2025	751	3 755
2025-2030	912	4 560
2030-2035	1 061	5 305
2035-2040	1 061	5 305
2040-2045	1 061	5 305
2045-2050	1 061	5 305
Total, 1995-2050		50 460

Source: United States Census Bureau, Internet release date: 13 January 2000, table E.

TABLE 4.   TOTAL PROJECTED POPULATION, UNITED STATES CENSUS BUREAU SERIES:
LOWEST SERIES (L.S.), MIDDLE SERIES (M.S.) AND HIGHEST SERIES (H.S.)
(*In thousands as of 1 July; resident population*)

Year	Population			Average annual percentage change		
	L.S.	*M.S.*	*H.S.*	*L.S.*	*M.S.*	*H.S.*
1998 (estimate)	270 299	270 299	270 299	-	-	-
2000.	274 853	275 306	275 816	0.84	0.92	1.01
2025.	308 229	337 815	380 397	0.46	0.82	1.29
2050.	313 546	403 687	552 757	0.07	0.71	1.49
2100.	282 706	570 954	1 182 390	-0.21	0.69	1.52

Source: United States Census Bureau, Internet release date: 13 January 2000, table A.

In all such cases, the projected totals of the projections released in January 2000 exceed by a substantial margin the comparable projected numbers released in 1996. In all three variants, the projected numbers for 2050 are at least 10 per cent larger.

3.   *Projected changes in age composition*

As is well known, the United States (along with only a small number of other countries, including Canada, Australia and New Zealand) experienced a far larger and longer-lived baby boom than did most industrialized countries after the Second World War. The United States baby boom extended over nearly two decades, from 1947 to 1965. Fertility rates did not peak until 1957, and the largest birth cohort was not seen until 1959. As a result, the age structure of the United States is characterized by a baby-boom bulge in its age composition that is both higher in amplitude and wider as to its current age range than in most other such countries. In 2000, the large baby-boom cohorts are (roughly) in the age range 35-54. If one is willing to accept the arbitrary age boundary of 65 as indicative of entry into "aged dependency" (but see discussion, below), this implies that the "dependent" category will begin to grow rapidly in size around 2011, and the largest cohorts will enter this age category in the middle of the third decade of the twenty-first century.

Thus, if measures such as the "aged dependency ratio" (defined as the number aged 65 years or over divided by the population aged 15-64, expressed as a percentage) are used to assess demographic ageing, it follows that such ratios can be expected to increase rapidly after 2010. Such a trend can indeed be seen in the Census Bureau projections. In the middle series, the aged dependency ratio, so defined, is projected to rise from 19.1 per cent in 2000 to 33.9 per cent in 2050 (United States Census Bureau, 2000, table F).

The projection variants on international migration also differ in this regard. However, although the quantitative differences in the migration assumptions are quite large among the variants, the impacts on the aged dependency ratio are relatively modest: whereas in the middle-migration variant this ratio rises from 19.1 in 2000 to 33.9 in 2050, in the high-migration variant the increase is from 19.1 to 30.3, and in the low-migration variant from 19.2 to 36.1 (United States Census Bureau, 2000, table F). In short, the trajectory of this ratio is driven primarily by the lagged effects of the post-war baby boom.

4. *Comparisons of United States Census and United Nations assumptions*

The assumptions about fertility, mortality and net immigration embodied in the two projection series differ quite substantially. The fertility assumptions of the United Nations projections for the United States population are summarized in table 5. Though the time intervals differ somewhat, these may be compared in rough terms with the fertility assumptions adopted by the United States Census Bureau, as set out in table 1 above.

As may be observed, the United Nations fertility assumptions are generally lower than the Census Bureau assumptions. For example, the "low variant" United Nations assumptions in 2025-2030 and again in 2040-2050 for total fertility rate (per woman) are 1.50, whereas the "lowest series" Census Bureau assumptions for 2025 and 2050 are 1.865 and 1.80, respectively. Similarly, the United Nations fertility assumptions in the "medium variant" for these same years are 1.90 and 1.90, versus 2.21 and 2.22 in the Census Bureau projections.

The differences in assumptions about future mortality may be examined by comparing table 6 with table 2. Here the assumptions are quite close for the periods around 2000 and 2025, but for the later period the United Nations assumptions about life expectancy are considerably lower than those of the United States Census Bureau.

Finally, the two projection series also differ substantially in their assumptions about the magnitudes and trajectories of future net migration. Table 7 presents the two sets of "middle" assumptions side by side. The United Nations projections are set a constant 760,000 per year over the projection period. Meanwhile, the Census Bureau's experiment with allowing limited feedback to produce rises and falls in net migration, coupled with the specific feedback assumptions adopted in this regard, produces an initial short-term rise in net migration, followed by a two-decade-long decline, and by a subsequent increase to 2030, at which point the Census migration assumption is held constant. It should be noted that the cumulative effect of such differing assumptions is quite substantial over the 55-year period in question. Overall, the assumed net flow of immigrants to the United States is 8.66 million higher in the Census projections than in those produced by the United Nations—a difference of over 20 per cent.

B. CONSEQUENCES

Before entering into any discussion of possible consequences of such projections, it is essential to underline just how uncertain the future demography of the United States truly is beyond the short term. Here one must be both clear and forceful: the uncertainties are many in number, and large in magnitude.

TABLE 5. UNITED STATES FERTILITY ASSUMPTIONS IN UNITED NATIONS PROJECTIONS
(Total fertility rate (per woman))

	Low variant			Medium variant			High variant		
	2000-2005	2025-2030	2040-2050	2000-2005	2025-2030	2040-2050	2000-2005	2025-2030	2040-2050
	1.80	1.50	1.50	1.93	1.90	1.90	2.13	2.30	2.30

Source: Replacement Migration: Is It a Solution to Declining and Ageing Populations? (United Nations publication, Sales No. E.01.XIII.19), table A.15.

TABLE 6. UNITED STATES LIFE EXPECTANCY AT BIRTH IN UNITED NATIONS PROJECTIONS FOR 2000-2005, 2025-2030 AND 2040-2050
(In years)

	2000-2005	2025-2030	2040-2050
Total population (male)	74.2	77.3	78.8
Total population (female). ...	80.6	83.0	84.4

Source: Replacement Migration: Is It a Solution to Declining and Ageing Populations? (United Nations publication, Sales No. E.01.XIII.19), table A.15.

(Thousands)

	United Nations medium variant		United States Census middle series	
	Per year	*Sum*	*Per year*	*Sum*
1995-2000	760	3 800	915	4 575
2000-2005	760	3 800	951	4 755
2005-2010	760	3 800	872	4 360
2010-2015	760	3 800	713	3 565
2015-2020	760	3 800	734	3 670
2020-2025	760	3 800	751	3 755
2025-2030	760	3 800	912	4 560
2030-2035	760	3 800	1 061	5 305
2035-2040	760	3 800	1 061	5 305
2040-2045	760	3 800	1 061	5 305
2045-2050	760	3 800	1 061	5 305
Total, 1995-2050		41 800		50 460

The professionals at the United States Census Bureau are well aware that it is nearly impossible to establish credible long-term forecasts for at least two of the three key components of their projections—fertility and international migration—and even the more stable and predictable component of mortality trajectories is increasingly uncertain.

It should not be necessary to state this kind of caveat: the failure of past long-term demographic projections to correctly anticipate long-term trends is well known. Two of many possible examples might be offered. First, there was a broad consensus during the 1930s that the populations of countries such as the United Kingdom of Great Britain and Northern Ireland and Sweden could be expected to decline in size during the ensuing decades; yet in reality their populations grew substantially over that period. Second, no one correctly anticipated the sustained and powerful baby boom seen in the United States and some other industrialized countries during the 1950s and 1960s: a short-term post-war fertility spike was anticipated, of course, but not the two-decade boom actually experienced.

Still, if the past is any guide, these caveats will prove fruitless: those who wish to make quantitative statements about the second half of the twenty-first century will (correctly enough) consider well-done demographic projections to be the most credible forward looks available, far more soundly based than those based upon economic, social or technological anticipations. Notwithstanding the deep uncertainties attaching to such demographic projections, they will—with varying levels of enthusiasm—interpret them as realistic and well-founded forecasts. The subjunctive form implicit in any long-range projection—"if X were to occur, then the implications would be Y or Z"—will unwittingly slip into the predictive form "will".

So, let us repeat: when it comes to the demography of 2050, uncertainties abound. No one should misinterpret the United Nations or Census Bureau projections to be credible long-range forecasts.

Having emphasized these uncertainties, we can also acknowledge that some demographic trends are more likely than others. This is the case because certain specifiable demographic patterns involve powerful forces of inertia that last over a period of decades, and these allow us to discern some futures to be more likely than others.

First, all of the long-range projections, from the lowest to the highest, show substantial continuing growth in the United States population to the year 2050. The highest series shows dramatic numerical growth over this 50-year period: from an estimated 1998 population of approximately 270 million to one of 553 million in 2050; but even the lowest series also shows substantial growth from 1998 levels, from 270 million to 314 million (see table 4).

Second, nearly all of the demographic projections show that the United States population will experience a gradual shift over the next half-century towards an "older" age composition, a trend that often is called "demographic ageing". (For a sceptical comment on this usage, see below.) In this, the United States is like all other industrialized countries, and even most developing countries. The fact that fertility rates are nearly everywhere lower than their levels during the 1950s and 1960s implies such a shift towards an age composition with higher proportions in older ages and lower proportions in younger ages. Moreover, this pattern is amplified by increases in life expectancies at older ages during the same period.

The fact that United States fertility rates during the 1980s and 1990s have generally been higher than those of Europe and Japan suggests that phenomenon may be less dramatic in the United States than in these other regions and countries—at least when comparing proportions in the older age groups. At the same time, United States fertility rates were far higher during the 1947-1965 baby boom than they were in most other industrialized countries, and hence current rates, though higher than those in peer countries, represent substantial proportional declines from those of the recent past.

Nonetheless, it is nearly certain that "aged dependency" in the United States, as measured by the ratio of persons aged 65 years or over relative to those in the "working ages" of 20-64, will increase substantially. The shift now under way in age distribution in most industrialized societies is a truly powerful force that policy will ignore at its peril. Yet there are perils too in blinding ourselves—by mis-specifying the concept of "aged dependency" itself. The lower bound of this category was set rather arbitrarily at 65 years fully two thirds of a century ago, based primarily upon the entitlement age then set by law (also rather arbitrarily) for retirement under Social Security. Since the 1930s, both the life expectancy and the health/vitality experienced at age 65 have increased dramatically.

Since then, an odd statistical rigidity has been established. Though demographers are well aware that the "meaning" of age 65 has changed dramatically, demographic categories have not adjusted to these changing demographic realities. Demographic analyses and projections (including the most recent United Nations and United States Census Bureau projections) present calculations of the proportion aged 65 years or over—sometimes to several decimal places. Yet this traditional age boundary appears increasingly disconnected from the real ages at which people in industrialized countries make the transition from "productive working age" to "aged dependency". In part, such a fixed and unchanging age boundary in the context of dramatic change in underlying mortality and morbidity rates represents a proper reflection of the rigidities of statutory retirement age emanating from the policy domain. It also reflects an understandable desire by statistical agencies and users to maintain the definition continuity of statistical time series. Yet we must recognize that our world view of the implications of "demographic ageing" may be in the process of being distorted by our own increasingly misleading indicators.

Lest we mislead ourselves as well as others, there is a strong case to be made for development and tabulation of a series of alternative indicators of "aged dependency", to be calculated and presented alongside the time series based on the constant definition currently in use. For example, a second aged dependency ratio (aged dependency') could be calculated using an age boundary of 70 years (also arbitrary, but perhaps closer to emerging reality). Or an aged dependency" that varied with changing life expectancy could be constructed, for example, by holding constant not the age boundary itself, but instead the number of years of remaining life expectancy.[2] These additional series, examined in parallel with continuation of the current measure, would offer quantitative insights into the real meaning of demographic ageing.

As noted above, the implications of the age-structural changes under way are indeed powerful forces that carry deep and troubling policy implications. They present unavoidable challenges to some of the most well-established social inventions of the last century, and especially to the near-ubiquitous PAYE (pay-as-you-earn) State-run pension systems such as the United States Social Security system, and to publicly provided or tax-subsidized health-care systems. In addition, they carry powerful implications for the common but hardly universal pension and benefit systems provided by employers in many countries. Many thousands of pages have been written in recent years about these implications in the United States, but the space limitations here require that only the key points be summarized, and very briefly at that. One sophisticated and balanced analysis (Urban Institute, 1998) makes the following points:

- United States fertility rates, though high by the standards of peer countries, are substantially lower than the high levels experienced during the 1947-1965 baby boom;

- There are large unfunded commitments in the public sector for Social Security and health care for the elderly;

- Private employers also face rising costs for largely unfunded retiree health benefits, as well as for "defined benefit" pension plans;

- The retirement security of even those who have saved for themselves is also threatened by unanticipated increases in life expectancy at old ages;

- Both the public and the private sectors provide strong incentives for older workers to retire early, and these incentives have led to substantial declines in retirement age;

- "In 1950, the typical male retired at age 69. By 1994, the average male retiree was 64 years of age. Combined with longer lives, this means that the typical person . . . now expects to live close to one third of his or her adult life in retirement" (p. 4).

One might add that the United States, compared with peer industrialized countries, is relatively exposed by virtue of its weak capacities to control the escalation of health-care costs. This incapacity imposes special stresses on the Social Security system, for several reasons. First, it makes cost containment very difficult for the Medicare system (which provides health care to persons aged 65 years or over). Second, the tax on the working-age population for Medicare has been rising rapidly, in effect exacerbating the perceived tax burden of the related Social Security system. Third, the fact that most United States health insurance is provided by employers under group-rated policies tailored to their particular workforces means that older workers tend to increase employers' health insurance premiums, thereby bringing about incentives for them to encourage retirement at younger ages.

In addition to such impacts upon the Social Security system, the relative incapacity of the United States to contain health-care costs means that, without policy intervention, a shift towards an older age structure can be expected to increase significantly the share of United States GDP allocated to health-care expenditures, a share that already is the highest in the world even though the age structure of the United States is "younger" than that of many other industrialized countries. Though such a shift in age structure would also be expected to simultaneously lower the share of GDP allocated to expenditures on the youth population (especially those to education), there are no policy or economic mechanisms in place by which incremental transfers might take place from the younger to the older age groups. Institutional resistance to expenditure reductions might therefore be expected to result in aggregate increases in total allocations to education and health sectors. (Whether one considers such expenditures to be non-productive "consumption" or productive "investment in social capital" is a matter of strongly contested opinion.)

C. POLICY OPTIONS

As noted by many commentators, these are problems of a quite peculiar sort. They are challenges that result from *success*: in women's gaining effective control of their own fertility; in improving health and vigour at older ages; in raising Social Security pension levels to lift those dependent on them out of poverty; in providing the elderly with subsidized health-care services.

However, the foundations of some aspects of this success are fragile. United States retirees have experienced extraordinarily high "returns" (at least relative to their Social Security contributions, although the system is a PAYE rather than a "funded" one). However, these returns over the past decades have in fact been based not upon financial returns of their own contributions, but instead upon increasing tax rates on cohorts of younger workers that were themselves increasing in size owing to the post-war baby boom. These large cohorts will themselves begin to reach the statutory retirement age early in the second decade of this century, and for them the returns on their Social Security contributions are likely to be low. Moreover, some commentators speak darkly of a catastrophic collapse of the entire system, leading to broader economic crises, even disaster.

These are problems that, from an analytical perspective at least, have an array of clear and unambiguous solutions. If rates of "return" have gradually been increased for decades in a manner that cannot be sustained, this trend can be reversed. If strong incentives for early retirement have been effective in guiding retirement behaviours, these incentives can be modified. If health-care costs have been allowed to escalate in an unsustainable fashion, the policies that allowed such trends can be changed.

Yet the fact that solutions are available does not mean that they will prove politically feasible, or at least attractive. Decades of increasingly generous provision for retirement and for retirees may well have engendered powerful expectations among prospective retirees of more of the same. The demographic fact that the leading edge of the United States baby boom will not reach age 65 until the second decade of the twenty-first century, and that current projections show fiscal surpluses during the first decade, allows political leaders to avoid unpopular measures for a period representing much of their likely political careers. Yet the longer incremental actions to equilibrate the system are delayed, the more painful and costly will be the measures required.

There is no lack of proposals; indeed, they are so numerous that we can only list them here (the author's appended comments on some of these are enclosed within brackets):

- Raise "normal retirement age" (under laws passed in the 1980s, Social Security retirement age is scheduled to increase, but only very slowly—up from age 65 to age 67 by 2027);
- Increase "early retirement age", currently 62 with somewhat lower annual pension payments. Alternatively, the financial attractiveness of taking such early retirement could be reduced;
- Enact legislation to prohibit compulsory retirement (this was done in the United States in 1986, under the so-called Pepper Act);
- Change laws regulating private pension plans to increase the age at which their pensions can be paid out, or alternatively reduce the tax incentives available for plans allowing earlier retirement;
- Adjust public and private pension and tax policies to facilitate part-time retirement by older workers who wish to reduce but not end time commitment to work;
- Invest part of Social Security payments in market investments expected to yield higher returns than current United States government bonds (albeit carrying with them higher risks), either collectively or via individual accounts;

  [*Comment*: This was a major partisan issue in the 2000 Presidential campaign.]

- Modify the cost-of-living index applied to Social Security payments, on grounds that the current consumer price index exceeds true inflation rates;

- Increase the progressivity of Social Security pay-outs, so that the current higher pay-outs for lower-wage contributors are even higher;

- Find ways to contain the rapid escalation of health-care costs, especially for elderly persons;

  [Comment: In the United States, this is a hotly contended political issue, given the existence of strong political and interest-group opposition to government-supported or "single-payer" health insurance systems such as those in many other industrialized countries.]

- Increase taxation rates on working-age population to subsidize pension benefits of retired population, or increase subsidies drawn from general taxation sources;

  [Comment: Such increases would have to be very substantial to compensate for demographic age shifts under way in many countries, unless other changes were made at the same time.]

- Increase fertility rates on a sustained basis (for example, via direct financial incentives for additional births, or indirect pension or in-kind benefits: preferential access for mothers with many children to subsidized housing, or early retirement provisions); or measures to reduce the opportunity costs of additional childbearing;

  [Comment: Such policies have had modest impacts in authoritarian States such as the former communist countries of Eastern Europe, but only minimal impacts in liberal democracies such as France and Sweden.]

- Increased immigration, to increase the number of working-age contributors to PAYE pension systems;

  [Comment: Even very large immigration numbers typically have relatively little impact upon the fiscal stability of PAYE pension systems. Immigrants are themselves future beneficiaries of inadequately funded PAYE pension systems. Moreover, the net financial contribution of immigrants to PAYE pension systems depends upon their likely taxable earning levels, yet the skill/education levels of United States immigration flows are poorly matched to such a purpose and seem unlikely to change, given the stalemated politics of United States immigration policy.]

- Retain or enhance productivity of the existing workforce via investment in "lifelong learning" or continuous upgrading of skills and education of the workforce.

  [Comment: This is becoming increasingly feasible with the growth of high-quality education and training delivered "anytime, anywhere" over the Internet.]

[1] It must be noted that the Census Bureau thereby implicitly assumes that there will be no additional legalization programmes of any magnitude. Here, one must note that as this paper is being written, there is substantial legislative advocacy under way for a new, substantial legalization; the outcome of such advocacy cannot be predicted.

[2] In 1940, the life expectancy of a United States male aged 65 was 11.9 years, versus 15.6 years in 1997; for women, the comparable numbers were 13.4 years in 1940 versus 19.2 years in 1997. See Urban Institute (1998), figure 3.

REFERENCES

Lee, Ronald, and S. Tuljapurkar (1998). Population forecasting for fiscal planning: issues and innovations. Unpublished manuscript, September.

United States Census Bureau (2000). *Methodology and Assumptions for the Population Projections of the United States: 1999 to 2100*. Population Division Working Paper, No. 38 (http://www.census.gov). Washington, D.C.: United States Census Bureau, Population Division, Population Projections Branch.

Urban Institute (1998). *Policy Challenges Posed by the Aging of America*. Washington, D.C.: Urban Institute. Discussion briefing prepared for the Urban Institute Board of Trustees meeting, 20 May 1998. Contributing authors include Len Burman, Rudolph Penner, Gene Steuerle, Eric Toder, Marilyn Moon, Larry Thompson, Michael Weisner and Adam Carasso.

Van Hoorn, W., and N. Keilman (1997). *Birth Expectations and Their Use in Fertility Forecasting*. Eurostat Working Papers, No. E4/1997-4. Luxembourg.

POPULATION AGEING IN THE UNITED STATES OF AMERICA: RETIREMENT, REFORM AND REALITY

*Judith Treas**

Although the United States of America will experience significant popula-tion ageing in the twenty-first century, the demographic situation of the United States is distinctive. Because its immigration and fertility are comparatively high, it will not confront the population decline facing so many developed nations. Instead, the United States must deal with the succession of cohorts of uneven size. As the large baby-boom generation grows older, population age-ing will accelerate. Older persons will constitute a growing share of the United States population, albeit one that is not as large as the percentage projected for Europe. Because the Social Security retirement system has been the object of serious study and debate, it offers insights into the institutional implications of population ageing in the United States. The probable policy response—some reform package of lower benefits, higher taxes and higher retirement age—points up the difficult choices confronting pay-as-you-go retirement systems. The problems of mature retirement systems are not amenable to quick resolu-tion, if only because of the complexity of underlying structural and behavioural relationships as well as the uncertainty inherent in long-range projections.

DEMOGRAPHIC PROSPECTS

In contrast to that of other developed countries, the population of the United States is expected to grow *larger* as it grows *older*. According to the medium-variant projections of the United Nations (1999, p. 418), the Ameri-can population will increase from 278 million in 2000 to 349 million in 2050. United States fertility has not fallen to the levels of Europe, Japan and other developed nations (United Nations, 2000), where fertility is too low to offset deaths, replace the parental generation and avoid a decrease in population. The fertility of the United States is at or slightly below replacement. From 1989 to 1998, the total fertility rate (TFR) ranged between 2.0 and 2.1 annually (United States National Center for Health Statistics, 2000). By contrast, the TFR fell below 1.5 in developed nations such as Germany, Spain, Japan and the Russian Federation (United Nations, 2000).

The United States is a major receiving country for immigrants. In the 1990s, net international migration approached 1 million persons annually

---

*University of California, Irvine, California, United States of America.

(United States Census Bureau, 1999, p. 9). Immigration accounted for about one in five new Americans. Even with fertility somewhat below replacement, the current level of immigration to the United States is more than sufficient to keep the total and working-age populations from declining over the next 50 years (United Nations, 2001, chap. IV, sect. B.8 (*h*)). Immigrants will not prevent the long-run ageing of the population, except in the highly unlikely scenario of a tenfold increase in annual immigration levels. Although immigration is selective of young people, they offset population ageing only temporarily, because young immigrants eventually grow old.

Future fertility in the United States may fluctuate in response to cyclic forces, but dramatic fertility declines to very low levels appear unlikely. Americans have not experienced fertility markedly below replacement levels, despite high levels of maternal employment combined with low levels of State subsidies for child-rearing (Treas and Widmer, 2000). Immigration is also expected to sustain fertility levels in the United States. Immigrants from developing countries with higher fertility acculturate slowly with respect to the family formation patterns of native-born Americans. Population projections by the United States Census Bureau assume Hispanic and Asian and Pacific islander fertility will converge to national levels only very gradually over the long term (Hollmann, Mulder and Kallan, 2000).

Of course, the historical record cautions against complacency about the future course of American fertility. The 1946-1964 baby boom was the unexpected result of rising living standards in the United States. Although many countries saw fertility increase after the Second World War, few experienced a sustained elevation in fertility like that of the United States, where about 4 million infants were born each year. Since the baby boom was followed by a baby bust, fertility swings created a bulge in the age structure that has had significant implications for population ageing.

The initial effect of the baby boom was to make the United States population younger. Then, as the baby boomers grew up and grew older, the median age of the population climbed from 28.0 years in 1970 to 35.7 in 2000 (United States Census Bureau, 1999, p. 14). Today, support ratios remain favourable, because there are baby boomers who are workers, taxpayers and caregivers for an older generation. For every person aged 65 years or over, there are about five younger persons aged 15-64. The older population is growing slowly as the small cohorts born during the Great Depression of the 1930s move into old age. In 2011, however, the first baby boomers will turn 65 years of age. The growth of the older population will accelerate markedly. Also contributing to ageing are mortality declines, especially at the older ages, which raised 1997 life expectancy at age 65 to 15.8 years for men and 19.0 for women (United States Census Bureau, 1999, p. 93). Between 2000 and 2050, the share in the total population of persons aged 65 years or over will increase from 12.5 to 21.7 per cent, according to medium-variant projections (United Nations, 2001, table A.15). Even as the United States undergoes unprecedented ageing, it will remain young compared with Europe where the share in the total population of the population aged 65 years or over will increase from 14.7 to 27.6 per cent over the same period (United Nations, 2001, table A.17).

The challenge of ageing populations arises because older people, especially those in advanced old age, become too sick, frail or disabled to take care of themselves. They need economic support, health care and assistance with activities of daily living. Although family members take care of older people, population ageing places greater demands on public resources as well. For example, under intermediate assumptions, Social Security costs in the United States are projected to rise from 4.2 per cent of gross domestic product (GDP) to 6.8 per cent in 75 years (Board of Trustees, Federal Old-Age Insurance and Survivors and Disability Insurance Trust Funds, 2000, p. 3). The dilemma of an ageing population is that the increase in younger adults does not keep pace with the growth of the older population. There are more old people in need of help and fewer working-age adults to help them.

Each year, Social Security actuaries prepare short-range (10-year) and long-range (75-year) projections of the financial status of the system. The projections, based on assumptions determined by the Board of Trustees that governs Social Security, point to disturbing, long-range financial problems. Using intermediate assumptions, estimates indicate that the annual Social Security deficit will amount to 2.2 per cent of GDP in 75 years (Board of Trustees, Federal Old-Age Insurance and Survivors and Disability Insurance Trust Funds, 2000, p. 3). Although Medicare, the federal health insurance programme for older Americans, faces even more pressing problems, its mix of public and private health-care financing does not generalize to other nations. Social Security offers a more instructive example of policy issues facing ageing populations, because it is similar in broad outline to the pay-as-you-go retirement systems in many other developed countries.

Current workers in the United States support current retirees through the payroll taxes paid by the workers and their employers. Social Security (OASDI) actually consists of two programmes, Old-Age and Survivors Insurance (OASI) and Disability Insurance (DI), each of which maintains its own trust fund account with the United States Treasury. According to intermediate projections (Board of Trustees, Federal Old-Age Insurance and Survivors and Disability Insurance Trust Funds, 2000), the trust funds will grow larger in the short run as baby boomers pay into the system. The first baby boomers will begin to leave the labour force even before reaching age 65 in year 2011. Because disability insurance covers workers who are not yet old enough for retirement benefits, the disability trust fund will peak as early as 2005 and be exhausted altogether by 2023. By 2015, the expenditures for the combined OASDI programmes will exceed income from payroll taxes. By 2024, these expenditures will exceed not merely taxes, but taxes plus interest on the trust funds. It will be necessary to spend the trust fund principal to pay benefits. OASDI will be exhausted by the year 2037, only eight years after the last baby boomer turns 65. After 2030, costs as a percentage of taxable payroll will level off and even decline slightly owing to smaller cohorts of retirees. A big gap will remain between costs and income, however, and costs are projected to rise again slowly in the middle of the twenty-first century owing to increases in life expectancy.

Without legislative changes, benefits will eventually exceed tax income, reserve funds will be spent, and the system will eventually be unable to meet its obligations. As a consequence of the persistent drumbeat of troubling projections, the American public is aware that Social Security faces serious financial difficulties. Only 7 per cent of American workers surveyed in 2000 stated that they were "very confident" that Social Security would continue to provide benefits equal to those received by current retirees (Employee Benefit Research Institute, 2000).

FIXING SOCIAL SECURITY

Although the Social Security problem stems from a demographic imbalance of generations, a demographic fix, propping up old-age support ratios by raising fertility and immigration, is not very feasible. First, pronatalist policies have had little success in raising fertility in democracies. Second, even if this were politically feasible, the American economy could not readily absorb the 10.8 million immigrants estimated to be needed annually to maintain current old-age support ratios until 2050 (United Nations, 2001, table 25, scenario VI). Nor can a mature Social Security system rely on the strategy that served it well in the 1950s, that is to say, maintaining support ratios by bringing in new categories of workers who accept taxes in exchange for future benefits. Fully 96 per cent of paid civilian workers are already covered by Social Security (Ways and Means Committee, United States House of Representatives, 1998).

In hindsight, a system that requires each generation to fully fund its own retirement would be preferable to a pay-as-you-go system, because retirement financing would not be directly affected by deteriorating old-age support ratios. Proposals for compulsory individual retirement accounts move in this direction, but someone still needs to pay for current retirees and for low-income workers who cannot save enough for old age. Projected Social Security deficits have prompted serious consideration of a number of ideas (for example, income and assets tests for benefits, investing trust fund reserves in private markets) that would once have been considered radical (Kingston and Quadagno, 1997). If pay-as-you-go retirement systems are to remain solvent, however, policy makers cannot avoid some combination of lower benefits, higher taxes, and higher age of eligibility for benefits.

These are painful courses of action. They call for some group—whether workers, retirees, or both—to make sacrifices sooner or later. The United States has tried all three strategies before. Payroll taxes were raised many times—most recently in 1990. Benefits were effectively cut in the 1980s when cost-of-living adjustments for recipients were delayed. And the normal retirement age for full benefits is being raised gradually from 65 to 67. Early retirement benefits continue to be available from age 62 although the actuarial reduction is greater (Ways and Means Committee, United States House of Representatives, 1998, p. 20). Financial projections indicate that more needs to be done.

One can argue that it is only fair to reduce benefits, because the economic circumstances of retirees are so much better than they were in the past. Forty years ago, one third of Americans aged 65 years or over fell below the federal poverty line. By 1998, only 10.5 per cent were poor (Dalaker, 1999, p. xiii). Current retirees have benefited from private pensions, from appreciation in home values, and from higher lifetime wages that permitted them to save for retirement. Unfortunately, this argument for benefit cuts overlooks the fact that Social Security is the primary reason that many older Americans lead reasonably secure lives. OASDI makes up 48.2 per cent of the income of elderly individuals who live alone, for example (Ways and Means Committee, United States House of Representatives, 1998, p. 1041). If Social Security and other government benefits were eliminated tomorrow, half of all persons 65 years of age or over would live in poverty (United States Census Bureau, 1993, table 2).

There are, however, several options for cutting benefits while protecting low-income elderly people. The formula used to calculate benefits could be made more progressive so that only those workers with high earnings would have their benefits cut. Another approach is to cut everyone's retirement benefits, but to compensate the poor for their loss of income by expanding public assistance. (The federal Supplemental Security Insurance (SSI) programme supports the low-income aged, but this means-tested programme has strict income and asset limits.) Social Security itself might become a means-tested programme: benefits could be reduced or eliminated for affluent retirees with high incomes and substantial assets. Even if no benefits were cut, the high-income elderly could have more of their benefits taxed away.

The political risk is that these measures may undermine public support for Social Security as a universal social insurance programme. Americans remain more sceptical of welfare programmes than most Europeans, for whom citizenship confers more rights to State support. As a right earned by working, Social Security has none of the stigma attached to public assistance programmes in the United States. The Welfare Reform and Personal Responsibility Act of 1996 demonstrated that United States needs-based poverty programmes are vulnerable to major cuts. The 1989 repeal of Medicare catastrophic coverage showed that middle-class retirees are unwilling to bear the burden of supporting low-income older people.

RAISING TAXES

Raising taxes is another budget-balancing strategy for public retirement systems. One way to measure the long-range Social Security deficit is as a percentage of payroll subject to OASDI taxes. According to intermediate projections by the Board of Trustees, Federal Old-Age Insurance and Survivors and Disability Insurance Trust Funds (2000, p. 3), the deficit for Social Security programmes is 1.89 per cent of taxable payroll in the next 75 years. Payroll tax rates are 6.2 per cent each, from employees and employers, on covered earnings up to a specified maximum amount ($72,600 in 1999) (Board of Trustees, Federal Old-Age Insurance and Survivors and Disability Insurance Trust Funds, 2000, table I.C.2). The maximum is indexed annually to the average wage for all workers. Social Security recipients with adjusted gross incomes above specified levels pay income tax on up to 85 per cent of their benefits, and these taxes are credited to the OASDI and Medicare trust funds.

There is no lack of precedents for Social Security tax increases. The OASDI tax rate has been raised 20 times since 1949, when it stood at 1 per cent of taxable earnings (Board of Trustees, Federal Old-Age Insurance and Survivors and Disability Insurance Trust Funds, 2000, table II.B.1). In addition to increasing the tax rate, additional revenue can be generated by removing the earnings maximum for payroll taxes and by increasing the percentage of Social Security benefits subject to income tax. Both economic and political considerations determine the extent to which tax increases can resolve the issues of ageing populations.

THE CASE FOR RAISING RETIREMENT AGES

The cost of old-age benefits has increased, in part, because retirees collect benefits longer. This results from increases in life expectancy at older ages coupled with declines in the age at which American workers retire (figure I). Most United States workers today choose to retire before the normal retirement age of 65, taking the actuarially reduced benefits that become available at age 62. Although the mean age for electing retirement benefits was 70 years in 1945, it declined sharply until the 1980s and stood at 63.6 years in 1995 (Ways and Means Committee, United States House of Representatives, 1998, p. 21). In addition, between 1940 and 1997, life expectancy at age 65 increased by 3.6 years for men and 5.7 years for women (Board of Trustees, Federal Old-Age Insurance and Survivors and Disability Insurance Trust Funds, 2000, p. 63). According to the Social Security Advisory Board (1999), a normal retirement age (NRA) of 71 years for receipt of full benefits, rather than 65, would be consistent with the remarkable increase in life expectancy.

Improvements in the life expectancy, health and functioning of older people offer a persuasive argument for raising the age at retirement and perhaps indexing it (for example, to life expectancy at age 65 or to disability-free life expectancy). During the 1980s, the health of older Americans improved markedly (Manton, Corder and Stallard, 1993). Under most scenarios, the "health-adjusted" ratio of persons aged 20-64 to chronically disabled persons aged 65 years or over is projected to remain above the 1994 level, assuming a continuation of recent trends—a 1.5 per cent decline annually in chronic disability for older people (Singer and Manton, 1998). Better health has translated into greater ability to work, as reported by persons aged 50-69 in 1982 and 1993 (Crimmins, Reynolds and Saito, 1997). Surprisingly, this improvement occurred primarily among the retired population, not among those still in the labour force. This finding is consistent with the observation that health has become less important to the retirement decision over time (Costa, 1996).

Figure I. Mean age at receipt of Social Security retirement benefits and total length of life for persons aged 65: United States of America, 1940-1995

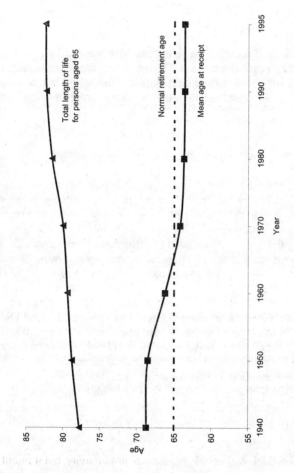

Sources: Ways and Means Committee, United States House of Representatives, *Green Book* (Washington, D.C., Government Printing Office, 1998), p. 21; Federal Interagency Forum on Aging, *Older Americans 2000: Key Indicators of Well-Being* (Hyattsville, Maryland, 2000), p. 70; National Center for Health Statistics, *Health: United States, 2000* (Hyattsville, Maryland, 2000), table 28.

Social Security was enacted in 1935 to insure workers against a time when they would become too old and too disabled to support themselves through their own labour. Today, most workers in the United States retire at a younger age and in good health. Workers look forward to leaving the labour force, having more free time, and taking advantage of the leisure activities for older people that have developed around the institution of retirement. In short, the United States, like other developed countries, has developed a "retirement culture". Leisure values promote labour-force exits as surely as the availability of retirement income. The serious financial problems confronting the system, however, create pressures for Social Security to return to its mission of insuring against old-age infirmity, leaving the responsibility to save for early retirement to individuals, if that is their preference.

PROPOSALS FOR RAISING RETIREMENT AGES

In 1983, the United States Congress took the first step towards raising retirement ages. Changes in the NRA are being phased in gradually from age 65 to age 66 between 2000 and 2005 and then from age 66 to age 67 between 2017 and 2022. Higher NRAs and different phase-in periods have been proposed. Eliminating the break in NRA increases (scheduled for 2005-2017) is projected to reduce the long-range deficit by 5 per cent (Goss and Wade, 1998, cited in Rix (1999)). Quickly raising the NRA to age 73 is projected virtually to eliminate the deficit (American Academy of Actuaries, 1997, cited in Rix (1999)). Without putting too much emphasis on particular proposals, it is clear that any serious reform of public retirement systems must consider the age at which workers retire. Raising the retirement age to 74 would maintain 1995 old-age support ratios (United Nations, 2001, chap. IV, sect. B.8 (h)), but these ratios generate a big OASDI surplus. Thus, most proposals focus on modest increases in the retirement age to 70 or younger.

The United States Government Accounting Office (1999) concluded that a higher retirement age would reduce the cost of lifetime benefits. A large increase in retirement age that is phased in rapidly would have a bigger financial effect than a small one phased in over a longer period of time. Assuming that an older eligibility age results in workers' waiting longer to retire, the measure would also raise the amount of payroll taxes that are paid into the system. Savings to the OASI Trust Fund would be partially offset by greater demands on the DI Fund, because some people in poor health would choose to receive disability benefits rather than wait until they are old enough to retire (United States Government Accounting Office, 1999). The existence of greater numbers of older workers might increase productivity, but it might also result in higher unemployment. Older workers with very low earnings, those who become unemployed, and those in poor health who do not meet the strict eligibility standards for disability benefits would have a longer struggle before qualifying for retirement benefits. This burden would fall disproportionately on already disadvantaged populations, including African-American, Hispanic and blue-collar workers.

The impact of policy changes in retirement age depends on whether workers have other financial resources that permit early retirement, whether they are willing and able to work longer, and whether employers want to retain older employees. Workers without other sources of retirement income will delay retirement in response to a higher retirement age for Social Security. Relying on assets and private pensions, other workers will continue to retire before they are eligible for Social Security. Because many American workers have employer-provided pensions with "defined benefit" formulas encourage-ing early retirement (Wise, 1997), NRA changes may have less effect in the United States than in countries where retirees depend more on public benefits. Private pension plans allow a worker to retire early by paying a larger pension that is reduced when the retiree becomes old enough to collect Social Security. Unless the earliest eligibility age (EEA) for Social Security is raised so that the employer has to subsidize early retirement longer, employers will have little incentive to eliminate early retirement inducements.

Despite the popularity of early retirement, there are indications that older Americans are willing to work, especially part-time (Treas, 1995). The labour-force participation of men aged 65 years or over levelled off in the 1980s, ending decades of declines (figure II). Older women's labour-force participa-tion held steady and then increased from the mid-1980s. With the rise in fe-male labour-force participation, each cohort had a higher proportion of women working at the threshold of old age than did the cohort that had gone before. Increasingly, older people take a job bridging from career to full-time retire-ment. Between 1984 and 1993, growing proportions of men under age 65 were working while receiving income from a pension (Herz, 1995). In a nationally representative sample, 75 per cent of workers expect employment to be an in-come source in retirement (Employee Benefit Research Institute, 2000, p. 7).

To be sure, older workers face barriers to employment, including em-ployer discrimination, a shortage of attractive part-time jobs, and lower pen-sion accruals (Herz and Rones, 1989). Employer reservations range from higher health insurance costs for older employees to concerns that older workers are less flexible, are less willing to learn new technologies, and lack the latest job skills (American Association of Retired Persons (AARP), 2000). Particularly since recent cohorts of elderly Americans are better edu-cated than earlier ones, a tight labour market may encourage employers to offer retraining, flexible schedules, and other programmes for older work-ers. Conversely, corporate downsizing and high unemployment work against older workers (Quinn and Burkhauser, 1994).

CONCLUSIONS

The United States has distinct advantages in dealing with population age-ing. Its percentage elderly is not projected to grow as large as in other devel-oped countries, and it does not have to cope with population decline. Its public retirement provisions are less generous. Its systems of private and secondary pensions are better developed. Several decades of painful restructuring have resulted in a sustained economic expansion that is generating the tax surplus to address major societal problems. Like many other countries with ageing popu-lations, the United States has a pay-as-you-go public retirement system and deteriorating old-age support ratios. Having gained additional years of health

Figure II. Labour-force participation by age and sex: persons aged 55-69, United States of America, 1963-1999

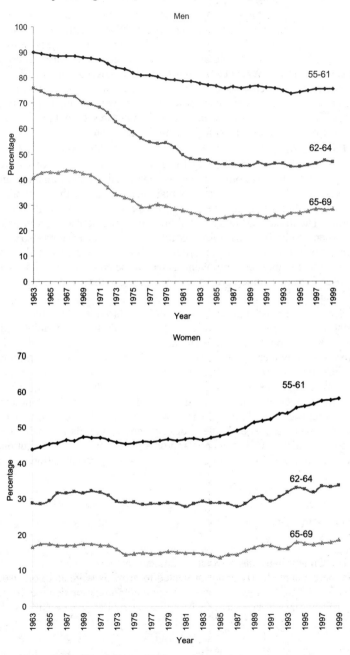

Source: United States Census Bureau current population surveys.

and life, older persons have chosen to lengthen their retirements, rather than to extend their work lives.

The challenges of ageing populations are too complex for simple solutions. Comprehensive reforms to pay-as-you-go retirement systems will need to call on some combination of approaches, including benefit cuts, tax increases, and increases in retirement age. The Social Security Amendments of 1983 contained 13 distinct provisions intended to build trust fund reserves, including covering new federal employees, taxing benefits, delaying benefit increases, and scheduling increases in retirement age (Ways and Means Committee, United States House of Representatives, 1994, p. 40). These measures did not prove adequate, but the experience offers useful lessons for ageing populations.

First, the long-run consequences of comprehensive reform packages for public programmes are difficult to forecast. Various elements of any reform are apt to affect the economy as well as individual decision-making, and the different parts of reform programmes may well interact with one another. Effectiveness will depend on how well policies are coordinated with other programmes. The impact of higher Social Security retirement age is apt to depend on whether the eligibility ages for Medicare and private pensions also increase. Because the consequences often differ for different segments of the population, income distribution consequences need to be considered: Who gains and who loses from new policy provisions, and how can the disadvantaged be protected from loss?

Second, the most sophisticated projections provide only a moving target for long-range solutions. The projections of OASDI budget deficits are based on assumptions about a host of economic and demographic factors, including future wage growth, rates of return on trust fund assets, fertility, immigration, life expectancy, labour-force behaviour etc. Small changes in assumptions—due to changing conditions, better understanding of the relationships between variables, or increased methodological sophistication—can compound into large discrepancies between old and new projections. It is possible to address some contingencies (for example, indexing benefits to inflation and retirement age to life expectancy), but change and uncertainty mean that institutional reform will require ongoing monitoring, evaluation and modification.

REFERENCES

American Academy of Actuaries (1997). *Raising the Retirement Age for Social Security*. Washington, D.C.: American Academy of Actuaries.

American Association of Retired Persons (AARP) (2000). *American Business and Older Employees: A Summary of Findings*. Washington, D.C.: AARP.

Board of Trustees, Federal Old-Age Insurance and Survivors and Disability Insurance Trust Funds (2000). *Annual Report*. Washington, D.C.: Government Printing Office.

Costa, Dora L. (1996). Health and labor force participation of older men, 1900-1991. *Journal of Economic History* (Wilmington, Delaware), vol. 56, No. 1, pp. 540-552.

Crimmins, Eileen M., Sandra L. Reynolds and Yasuhiko Saito (1997). Trends and differences in health and the ability to work. *Social Security Bulletin* (Washington, D.C.), vol. 60, No. 3, pp. 50-52.

Dalaker, Joseph (1999). Poverty in the United States: 1998. *Current Population Reports*, Series P60-207. Washington, D.C.: Government Printing Office.

Employee Benefit Research Institute (2000). *The 2000 Retirement Confidence Survey Summary of Findings*. Washington, D.C. (http://www.ebri.org/rcs/2000/2000_results.htm/). Accessed on 2 August 2000.

Goss, Stephen C., and Alice H. Wade (1998). Estimated long-range OASDI financial effect of various reform provisions request by AARP. Memorandum prepared by the Office of the Chief Actuary, Social Security Administration, June 25.

Herz, Diane (1995). Work after early retirement: an increasing trend among men. *Monthly Labor Review* (Washington, D.C.), vol. 118, No. 9, pp. 13-20.

_____, and Philip L. Rones (1989). Institutional barriers to employment of older workers. *Monthly Labor Review* (Washington, D.C.), vol. 112, No. 4, pp. 14-21.

Hollmann, Frederick W., Tammany J. Mulder and Jeffrey E. Kallan (2000). Methodology and assumptions for the population projections of the United States, 1999-2100. *Population Division Working Paper* (Washington, D.C.), No. 38, pp. 1-24.

Kingston, Eric R., and Jill Quadagno (1997). Social Security: marketing radical reform. In *The Future of Age-Based Public Policy*, Robert B. Hudson, ed. Baltimore, Maryland: The Johns Hopkins University Press, pp. 117-133.

Manton, Kenneth G., Larry S. Corder and Eric Stallard (1993). Estimates of changes in chronic disability and institutional incidence and prevalence rates in the U.S. elderly population from the 1982, 1984 and 1989 National Longitudinal Mortality Study. *Journals of Gerontology: Social Sciences* (Springfield, Illinois), vol. 48, No. 10, pp. S153-166.

Quinn, Joseph F., and Richard Burkhauser (1994). Retirement and labor force behavior of the elderly. In *Demography of Aging*, Linda G. Martin and Samuel H. Preston, eds. Washington, D.C.: National Academy Press, pp. 50-101.

Rix, Sara E. (1999). Social Security reform: rethinking retirement-age policy—a look at raising Social Security's retirement age. Washington, D.C.: AARP Public Policy Institute.

Singer, Burton H., and Kenneth G. Manton (1998). The effects of health changes on projections of health service needs for the elderly population of the United States. *Proceedings of the National Academy of Sciences* (Washington, D.C.), vol. 95, No. 26, pp. 15618-15622.

Social Security Advisory Board (1999). *Forum on Implications of Raising the Social Security Retirement Age*. Washington, D.C.: Social Security Advisory Board.

Treas, Judith (1995). Older Americans in the 1990s and beyond. *Population Bulletin* (Washington, D.C.), vol. 50, No. 2, pp. 1-46.

_____, and Eric D. Widmer (2000). Married women's employment over the life course: attitudes in cross-national perspective. *Social Forces* (Chapel Hill, North Carolina), vol. 79, No. 4, pp. 1409-1436.

United Nations (1999). *World Population Prospects: The 1998 Revision*, vol. I, *Comprehensive Tables*. Sales No. E.99.XIII.9.

_____ (2000). *Below Replacement Fertility: Population Bulletin of the United Nations* (New York), Special Issue Nos. 40/41. Sales No. E.99.XIII.13.

_____ (2001) *Replacement Migration: Is It a Solution to Declining and Ageing Populations?* Sales No. E.01.XIII.19.

United States Census Bureau (1993). Measuring the effect of benefits and taxes on income and poverty. *Current Population Reports*, Series P60-186RD, Washington, D.C.: Government Printing Office.

_____ (1999). *Statistical Abstract of the United States: 1999*. Washington, D.C.: Government Printing Office.

_____ (2000). *National Population Projections. I. Summary Files*, No. NP-T1 (http://www.census.gov/population/ww/projections/natsum.html). Revised 12 February 2000; accessed 3 August 2000.

United States Government Accounting Office (1999). *Social Security Reform: Implications of Raising the Retirement Age: Report to the Chairman and Ranking Minority Member, Special Committee on Aging, U.S. Senate*, Report No. GAO/HEHS-99-112, Washington, D.C.

United States National Center for Health Statistics (2000). Births: final data for 1998. *National Vital Statistics Reports* (Washington, D.C.), vol. 48, No. 3, p. 27.

Ways and Means Committee, United States House of Representatives (1994). *1994 Green Book*. Washington, D.C.: Government Printing Office.

_____ (1998). 1998 *Green Book*. Washington, D.C.: Government Printing Office.

Wise, David A. (1997). Retirement against the demographic trend: more older people living longer, working less, and saving less. *Demography* (Silver Spring, Maryland), vol. 34, No. 1, pp. 83-95.

LOOKING FOR EUROPEAN DEMOGRAPHY, DESPERATELY?

*Patrick Festy**

According to the United Nations population projections (1998 revision, medium variant), the European population would have reached a maximum by the end of the twentieth century and would continuously decline in the following five decades, at an ever-increasing rate. From 730 million people in 2000, it would have lost 100 million by 2050, despite a rise in fertility (the total fertility rate (TFR) would have gained 0.35 child per woman, having risen from 1.42 in 1995-2000 to 1.77 in 2045-2050), a prolonged life expectancy at birth (from 73.3 to 80.1 years) and some immigration (see United Nations, 1999, part one, table A.1, Europe). Ageing would be the other major feature, with a decline in the proportion of children under age 15 (from 17.5 per cent in 2000 to 14.4 per cent in 2050) and a rise in the proportion of elderly people aged 65 years or over (from 14.7 to 27.6 per cent).

Of course, these results are correct, in other words, population trends in numbers and age structure are consistent with the values taken by the components of the demographic movements: fertility, mortality and migration. The latter are just assumptions, which we will not contest; but, in fact, there were no projections, through assumptions and calculations, made for Europe: only projections for each national population, then an aggregation that resulted in a European total. Aggregations of births, deaths or migrants can be seen as the result of European levels of fertility, mortality and migration applied to European population, but they were not reached this way. Consequently, we will not question these implicit global assumptions and wonder whether they are reasonably likely or not; instead, we will question the process of aggregation and wonder whether demographic levels in European countries are homogeneous enough for their sum to be considered meaningful. Our analysis of the diversity of demographic situations in Europe will reveal different configurations of family or health elements, with various policy implications.

Europe is a large puzzle of 47 countries which would be too difficult to understand if we had no simplification scheme, ab initio. We will assume that there are two Europes, a Western one, whose population numbers are dominated by the European Union (EU), and an Eastern one, which includes the Russian Federation as a major member. A widely shared view is that the demographic regime that prevails currently in Western Europe (the "second demographic transition" model, perhaps) should extend to the Eastern part in the future, thus resulting in converging trends between the two regions. By

---

*Institut National d'Études Démographiques (INED), France.

1995, there were 728 million people in Europe, of which slightly more than one half lived in the 15 countries of EU (372 million persons).

However, EU is itself diverse. An opposition is generally set up between the North and the South, with the idea of a possible diffusion from North to South of family patterns and health systems, likely to have a strong incidence on demography. Four countries dominate EU by their population numbers: Germany with more than 80 million in 1995, and France, Italy and the United Kingdom of Great Britain and Northern Ireland with nearly 60 million each. We will concentrate most of our analyses on them, before we contrast EU with the rest of Europe, where the Russian Federation (nearly 150 million persons) will be given a major role.

In recent years (1990-1995), the TFR was 1.57 children per woman in Europe; life expectancy at birth was 72.6 years for both sexes. EU had a lower fertility than the rest of Europe (1.50 against 1.64), but a higher life expectancy (76.5 against 68.7 years). Inside EU, there were marked differences in fertility, with low rates in Germany and Italy (more generally, in Central and Southern Europe) and relatively high rates in France and the United Kingdom (and in Northern Europe). Disparities within EU were wide enough for the figure for the Russian Federation (and the average for the rest of Europe) to be inserted in the EU 1.28-1.78 bracket. In contrast, life expectancies were very similar in the above-mentioned four Western European countries and the distance was large between them and the Russian Federation (table 1).

There is a global diversity in fertility levels, throughout Europe, with a limited gap between East and West. There is a clear divide in mortality, with much more favourable levels in EU than in the rest of Europe. From a slightly different perspective, EU is diverse on fertility, but fairly homogeneous on mortality.

A.   DIVERSITIES IN EUROPE ON FERTILITY

1.   *Diversity in the European Union on fertility*

Low period fertility indices can partly be explained by tempo effects: fertility is low now, because people prefer to postpone the births they will have to later (better?) times. An increase in the age at birth is a signal for this movement, which also results in period rates being lower than cohort rates.

TABLE 1.   FERTILITY AND MORTALITY INDICATORS IN EUROPEAN REGIONS AND SOME COUNTRIES, 1990-1995

| | European Union | | | | | Rest of Europe | |
	Total	France	Germany	Italy	United Kingdom	Total	Russian Federation
Total fertility rate (number of births per woman)	1.50	1.72	1.30	1.28	1.78	1.64	1.55
Life expectancy at birth (in years, for both sexes) . .	76.5	77.1	76.0	77.2	76.2	68.7	66.5

Source: *Replacement Migration: Is It a Solution to Declining and Ageing Populations?* (United Nations publication, Sales No. E.01.XIII.19), tables A.1, A.3, A.5, A.11, A.13, A.17 and A.19.

The total number of children to women in birth cohorts can remain unaffected, while postponement results in a lowering of contemporary fertility. A possible explanation for divergences in period fertility within EU could be linked to differentials in these tempo effects.

It is not really the case. Mean ages at birth are rather similar throughout Western Europe. Still more importantly, the four more populated EU countries share the movement towards later childbearing; only Italy emerges with an amplified increase in mean age at birth. Cohort fertility rates, which result in period rates when combined with tempo variations, are nearly as diverse as period rates have already been shown to be (table 2).

Diversity in EU fertility is not just a postponement effect that would explain short-term movements and levels of period indices. It is a lasting phenomenon, written in cohort histories and likely to be maintained in the future. Reasonably enough, the United Nations population projections have taken some account of that reality.

Low fertility can also be linked to the movement away from marriage, which many Western European countries have experienced for the recent decades. Of course, marriage is no longer a precondition for childbearing in most of these populations, but it remains true that married couples have a higher fertility than non-married people, even those who live in a "marriage-like" cohabitation.

This time, the decomposition is very efficient—not because of marriages, the proportion of which is low but not very different throughout EU, but because of the proportion of children born from married parents, which is low where total fertility is relatively high and high where the TFR is especially low. When children born in wedlock are referred to ever-married women, the fertility index so calculated is much more uniform throughout EU countries than the TFR itself. That index is lower than the TFR in France and the United Kingdom; it is higher than the TFR in Germany and Italy. The range for the TFR is 0.50 child (from 1.28 to 1.78); that for the marital fertility index is but 0.11 (from 1.41 to 1.52) (table 3).

The countries with the highest TFR, France and the United Kingdom, are those in which low nuptiality has been compensated for by the rise of fertility out of marriage. In the countries with very low period fertility, the decline in marriages has been directly consequential for fertility, because marriage remains *the* place for childbearing, without any substitutes for it. We must go on

TABLE 2.   TEMPO AND QUANTUM COMPONENTS OF PERIOD FERTILITY RATES IN
COUNTRIES OF THE EUROPEAN UNION

		France	Germany	Italy	United Kingdom
(a)	TFR (birth cohort 1963) (births per woman)......	2.02	1.57	1.57	1.89
(b)	Mean age at birth (birth cohort 1963) (years)	28.0	27.5	28.4	28.0
(c)	Variation in mean age at birth (birth cohort 1958-1963) (years).........................	+0.6	+0.6	+1.0	+0.5
(d)	Expected period TFR [$a(1 - c/5)$] (births per woman)	1.78	1.38	1.26	1.70
(e)	Actual TFR (1990-1995) (births per woman)	1.72	1.30	1.28	1.78

Sources: United Nations (2001); Conseil de l'Europe, *Évolution démographique récente en Europe, 1999* (Strasbourg, France, 1999).

	France	Germany	Italy	United Kingdom
(a) Total fertility rate (1990-1995) (births per woman)......................	1.72	1.30	1.28	1.78
(b) Proportion of ultimately married women (birth cohort 1963).......................	0.75	0.80	0.83	0.81
(c) Proportion of children born from married parents (1990-1995)......................	0.66	0.87	0.93	0.69
(d) Estimated number of "legitimate" births to ultimately married women [$a \times c/b$]	1.52	1.41	1.43	1.52

Sources: United Nations (2001); and Conseil de l'Europe (1999).

developing our discussion along these lines, to understand trends and diversities in EU.

(a)   *Decline in marriages*

Marriage has declined throughout Western Europe. The Nordic countries, France and the United Kingdom have experienced dramatic changes. In Sweden, the proportion of men and women who will definitely not marry will reach some 40 per cent in recent birth cohorts and women who do marry will not do so before the average age of 27.5 years; in Finland, France and Norway, the proportion of never-married will climb up to 30 per cent and the mean age at first marriage for women will rise to 26.5 years. By contrast, the Mediterranean countries are facing mild transformations: the proportion of never-married women has not yet reached 20 per cent in Italy in the 1960s birth cohorts; Portugal, still further from Sweden, has exhibited only very recently a decline in period marriage rates which has hardly affected birth cohorts (*L'Observatoire Démographique Européen* (1998)).

With respect to Northern and Southern Europe, the central part of the region (Austria, Germany and Switzerland) is in a median position. The global picture is that of a regular gradation, which evokes the idea of a geographical diffusion of a matrimonial model from North to South.

(b)   *Rising number of divorces*

Divorces have been more and more numerous throughout Western Europe for the last three decades. The 1970s were also a period of changes in family laws which made the access to divorce easier almost everywhere, through more rapid and simplified procedures. However, comparing the magnitude of juridical and statistical changes, or the tempo of reforms and numbers, suggests that the evolution of attitudes and behaviours came first and resulted in legislative action, rather than the other way around.

Levels of divorce rates, like marriage trends, gradually decline from Northern to Southern Europe. According to the most recent period rates, 40 to 50 per cent of marriages will be concluded by a divorce in the Scandinavian countries and the United Kingdom, 30 to 40 per cent in the central and western parts of the region, and less than 20 per cent in the Mediterranean countries.

(c)   *The spread of cohabitation*

A declining number of marriages and a rising number of divorces do not mean that couples refuse to live together any longer. Everywhere in Western Europe, informal living arrangements have developed, with men and women living "like husbands and wives" without being married.

The spread was exceptionally rapid in Sweden, where the marriage burst and the divorce boom were so sudden. As many as 80 per cent of women born in the early 1950s had chosen cohabitation as their first form of living together before age 25. The proportion rose to 90 per cent in the following cohorts, but there already remained little room for any further evolution. A few years have been enough for cohabitation to become not only predominant but almost exclusive and for marriage to be left with a residual importance.

Trends were more gradual and slightly time-lagged in the rest of the Nordic countries. Then came the time for Western countries like France, Germany and the United Kingdom. Levels are coming closer and closer to those recorded by Sweden: 90 per cent of the women in Finland and 70 to 80 per cent of those in the other countries have chosen cohabitation as their entry gate into conjugal life.

By contrast, the movement has hardly started in the Mediterranean countries. Some increase has occurred across cohorts, but as few as 10 to 20 per cent of young women have chosen cohabitation for their first experience of living together in Italy, Portugal and Spain. Marriage remains heavily predominant in these countries. Maybe convergence towards higher cohabitation levels is on the way, but there remains a long way to go (Macura, Sternberg and Garcia, 2000).

(d)   *Marriage, couples, children*

The proportion of couples who *conceived* a child out of wedlock and who married before the end of pregnancy, so as to legitimize their child, was high everywhere in Western Europe by the 1960s: about 60 per cent; but trends since then have been divergent. In Northern Europe, France and the United Kingdom, the proportion has sharply declined: to 10 per cent or less; in contrast, in Southern Europe, high levels have been maintained, like the ones in the 1960s: for instance, in Italy, unmarried couples turn to marriage 6 times out of 10 when a pregnancy occurs. In between, but very close to the Mediterranean countries, Central Europe has experienced a limited decline in the nuptiality of pregnant unmarried women: in Germany (western Länder) and Austria, more than half of conceptions out of wedlock result in a marriage before the end of the pregnancy. The case of Germany is all the more remarkable inasmuch as an increased proportion of children *born* from unmarried parents are legitimized later: more than 40 per cent against 30 per cent by the end of the 1970s. The movement in France is in the reverse direction. Three quarters of children conceived out of marriage are integrated into marriage, before birth or after, in Germany; the proportion is more than double that for France, while the two countries were at the same high level 25 years ago.

On this point, there is a clear-cut distinction between the North-Western part of Europe and the Central and Mediterranean countries. It is quite different from what has occurred in nuptiality trends, but very similar to the fertility divide. Central Europe and Southern Europe had already experienced sharp fertility declines when nuptiality still maintained relatively high levels. In these countries, marriage remains the highly favoured frame for family-building and a very limited space has been left for fertility outside its traditional, legitimate form. No compensatory mechanism has been able to work interposed between declining births from married parents and rising births from unmarried ones.

(e) *Implications*

Differential fertility within EU does not result only in unequal rates of population growth and population ageing. It also has social implications linked to the very significance we have just analysed.

By 2050, population numbers in France and the United Kingdom will still be over their 2000 mark; Germany will have lost 9 million persons and Italy 16 million. The proportion of elderly people aged 65 years or over will reach 25 per cent in France and the United Kingdom, 28 per cent in Germany, and 35 per cent in Italy, instead of remaining at their levels of fifty years earlier, namely, 16 per cent in France, the United Kingdom and Germany, and 18 per cent in Italy. The rapidly declining and ageing Italian population makes a large difference in contrast with the stabilized numbers and the slowly increasing proportions in France and the United Kingdom.

However, it could be still more important to note that children in Italy will probably be born and raised in marriage, while those in France and the United Kingdom will have experienced more informal and more unstable family links, through cohabitation, separation, reconstituted families and so on. One step further would lead us from "more informal" to "weaker"; but some sociologists suggest that things evolve the other way around, from "more informal" to "more personal" then "stronger": Cohabiting fathers who care to recognize their children will be closer to them than married fathers who receive their paternal authority automatically from their marital status. We are unable to add arguments in one direction or another, but the issue is crucial for the future of our societies, which are based on an intergenerational contract. Parents contribute to the education of their children with the implicit hope that they will be rewarded later, when the generation of their children supports them in their older ages. It has been admitted up to now in Europe that the most effective way to get this exchange to work is to rely mostly on private transfers from adults to their young children and to have public systems to transfer resources from the active to the inactive population or from the healthy to the unhealthy people.

Let us take two realistic case studies, which oversimplify the situation various EU countries will face in the future. Will children take in charge similarly their dependent fathers in their old age, whether these raised them, together with their spouses, or paid a reasonably generous child support after their divorce? Will they be efficient caregivers for their elderly parents, whatever their present situation: still married to their only spouse, separated from him (her) or living with a second (third ...) partner?

Answers to these questions are important not only for these individuals but for society as a whole. If marital status does matter, for better or worse, the difference between two countries like France and Italy will probably be much greater in 2050 than that reflected in population numbers. Present disparities in their fertility trends and levels point to disparities in family systems, which should exclude aggregation and globalization.

2. *Eastern-Western European fertility differentials*

Fertility levels in Eastern Europe, exemplified by the Russian case, are not very different from those in EU. More precisely, period rates for 1990-1995 or cohort rates for women born in 1963 are midway between the relatively high levels in France and the United Kingdom and the extremely low levels in Germany and Italy (table 4).

Discrepancies are elsewhere. First, mean age at childbirth is much lower in the Russian Federation: an enormous three-year gap with respect to the Western countries, which are fairly homogeneous on this point. Second, mean ages were still declining in the Russian Federation when that trend had been reversed for a long time in EU countries. Third, cohort rates, variations in mean age at childbirth and period rates apparently failed to be consistent in the Russian Federation, but the expected TFR should have been compared with earlier actual rates, because of earlier childbirth.[1]

Other discrepancies are linked to the marital and non-marital components of total fertility. EU is diverse on that point because of the unequal contribution of unmarried parents, substantial in France and the United Kingdom and very limited in Germany and Italy; the Russian Federation stands in the middle but diverges substantially by virtue of the high proportion of ever-married persons

TABLE 4. TEMPO AND QUANTUM COMPONENTS OF PERIOD FERTILITY RATES
IN THE RUSSIAN FEDERATION AND COUNTRIES OF THE EUROPEAN UNION

	France	Germany	Italy	United Kingdom	*Russian Federation*
(*a*) TFR (birth cohort 1963) (births per woman)	2.02	1.57	1.57	1.89	**1.71**
(*b*) Mean age at birth (birth cohort 1963) (years).................	28.0	27.5	28.4	28.0	**24.7**
(*c*) Variation in mean age at birth (birth cohort 1958-1963) (years)	+0.6	+0.6	+1.0	+0.5	**-0.6**
(*d*) Expected period TFR [*a* (1 - *c*/5)] (births per woman)...................	1.78	1.38	1.26	1.70	**1.92**
(*e*) Actual TFR (1990-1995) (births per woman)	1.72	1.30	1.28	1.78	**1.55**

Sources: United Nations (2001); and Conseil de l'Europe (1999).

(table 5). That specificity is reinforced by the prevalence of young ages at marriage, which is consistent with early childbirth.

More generally, family-building in the Russian Federation differs from the Western models through the coexistence of three traits:

(*a*) Marriage is frequent and takes place at young ages. This ancient specificity is shared by all the populations east of the Saint Petersburg–Trieste line, already drawn by J. Hajnal. The political and economic crisis of the 1990s has resulted in a sharp decline in marriage rates, but it could be a short-term reaction to acute uncertainties. Some people thought that early marriage was a way for young persons to procure some facilities like independent housing during the Soviet period, but this is an oversimplification which severely underestimates the importance of a deeply rooted practice of young marriage in the Russian Federation;

(*b*) Divorce is frequent too. Half of marriages result in a divorce. By the mid-1960s, after a limited reform of the judicial procedure, numbers have skyrocketed to 30 divorces per 100 marriages, at a time when there were 10-15 per 100 marriages in most Western countries. A continuous rise since that period has put divorce frequency in the Russian Federation at one of the highest levels in the world, with Sweden and the United States of America;

(*c*) The combination of early and frequent marriage with a high divorce rate is very unusual. In Western Europe, the rise in divorce has paralleled the decline and delay in marriages. It is made possible in the Russian Federation by the existence of a dense family network, which interferes continuously with the daily life of couples and families. The cohabitation of different adult generations in the same household (young couples frequently live with parents or in-laws) and the intergenerational support (child-sitting, shared food, financial aid etc.) are not only the result of economic difficulties but also the product of old traditions, brought from rural settings to modern urban sites. Cohabitation in the same household not only helps solve the housing shortage but also permits early marriage to be a first step towards material independence; it is also one of the safety nets offered to former spouses after their divorce. Most importantly, it gives the young generation a stable framework for their socialization after the separation from their parents.

TABLE 5. MARRIAGE AND MARITAL FERTILITY COMPONENTS OF FERTILITY RATES
IN COUNTRIES OF THE EUROPEAN UNION AND THE RUSSIAN FEDERATION

	France	Germany	Italy	United Kingdom	*Russian Federation*
(*a*) Total fertility rate (period 1990-1995) (births per woman).	1.72	1.30	1.28	1.78	**1.55**
(*b*) Proportion of ultimately married women (birth cohort 1963)	0.75	0.80	0.83	0.81	**0.91**
(*c*) Proportion of children born from married parents (period 1990-1995)	0.66	0.87	0.93	0.69	**0.83**
(*d*) Estimated number of "legitimate" births to ultimately married women [*a* × *c*/*b*]	1.52	1.41	1.43	1.52	**1.41**

Sources: United Nations (2001); and Conseil de l'Europe (1999); and A. Avdeev and A. Monnier, "La nuptialité russe: une complexité méconnue", *Population*, Nos. 4-5 (1999).

The family network is probably the central part of the Russian family system, with important implications for the future when the ageing of the society increases the weight of the elderly and puts more pressure than ever on families. Private solidarity will find traditional channels more easily accessible than in most Western European countries. The heavy strain currently being put on family networks by the transition to market economy must be watched with great concern.

B. DIVERSITIES IN EUROPE ON MORTALITY

1. *Diversity in the European Union on mortality*

Contrary to what has been just shown concerning fertility, there is a remarkable homogeneity in mortality levels throughout EU. We have already exhibited life expectancies at birth in table 1, but even such a volatile index as the infant mortality rate has a limited range of values: in the four more populated EU countries in 1997, it was as low as 4.7 per 1,000 in France and as high as 5.9 per 1,000 in the United Kingdom, at the two extremes.

A classical decomposition of life expectancy by age and sex does not introduce major changes in that preliminary observation. Differentials between men and women are somewhat more contrasted than average life durations, ranging from 5.2 years in the United Kingdom to 7.9 in France. The gap between the two extremes has increased since the 1980s, because male over-mortality declined more rapidly in the United Kingdom, but these discrepancies are long-lasting and relatively moderate. EU countries are all characterized by an important male excess mortality. Similarly, differentials associated with age are limited: for instance, the expectation of life at age 65 is lower in France than in Germany and Italy, but the difference never exceeds two years. On all these aspects, the homogeneity of EU countries cannot be questioned. All of them have a long survival; in technical terms, their survivorship curve declines so late that the area under the curve looks like a rectangle (table 6).

A long survival has direct consequences for numbers and age structure in any population, but its impact on the other features of the society are at best indirect. For instance, the distinction between actives and non-actives is linked with age, and demographers often contrast people in working age with those out of that bracket, but the divide between active and inactive people is more pertinent for social policy. The most direct and socially pertinent associate with age and mortality is health. Mortality is just an indication of a more important issue: how healthy are the survivors? That is the reason for the increasing popularity of the decomposition of life expectancy into "good" and "bad" years, the latter ones being costly for individuals and the society.

The decomposition according to health status gives some contradictory results. A large portion of life is free of any disability and the average number of these good years are distributed among the EU countries as life expectancies are: France and Italy are in a slightly better position than Germany and the United Kingdom. However, disparities between the first and second group

379

of countries are larger (4.0 years between France and Germany in respect of disability-free life expectancy, instead of 1.5 years in respect of life expectancy at birth): not only is life longer, but it is also better in France, with only 15.4 years with some disability against 17.9 in Germany. Unfortunately for the French people, their bad years are much worse than in Germany, with 7.9 years of severe disability instead of 5.2. Taken at face value, this last indicator leads to the following conclusions: the most costly years of life are more numerous in France and Italy than in Germany and the United Kingdom, as if longer life expectancies had been gained in bad physical conditions. Years of severe disability weigh so heavily on the health budget that we could no longer consider all these countries homogeneous. What a pity these data look so unreliable; they would be so valuable for policy-making (table 7)!

Let us conclude with a result obtained for the Netherlands. By age 65, people still have 6.5 disability-free years to live and 10 additional years in disability. If cancer were eliminated, they would gain disproportionately more bad years than good ones (respectively, 1.6 and 0.6); if heart diseases were eliminated, they would maintain the balance between bad and good years (respectively, 1.7 and 1.2); if arthritis and back complaints were eliminated, their total life expectancy would remain unchanged, but they would transform bad years into good ones (an estimated 0.9) (W. J. Nusselder and others, 1996). Longer life can be a proxy for healthy life for demographers, but it should not be one for politicians.

2. *Eastern-Western diversity on mortality*

The East-West divide on life expectancy is so clear-cut that it hardly deserves any comment. It is a relatively recent phenomenon, which started in the mid-1960s and which has continuously amplified since. Some improvement in the Russian situation after 1995 stopped in 1999 (owing to an epidemic of flu).

In 30 years, the male situation has progressively deteriorated, while the female one has stagnated. It has resulted in an ever-growing excess mortality for men: the differential between men and women, which was already important in the 1960s, is now over 13 years, twice as great as that in France (table 8).

Most of the deterioration has been concentrated in the adult ages, with a possible improvement at young ages and a slower-than-average worsening for the elderly; but the data quality can probably be questioned at these ages. Nevertheless, excess mortality over age 65 is not much different from that in France and the United Kingdom. The quality of survival at working ages has probably declined sharply for the last decades.

Causes of death point to two factors responsible for the gap between Eastern and Western countries: heart disease and violence (table 9). The former played a major role in decennial trends and differentials. A slow rise in frequency thereof in the Russian Federation contrasted with a sustained decline in France and the United Kingdom. The advantage of the French population has been gradually increased; the United Kingdom, which hardly did better than the Russian Federation in 1970, has followed the French example. Costly

TABLE 6. AGE AND SEX COMPONENTS OF LIFE EXPECTANCY AT BIRTH
IN COUNTRIES OF THE EUROPEAN UNION (1995)

	France		Germany		Italy		United Kingdom	
	Men	Women	Men	Women	Men	Women	Men	Women
Life expectancy at birth (years)	73.2	79.7	73.9	81.8	74.6	81.0	74.3	79.5
Men-women differential	6.5		7.9		6.4		5.2	
Life expectancy at 65 (years)	14.7	18.4	16.1	20.6	15.5	19.4	14.8	18.3
Men-women differential	3.7		4.5		3.9		3.5	

Source: Conseil de l'Europe (1999).

TABLE 7. HEALTH COMPONENTS OF LIFE EXPECTANCY AT BIRTH
IN COUNTRIES OF THE EUROPEAN UNION (1994)

	France	Germany	Italy	United Kingdom
Life expectancy at birth (years)	77.7	76.2	77.5	76.6
Disability-free life expectancy (years)	62.3	58.3	60.5	59.9
Mean number of years in mild disability	7.5	12.7	11.2	12.7
Mean number of years in severe disability	7.9	5.2	5.8	4.0

Source: J. M. Robine and others, "Les espérances de santé dans l'Union européenne: analyse des données du Panel des Ménages de la Communauté européenne", Réseau Espérance de Vie en Santé (REVES) paper, No. 320, octobre 1998.

TABLE 8. AGE AND SEX COMPONENTS OF LIFE EXPECTANCY AT BIRTH IN THE
RUSSIAN FEDERATION AND COUNTRIES OF THE EUROPEAN UNION (1995)

	France		United Kingdom		Russian Federation	
	Men	Women	Men	Women	Men	Women
Life expectancy at birth (years)	73.2	79.7	74.3	79.5	58.3	71.7
Men-women differential	6.5		5.2		13.4	
Life expectancy at 65 (years)	14.7	18.4	14.8	18.3	10.8	14.9
Men-women differential	3.7		3.5		4.1	

Source: Conseil de l'Europe (1999).

TABLE 9. CAUSE-OF-DEATH COMPONENTS OF STANDARDIZED MORTALITY RATES
IN THE RUSSIAN FEDERATION AND COUNTRIES OF THE EUROPEAN UNION
(Per hundred thousand)

	France (1992)		United Kingdom (1992)		Russian Federation (1993)	
	Men	Women	Men	Women	Men	Women
Infectious diseases	28	11	5	4	33	7
Cancer	360	158	324	210	361	160
Diseases of circulatory system	332	209	554	350	1 292	839
Diseases of respiratory system	86	40	144	82	168	86
Diseases of digestive system	56	31	35	29	63	29
Other diseases	100	74	106	88	83	55
Injury, poisoning, violence	114	51	46	20	400	95
TOTAL	1 075	575	1 214	782	2 401	1 235

Source: V. Shkolnikov, F. Meslé and J. Vallin, "La crise sanitaire en Russie", Population (juillet-octobre 1995).

techniques and health care for the elderly have been responsible for progress in Western Europe, but they could not be afforded in the East.

Violent deaths are directly linked to alcoholism. Ups and downs in their numbers coincide with the anti-alcoholism campaigns. Together with alcohol, the worsening of economic conditions and the deterioration of the political system are responsible for these trends. Divergences with EU countries on this point exhibit consequences of more general differences in ways of living.

There are such deep structural differences between Eastern and Western Europe in respect of mortality that a real convergence cannot be expected in the short or even the medium term. Once more, the aggregation of populations with so very different health conditions, and, probably, health determinants and systems, looks like a statistical artefact. Ageing, which will be equally important in the Eastern and Western parts of Europe, can hardly be considered a single issue, when such different answers are likely to be given by societies.

CONCLUSION

The European population will probably decline in the next five decades by 100 million out of 730 million. The group of people aged 65 years or over will grow in numbers and, still more, in proportions, up to 27.6 per cent in 2050. A slowly rising fertility (from 1.4 to 1.8 children per woman) and a continuously prolonged life expectancy, up to 80 years, will fuel these movements. But does that population exist or is it just a statistical aggregate?

There is much diversity in the European family. Intergenerational links, which will play a crucial role in ageing societies, have become more and more personal in the Nordic countries, France and the United Kingdom, while they stayed deeply anchored in marriage in the Mediterranean countries or embedded in dense networks in Eastern Europe, especially in the Russian Federation. Not only does that variety result in different fertility levels, but it also has differentiated implications for socio-economic issues. Private solidarity is stronger when one moves from personal-type to marriage-type and then network-type families, and the need for social solidarity will be more intense when the forms of private solidarity are more problematic. If this diversity was to be maintained during the next 50 years, the tackling of the ageing problem would probably imply differentiated answers throughout Europe.

On health matters, diversity leaves room for an East-West divide. While most European countries have experienced a substantial increase in life expectancy since the 1970s, the Eastern countries have stagnated, owing to the collapse of their health system and economic regime. There is some uncertainty as to the quality of life gained during that phase of costly struggle against cancer and heart diseases. The statistical indices should give more consideration to these aspects, so that politicians will be in a better position if a choice is to be made between more years of survival and better years of life. It is doubtful whether countries in so very different stages of their health transition would give similar consideration to this topic.

All European countries in the future will share ageing, but the diversity in the components of demographic change throughout Europe precludes any hastily generalization. Policy implications of that diversity will mean national or regional adaptations to long-lasting socio-economic systems.

NOTE

[1]Actual TFR in the previous four-year period, 1986-1991, was 2.02.

REFERENCES

Conseil de l'Europe (1999). *Évolution démographique récente en Europe*, 1999. Strasbourg, France.

Macura, M., Y. Mochizuki Sternberg and J. Lara Garcia (2000). Europe's fertility and partnership: selected developments during the last ten years. Paper presented at the Fertility and Family Surveys (FFS) Flagship Conference, Brussels, May 2000.

Nusselder, W. J. (1996). The elimination of selected chronic diseases in a population: the compression and expansion of mortality. *The American Journal of Public Health*, vol. 86, No. 2, pp. 187-194.

Observatoire Démographique Européen (1998). Évolution récente de la nuptialité féminine en Europe occidentale. *L'Observatoire Démographique Européen vous informe*, No. 7 (janvier).

United Nations (1999). *World Population Prospects*, vol. I, *Comprehensive Tables*. Sales No. E.99.XIII.9.

_____ (2001). *Replacement Migration: Is It a Solution to Declining and Ageing Populations?* Sales No. E.01.XIII.19.

EUROPE'S DEMOGRAPHIC ISSUES: FERTILITY, HOUSEHOLD FORMATION AND REPLACEMENT MIGRATION

*Ron Lesthaeghe**

INTRODUCTION

The present paper is meant to give a general overview of recent trends in fertility and in patterns of household formation, and to speculate about future demographic developments. We apologize for the fact that not enough attention is being paid to Eastern European changes, but the situation in this area is such that it really requires a special background paper.

Since the outcome of the fertility analysis is that sub-replacement fertility is not likely to disappear, we equally need to address policy responses that cope with the consequences of several decades of low fertility. This will inevitably bring us to discussing the issue of replacement migration. This topic will be analysed both in terms of its own efficiency (or lack thereof) and in the context of other policy measures addressing the problem of an ageing labour force and of ageing in general.

I. FERTILITY

1.1 *Trends in period fertility indicators*

The historical fertility transition, that is to say, "the first transition", was characterized by increased fertility control that predominantly manifested itself by fertility reductions at older ages. The degree of control typically followed a learning curve with contraceptive efficiency increasing monotonically with age (Coale and Trussell, 1974), with parity (Henry, 1953) or with marriage duration (Page, 1977). This reduction at older ages led to declines in the mean age at childbearing (MAC), a trend that was reinforced in Western countries by declining mean age at first marriage (MAFM) as well. More recent elements contributing to this historical pattern were the adoption of efficient forms of contraception (hormonal, intrauterine devices (IUDs)), which, particularly during the 1960s and 1970s, eliminated most unplanned pregnancies at older ages and further reduced fertility beyond age 30. In other countries, and especially in Eastern Europe, access to legalized abortion fulfilled a similar function.

*Interface Demography, Department of Social Research, Vrije Universiteit Brussel, Brussels, Belgium.

The "second demographic transition", by contrast, is characterized by the adoption of efficient contraception at early ages and therefore by the overall postponement of parenthood. The contraceptive learning curve is now rising very steeply at young ages (typically before age 20) and has become much less a function of union duration or parity. Together with the postponement of marriage and the adoption of new living arrangements, fertility now declines prior to age 30. This general postponement is the hallmark of the second demographic transition as far as the fertility pattern is concerned. During this phase, period total fertility rates (PTFRs) decline below the replacement level and record low levels are being reached. As is well known (see, for example, Ryder, 1980), such a tempo shift in fertility is a strong factor in producing an extra steep decline of period fertility indicators. Particularly when newly incoming cohorts postpone at a growing rate compared with their immediate predecessors, there will be an enhanced depressing effect on the PTFR. Once this trend is set in motion, two questions arise that are of direct relevance for future trends: (a) To what extent and for how long will such a tempo shift be maintained by newly arriving cohorts? (b) To what degree will cohorts recuperate after age 30 for fertility forgone during their twenties? An end to the tempo shift, or even a reduction in the speed of postponement among younger cohorts, definitely has the potential of raising the PTFR (cf. Bongaarts and Feeney, 1998), but the magnitude of this "end of postponement" effect strongly depends on the degree of fertility recuperation past age 30 (cf. Lesthaeghe and Willems, 1999). The adjusted PTFR proposed by Bongaarts and Feeney illustrates the effect of "pure postponement" calculated in the absence of changes in parity-specific period total fertility rates (PTFRs). Inadequate recuperation at older ages will depress these parity-specific PTFRs, and this will add a quantum effect to the tempo effect. If postponement leads, to some degree, to a cancellation of a first or next birth, the tempo effect will feed a negative quantum effect. Consequently we need to inspect recent cohort patterns of fertility for clues regarding changes in the pace of postponement among younger women and regarding patterns of subsequent recuperation among cohorts that have reached the older ages. In a later section, we shall concentrate on these issues in greater detail (see also Frejka and Calot, 2000; and Lesthaeghe and Moors, 2000).

During the second demographic transition, the ages at first sexual intercourse have declined for both sexes. This was obviously a part of the "sexual revolution" and of the more general normative and ethical changes occurring since the 1960s. However, the learning curves regarding contraceptive use-effectiveness do not exhibit the same steepness at young ages in all populations. In several countries, distinct subpopulations with slower learning have emerged, and they exhibit high teenage pregnancy rates often followed by high teenage fertility as well. Already in the late 1960s, a rise in prenuptial conceptions followed by precipitated ("shotgun") marriages occurred in many countries. Sex was learned faster than modern contraception. However, by the mid-1970s, nothing of this bulge was left in many Western European nations. In others, though, this pattern has been maintained for much longer or has been on the rise. In such instances, it has led to a high incidence of teenage lone motherhood and it is associated with increased child poverty (cf. Bradbury and Jäntti, 1999). The presence of such subpopulations is readily detectable from a bump prior to age 25 in period age-specific fertility distributions (Chandola and others, 1999), from the presence of young lone mothers living either on their own (in the West) or in their own parental household (in the East) and from the proportions of children currently being raised in lone-parent households typically headed by mothers under age 25.

These features are furthermore contingent on two other demographic variables, namely, the nuptiality patterns as they existed prior to the 1960s and have evolved since then, and the path followed during the phase of contraceptive modernization.

With respect to the first factor, the old cleavage along the Hajnal line, dividing Europe in a western and an eastern half, is of significance again. In the West, the MAFMs rose after 1965, whereas they remained low in the East. Communist policies, reserving housing for married couples, stimulating female labour-force participation and eliminating unemployment, produced stable living conditions which contributed to the maintenance of the historical pattern of earlier marriage. At present, the issue is whether the features of the Western second demographic transition are currently spreading to Eastern Europe as well: are ages at first marriage increasing as a result of the development of alternative and often temporary childless living arrangements? If so, these countries too would have a postponement effect over and above that caused by the events of 1989.

The second factor, namely, the modernization of contraception, equally produces an East-West divide, with Eastern Europe relying much more on abortion and on traditional methods of contraception (non-supply methods). "Roller-coaster" policies with waves of liberalization and restrictions concerning access to abortion (see, for example, Stloukal, 1998) combined with the lack of support for hormonal contraception have left the East with significantly lower contraceptive use-effectiveness and a considerable "unmet need" (Klijzing, 2000). Hence, during the 1970s and 1980s, Eastern European countries still faced the problem of unplanned pregnancies for women at older ages, and still had ample room for fertility declines at ages above 30. Eastern European countries are typically more than a decade behind the Western ones in making the pattern shift in fertility: fertility rates after age 30 were still declining (and often these prior to age 30 increasing) before 1980, when Western patterns had definitively shifted to the postponement and subsequent partial recuperation pattern (Lesthaeghe and Moors, 2000). At present, the question for Eastern Europe is again whether they will be following this Western pattern. Since 1990, most Eastern countries have had rapidly falling fertility at all ages, and only in Hungary, Slovenia and Croatia are there signs of fertility rises after age 30 (Lesthaeghe and Moors, 2000).

A first synoptic picture of the current situation is offered in table 1 and figure I through a set of classic indicators: the PTFR, the mean age at first childbearing (MAC1), the teenage fertility rate, the number of abortions per 100 live births and the percentage of births out of wedlock. The data pertain to the period 1995-1997. At present, only 3 of the 35 countries considered are at replacement-level fertility or close to it: Iceland, the United States of America and New Zealand. Of the 18 Eastern European populations except east Germany,

			PTFR	MAC1	Fertility rate per thousand (age group 15-19)	Abortions/ 100 live births	Percentage non-marital births
		A. *Southern*					
ITA	Italy		1.22	27.9	7	25	8
SP	Spain		1.15	27.8	8	13	13
GRE	Greece		1.32	26.6	13	12	3
POR	Portugal		1.46	25.8	21	..	20
		B. *Eastern*					
BUL	Bulgaria		1.09	22.8	45	130	30
CRO	Croatia		1.69	25.2	20	29	7
CZR	Czech Republic		1.17	24.1	18	51	18
EST	Estonia		1.24	23.4	29	127	52
HUN	Hungary		1.38	23.4	28	73	25
LAT	Latvia		1.11	23.5	21	48	35
LIT	Lithuania		1.39	23.1	32	71	17
MOL	Moldova (Republic of)		1.60	22.4	53	89	17
POL	Poland		1.51	23.1	20	2	11
ROM	Romania		1.32	23.1	41	213	22
RUS	Russian Federation		1.28	22.8	40	179	25
SLO	Slovenia		1.25	25.6	9	54	32
MAC	The former Yugoslav Republic of Macedonia		1.90	..	39	45	9
YUG	Yugoslavia		1.80	24.7	30	72	18
SLK	Slovakia		1.47	..	31	41	14
BLR	Belarus		1.39	..	39	81	15
UKR	Ukraine		1.40	..	54	153	14
GDR	Germany (east)		0.95	27.3	8	32	44
		C. *Western*					
AUS	Austria		1.36	26.7	15	25[a]	29
BEL	Belgium		1.59	27.5	9	10	18
FRA	France		1.71	28.3	7	21	39
FRG	Germany (west)		1.39	28.4	10	14	14
IRL	Ireland		1.92	27.0	17	10[b]	27
LUX	Luxembourg		1.71	28.5	7	10	17
NL	Netherlands		1.55	29.0	4	11	19
SWI	Switzerland		1.48	28.3	4	..	8
UK	United Kingdom		1.71	26.7	30	24	37
		D. *Northern*					
DK	Denmark		1.75	27.7	8	25	46
FIN	Finland		1.74	27.7	9	26	37
ICE	Iceland		2.04	25.0	25	19	65
NOR	Norway		1.86	27.0	13	23	49
SWE	Sweden		1.53	27.4	7	34	54
		E. *Non-European*					
CND	Canada		1.64	26.8	25	28	30
USA	United States		2.06	24.8	58	38	32
AUL	Australia		1.77	26.8	21	36	23
NZ	New Zealand		2.04	..	34	24	41
JPA	Japan		1.44	27.9	4	29	1

Sources: Council of Europe (1999), tables T3.2, T3.3 and T3.4 and country tables xx-2; United Nations *Demographic Yearbook* (various years); personal communications from H. Kojima and P. McDonald; and A. Monnier (1999).

[a]Estimates based on Fertility and Family Surveys (Austria).

[b]Estimates based on D. Coleman (1999).

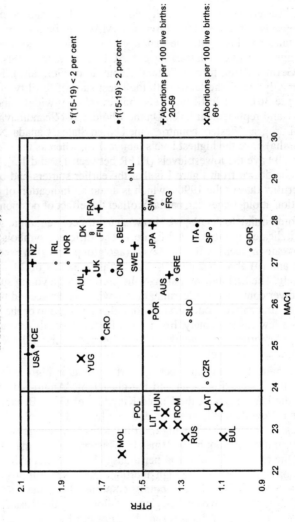

Figure I. Period total fertility rates (PTFRs) and mean ages at birth of first child (MAC1), 1996-1997

○ f(15-19) < 2 per cent

● f(15-19) > 2 per cent

✛ Abortions per 100 live births: 20-59

✗ Abortions per 100 live births: 60+

9 have an early reproductive pattern with MAC1 below age 24. However, this early start of reproduction has not prevented them from having steep PTFR declines during the 1990s. Only two countries, Yugoslavia (including Kosovo) and Croatia, have PTFRs close to 1.7 or just above it. Eight Eastern European countries have PTFRs lower than 1.5 and three dipped below 1.3 children. In this set, we have not included the former German Democratic Republic, which had a PTFR value of barely 0.95 in 1996.

The Western countries have developed much later ages at childbearing. There are only three countries for which MAC1 is below 26: Iceland, the United States and Portugal. The majority of countries are located within the 26-28 range, and five countries have MAC1 values above 28: Switzerland, France, Germany (the former Federal Republic of Germany), Luxembourg and especially the Netherlands with the latest start of fertility of all (MAC1 close to age 30). The fertility levels, however, vary widely and range between 1.1 and replacement level. On the whole, most Scandinavian countries and non-European Western countries (the United States, Canada, New Zealand and Australia) have the highest levels (above 1.6), whereas the Mediterranean countries all have the lowest levels (PTFR between 1.1 and 1.5). The general lesson to be drawn from figure I is that the earlier starters had by no means higher fertility during the 1990s, which is again an indication of the fact that recuperation at older ages can partially offset the effect of postponement.

Before turning to details, we also wish to attract attention to several other features indicated in table 1 and figure I. The different symbols used in the figure indicate (*a*) teenage fertility levels (age group 15-19) in excess of 20 per thousand and (*b*) abortions per 100 live births in excess of 20 and above 60 respectively. The first indicator signals the presence of a young subpopulation with a slower contraceptive learning curve, whereas the second one indicates a slower contraceptive modernization for either a subgroup or the entire population. In a few cases, namely, Ireland and Portugal, legal restrictions are the cause of low abortion rates, but these two countries exhibit a slower contraceptive modernization as well.

The countries with high teenage fertility and/or high abortion figures are typically Eastern European and the cluster of "Anglo-Saxon" countries (namely, the United States, the United Kingdom of Great Britain and Northern Ireland, New Zealand, Australia and to a lesser degree also Canada). The United States in particular has high fertility rates for teenage women (58 per thousand), and this cannot be explained by a history of early marriage as is, for instance, the case for Ukraine (54 per thousand) or the Republic of Moldova (53 per thousand). Particularly high abortion figures are still prevailing in the late 1990s in a set of former communist countries. Romania leads this group (213 abortions per 100 live births), closely followed by the Russian Federation (179) and Ukraine (153); but several other Eastern European or Baltic countries equally have abortion figures in excess of 100 live births: Bulgaria (130), Estonia (127) and Latvia (123). High abortion figures by Western standards, that is to say, above 25 per 100 live births, are found in the United States (38), Australia (36), Sweden (34), Japan (29) and Canada (28). Evidently, not all Western countries have "perfectly contracepting" populations.

1.2. *Cohort fertility in Western countries and expectations for the future*

The picture presented so far only gives a synoptic cross-sectional view of what is essentially unfolding at the cohort level. Also, recent cohort trends provide better clues about the more likely future developments. There are two ways of representing cohort fertility. The first one typically looks at cumulative cohort fertility, either directly or in the form of deviations from a benchmark cohort. The latter form brings out the postponement and recuperation features in a very telling way (see, for example, Frejka and Calot, 2000). The second method focuses on the evolution of the separate age-specific fertility rates for each cohort without cumulation, and this is ideally suited to bring out acceleration in trends or period-linked distortions. Such distortions show up in the diagonal location of peaks and troughs. In what follows we shall refrain from presenting long series of graphical representations since the first set (deviations from a benchmark cohort) is given and discussed in Frejka and Calot (2000, figures 3A through 3D), and the second set (cohort age-specific rates) is presented and commented upon in Lesthaeghe and Moors (2000, figures 5 to 20). Instead, we will only present four indicators of cohort fertility change in table 2.

The first indicator (A) captures the magnitude of the trough produced by postponement by measuring the cumulative deficit in the number of children by age 30 for the cohorts reaching adulthood (that is to say, ages 15-19) in 1985 compared with the offspring at that age realized by the cohorts reaching adulthood in 1960. Using the graphical method of cumulative deviations from a benchmark cohort, this indicator corresponds to line A in figure II (the Netherlands example). The second indicator (B) measures the extent of past recuperation for the latest cohort reaching age 40, by measuring the distance to replacement fertility (cohort total fertility rate (CTFR) = 2.08). This corresponds to line B in figure II. Obviously, these two indicators already give a more "historical" view of the Western postponement and partial recuperation patterns.

The third indicator (C) measures how much further the cumulated deficit by age 30 has advanced in the cohorts reaching adulthood in 1985 compared with their predecessors of 1975. Large figures indicate a speeding up of postponement in the late 1980s and early 1990s. This indicator corresponds to distance C in figure II. Finally, the fourth indicator (D) shows to what extent the younger cohorts reaching adulthood in 1990 (see line D in figure II) have slipped further back by age 25 compared with their predecessors of 1980. This indicator gives a higher relative weight to teenage fertility and its trend, but it also brings out whether the postponement trend has been accelerating or decelerating during the 1990s. This is of particular importance for understanding and even predicting the eventuality of emerging increases in PTFRs. As indicated earlier, such a slowing down of postponement among incoming cohorts, in tandem with even only partial recuperation among older ones, is capable of producing modest rises in period total fertility levels.

Obviously, the forecasting of future PTFRs is highly dependent on yet unknown degrees of recuperation past age 30 for cohorts reaching adulthood

TABLE 2. INDICATORS OF POSTPONEMENT AND RECUPERATION OF COHORT FERTILITY IN WESTERN COUNTRIES

	Past trend (A, B)		Recent postponement (C, D)	
	A. Trough produced by postponement: cumulated deficit by age 30 for cohort reaching 15-19 in 1985 relative to predecessor of 1960	B. Recuperation: cumulated deficit by age 40 for cohort reaching 15-19 in 1975 relative to replacement fertility (=2.08)	C. Recent postponement: cumulated deficit by age 30 for cohort reaching 15-19 in 1985 compared with predecessor of 1975	D. Youngest cohort: cumulated deficit by age 25 for cohort reaching 15-19 in 1990 compared with predecessor of 1980
1. Northern Europe				
Sweden	-0.66	+0.02	-0.11	-0.09
Norway	-0.55	-0.04	-0.15	-0.12
Finland	-0.33	-0.19	-0.13	-0.21
Denmark	-0.65	-0.22	-0.14	-0.12
2. Western Europe				
2 (a) France	-0.71	+0.02	-0.36	-0.25
United Kingdom	-0.76	+0.01	-0.25	-0.09
2 (b) Netherlands	-0.90	-0.25	-0.31	-0.10
Belgium	-0.55	-0.22	-0.19	-0.11
2 (c) Germany (FRG)	-0.58	-0.50	-0.24	-0.04
Austria	-0.58	-0.36	-0.27	-0.20
Switzerland	-0.64	-0.35	-0.24	-0.04
3. Southern Europe				
Spain	-0.87	-0.27	-0.53	-0.30
Italy	-0.80	-0.36	-0.44	-0.26
Portugal	-0.53	-0.23	-0.32	-0.30
Greece	-0.42	-0.18	-0.21	-0.43
4. Other				
Australia	-0.82	+0.12	-0.35	-0.16
Canada	-0.73	-0.22	-0.20	-0.09
United States	-0.51	-0.10	-0.03	-0.02
Japan	-0.74	-0.25	-0.45	-0.10
Ireland	-0.88	+0.38	-0.85	-0.22
Iceland	-0.75	+0.37	-0.18	-0.23

Sources: Calculated from series of age-specific fertility rates in Council of Europe (1999), country-specific tables x-3, and United Nations *Demographic Yearbooks*, various years.
NOTE: Multiplication by 100 gives the deviations in number of children per 100 women.

392

Figure II. The Netherlands—completed cohort fertility by age

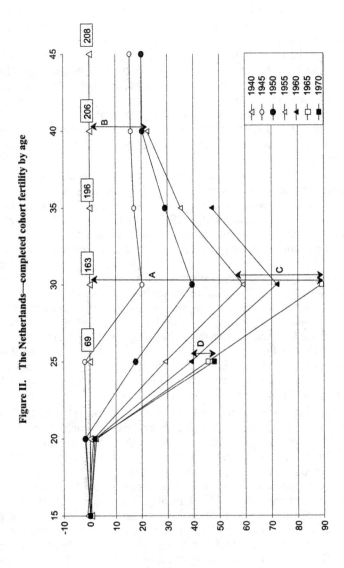

after 1985, and from this point of view their age-specific fertility rates (ASFRs) in age groups 30-34 and 35-39 need close monitoring as well.

The four indicators provide only a summary and are not a substitute for the full picture of cohort fertility experiences; but they are still useful in comparing and classifying the experience of Western countries. Table 2 presents the results.

The first group that can be distinguished are the Scandinavian countries. The troughs (indicator A) are small (Finland) to modest (Sweden, Norway, Denmark) and the latest cohorts reaching age 40 have brought their CTFRs close to replacement level (Sweden and Norway) or leave a modest deficit only (about -0.20 in Finland and Denmark). Also, the indicators C and D of more recent postponement show modest levels, and this and the steadily rising fertility after age 30 are the main reasons why Scandinavian period fertility levels remained fairly high by European standards. Among these populations, the position of Sweden is special given the strong period distortion induced around 1990.

The second group is made up of Western European countries, but these exhibit quite a bit of heterogeneity. France and the United Kingdom, with almost diametrically opposed family policies, have been nearly identical twins as far as their PTFRs are concerned: in 1970 this indicator was 2.47 in France and 2.45 in the United Kingdom, and in 1997 both populations had a PTFR of 1.71. The largest difference in PTFRs was barely 0.12 children in 1975. From table 2 it also appears that the cohort "trough" (A) was very similar, and that the latest cohorts reaching age 40 made it exactly to replacement-level fertility in both countries (B). The main difference between them is that the United Kingdom could realize this at the expense of much higher teenage fertility. This shows up in indicators C and D as well: postponement during the 1990s progressed faster in France than in the United Kingdom, and it could very well be that the PTFR in France could dip below the 1.70 level. The crucial element here is again future recuperation. Incidentally, the same could happen to the United Kingdom, since the rise in the ASFRs past age 30 is slowing down more in the United Kingdom than in France.

The next set of twins comprises the two Low Countries, namely, the Netherlands and Belgium: their PTFRs have not deviated from each other for more than 0.10 children since 1975. However, the Netherlands has had a massive postponement effect (indicator A = -0.90), whereas that of Belgium has been much more modest (A = -0.55); but the recuperation effect has been equally impressive in the Netherlands, and in both countries the latest cohorts reaching age 40 fall short of replacement CTFR by about 0.25 children. In the Netherlands, this record postponement did continue at a respectable speed for cohorts reaching adulthood around 1985 (C). In both countries, the youngest cohorts still have lost ground by age 25, but at a much slower speed than before. Very recent PTFR estimates for Belgium (Deboosere and others, 2000) indicate a modest rise (from 1.55 in 1995 to about 1.63 in 1999), which could be partially due to this reduced pace of postponement.

The third set of Western European countries is made up of western Germany (former Federal Republic of Germany), Austria and Switzerland. They all experienced a more moderate postponement-induced trough (A), but compared with the other countries in the second group, the latest cohort reaching age 40 failed to recuperate at older ages to a much larger degree. These older cohorts were 0.33 to 0.50 children short of replacement CTFR (see B). The cohorts reaching adulthood in the 1980s nearly produced half of the overall postponement effect (compare A with C), and they would have to display a major recuperation effect to come even close to a CTFR of 1.60. In Germany and Switzerland, but not yet in Austria, the youngest cohorts have not significantly fallen back by age 25 compared with their predecessors that are 10 years older (D). Again, it is this delicate balance between a slowing down of postponement and the yet unknown degree of recuperation past age 30 that will determine whether the already low PTFRs in these countries will slide further down or stabilize.

The third group is made up of the Southern European countries, and they all had, although starting at different times, very large postponement effects with weak recuperation. The "pioneers" of the new fertility regime in the third group were Italy and Spain, and they have the largest troughs (-0.80 and -0.87 respectively) after the Netherlands (-0.90) and Ireland (-0.88) (see A). Also, the latest cohorts reaching age 40 had a weak recuperation, and the CTFR fell to about 1.70 in Italy and 1.80 in Spain for them. These figures are very likely to drop. Half or more than half of the trough is produced by cohorts reaching adulthood in the mid-1980s (C), and, even more significantly, the very youngest cohorts, followed until age 25, are dropping further behind (D = -0.26 and -0.30 respectively). In Portugal and Greece, the evolution started later, and hence both the trough (A) and the deficit for the older cohorts relative to replacement-level fertility (B) are smaller than in Italy or Spain, but the postponement among the youngest cohorts is still fully developing (see D). Already by age 25, Greek cohorts reaching adulthood in 1990 are 0.43 children behind the offspring realized at this age by their predecessors of 10 years before. Hence, in the absence of any miraculous recuperation effect, CTFRs in Southern Europe are very likely to drop considerably, and possibly to levels of about 1.5 in Italy, 1.6 in Spain and 1.7 in Greece and Portugal. PTFRs are more likely to decline further than to stabilize, unless a rather spectacular recuperation at older ages occurs in the next decade.

The fourth group is a highly heterogeneous collection. Canada has a cohort profile that comes close to that of the Low Countries with modest recuperation for the oldest cohort (B = -0.22) and a slowing down of postponement as well (D = -0.09). Australia is more like the France–United Kingdom tandem, with a deeper trough but with strong recuperation in the past, even to the point of still exceeding the replacement fertility level (B). However, the recent postponement trend is stronger than in Canada and about equal to that of France. The Japanese experience fits that of Southern Europe in the past: a large postponement trough at age 30 (A), followed by inadequate recuperation and hence a recent CTFR of about 1.80 (B). Much of this postponement occurred after 1985 (see C), but the lag produced by the youngest cohort reaching age 25 is much smaller than in Southern Europe (D = -0.10 only).

The United States is very atypical in the sense that it is the country with the weakest marks of the Western postponement syndrome. Its postponement trough at age 30 compared with cohort fertility at that age 25 years earlier is fairly small (A = -0.51), the latest cohort attains replacement-level fertility and the cohorts reaching adulthood since the mid-1980s have exhibited virtually no postponement at all (C = -0.03 and D = -0.02). Behind this striking stability in cohort fertility profiles, however, large educational differences are to be found in the United States (cf. Rindfuss and others, 1996), with the least educated not following the postponement-recuperation pattern of the most educated.

Finally, Iceland and Ireland still had PTFRs above replacement level in 1990 (2.3 and 2.1, respectively) and had modest declines since (to 2.0 and 1.9 in 1997). Nevertheless, past fertility levels were still sufficiently high for a large postponement effect (A = -0.75 and -0.88, respectively) not to threaten cohort replacement fertility: the latest cohorts reaching age 40 still had 0.37 and 0.38 children, respectively, in excess of the replacement level. However, postponement is much more recent in Ireland (compare C with A) which explains the much faster decline of the PTFR from considerably higher levels than in Iceland during the 1980s. At present, postponement among the youngest cohorts is progressing at a similar speed in the two countries, but Ireland still had declining fertility rates at ages above 30 till 1994, whereas Iceland has been displaying a rise since 1985.

1.3 Cohort fertility in Central and Eastern Europe

As is well known, the sudden political changes of 1989 marked a decisive turning point in the fertility trends of former communist countries. Of the 18 emerging nations, 15 had PTFRs above 1.80 in 1990 and 10 had PTFRs above replacement level. By 1993, 13 had PTFRs below 1.70 and 8 below 1.55. The PTFR drop was particularly pronounced in the former German Democratic Republic (PTFR in 1993 of barely 0.78), the Russian Federation (1.39), Slovenia (1.34), Bulgaria (1.46), Estonia (1.45), Romania (1.44), Latvia (1.51), Croatia (1.52) and Ukraine (1.55). In several countries, however, and most noticeably in the former Yugoslav republics, the decline had started earlier. For instance, Croatia and Slovenia started a Western-like postponement with the cohorts reaching adulthood after 1975. Also Bulgaria had declining fertility before age 30 starting with such early cohorts. Evidently, a number of communist countries had initiated the postponement phase well before the events of 1989.

The magnitude of the cohort fertility declines in the former communist countries can be appreciated from the indicators in table 3. D (as in table 2) gives the cumulated deficit of the cohorts reaching adulthood (ages 15-19) in 1990 compared with that of their predecessors of 1980 at the same age (see also D in figure III, with respect to the Bulgarian example). This youngest cohort started procreation almost entirely after 1989, and it is being compared with the cohort that started mainly in the 10 years preceding the end of the old regime. C and E (see also lines in figure III) show the deficit for older cohorts that had their fertility both before and after the events of 1989, and each of them is being compared with their respective predecessors that are 10 years older and had most or all of their fertility before that date.

		C. Middle cohort: cumulated deficit by age 30 for cohort reaching age group 15-19 in 1985 compared with predecessor of 1975	D. Youngest cohort: cumulated deficit by age 25 for cohort reaching age group 15-19 in 1990 compared with predecessor of 1980	E. Oldest cohort: cumulated deficit by age 35 for cohort reaching age group 15-19 in 1980 compared with predecessor of 1970
1.	Central and Eastern Europe			
	Germany[a]	-0.24	-0.33	+0.06
	Poland	-0.24	-0.36	-0.08
	Czech Republic	-0.25	-0.47	-0.11
	Slovakia	-0.23	-0.41	-0.11
	Hungary	-0.13	-0.39	+0.05
	Romania	-0.58	-0.51	-0.28
	Bulgaria	-0.31	-0.44	-0.19
2.	Former Soviet Union			
	Russian Federation	-0.20	-0.20	-0.11
	Ukraine	-0.16	-0.23	-0.16
	Belarus	-0.23	-0.19	-0.15
	Republic of Moldova	-0.30	-0.22	-0.13
	Estonia	-0.21	-0.33	-0.01
	Latvia	-0.12	-0.30	+0.01
	Lithuania	-0.17	-0.18	-0.11
3.	Former Yugoslavia			
	Slovenia	-0.39	-0.47	-0.10
	Croatia	-0.24	-0.33	-0.06
	Former Yugoslavia	-0.21	-0.24	-0.03
	FYR Macedonia[b]	-0.13	-0.14	-0.10
	Bosnia and Herzegovina	..	..	..

Source: Calculated from series of age-specific fertility rates in Council of Europe (1999).

NOTE: Indices C and D are the same as in table 2; multiplication by 100 gives the deviations in number of children per 100 women.

[a]German Democratic Republic.

[b]The former Yugoslav Republic of Macedonia.

By age 25, large fertility deficits are recorded for the "post-communist" cohorts in excess of 0.40 children in five countries: Romania (-0.51), the Czech Republic and Slovenia (-0.47), Bulgaria (-0.44) and Slovakia (-0.41). Very often, they also have sizeable reductions by age 30 for the cohort that reached adulthood in 1985, and particularly Romania, Bulgaria and Slovenia stand out in this respect. The declines in cohort fertility in the former parts of the Soviet Union are generally more modest than in the other Central and Eastern European countries, but among the former Soviet republics, the declines for the youngest cohort are highest in the two Baltic States of Estonia (-0.33) and Latvia (-0.30). In the republics of the former Yugoslavia, there is a clear north-south gradation with the strongest reaction in Slovenia and the smallest in the former Yugoslav Republic of Macedonia.

More generally, there seems to be a stronger reaction in countries that had higher standards of living and/or were more oriented towards the West, with Romania being the major exception. Hence, it is not so much absolute

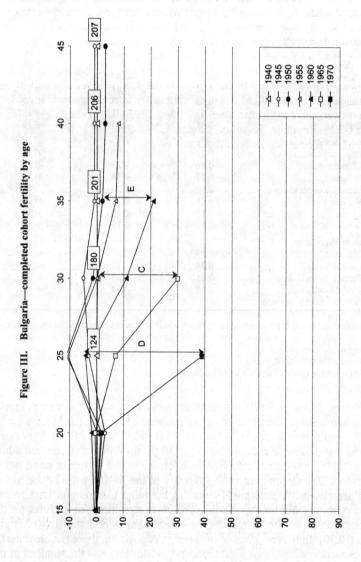

Figure III. Bulgaria—completed cohort fertility by age

deprivation (that is to say, actual living standards) as relative deprivation (measured against Western living styles and consumption aspirations) that seems to account for the more pronounced fertility reduction of younger cohorts after 1989. Nevertheless, it is the overall postponement for all cohorts and at all ages that has driven down the PTFRs in these populations.

Future PTFR levels are likely to remain depressed, but a rise could be envisaged when the younger "post-communist" cohorts decided to make up, at least partially, for currently postponed births. Given the historically rather narrow variance in the parity distributions (cf. Barkalov, 1999) and little progression beyond the second child, older cohorts are more likely to stop and take unrealized fertility for granted. A minor factor operating in the opposite direction—but socially a felicitous one—is the decline in teenage fertility and the end of the "teenage fertility bulge" that many former communist countries had experienced, roughly between 1975 and 1995 (for example, early bulges in the Czech Republic, Hungary, Romania, Slovenia and Croatia, and a later bulge in the former Soviet republics).

1.4 *Family policies (European Union) and experience with fertility policies (former German Democratic Republic, Russian Federation, Sweden)*

The overview of family policies during the 1990s is unfortunately limited to the 15 European Union (EU) countries, and a set of indicators is given in table 4. The first two indicators pertain to the length of maternity leave and the associated benefits expressed as a percentage of female wages. The second pair of indicators give the amount of child allowance benefits and the use of child day-care facilities for children between ages 3 and 5. The last pair gives the overall income transfers in euros (tax benefits included) per child for a household with three children and one earner and for a household with two children and two earners respectively.

The Scandinavian EU members have a long-standing policy of granting extensive maternity leaves (for example, 65 weeks in Sweden and 44 in Finland) with benefits covering 75-90 per cent of earnings. The maternity leave in Denmark is shorter, but still about twice the duration granted in the other EU States (commonly 14-16 weeks). At the tail of the distribution are the United Kingdom and Greece where the maternity leave benefits cover only 45 and 50 per cent, respectively, of monthly wages. The model form in EU, however, is the income supplement provided by child allowances. These correspond to more than 7 per cent of male wages in manufacturing in Austria (11.3), Belgium (10.4), Luxembourg (8.3), the Netherlands (7.4), Sweden (7.2) and France (7.1), although such income supplements have remained substantially below the EU average in Ireland (3.0), Spain (0.3) and Italy (0.0). Use and availability of day-care facilities for pre-school children (ages 3-5) are high in Belgium and France (96 per cent of children), Italy (86 per cent), Denmark (85 per cent) and Sweden (80 per cent), but still low in the Netherlands and Luxembourg (55 per cent) and Finland (50 per cent) and particularly low in the United Kingdom and Portugal (35 per cent). Taking also into account tax benefits for children and various other subsidies for families with children,

TABLE 4. OVERVIEW OF FAMILY POLICY INDICATORS IN THE EUROPEAN UNION

	Duration of maternity leave (weeks), 1996	Maternity leave benefits (percentage of salary), 1996	Children allowance (percentage of male wages in manufacturing), 1990	Percentage of children aged 3-5 in day care, 1998	Net monthly contribution per child (euros)	
					(a) Three children: 1 earner, 1996	(b) Two children: 2 earners, 1996
Sweden	65	75	7.2	80	514	151
Finland	44	80	6.2	50	389	210
Denmark	28	90	5.2	85	191	128
Germany	14	100	4.9	65	323	184
Netherlands	16	100	7.4	55	178	-2
Belgium	15	80	10.4	96	463	266
Luxembourg	16	100	8.3	55	510	766
Austria	16	100	11.3	..	332	199
France	16	84	7.1	96	517	229
United Kingdom	18	45	6.3	35	484	119
Ireland	14	70	3.0	..	389	8
Spain	16	100	0.3	65	43	13
Italy	20	80	0.0	86	210	-68
Portugal	14	100	4.9	35	32	36
Greece	16	50	3.2	65	-338	-155

Sources: De Santis (1999), Ditch and others (1998), Gauthier (1996) and van Solinge and others (1998).

single-earner families with three children and an income at 50 per cent of the male average are benefiting most (provided that they pay taxes) in France (517 euros per month), Sweden (514 euros per month), Luxembourg (510 euros per month), the United Kingdom (484 euros per month) and Belgium (463 euros per month), and least in Spain (43 euros per month), Portugal (32 euros per month) and particularly in Greece where they suffer a loss (-338 euros per month). In most countries, such transfers remain positive for dual-earner families with two children and an income at par with 150 per cent of male average earnings. In Luxembourg, they benefit even more than much poorer families (766 euros per month), and in Greece their loss is smaller (-155 euros per month). In the Netherlands, Ireland, Italy and Portugal, such children-related transfers have become negligible for such better-off families.

A simple multiple regression indicates that these incentives and transfers are related to the PTFR. In this regression, we have used the duration of maternity leaves weighted by the proportion of guaranteed income (MATPAY) and the average of the transfers paid to the two types of families used in table 4 (TRANSF). The regression equation is

100 x PTFR	= 138.3	+	0.06 TRANSF	+	0.14 MATPAY
Beta-coefficient	=		0.55		0.07
t	=		2.27		0.27
significance	=		0.03		ns
adjusted R square	=	0.21			

The addition of the percentage of children ages 3-5 in day care did not produce any positive effect. Since the ranking of countries according to PTFR and their family policies has remained almost the same since the mid-1980s, these regression results for 1996 measurements have a more general validity. Despite an overall significant correlation, an extra monthly transfer of 100 euros would increase 100 x PTFR by 6 percentage points only and an extra 10 weeks of maternity leave at full pay by only 1.4 percentage points. These calculations are of course simply illustrative since the populations in the various countries are accustomed to their national policies and individuals do not yet compare themselves across national boundaries in EU.

Experiments with actual policy interventions produce more convincing results. The former German Democratic Republic, the Russian Federation and Sweden provide examples. The effects can be followed in table 5 in the cohort age-specific fertility rates.

In the former German Democratic Republic, a clear dip in fertility was produced immediately after the liberalization of abortion in 1972, showing that a substantial proportion of pregnancies had been unintended. In 1976, this policy was reversed and pronatalist legislation was passed that prolonged maternity leaves and increased maternity payments of up to one year for working mothers with at least two children (cf. Büttner and Lutz, 1990). This had a positive effect of a considerable magnitude, but by the beginning of the 1980s the cohort fertility profiles simply resumed their downward trend. Immediately after the *Wende*, this trend accelerated and produced record low PTFRs with the absolute trough of 0.77 being reached in 1994.

401

TABLE 5. COHORT AGE-SPECIFIC FERTILITY RATES IN THREE COUNTRIES WITH FERTILITY POLICY INTERVENTIONS

ASFR at age	Cohort aged 15-19 in:								ASFR max/ASFR previous cohort
	1960	1965	1970	1975	1980	1985	1990	1995	
1. Former GDR									
15-19	42	79	43	33	39	31	23	8	1.18
20-24	184	187	144	183	158	135	55		1.27
25-29	112	88	114	110	100	66			1.30
30-34	30	42	39	36	28				1.40
35-39	42	39	10	9					-
40-44	2	2	2						
									Mean = 1.29
2. Russian Federation									
15-19	27	25	30	35	44	47	56	46	1.07
20-24	148	153	159	158	166	157	114		1.05
25-29	116	108	102	118	93	67			1.16
30-34	60	52	63	48	30				1.21
35-39	22	25	19	11					1.14
40-44	4	4	2						-
									Mean = 1.13
3. Sweden									
15-19	35	49	34	29	16	11	14	9	1.27
20-24	141	120	115	96	82	99	66		1.21
25-29	129	123	124	132	156	126			1.18
30-34	64	71	89	110	99				1.24
35-39	25	30	41	44					1.37
40-44	6	7	7						
									Mean = 1.20

Source: Council of Europe (1999), country-specific tables X-3.

NOTE: ASFR per 1,000 women.

In the former Union of Soviet Socialist Republics (USSR), there has been a clear effect of the pronatalist policies of 1981 as well. Then, the equivalent of 30-60 per cent of the average salary was granted at each new birth, maternity leave was prolonged to up to a full year with partial salary (20 per cent only) or longer without remuneration, and access was given to favourable loans (Avdeev and Monnier, 1994). At that time, cohort ASFRs rose on average by 13 per cent (see table 5) and PTFRs stayed above replacement level for seven years. After 1989, however, this effect was simply wiped out, and a steep decline in PTFRs started.

In Sweden, a similar fertility rise occurred in the late 1980s, bringing the PTFR back to 2.14 in 1990, the highest level since the 1960s. The direct cause of this was an extra prolongation of the already long maternity leave. It enabled women to cumulate two maternity leaves by closely spacing two successive births. Cohort ASFRs then rose on average by 20 per cent and these rises are rather similar for all age groups (see table 5) (Hoem and Hoem, 1997; Andersson, 1999). Subsequent cutbacks in social provisions and rising unemployment—a novelty in Sweden—produced a backlash (Hoem, 1998). Also, many couples had reached their desired final family size a bit earlier than otherwise anticipated, and all cohorts irrespective of age curtailed fertility after 1990. The Swedish PTFR then dropped steadily to 1.53 in 1997. In Sweden's Nordic neighbours, such a policy induced a bulge, and their PTFRs continued to increase steadily to levels of at least 1.80 in the mid-1990s, mainly as a result of strong recuperation effects at older ages.

These three cases illustrate that policy interventions in either direction can have very noticeable effects on period total fertility, but that these seldom last for more than five years. Cohorts adjust to such period stimuli by either postponing births or by moving them forward, only to resume a more stable long-term fertility trend thereafter. Clearly, the other societal changes of a socio-economic or cultural nature are far stronger determinants. The lesson learned by other countries is that pronatalist fertility policies are costly, given their temporary effect. To sustain fertility for a substantially longer period, such incentives would need to "snowball" for the next 15 years or so until the expenditure becomes so large that it runs directly into competition with the increasing costs of ageing. Beside this, there are of course interventions that were never tried before. One of them is to make pensions in the pay-as-you-go system partially dependent on procreation as well as on production, that is to say, on the number of children as well as on past earnings. However, it is highly questionable whether Western publics or politicians are ready to accept this logic of unfunded pensions.

II. HOUSEHOLD FORMATION

2.1. *Home-leaving and household formation: destandardization and diversity*

The most salient characteristics of Europe's "second demographic transition" are all associated with the destandardization of patterns of home-leaving and household formation. Destandardization refers to the fact that the classic ordering of transitions during the life course, and particularly in age bracket 18-30, has been altered. The sequence of first finishing school, subsequently entering into the labour force, then home-leaving via marriage and finally becoming a parent is being reordered in ever-larger segments of the population. New phases of single living, sharing dwellings with age mates, premarital cohabitation and parenthood prior to marriage with or without a partner have been added, and these can occur before the end of education or before the entry into the labour force as well.

The destandardization is predicated on both structural and cultural factors (cf. Liefbroer, 1999), but these tend to act differentially on the various ingredients of the new patterns. Moreover, historical context matters quite a bit and developments are strongly path-dependent. Diversity should therefore not come as a surprise. A list of determinants would include the following:

(*a*) The prolongation of education and the "democratization" of access to higher education. Advanced education has a mechanistic effect in postponing home-leaving or marriage, but it also produces a cluster of additional effects such as increased female economic autonomy, decreased reliance on economic support from male partners, a longer search on the marriage market in systems with educational homogamy (cf. Oppenheimer, 1988) and shifting value preferences;

(*b*) The emergence of a more libertarian culture with greater tolerance for alternative lifestyles, which has followed in the wake of the overall weakening of authority and trust in institutional regularization. As such, this feature is a correlate of the cohortwise progression of the so-called post-materialist value orientations which stress grass-roots democracy, self-actualization, tolerance and ethical autonomy (cf. Inglehart, 1970; Lesthaeghe and Surkyn, 1988). The innovators of premarital cohabitation have often been persons with sympathies for the new left during the 1960s and 1970s (Lesthaeghe and van de Kaa, 1986) and, even today, premarital cohabitation has remained a correlate of secularism, tolerance for minorities, relativism in ethics, gender equality, non-conformist education values, and a preference for leftist or green parties in countries such as Germany, France, the Netherlands and Belgium (Lesthaeghe and Moors, 1995, 1996);

(*c*) The expansion of the welfare State, which has fostered earlier partial or complete economic independence of younger people via income supplements (for example, study allowances, reduced tuition, guaranteed minimum incomes or other social security benefits) or via specific services and facilities often destined for particular groups (for example, students, lone mothers). Earlier independence and premarital cohabitation have to some degree been State-subsidized and have expanded most in nations with advanced welfare systems (Scandinavia, the Netherlands) and least in nations where young adults are mostly dependent on parental resources (Southern Europe). This also implies that the spread of early single living and cohabitation is more dependent on the type of development of the welfare State than on the growth of economic prosperity in general;

(*d*) The intergenerational transmission of family instability has also repeatedly been identified as a crucial factor associated with earlier home-leaving, single living, cohabitation and lone motherhood. Not only is the actual experience of problems in the parental household, such as divorce or re-marriage, a correlate of these phenomena (see, for example, Kiernan, 1992; Cherlin and others, 1995), but also weaker familistic values in the parental generation seem to be transmitted across generations (see, for example, Axinn and Thornton, 1991). As a consequence, certain social strata can generate sub-cultures in which family instability becomes a characteristic trait;

(*e*) Growing labour-market flexibility leading to less secure and less structured career development also seems to be associated with the destand-ardization of the life course in young adulthood. Premarital cohabitation and the postponement of parenthood are responses to periods of job insecurity or interim phases during the period of career development (see, for example, Easterlin and others, 1990; Kravdal, 1999).

To this basic list, another set of features can be added that are of impor-tance in more specific settings:

(*a*) Cycles characterized by weakened economic opportunities for new cohorts, with increased youth unemployment leading to prolonged economic dependence on the parental household (for example, in Southern Europe dur-ing the 1980s);

(*b*) Unfavourable housing conditions, caused either by a structural housing shortage or by high rents or high purchase prices (see, for example, Miret-Gamundi, 1997);

(*c*) Rising consumerism leading to higher aspirations with respect to material comfort and to higher minimal material standards for establishing a new household (Easterlin, 1976; Crimmins and others, 1991);

(*d*) Mechanisms of social diffusion that either foster or inhibit the spreading of alternative lifestyles or patterns of household formation from the early innovators to other strata of the population. These factors are often tied to the social stratification system (see, for example, Kohn, 1977) and to param-eters of social cohesion;

(*e*) More idiosyncratic or culture-specific factors, such as the survival of three-generation households in Eastern Europe, or the rise of individual and autonomous partner choice replacing arranged marriages in Japan (cf. Ogawa and Retherford, 1993; Tsuya and Oppenheim-Mason, 1995; Retherford and others, 1996).

2.2. *The household position of young women in Europe*

The differences in patterns of household formation across countries can be documented by comparing the household positions of women aged 20-24. It is in this age group that the unfolding of the life course starts. In what follows we shall make use of the results of the Fertility and Family Surveys (FFS) for the 1990s and various other sources that give orders of magnitude of premarital cohabitation (Kiernan, 1999a, 1999b).

First of all, the plotting of the percentage of non-marital births to all births against the proportion of young women cohabiting, as shown in figure IV, reveals that there are essentially four patterns:

(*a*)   Low extramarital fertility coupled with a low incidence of premarital cohabitation: this pattern is found in the Mediterranean countries, in Poland and in Japan. In these instances, the proportion of extramarital births is below 15 per cent and there are fewer than 5 per cent of women aged 20-24 currently cohabiting. However, in Spain and even more in Portugal, the percentage of non-marital births has steadily increased to Western European levels. Italy is the most striking counter-example: despite rapid rises in female education, premarital cohabitation has hardly followed the European trend. However, the mean ages at first marriage in all Mediterranean countries have risen quite substantially, as in the other Western nations;

(*b*)   Low prevalence of cohabitation but high non-marital fertility: this pattern is typically the lone-mother variant and it is encountered in Eastern European countries, but also in Portugal, Ireland, the United Kingdom and the United States. However, not all lone mothers must show up in their own separate household; they can also be co-residents in their parental household, which then comprises three generations. FFS published data do not permit the identification of such arrangements, and it may well be that the lone-mother phenomenon in Eastern Europe is underestimated as a result. The bulges of teenage fertility, referred to earlier, further fuel the suspicion that such three-generation households with lone mothers may be more common in Eastern Europe. Also, women may pass through the lone-mother stage for a shorter time-span and then move into marriage at an earlier age. This would equally lead to a combination of higher non-marital fertility and low premarital cohabitation in tandem with earlier mean ages at marriage;

(*c*)   High prevalence of cohabitation but low non-marital fertility: this combination is typical for the more conservative Western European populations where cohabitation has risen but where parenthood is postponed until after a formal marriage. This pattern is found in Switzerland, where a quarter of young women are currently cohabiting but in combination with less than 10 per cent of births being out of wedlock. Belgium, the Netherlands and West Germany also tend to follow this pattern, but extramarital fertility has risen well above the 10 per cent level during the 1990s. These countries are gradually moving towards the next type;

(*d*)   High prevalence of cohabitation combined with parenthood: this combination has been typical for a long time now in the Scandinavian countries, with Sweden, Denmark and also Iceland being outliers with more than 40 per cent of young women currently in a cohabiting union. A number of other Western countries, such as France and Canada, and a Baltic country, Estonia, have followed in this direction at a respectable pace. In these cases, most non-marital fertility occurs within cohabiting couples, and these tend either to be more stable or to be quickly succeeded by partner changes and transitions to a next consensual union.

More detailed data for 20 FFS countries are brought together in table 6. For these countries, we are able to make a distinction between the following household positions of women aged 20-24:

Figure IV.   Percentage of non-marital births by percentage of women aged 20-24 cohabiting, 1996-1997

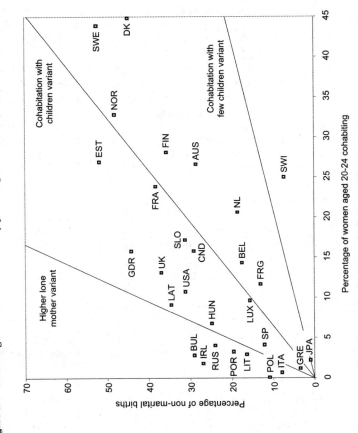

TABLE 6. DISTRIBUTION OF WOMEN AGED 20-24 ACCORDING TO HOUSEHOLD POSITIONS, FERTILITY AND FAMILY SURVEYS (FFS) COUNTRIES IN THE 1990S

(*Percentage*)

	Resident with parents[a]	Living alone	Cohab. no children	Cohab. with children	Lone mother (not co-residing)	Married no children	Married with children
A. Southern Europe							
Italy	87	1	1	0	0	4	7
Spain	71	1	3	1	2	6	13
Portugal	75	1	3	0	4	8	18
Mean	79	1	3	0	2	6	13
B. Eastern and Central Europe							
Bulgaria	50	1	2	2	5	8	33
Poland	55	1	0	0	3	14	37
Latvia	54	7	5	4	11	7	29
Lithuania	51	6	2	1	5	14	38
Slovenia	54	3	8	9	4	4	25
Hungary	46	3	4	3	4	12	34
Mean	52	4	4	3	5	10	33
C. Western Europe							
Belgium/Flanders.	54	3	10	2	1	23	9
Netherlands	44	15	20	1	1	10	6
France.	41	17	19	5	4	6	8
Canada	37	9	13	3	7	9	10
Austria	38	12	20	7	6	4	8
Switzerland	36	17	24	1	1	8	7
Germany (former GDR)	30	15	8	8	6	5	27
Germany (former FRG)	37	22	11	1	2	7	12
Mean	40	14	16	4	4	9	11
D. Northern Europe							
Norway[b]	16	18	21	12	5	9	16
Sweden[b]	8	27	32	12	5	4	19
Mean	12	23	27	12	5	7	17

Source: FFS country reports, appendix table 4.

[a]For those residing with parents, we do not know whether they are single or not (that is to say, couples with or without children, lone mothers). Owing to the status of the entries in this column, the row totals are not equal to 100 per cent.

[b]At age 23, rather than for age group 20-24.

(*a*) Resident in the parental household, which is mostly as a single person in Western Europe, but could also be as a lone mother or as a married person in Eastern Europe;

(*b*) Living alone, that is to say, without partner or children;

(*c*) Cohabiting without children, that is to say, not currently married but with a partner;

(*d*) Cohabiting with children;

(*e*) Lone mother, that is to say, without partner but with children and living in a separate household;

(*f*) Married without children, and forming a separate household;

(*g*)   Married with children, also forming a separate household.

In table 6, averages are also calculated for each of the geopolitical areas, and these reveal the differences between four "families" of countries. The Southern European group is characterized by very high proportions of women aged 20-24 (about 80 per cent) still co-resident in the parental household, by a direct move into marriage, and by few women passing through the intermediate stages of living on their own or cohabiting. These are also countries where students of either sex (aged 15-24) are more than 90 per cent dependent on parental support and more rarely draw supplementary incomes from scholarships (less than 5 per cent) or from jobs (less than 20 per cent) (Organisation for Economic Co-operation and Development (OECD), 1999).

The Eastern European group also has a predominant pattern of home-leaving via marriage and, given a long tradition of early marriage, this cluster has the highest proportion of young married mothers as well. The percentages in the intermediate living arrangements, namely, living alone, cohabiting or being a lone mother, are slightly higher than in Southern Europe. It seems that these features may be spreading more rapidly eastward than southward.

The Western European cluster has a pattern of home-leaving that is essentially as early as in Eastern Europe, but the transition is not to marriage but to alternative living arrangements. In these countries, the prevalence of cohabitation with or without children is often higher than that of marriage for women 20-24 (for example, in the Netherlands, France, Austria and Switzerland). In these countries, the late ages at marriage and at parenthood are strongly related to the extra time spent in these intermediate household positions. Moreover, economic dependence on parents among young adults is much lower than in Southern Europe: a quarter to half derive supplementary incomes from jobs (Germany, 41 per cent; and United Kingdom, 46 per cent) and from 10 to over 40 per cent of students (for example, the Netherlands, 44 per cent) have State fellowships (Organisation for Economic Co-operation and Development (OECD), 1999). Only Belgium has a more conservative pattern of stronger reliance on parents (88 per cent), as its fellowship programme withered away during the 1980s and as part-time jobs remained rare until the mid-1990s.

Finally, the Northern European populations are characterized by the earliest home-leaving pattern of all, and by transitions either to living alone or to cohabitation. Moreover, procreation has been detached from the preconditions of marriage and, as a consequence, fertility postponement during the last two decades has not been as strong as in many Western European countries. Such early independence has also been fostered by social policies. Among students, large proportions benefit from State fellowships (35 per cent in Finland, 46 per cent in Denmark) and many secure income supplements in the large part-time job market (Sweden 30 per cent, Finland 37 per cent and Denmark 59 per cent) (Organisation for Economic Co-operation and Development (OECD), 1999).

The above pattern indicates that the growth of alternative living arrangements is predicated not only on historical traditions but also on welfare State policies towards youths and young adults (State fellowships, subsidized housing and/or transportation) and on an earlier deregulation of the labour market (availability of part-time jobs). These policies may not have been intended to stimulate the growth of alternative living arrangements, but over the years they did produce such a result.

To sum up, policies that were clearly intended to change fertility trends have so far not been able to do so in the longer run, but more general policies supporting students, combined with educational expansion, have provided an extra prop for the growth of alternative living arrangements.

III. REPLACEMENT MIGRATION

3.1. *Old lessons from basic demography*

The issue of replacement migration is by no means a new topic in formal demography. In 1972, for instance, A. J. Coale started with the reverse problem for the United States: assuming an initial stationary population and a fixed number of immigrants (with a fixed age composition), he asked by how much native American fertility would have to decline in order to offset the impact of immigrants and their fertility, the aim being the maintenance of a stationary population with the same annual number of births. At that time, the United States was obviously worried about rapid population expansion, and zero population growth (ZPG) was viewed as a national target. Replacement migration deals with the mirror image of Coale's problem, and the application of his calculations yields the results presented in table 7. In this table, we have computed (Lesthaeghe and others, 1988, 1991) what the fertility of native women (TFR_n) would need to be, given three levels of fertility of immigrants (TFR_f) and four levels of immigration, expressed as a percentage of the fixed birth stream (I/B). The current birth stream of EU is 3.89 million, and an annual immigrant intake of 10 per cent of that number would suffice to maintain a stationary population if immigrant women had replacement fertility ($TFR_f = 2.1$) and native women had a TFR_n of 1.94. If TFR_n drops to 1.84 children, while TFR_f stays at 2.1, the immigrant intake needs to be 20 per cent of the birth stream. Obviously, if fertility of immigrants is higher and remains at that level, the TFR_n of natives can be lower. For instance, with I/B ratio of 20 per cent and a constant TFR_f of 3.0 children, the TFR_n is allowed to drop from 1.84 to 1.75. Applied to EU, if the TFR_n is 1.59, a stationary population could be maintained if foreign women have a constant TFR_f of 3.0 and if the annual intake of immigrants is slightly over 1 million per year. Similarly, with a TFR_n of 1.62, EU would need an annual intake of just over 1.5 million immigrants if these had replacement fertility. Incidentally, this theoretical outcome is very close to the simulation results of the United Nations (2001; see also table 8, column 1): around 2040, about 1.42 million immigrants per year will be needed to maintain the EU population size at its present level. The orders of magnitude are hence quite clear: the annual number of immigrants in EU will have to rise and then stay well above 1 million in order to compensate for sustained low native fertility corresponding to a TFR_n of about 1.6 children, given that immigrants themselves maintain their own fertility at replacement levels or slightly higher (up to $TFR_f = 3.0$). For this immigration to be cut down to 20 per cent of the birth stream or to about 0.8 million per year, the EU native TFR

TABLE 7. FRACTIONS OF THE ANNUAL BIRTH STREAM THAT WOULD NEED TO BE FILLED BY IMMIGRANTS (I/B) IN ORDER TO MAINTAIN A STATIONARY POPULATION, GIVEN VARIOUS TOTAL FERTILITY RATES OF LOCALLY (TFR_N) AND FOREIGN-BORN (TFR_F) WOMEN

TFR_f fertility, foreign-born women	TFR_n fertility, native women	I/B: required number of immigrants as percentage of birth stream	Implied annual number of immigrants to EU in order to maintain current birth stream (3,892,000)[a]
2.1	1.94	10	389 200
3.0	1.90	10	
4.0	1.85	10	
2.1	1.84	20	778 400
3.0	1.75	20	
4.0	1.64	20	
2.1	1.73	30	1 167 600
3.0	1.59	30	
4.0	1.44	30	
2.1	1.62	40	1 556 800
3.0	1.44	40	
4.0	1.24	40	

Source: Lesthaeghe and others (1988).

[a]In order to maintain a stationary EU population of its current size (in other words, 372 million) and with a life expectancy for both sexes of 80 years, the birth stream would need to be 4,655,500 per annum instead of the 3,892,000 births used here. With this assumption for life expectancy and the latter-mentioned birth stream, the EU stationary population would only be 311 million instead of 372 million.

would have to rise to about 1.8 children. From the previous section on cohort fertility, it is clear that this is not likely to occur in the next decade.

So far, total population size has been the only criterion. Other authors have looked at different constraints, imposing age structure criteria as well. From then onward, more serious problems are encountered, as already signalled, for instance, by Bodart and others (1977) and by Blanchet (1988). The latter author showed how the criterion of a fixed ratio of persons aged 20-60 to persons 60+ leads to exploding cyclic net migration rates. For instance, the French migration rate would have to increase first to about +20 per thousand by 2010 until 2030, then decline to about -15 per thousand by 2040 and then rise again in 10 years to +30 per thousand in 2050. With a cycle of about 35 years, a new peak would be produced in 2085, but with a net migration rate of +50 per thousand. For comparison, the French net migration averaged only 0.9 per thousand in the 1990s and, at peak level, it was only 3.5 per thousand in 1970. Furthermore, the French population would expand to about 120 million by 2080 as well, which is more than twice its current size. For EU as a whole, the outcomes of the United Nations simulation with a constant "potential support ratio" (PSR = population 15-64/population 65+) is of necessity in line with Blanchet's prediction (see table 8, series C): the annual number of immigrants oscillates between 6 million and 20 million during the next half-century for EU and between 6 million and 22 million for the other European countries

TABLE 8. AVERAGE ANNUAL NUMBER OF IMMIGRANTS NEEDED TO MEET THREE DEMOGRAPHIC CRITERIA, AND RESULTING POPULATION SIZES, EUROPE, 2000-2050

	Criteria					
	A. Constant population size		B. Constant size age group 15-64		C. Constant ratio 15-64/65+	
	Annual number of immigrants needed[a] (thousands)	Index population size[b]	Annual number of immigrants needed (thousands)	Index population size	Annual number of immigrants needed (thousands)	Index population size
1. European Union						
2000	263	100.0	396	100.0	6 171	100.7
2010	663	100.0	1 596	100.3	9 012	123.8
2020	869	100.0	2 424	103.5	12 947	151.9
2030	1 216	100.0	2 407	108.9	20 346	200.9
2040	1 416	100.0	1 063	112.2	16 483	266.5
2050	-	100.0	-	112.4	-	329.8
2. Other European						
2000	800	100.0	-396	100.0	6 239	100.8
2010	487	100.0	2 046	96.7	8 222	103.4
2020	1 010	100.0	2 423	101.7	16 870	137.0
2030	1 155	100.0	1 104	104.9	9 764	183.6
2040	1 249	100.0	2 467	106.4	22 380	227.1
2050	-	100.0	-	111.4	-	318.6

Source: United Nations (2001), tables A.18 and A.20.

[a]Average number per annum during the next five years (thousands).

[b]Index = 100 corresponds to 372 million in EU and 351 million in the rest of Europe.

combined. Moreover, the populations of EU and of the rest of Europe would have more than tripled by 2050. In the United Nations simulation, this is exacerbated by the hypothesis that migrants instantaneously adopt the low fertility of the host population (United Nations, 2001, p. 15), so that this scenario corresponds indeed to the filling of the "Tonneau des Danaïdes" (a bottomless cask) (Leridon, 2000). From this, it is clear that an instantaneous reaction via immigration with respect to maintaining a constant PSR at all times is plainly impossible.

As already indicated by Blanchet (1988) and supported by simulations for several countries (Wattelar and Roumans, 1990), the only feasible way of tackling the problem is to focus on a long-term demographic objective and to abandon any attempt at equilibrating age structure characteristics on an annual basis. Hence, one could envisage the longer-term maintenance of the volume of the potential active population or aim at a PSR of the order of 2.5 or 3 potentially active persons per person 65+ via a constant immigration rate. This would avoid such unrealistic population growth rates, but would still imply annual migration intakes that are substantially larger than the ones witnessed in EU over the last four decades. As a consequence, the two other projections performed by the United Nations are less unrealistic—but unfortunately those did not capture the attention of the media. We are referring here to the simulation with constant population size (projection A in table 8) and with a constant size for age group 15-64 (projection B).

Aiming at a constant population requires the smallest intake of immigrants, but the numbers still increase to a total of 1.4 million per annum for 2040-2045 for EU and to 1.25 million per annum for the rest of Europe for the same period. Furthermore, these numbers would continue to increase given the United Nations hypothesis of migrants' instantaneous adoption of sub-replacement fertility upon entry. Obviously, such a further increase can be avoided if immigrants maintain a TFR_f above 2.1 (see table 7). The drawback of this scenario is that the PSR for EU drops from 4.1 in 2000 to 3.1 in 2020 and further to 2.2 in 2050, and, concomitantly, that the proportion aged 65+ rises from 16.5 per cent in 2000 to 21.0 per cent in 2050. Ageing of the total population and ageing of the labour force itself cannot be stopped, but they can be limited. In the absence of migration, the proportion of age group 65+ in EU in 2050 would reach 30 per cent, assuming a relatively optimistic course of fertility corresponding to the United Nations medium variant.

The United Nations scenario aiming at a constant size for age group 15-64 requires a far more rapidly rising intake of immigrants to a very high level of 2.8 million per annum in the period 2025-2030 for EU. Thereafter, the numbers drop to just over a million in the middle of the century, but they would increase very substantially again when the record intake of the years 2020-2029 crossed the age boundary of 64 about 40 years later. Here we are again forcefully encountering the problem of self-perpetuating and ever-amplifying cycles. The gain in terms of the PSR are minimal compared with the previous set aiming at a constant overall population size: the PSR still declines from 4 in 2000 to 3.17 (compared with 3.07) in 2020 and to 2.41 (compared with 2.21) in 2050. The proportion 65+ stabilizes at 24.7 per cent in 2050 in projection B compared with 26.3 per cent in projection A. Also, in the former scenario, there is a modest overall population increase by 2050 of 12.4 per cent. To keep the PSR with the United Nations definition at 4 for EU, the minimum actual age at leaving the labour force would have to rise to about 74 years in scenario A and to about 72 years in scenario B. With zero migration, this age would be 76 years (United Nations, 2001, table A.20).

Once more it becomes obvious that immigration cannot stop ageing and that there is a steep price to be paid for all the past years of sub-replacement fertility. Also, record numbers of immigrants between 1.0 million and 2.5 million per year in EU can only modestly alleviate the ageing problem.

3.2. *More detailed simulations of total labour supply*

P. McDonald and R. Kippen (2001) provide different scenarios in which not only the migration parameter is allowed to vary but also fertility and labour-force participation. We have summarized their results in table 9 by means of index = 100 for the current levels of the total labour-force supply (TLFS) and the total population size (TPOP), respectively.

In scenario A, all three parameters—the total fertility rate (TFR), the annual number of immigrants (ANM) and the labour-force participation rates (LFPR)—are held constant at the current levels. In each of the other scenarios, one of these three parameters is allowed to vary. In scenario B, the annual intake of immigrants leads to a net migration rate equivalent to 0.5 per cent of the present population size and is kept constant thereafter. For EU as a whole, this corresponds to an intake of no less than 1.86 million per annum. Hence, the hypothesis squarely falls in the category of record immigration assumed by the United Nations (cf. table 8, hypothesis B) and the intake is even larger than the numbers needed to maintain a stationary population with low native fertility (cf. table 7). Nevertheless, an annual intake of 0.5 per cent of current population size corresponds approximately to the immigration stream of Canada or Australia. We also suspect that the authors assume instant adaptation of immigrant fertility to that of the host country.

In scenario C, the labour-force participation rates are increased over a period of 30 years. For men, this implies a rise in LFPRs after age 35 to the levels that prevailed in 1970. For several EU countries (for example, Belgium, France and Finland), such a return means a very substantial drop in non-activity rates for men older than 55 years of age, but in a number of other countries (for example, Denmark, Sweden, Norway and Switzerland), this is a rather "light hypothesis" (cf. Punch and Pierce, 2000, p. 55). For women, the LFPRs increase to the current Swedish levels, equally over a period of 30 years. In full-time equivalents, this implies a substantial rise of female labour-force participation for countries such as Italy, Spain, Greece, Belgium and the Netherlands, but also for EU as a whole when compared with the United States (Punch and Pierce, 2000, p. 68). Scenario D, finally, assumes a TFR rise to the level of 1.80 children over a period of 10 to 15 years. This is a strong assumption for European populations that have at present TFR levels below 1.50.

	A. TFR constant ANM constant LFPR constant	B. TFR constant ANM = 0.5 per cent of population LFPR constant	C. TFR constant ANM constant LFPR rise to 1970/Swedish benchmark	D. TFR rise to 1.8 ANM constant LFPR constant
1. Low-fertility countries				
Italy TLFS 2025	82	96	112	83
TLFS 2050	60	82	82	78
TPOP 2050	77	98	77	96
Spain TLFS 2025	88	102	118	90
TLFS 2050	59	85	81	76
TPOP 2050	74	102	74	94
Germany TLFS 2025	86	94	103	88
TLFS 2050	69	86	83	83
TPOP 2050	83	100	83	99
Japan TLFS 2025	82	104	99	89
TLFS 2050	68	100	78	75
TPOP 2050	76	112	76	87
2. Medium-level-fertility countries				
United Kingdom TLFS 2025	100	116	112	100
TLFS 2050	89	121	101	92
TPOP 2050	97	129	97	100
France TLFS 2025	98	117	114	98
TLFS 2050	84	123	102	89
TPOP 2050	102	136	102	103
Sweden TLFS 2025	98	111	100	98
TLFS 2050	86	109	87	95
TPOP 2050	93	117	93	103
Netherlands TLFS 2025	93	104	119	94
TLFS 2050	86	103	109	92
TPOP 2050	100	119	100	106
3. High-fertility country				
United States TLFS 2025	115	122	124	114
TLFS 2050	126	143	136	116
TPOP 2050	135	151	135	122

Source: McDonald and Kippen (2001), computed from graphs and tables.

NOTE: "Current levels" refer to 1995 for France, Sweden, Germany and Italy; to 1997 for the United Kingdom; to 1998 for the Netherlands; and to 1999 for Japan and the United States of America.

TFR = total fertility rate; ANM = annual migration rate; LFPR = labour-force participation rate.

A number of conclusions are already clear before turning to the results. Obviously, the rising fertility hypothesis can produce results only in the longer run: it takes 20 years for children to enter the labour force. The immigration and labour-force participation scenarios are by definition more important in the shorter run, but the latter can only have a temporary effect. Once the labour-force participation benchmarks are reached, there are no further gains from this intervention, and the demography of low fertility will simply take over. Hence, it comes as no surprise that rising participation rates are often offered as a solution, particularly if the time-horizon is restricted to 2020 or 2025 (see, for example, Feld, 2000), but one is quite mistaken to assume that this factor can prevent a decline in the labour supply thereafter. The time path of the effect of each intervention is therefore of major importance as well.

The results of the McDonald and Kippen scenarios are presented for selected countries grouped according to their past fertility levels, since the outcomes illustrate equally the price to be paid for sustained low fertility. With all three input parameters maintained at current levels (scenario A in table 9), the labour-force supplies in countries such as Italy, Spain, Germany and Japan would fall to about 85 per cent of their current level by 2025 and to about 65 per cent by 2050. In Italy and Spain, the reduction would be larger still (index = 60 and 59, respectively), reflecting their very low fertility. Also, the overall population size would be reduced to about three quarters of current size by 2050. Immigration scenario B prevents much of such a drop in the labour-force supply, but it can stop it entirely only in Japan where it would also lead to 12 per cent population growth. Hence, in this group Japan is the only case for which a slightly lower fixed migration intake could suffice. In scenario C, the rises in labour-force participation rates produce the expected shorter-run effect by 2025, but no longer thereafter, and then least of all in Japan. Also, the population decline can obviously not be avoided by this intervention. Rising fertility, finally, would fail to produce an effect before 2025, but would limit the damage by 2050. Population sizes would still be smaller too, given that the TFR of 1.80 is inadequate for replacement.

In the next group, comprising the United Kingdom, France, Sweden and the Netherlands, the outcomes of scenario A are less dramatic: until 2025, there would be only small reductions in the labour-force supply, and by 2050 the fall would be limited to about 15 per cent of the current level. The immigration scenario with a fixed intake of 0.5 per cent of current population size is also overshooting the target since it would produce an increase both in labour-force supply and in population size. Clearly, this parameter could be scaled down below the 0.5 per cent assumption. Rising LFPRs would also correct the situation and actually do so until 2050, except in Sweden where these rates are at present already high enough. Rising fertility would also limit the drop in labour supply to 5-10 per cent but, compared with the LFPR rises of the previous scenario, this would be less efficient by 2050 in France, the United Kingdom and the Netherlands, and more efficient in Sweden and other EU countries with a current high level of labour-force participation.

Finally, in the United States no interventions are needed: even at fixed current parameter values, the labour supply will expand and so will the total population. The United States therefore maintains a considerable demographic advantage over EU and Japan. Furthermore, the United States could even benefit from raising current LFPRs and from less immigration since this would lead to a larger labour force relative to overall population growth. Also, even if fertility drops from replacement level at present to a TFR of 1.80, both American labour supply and total population size would continue to expand over the next half-century.

To sum up, rises in LFPRs are clearly most beneficial in the shorter run for maintaining the labour supply at acceptable levels in most EU countries, and particularly in those where such participation rates were allowed to shrink for men older than 50 and/or where female participation rates expressed in full-time equivalents are still too low. On the other hand, this policy is likely to be detrimental for reversing the fertility trend, so that rising LFPRs are not a remedy for overall population ageing and for containing its costs. Also, in the longer run, the marginal benefits of raising LFPRs will decline and then the sheer dynamics of a shrinking and ageing population will take over. In order to prevent these longer-term effects, the remedies will need to be demographic and to take the form of increased immigration and/or rising fertility. Since below-replacement fertility has proved to be difficult to reverse, EU will have to envisage a gradual increase of its immigrant intake to a level of about 1.0 million per annum from about 2025 onward. This is lower than what was envisaged by the United Nations or by the McDonald and Kippen simulations, but still substantially higher than the recent migrant flows into EU. The actual number of immigrants needed will furthermore strongly depend on foreign-born fertility levels as well, and from this point of view migration of couples or families is to be preferred over migration streams of singles or streams with a strong sex imbalance. Also from the point of view of migrants' skills, European immigration policies need to become more flexible and more responsive to specific needs. This favours the "green card" approach, like that, for instance, adopted in Germany (as of August 2000).

The situation in Eastern and Central Europe is considerably more precarious than in EU. Of the 17 countries therein, 11 already have negative rates of natural increase and 9 have negative net migration rates for the period 1990-1997 as well. In fact, only the Russian Federation and Slovenia have managed to correct their natural deficit at least partially through a positive migration balance during the 1990s. Given the economic situation in Eastern and Central Europe, the demographic picture is not likely to be substantially altered in the near future, and also a potential entry into EU for some of them is likely to produce more emigration in the short run. Only a major economic recovery can then stem the tide.

CONCLUSIONS

The analysis of recent developments in cohort fertility profiles indicates that a return of European fertility levels to, or close to, replacement level is not in the making. Even if the pace of postponement in Western countries slows down or stops altogether, only a modest rise in TFRs is to be envisaged. This rise, furthermore, strongly depends on the amount of fertility recuperation at older ages (that is to say, past age 30) and, except for the Scandinavian countries, this recuperation has been inadequate, and strongly so in a number of large EU countries (Spain, Italy, Germany). In Eastern and Central Europe, the steep fertility decline is predominantly a feature of the 1990s, and has been caused by a fertility reduction in all cohorts, irrespective of the stage of family-building or age. Also in these countries, the degree of fertility recuperation, particularly for the post-communist generations, will be crucial in establishing more acceptable levels of period fertility. Finally, policy measures directly aimed at influencing fertility have had clear, but only temporary effects, and also sustained policies producing sometimes large income transfers in favour of families with children have not had any substantial effects either.

Another salient feature of European demographic development is the growth of "unconventional" household types and the destandardization of the sequence of life course events in young adulthood. In this respect, strong national and even subnational differences prevail, and these have, at least in Western countries, been enhanced, intentionally or not, by social policies in favour of the expanding student populations. With respect to the growth of such "intermediate stages" in household formation, two features warrant particular attention: teenage fertility and the growth of lone-parent households. Compared with the United States, European countries have managed either to contain the incidence of these phenomena or to reduce the negative social effects. The United Kingdom, however, provides the most important exception to this observation. In Central and Eastern European countries, the incidence of lone-mother households may not yet be measured adequately, possibly because of co-residence of such mothers with their own parents; but virtually all of these countries have experienced a teenage fertility bulge, earlier in Central Europe and more recently in the Commonwealth of Independent States (CIS) countries. Fortunately, also in the latter, current teenage fertility rates have been falling since the middle of the 1990s.

The prospect of long-term sub-replacement fertility had to revive the issue of replacement migration sooner or later. In this respect, the United Nations (2001) report drew widespread media attention all over Europe, but the unfortunate feature was that the media zoomed in on the results of only one simulation, namely, the one maintaining a constant PSR at all times until 2050. Much earlier formal demographic analysis (see, for example, Blanchet, 1988) had indicated that such age structure equilibration leads to impossible outcomes, in contrast with longer-term views with less stringent constraints. However, the latter still lead to record immigration intakes of over 1.0 million per annum from 2025 onward for EU as well as for the remainder of Europe. Moreover, the efficiency of such a replacement migration remains limited if not complemented by other measures such as the rise of labour-force participation rates. The latter is particularly needed in countries, both in and outside EU, that have had a considerable reduction in male activity rates above age 50 or have a small female labour-force participation expressed in full-time equivalents. Finally, replacement migration into EU needs to be directed especially towards the countries with the largest fertility deficit, including Italy and

Spain, which have only more recently become immigration countries. Hence, the million or so extra immigrants should by no means be spread evenly within EU territory.

To sum up, replacement migration is not to be viewed as the sole solution for Europe's ageing problem, nor is it to be relegated to oblivion altogether. It can be an ingredient in a far more diversified approach in which numerous other measures have their place, and also more time-specific effects. In this respect, economic measures or measures that restructure social security arrangements are powerful pain relievers, but their effects do not last. One cannot raise activity rates beyond 100 per cent, nor can one increase the age at leaving the labour force much beyond 65 years in economies where globalization means increased flexibility and where fast technological evolution is synonymous with greater reliance on younger labour vintages. One can disconnect the evolution of pensions to some degree from that of productivity or economic growth, but not to the extent of creating new poverty. In other words, we can buy time for another quarter of a century or so by implementing economic measures—which are necessary at any rate—but in the longer run, we still have to envisage the inevitable consequences of not altering the demographic recruitment parameters, namely, fertility and migration. With a time-horizon beyond 2025, one has to realize that the effects of economic measures—if taken in time—will gradually wear off and that the laws of formal demography—just like those of gravity—will simply continue to operate.

REFERENCES

Andersson, G. (1999). Trends in childbearing and nuptiality in Sweden, 1961-1997. *Stockholm Research Reports in Demography* (University of Stockholm), No. 133.

Atoh, M. (1994). The recent fertility decline in Japan: changes in women's roles and status and their policy implications. In *The Population and Society in Post-war Japan*. Tokyo: Population Problems Research Council, pp. 49-72.

Avdeev, E., and A. Monnier (1994). A la découverte de la fécondité russe contemporaine. *Population*, vol. 49, Nos. 4-5, pp. 859-902.

Axinn, W., and A. Thornton (1991). Mothers, children and cohabitation: the intergenerational effect of attitudes and behavior. *American Sociological Review*, vol. 58, pp. 233-246.

Baizan Munoz, P. (1998). Transitions vers l'âge adulte des générations espagnoles nées en 1940, 1950 et 1960. *Genus*, vol. 54, Nos. 3-4, pp. 233-263.

Barkalov, N. B. (1999). The fertility decline in Russia, 1986-1996: a view with period parity-progression ratios. *Genus*, vol. 55, Nos. 3-4, pp. 11-60.

Blanchet, D. (1988). Immigration et régulation de la structure par âge d'une population. *Population*, vol. 43, No. 2, pp. 293-309.

Blossfeld, H. P., and A. De Rose (1972). Educational expansion and changes in entry into marriage and motherhood: the experience of Italian women. *Genus*, vol. 47, Nos. 3-4, pp. 73-88.

Bodart, P., and others (1977). Migrations et politiques démographiques: quelques résultats de modèles avec consignes. *Population et Famille*, vol. 40, No. 1, pp. 77-96.

Bongaarts, J., and G. Feeney (1998). On the quantum and tempo of fertility. *Population and Development Review*, vol. 24, No. 2, pp. 271-291.

Bradbury, B., and M. Jäntti (1999). Child poverty across industrialized nations. *Innocenti Occasional Papers*. Florence, Italy: United Nations Children's Fund.

Büttner, T., and W. Lutz (1990). Estimating fertility responses to policy measures in the German Democratic Republic. *Population and Development Review*, vol. 16, No. 3, pp. 539-555.

Castro Martin, T. (1992). Delayed childbearing in contemporary Spain: trends and differentials. *European Journal of Population*, vol. 8, No. 3, pp. 217-246.

Chandola, T., and others (1999). Recent European fertility patterns: fitting curves to "distorted" distributions. *Population Studies*, vol. 53, No. 3, pp. 317-329.

Cherlin, A., and others (1995). Parental divorce in childhood and demographic outcomes in young adulthood. *Demography*, vol. 32, pp. 299-318.

Clarkberg, M., and others (1993). Attitudes, values and the entrance into cohabitational unions. University of Chicago, Chicago, Illinois (National Opinion Research Center (NORC) research report).

Coale, A. J. (1972). Alternative paths to a stationary population. In *Demographic and Social Aspects of Population Growth*, C. Westoff and R. Park, eds. Washington, D.C.: Commission on Population Growth and the American Future, pp. 598-603.

_____, and R. Treadway (1986). A summary of the changing distributions of overall fertility, marital fertility and poportions married in the provinces of Europe. In *The Decline of Fertility in Europe*, A. J. Coale and S. C. Watkins, eds. Princeton, New Jersey: Princeton University Press, pp. 80-152.

Coale, A. J., and T. J. Trussell (1974). Model fertility schedules: variations in the age structure of childbearing in human populations. *Population Index*, vol. 40, No. 2, pp. 185-258.

Coleman, D. A. (1999). Ireland north and south: perspectives from social science. *Proceedings of the British Academy*, vol. 98, pp. 69-115.

Conrad, C., and others (1996). East German fertility after unification: crisis or adaptation? *Population and Development Review*, vol. 22, No. 2, pp. 331-358.

Council of Europe (1999). *Recent Demographic Developments in Europe*. Strasbourg, France: Council of Europe Publications.

Crimmins, E., and others (1991). Preference change among American youth: family, work and goods aspirations, 1978-1986. *Population and Development Review*, vol. 17, pp. 115-133.

Dalla Zuanna, G., and others (1998). Late marriage among young people: the case of Italy and Japan. *Genus*, vol. 54, Nos. 3-4, pp. 187-232.

De Santis, G. (1999). *Le politiche natalista dei paesi industrializatti: démographie: analyses et synthèse*. Paris and Rome: INED and La Sapienza.

Deboosere, P., and others (1997). *Familles et ménages*, Census Monograph, No. 4. Brussels: National Institute of Statistics.

_____ (2000). *Evolutie van de nationale, regionale en gemeentelijke vruchtbaarheid in België, 1989-1999*. Brussels: Vrije Universiteit Brussel.

Ditch, J., and others (1998). *A Synthesis of National Family Policies*. York, United Kingdom: European Observatory on National Family Policies, University of York, and the European Commission.

Easterlin, R. (1976). The conflict between aspirations and resources. *Population and Development Review*, vol. 2, No. 3, pp. 417-425.

_____, and others (1990). How have American baby boomers fared? Earnings and economic well-being of young adults, 1964-1987. *Journal of Population Economics*, vol. 3, No. 4, pp. 277-290.

Espenshade, T. (1986). Population dynamics with immigration and low fertility. *Below-Replacement Fertility in Industrial Societies*, K. Davis and others, eds. New York: The Population Council.

Eurostat (1997). Beyond the predictable: demographic changes in the EU up to 2050, Statistics in Focus: Population and Social Conditions, 1997-7. Luxembourg.

Feld, S. (2000). Active population growth and immigration hypotheses in Western Europe. *European Journal of Population*, vol. 16, No. 3, pp. 3-40.

Frejka, T., and G. Calot (2000). The cohort fertility story: industrialized countries in the second half of the twentieth century and in the early twenty-first century. Presented at the annual meetings of the Population Association of America, Los Angeles, California.

Gauthier, A. H. (1996). *The State and the Family: A Comparative Analysis of Family Policies in Industrialized Countries*. Oxford: Clarendon Press.

Henry, L. (1953). *Fécondités des mariages: nouvelle méthode de mesure.* Cahier de l'Institut National d'Études Démographiques, No. 16. Paris: Presses Universitaires de France.

Hobcraft, J. (1996). Fertility in England and Wales: a fifty-year perspective. *Population Studies,* vol. 50, No. 3, pp. 485-524.

_____, and K. Kiernan (1995). Becoming a parent in Europe. In *Evolution or Revolution in European Population,* European Conference Proceedings. Milan: Franco Agnelli Publishers, pp. 27-61.

Hoem, B. (1998). Entry into motherhood in Sweden: the influence of economic factors on the rise and fall in fertility, 1986-1997. Paper presented at Conference on Lowest Low Fertility, Rostock, Max Planck Institute for Demographic Research.

_____, and J. Hoem (1997). Fertility trends in Sweden up to 1996. *Stockholm Research Reports in Demography* (University of Stockholm), No. 123.

Inglehart, R. (1970). *The Silent Revolution.* Princeton, New Jersey: Princeton University Press.

Kiernan, K. (1992). The impact of family disruption in childhood on transitions made in young adult life. *Population Studies,* vol. 46, No. 2, pp. 213-234.

_____ (1999a). Cohabitation in Western Europe. *Population Trends* (London, Office for National Statistics), vol. 96, pp. 23-32.

_____ (1999b). European perspectives on non-marital childbearing. Paper presented at Conference on Non-Marital Childbearing, Madison, Wisconsin.

Klijzing, E. (2000). Are there unmet family planning needs in Europe? *Family Planning Perspectives,* vol. 32, No. 2, pp. 74-81.

Kohn, M. L. (1977). *Class and Conformity: A Study in Values.* Chicago, Illinois: University of Chicago Press.

Kravdal, O. (1999). Does marriage require a stronger economic underpinning than informal cohabitation? *Population Studies,* vol. 53, No. 1, pp. 63-80.

Kuijsten, A. (1996). Changing family patterns in Europe: case of divergence? *European Journal of Population,* vol. 12, No. 2, pp. 115-143.

_____ (1999). Households, families and kin networks. In *Population Issues: An Interdisciplinary Focus,* L. V. Wissen and P. Dijkstra, eds. New York: Plenum Press, pp. 87-122.

Leridon, H. (2000). Vieillissement démographique et migrations: quand les Nations Unies veulent remplir le tonneau des Danaïdes ... *Population et Sociétés* (Paris, INED), No. 358, pp. 1-4.

Lesthaeghe, R. (1995). The second demographic transition: an interpretation. In *Gender and Family Change in Industrial Countries,* K. O. Mason and A. M. Jensen, eds. Oxford: Clarendon Press, pp. 17-62.

_____ (1998). On theory development: an application to the study of family formation. *Population and Development Review,* vol. 24, No. 1, pp. 1-14.

_____, and G. Moors (1995). Living arrangements and parenthood: do values matter? In *Values in Western Societies,* R. de Moor, ed. Tilburg, Netherlands: Tilburg University Press, pp. 217-250.

_____ (1996). Living arrangements, socio-economic position and values among young adults: a pattern description for France, Germany, Belgium and the Netherlands. In *Europe's Population in the 1990s,* D. Coleman, ed. Oxford: Oxford University Press, pp.163-221.

_____ (2000). Recent trends in fertility and household formation in the industrialized world. *Review of Population and Social Policy,* vol. 9, pp. 1-49.

Lesthaeghe, R., and J. Surkyn (1988). Cultural dynamics and economic theories of fertility change. *Population and Development Review,* vol. 14, No. 1, pp. 1-45.

Lesthaeghe, R., and D. van de Kaa (1986). Twee demografische transities? In *Groei en Krimp,* D. van de Kaa and R. Lesthaeghe, eds. Deventer, Netherlands: Van Loghum-Slaterus, pp. 9-24.

Lesthaeghe, R., and P. Willems (1999). Is low fertility a temporary phenomenon in the European Union? *Population and Development Review,* vol. 25, No. 2, pp. 211-228.

Lesthaeghe, R., and others (1988). *Are Immigrants Substitutes for Births?* Brussels: Interface Demography, Vrije Universiteit Brussel.

_____ (1991). Sind Einwanderer ein Ersatz für Geburten? *Zeitschrift für Bevölkerungswissenschaft,* vol. 17, No. 3, pp. 281-314.

Liefbroer, A. (1991). The choice between a married or unmarried first union by young adults. *European Journal of Population*, vol. 7, No. 3, pp. 273-298.

_____ (1998). Understanding the motivations behind the postponement of fertility decisions: Evidence from a panel study. Paper presented at Conference on Lowest Low Fertility, Rostock, Max Planck Institute for Demographic Research.

_____ (1999). From youth to adulthood: understanding changing patterns of families formation from a life course perspective. In *Population Issues: An Interdisciplinary Focus*, L. Van Wissen and P. Dijkstra, eds. New York: Plenum Press, pp. 53-85.

McDonald, P., and R. Krippen (2001). Labor supply prospects in 16 developed countries, 2000-2050. *Population and Development Review* (New York, New York), vol. 27, No. 1 (March), pp. 1-32.

Mérenne, B., and others (1997). La Belgique: diversité territoriale. *Bulletin du Crédit Communal*, No. 202 (1997/4). Brussels: Federal Agency for Scientific, Technical and Cultural Cooperation.

Micklewright, J., and K. Stewart (1999). *Is Child Welfare Converging in the European Union?* Innocenti Occasional Papers, EPS 69. Florence, Italy: United Nations Children's Fund.

Miret-Gamundi, P. (1997). Nuptiality patterns in Spain in the eighties. *Genus*, vol. 53, Nos. 3-4, pp. 185-200.

Monnier, A. (1999). La conjoncture démographique: l'Europe et les pays développés d'outre-mer. *Population*, vol. 54, Nos. 4-5, pp. 747-773.

Moors, G. (1999). Values and living arrangements: a recursive relationship. In *Ties That Bind: Perspectives on Marriage and Cohabitation*, L. Waite and others, eds. Hawthorne, New York: Aldine de Gruyter (in press), chap. 11.

Ogawa, N., and R. Retherford (1993). The resumption of fertility decline in Japan, 1973-1992. *Population and Development Review*, vol. 19, No. 4, pp. 703-741.

Oppenheimer, V. K. (1988). A theory of marriage timing. *American Journal of Sociology*, vol. 94, pp. 563-591.

Organisation for Economic Co-operation and Development (OECD) (1999). *Preparing Youth for the 21st Century*. Paris.

_____ (1999). Trends in international migration. Paris.

Page, H. J. (1977). Patterns underlying fertility schedules: a decomposition by both age and marriage duration. *Population Studies*, vol. 31, No. 1, pp. 85-106.

Péron, Y., and others (1999). *Canadian Families at the Approach of the Year 2000*. Ottawa: Statistics Canada.

Philipov, D., and H.-P. Kohler (1998). Timing and quantum effects on fertility in Bulgaria, the Czech Republic and Russia. Paper presented at Conference on Lowest Low Fertility, Rostock, Max Planck Institute for Demographic Research.

Punch, A., and D. L. Pearce (2000). Europe's population and labour market beyond 2000. *Population Studies*, No. 33 (Strasbourg, France: Council of Europe).

Retherford, R., and others (1996). Values and fertility change in Japan. *Population Studies*, vol. 50, No. 1, pp. 5-26.

Rindfuss, R., and others (1996). Education and the changing age pattern of American fertility: 1963-1989. *Demography*, vol. 33, No. 3, pp. 277-290.

Ryder, N. (1980). Components of temporal variations in American fertility. In *Demographic Patterns in Developed Societies*, R. W. Hiorns, ed. London: Taylor and Francis, pp. 11-54.

Statistics Canada (1997). *Report on the Demographic Situation in Canada, 1996*. Ottawa: Ministry of Industry.

_____ (1998). *Report on the Demographic Situation in Canada, 1997*. Ottawa: Ministry of Industry.

Stloukal, L. (1998). An APC-analysis of demographic responses to population policy measures: the case of the Czech and Slovak Republics, 1960-1990. *Genus*, vol. 54, Nos. 1-2, pp. 87-121.

Tsuya, N., and K. Oppenheim-Mason (1995). Changing gender roles and below-replacement fertility in Japan. In *Gender and Family Change in Industrialized Countries*, K. Oppenheim-Mason and A.-M. Jensen, eds. Oxford: Clarendon Press, pp. 139-167.

United Nations (1999). *World Population Prospects: The 1998 Revision,* vol. I, *Comprehensive Tables.* Sales No. E.99.XIII.9.

_____ (2001). *Replacement Migration: Is It a Solution to Declining and Ageing Populations?* Sales No. E.01.XIII.19.

United Nations Children's Fund (1999). *After the Fall: The Human Impact of Ten Years of Transition.* Florence, Italy: International Child Development Centre.

van de Kaa, D. J. (1987). Europe's second demographic transition. *Population Bulletin,* vol. 42, No. 1, pp. 1-38. Washington, D.C.: Population Reference Bureau.

_____ (1997). Options and sequences: Europe's demographic patterns. Nethur-demography paper, University of Amsterdam.

van Imhoff, E., and N. Keilman (1991). *LIPRO 2.0: An Application of a Dynamic Demographic Projection Model to Household Structure in the Netherlands.* The Hague: Netherlands Interdisciplinary Demographic Institute.

van Solinge, H., and others (1998). *Population, Labour and Social Protection in the European Union.* The Hague: Netherlands Interdisciplinary Demographic Institute.

Wattelar, C., and G. Roumans (1990). L'immigration, facteur d'équilibre démographique? *Futuribles* (juillet 1990), pp. 3-23.

Zakharov, S. (1998). Fertility trends in Russia and the European new independent States: crisis or turning point? Paper presented at Conference on Lowest Low Fertility, Rostock, Max Planck Institute for Demographic Research.

Zakharov, S. V., and E. I. Ivanova (1996). Fertility decline and recent changes in Russia: on the threshold of the second demographic transition. In *Russia's Demographic Crisis,* J. Da Vanzo, ed. Santa Monica, California: Rand Conference Proceedings, pp. 36-83.

DEMOGRAPHIC AGEING, EMPLOYMENT GROWTH AND PENSION SUSTAINABILITY IN THE EUROPEAN UNION: THE OPTION OF MIGRATION

*Constantinos Fotakis**

A. INTRODUCTION

Higher life expectancy and lower fertility rates have been the driving forces behind a secular trend towards population ageing. Although this trend is not new, it is set to further intensify because of the post-war baby boom. Demographic ageing raises important challenges for all those institutions and policies established in the middle of the last century when the demographic perspective was very different. Policy makers and politicians have tended to underestimate the cumulative impact of these demographic trends. However, there is an increasing awareness as Europe approaches the critical decades when the bulk of the ageing baby boomers will start moving out of the labour market, that this trend is important and irreversible within the foreseeable future. Family-friendly policy measures could still provide some attenuation effects in the long run, but even in the most family-friendly European Union (EU) countries, fertility rates are currently too low to prevent population ageing.

Today, there is a growing awareness in EU that there are at least two major policy issues in relation to population ageing. These are the ageing of the workforce and the risk of growing imbalances in the financing of social protection. These issues remain manageable for all member States for some more years depending on the national situations. Then the trends accelerate in pace and raise serious questions about the capacity of the existing institutions to handle the impact.

Immigration is considered one of the potential means to address the demographic challenge. In fact, it has always been an important feature of social, economic and cultural change in Europe. The European countries have long played a major part in migratory movements both as sending and as receiving countries. The final decade of the twentieth century has been characterized by an unprecedented rise in forced and voluntary migrations throughout the world and they have also had a major effect in Europe.

Today, in view of a rapidly changing economic and demographic situation, the debate on migration policies becomes a major issue in EU. There is a growing awareness that the restrictive immigration policies of the past 25 years

*European Commission, General Directory of Employment and Social Affairs, Brussels, Belgium.

are no longer relevant to the economic and demographic situation in which the Union now finds itself. Some European policy makers think that it is now the appropriate moment to review the longer-term needs for EU as a whole, to estimate how far these can be met from existing resources and to define a policy for the admission of third-country nationals to fill those gaps that are identified. This will also provide an opportunity to reinforce policies to combat irregular work and to ensure that employers comply with existing labour legislation for third-country nationals who work for them.

The European Council, in Tampere in October 1999,[1] agreed that with the coming into force of the Amsterdam Treaty, the Union should develop a common asylum and immigration policy. It is therefore of particular importance to examine current trends and reflect on the related policies.

The present paper briefly presents some of the issues related to the debate on immigration in EU today. It also attempts to provide some insight on possible future needs.

B. THE IMPLICATIONS OF THE DEMOGRAPHIC TRENDS IN THE EU LABOUR MARKET

Since 1990, age group 15-29, from which entrants into the labour market are drawn, has been decreasing rapidly. Furthermore, the average age of the labour force, which had remained quite stable at about 40 years over several decades, has started to increase since 1995 at a speed of 1 year every 7 years. Finally, the 65+ cohort will start growing rapidly in the next five years. As a result, labour capacity will be considerably reduced in EU over the next decades, particularly after 2015. However, it should be noted that the situation in the EU labour market is quite different from that in the United States of America and Japan. Europe faced several employment crises between the middle of the 1970s and the middle of the 1990s resulting in a relatively poor activity and employment record. Over the last three years, there are signs of a lasting recovery trend. However, unemployment is still as high as 9.5 per cent, compared with 4.5 per cent and 4.1 per cent in the United States and Japan, respectively. Furthermore, the EU average employment level is as low as 62 per cent. Table 1 shows the employment rates for each of the main age/sex groups for each member State in 1999. EU employment rates are considerably lower than those in the United States (74 per cent) and Japan (70 per cent). Only the Scandinavian countries and some specific regions have employment rates exceeding 70 per cent. At the other end of the scale, there are countries and regions (Greece, Spain, southern Italy) with employment rates at around 50 per cent.

There are 15 million people in Europe currently looking for a job. There would be more than another 15 million people available for the labour market if all member States reached the employment rate of the best-performing European countries or of the United States. In other words, the other side of Europe's weakness in respect of having a low employment record entails the availability of its considerable employment potential. If employment rates were similar to those of the best-performing European countries or those of the United States,

TABLE 1. EMPLOYMENT RATES FOR EU MEMBER STATES BY GENDER AND AGE GROUP IN 1999

(*Percentage*)

	Males 15-24	Males 25-54	Males 55-64	Total males 15-64	Females 15-24	Females 25-54	Females 55-64	Total females 15-64	Total 15-64
EU	42.2	86.2	47.3	71.6	35.1	64.5	27.0	52.6	62.1
Denmark	69.6	89.3	60.1	81.3	63.0	79.3	47.5	71.6	76.5
Germany	48.6	86.6	46.9	72.4	43.9	69.9	28.7	57.1	64.8
Portugal.	47.9	89.8	62.3	75.7	38.5	72.2	41.6	59.5	67.4
United Kingdom . . .	57.1	86.5	59.4	76.9	52.8	72.5	39.8	63.7	70.4
Netherlands.	62.8	91.4	48.8	80.3	62.5	69.4	22.0	61.3	70.9
Luxembourg	33.3	92.0	38.1	74.5	29.2	61.5	19.0	49.6	52.9
Austria.	59.0	89.6	41.5	76.7	50.6	73.0	17.7	59.8	68.2
Sweden	35.6	83.5	67.3	72.1	35.0	80.1	61.8	68.9	70.5
France	29.9	86.0	31.9	67.5	23.3	68.6	24.9	53.5	60.4
Belgium.	27.4	86.1	35.1	67.5	23.3	66.3	14.7	50.2	58.9
Finland	47.2	83.3	40.7	70.2	43.0	77.5	37.8	64.6	67.4
Italy.	30.3	84.3	40.8	67.1	20.9	49.5	15.1	38.1	52.5
Ireland	49.9	86.4	61.1	73.5	43.0	60.2	25.6	51.4	62.5
Spain	35.2	84.2	52.2	67.6	27.8	23.1	47.5	19.1	52.3
Greece	34.1	89.1	55.8	71.6	22.2	51.6	23.7	40.3	55.6

Source: Eurostat, 1999-based Population Scenarios (1999).

this would amount to an additional 33 million jobs in Europe. This can been seen as Europe's "full employment" potential. As shown in table 1, this employment "gap" does not lie with prime-age men. The EU employment level of men aged 25-54 (86 per cent) is equivalent to that of the United States of America (88 per cent). The main divergence in employment rates can be ascribed to female employment participation. In Europe, only 50 per cent of all women aged 15-64 are in employment. If the employment rate of women in Europe were to equal that of the United States, this would imply 21 million additional jobs.

In fact, the services sector, on the demand side, and female employment, on the supply side, are the key to improving performance. The success in mobilizing inactive human resources represents the main policy priority for the next years, since most EU member States will still have unused labour capacities for at least 10-15 years. Nevertheless, it is worth noting that the ageing of the working-age population implies that participation levels will be more and more influenced by the activity patterns of the older generations that are increasing in size. The question of maintaining older people in employment becomes an increasingly important policy issue since early retirement has become, over the last two decades, a well-established practice.

C. THE LINK AMONG DEMOGRAPHIC AGEING, EMPLOYMENT GROWTH AND PENSION SUSTAINABILITY

In its effort to further reduce unemployment, the Lisbon European Council in spring 2000[2] established that, on the basis of a sustainable economic growth of 3 per cent of gross domestic product (GDP), member States should move towards a total average employment rate of 70 per cent, and over 60 per cent for women, in 2010. To achieve this goal, the rise in the current levels of activity among women and older workers will be crucial. An integrated policy of technology-driven productivity growth, more and better jobs, and a strategy for human resources development have been proposed.

The European Council also underlined the need to modernize social protection. Within this context, the link between employment and the pension systems is of critical importance. On the one hand, pension systems play a role in encouraging or sometimes discouraging employment. On the other hand, changes in the number of people in employment have a powerful impact on the financial balance of pension systems.

The pressure on pension systems and public finances mainly stems from the situation of a growing dependency. During the period 1995-2015, the population above the standard retirement age, 65 years, will increase by 17 million (30 per cent). Within this group, the very old, those over age 80, will increase by 5.5 million (39 per cent). Pension systems will have to become less sensitive to demographic and other societal changes.

However, in policy terms, it is not the demographic old-age dependency ratio that matters for the sustainability of pensions, but the economic dependency ratio. The importance of this link is explored in the following simulation. The economic dependency ratio consists in the ratio between economically active people and dependent people. For the purpose of this analysis, the number of people in age group 65+ divided by the number of people in employment represents a reasonable proxy of the old-age economic dependency ratio. Figure I compares the trends in the demographic and economic dependency ratios at the EU level. The gap between the demographic and the economic dependency ratio provides a measure of the existing margins of employment growth compared with the state of full employment. If employment in EU grows over the next years according to the targets set in Lisbon, then, as shown in figure I, the decline of the economic dependency ratio will be much slower than that of the demographic dependency ratio.

D. HOW MANY (... ADDITIONAL) WORKERS ARE NEEDED IN THE UNION ?

1. *The question examined*

This simulation aims to find out whether mobilizing the unused potential of the EU working-age population could suffice to offset the impact of the demographic trend. Alternatively, it attempts to provide a rough estimate of the volume of working-age population needed to satisfy the employment growth and pension sustainability objectives set out in the form of the following two conditions:

I.   Employment growth should attain the target level corresponding to an average employment rate of 70 per cent set at the Lisbon summit, and it will then continue growing at a pace leading to a rate of 78 per cent[3] in 2040;

II.   Employment growth should be sufficient to keep economic dependency of each of the member States constant at the corresponding 1999 national levels throughout the period 1999-2040.

2. *Methodology and assumptions*

The simulation is built upon the baseline scenario of the 2000 revision of the Statistical Commission of the European Communities (Eurostat). The time period covered extends from 2000 to 2040. In particular, the aim of this simulation is to find what are the requirements in terms of employment level in order to satisfy condition I for employment growth and condition II for the sustainability of pensions.

The assumptions made are the following:

• The rate of productivity growth is set at 1.8 per cent throughout the period. The figure is based on the current three-year projections of the European Commission;

• The effort towards attaining the employment level of 70 per cent at the EU level in 2010 is distributed among the member States, taking into account their present age/sex employment levels and their corresponding activity rates;[4]

Figure I. Member States of EU (EU-15): future trends in the demographic and economic dependency ratios

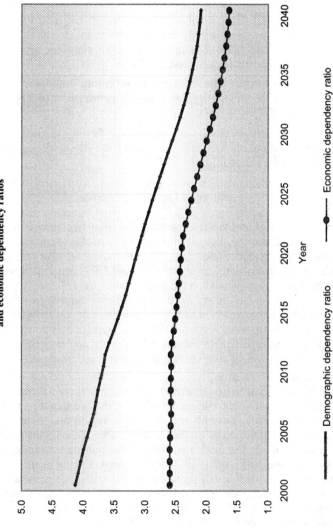

Sources: Eurostat and European Commission.

- The labour demand keeps sufficiently strong to absorb not only the available employment resources but also the immigration needed to satisfy the two employment growth conditions throughout the period until 2040;

- The number of pensioners equals the number of persons in age group 65+, while the number of contributors is equal to the number of people in employment. The ratio of these two variables represents, in this exercise, the economic dependency ratio;

- The only means to satisfy the two conditions set is employment growth. All other policies options (level of pensions, age of retirement etc.) are kept unchanged;

- The age structure of the additional labour entries (immigrants) needed is equal to the average age structure of the immigrants observed at EU level in 1998;

- The behaviour of immigrants in terms of fertility, employment rate and retirement is the same as that of the rest of the working-age population at the national level.

3. *Findings and policy implications*

This simulation shows that the objective of employment growth set in Lisbon could have a substantial, though temporary, positive effect on the sustainability of pensions for member States. Important differences are observed between the member States in terms of their ability to sustain 1999 economic dependency levels by increasing employment on the basis of condition I. Table 2 shows how long each member State could sustain the level of employment growth needed with its available labour reserves to maintain the economic dependency ratio at the corresponding national levels of 1999. The immigration flows built into Eurostat projections represent an average net inflow of approximately 650,000 people per year. It is widely accepted that this figure is underestimated.

Table 2 presents a diverging situation. Germany is facing immediate problems, while at least two other member States, Austria and Denmark, will also face pressures within the current decade. It is also worth noting that some countries (Greece, Italy, Luxembourg, Portugal, Ireland and Belgium) will face a relatively long period of gradual deterioration of their situation, while in some others (mainly Denmark and Finland) the transition from balance to imbalance will take place within two to three years. Finally, some countries may have some additional labour capacities owing to the high number of part-timers. The most typical example is the Netherlands. These countries may have some further possibilities of sustaining the level of their economic dependency ratio by progressively converting part-time to full-time jobs.

Nevertheless, by 2020 the majority of the member States will be faced with pressures in their economic dependency ratio that could not be managed by employment growth unless the Union increases its employment capacity through a substantial growth of immigration or undergoes substantial reforms of its social protection systems.

TABLE 2. HOW LONG EMPLOYMENT GROWTH COULD MAINTAIN ECONOMIC DEPENDENCY AT AROUND THE 1999 LEVELS WITHOUT ADDITIONAL IMMIGRATION

Country or group	Until
Austria	2006
Belgium	2016
Denmark	2006
Finland	2011
France	2013
Germany	2001
Greece	2020
Ireland	2020
Italy	2020
Luxembourg	2020
Netherlands	2012
Portugal	2017
Sweden	2012
United Kingdom	2014
European Union	2012

Source: Calculations based on Eurostat, 1999-based Population Scenarios (1999).

The situation at the EU level is presented in figure II. The higher lines denote the level of employment required to satisfy the two conditions mentioned earlier. The lower line shows the level of employment required to satisfy only the first condition relating to the employment target of Lisbon. Finally, the difference between the two lines (middle line) represents the additional amount of employment needed to cover the resulting pensions rights of the additional labour inflows required. A new migration-boom effect will be born. Future generations will have to deal with it some 30 years later.

According to this simulation, to maintain the EU level, the average economic dependency ratio at the 1999 level (2.6) would require approximately 120 million additional workers corresponding to an additional total immigration of some 170 million people.[5] These figures show the difficulty of maintaining the sustainability of pension systems through employment growth and migration without any further policy action.

For those member States having an economic dependency ratio much higher than the EU average (namely, Ireland (3.69), Netherlands (3.56), Denmark (3.5) and Finland (3.1)), a plausible approach would be to opt for reforms in their pension systems in order to lower the level of the economic dependency ratio at which their pensions system attains equilibrium. This would also lead to a higher convergence of the national levels of the economic dependency ratio across the Union. It could also substantially delay the need of these countries for immigration. Inversely, those member States that are found to be already below the EU average level of the economic dependency ratio may look

431

Figure II. Employment levels required to meet employment and pension sustainability conditions in EU, 2000-2040

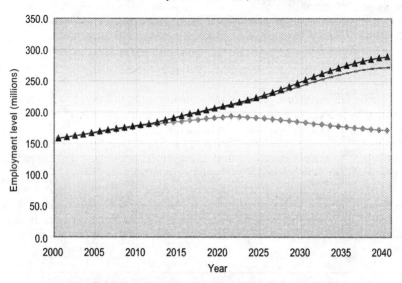

------- Optimal utilization of the available EU employment potential (employment rate at 70 per cent in 2010 and at 78 per cent in 2040)

------- Employment beyond this level is needed to cover additional immigrants' pension rights

—▲— Employment levels needed to keep economic dependency ratio at 1999 average level (economic dependency ratio = 2.6)

Sources: Eurostat and European Commission.

for higher employment levels either by a better utilization of their workforce or, in the case of low labour reserves, by the development of a more active immigration policy. However, these conclusions should be interpreted with considerable caution given the complexity of the issues, the high degree of uncertainty associated with the set of economic assumptions over the long term and the difficulty of establishing full comparability between member States.

E. SOME ADDITIONAL DIMENSIONS OF THE DEMOGRAPHIC IMPLICATIONS IN RESPECT OF THE EU LABOUR MARKET

Although this paper deals with issues and policies of the Community with its present membership, it is important to recognize the significant implications for employment policies that an enlarged Union will represent. In addition, analysing trends and setting objectives for employment based on aggregate data may be misleading since this does not take account of the very high diversification of labour-market situations at the regional level. Also, it does not consider the risk of growing skill mismatches. Consequently, although EU may still have at hand, at the aggregate level, the necessary resources to face demographic ageing over the next 10-15 years, important shortages and/or mismatches may arise much earlier at the regional or sectoral level. It is thus necessary to briefly discuss these issues.

1. *Migration and enlargement*

No clear prediction can be made as to how migration trends will develop during the process of enlargement of EU. It is expected that there would be a substantial migration flow from the Eastern European countries to the rest of EU immediately after the introduction of the free movement of persons. This is likely to be characterized by a peak in movement in the short term, levelling out over 10 years to below 150,000 people per annum.

The extent and type of transition period constitute a crucial aspect in determining the size of future migration in the enlarged EU, since this is one mechanism for managing the balance of factors involved in migration. Important among these are labour-market demand and wage differentials and they are supplemented by geographical and cultural considerations as well as by established patterns of migration. However, experience has shown that an assessment of wage differentials must always be accompanied by an assessment of the cost of living, which acts as a balancing factor.

The impact of labour migration in the enlarged EU is dependent on wage differences. It is currently estimated that wage equalization between the 10 Central and Eastern European countries and EU will be reached in about 30 years, and as this is reached, movement will reflect more and more the current patterns of movement between member States. The movement of highly skilled workers will increase as flexibility increases and multinational companies move employees throughout Europe. "Labour tourism" (short-term income-seeking workers and contracted temporary workers) will also continue to develop as companies take advantage of labour that is cheaper than indigenous labour, and low-level cross-border trading will also increase as transborder economic regions develop.

2. *The regional trends*

The regional situation in EU is quite diversified. Some of the regions in southern Scandinavia, northern Italy, a substantial part of England, central Portugal and southern Germany combine sustained economic growth with relatively high employment rates sometimes ranging beyond 70 per cent, and a fast-declining demographic trend. This implies that their ability to compensate for the demographic effects, over the next decades, will be limited. Mismatches and local scarcity of human resources might prove a serious challenge for economic growth in these parts of Europe, already during the current decade.

While these regions do not have any labour reserves, other regions, often within the same country, either face particular difficulties in activating their unused employment potential or suffer from regional decline. Several member

States (Italy, Spain, Portugal, France and Greece) show situations of increasing regional disparities, with some of their regions below 80 per cent and others above 120 per cent of their national average employment rate. The extension of EU membership to countries of Eastern Europe may aggravate this situation in the Union so enlarged.

Could intra-European mobility help improve employment and growth performance? The reversal of demographic trends that so clearly differentiate Europe's regions naturally also raises this question. Increased labour mobility is one way of dealing with regional imbalances. Mobility has both an occupational and a geographical dimension. Occupational mobility—training and retraining of the workforce—and geographical mobility are important factors for adjustment to the changing labour-market conditions.

Despite the important progress made in the liberalization of the free movement of persons over the last decades in EU, Europeans have still tended to move less than in the early post-war period. Geographical mobility between member States is limited to 0.1 per cent per year. Nevertheless, the scale of labour mobility between regions is bigger, at about 1.5 per cent a year, though with large variations between regions. The increased participation of women in the labour market might have been one of the reasons explaining this lack of geographical mobility, as mobility in many cases concerns two people with professional careers. Some further important reasons to be considered are the increasing welfare standards across even the poorer EU regions and the growing instability of jobs.

The issue of mobility will be increasingly important over the coming 10-20 years. It is expected that in the near future, the socio-economic and institutional environment in Europe will be more favourable for geographical mobility. Growing economic integration, together with improved economic performance, will certainly contribute to this trend. As mentioned before, the enlargement of EU to Eastern European countries will also contribute to an increased mobility. However, given that most of the candidate countries face similar or even stronger demographic ageing trends, this mobility might be a source of increasing regional demographic and economic imbalances.

In the long run, rapid technological change and, particularly, the expected progress in telecommunications, networking and transport could help improve the allocation of human resources and may decrease the need for geographical mobility.

3. Skill mismatches and unsatisfied labour demand

Skill mismatches may also grow as a result of the decrease of labour reserves and for at least two further reasons as well.

(a) The acceleration of technological progress

Rapid changes in technology create new demands for skills and competencies across most economic sectors. The young people entering into the labour market are indeed more highly educated in general terms. However, technological progress seems to be bringing about a polarization of the skills mix. The employers demand specialized workers, whereas the workers offer a medium to high, but generic, educational level. Already, today, 80 per cent of European enterprises consider information technology skills development to be their number one training priority. A new economy is emerging, with technologically more advanced enterprises, and a growing services sector, often delivered by new small firms. In large and small enterprises, new demands are being made upon workers, with the technologies creating more of a process-driven rather than a function-driven workplace. EU has yet to respond to this shift in demand. Five hundred thousand information technology jobs could not be filled in 1998 owing to the lack of qualified applicants. Without urgent action the direct job growth forgone will rise to 1.6 million by the year 2002.

(b) *The growing need for new types of services*

The shortage of highly skilled information society specialists is not the only aspect of the shift in skills demand. Skills shortage problems will spread out and affect other growing sectors that are being developed based on cross-disciplinary applications of information and communication technologies (ICT). This mainly refers to the service sector. Over 54 per cent of the working-age population in the United States works in the service sector. In Europe, the proportion is just 40 per cent. This difference amounts to 36 million jobs. Differences are to be found in all parts of the service sector—distribution, financial services, hotels and restaurants, leisure, and communal services such as education, health and social services. Communal services alone represent 10 million jobs. Demographic ageing and increasing prosperity will certainly accelerate the growth of these services in the future.

(c) *The household needs and the underground economy*

Trends in demography and the family also increase the need for services to people. As more women—traditionally the main carers—are entering employment, fewer people are available to care for family dependants and particularly for the increasing number of the very old. In fact, the 80+ population group is expected to double over the next 15 years. Over the last decades, a considerable number of these types of jobs have been created in EU member States. The trend is expected to continue, since female participation in the labour market is far from complete and changes in the structure and composition of the household are expected to further increase these needs. It is worth noting that the formal labour market has failed in most member States to satisfy this demand, which is mostly covered by immigrants within the underground economy.

In fact, the growth of illegal immigration, over the last years, has been encouraged by the underground economy, particularly in Mediterranean member States. This trend mainly refers to temporary or seasonal employment primarily in agriculture, construction and the services sector. The trend is also observed even in regions with higher unemployment. There are a number of causes to explain this, ranging from institutional rigidities, particularly the relatively high level of non-wage costs in the formal sector, to social attitudes.

Moreover, some member States, mainly in southern Europe, appear to be more tolerant of large informal sectors than their Scandinavian counterparts.

However, the issue seem to be ever broader. Both illegal and legal immigrants are more vulnerable than national workers. They are often ready to make concessions concerning their wage and other work-related rights. This may be a source of increased competition with the national workers, particularly when employment is stagnant. The issue is more important among the low-skilled workers. This is precisely the kind of argument often used in support of policies to limit recruitment of new immigrants.

F.   SOME FURTHER CONCLUDING REMARKS

This analysis allows for some conclusions but it also raises several issues for further debate.

Certainly, population ageing will have a major impact on the labour market with the arrival of the baby boomers at the age of retirement, and this will be a lasting trend. The problem of labour shortages seems to be limited at least for the next 10 years to some specific sectors of the economy and some regions of Europe. Unlike the United States, EU has had over the last three decades a poor record in respect of job creation. Today, EU still has considerable employment reserves owing to relatively high unemployment and low activity levels compared with those of the United States and Japan. The paradox is that this weakness of Europe represents, at the same time, its force (compared, for instance, with the case of Japan) in facing the demographic challenge. The reserve employment potential of EU represents a total of more than 30 million people which with appropriate policies could become a source of further employment growth in the next 10-15 years. These labour reserves mainly consist of females and males in the older age group. However, given the importance of demographic ageing, Europe may progressively face a more generalized labour scarcity, but in any case not before 2020.

Future enlargement may further complicate the issue. Although this paper mainly focuses on issues and policies of the Community with its present membership, it is important to recognize the significant implications for employment policies that an enlarged Union will create. The existing differential in economic terms is expected to generate a considerable inflow of immigrants from these candidate countries. However, such countries are also faced with similar demographic problems. Employment reviews are being carried out in candidate countries at present, with a view to gaining a better understanding of the situation and the possible future trends.

An additional element of uncertainty is related to the future evolution of productivity. The limited growth of productivity over the last two decades despite the information revolution has puzzled economists. A substantial increase of productivity in the future may modify significantly the policy debate on future employment trends.

The sustainability of the European pension systems seems to be an additional and perhaps more important issue in the long run because of the speed with which its seriousness will develop once the baby-boom generation crosses the age of retirement. The policy makers are faced with different options. Containing public spending on pensions by rendering pension schemes less sensitive to demographic changes is one of the options. This option is often complemented by suggestions regarding important reforms in the pay-as-you-go systems[6] or a shift to a funded system. The latter in fact may ultimately imply, inter alia, investing in countries with higher potential in human resources and higher economic growth.

Covering the growing imbalances by targeting higher and higher employment levels through migration represents another option. This approach privileges the need to sustain growth within the developed world. The different options are not mutually exclusive. Different policy mixes can be considered in an effort to maintain the high welfare standards of the EU social models without harming either European society or the developing countries. Besides, rapid and radical policy changes in either direction might imply increased transition costs and unpredictable social implications.

Finally, a last consideration concerning the long run. Rapid technological change and particularly the expected progress in telecommunications, networking and transport may increase the importance of the intangible economy, reducing the need for geographical mobility of the workforce. Nobody can say today with certainty whether or not in 30 years from now the European economy would need all of these millions of immigrants.

Nevertheless, over the next 20 years, migration could make a substantial contribution towards offsetting mismatches and part of the demographic decline, provided that there is a sustained rate of employment growth commensurate with this extra labour supply. In the absence of sustained employment growth, migration inflows could not have the expected positive balancing effect in the labour market and social protection.

The key role of employment growth has been underlined by the EU policy makers. Significant policy initiatives were taken since 1997 in the context of the Common Employment Strategy[7] designed to improve employability, adaptability and equal opportunities and to promote entrepreneurship with a view to achieving job creation in existing and new enterprises. In addition, in spring 2000, the Lisbon European Council outlined an integrated approach that should encompass a wide range of policies including the need to modernize the European social model and, in particular, its developed systems of social protection. This strategy combined with a broader mobilization of all economic and structural policies, operating more and more in a mutually supportive way, is expected to increase the performance of EU over the next years. In fact, over the last three years, there have been encouraging signs of improvement in the fight against unemployment.

In conclusion, assessing the needs of immigration for EU is a quite complicated issue that cannot be dealt with by taking into account only the demographic trends. There are many other considerations. Besides, each country of the Union represent a different situation not only because the demographic patterns are different but also because each of them faces its own socio-economic reality. Economic and social institutions are often different, too.

Today, the political momentum tends to be in favour of a managed increase in legal immigration.[8] In order to manage migrant flows successfully and to cut illegal migration, EU intends to adopt a coordinated approach focusing its attention on all aspects of the migratory system in close partnership with the countries of origin. In addition, EU intends to promote effective integration measures for the new immigrants, ensuring them decent living and working conditions and the development of anti-discrimination policies,[9] which could in turn reinforce their socio-economic contribution to the host society.

NOTES

[1]Presidency conclusions (1999) of the Tampere European Council, 15 and 16 October 1999 (*www.presidency.finland.fi/frame.asp*). Accessed on 1 August 2000.

[2]Presidency conclusions (2000) of the Lisbon European Council, 23 and 24 March 2000 (*www.portugal.ue-2000*). Accessed on 1 August 2000.

[3]Seventy-eight per cent is considered to be the maximum level of employment that can be sustained over a long period. It is comparable with the labour performance observed in the United States of America and Japan during periods of sustained economic growth.

[4]The EU employment target of 70 per cent for 2010 is set for each of the member States as follows: Austria (73.0 per cent), Belgium (66.0 per cent), Denmark (79.7 per cent), Germany (71.2 per cent), Greece (66.0 per cent), Spain (66.7 per cent), France (67.0 per cent), Ireland (72.9 per cent), Italy (63.3 per cent), Luxembourg (67.9 per cent), Netherlands (78.7 per cent), Portugal (74.9 per cent), Finland (73.2 per cent), Sweden (75.8 per cent), United Kingdom (75.0 per cent). In 2040, all countries are assumed to converge to 78 per cent.

[5]Assuming that the immigrants have the same activity rates as the EU population. This is perhaps unrealistic for the first years. However, given the assumption about a gradual increase of the employment rate up to 78 per cent, the assumption becomes overall quite plausible.

[6]According to an internal Commission study, a gradual average increase in the effective retirement age of nine years would be required to compensate for the demographic effect on EU pension systems between 1999 and 2030.

[7]For more information, see European Commission, Employment Guidelines, 1999, and Employment Guidelines, 2000.

[8]See European Commission Communication COM (2000). 755 final: Towards a common asylum procedure and a uniform status throughout the Union of persons granted asylum. Brussels, 22 November 2000; and European Commission Communication COM (2000). 755 final: On a Community immigration policy, Brussels, 22 November 2000.

[9]See Council Directive 2000/43/EC: Implementing the principle of equal treatment between persons irrespective of racial and ethnic origin, of 29 June 2000.

DEMOGRAPHIC CHANGE AND THE POTENTIAL CONTRIBUTION OF INTERNATIONAL MIGRATION

*International Organization for Migration**

INTRODUCTION

The publication in 2001 of the report of the Population Division of the United Nations Secretariat entitled *Replacement Migration: Is It a Solution to Declining and Ageing Populations?* (United Nations, 2001) has stimulated renewed debate about policies and programmes relating to international migration. It has encouraged many to think again about the demographic implica-tions of current migration policies. The enormous public reaction to the report indicates the level of interest about international migration issues around the world.

However, discussion of the ways in which Governments might offset population ageing and population decline is not new. For example, more than 10 years ago, the Organisation for Economic Co-operation and Development (OECD), in a report entitled *Ageing Populations: The Social Policy Implica-tions*, concluded that "the influx of immigrant workers would need to be very large to fully compensate for shrinkage of the working-age population in many European countries" (Organisation for Economic Co-operation and Develop-ment, 1988, p. 58).

In the present paper, we shall briefly discuss some of the arguments ad-vanced in the United Nations report on replacement migration and consider some of the implications of the study for international migration policies. This paper does not discuss in any detail the range of other social and economic policies that could be adopted to offset population ageing and population de-cline. These measures include: raising fertility rates, increasing labour sup-ply, improving the training and education levels of the existing workforce, reducing unemployment, and reforming the financing of health-care and pen-sion systems (see Organisation for Economic Co-operation and Development, 1988, 1991; Coleman, 1992, 1995; Feld, 2000; Tapinos, 2000).

In our discussion of the demographic implications of international migra-tion and our review of migration policy approaches, we have drawn on some of the findings from *World Migration Report* (United Nations and International Organization for Migration, 2000a), which reviews recent trends in migration in every region of the world and is published in English and French.

---

*International Organization for Migration, Geneva, Switzerland.

We have highlighted some of the findings of the *World Migration Report* for Western Europe, since it is in this region that policy makers are first likely to be confronted with population ageing and population decline. Japan also faces similar problems; for a discussion of the challenges facing Japan see D. Papademitriou and K. Hamilton (2000).

Explicit demographic considerations have generally not been a key objective of migration policies in Europe (Organisation for Economic Co-operation and Development, 1991). Governments have tended to think about the short term, but population ageing and population decline are gradual and long-term trends. Given high unemployment over the last decade, few Governments in Europe have promoted permanent immigration for demographic or other reasons. However, as discussed below, there are signs that several European countries are beginning to develop new initiatives to attract labour migrants both for economic and for demographic reasons.

REPLACEMENT MIGRATION

In its study on replacement migration, the United Nations defines "replacement migration" as "the international migration that would be needed to offset declines in the size of population and the declines in the population of working age, as well as to offset the overall ageing of a population" (United Nations, 2001, executive summary, second paragraph).

For the eight countries—France, Germany, Italy, Japan, the Republic of Korea, the Russian Federation, the United Kingdom of Great Britain and Northern Ireland and the United States of America—and the two regions—Europe and the European Union (EU)—examined in the study, the size of replacement migration needed was calculated, while the possible effects of replacement migration on the population size and age structure for these countries were investigated. The study estimates that in order to keep constant the size of the working-age population, many countries will need to increase migration flows substantially.

The United Nations study concludes that:

"The projected population decline and population ageing will have profound and far-reaching consequences, forcing Governments to reassess many established economic, social and political policies and programmes, including those relating to international migration" (United Nations, 2001, executive summary, major finding 4).

In the United Nations study, estimates of the scale of migration that may be required to offset population ageing and population decline are mainly discussed in aggregate terms, assuming a permanent flow of migrants. The report asks how many more migrants will be needed to reduce population decline and population ageing and how migration will affect the ratio of persons of working age (15-64) to older persons (65 years or over).

Both migration and support ratios are defined in fairly simple terms in the calculations made in the study. The support ratio, that is to say, the number of persons of working age (15-64) compared with those aged 65 years or over, is not an accurate measure of the dependency ratio, since this requires consideration of how many people of working age are likely to be economically active. There is also no discussion in the study of replacement migration of how the effect of migration might vary according to the age and sex profile of the migrant population, the duration of migration, whether it may be temporary or permanent, and the socio-economic characteristics of migrants (sex, age, skill, occupation, industry etc.).

However, even given that the profile of migrants may vary, most studies show that a very large number of international migrants—a number far larger than is currently the case—would need to enter each year to offer a significant benefit, given the rapid ageing and low fertility rates of many countries (United Nations and International Organization for Migration, 2000a, p. 26). The likely political acceptance of such findings is not discussed in the United Nations study. To what extent are developed countries, and the countries of Western Europe in particular, prepared to accept such a substantial increase in migration?

NEW DIRECTIONS FOR EUROPEAN MIGRATION POLICY IN RESPONSE TO DEMOGRAPHIC CHANGE?

International migration does have a beneficial effect on the ageing of a population as immigrants tend to be younger than the host population, and female international migrants coming from developing countries generally have higher fertility rates. Even though migrants' fertility rates do come down after residing in the new country for some period, in the interim they contribute to population growth. However, eventually immigrants also become old, so the demographic benefits of migration can be short-term. An influx of foreign workers may swell the ranks of those contributing to social security systems, but by so doing they acquire benefit entitlements and so eventually increase the size of the beneficiary population (Organisation for Economic Co-operation and Development, 1988). For this and other reasons, policy makers may prefer temporary rather than permanent labour migration.

Other often-cited potential benefits of migration include the provision of a service workforce to care for the elderly, and the creation of a younger and more dynamic workforce to offset the perceived loss of productivity and flexibility associated with an ageing workforce (Coleman, 1992).

In most countries of Western Europe, authorized immigration either levelled off or declined by the mid-1990s, as Governments introduced tighter immigration controls and more restrictive entry policies (United Nations and International Organization for Migration, 2000a, p. 191).[1] Net migration into EU fell from a peak of 1.35 million in 1992 to 378,687 in 1998. By contrast, the United States has continued to favour immigration. It receives almost 1 million legal immigrants a year, making it the largest recipient of foreigners welcomed into another country as permanent residents.

Government attempts to restrict irregular immigration, whether into Western Europe, North America or Japan, have met with mixed success. For example, in Japan the number of foreign workers is estimated to have increased from 260,000 in 1990 to 630,000 in 1996, of whom 45 per cent in the latter year were deemed overstayers.

In Europe, the number of asylum-seekers rose from 226,000 in 1996 to 430,000 in 1999. Although this increase was due to a significant extent to the conflict in Kosovo, there are, among this group of asylum-seekers, many economic migrants who in the absence of other legal immigration options seek entry to Europe via the asylum system.

Even in a time of economic crisis, there remains a key role for foreign labour. Irregular migration remains a persistent and growing problem in Europe. In 1998, it was estimated that there were 3 million unauthorized migrants in Western Europe, at a time when there were some 18 million non-nationals residing in the 15 member States of EU. Thus, perhaps up to 1 in 7 of all migrants in Europe are unauthorized.

The high number of irregular migrants, most of whom are engaged in low-paid and low-skilled work, indicates that there is a considerable demand for migrants in Europe even though unemployment rates remain high in many EU countries. Some countries have accepted this fact and have introduced regularization programmes. During the 1990s, Spain, Italy, Portugal, Greece and France all enacted amnesty programmes for unauthorized migrants. Such programmes, although not implemented explicitly for demographic reasons, may nonetheless help to offset the cost of population ageing in the short run, by bringing more workers into the social security system.

Recent efforts by EU States to develop a common migration policy have not come easily. States are reluctant to relinquish national control over immigration. Their main immigration concern is restricting the entry of groups from outside the EU whose socio-economic and/or political integration they see as problematic.

While concerns about the management of non-EU migration flows continue to dominate discussions of immigration within Western Europe, the demographic realities of an ageing population—as well as the economic demands of a global marketplace—are of increasing importance (United Nations and International Organization for Migration, 2000a, p. 192).

The year 2000 may come to be recognized as having marked a watershed in the history of migration in Europe. For the first time in many years, several European Governments, including those of Austria, Germany, Italy, Spain and the United Kingdom, have begun to talk about the benefits of economic migration and, even more significantly, have begun to take action to recruit more migrants, especially skilled workers. As OECD predicted nearly 10 years ago, restrictive migration policies in Europe are unlikely to change solely in response to population ageing since this is a gradual and long-term trend (Organisation for Economic Co-operation and Development, 1991). However, the new initiatives outlined below are not triggered only by labour-market pressures. They are also linked to demographic changes such as smaller youth cohorts entering the labour force. They also concern the recruitment of foreign workers to some sectors of employment that have ageing workforces, such as agriculture and the health service. Thus, these measures may also help to remedy a growing demographic imbalance resulting from an ageing and declining population.

Policy approaches vary, however, and there is no common European approach to these new challenges. While some countries have introduced regularization programmes, as mentioned above, others have targeted skilled workers. The latter programmes tend to be temporary, whereas regularization programmes provide the opportunity for migrants to remain in a country permanently. While some countries have tried mainly to recruit small numbers of highly skilled workers, others have been more concerned about regularizing the employment of large numbers of low-paid and unskilled workers. Those who favour the recruitment of the highly skilled argue that it provides a means of selecting the migrants who are most needed for economic reasons. This approach may also have demographic advantages, to the extent that the workers concerned are employed under temporary labour contracts. However, temporary worker programmes have proved difficult to manage in many countries, as many temporary workers have been unwilling to return home at the conclusion of short-term contracts (for an extensive discussion and comparison of such programmes, see Organisation for Economic Co-operation and Development, 1999). Yet, the dictates of today's economy—with the growth in international trade multinational operations, and contract labour even in highly skilled sectors—make it likely that there will be a continued demand for temporary labour migration.

Some examples of different Western European approaches and recent new labour migration initiatives are given below.

Italy

After many years of being a source country, Italy has rapidly become a target country for labour migrants, many of whom are in an irregular situation. One study, for example, suggests that Italy "hosts probably the largest proportion of illegal immigrants in Western Europe" (Ghosh, 1998, p. 12). In August 2000, the largest Italian farmers' federation, *Coldiretti*, called for 65,000 migrants to be allowed to work in Italy in 2000.[2] Foreign seasonal workers were needed, said its President, Paolo Bedoni, to harvest cereals, grapes and vegetables—low-paid work that Italians, despite an unemployment rate of 11 per cent, are reluctant to do.

The Italian Minister for the Interior, Enzo Bianco, said in July that Italy "urgently needs a labour force and new vital energy because it is growing old very quickly. If Italy wants to develop and grow, it must turn to immigrants, who can act as a lifeblood."[3]

The Italian Parliament, under pressure from northern Italian businesses complaining of labour shortages, is under pressure to grant legal status to more unauthorized foreigners. In 1999, 56,500 foreigners were regularized. The head of the Eurispes think tank in Rome asserted that Italy needs immigration and should accept immigrants via front-door legal immigration rather than legalize some of the illegals in the country.

An example of the type of measure that might be more widely considered is an initiative being implemented by the International Organization for Migration (IOM). The Italian Government recently called upon IOM for assistance in recruiting and training labour migrants from Albania. IOM is currently offering technical assistance to the Italian and Albanian Governments in the form of a pilot project targeting 5,000 Albanians interested in training or work opportunities in Italy.

Germany

Germany, in contrast with Italy, has not implemented regularization programmes. Instead, it has started to open up more legal migration channels. On 1 August 2000, Germany introduced a new so-called green card programme allowing up to 20,000 foreign information technology specialists to work in the country for a period of up to five years, with the possibility of the extension of these permits. Applicants must have a university qualification or the promise of a salary of at least 100,000 deutsche mark (50,000 United States dollars) a year. The head of the Federal Labour Office reported in August that 5,486 people had already applied for a special permit to work in Germany under the scheme. This is the first time Germany has formally opened its doors to economic immigrants since it invited "guest workers" from Turkey and other parts of Southern Europe to help rebuild its economy after the Second World War, although Germany has accepted temporary workers from Eastern Europe for some time (see below).

In March 2000, the German Foreign Minister, Joschka Fischer, issued a memo urging German consulates to relax visa restrictions so as to make it easier for foreign professionals to come to Germany. Another significant change is that asylum-seekers who have been prohibited from working since 1997 would from autumn 2000 be expected to be allowed to work after 12 months in Germany.[4]

Most business leaders support the green card programme and want to see easy-entry programmes expanded to cover other industries and occupations. However, the change in policy by the German Government reopened larger debates about immigration, and about whether the new green card programme should be linked to a further tightening of Germany's asylum and deportation policies.

The opposition parties argue that Germany accepts enough immigrants already but they are not the ones most needed for the economy. Germany now receives about 300,000 immigrants a year: 100,000 asylum-seekers, 100,000 ethnic Germans and 100,000 family unification immigrants. Instead of taking in newcomers who need Germany, they argue, Germany should be attracting newcomers that it needs, such as computer specialists. The way to do this without increasing overall immigration, they argue, is to further restrict asylum and to limit family unification.

There are also signs of a growing awareness of the need to recruit more skilled foreign workers in Great Britain. On 11 September 2000, the United Kingdom Immigration Minister, Barbara Roche, made a well-publicized speech[5] on the benefits of economic migration, suggesting that Great Britain should, for both economic and demographic reasons, consider recruiting more foreign skilled workers from abroad. Referring to population ageing in the United Kingdom, Ms. Roche argued that "migration is one of a range of measures that could help ease the economic impact of such demographic change".

Ms. Roche further argued, referring to the experience of the United States during the 1990s, that economically driven migration can bring substantial overall benefits both for growth and for the economy. She referred to skill shortages in many sectors of United Kingdom industry. The United Kingdom National Health Service, which is the largest employer in the country, and which devotes a high percentage of its funding to providing health care for the elderly, has already begun to recruit nurses from abroad and already relies heavily on foreign doctors. Nearly one third of doctors in the United Kingdom were born abroad and nearly one third of nurses in inner London were trained outside the United Kingdom.

In June 2000, the tragic deaths of 58 Chinese discovered in a container at Dover, England, once again highlighted the problem of irregular migration in Europe and led to calls for tougher measures to restrict immigration. Ironically, in the same month, the United Kingdom authorities reported that, faced with a severe shortage of some 17,000 nurses, the National Health Service had decided to begin discussions with the Chinese authorities on the terms and conditions of receiving Chinese nurses as "trainees" in the United Kingdom.

The *weekly* number of foreign nurses applying to register in the United Kingdom has risen from 70 five years ago to some 1,000 today. Critics of the policy of recruiting nurses from abroad argue that there is no serious shortage of qualified nurses in the United Kingdom. The real problem is that, for qualified nurses in the United Kingdom who wish to work in hospitals, the wages offered are too low (*Migration News Sheet*, June 2000). Along with nurses, the United Kingdom is also faced with a shortage of workers in other low-paid jobs in the public sector such as teachers and social workers. Such posts are increasingly filled by South Africans, Scandinavians and Belgians.

NEGATIVE PUBLIC PERCEPTIONS OF MIGRATION

Although the measures outlined above are fairly modest, public reaction to further immigration has been rather negative. For example, in Germany, most opinion polls find that 55-65 per cent of Germans oppose the green card programme. A poll published in the newspaper *Die Woche* in July 2000 showed that 63 per cent of those asked thought that Germany did not need any more immigrants.

Earlier this year *The Economist* commented that:

"The European popular imagination, it seems, is gripped by panic about foreigners: that there are too many of them pouring in, that there is certainly no need for any more. In short, that Europe is 'full up'" (6 May 2000).

Too often, migration, like the impact of ageing, is seen as a burden on advanced industrialized societies. Much of the public debate about migration and ageing in recent years has been conducted in negative terms. International migration, especially in Europe, has for many years been viewed as something that must be restricted and controlled. Similarly, much of the debate about population ageing concerns ways to reduce the costs of an ageing society. New migrants are often portrayed as a burden on receiving countries even though many studies have shown that migrants bring great economic and social benefits to these countries and contribute to their cultural diversity. There are many good economic arguments for immigration, including the energy, entrepreneurialism and fresh ideas that migrants bring. Similarly, the fact that more people are living longer is too often seen as a worrying trend, rather than as a positive one offering great opportunities for older people themselves and for the societies they are living in.

There are also tremendous fears in some European countries of the migration consequences of EU enlargement. Many people simply fear being swamped by a new wave of migration from the East. This was reflected in a recent Danish election campaign poster warning of the imminent arrival of 40 million Poles following EU enlargement eastward (United Nations and International Organization for Migration, 1998).

Significant changes in migration policy in Europe are unlikely to occur without greater efforts being made to educate public opinion about the benefits of migration. One of the ways in which this might be achieved is through awareness-raising information campaigns which would challenge some of the current misconceptions about migration in Europe.

WHAT ARE THE POSSIBLE CONSEQUENCES OF "REPLACEMENT MIGRATION" FOR SENDING COUNTRIES?

If Europe, the United States and Japan begin to recruit substantially greater numbers of migrants, especially skilled workers, what are the likely consequences for sending countries? There has been little discussion of the possible consequences of "replacement migration" for developing countries and countries in transition, many of which also have declining or ageing populations.

The effects of international migration are complex for both source and destination countries. Their impacts cannot be characterized as solely positive or negative. Often, the same factors that create benefits can also produce costs. To give a seemingly simple example, brain drain of highly skilled migrants is often described as a loss to the source country and benefit—brain gain—to the destination country. However, if the migrants help link companies in the home country with business opportunities in the new location, both countries may benefit. On the other hand, if the destination country does not utilize the skills brought by the migrants in its workforce, then the migration may well create negative impacts for both societies (United Nations and International Organization for Migration, 2000a, p. 22). The range and complexity of international migration flows, and the fact that the scale of these flows is often underreported, make it difficult to assess the full impact of international migration on either receiving or sending countries.

Since many of the principal countries of emigration have large and growing populations, international migration generally has little effect on overall population. The number of migrants relative to total population size is small in countries such as China, India, Mexico and the Philippines (United Nations and International Organization for Migration, 2000a).

However, a number of countries have experienced the emigration of a sizeable portion of their populations. For example, an estimated 300,000-450,000 Albanians (10-14 per cent of the population) left the country in the early 1990s when removal of prior exit controls coincided with recurrent economic and political crises.

The effects of emigration on sending countries will vary according to the skill level of emigrants. The loss of unskilled and semi-skilled workers can usually be made up relatively cheaply and quickly, but the loss of highly educated professional workers is a more serious problem. Some countries have lost significant proportions of skilled workers. For example, between 1960 and 1987, sub-Saharan African countries are estimated to have lost 30 per cent of their highly skilled manpower, chiefly to Western Europe (Stalker, 1994).

It is likely, however, given EU enlargement, that a high proportion of immigrants to Western Europe in the future will come from Central and Eastern Europe. Currently, average wage levels in the Central and Eastern European candidate countries are about a quarter of those in EU at purchasing power parities, and the gap is not expected to close significantly in the short term. Germany already recruits large numbers of temporary contract workers under bilateral quota agreements with some 13 countries in Central, Eastern and South-Eastern Europe (United Nations and International Organization for Migration, 2000a). As a result of EU enlargement, there is likely to be an increase in East-West migration (and West-East migration), although it is unlikely to be on the massive scale that some fear. A recent European Commission study suggests that Germany can expect an inflow of 220,000 migrant workers a year after EU admits new members from Central and Eastern Europe.[6] This is approximately two thirds of the total expected inflow to EU from Central and Eastern Europe. However, research conducted by IOM suggests that much of the migration from Central and Eastern Europe will be temporary, with many workers maintaining their houses, families, pensions and health insurance in their home countries (United Nations and International Organization for Migration, 1998). Based on the experiences of past rounds of enlargement, this labour migration is likely to help promote economic growth in the Central and Eastern European region, eventually leading to declining emigration (Salt and others, 1999).

Alone, replacement migration is unlikely to be a solution to declining and ageing populations but, together with other measures, it could be an important way in which Governments could better respond to these demographic challenges. However, it seems unlikely at present that States in Western Europe are prepared to promote a substantial increase in permanent immigration. What is more likely is that there will be more selective and temporary labour migration into Western Europe, specifically to meet skill shortages in certain occupations and industries. This type of migration could also have demographic benefits, as migrant workers contribute to social security costs, fill jobs in areas providing services to the elderly, and help reduce the ageing of the workforce.

As we have seen, there are recent signs of a shift in government thinking in several Western European countries in favour of more selective labour migration. However, even these modest attempts to increase temporary and skilled labour migration have not been popular in Europe. If selective labour migration schemes are to be successful, Governments will have to give greater priority to educating public opinion about the potential benefits of migration. This will require information campaigns, using the mass media, to better inform the European public about migration issues.

Despite restrictive immigration policies, there has been considerable irregular labour migration into Western Europe over the last decade—even during times of high unemployment. Hundreds of thousands of migrant workers are already employed illegally in Western Europe. Most of these workers are low-skilled and low-paid. More countries are likely to begin to accept that their economies need these workers, and that their status should be regularized. This would produce demographic benefits as well. By regularizing the workers' status, several European States have brought these workers into their social security and health insurance systems in recent years. Many also believe that the creation of more regular channels for labour migration into Europe could help to reduce irregular migration pressures and the smuggling and trafficking of migrants (United Nations and International Organization for Migration, 2000b).

Finally, if immigration is to increase in Western Europe, it is important that this does not lead to costs for developing countries and countries in transition, many of which also have ageing and declining populations. A managed approach to migration requires the cooperation of both source and destination countries. In an increasingly interconnected world, cooperation among countries is essential in addressing such global issues as international migration.

NOTES

[1]Migration to Western Europe increased sharply in 1999, despite restrictive policies, because of the conflict in Kosovo which resulted in the displacement of nearly 1 million ethnic Albanians.

[2]See *The Economist*, 5 August 2000, p. 32.

[3]Ibid.

[4]*Migration News, Europe*, vol. 7, No. 8 (July 2000).

[5]"UK migration in a global economy", draft speech by Barbara Roche, Member of Parliament, Immigration Minister, Home Office, 11 September 2000.

[6]See "Germany faces large influx of migrant workers", *Financial Times*, 20/21 May 2000.

REFERENCES

Coleman, David (1992). Does Europe need immigrants? population and work force projections. unexplored options *International Migration Review* (New York), vol. 26 (summer).

_____ (1995). International migration: demographic and socio-economic consequences in the United Kingdom and Europe. *International Migration Review*, vol. 29, No. 1.

Feld, Serge (2000). Active population growth and immigration hypotheses in Western Europe. *European Journal of Population*, vol. 16, pp. 3-40.

Ghosh, Bimal (1998). *Huddled Masses and Uncertain Shores: Insights into Irregular Migration.* The Hague: Martinus Nijhoff Publishers.

Organisation for Economic Co-operation and Development (1988). *Ageing Populations: The Social Policy Implications.* Paris: OECD.

_____ (1991). *Migration: The Demographic Aspects.* Paris: OECD.

_____ (1999). *Trends in International Migration.* Paris: OECD.

Papademitriou, D., and K. Hamilton (2000). *Reinventing Japan: Immigration's Role in Shaping Japan's Future.* Washington, D.C.: Carnegie Endowment for International Peace.

Salt, J., and others (1999). *Assessment of Possible Migration Pressure and Its Labour Market Impact following EU Enlargement to Central and Eastern Europe*, part 1. London: HM Stationery Office.

Stalker, Peter (1994). *The Work of Strangers.* Geneva: International Labour Organization.

Tapinos, George (2000). *Le rôle des migrations dans l'attenuation des effets du vieillissement démographique.* Paris: OECD, Groupe de travail sur les migrations. 19-20 juin.

United Nations (2001). *Replacement Migration: Is It a Solution to Declining and Ageing Populations?* Sales No. E.01.XIII.19.

_____ and International Organization for Migration (1998). *Migration Potential in Central and Eastern Europe.* Sales No. E.98.III.S.18.

_____ (2000a). *World Migration Report, 2000*, Susan Martin, ed. Sales No. E.00.III.S.3. Chapter on Western Europe and the Mediterranean prepared by Sarah Collinson.

_____ (2000b). *Migrant Trafficking in Europe: A Review of Migrant Trafficking and Human Smuggling in Europe.* Sales No. E.00.III.S.4.

ON POLICY RESPONSES TO POPULATION DECLINE

*Paul Demeny**

We are discussing, and will be discussing during the next three days, issues related to the questions of population ageing and population decline.

Seen from the perspective of this glass building—even from this basement conference room—these are not the most troubling global population problems.

Let me mention two of those, picking the most obvious.

During the next 50 years, the net addition to population size in the world's less developed countries, United Nations projections tell us, will be somewhere between 1.5 billion and 4.4 billion. Even the lower figure has less than happy implications for the prospect of a speedy reduction of global poverty and the prospect of economic development at large.

The United Nations also estimates that some 35 million people today are infected with the human immunodeficiency virus (HIV) or suffering from acquired immunodeficiency syndrome (AIDS), with a current annual death toll of nearly 3 million. This is an unmitigated, and growing, demographic disaster, concentrated today mostly in Africa. It is also a human tragedy with few precedents.

These issues need urgent and sustained attention from the international system.

Does the existence of these problems diminish the importance of the issues on the agenda of this meeting?

Not at all. Indeed, the United Nations, and in particular the Population Division of the United Nations Secretariat, under the leadership of Joseph Chamie, should be congratulated for putting a searchlight on issues that until now received little recognition at international population forums. More to the point, with few exceptions, they have also been swept under the rug by Governments in the countries directly affected and they are ignored by public opinion. We have a case here of an attention deficit disorder writ large.

This ostrich-like stance can be in part explained, although not excused, by the fact that the most startling aspect of the issue at hand—population decline—is still largely masked by the transient momentum provided by existing demographic features: results of relatively high past fertility and increasing life expectancy.

---

*The Population Council. Remarks prepared for the panel discussion.

Admittedly, the future, even the demographic future, cannot be predicted with great accuracy.

But as the calculations of the United Nations show by most plausible assumptions, population decline will affect numerous countries in the coming decades. Very likely, it will do so at an accelerating pace. At present, the countries affected are sliding, as it were, on a gently sloping downward course in population numbers. After a decade or two, the steepness of the decline is virtually certain to greatly increase.

Population decline, in combination with population ageing and with increasing loss of relative demographic weight within the family of nations, points to a future with some distinctly unpleasant features—economic, social, cultural and geopolitical—for the countries affected.

If so, countermeasures need to be considered, sooner rather than later. Delay will make any plausible remedy far costlier than a timely response.

Broadly speaking, possible remedies are of three types.

The first involves institutional reforms and fiscal arrangements affecting intergenerational relationships. Their aim is to ease economic and social accommodation to an age structure in which the proportion of older persons is greater than is the case today. No one would dispute the legitimate role of government in this domain.

The second has to do with immigration policy. By permitting a larger influx of economically active foreigners, a country can gain at least a temporary rejuvenation of the age structure, and can slow, or at least mitigate, the numerical shrinkage of population size that might otherwise ensue. Regulation of immigration is recognized in international law as the sovereign right of each nation. Determining the rules of the game on immigration that are considered best by the citizenry is a routine function of the political process.

The third type of measure would seek to counteract population ageing and population decline by increasing the birth rate.

I will comment only on the most difficult and controversial among the three—the last one: policies seeking to raise fertility.

The legitimacy of interference with parental decisions about the number of children, unlike that of government involvement in pension reform or immigration control, is not readily accepted in a democratic polity.

Governments, of course, do many things that may influence choices about having or not having children. Some social policies, like family allowances or tax breaks based on the number of dependent children, are perceived as having a pronatalist effect.

However, in virtually all democracies, Governments profess to shape such policies exclusively with welfare and equity considerations in mind. They explicitly disavow any intent to increase the birth rate. Children are home-produced goods. Even apostles of a solicitous and overbearing nanny State tend to hold that it is not the Government's business to tell people how many children they should have.

Yet the potential flaw in this stance is evident. The sum total of individual choices may or may not add up to what is in society's best interest. Parental decisions on the number of children they have may result in positive aggregate growth that is socially too high, or negative growth that is recognized as socially harmful. These are situations that economists describe as market failure. Even on pure Adam Smithian principles, there is then a potential case for collective remedial action.

But do Governments, or for that matter any one of us, know what is too-low or too-high fertility? Do we know the optimum population size and the optimum population change?

Over the long term, there is a simple, if somewhat vacuous, answer to this question. The answer is zero growth, that is to say, fertility at replacement level. It consists in 2 children per woman on average, or very slightly more than 2 children in order to compensate for mortality—very low in modern populations—between birth and early adulthood. Fertility higher than this eventually results in impossibly high numbers. Fertility lower than this eventually leads to extinction.

For time-horizons that may realistically be considered in policy decisions—perhaps spanning the length of one generation and fading to indifference by the end of two—the answer demands quantitative distinctions. I will make reference only to populations relevant in the present context, that is to say, those where fertility is below replacement level. My comments are necessarily stylized and lacking in the documentary detail that could support bottom-line summary judgement. I will make references to actual countries for rough orientation only. We may distinguish three cases.

In some countries—let's call them category I—fertility is only moderately below replacement level. Among the countries considered in the United Nations study of replacement migration (United Nations, 2001), the prototypical case, of course, is the United States of America; but the lower bound of moderate fertility may be defined, somewhat optimistically, as a total fertility rate (TFR) of 1.7. If so, France and the United Kingdom are also within this band, along with some Northern European countries. It would be difficult to be alarmed about the demographic prospects of such countries. In any event, policies with the primary aim of increasing the birth rate could hardly command consensus and strong political support for vigorous action.

To be sure, the ongoing shifts towards an age structure characterized by an increasing proportion of the aged and especially of the very old—both terms understood as conventionally defined—are bound to pose problems of adjustment; but the difficulties inherent in such adjustment should be well within the capacity of modern affluent industrialized societies to overcome. Immigration policy in these situations would be inappropriately seen as a demographically commanded medicine; decisions on immigration matters should be guided by other considerations of national interest and preference. These decisions may be consistent with a generously welcoming open door policy, or with virtually no permanent net immigration at all.

Social policy, likewise, would have little reason to be focused on concern with population growth, as distinct from concern with population quality—the proper upbringing of children who do get born as a result of parental choice. Demographic targets, like maintaining a constant level of population of labour-force age—again, as conventionally defined—let alone preserving a status quo with respect to a support ratio (a ratio between those of working age and those of retirement age set by fiat), have no special normative significance. Should below-replacement fertility be entirely ignored in category I countries? Well, not quite. A degree of demographic decompression—falling population numbers—may be easily tolerated, even mildly welcome. Numbers alone do not make countries great. In terms of cultural, artistic and even scientific productivity and influence, a country's greatness need not depend on whether it is a country of 50 million rather than 40 million. Still, indifference to the matter of demographic change would be warranted only if there was a realistic prospect of eventual spontaneous recovery to higher fertility—to, or close to, replacement proper. Absent such a prospect, it would be reasonable to expect an increasing bias towards favouring social policies that are at least implicitly pronatalist.

In the present intellectual climate, it is easy to predict that such policies would be patterned along the lines of what may be described as the Swedish model. The essence of the model is substantial transfer of child-rearing costs and activities from the family to the community so as to make childbearing more compatible with women's labour-force participation. Supplementary elements in the prescription are efforts towards cultural change aimed at greater involvement of men in roles traditionally considered female. This recipe is now widely accepted as the most potent—and, one might add, only politically correct—antidote to low fertility.

There are problems with the recipe. One of these, apart from its high cost and inefficiency, is its lopsided commitment to a particular style of child-rearing arrangement. Those who would prefer a more traditional pattern of family-building would have difficulty opting out of the model unless they were financially well off. More to the point in the present context, international comparisons of the correlation between the intensity of the model's application and the actual level of aggregate fertility provide at best very weak support for its effectiveness in raising the birth rate or keeping it relatively high.

Thus, while category I countries have no cause for alarm, the matter does need watching. After all, over a period of 50 years—not a long time in the life of a nation—a TFR of 1.7, in the absence of net immigration and apart from transitory momentum effects, would make a population lose some 30 per cent of its original stock.

I skip over category II for the sake of brevity. Among the populations considered in the United Nations study, Japan and the Republic of Korea may fit therein, as does the European Union (EU) in toto—with TFRs in the neighbourhood of 1.5. The steepness of incipient population decline is obviously much higher, with the prospect of 1 per cent population loss per year and the peculiar age distribution that goes with such a pattern. If nothing else, the prospect should generate intensive soul-searching and policy debates.

Finally, category III. In the United Nations study, it is represented by two countries: Italy and Germany, with TFRs of 1.2-1.3. I omit the Russian Federation: the cataclysmic transformations of that country's economic and social order during the last decade make even tentative interpretations hazardous.

However, Italy and Germany are, of course, not alone in their category; one might add such countries as Greece, Spain, the Czech Republic and Hungary. Others are not far behind. Such low levels of fertility as are exhibited in these countries, in some cases now extending over decades, have no precedent in populations of comparably large national entities. Italians, one might expect, would loudly broadcast the alarm: Rome, we have a problem. Or if they do not do so, perhaps Brussels should. As things stand, among forums of some international visibility, only the Population Division of the United Nations Secretariat seems to be emitting warning signals.

What are the policy choices in such a situation?

A possible choice, as I noted, is sticking to the stance of laissez-faire, as far as fertility is concerned. The situation, optimists may hold, could be temporary—an aberration that will in due course right itself. Italy may rejoin the United Kingdom or France as a demographically passably normal country. Others, of more pessimistic bent, might suggest of course that, to the contrary, category III countries are in the vanguard of a socio-economic and cultural transformation and it is the others, now still with fertility only moderately below replacement, that are the laggards. Eventually they, too, will follow the Italian pattern, leading towards precipitous decline in population size. It is possible to find arguments that lend some support to the optimistic scenario; but betting the country's future on spontaneous adjustment places uncomfortably high demand on sheer good luck.

More likely, Governments in Italy-like situations will eventually respond with garden-variety pronatalist polices, along the lines of the Swedish model or pushed beyond it. Perhaps that will work; more likely it will fall far short of its hoped-for effectiveness. The remedy offered by the model is increasing socialization of child-rearing, with the attendant escalating tax burdens of the welfare State. Its logic is that people pay through the government not just for each other's doctors, nurses, medicines, schools and assorted traditional public services, but also for what international documents nowadays delicately refer to as child-minders, thereby avoiding the somewhat sexist term "mother". This may work to some degree, or it may prove counterproductive. Why have a child, or more than one, or more than two, if, after a paid maternity leave, someone else will be de facto raising that child? For that matter, why get married? Having a job and a cat and a bit more discretionary pocket money after the taxes are paid may be just as satisfactory, or more so.

Is compensating for the demographic deficit through immigration an option? Theoretically it is, as long as there is a vast potential pool of immigrants, which there is. However, as the United Nations calculations clearly demonstrate, counterbalancing shrinking numbers implied by category III–type fertility would require an influx of such magnitude as to be radically inconsistent with maintaining not only ethnic and cultural continuity but arguably also economic and social stability. Preferred and allowed immigration might be large by today's standards, but could not be commensurate with what the United Nations calls replacement migration.

Thus, absent other solutions, we are left with the prospect of declining numbers and with an age structure resembling not a rectangle, let alone a pyramid, but rather a light bulb standing on its base, or a pear standing on its stem. Is this a disaster?

Well, it depends. Seen in isolation, the old-age support problem would present an unsolvable task. But I live in Connecticut, a state that lost population between 1990 and 1999—not very rapidly, but it did. So did Rhode Island and North Dakota. Life can be pleasant in these states, albeit perhaps a bit lacking in local entertainment in the last-named state, with the average age of farmers hovering around 60. These states are part of a broader political entity within which goods, money and people can freely flow.

But so is, to a large and increasing degree, Italy. Its standard of living depends on international trade, and its pensioners, especially its future pensioners, will increasingly look for the fruits of their foreign investments—not just from Wall Street but from bonds that helped to build skyscrapers in Shanghai and factories in Indonesia. The transition problems for those now nearing retirement, however, will be severe.

As to Italy's national borders, they are already open to unlimited immigration from EU, a community of nearly 400 million people, all characterized by below-replacement fertility. Note in this context that the numerical results of the calculations in the United Nations replacement migration report crucially depend on the stipulated age distribution of the international migrants. This is assumed to replicate the age distribution of migrants to the main immigration countries, a distribution shaped by the magnet of the dynamic economic growth and labour-absorptive capacity of the receiving countries, most notably the United States. Thus, for instance, the proportion of immigrants over age 65 according to the United Nations is less than 3 per cent of the total number of migrants.

This assumption may be completely unrealistic in the case of low-fertility countries. EU may decide to reduce immigration to a very small number; it could do so, albeit at some cost. Would this be the end of immigration to Italy? Not likely. Its immigrants (if the word "immigrants" still applied in the new context) would come from places like Glasgow, Hamburg and Helsinki, and they would be looking for sunny skies in their post-retirement seventies and eighties. While its total population was shrinking, Italy's age structure would come to resemble that of Sun City, Arizona.

While Italy was coasting towards regaining the population size it enjoyed at the time of the high Renaissance—about 10 million—it could still have not just coupon-clippers but also a flourishing, productive economy. Export of architectural design and high fashion, or of opera singers, does not require large numbers—it requires competitiveness in quality. Tourism, a fabulous money-earner, is a bit more labour-intensive, but could still prosper by displacing less productive segments of the Italian labour force. A less crowded Italy would give tourism an extra attraction.

Thus, not all is lost when population nosedives. Given the uncertainties of the international environment, it would of course be wise for a numerically dwindling Italy to be a generous supporter of that ever-planned European Rapid Reaction Force or, better yet, to make sure that it remains safely under the North Atlantic Treaty Organization's (read America's) defence umbrella. By mid-century, the world, or at least its northern tier, might be a United States and China–managed co-prosperity sphere. The type of risks that French would-be retirees took 100 years ago when they invested in tsarist railroad bonds might be greatly reduced as a result. By mid-century, even Chinese millionaires will have discovered the charms of Tuscany and their retirement there in their second homes will be welcomed. Italy could end up being very short of home-grown children, yet prosperous.

This hypothetical Italian model might be applicable in a number of other places, too—not just demographic pygmies like Monaco or Luxembourg, but also EU as a whole and Japan. Success, however, would typically require possession of special human and natural assets. Owning ancient ruins, for example, is distinctly helpful. More to the point, the recipe is workable only for countries in the vanguard of the ageing process. Further down the line, relying on rents from distant lands that pay the proceeds from past investments will be increasingly difficult—in current American parlance, a risky scheme indeed. And those countries at the end of the line have no access to such a solution. With descendants scarce, perhaps most of their aged will have to rely on robots for their daily care.

And even for our hypothetical Italy, from high Renaissance population size the direction of change would point towards the sixth century—towards the demographic vacuum that followed the collapse of the Roman Empire. A dismal prospect, by most odds. Countries that are short of Italian-style human and natural assets and wish to stay in business long-term might be advised to try to reverse their demographic fortunes now.

What can they do? There are a number of options outside the familiar armamentarium of pronatalist welfare State measures that have not been tried yet offer considerable promise. Such measures would seek structural reforms that would not rely primarily on dispensing money and resources. Rather, they would seek to change institutional arrangements so as to reinforce parental responsibility for and authority over children; strengthen the economic security of women within the family; allow parents to benefit directly from having raised children (for example, through reallocation of social security contributions of working persons in existing pay-as-you-go arrangements directly to their living parents); and make the political system more responsive to the young generation's interest (for example, by granting extra voting rights to adults for their minor children).

I will comment here on only one, more radical, approach, but one that would certainly require considerable financial expenditure on the part of the government, not fully compensated by savings on other policies that would be eliminated or cut back. I know that some will find the ideas I am about to outline unpalatable for reasons that have nothing to do with money. I offer what follows, described in rudimentary fashion, not as a proposal for adopting a policy, but as a plea for discussion and reasoned criticism.

As is well known, the present low-fertility regime gravitates towards a highly compressed distribution of women by the number of their offspring. Let us assume, for the sake of a simplified illustration, that the regime can be described as follows: at the end of the childbearing years, 20 per cent of women end up childless, 40 per cent with 1 child, and 40 per cent with 2 children. The TFR in such a population—the number of children women have on average—is of course 1.2. This happens to be the present level of Italian fertility. It is a fertility level far below replacement, pointing to rapid population decline in the long run.

Standard pronatalist policies seek to increase this average by mounting a full-front attack: trying to reduce voluntary childlessness, encourage single-child women to have a second, and, hopefully, persuade women with two children to have a third child. In this endeavour, policies thus far have conspicuously failed. Incentives could manipulate the timing of children, but not what counts for population reproduction: ultimate family size. The policies are also vastly inefficient: they subsidize behaviour that would by and large be forthcoming even in the absence of subsidies.

Now consider a two-tier, bifurcated fertility regime, composed of women whose fertility is the one just described, and of a second tier: women with a substantially higher family size. Suppose that the first group comprises 70 per cent of all women. How many children would the remaining 30 per cent have to have, on average, to bring overall fertility exactly to replacement level? The answer is 4.

Could 30 per cent of couples be persuaded to raise 4 children apiece—typically their own or, if necessary, adopted ones? Certainly not in response to pleas from presidents and prime ministers to have children for the good of the mother country.

Could even the most vigorous efforts in the service of the accepted goal of "permitting women to combine jobs and children" do the trick? Certainly not. Raising children *is* a job. Women and, more rarely, men do commonly and bravely carry two jobs: the "job" job and that extra child-rearing job, but not if the latter involves four children. That is a full-time job in every sense of the word, and then some.

But at present it is an unpaid job, or paid, in material terms, in small change and with the rider of decreased financial security to boot. Would 30 per cent of potential parents be willing to undertake rearing four children as a career if the job was adequately compensated? The answer would be testable in the market; with confidence it can be predicted that the requisite supply could be recruited. Motherhood is much praised in poetry and songs: indeed, as a challenging yet psychologically rewarding avocation it would easily surpass or compete with most regular jobs, whether in industry, the services or the professions. But parenting would need material recognition to make it fully competitive with jobs in the formal labour market.

The scheme would also need appropriate institutional framing. It would be reasonable to take a leaf in this regard from time-tested models for successful child-rearing. The goal of any politically acceptable pronatalist policy must be not simply to raise the birth rate but to produce more babies who grow up to be productive and responsible members of their society. This would suggest that the paid parental job option could be offered to young married couples who had met certain minimal criteria of education and other characteristics and were willing to make a commitment to raise a "large" family—albeit that "large", if the number of children is just 4, is not quite an appropriate characterization by historical standards. Such couples would also have to consent to rules that would make dissolution of the marriage difficult, as long as a minor child was present. But some models of a more contemporary-liberal bent could also be readily envisaged.

The whiff of eugenics would inevitably be detectable in such a scheme, but rules accepted socially as fair could be worked out. For instance, one legitimate objective might be that the educational composition and ethnic background of such volunteers should replicate the average composition of young persons of similar age, say, 25. To arrive at that result, differentiated salary levels would be both necessary and just. Couples would have to be carefully screened for aptitude and fitness for child-rearing. However, applicants are similarly screened for any responsible job—whether it be that of firefighter, lawyer, teacher or policeman. With proper selection, once accepted for the scheme, monitoring of performance would be typically lighter than is the case in the formal labour force. Dropout rates would be also low. As the family grew, so would remuneration brought by the at-home parent to this now normal two-earner family, is as much the case for ordinary professional jobs and ordinary two-earner families. The salary accruing to the at-home parent would be subject to the same rules concerning social security and taxation as in the formal labour force. As children left the household, parental responsibilities would decrease, and so would the salary. Some caregivers at that point might elect to enter the formal labour force, but they need not do so. At that time, regular retirement age would be fairly close at hand.

I conclude simply by saying that populations that are disinclined to accept their numerical decline have available to them unexplored options that could assure a sufficient number of home-grown children to satisfy their preference. They may still wish to welcome immigrants for a number of good reasons. Population replacement need not be one among them.

REFERENCES

United Nations (2001). *Replacement Migration: Is It a Solution to Declining and Ageing Populations?* Sales No. E.01.XIII.19.

كيفية الحصول على منشورات الأمم المتحدة

يمكن الحصول على منشورات الأمم المتحدة من المكتبات ودور التوزيع في جميع أنحاء العالم . استعلم عنها من المكتبة
التي تتعامل معها أو اكتب إلى : الأمم المتحدة ، قسم البيع في نيويورك أو في جنيف .

如何购取联合国出版物

联合国出版物在全世界各地的书店和经售处均有发售。请向书店询问或写信到纽约或日内瓦的
联合国销售组。

HOW TO OBTAIN UNITED NATIONS PUBLICATIONS

United Nations publications may be obtained from bookstores and distributors throughout the
world. Consult your bookstore or write to: United Nations, Sales Section, New York or Geneva.

COMMENT SE PROCURER LES PUBLICATIONS DES NATIONS UNIES

Les publications des Nations Unies sont en vente dans les librairies et les agences dépositaires
du monde entier. Informez-vous auprès de votre libraire ou adressez-vous à : Nations Unies,
Section des ventes, New York ou Genève.

КАК ПОЛУЧИТЬ ИЗДАНИЯ ОРГАНИЗАЦИИ ОБЪЕДИНЕННЫХ НАЦИЙ

Издания Организации Объединенных Наций можно купить в книжных магазинах
и агентствах во всех районах мира. Наводите справки об изданиях в вашем книжном
магазине или пишите по адресу: Организация Объединенных Наций, Секция по
продаже изданий, Нью-Йорк или Женева.

COMO CONSEGUIR PUBLICACIONES DE LAS NACIONES UNIDAS

Las publicaciones de las Naciones Unidas están en venta en librerías y casas distribuidoras en
todas partes del mundo. Consulte a su librero o diríjase a: Naciones Unidas, Sección de Ventas,
Nueva York o Ginebra.

Litho in United Nations, New York
01-72258—December 2004—6,445
ISBN 92-1-151364-2

United Nations publication
Sales No. E.02.XIII.4
ST/ESA/SER.N/44-45